Critical Approaches to Television

- content analizes Ideologiciel
  see if this match with News
  Relate PaleoTV, Neo TV with
     dinamics of today
  Name "Framing"?

Critical Approaches to Television

Leah R. Vande Berg
California State University, Sacramento

Lawrence A. Wenner
University of San Francisco

Bruce E. Gronbeck
University of Iowa

HOUGHTON MIFFLIN COMPANY   Boston   New York

Sponsoring Editor: George T. Hoffman
Editorial Assistant: Kara Maltzahn
Production/Design Coordinator: Deborah Frydman
Manufacturing Manager: Florence Cadran
Marketing Manager: Pamela J. Laskey

Cover Design: Diana Coe
Cover Image: James Porto/FPG International

Acknowledgments appear on page xix.

Printed in the U.S.A.

Library of Congress Catalog Card Number: 97-72558

ISBN: 0-395-76641-9

3456789-DH-03 02 01 00 99

Contents

6   Text-Centered Approaches to Television Criticism   *93*

 *Alternative Contents*

Preface

Television, the prototypical mass medium, has been pivotal to the progress of electronic communications in the twentieth century. In the early days of television people had to leave home to see a motion picture, but TV hooked them together in their parlors and kitchens. Radio joined people, too, of course, but without the informational and emotional impact provided by pictures. Television exposed Americans not only to their local business advertising on the evening news but also to aboriginal peoples from halfway around the world. Marshall McLuhan talked in the 1960s about the Global Village to capture metaphorically the sense of proximity and instantaneousness of associations that accompanied relationships constructed through electronic communications. With its channels multiplying from the original VHF (very high frequency) dozen to the hundreds now available via DDS (direct satellite systems), television beams into every corner of our lives, through its news and entertainment channels, cooking shows, home shopping networks, sports extravaganzas, sound-only channels, movie outlets for every taste, religious experiences, foreign programming, cartoons, and even nonstop weather information and wisdom. Television is parent, financial adviser, friend, moralist, distraction, and, perhaps above all, teacher to us all—or at least to the ninety-nine percent of us in the United States with television sets.

Whether you like it or not, significant portions of your life are probably centered on television. Even if you don't watch TV, most of the people you come in contact with use it for surveillance, authority, and entertainment. As television turned into a consumer product especially in the United States some fifty years ago, it was popularly called a "window on the world." We have learned by now, however, that the window doesn't have clear glass: in part it's reflective, showing you part of yourself; in part, distortive, selecting and even recontextualizing what you're looking at; in part, fantasy, showing you an environment that never was or can be. Reflection, distortion, and fantasy are aspects of your viewing, whether you're looking at *Rugrats, The Wide World of Sports, One Life to Live, Mad About You,* or *The Evening News with Dan Rather.*

This book has been written and assembled to help you analyze television culture sensitively, systematically, and expertly. To confront television for what it is and what it can do to you, you must be able to distance yourself from the concept of "watching a little TV" by monitoring your own reactions to what has been constructed for you in sight, sound, and symbols. You'll understand television's ways and importance—*understanding* is the primary outcome of good criticism—only by studying the people who think up and construct programs, the coding systems used for a TV program, the descriptive and valuative content of what you see, characteristics of people who view and draw sustenance from TV, and the industrial behemoths that profit from your relationship with "The Box." This book seeks to make you a good television critic.

This book started out as *Television Criticism: Approaches and Applications*, written and edited by Leah Vande Berg and Lawrence Wenner in 1991. It was conceived of as a textbook and reader, a book with both methodologically oriented how-to-do-it instruction and samples of television criticism. Those who used it applauded the concepts behind the effort but wanted more about general criticism, specific television criticism, various approaches to critical analysis, and writing.

So that's what we did when we wrote *Critical Approaches to Television*. Several new features stand out in this version of the book, and the strengths of its predecessor remain. Here are some of the features that make *Critical Approaches to Television* the most comprehensive textbook and reader on media criticism available today:

- The title *Critical Approaches to Television* emphasizes the book's focus on various sorts of understandings television critics try to engender through their writing.
- A third author-editor, Bruce Gronbeck, was brought in to add breadth of vision, depth of background, and pedagogical-authorial experience to the team.
- The four introductory chapters expand students' orientations to criticism as an intellectual activity, to television criticism as a site for thinking and analysis, and to critical writing as a special challenge. These chapters provide a background and foundation for critically analyzing television.
- *Critical Approaches to Television* has two tables of contents: the primary Contents is assembled around approaches to criticism, and the Alternative Contents is organized by television genre (type of program). The book offers organizational possibilities based on the two principal ways a course in media criticism is taught.
- The sample essays are organized by six general approaches—auteur-, text-, audience-, context-, culture-, and institution-centered. Substantial introductions to the approaches help prepare inexperienced critics for using them. Each introduction to a particular approach to criticism treats its assumptions, general vocabulary, and special writing challenges and finishes by orienting analyses to the sample criticisms that follow.
- Essays have been updated where appropriate. Television is an ephemeral medium, with shows coming and going even in midseason. Most of the authors were asked to work on examples of television from the nineties, but we included analyses of older programs such as *Cheers* and *Roots* because they are so instructive and so widely available in syndication or video.

- A new final chapter has been designed for end-of-the-term discussions about where criticism and even television itself have been this half-century and what their social roles will be in the future.

We have brought together the most current ideas about television criticism generally and specifically in a reader accessible to undergraduates but mindful of the metacritical issues of particular interest to graduate students. We have presented classic and contemporary television shows to provide both a historical and a critical context for your understanding and writing. We have maintained a level of theoretical-conceptual and critical-interpretive analysis appropriate to college-level instruction in the liberal arts even as we've recorded enough how-to-do-it advice to jump-start the beginning writer.

We have been helped in our endeavor by many. Special thanks are due the anonymous reviewers of both the earlier version of the book and its current version: Michael J. Porter (University of Missouri), Harry W. Haines (Trinity University), Barry Brummett (University of Wisconsin-Milwaukee), Robert Schrag (North Carolina State University), Christopher Francis White (Sam Houston State University), Raymond Gozzi Jr. (Ithaca College), and Barbie Zelizer (Temple University). We thank, too, the authors of the sample essays; they responded with enthusiasm and expertise to our requests to revise and reform their work in ways appropriate to a textbook. Houghton Mifflin took over this book when it was being reborn. Acquisitions Editor Margaret Sewell helped us start the reconceptualization, and George Hoffman aided us in its completion. Thanks to Kara Maltzahn for representing the company in developing the book, and to Andrea Cava for overseeing the editorial production and shepherding us through the revision process. Thanks also to interior book designer George McLean, to the photo researcher Linda Finigan, to production/design coordinator Deborah Frydman, and to the manufacturing manager Florence Cadran. The marketing expertise of Pamela Laskey aided us in getting the book into your hands. Houghton Mifflin put together a powerful instructional textbook.

We offer our deepest thanks to the former teachers and students who used the book and cared enough to give us good advice on how to improve it. Only by meeting the needs of students and their mentors is any textbook worth the effort that goes into its making. The users we've come to know over the nineties have inspired and directed our work. We appreciate their loving attention and exhortation. We hope that they like it even better.

We hope that you become someone who'll never again "watch a little TV" without first engaging your critical facilities. Students often tell us that their television viewing has been ruined by this course because they find themselves analyzing and assessing the stuff they view. Life as a couch potato is no more. We smile knowingly when we hear that, telling them that it's all right. College education is supposed to disturb your ability to live life in a business-as-usual sort of way; it's supposed to alert and deploy your critical defenses.

Adopting critical attitudes as you look at life, even life in front of a TV set, doesn't really ruin it. Rather, they allow you to enjoy life on two levels—the mundane and the critical, life-as-experienced and life-as-reflected-upon.

So read this book and carry out the class discussions and writing assignments enthusiastically. If you do, you ought be able to double your television-viewing pleasure.

LEAH R. VANDE BERG
LAWRENCE A. WENNER
BRUCE E. GRONBECK

 *Acknowledgments*

From *Television's Second Golden Age: From Hill Street Blues to Picket Fences* by Robert J. Thompson. Copyright © 1996 Robert J. Thompson. Reprinted by permission of The Continuum Publishing Company.

Lawrence A. Wenner, "The Dream Team, Communicative Dirt, and the Marketing of Synergy" from *Journal of Sport & Social Issues*, Vol. 18, No. 1, pp. 27–47. Copyright © 1994 by Sage Publications. Reprinted by permission of Sage Publications.

Glenn C. Geiser-Getz, "*COPS* and the Comic Frame: Humor and Meaning-Making in Reality-Based Television" from *Electronic Journal of Communication*. Copyright 1995. Reprinted by permission of the Electronic Journal of Communication/La revue electronique de communication.

Robert Schrag, "From Yesterday to Today: A Case Study of *M*A*S*H*'s Margaret Houlihan" from *Communication Education*, Vol. 40 (1991), pp. 112–115. Copyright © 1991 by the Speech Communication Association. Reproduced by permission of the publisher and the author.

Heather L. Hundley, "The Naturalization of Beer in *Cheers*" from *Journal of Broadcasting & Electronic Media*, Vol. 39 (1995), pp. 350–359. Copyright 1995. Reprinted by permission of the National Broadcast Association.

Bonnie J. Dow, "Femininity and Feminism in *Murphy Brown*" from *Southern Communication Journal*, Vol. 57, No. 2 (1992), pp. 143–155. Printed with permission of the Southern States Communication Association and the *Southern Communication Journal*.

Lauren R. Tucker and Hemant Shah, "Race and the Transformation of Culture: The Making of the Television Miniseries *Roots*" from *Critical Studies in Mass Communication*, Vol. 9 (1992), pp. 325–336. Copyright © 1992 by the Speech Communication Association. Reproduced by permission of the publisher.

Critical Approaches
to Television

PART I

THEORETICAL FOUNDATIONS AND CRITICAL CONTEXTS

The Context of Criticism: Television and Society

Television is ubiquitous. We watch it in Laundromats, bars, hospital waiting rooms, living rooms, and even minivans. Television's programs are available 24 hours a day, and we don't have to drive to a theater, stand in line, and buy a ticket to watch them. That's part of the reason why the TV set in the average American home is turned on for viewing 7 hours and 15 minutes a day. One result is that by the time most of you graduated from high school, you had spent far more time with this electronic storyteller—approximately 20,000 hours—than with your classroom instructors—11,000 hours! (*Broadcasting & Cable Yearbook,* 1994; Kline, 1993).

The goal of this book is to help you develop the critical viewing skills to explore the meanings and pleasures you have created through your interactions with television. We believe that for you, as it was for us, becoming a more informed and articulate critic of television will change your sense of self, your tastes, and your perception of television as a uniquely powerful social and cultural force.

The Powers of Television

Indeed, television's pervasive cradle-to-grave presence and its potential powers have been regarded by both critics and social scientists as sufficiently important reasons for subjecting the medium and its contents, uses, and effects to extensive scrutiny (see, for example, Gerbner, Gross, Morgan, & Signorielli, 1994). Among television's powers are the power to entertain, to inform, to educate and socialize, and to create community and consensus.

The Power to Entertain

One of the most common reasons people watch television, according to researchers who study television's uses and effects, is for entertainment or diversion (Zillmann, 1982; Zillmann & Bryant, 1985). Television is a prolific provider of diversion, escape, and entertainment that requires no literacy, no mobility, and no direct purchase; indeed, children begin watching this tirelessly entertaining babysitter long before they can talk or read (see Gerbner, Gross, Morgan, & Signorielli, 1994).

For many of us, lounging on the couch watching episodes of *Friends, Seinfeld,* or *Frasier* is a convenient, inexpensive way to relax after a stress-filled day of tests, work, and driving before starting in on the evening's tasks. However, television's power to entertain includes not only the capacity to divert and relax us but also the power to cheer us up. Zillmann and Bryant (1994) note that not only do adults turn to television entertainment programs when they need some cheering up, but that children as young as four use television to change their bad moods into good moods (see Masters, Ford, & Arend, 1983).[1]

The Power to Socialize and Educate

When you think about television as a socializing agent or teacher, your first response may be to think about the studies on the efficacy of *Sesame Street* and *Mister Rogers' Neighborhood* in preparing children for school by helping them to learn the alphabet, simple rules of social courtesy, and intercultural cooperation (Silverman & Sprafkin, 1980). With a little more thought you might also mention educational PBS documentaries like Ken Burns's *Baseball* or Bill Moyers's *A Walk Through the Twentieth Century, The Power of Healing,* and *The Language of Life;* PBS science series *Nova* and *Nature;* and the programs on such cable outlets as the Discovery Channel. However, if we understand education in the larger sense to mean the acquisition of knowledge—including social, cultural, political, economic, scientific, philosophical, and religious information, generalizations, theories, and facts—then *all* television is educational. As Gerbner, Gross, Morgan, and Signorielli (1994) put it:

> Television is the source of the most broadly shared images and messages in history. It is the mainstream of the common symbolic environment into which our

children are born and in which we all live out our lives. . . . Transcending historic barriers of literacy and mobility, television has become the primary common source of socialization and everyday information (mostly in the form of entertainment) of otherwise heterogeneous populations. (pp. 17–18)

From television's continuous and coherent use of visual, musical, aural/oral, and narrative codes we learn to "read" television and movie visual texts: we learn to identify (or decode) certain visual indicators as flashbacks, dream sequences, and simultaneously occurring events (created through editing techniques that Christian Metz, 1974, calls *alternating syntagms*). We learn the power of the camera's "gaze" (Mulvey, 1975, 1989; Vande Berg, 1993); we learn to read musical soundtracks as signaling danger, suspense, humor, discovery, romance, or grief; and we learn from the laugh tracks what we are supposed to regard as funny and to anticipate when something humorous is about to happen (see Altman, 1986).

From the characters in television programs, performers in music videos, and actors' guest appearances, we can acquire social knowledge and cues about contemporary hairstyles and clothing styles (e.g., Madonna's underwear as outerwear and *Beverly Hills 90210*'s Dylan's James Dean hairstyle), language use (e.g., Beavis and Butthead's "Hey, dude"), and behavioral mannerisms (e.g., baseball player Glenn Burke's "high five"). From soap operas, medical dramas, and made-for-television movies, we learn facts about heart disease, incest, and AIDS. From police and legal dramas, we learn about the criminal justice and judicial systems—what our Miranda rights are, what arrest procedures typically are like, and what prosecuting and defense lawyers do. Situation comedies and dramas can teach us about contemporary social values and attitudes toward sex, family, and school, and can provide glimpses of various occupations.

Television's fictional and nonfictional entertainment also serve a socializing function by celebrating some characters and their deeds as admirable and heroic while ignoring and failing to cover other groups, thereby signifying their lower social status. Television can help demonize or canonize cultural heroes, create and destroy cultural myths, and shape people's perceptions and attitudes. For example, television coverage of John F. Kennedy in the 1960s and subsequent assassination-anniversary pilgrimage specials and made-for-television movies such as *Kennedys Don't Cry, Four Days in November,* and *JFK: That Day in November* helped create and maintain the American Camelot myth (Vande Berg, 1995). Television series about war (*Hogan's Heroes, M*A*S*H, China Beach,* and *Tour of Duty*), television series about doctors (from *Marcus Welby, M.D.* to *St. Elsewhere* to *ER* and *Dr. Quinn: Medicine Woman*), and television series about cops (from *Car 54* to *Miami Vice, Hill Street Blues, Homicide: Life on the Streets,* and *NYPD Blue*) affect our understanding of history and contemporary culture (see, for example, Real, 1996, pp. 208–236).

Hijinx at the 4077th M*A*S*H

*During its 11-season run from 1972 to 1983, M*A*S*H showed viewers the horrors and heroes of war and, as Schrag's Chapter 8 essay explains, the personal growth and evolution of "Hot Lips" Houlihan into the self-respecting, self-actualized Margaret.*

The Power to Create Community and Consensus

Television also helps create community and consensus and teaches us the lessons of history. For instance, some 130 million American television viewers watched Alex Haley's *Roots* (McNeil, 1991), and at least as many tuned in to find out who shot *Dallas*'s J.R. and to say "Goodbye, Farewell and Amen" to their friends on *M*A*S*H*. Thanks to television, almost every adult American knows what "the real thing" is and that "Air Jordan" is not the name of a commercial airline.

Indeed, many of us regard our favorite television series and characters as familiar friends whom we look forward to seeing each week. Scholars call this aspect of television its *parasocial function* because although it isn't really social interaction, for many people, watching a favorite character or cast of characters serves as a partial functional replacement for social relationships (Horton & Wohl, 1956). In fact, many viewers apparently read the characters in television series quite realistically. For example, actor Tim Busfield, who played Elliot Weston on the prime-time serial *thirtysomething*, recalls a time when he was slapped in the face in a grocery store by a woman who told him that Elliot should not have left his wife (Zehme, 1989, p. 75). This incident happened, in part, because television uses social codes to create a sense of realism or verisimilitude (see Heide, 1995).

Television also helps to create community by providing viewers with grist for social interactions. This *social utility function* of television can be seen, for example, in our work environments when we stop for a cup of coffee and engage in conversations with coworkers about what happened on last night's *Friends* or *Seinfeld* episode or Sunday night's *X-Files*.

The Power to Inform

Closely related to television's power to educate and socialize is its power to inform. Television news and public affairs programming provide *surveillance* of our physical environment—functioning as an early-warning system about everything from tomorrow's rain predictions and tornado warnings to proposed actions by the U.S. Congress and state legislatures, terrorist attacks, and global warming. It was from television that many Americans learned that President Kennedy had been shot, and it was on television that we watched the *Apollo* astronauts walk on the moon and the *Challenger* explode.[2] Because so many more events occur than can possibly be covered in any one newscast (or any one newspaper or news magazine, for that matter), television confers status on those events, individuals, and ideas it does choose to cover and marginalizes or symbolically annihilates those persons, events, ideas, issues, and problems to which its national and local executives decide not to give air time. Although television critics recognize that such gatekeeping is an essential part of television's continued functioning, critics also recognize that television's *status conferral* power is a dimension of television's information provision and, thus, that it is very important to constantly and critically examine television's gatekeeping choices.

Although many media studies scholars have focused on television's power to set viewers' political agendas—not by telling them what to think or how to vote, but by telling them what to think *about* (Fan, Brosius, & Kepplinger, 1994; McCombs & Shaw, 1972), far fewer media studies scholars have explored television's *agenda-setting function* in the social and cultural areas of music and fashion, language use, behavioral mannerisms, myths, ideologies, and social norms.

Dr. Mike, Sully, Brian, Matthew, and Colleen from *Dr. Quinn: Medicine Woman*

Dr. Mike's adopted daughter, Colleen, has been played by two different actors. Projansky's Chapter 9 essay argues that the different bodies of these two characters and their different relationship to Dr. Mike reveal how this series attempts to balance feminism and idealized femininity.   (Archive Photos/© 1993 CBS, Inc.)

Characteristics of the Medium of Television

Television has the power to entertain, inform, and socialize because it is simultaneously an industry, an electronic apparatus, and a collection of extremely diverse programs or texts—a 24-hour flow of words and images.

Television as Industry

That television is an industry means that it is a complex of organizations and individuals whose primary goal is economic profitability and only secondarily aesthetic excellence or public service. By 1994, for example, the U.S. television industry included one public and six commercial television networks, about 1500 operating television stations, 11,800 operating cable television systems reaching about 58 million subscribers or some 62.4 percent of all U.S. households, plus scores of program production companies, advertising agencies, talent agencies, and so on. For the television networks and cable outlets (which typically purchase programs from program creators to distribute to their owned and affiliated stations/systems) and advertisers, programming is merely the filler between the truly important television content—the advertisements. And in 1994 the average 30-second prime-time television network commercial announcement cost $100,000, and 30-second spots on top-rated TV series cost $325,000. Of course, for the 1997 Super Bowl 30-second announcements, advertisers paid up to $1.3 million to reach the estimated 121 million people viewing this sports event (*Broadcasting & Cable Yearbook,* 1995, p. xxi; "Super Bowl," 1997).

Because broadcast television requires no direct out-of-pocket purchase we tend to think of it as free, but that is far from the case. Programs are financed by selling time to product producers for promoting their products within and between programs. The more viewers, or sometimes the more "quality" viewers with large disposable incomes, who watch a particular program, the more the advertisers are willing to pay the networks to try to reach those viewers with product promotions. Hence, as you see, what is really being sold is us— the viewers. One important implication of commercialism for television criticism is that television stations, broadcast networks, and cable channels assess the goodness of a program in terms of the Nielsen aesthetic standard—that is, how many viewers does the program attract—rather than a medium-based aesthetic standard—how well does the program utilize the unique characteristics of the television medium.

Television as Appliance

When we think of television, we also think of the appliance that sits in our living rooms (and bedrooms, dens, kitchens, and even our RVs). Our expectations of our television appliance are similar to expectations we have of such other household appliances as the refrigerator, microwave, dishwasher, and air conditioner: we expect it to provide us with a range of services of our choosing, upon demand, at any and every hour of the day or night. However, although we may reasonably expect to find a book we like among the 10,000 offerings on the shelves at a bookstore like Barnes & Noble any time we saunter in, without an equivalent number of channels, it is unreasonable to apply the same criteria to television. Thinking of television as a set or appliance, then, can lead to just such unreasonable expectations. Furthermore, television's commonplace ordinariness is one reason that many viewers, critics, and educators have been slow to take television seriously as an art form and slower still to train students in elementary, secondary, and postsecondary classes to critically analyze television in the same way students are taught to analyze literature.

Television as Flow

Another key characteristic of television is *flow*—its constantly changing yet seamless stream of images and sounds (Williams, 1974). Television programs are interwoven with advertisements, public service announcements (PSAs), station identifications, program promotions, bumpers, teases, and other materials designed to provide a constant flow of sight and sound. Since about 1976, thanks to videocassette recorders, we have had a means of arresting this flow and capturing the ephemeral, fleeting televisual experiences for closer study. However, the nonstop stream of programs on all 40 to 120 cable television channels makes television criticism extremely challenging—and never dull.

Television as Provider of Program Fragments

If part of what contemporary theorists mean by postmodernism is the fragmentation of temporal, linear narrative, disjointed plots and incoherent character development, television is the quintessential postmodern art form (see Collins, 1992). That is, despite television's perpetual flow of images and sounds, television comes to us in fragments. It is, as Gronbeck (1984) has noted, "a series of islands, a patch here and patch there . . . chopped into 20-, 60-, and 90-minute narratives, each broken down into acts or episodes running anywhere from three to twenty minutes apiece, thanks to commercials" (p. 8). Most television programs are episodic, meaning that each series—like *Baywatch, Dr. Quinn: Medicine Woman, Seinfeld,* and *Spin City*—comes to us in 20 to 22 weekly installments. Each weekly episode is a different, complete-in-itself narrative featuring the program's recurring characters. Furthermore, the structure of each weekly installment is also predictably fragmented into acts that include the introduction of the week's special situational problem, rising action, falling action, and denouement. Each of these acts, of course, ends on a note of imminent suspense or romance designed to make sure we are there watching after the commercial breaks.

On the other hand, some television programs are serial, meaning that the story line is not resolved at the end of each week's episode, but instead continues from week to week. Still, even serial television shows are fragmented (ending at peaks of action and emotion in order to keep viewers coming back week after week to see what happens). For example, daytime soaps such as *Days of Our Lives* and prime-time serials such as *NYPD Blue* or *ER* are broken up into weekly installments that usually end on a note of suspense designed to draw us back the following week to see what happens. Indeed, to deal with such fragmentation in continuing story lines, television writers have developed a number of aesthetic strategies ranging from an announcer's introduction, reviewing preceding weeks' stories ("Last week on *Melrose Place*") and explicit voice-over narration (e.g., *Wonder Years'* adult Kevin Arnold introducing the week's look back at his life in junior high and high school in the late 1960s and early 1970s) to what Robert C. Allen (1987) terms *interepisodic redundancy* (e.g., having one character tell another character what happened previously, thereby catching up both the character and the viewer on previous events that they did not witness).

The Need for Critical Analysis of Television

It is precisely because television is all of these things—industry, mundane appliance, flow of images and sounds, and narrative fragments—that critical analysis of television is needed. Thirty-five years ago, Moses Hadas noted that

> In literature, as we have observed, there is a tangible critical climate, guided and made articulate by professional critics, perhaps, but shaped by all who take books seriously and write and talk about them. The critical climate, in turn, determines what books are made available. . . . A similar climate must be created for television; all who take education seriously in its larger sense—and not the professed critics alone—should talk and write about television as they do books. (1962, p. 19)

Hadas's comments express several reasons why it is important for you to become serious television critics: becoming a more articulate critic of television will help you interpret and understand your television-viewing experiences and those of your friends, neighbors, and children. Learning and practicing television criticism will enable you to critically evaluate the subtle and overt ways in which encounters with television programs can shape aesthetic tastes; ethical, social, and cultural values; and political and ideological perspectives. Your understanding of the TV industry will change as you begin to study the various ways in which the TV industry packages, markets, and positions *you* as the commodity that is being sold, and so will your sense of yourself. Learning to use the various tools of criticism will help you discover how television's technical, social, conventional representational, and ideological codes work to position you to see and create some "preferred" meanings rather than "oppositional" meanings from the structured program elements.[3] And practicing television criticism will enable you to explain knowledgeably and articulately to others how and why some programs, series, and stories have engaged you, emotionally moved you, angered you, and amused you while others have annoyed, depressed, and manipulated you (and them).

By learning how to practice television criticism, you will be helping to create a critical climate within which television is taken as seriously as books. As we have explained in this chapter, it is important to create such a critical climate because television, like books, is a powerful cultural and social force. Indeed, many educators believe that media literacy is a basic skill like reading and math, and they believe that all high school students should have to take classes that teach students how to "read television" in the same way that secondary students now take classes in which they learn to read writers like William Shakespeare, William Faulkner, and Flannery O'Connor. The goal of such television criticism classes is to enable people to become informed, everyday critics who can use critical tools to systematically examine the social, cultural, aesthetic, and political meanings of television programs and to share these insights with other television viewers, with television program creators and industry decision makers, and with other television-studies students, scholars, and professionals.

Serious, careful television criticism provides informed, insightful explanations of particular television texts or groups of texts. It locates a text or a group of texts in one or more contexts, thereby encouraging and enabling viewers to understand their experiences with television in new and different ways. Serious television criticism invites viewers (or readers) of television to undertake new evaluations of their television experiences—sometimes appreciative, sometimes depreciative—in light of systematic, substantive, stylistic criteria that it articulates for the reader. As you can see, television critics are interpreters, teachers, and social and intellectual catalysts all rolled into one. In fact, because television criticism essays simultaneously provide a critical analysis and teach through example how to perform similar types of critical analyses on other television programs (or texts), all television criticism provides a pedagogical service.

Most of us who read and practice writing television criticism believe that if there were more informed, serious criticism and less unconsidered opining about television in newspapers, in magazines, and in books and classrooms, the television industry and the public would take television criticism and the television medium seriously—like the theater and literary communities have for decades—to the great benefit of both. Indeed, given that according to Kubey and Csikszentmihalyi (1990, p. 1), today alone some 3.5 billion hours will be spent watching television around the world, don't you think it's about time you started thinking critically about television?

The remainder of the book is designed to help you begin practicing television criticism. Chapters 2 and 3 provide a brief background and history of television criticism; they also discuss what television criticism is and what it isn't. Chapter 4 describes the general structure of critical essays about television. This material can serve as a template that you can use to examine how the sample critical essays in Chapters 5 through 10 are constructed and also as a model for writing your own television-criticism essays. Part II (Chapters

5–10) introduces you to six general types of criticism. Each chapter begins with a methodological essay that explains the assumptions underlying each approach (or method), defines the central terms and concepts, and discusses some of the questions critics using each method ask and try to answer about television. Then, after these methodological essays, we provide sample critical essays that illustrate how some critics have used these methods to analyze particular television programs or sets of programs. Finally, Chapter 11 summarizes some of the connections among the chapters and offers some suggestions about the future of television and television criticism.

We sincerely hope you enjoy reading these chapters and trying your hand at practicing television criticism as much as we have enjoyed writing these chapters and our own television-criticism essays.

NOTES

1. The therapeutic powers of television entertainment do have some limitations, however. For example, researchers have found little support for television's cathartic power—that is, the ability to harmlessly discharge accumulated aggressive impulses merely by watching televised violence (see Gunter, 1994). In fact, the accumulated research on television suggests that viewing television entertainment can have some less-than-therapeutic effects as well. For instance, researchers have found a strong, positive correlation between watching a large number of violent television programs and approving the use of aggression to solve conflicts, and they have found that this relationship persists even when such other contributing factors as education level, social class, aggressive attitudes, parental behavior, and sex-role identity are controlled. Among some of the recent research that has consistently found such positive correlations are studies by Freedman, 1984; Huesmann, Lagerspetz, and Eron, 1984; Joy, Kimball, and Zabrack, 1986; Liebert and Sprafkin, 1988; and Williams, 1986.
2. See, for example, Barbie Zelizer (1992) and Bradley S. Greenberg and Edwin Parker's (1965) studies of the JFK assassination coverage, as well the Fall 1986 special issue of *Central States Speech Journal*, which is entirely devoted to coverage of the space shuttle *Challenger* disaster.
3. As we mention in Chapter 6, Stuart Hall, a British professor and scholar who studies culture and media, has explained that there are three ways that we can "read" or decode television texts: through a *dominant* reading, we understand the text's signs in virtually the same way as the text's producer(s) intended; through a *negotiated* reading, we understand the producer(s)' encoded meanings but adjust some of them to better fit with our particular social experience, knowledge base, and position in society; and, through an *oppositional* reading, we reverse the producer(s)' understanding (e.g., treating a serious moment as laughable).

REFERENCES

Allen, R. C. (1987). *Speaking of soap operas.* Chapel Hill, NC: University of North Carolina Press.

Altman, R. (1986). Television/sound. In T. Modleski (Ed.), *Studies in entertainment: Critical approaches to mass culture* (pp. 39–54). Bloomington, IN: Indiana University Press.

Broadcasting & Cable Yearbook. (1995). Year in review: Broadcasting and cable, 1994 (p. xxi). New Providence, NJ: Bowker.

Collins, J. (1992). Postmodernism and television. In R. C. Allen (Ed.), *Channels of discourse, reassembled: Television and contemporary criticism* (2nd ed., pp. 327–353). Chapel Hill, NC: University of North Carolina Press.

Fan, D. P., Brosius, H., & Kepplinger, H. M. (1994). Predictions of the public agenda from television coverage. *Journal of Broadcasting & Electronic Media, 38,* 163–178.

Freedman, J. L. (1984). Effect of television violence on aggressiveness. *Psychological Bulletin, 96,* 227–246.

Friedrich-Cofer, L., & Huston, A. C. (1986). Television violence and aggression: The debate continues. *Psychological Bulletin, 100,* 364–371.

Gerbner, G., Gross, L., Morgan, M., & Signorielli, N. (1994). Growing up with television: The cultivation perspective. In J. Bryant & D. Zillmann (Eds.), *Media effects: Advances in theory and research* (pp. 17–42). Hillsdale, NJ: Lawrence Erlbaum.

Greenberg, B. S., & Parker, E. (Eds.). (1965). *The Kennedy assassination and the American public.* Palo Alto, CA: Stanford University Press.

Gronbeck, B. E. (1984). *Writing television criticism* (Modules in mass communication series). Chicago: Science Research Associates.

Gunter, B. (1994). The question of media violence. In J. Bryant & D. Zillmann (Eds.), *Media effects: Advances in theory and research* (pp. 163–212). Hillsdale, NJ: Lawrence Erlbaum.

Hadas, M. (1962). Climates of criticism. In R. L. Shayon (Ed.), *The eighth art* (pp. 15–23). New York: Holt, Rinehart, Winston.

Heide, M. (1995). *Television culture and women's lives:* thirtysomething *and the contradictions of gender.* Philadelphia: University of Pennsylvania Press.

Horton, D., & Wohl, R. R. (1956). Mass communication and para-social interaction: Observations on intimacy at a distance. *Psychiatry, 19,* 215–229.

Huesmann, L. R., Lagerspetz, K., & Eron, L. D. (1984). Intervening variables in the television violence-viewing-aggression relation: Evidence from two countries. *Developmental Psychology, 20,* 707–716.

Joy, L. A., Kimball, M., & Zabrack, M. L. (1986). Television exposure and children's aggressive behavior. In T. M. Williams (Ed.), *The impact of television: A natural experiment involving three towns* (pp. 303–360). New York: Academic Press.

Kline, S. (1993). *Out of the garden: Toys and children's culture in the age of TV marketing.* London & New York: Verso.

Kubey, R., & Csikszentmihalyi, M. (1990). *Television and the quality of life: How viewing shapes everyday experience.* Hillsdale, NJ: Lawrence Erlbaum.

Liebert, R. M., & Sprafkin, J. (1988). *The early window: Effects of television on children and youth* (3rd ed.). New York: Pergamon.

Masters, J. C., Ford, M. E., & Arend, R. A. (1983). Children's strategies for controlling affective responses to aversive social experience. *Motivation and Emotion, 7,* 103–116.

McCombs, M. E., & Shaw, D. L. (1972). The agenda-setting function of mass media. *Public Opinion Quarterly, 36,* 176–187.

McNeil, A. (1991). *Total television* (3rd ed.). New York: Penguin.

Metz, C. (1974). *Film language: A semiotics of the cinema.* M. Taylor (Trans.). New York: Oxford University Press.

Mulvey, L. (1975). Visual pleasure and narrative cinema. *Screen, 16* (3), 6–18.

Mulvey, L. (1989). Afterthoughts on "Visual pleasure and narrative cinema" inspired by King Vidor's *Duel in the Sun* (1946). In *Visual and other pleasures* (pp. 29–38). Bloomington, IN: Indiana University Press.

Real, M. R. (1996). *Exploring media culture: A guide.* Thousand Oaks, CA: Sage.

Silverman, L. T., & Sprafkin, J. N. (1980). The effects of *Sesame Street*'s prosocial spots on cooperative play between young children. *Journal of Broadcasting & Electronic Media, 24,* 135–147.

Super Bowl ads hitting $1.3 million. (1997, January 8). *Sacramento Bee,* pp. F-1, F-4.

Vande Berg, L. R. (1993). *China Beach,* Prime time war in the postfeminist age: An example of patriarchy in a different voice. *Western Journal of Communication, 57,* 349–366.

Vande Berg, L. R. (1995). Living room pilgrimages: Television's cyclical commemoration of the assassination anniversary of John F. Kennedy. *Communication Monographs, 62,* 47–64.

Williams, R. (1974). *Television: Technology and cultural form.* London: Fontana.

Williams, T. M. (Ed.). (1986). *The impact of television: A natural experiment in three communities.* New York: Academic Press.

Zehme, B. (1989, June 1). *thirtysomething:* The real-life angst and ecstasy behind TV's most serious series. *Rolling Stone,* 70–72, 75–76.

Zelizer, B. (1992). *Covering the body: The Kennedy assassination, the media, and the shaping of collective memory.* Chicago: University of Chicago Press.

Zillmann, D. (1982). Television viewing and arousal. In D. Pearl, L. Bouthilet, & J. Lazar (Eds.), *Television and behavior: Ten years of scientific progress and implications for the eighties: Vol. 2. Technical reviews* (pp. 53–67). Washington, DC: U.S. Government Printing Office.

Zillmann, D., & Bryant, J. (1985). *Selective exposure to communication.* Hillsdale, NJ: Lawrence Erlbaum.

The Nature of Television Criticism

> Shall we allow the children to hear any stories that chance to be told by anyone without distinction and to take into their souls teachings that are wholly opposite to those we wish them to be possessed of when they are grown up?
>
> —*The Republic*, Book II, 377B

Although the language is a bit stilted and formal, in any given week you could easily find this quotation or one very similar to it at the beginning of a *Time* or *Newsweek* article on concerns about what is being shown on television. However, these words were written by teacher/philosopher Plato some 2300 years ago.

In this quotation, Plato is expressing his concern about the functions of popular culture (in his case, drama) in society. This issue was a hot one between 429 B.C. and 386 B.C. Plato's contemporary, Aristophanes, wrote a play titled *The Frogs* that dealt with the same issue. In *The Frogs*, Aristophanes weighed the question of which of two "great" playwrights should be brought back from the dead. One candidate was the playwright Aeschylus, whose plays illustrated the view that art should present life as it ideally should be—through themes, actions, and subjects that morally uplifted audiences and instructed them in proper social and personal ethics: a view not unlike that represented in "wholesome" or "family" television series like *Touched by an Angel, Cosby,* or *Dr. Quinn: Medicine Woman.* The other candidate under consideration was Euripides. Euripides' plays illustrated the opposing view that art should present life realistically—through gritty depictions of crime, corruption, and immorality—life as it is on the streets: a view of popular art and culture that is illustrated in current television programs like *NYPD Blue, ER,* and *Homicide: Life on the Streets.*

Although Aristophanes eventually decided to bring Aeschylus and not Euripides back from the dead, the debate did not end there. Nearly 400 years later, in 65 B.C., Horace offered an alternative aesthetic standard; he argued that artistic works should both teach (i.e., be morally uplifting) and delight.

One recent example of this debate occurred during the 1992 presidential campaign. On May 19, 1992, shortly after the Los Angeles uprisings, Vice President Dan Quayle delivered a speech in San Francisco in which he blamed the uprisings on the collapse of traditional family values (especially among African Americans) and argued that the television series *Murphy Brown* had further contributed to their erosion: "It doesn't help matters when prime-time TV has Murphy Brown . . . mocking the importance of fathers by bearing a child alone and calling it 'just another lifestyle choice.' " The next day the *New York Times* carried the story (about the vice president of the United States attacking a television situation comedy that presented a single woman grappling with learning that she was pregnant and whether to have the child or an abortion) and a photograph on its front page. Included in the *New York Times* story was this response by Diane English, the creator and producer of *Murphy Brown*: "If the Vice President thinks it's disgraceful for an unmarried woman to bear a child, and if he believes that a woman cannot adequately raise a child without a father, then he'd better make sure abortion remains safe and legal" (see Fiske, 1994, pp. 21–23).

As this example illustrates, the argument about whether popular culture should present life realistically or idealistically, whether it should teach or delight or both, has continued to simmer in the centuries since Plato and Horace. In media studies this debate has come to be known as the mass society/popular culture debate. The brief historical overview of this debate in the next section provides you with a context for better understanding past eruptions of it as well as contemporary clashes—like that between Dan Quayle and Murphy Brown.

The Mass Society/Popular Culture Debate:
A Historical Overview

Concern about the potential impact of popular culture on ordinary citizens became particularly controversial in Western European societies as medieval religious and monarchical empires began to crumble. Until the beginning of the 19th century, the educated (reading) public consisted primarily of male

Angel Grove's Mighty Morphin' Power Rangers

In the mid-1990s the Power Rangers were the number one program with children in every time period in which this syndicated series appeared. In 1994 Power Rangers action figures and other merchandise sales topped $1 billion. In fact, when the Power Rangers made a personal appearance at Hollywood's Universal Studios, traffic was backed up for 10 miles on the Hollywood freeway as the cars of the 35,000 children and parents who attended the event arrived.

scholars, male clergy, and male members of the elite socioeconomic classes. As Gans (1974) succinctly summarizes:

> During the preindustrial era, European societies were divided culturally into high and folk culture. The latter was sparse, homemade, and, because peasants lived in isolated villages, largely invisible. The former was supported by the city-dwelling elites—the court, the nobility, the priesthood, and merchants—who had the time, education, and resources for entertainment and art and were able to subsidize a small number of creative people to produce culture for them. Both artists and in-

tellectuals were close to the sources of power and some shared the prestige and privileges of their employers and patrons. Because of the low social status and geographical isolation of folk culture, they also had a virtual monopoly on public and visible culture. (pp. 52–53)

Indeed, prior to the end of feudal Europe and the emergence of modern industrial societies, cultural contact between the elite classes and the masses was extremely limited; furthermore, there was no middle class of shopkeeper merchants, tradespeople, doctors, and lawyers to bridge the gap (see Lowenthal, 1959). However, with the death of feudalism, the demise of the all-powerful religious states, and the rise of industrialism came economical, political, and technological changes that forced peasants from the countryside into the cities. There, with newly found free time and some disposable income, these laborers joined other working-class consumers of popular culture.

Painters, sculptors, dramatists, composers, and writers were among the artists who lost their privileged standing as well as their source of support when the power and economic resources of their aristocratic patrons declined. These artists were forced to look elsewhere for audiences and patronage. What they found was the growing popular culture market made up of these newly urbanized peasants and the growing middle class. Many of these artists were themselves impoverished members of the aristocratic class; however, even those who weren't tended to think of themselves as artistic geniuses. As a result, they often did not share common social, political, or aesthetic interests or tastes with their new-found working audiences. For these artists, the loss of their courtly patronage and their subsequent need to rely on the popular (mass) market meant dependence on less-educated, lower-status audiences. "In this process the artists forgot the subordination and humiliation they had often suffered at the hands of their patrons . . . and had only contempt for the new publics on whom they depended for economic support, even though these offered artists greater rewards and more freedom than they had before" (Gans, 1974, p. 53).

One way the artists compensated for this loss of prestige was to develop the "cult of the artist as genius." This image, which later became romanticized (the artistic genius starving in his—rarely her—garret tower in order to remain faithful to his/her inner vision), provided artists and "high culture" with the prestige it lost when the aristocracy, and its leisure pastimes, declined (Gans, 1974; Lowenthal, 1959). Not surprisingly these artists' former patrons—the educated, sociocultural elites—also publicly decried these changes in their privileged world, and they also resurrected the form of the popular culture critique Plato had expressed. These social elites translated their loss of power, autonomy, and prestige into the view that society as a whole was deteriorating. Some dispossessed elites (social conservatives) argued that the general public would be corrupted by exposure to this popular art, for the public would become unwilling to accept its appropriately subordinate station in life. The elites saw popular culture as a potent force in advancing a social revolution that would result in their loss of control—not only over what was considered art, and good taste, but over economic, educational, and political institutions as well. In contrast, socialist critics feared that popular culture would have the opposite effect—that consuming popular culture products would numb an ordinary working person into becoming a complacent couch potato (i.e., would create a mass society of undifferentiated and indifferent blobs) and cause the demise of authentic folk culture.

The debate continued when sensationalized dime novels, affordable by the newly literate working classes and middle classes, appeared in England and in the United States from about 1860 to 1901. In fact, the popular culture/mass society debate flared up with renewed vigor with the introduction of new popular culture forms—movies and jazz—in the early decades of the 20th century. Both movies and jazz music were reviled by many social elite and educated classes as potential threats to public morality as well as to "real" art.

Conservative, liberal, and radical groups all have charged that forms of popular culture—including film, popular musical genres, and television—would have the direst social and cultural consequences (see Real, 1976). Among the most outspoken participants in the mass society/popular culture debate that seethed from the 1930s through the 1950s were Dwight Macdonald, Edward Shils, and C. Wright Mills (Carey & Kreiling, 1974; Himmelstein, 1981). Macdonald (1957) argued that popular culture was a blight on the aesthetic landscape that debased high art, and Mills (1956) argued that the media are tools through which the power elite manipulate the masses and destroy democratic community life.

Underlying Mills's critique of popular culture is the belief that the mass media have contributed to the decline of the *gemeinschaft* society—that is, the type of society in which social bonds between people are based on tradition, friendship, reciprocal sentiments, kinship, and geographic proximity. He argued that the media have fostered instead a *gesellschaft* society—a society in which people relate to others impersonally and anonymously through social bonds based on buyer–seller contract types of relationships (Tönnies, 1957). In other words, Mills and other popular culture critics who share this view believe that the mass media are helping to turn "the public" into a "mass"—a collection of geographically and psychologically isolated individuals whose anonymity, lack of interaction with each other, and lack of shared involvement in community organizations leaves them relatively free from informal, binding social obligations and turns them into a mass that can be far more easily manipulated because there are fewer interpersonal social checks and balances (Lowenthal, 1959).

Like Euripides, other writers, scholars, and critics have defended popular cultural forms, including television and film. For example, Edward Shils (1960) argued that popular culture had not debased people's taste or exploited aesthetic reception any more than "brutal culture." In fact, Shils claimed that the term *mass culture* itself was problematic "because it refers simultaneously to the substantive and qualitative properties of the culture, to the social status of its consumers, and to the media by which it is transmitted . . . [and] begs the important questions [of] whether the mass media can transmit works of superior culture. . . . Also, it does not consider the obvious fact that much of what is produced in the genres of superior culture is extremely mediocre in quality." (p. 291)

Television and the Mass Society/Popular Culture Debate

Although some of the vocabulary and terms used to critique and defend popular culture have changed, these same concerns have been—and still are—raised about television. Some critics argue that not only has television turned viewers—especially watchers of a lot of television—into passive couch potatoes, it also has cultivated in them attitudes of "learned helplessness" (Levine, 1977). These opponents of popular culture assert, for example, that as a result of the view that they can do nothing to change the way things are, many television viewers have substituted watching politics on television for active civic participation, including voting.

Still other critics have used the work of communication scholar George Gerbner and his colleagues to argue that television is contributing to the deterioration of the quality of our social life because heavy television viewing "cultivates" the view that the world is a mean and scary place. These critics fear that viewers who watch the nonstop parade of crime, corruption, and danger in television dramas and news eventually become afraid to venture out, afraid to interact with fellow citizens, and afraid to help others in distress (Gerbner, Gross, Morgan, & Signorielli, 1986). Indeed, these critics of television as a form of popular culture point to the 1964 Kitty Genovese case as a classic example of television's cultivation of learned helplessness and the mean-world syndrome because several dozen people at home, many watching TV, heard her scream when she was attacked and stabbed repeatedly as she walked down a city street. No one was willing to open his or her apartment door to respond to Ms. Genovese's cries for help. Ultimately she died, and people interviewed later explained that they were afraid to get involved.

Defenders of popular culture, on the other hand, argue that mass-mediated popular culture forms like television have far more benefits than deficiencies. For example, Marshall McLuhan, a well-known 20th-century defender of mass-mediated forms of popular culture, predicted (in his 1964 book *Understanding Media*) that rather than destroying our sense of community, the mass media would retribalize the world. McLuhan argued that the mass media would create less insular, less xenophobic societies—in fact, a global village through which we could achieve instantaneous visual and verbal communication with fellow humans across the hemispheres.

Another contemporary defender of television as popular culture, Walter Karp, urges us not to worry about violence in television cartoons. Karp (1987) argues that sanitizing the violence out of cartoons would be a serious disservice to children. Following G. K. Chesterton and child psychologist Bruno Bettelheim (1976), Karp maintains that children's television cartoons should tell scary stories about lonely but eventually triumphant heroes because the characters' "isolation mirrors the isolation every child feels in the face of his real terrors" and their "ultimate triumph provides the heartswelling promise that the child, too, will find inner strength" from the belief that "monsters can be slain, injustice remedied, and all obstacles overcome on the hard road to adulthood" (pp. 437, 438). In short, Karp argues that television viewing of violent cartoons, like reading violent fairy tales, can be therapeutic for children. These defenders of television point out that although only very limited social-scientific support has been found for the catharsis theory (Gunter, 1994), neither has social science been able to pinpoint just which social problems television alone (or even primarily) is responsible for (see, for example, the five-volume report of the Surgeon General's Scientific Advisory Committee on Television and Social Behavior, 1972).

A second critique of television as a contemporary popular culture form is that television texts are produced by a group of individuals and not by a single artist expressing her or his unique creative vision within an established aesthetic tradition. This criticism, based on the traditionally literary romantic "cult of the artist as hero," looks down on television texts because they lack the individuality of art produced by a single artist. These critics claim that popular art forms, like television, debase "real art" because they substitute commercialized, standardized, assembly-line products that reduce audience members to mere consumers for individualized expressions of artistic vision.

This critique implies a comparison and contrast among four different types of art. *Popular art* is defined as works that combine familiar conventional forms expressive of common cultural experiences with creative originality and individual stylization. Examples of popular art include William Shakespeare's plays (in his day, of course; today, they are considered "elite art"), the Beatles' music, and Steven Bochco's television police/law series like *Hill Street Blues, NYPD Blue,* and *Murder One.*

Mass art, like popular art and much of elite art, is commercially distributed. However, these standardized forms are hybrids that lack the complex individualism typical of elite art, the shared traditions of folk art, or the unique mixture of these qualities that popular art has. Examples of mass art include the Kathy Lee Gifford holiday TV specials and collectible Elvis Presley plates such as those advertised in *TV Guide.* Mass art is created solely as a money-making venture designed to please the average taste preferences of the mass market. As Raymond Williams explains, in contrast to elite, folk, and popular culture that are created "by a people," mass culture is created "for a people by an internal or external social group and embedded in them by a range of processes from repressive imposition to commercial saturation" (1974, p. 15).

Folk art includes individually performed or created but technically and thematically unsophisticated works produced as variations on common grass roots or local traditions that the artist and audience share. The music of Joan Baez and Peter, Paul, and Mary and quilts hand sewn by individuals not employed by a corporation are examples of folk art.

In contrast, *elite art* consists of those unique thematically and technically complex creative forms produced by an identifiable artist in accordance with (or in opposition to) an accepted canon of works and within a conscious aesthetic context (Real, 1976). Examples of elite art include the music of Mozart, the paintings of Edward Hopper, the novels of James Joyce, the movies of François Truffaut and Jean Renoir, and such television productions as the BBC's *I, Claudius*. Given these definitions, you should not find it surprising that all but elite art are regarded as artistically deficient by critics of popular culture.

On the other hand, however, are defenders of popular culture or popular art (including television). In defense of collective art forms like television and film (which require a group or collective effort to create), these critics point out that to reject artistic creations merely because they are created by a group rather than a lone individual artist is an elitist prejudice. They point out that such a snobbish view is not compatible with the democratic notion of respect for the plurality of ideas, tastes, and traditions. Indeed, these defenders of televised popular culture point out that although Steven Bochco did not single-handedly create and complete *Hill Street Blues,* neither did Michelangelo single-handedly paint the ceiling of the Sistine Chapel. Both had helpers (see Gans, 1974). Further, these defenders also remind popular culture detractors that the same shared values and ties that bind both elite and folk artists to their publics can also join popular culture creators and their audiences (see, for example, Heide's [1995] ethnographic study of *thirtysomething* viewers).

Opposers of popular culture counter this contention with the claim that pop culture (like television and rock music) steals artists and ideas away from high culture. As a result of this talent and idea drain, high art (the individualized expressions of novelists, painters, etc.) loses potential creators to formulaic productions, and terminally derivative popular culture flourishes. In support of this argument the critics bemoan the fact that a number of well-known literary figures were lured into writing original teleplays for the well-paying television medium (rather than novels or Broadway plays). These popular culture detractors point to John Cheever (*The Shady Hill Kidnapping*) and Paddy Chayefsky (*Marty*) whose time spent writing (and also acting and directing) for television meant less time for their work in "serious" art forms like the novel and the theater. Defenders of popular culture, however, point out that it was not until the Renaissance that originality of subject matter, form, and technique became the aesthetic standard. Prior to that period, imitation of classical models with only minor innovations was the dominant aesthetic standard. Furthermore, when defenders of popular culture feel particularly feisty about the social class distinction implied in this critique, they sarcastically point out that a number of high art forms also are *highly* conventionalized (sometimes they go so far as to say "derivative")—for example, the sonnet and haiku.

Another defense offered by supporters of television culture is that aesthetic standards (what is regarded as artistically good) change over time. They point out, for instance, that in his era Shakespeare's plays were considered popular entertainment, not high art. Shakespeare wrote for a broad popular audience, not merely the aristocratic classes (Craig, 1961). Similarly, these supporters point out that, like television soaps and series, Charles Dickens's serialized novels (now studied as classics in literature classes) and Jane Austen's "feminine" novels of manners once were looked down upon by literary doyens. These defenders of popular culture also point out that the only reason high-art snobs have access to elite art works such as John Donne's "The Canonization," or Edmund Spenser's "Epithalamion" is because these poems have been reprinted in *mass-produced* and *mass-distributed* books by relatively anonymous publishers for a large, geographically dispersed, and heterogeneous audience.

Finally, defenders of mass-mediated culture argue that distinctions between elite art, folk art, popular art, and mass art are problematic because essentially they are merely pretexts for social class distinctions. Sociologist Herbert Gans (1974) effectively summarizes the ideological issues underlying the mass society/popular culture debate:

> The so-called mass culture critique is important because it is concerned with far more than media fare and consumer goods. It is really about the nature of the good life, and thus about the purpose of life in general, particularly outside the work role. It is also about which culture and whose culture should dominate in society, and represent it as the societal or national culture in the competition between contemporary societies and in the historical record of cultures or civilizations. As such, the mass culture critique is an attack by one element in society against another: by the cultured against the uncultured, the educated against the uneducated, the sophisticated against the unsophisticated, the more affluent against the less affluent, and the cultural experts against the laity. In each case, the former criticize the latter for not living up to their own standard of the good life. (pp. 3–4)

Cultural forms (like paintings, television programs, films, novels) don't just appear; they grow out of the values and aesthetic standards of a society. As Gans (1974) explains, in homogeneous societies where there is little diversity, there is often only a single standard of beauty, style of art, and so on. In heterogeneous Western societies, however, there are a number of aesthetic standards, or what Gans calls different "taste cultures": people do not all agree on a single view of what is pleasurable, desirable, and beautiful. Furthermore, not everyone is content to accept that other people's aesthetic tastes are as valid as his or her own. Typically those who wish to impose their values—including aesthetic values—on everyone else are those with the greatest economic, social, and political power. Thus, "although most taste cultures are not explicitly political, all cultural content expresses values that can become political or have political consequences" (Gans, 1974, p. 103).

As Gans's quotation points out, many critics of mass and popular culture are members of the upper socioeconomic classes who value elite culture (sometimes called "high" to indicate the view that they are better) because the education and/or wealth generally needed to have access to elite culture and an appreciation for "high art" historically has been available to a relatively small, select subset of the society. Thus, for these critics, the limited access to elite cultural works or possession (in the case of paintings, for example) of elite art is a reflection and affirmation of the socioeconomic and cultural status and power of these elites.

Television and Other Cultural Forms

Defenses of popular culture do not ignore that there are differences among forms of popular culture as a result of their different mediums of expression (the printed page, film, television, live theater, etc.). Television programs, for example, are far more ephemeral than are novels or even films. Indeed, even with three of four U.S. homes possessing videocassette recorders (see *Broadcasting Yearbook,* 1990), most first-run television episodes air only twice during a year—unlike newly released films that have multiple daily screenings or books of which multiple copies usually can be accessed at any time. So, if you happen to miss an episode of a television series or if your VCR malfunctions, you may not be able to see that episode for a long, long while—unless a friend happened to tape it. Although libraries house copies of books, and most films are available on videotape or in archives, there are no comparable repositories of old television programs. Even the Museum of Broadcasting in New York City has only selected episodes of selected series.

Another difference between television and film is that television programs are most typically viewed in the home and in a fragmented, distracted way. According to Kubey and Csikszentmihalyi (1990), about two-thirds of the time when we are watching television, we are also engaged in other activities—work, housework, eating, talking, reading, caring for children, doing schoolwork, needlework, or hobbies. Additionally, LoSciuto (1972) found that two-thirds of the time we view television in the presence of at least one other person, who may periodically enter and leave the room, talk with us, and engage in other activities. This observation led him to conclude that "most television viewing is a rather chaotic and discontinuous phenomenon, highly influenced by whoever happens to be in the room" (p. 59).

In contrast to the typically inattentive and distracted nature of television viewing, when we speak of viewing films, we are referring to going to a film theater. There we sit in a quiet, dark room with others who are doing what we are doing—concentrating on the images being projected from behind our heads onto the large screen in front of us. Film viewing, then, is characterized by a continuous, focused engagement with the large, loud, vivid audiovisual narrative playing on the screen. Indeed, this analogy between film viewing and dreaming has led many film theorists and critics to use psychoanalytic theories to explain our relationship with films.

In spite of the differences between the ways we experience films and television, however, Peter Wood (1976) argues that television may be a reflection of the fantasies—"the collective dream life of society as a whole." Wood suggests that television is like dreams in that each "is highly visual . . . highly symbolic . . . involves a high degree of wish-fulfillment . . . appears to contain much that is disjointed and trivial . . . has an enormous and powerful content which is quickly forgotten . . . and makes both overt and covert use of material from our recent experiences" (pp. 19, 21–23). If this is so, he argues, the content of our collective dreams certainly deserves serious critical analysis by television critics.

The Emergence of Television Criticism

Television initially received little or no critical attention by critics in the popular press—in part because television was viewed (by newspaper owners) as competing with newspapers for the public's attention (and advertising dollar). Indeed, from the 1950s through the present, trade publications like *Broadcasting* or *Variety* have chronicled television's industrial, production, or regulatory news, but most newspaper writers assigned to the television beat—unlike those writers assigned to review books, art exhibitions, and theatrical productions—have not treated television "texts" with the same serious attention that other cultural texts have received (Himmelstein, 1981).

Among the journalistic writers and critics who did give serious critical attention to television as an important social and aesthetic force, and who provided thoughtful critical commentary on television texts, were Laurence Laurent, John J. O'Connor of the *New York Times,* and Michael Arlen of *The New Yorker.* More recently, this list has included Pulitzer prize-winning media critics Tom Shales of *The Washington Post* and Howard Rosenberg of the *Los Angeles Times,* as well as David Zurawick of the *Baltimore Sun,* Thomas Feran of the Cleveland *Plain Dealer,* and David Bianculli of the New York *Daily News.*

In fact, until the mid-1970s little serious critical analysis of television could be found in either popular periodicals or scholarly journals and books. David Thorburn (1985), for example, reminds those of us a little too young to

The "Cheers" bar, where "Everybody Knows Your Name"

The humor and camaraderie evident here are two of the strategies through which Cheers *naturalizes beer drinking, as Hundley's Chapter 9 essay explains.*   (Fotos International/Archive Photos.)

remember, that in the 1950s academics hid the fact that they watched television from their colleagues for fear they would be ridiculed.

Television acquired some measure of respectability, however, with Marshall McLuhan. McLuhan was a brilliant, outrageous popular culture and media studies scholar from Canada. When he was given a prestigious University chair and a six-figure salary (which was even more money 25 years ago than it is today) for his books on popular culture, popular culture studies, and television studies in particular, acquired a new legitimacy and respectability. Shortly thereafter, American studies scholars and literary critics from prestigious universities, such as John Cawelti (1971, 1976) at the University of Chicago, began to write seriously about popular film and television. And when the popular literature division of the national scholarly English literature association, the Modern Language Association, began publishing the *Journal of Popular Culture* in 1967, popular culture (and television) criticism had become almost academically respectable (Gronbeck, 1986, p. 335).

A few years later, America's first serious academic critic to focus on television, Horace Newcomb, published his book-length genre study, *TV: The Most Popular Art* (1974). The 1976 publication of his first anthology of critical essays on television, *TV: The Critical View,* provided a scholarly foundation for the newly emergent area of television criticism. This attention to television by serious scholars in the mid-1970s coincided with what Newcomb (1986) has termed *television's renaissance*. This period included Larry Gelbart and Gene Reynold's *M*A*S*H*, MTM's[1] *The Mary Tyler Moore Show*, Norman Lear's *All in the Family* and *Maude*, and Garry Marshall's *Happy Days*. As Newcomb put it, "for richness and complexity, challenge and delight" these popular culture texts were definitely worth taking seriously and writing critically about (1986, p. 220).

Soon other American scholars also began writing serious television criticism. Two influential edited collections, Adler and Cater's (1976) *Television as a Cultural Force* and Cater and Adler's (1975) *Television as a Social Force*, reprinted television criticism papers that had been presented at conferences on television studies sponsored by the Aspen Institute for Humanistic Studies. Michael Real introduced American scholarly television critics to cultural studies when he published *Mass-mediated Culture* (1976), and noted rhetorical critic Bruce Gronbeck turned his attention from parliamentary rhetoric to the criticism of television (1978, 1979, 1984). As a result, an increasing number of communication studies departments in U.S. universities began offering courses at the undergraduate and graduate level in television criticism.

Also in 1978, a group of young journalistic critics, university trained in television and film criticism and concerned about the quality of television programming, created the Television Critics Association. Today the association publishes a bimonthly *TCA Newsletter* that includes interviews with writers, producers, directors, and network and cable executives, as well as samples of members' critical columns. It holds semiannual meetings and panels during the members' twice-yearly junkets to Universal City to view the next season's lineups offered by the networks, public television, and independent production companies.

Scholarly conferences such as the Television Drama Conferences at Michigan State University in the early 1980s, the 1984 University of Iowa Television Criticism Symposium (organized by Bruce Gronbeck), the Visual Communication Conferences (brainchild of Robert Tiemans of the University of Utah and Herb Zettl of San Francisco State University), and the feminist Consoleing Passions conferences all have contributed to the development and legitimization of television criticism as a significant area of study.

British and Australian Popular Culture, Media, and Television Criticism

Meanwhile, a different type of serious analysis of popular culture was developing in Great Britain. Beginning in the 1960s in Great Britain, an approach to the analysis of popular culture that blended several strands of critical and social theory emerged in the writings of Raymond Williams, Stuart Hall, and John Thompson. British Cultural Studies, as this approach came to be called, crossed the Atlantic in the early 1970s and further stimulated the fledgling

American television criticism studies. Especially influential for the evolution of U.S. television criticism was a work by two of the second generation of British Cultural Studies scholars, John Fiske and John Hartley—*Reading Television* (1978).

Arguably, the publication of John Fiske's *Television Culture* in 1987 truly marked television criticism's coming of age. Like Fiske and Hartley's (1978) and Gronbeck's (1984) earlier works, Fiske's *Television Culture* begins with the assumption that television is a subject worthy of serious critical study. Unlike contemporary antitelevision, antipopular culture critics such as Neil Postman, however, Fiske argues that television is "so popular, that is, capable of offering such a variety of pleasures to such a heterogeneity of viewers, because the characteristics of its texts and of its modes of reception enable an active participation in that sense-making process which we call 'culture' " (Fiske, 1987, p. 19). Fiske's (1987) textual study of television combined the study of codes (a rule-governed system of signs, or symbols, which convey meaning), discourses (systems of representation that convey shared meanings about topics), and audiences (socially situated readers of television texts who actively negotiate the meanings encoded into television texts). He argued that a far more useful understanding of why television and popular culture are so popular (and important to study) is produced when we think of television texts as "provokers of meaning and pleasure" rather than as makers of meaning (i.e., transmitters of transparent meanings).

Fiske's book began a new era of television criticism by elegantly incorporating multiple approaches (neo-Marxist/ideological, semiotic/structural, feminist, psychoanalytic, screen theory, auteur, institutional, and audience ethnographies) into studies of gender, class, and race in media. His recent book, *Media Matters* (1994), has extended these concerns even further and reconnected television criticism and social criticism.

Now that you realize how exciting (and respected) television criticism has become, it's time to talk about what exactly (television) criticism is and what it is not.

What Criticism Is

Criticism involves organizing; systematically and thoroughly describing, analyzing, and interpreting; and evaluating the patterned relationships among symbols in order to share an informed perspective with others. All criticism has three absolutely necessary components: (1) a thesis statement that expresses the central, overarching interpretation, critical insight, or evaluation the rest of the criticism essay expands on; (2) the development of that thesis or interpretive proposition through logical arguments; and (3) concrete and specific supporting evidence (including examples from television programs;

dialogue, plot and scene descriptions, and other details from specific episodes; quotations from other critical analyses or theoretical articles that define critical concepts and/or illustrate their application to other television texts; testimony from expert and authoritative sources; etc.). Without any one of these, an essay is not criticism.

As Wander and Jenkins (1972) aptly put it, "Criticism, at its best, is informed talk about matters of importance" (p. 450). This definition of television criticism contains several implicit assumptions. The first and most basic assumption is that television is a popular art form that is potentially just as socioculturally and aesthetically meaningful and important as works of literature, theater, painting, music, and the other popular and fine arts, and therefore, it is just as deserving of serious, critical analysis as they are. Second, this definition assumes that television criticism, like criticism generally, is *epistemic*. By this we mean that the acts of reading and writing critical analyses of television generate knowledge and understanding of what television texts are, what meanings television texts provoke, and the nature of the relationships among television, society, and ourselves. As Sonja Foss (1989) explains, "The notion that reality is created through critical discourse means that reality is not fixed. It changes according to the symbols we use to talk about it. What we count as 'real' or 'knowledge' about the world depends on how we choose to label and talk about things" (p. 4).

Critics use a variety of tools, called *methods* or *approaches,* to talk about and analyze television. Critical methods (or approaches) are simply sets of technical vocabularies, analytical constructs, and normative assumptions that allow critics to organize their observations and communicate their insights and interpretations systematically and efficiently. As Gronbeck (1980) points out, critical methods are really shared codes that critics and their readers have learned to understand and use. However, no matter what method (e.g., genre criticism, feminist criticism) or critical construct (e.g., discourse, cultural values, neocolonialism) the critic uses to develop and explain his or her interpretation, all critical essays must have the three absolutely necessary components listed above.

Television critics do write differently as they address one of three audiences: (1) the academic audience of students, television and communication scholars, and other academics; (2) the television-industry audience, composed of writers, directors, producers, and program decision makers; and (3) the general public. The principal differences in the criticism written for these audiences is in the amount of supporting argumentation, the nature and amount of supporting evidence cited, and the extent to which the method and theoretical assumptions that the critic used to arrive at the critical interpretation are explicitly laid out for the reader. The essays in this book were written for the academic audience of students like you, television and communication scholars, and other academics.

What Criticism Is Not

It should be clear from the preceding discussion that television criticism is *not* everyday, unsupported opinions—whether by ordinary viewers, paid journalists, Hollywood executives, or university students and professors. It should also be clear that criticism is not necessarily negative; criticism can be appreciative as well as depreciative, systematic, close analysis.

Criticism also is not history. Although a critical essay may trace the evolution of a genre of television programming or map the relationships among the medium of television, programs airing during a particular era, regulatory policies, and societal events, television critics write such essays for different reasons than historians do. In contrast to the historian, who focuses on questions of what and why, the critic is more concerned with how and what does it mean. As Gronbeck (1980) put it, the critic "is more concerned with generating than finding meaningfulness" (p. 13). Criticism, then, is concerned with providing insightful interpretations that stimulate viewers to look at a television program (or text) in a new and different way.

Critics do sometimes count things (see, for example, Porter, 1987); however, criticism is *not* social-scientific hypothesis testing. Unlike the social scientist, whose larger interest is in making predictions about how things work in order to control them, the critic's primary interest is in post hoc explanations of meaning construction. That is, the critic's goal is to better understand television texts as meaningful sociocultural, symbolic forms and forces.

Finally, criticism is not theory. A well-written critical analysis can and often does move beyond interpreting the particular program/text, event, or experience to make a contribution to our general theoretical understanding about the processes of meaning production and audience reception at work in television programs. However, the *primary goals* of criticism are understanding, explanation, and appreciation. They are not theory building. Thus, although critical essays often advance critical television theory, criticism is not constructed or delivered as a theoretical treatise.

Standards for Evaluating Serious Television Criticism Essays

Understanding what television criticism is (and what it is not) helps us identify appropriate (and inappropriate) standards to use in evaluating the merits of television criticism essays. For example, since television criticism is not social-scientific research, the social science standards of validity, reliability, and significance—whether a main effect at the specified level of statistical significance was found—are *not* appropriate standards for evaluating the merits of a serious television criticism essay. Similarly, since criticism is systematic, informed analysis and not unsupported personal diatribes, the personal bias standard (i.e., do the central critical proposition and the writing seem right or wrong according to my individual biases as a reader) is *not* an appropriate standard.

Four Criteria for Evaluating Television Criticism Essays

The appropriate standard for evaluating the merits of television criticism essays (or any other type of critical argument) should be the thoroughness with which the critique meets the following criteria:

1. Does it possess internal consistency?
2. Does it provide sufficient, appropriate evidence for the claims implied by the thesis and advanced in the essay?
3. Does it offer a plausible rationale for its cultural, critical, theoretical, or practical significance?
4. Does it cause an astute reader to accept the critical interpretation or explanation argued for in the essay as a *reasonable* one?

Let's talk about each of the four criteria that make up our evaluative standard.

Internal Consistency. Internal consistency refers to the goodness of fit among the central critical proposition (the critical interpretation or thesis that the rest of the essay develops and supports), the arguments, the evidence used to support the arguments, and the general conclusions or implications the critic draws from the results of her/his analysis. All of these elements of the critical essay must follow logically from the essay's thesis or central interpretation—whether this is in the form of a question or an assertion.

Evidence.   The criterion of ample, appropriate evidence is one of the important differences between criticism and everyday opinion. A critic must provide sufficient evidentiary support so that a reasonable reader can judge the plausibility of the critic's interpretation. Of course, there is no magic yardstick for deciding if the amount of evidence is sufficient to make the critic's argument plausible. However, the assumption is that the evidence provided is sufficient if you think it would convince an open-minded but demanding critical reader that this interpretation of the television text(s) is one a reasonable, educated person could arrive at.

Significance.   The cultural, critical, theoretical, or practical significance criterion requires that the critic explain to the reader why the time the critic spent to research, analyze, and write this particular critical essay was worthwhile. This criterion also requires the critic to provide a rationale, to explain why a reader would be well served by reading the results of the critic's analysis.

Reasonableness.   The final criterion is a statement about the nature and degree of persuasion that must be accomplished by the critical analysis. Notice that this criterion is not "The Truth" or "The Right Explanation," but merely that a critical analysis must provide one insightful interpretation arrived at by systematic, reasoned analysis. Criticism is systematic, but it is subjective, not objective.[2] The critic *is* the analytical instrument; critical theories and methods are just tools, as we noted earlier.

The reader does not have to be persuaded that an essay provides the definitive explanation or interpretation of a television text (or group of texts). Criticism assumes that there are multiple interpretations, or readings, of each television program. The reader also doesn't have to be persuaded to arrive at moral, aesthetic, or political agreement with the critic's beliefs and perspective. However, each critical essay does have to persuade a reader who approaches it with an open mind that the critic's interpretation is plausible, is sufficiently well supported, and is concerned with a socially, critically, aesthetically, or theoretically important issue, construct, or text. Essays that meet these standards are indeed good criticism.

Looking Ahead

In this chapter we looked briefly at the historical debate about popular culture and the development of television criticism. We also discussed a working definition of what television criticism is and what it is not. In Chapter 3 we discuss some of the ways in which television criticism can be classified, some of the problems critics face in choosing a critical approach, and how to get started writing your first television criticism essay. Then in Chapter 4 we provide a model or outline of what an ideal television criticism essay might look like—what its parts are and how it is organized—recognizing that models are general blueprints, not rigid molds.

NOTES

1. MTM is the acronym for the Mary Tyler Moore Company, an independent Hollywood production company established in 1970 to produce programs on commission for the network systems. It was started by Mary Tyler Moore, her manager Arthur Price, and her then-husband Grant Tinker (who left MTM in 1981 to become CEO and Chair of the board of NBC). MTM was (and still is) known in television and academic circles for its "quality television" series and the "quality audiences" its programs attracted (see Feuer, Kerr, & Vahimagi, 1984). Among the many illustrious writer/producer alumni who did apprenticeships at the MTM sitcom and drama academy before going off on their own were James Burrows and Glen and Les Charles (from MTM's *Mary Tyler Moore Show, Phyllis,* and *The Bob Newhart Show,* to *Taxi* and *Cheers*), Gary David Goldberg (from MTM's *Tony Randall Show* and *Lou Grant* to his *Family Ties, Brooklyn Bridge,* and *Spin City*), and Steven Bochco (from

MTM's *White Shadow, Paris,* and *Hill Street Blues* to his *L.A. Law, Hooperman, Doogie Howser, M.D., NYPD Blue,* and *Murder One*).

2. Indeed, as Tuchman (1978) and others have noted, objectivity is really just a strategic ritual for performing certain tasks efficiently and with a minimal number of challenges.

REFERENCES

Adler, R., (Ed.). (1976). *Television as a cultural force.* Aspen series on communications and society. New York: Praeger.

Aristophanes (1962). *The frogs.* (R. Lattimore Trans.). Ann Arbor: University of Michigan Press. (Original work circa 450–385 B.C.)

Arlen, M. J. (1977, November 23). The prosecutor. *The New Yorker,* 166–173.

Bettelheim, B. (1976). *The uses of enchantment: The meaning and importance of fairy tales.*

Broadcasting Yearbook, 1990. (1990). Washington, DC: Broadcasting Publishing Co.

Carey, J., & Kreiling, A. (1974). Popular culture and uses and gratifications: Notes toward an accommodation. In J. G. Blumler & E. Katz (Eds.), *The uses of mass communication: Current perspectives on gratifications research* (pp. 225–248). Beverly Hills, CA: Sage.

Cater, D., & Adler, R. (Eds.). (1975). *Television as a social force: New approaches to criticism.* New York: Praeger. (Published with the Aspen Institute Program on Communications and Society).

Cawelti, J. G. (1971). *The six-gun mystique.* Bowling Green, OH: Bowling Green University Popular Press.

Cawelti, J. G. (1976). *Adventure, mystery, romance: Formula stories as art and popular culture.* Chicago: University of Chicago Press.

Craig, H. (Ed.). (1961). *The complete works of Shakespeare.* Glenview, IL: Scott, Foresman.

Feuer, J., Kerr, P., & Vahimagi, T. (1984). *MTM "quality" television.* London: British Film Institute.

Fiske, J. (1987). *Television culture.* London/New York: Methuen.

Fiske, J. (1994). *Media matters: Everyday culture and political change.* Minneapolis: University of Minnesota Press.

Fiske, J., & Hartley, J. (1978). *Reading television.* London/New York: Methuen.

Foss, S. (1989). *Rhetorical criticism: Exploration and practice.* Prospect Heights, IL: Waveland.

Gans, H. (1974). *Popular culture and high culture: An analysis and evaluation of taste.* New York: Basic Books.

Gerbner, G., Gross, L., Morgan, M., & Signorielli, N. (1986). Living with television: The dynamics of the cultivation process. In J. Bryant & D. Zillmann (Eds.), *Perspectives on media effects* (pp. 17–40). Hillsdale, NJ: Lawrence Erlbaum.

Gronbeck, B. E. (1978). Celluloid rhetoric: On genres of documentary. In K. K. Campbell & K. M. Jamison (Eds.), *Form and genre: Shaping rhetorical action* (pp. 139–162). Falls Church, VA: Speech Communication Association.

Gronbeck, B. E. (1979). Television criticism and the classroom. *Journal of the Illinois Speech-Theatre Association, 33,* 1–12.

Gronbeck, B. E. (1980, November). *Meaning and epistemic claims in criticism.* Paper presented at the annual meeting of the Speech Communication Association, New York, NY.

Gronbeck, B. E. (1984). *Writing television criticism.* (Modules in mass communication series). Chicago, Science Research Associates.

Gronbeck, B. E. (1986). The academic practice of television criticism. *Quarterly Journal of Speech, 74,* 334–347.

Gunter, B. (1994). The question of media violence. In J. Bryant & D. Zillmann (Eds.), *Media effects: Advances in theory and research* (pp. 163–212). Hillsdale, NJ: Lawrence Erlbaum.

Heide, M. J. (1995). *Television culture and women's lives: thirtysomething and the contradictions of gender.* Philadelphia: University of Pennsylvania Press.

Himmelstein, H. (1981). *On the small screen: New approaches in television and video criticism.* New York: Praeger.

Horace. (1919-1974/65-8 B.C.). Ars poetica (N. DeWitt, Trans.). In A. Preminger, O. B. Hardinson, Jr., & K. Kerrane (Eds.), *Classical and medieval literary criticism* (pp. 158–170). New York: Frederick Ungar.

Karp, W. (1987). Where the do-gooders went wrong. In H. Newcomb (Ed.), *Television: The critical view* (4th ed., pp. 433–444). New York: Oxford University Press. (Reprinted from *Channels,* vol. 10, March/April 1984).

Kubey, R., & Csikszentmihalyi, M. (1990). *Television and the quality of life: How viewing shapes everyday experience.* Hillsdale, NJ: Lawrence Erlbaum.

Levine, G. F. (1977). "Learned helplessness" and the evening news. *Journal of Communication, 27* (4), 100–105.

LoSciuto, L. A. (1972). A national inventory on television viewing behavior. In *Television and Social Behavior* (pp. 33–86). Washington, DC: U.S. Government Printing Office.

Lowenthal, L. (1959). A historical preface to the popular culture debate. In N. Jacobs (Ed.), *Culture for the millions? Mass media in modern society* (pp. 28–42). Boston: Beacon Press.

Macdonald, D. (1957). A theory of mass culture. In B. Rosenberg & D. M. White (Eds.), *Mass culture: The popular arts in America* (pp. 59–73). Glencoe, IL: Free Press.

McLuhan, M. (1964). *Understanding media.* London: Routledge & Kegan Paul.

Mills, C. W. (1956). *The power elite.* New York: Oxford University Press.

Newcomb, H. (1974). *TV: The most popular art.* Garden City, NY: Doubleday.

Newcomb, H. (Ed.). (1976). *Television: The critical view.* New York: Oxford University Press.

Newcomb, H. (Ed.). (1979). *Television: The critical view* (2nd ed.). New York: Oxford University Press.

Newcomb, H. (Ed.). (1982). *Television: The critical view* (3rd ed.). New York: Oxford University Press.

Newcomb, H. (1986). American television criticism 1970–1985. *Critical Studies in Mass Communication, 3,* 217–228.

Newcomb, H. (Ed.). (1987). *Television: The critical view* (4th ed.). New York: Oxford University Press.

Newcomb, H. (Ed.). (1994). *Television: The critical view* (5th ed.). New York: Oxford University Press.

Plato. (1962). *The republic, Book II.* In A. Gilbert (Ed. & Trans.), *Literary criticism: Plato to Dryden.* Detroit: Wayne State University Press. (Original work circa 429–347 B.C.).

Porter, M. J. (1987). A comparative analysis of directing styles in *Hill Street Blues. Journal of Broadcasting & Electronic Media, 31,* 323–334.

Real, M. R. (1976). *Mass-mediated culture.* Englewood Cliffs, NJ: Prentice-Hall.

Shils, E. (1960). Mass society and its culture. *Daedalus, 89,* 228–314.

Thompson, R. J., & Marc, D. (1992). *Prime time, prime movers.* Boston: Little, Brown.

Thorburn, D. (1985, April). *An aesthetic approach to television criticism.* Paper presented at the University of Iowa Symposium and Conference on Television Criticism, Iowa City, Iowa.

Tönnies, F. (1957). *Gemeinschaft und gesellschaft* (Trans. by C. P. Loomis as *Community and Society*). East Lansing: Michigan State University Press. (Original work published in 1887.)

Tuchman, G. (1978). *Making news: A study in the construction of reality.* New York: Free Press.

U.S. Surgeon General's Scientific Advisory Report on Television and Social Behavior. (1972). Washington, DC: U.S. Government Printing Office.

Vande Berg, L. R. (1989). Dramedy: *Moonlighting* as an emergent generic hybrid. *Communication Studies, 40,* 13–28.

Vande Berg, L. R., & Wenner, L. A. (Eds.). (1991). *Television criticism: Approaches and applications.* White Plains, NY: Longman.

Wander, P., & Jenkins, S. (1972). Rhetoric, society, and the critical response. *Quarterly Journal of Speech, 58,* 441–450.

Williams, R. (1974, November 23). On high and popular culture. *The New Republic,* 15.

Wood, P. (1976). Television as dream. In R. Adler & D. Cater (Eds.), *Television as a cultural force* (pp. 17–36). New York: Praeger. (Published with the Aspen Institute Program on Communications and Society).

Critical Approaches to Television Discourse: An Overview

Had enough, left,
        with his sins, with his virtues, long
    howled the dog on the grave, then died,
the way dogs die, of hunger.

The house stood empty, the wife
        ran away long ago
    with Fredriksson, the children
were out in the world, one far away in America.

The family was consumptive, predisposed
        to madness, an aunt had seen
    Jesus on the roof of the potato cellar,
from then on awaited the coming of the groom.

                —Matti Rossi, "Tragedy, Finnish Style"

The first three stanzas of Rossi's poem (1965/1992), as well as its other verses, present us with approaches to plots for domestic tragedies—suicide, abandonment, and madness. Also mentioned are murder, mental illness while living outside of Finland, and marrying outside one's ethnic origin. The poem ends with a vision of the Finnish countryside: "The rowan trees have bloomed. A lot of berries,/the winter will be severe. Wild roses/wave in a circle against the wall/of the house. The door stands open. The curlews cry/in the marsh." The countryside endures in spite of human degradation. The regularities of life, even the sordid human tragedies, spin on relentlessly ("The door stands open"), in counterpoint to the odd twists of individuals' fates. And yet, of course, the real interest we have in this poem flows from the personal biographies of depressed fathers, mothers seeking fulfillment, and aunts looking for Jesus on the doors of potato cellars.

"Tragedy, Finnish Style" illustrates some important features of how critics approach the analysis of discourses—poems, essays, novels, TV programs, films—at the dawn of the 21st century. The poet seeks to understand a primary concept or object: tragedy as experienced by Finns. Likewise, the critic wishes to comprehend a primary concept or object—some kind of *text* (a novel, newspaper story, TV program) or *discourse* (a kind of subject matter such as talk about gender relations or the welfare system) that is enjoyable, interesting, frustrating, infuriating, or in some other way engaging. But a concept or even an object is never experienced in general, abstractly. Rather, it is experienced only in concrete or manifest ways. You understand Finnish tragedy only by seeing the lives of particular Finns. You don't ever experience the presidency—only the actions of particular presidents—Reagan, Bush, Clinton. Likewise, you don't experience television abstractly, generally; instead, you experience particular programs in concrete ways. You may watch cartoons with a sense of nostalgia, a sense of your lost youth. Soaps may pressure you to rearrange your class schedules so that you don't miss them. You may enjoy watching some sitcoms now and then but feel no urge to reorient your life around them. You perhaps watch football or baseball only when the Bears (or White Sox) are playing the Lions (or Tigers).

If television criticism is to be a valuable intellectual enterprise, therefore, we must know what kinds of texts or discourses comprise the televisual experience and try to understand all the concrete ways in which those texts or discourses can be approached. The purpose of this chapter is to examine some of the ways in which television discourses have been approached by critics so that we can offer an informed and reasonable scheme for talking about types of television criticism in the rest of this book.

Three Ways to Classify Types of Television Criticism

The work of television critics can be divided in multiple ways; three approaches to the classification of types of criticism, however, have dominated the history of televisual studies. Horace Newcomb (genre), Raymond Williams (pluralism), and the editors of the Aspen Institute Program's Workshop on Television (critical perspectivism) each featured a different method for classifying the work of TV critics.

Horace Newcomb: Subject Matter

In his 1974 book, *TV, The Most Popular Art,* Horace Newcomb followed a time-honored practice of literary studies: he classified approaches to criticism by types of television program. Just as you're likely to see literary criticism divided by type of literature (poetry, drama, novels, essays), so Newcomb showed his readers how to do critical analyses of different kinds of TV programs. He reviewed the principal genres of shows: situation and domestic comedies, Westerns, mysteries (police and detective shows), doctors and lawyers (professional shows), adventure shows, soap operas, news/sports/documentary, and what he called new shows (shows that defied generic classification because they mixed elements from several genres).

For each of these genres, Newcomb suggested formulaic ways of analyzing that sort of program, by examining *character types, plots,* and *the environment (setting).* By studying character, plot, and setting, Newcomb argued, we are able to understand *television formulas,* that is, the habitual ways particular types of programs are put together. His interest in formulas came not from a desire to put down television as predictable and simplistic, but from a hope that they can help us better understand our culture—the beliefs, attitudes, hopes, and fears of a citizenry—as it is presented to us daily by TV. Newcomb articulated his goal in this way:

> Each chapter deals with a separate formula or with a group of related formulas. While we explore the sense of cultural significance, it is also possible to define a set of artistic techniques, aesthetic devices that contribute to some unique capabilities on the part of television. The things that television does best are directly related to the most formulaic and popular works. They are developed in various ways by the various formulas we examine and build into a set of possibilities that allow television, like other media, to go beyond the popular and into works of great artistic complexity and cultural significance. (1974, pp. 23–24)

Newcomb's interest in the artistry of television led him to conclude the book with a chapter titled "Toward a Television Aesthetic," where he discussed television as a medium characterized by *intimacy, (dis)continuity,* and *history.* Our sense of intimacy, he noted, was due in part to the smallness of the screen, and in part to the ways in which good directors shoot a TV show, with many closeups that rely on concreteness of detail and the emotional impact of direct involvement. Second, the lack of continuity on most television programs—the characters of most shows seemingly have no memory of what happened in previous weeks—means that television creates no artistic probability and little analytical force. Because episodic shows end with their problems neatly resolved on a weekly basis, there is little chance for sophisticated studies of human turmoil, except in some multipart specials such as *Roots, Civil War,* or *Masterpiece Theatre* episodes. The lack of continuity limits television's serious effect in our lives, according to Newcomb. And third, television

First Lady Hillary Rodham Clinton chats with Oprah Winfrey on her daytime syndicated talk show

Like most daytime talk shows, The Oprah Winfrey Show *deals with social rather than political issues. However, Banks and Tankel's Chapter 6 essay explains that unlike most other daytime talk shows, Oprah only occasionally deals with sexually oriented topics.*   (AP Photo/Oprah Winfrey Show, Steve Green, Pool.)

is strongly historical. Not only does the recent past provide the plots for most programs, but the more distant past—the mythic past of the United States—provides the underlying formulas for many stories. Television seeks whatever depth it has through myth (see Chapter 8).

Newcomb, in other words, classifies television programs by program type, or genre, and then asks critics to investigate the formulas typical of each type so that we can understand the breadth of television's different-yet-interesting aesthetic.

Raymond Williams: Pluralistic Criticism

In his 1974 book, *Television: Technology and Cultural Form,* Cambridge University professor Raymond Williams explored relationships between television as a governmentally regulated communications technology and television as a social experience. The book was written while he was at Stanford University, so he was able to compare British and American experiences with the technological and cultural form.

To Williams, it is important for critics to examine not only characteristics of a technology and the social uses to which a technology is put, but also the economic links between technology and social uses. A new communications technology, after all, is not developed unless someone can make money selling it, and then the actual delivery of communication messages must be paid for as well. Technology and culture are linked in societies by either economics in the case of democracies or politics in the case of fascist regimes (1974/1975, p. 24).

Williams was convinced, therefore, that no critic can adequately analyze television without examining (1) *the institutions of the technology* (governmental, economic, artistic), (2) *the forms of television* (the types of programs inherited from other media or newly developed for TV), (3) *the distribution and flow of programming* (how consumer markets are divided up and regulated through sequences of programs on a station or network), and (4) *the effects of the consumption of the technology by a society* (the way that television is used in particular societies and measurable effects of those uses). These four ideas are represented in the central chapters of the book.

In other words, Williams saw technological development and expansion, economic and political institutions, and the social uses of television locked up in direct relationships with each other. Criticism, therefore, had to be pluralistic: a combination of technological history, examination of economic and political controls, a content analysis of program offerings on different channels, the close study of "flow" of programs on specific days of specific weeks, and the social-scientific study of effects. According to Williams, a person cannot understand a television text without knowing something about the industry, where it fits in a day's scheduling, and the general social interests or needs that it seemingly addresses; one kind of criticism is inadequate. One's critical analysis of a TV program such as *COPS* could not proceed without an understanding of the economics of inexpensive (VHS system) production, the programming local channels need to supply between their news hour and the beginning of prime-time network fare, the formulaic aspects of cop shows, and the public's interest in law-and-order issues in the late 20th century.[1] Criticism that ignored some aspects of the television production and delivery system was flawed. Pluralism—many things at onceness—should characterize TV criticism.

No one (except Williams himself) has ever really executed this pluralistic analytical task, yet his influence on British and American television critics is immense. His insistence on tying together technologies, economics, politics, and social impact can be seen in studies of the political economy underlying programming, in studies of relationships between television as technology and television as social force, and in the new ethnographic studies of how real people make meaning from TV in real social situations. He and Newcomb together launched contemporary television criticism (Gronbeck, 1988).

Aspen Institute Program: Critical Approaches

The Aspen Institute for Humanistic Studies (Washington, D.C.) set up its program in 1971 to foster analysis of public broadcasting, government and media, and the sociocultural aspects of television. Under the directorship of Douglass Cater, the Aspen Institute Program launched workshops for researchers and critical scholars to explore television's role in society. Its first two publications were *Television as a Social Force* (1975) and *Television as a Cultural Force* (1976). The 1975 volume was sensitive to the economic, political, regulatory, and social aspects of television—primarily institutional studies. The 1976 volume was important in the history of TV criticism.

Richard Adler, associate director of the institute, opened the 1976 volume with a definition of television as a medium, citing four primary characteristics: (1) *diversity* (a great variety of types of programs shown weekly); (2) *intimacy* (we accept it uncritically as a familiar friend); (3) *flow* (television is composed of programs but viewed across time in larger or at least regularized ways, making it difficult for textual critics to know what to analyze); and (4) *simplicity* (a childish medium that, again, makes it difficult for critics to access it fairly). Adler also noted its small screen, which hampers television's ability to show spectacle, and its low-fidelity sound system, giving its music a thin quality. TV is much better for sports, news, and public affairs than it is for opera or spectacular movies (Adler, 1976).

The essays in the volume were highly diverse, reflecting not only different kinds of programs but, more important, different approaches to critical analysis. Peter Wood used a psychoanalytic approach to television as dream; Paula Fass explored television comedy as a part of our cultural equipment; Kenneth Pierce examined *All in the Family*'s mixing of comedy and news genres; David Thorburn viewed television programming as melodrama; and Robert Alley explored the morality documented in medical shows. The moral development of children as reflected in television shows was featured in Kevin Ryan's essay, and Sharon Lynn Sperry argued that the narrative form of news controls the way we experience the world.

In other words, the Aspen Institute Program suggested structurally that television programs could be studied through a variety of methods or approaches. The person who read Fass, Pierce, and Thorburn learned about three different critical approaches to situation comedies—or, in Adler's language, three different *mediations* (1976, p. 13) between TV and our lives. The *critical approaches view* of television program analysis was born that year.[2]

By now, most books on television criticism are variations and extensions of one of these three approaches: by subject matter, by multiple or pluralistic modes of attack, and by type of criticism. Types of criticism—critical approaches—receive the most emphasis in our times. For one thing, a types approach recognizes that criticism is a way of looking at the world, with each approach or type of criticism representing a different way of looking at a program or the medium. Cultural criticism places the program in its broadest social context, and psychoanalytic criticism, in its most secret and private dimensions; genre criticism is centered on the ways literatures can be classified, and feminist criticism, on the ways women are gazed upon and portrayed in series. The different critical approaches show us different questions people ask about their worlds. Examining *Roseanne* in these ways would help us understand the social force of its lower-class humor, the psychosexual dimensions of Roseanne's and Dan's relationship, the show's place in the history of sitcoms, and Roseanne's challenges to patriarchal structures. Multiple approaches reveal multiple facets of programs.

The critical approaches school of TV analysis is also popular because it puts primary emphasis on the television program: "the text." Most critics do their best work when faced with a text—with a musical score, a poem, a novel, a film, or a videotape of a TV program. Most critics have been trained to "read closely," to dissect particular aspects of texts. The critical approaches school of television criticism is generally textually oriented. We are not suggesting that it is easy to define what the text is (see Chapter 5)— only that textual analysis dominates television criticism, as this book illustrates.

Williams's concerns with history, the industry, and viewers' experiences cannot be forgotten. Of course not. Nor should Newcomb's early emphasis on types of programs be ignored. We must remember that *television* is an ambiguous word, referring to a technology, an industry, a piece of furniture, a life-long experience, and, yes, the specific programs you watch on Monday nights. Our explorations of television must reflect those ambiguities. The interests of Williams are reflected in the institutional studies in Chapter 10, and the Alternative Table of Contents is constructed around Newcomb's generic emphases.

Types of Television Criticism: Problems and Solutions

So we have arranged this book by critical approaches. Yet, one faces a series of obstacles when constructing any typology of critical approaches. The phrase *critical approaches* is ambiguous and abstract enough to need specification, and yet it must be broad enough to have some intellectual flexibility. To illustrate these requirements, consider three problems we confront when talking about critical approaches: essentialism, pluralism, and partiality.

Essentialism

Too often, critics assume that each type of criticism is a pure form that must be maintained in pristine condition when being used. If you are doing a psychoanalytic analysis of *NYPD Blues,* you might think that you should talk only in Freudian or Jungian terms and not mention cop shows as a genre or the aesthetic quality of the program. Or you might want to approach Michael Moore's *TV Nation* with an interest in the *auteur* ("author") of the program, given the strength of his personality and the relentlessness of his anti-institutional crusades, ignoring techniques of production or comments on the genre of the show. Drive such a thought out of your mind. In fact, many of the questions critics ask demand the use of analytical techniques from various types or schools of analysis.

Suppose you wanted to study the interesting narrative structure of *Highlander*—the way it uses a mythic past and future to frame its stories in the present. To study the unfolding of its stories, you would probably want to talk about its mythic background, the semiotics of its primary symbols (the swords, eyes as windows to near-eternal souls, distinctions between indoors and out-of-doors spaces), and even the adventure genre as a vehicle for exploring larger social issues of truth, goodness, and perseverance. Or if you asked the question "Why is the *Highlander* constructed the way it is?" you'd want to know something about the movies that preceded the program, the industrial practices involved in spinning off a TV program from films, the author and his or her background, and the special attractiveness of such a mythic-adventure show to audiences of the late 1980s and early 1990s, perhaps through interviews of regular viewers. The question "Why is the *Highlander* constructed the way it is?" requires the use of more than one critical approach if you are to offer a good answer to it. The point is this: although critical methods can be defined in pure forms, your critical studies should be guided by the questions you ask, not the methods you want to use.

Pluralism

Your problems in using a particular critical approach are complicated by the fact that none of them appears in only one form. So you might define *ideology* as (1) false consciousness, (2) a set of ideas held by a society to be true, and (3) discourse in the service of power. Each definition would suggest a different kind of analysis of, say, *Law and Order.* Exploring false consciousness in that program would lead you to look for pro-police and pro-lawyer values disguised as facts in the program. You might try to inventory American ideals about crime and punishment by examining statements made by citizens (and criminals) in particular episodes, and to study the ways that discourse is used to legitimate the criminal justice system, you might take apart the trials described in two or three episodes. Different definitions of *ideology* would seem to suggest different sorts of criticisms.

A pensive scene from Supreme Court Justice Clarence Thomas's 1991 Senate confirmation hearing

Television coverage of Justice Clarence Thomas's Senate confirmation hearings included testimony by Anita Hill and raised the nation's consciousness about sexual harassment and the politics of judicial appointments. However, as Scott's Chapter 9 essay argues, the hearings also rearticulated myths about African Americans and showed us the power of cultural stereotyping.   (AP/Wide World Photos.)

One of the ways that critical studies stay fresh and alive, actually, is through the construction of new definitions—new theories of language that ask critics to study something they weren't studying before those theories came along, for example, or new understandings of male–female relationships that tell us our old ways of looking at *Father Knows Best* or *The Donna Reed Show* in the 1950s disguised the real dynamics of family power. To look at a Western such as the classic *Bonanza* as an instantiation of frontier myth will get you into the program, probably, as it was constructed from 1959 to 1973; but to redefine that myth, not simply as a frontier story but as a patriarchal story, changes the direction of your mythic analysis in significant ways. Each critical approach described in this book must be thought of as *multidimensional*—as multivocal concepts. Although the world would be neater if a particular word had only one meaning, only multidimensionalism guarantees that all critics will not end up saying the same things.

Partiality or Perspectivism

A third problem created by the critical approaches theory of televisual analysis is that of partiality: each critical approach allows us to see only a part of a program. That is, each approach is but one perspective on an object. Consider the old story of the blind men of India. They came upon an elephant and asked each other what it was. The one holding the tail said, "Oh, it is a long, thin animal with a beard on one end." "No, no," said the second, holding the trunk; "it is long and round, not thin, but rather tubelike with air moving through it." The third having a foot said, "You're both crazy, for it's ponderous, flat, and armored with hard nails." Grabbing the ear, the fourth noted, "Heavens, no, it is flat, but soft and pliable, covered with an alluring fuzz." The fifth blind man, knowing that the rib cage he was feeling was for all the world like a giant drum, thought they were all witless. And so the dispute went on into the night, as each man was doubly blind: blind by nature and blinded by the perspective he had on the elephant, controlled as it was by the part he first seized.

And so it goes with television program analysis. A feminist approach to *Martin* usually ends up ignoring the racial and class questions raised by that program. If you focus on the mythic dimensions of the Super Bowl, you might well ignore the economic force of the event. A narrative study of the evening news is interesting but may blind you to the kinds of people whose stories are never told by Dan Rather or Peter Jennings.

Examining only particular aspects or parts of something leads to the problem of *perspectivism:* each critical approach is a perspective, more or less a point from which to look at a program. And as the blind men of India found out, if you look at an elephant from only one point, you'll miss a lot. There's always a sense of incompleteness in a piece of criticism.

Overcoming the Problems

Essentialism, pluralism, and partiality can hamper your work as a critic, messing with your thinking about your intellectual tasks if you're not careful. So, what can you do?

The Centrality of "the Question."   First, critics always must remember that the question—the question that they want to answer in their papers—is central to criticism. The questions you ask help you select methods or approaches, suggest what aspects of a program to explore, and become the conclusions that are the outcome of good work. If you find yourself worrying more about critical methods than about critical questions, you've got your priorities mixed up. Saying that you want to do a cultural study of *The Simpsons* is likely to encourage you to focus on cultural approaches to criticism rather than on the show; instead, asking a culturally sensitive question—In what ways do the social parodies of *The Simpsons* sensitize Americans to their cultural excesses?—will keep your eyes on the program even as you pursue a cultural study.

Approaches and Audiences.   Another thing to think about is that the kind of study you do often defines its own audience, which is to say, a group of readers interested in the perspectives you take. If you're doing a feminist analysis, you're more likely to be read by other feminists than by farm hands. If a person despises the intricacies of semiotic analysis, he or she is unlikely to read a critical analysis of the sign systems used to suggest class in *Friends*. A focus on types of criticism, therefore, is as much a focus on audience interests—others' questions—as it is on critical machinery. Hence, you should expect most criticism to be partial—that's even the point!

An important point to remember about your work as a critic is that there in fact will be people who find it worthless. In the essays that follow in this book, too, there will be pieces you enjoy and works that you despise. (If you don't like any of them, you're probably in the wrong course!) In a sense, doing criticism is like participating in a late-evening chat-a-thon in a dorm room or on the World Wide Web. Criticism is strongly dialogic, a conversation about some text or event wherein particular aspects of that text or event are examined closely. If your favorite chat room is dealing with a topic you're not interested in, you sign off. The same is true about television criticism: you'll avoid the discussions of aspects of programs or approaches to them that you don't like. Criticism is *partial*, therefore, in two senses of the word: it's never a complete study of anything, and it produces kinds of knowledge of particular interest to only part of a population.

Centeredness.   If you think long about the importance of the guiding question and the audiences who might be interested in how someone answers it, you can see that critical approaches are not prisons within which you do criticism but rather centers from which you launch projects. You might start a context-centered study of *Green Acres, The Beverly Hillbillies,* and *Petticoat Junction,* asking the question "Why were these programs so popular in the 1960s?" Such a question would force you to probe the 1960s, the decade of revolution and of the breakdown of many political, economic, and social institutions. You'd probably soon discover that mere description of that context was not enough; you'd want to explore the ideological battles of that decade, seeing the popularity of comedies in a rural setting as a conservative backlash, and you might even want to talk a little semiotics—about rural characters as signs for innocence in the face of too much knowledge, for simplicity in the face of a growingly complex world, and for the guilelessness of the farm in the face of corrupted cities. (*Green Acres,* especially, often featured the corrupted city.)

The key here is to remember what your center is: the question, which ought to suggest kinds of analyses to you. Kenneth Burke (1945/1982) talked about the importance of understanding the container and the thing contained. Because of the question you ask, one type of criticism likely will be the container for your study. In the study of rural TV comedies of the 1960s, for example, a sociocultural exploration of the context, the 1960s, is the container. Other approaches can also be used to fill out the sociocultural container: the ideological study of the times (also a contextual analysis but of a different sort, as we point out in Chapter 8); the semiotic study of people and objects as significant signs or symbols (a kind of rhetorical analysis, as we discuss it in Chapter 6); and even a study of people who watched those shows (especially the middle- and lower-middle class, lower-income people who made up the bulk of their audiences) would provide parts of the answer to the question.

As another example, suppose you wanted to investigate the matter of image and issue ads in presidential campaigning. Your investigation could well be centered in a particular kind of textual study, a so-called genre study: image ads and issue ads as two genres. You even break those down farther into four genres or types of ads: positive and negative issue ads and positive (of self) and negative (of other) image ads. Sorting ads and defining each genre helps you find a center, but that's all. To talk about the power of such ads, for example, you might want to do a rhetorical or ideological analysis of the ads in each category; to talk about stylistic variations within each genre, you could do a sociocultural analysis of the times within which particular ads played; and to get at audience reactions to ads, some ethnographic work might be called for. Centers are starting points and the places where your framing questions live. You start at centers and inevitably return to them by the end of your critical essays, but you likely intercut other approaches to critical analysis along the way.

Centeredness, then, is the key to understanding what we are doing in this book. Not only can criticism be diffused so long as it is centered, but also our arrangement of critical approaches to television criticism is centered—in this case, centered on the classic communication model (Figure 3.1). That model suggests that the communication process—and television is assuredly a medium of one-to-many communication—can be examined in terms of the following:

Sender: the producers, directors, technicians, actors, and so on, who are the authors (*auteurs*) of television series and individual episodes

Messages: the *texts* of the programs, including verbal, visual (deep backgrounds, sets, costumes, icons, people), and acoustic (voice qualities, music) codes

Audiences: the *viewers* as understood by gender, race, class, and other social markers that can affect how they make meanings out of television programs

Situation: the *contexts* of a show, including the period in which it was developed and exhibited, the kinds of worlds (work, family, foreign, his-

FIGURE 3.1   **Critical approaches to television arranged by communication model**

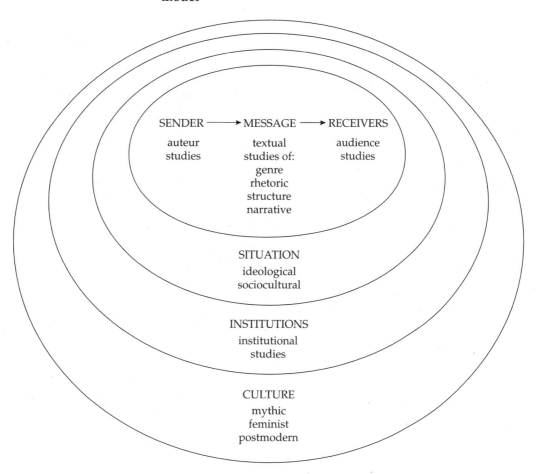

SENDER ⟶ MESSAGE ⟶ RECEIVERS

auteur   textual   audience
studies   studies of: studies
                genre
                rhetoric
                structure
                narrative

SITUATION
ideological
sociocultural

INSTITUTIONS
institutional
studies

CULTURE
mythic
feminist
postmodern

torical) it depicts, and the ideological dynamics of the program and the period in which it was shown

Institutions: the *primary* and *secondary institutions* (network, production house, government regulatory agency, economic sponsor) controlling or in other ways affecting the way programs are produced, exhibited, and watched

Culture: the *culture* of a program, including social structures, rules for living, definitions of social roles and how they are played, and the use of television in different societies

Don't worry: each of these descriptions is expanded significantly in later chapters of the book. But perhaps this listing helps you understand the rationale for the way this book is laid out—how it is centered. These are the centers for criticism, though, again, you should remember: just as you seldom talk about a message sender without saying something about the message, so, too, are you unlikely to do an auteur study of a television production company such as MTM Productions without mentioning some of its messages (programs) such as *The Mary Tyler Moore Show* and *Hill Street Blues*.

The Rest of the Book

The rest of this book, therefore, leads you through a types-centered approach to television criticism. An array of types—not all types, of course, and not all variations of each type—is offered. We discuss each type in terms of its origin, some of the variations available within it, its operating assumptions about the world of television, and its problems or potential shortcomings. Then, along with some short headnotes, we present sample critical essays that show you how at least a few people have worked within the assumptions of a particular approach. You can skip around, not necessarily reading the chapters in order, because the approaches are more or less independent of each other. That's the way it is with perspectives; any of the blind men of India could have spoken first.

As a result of reading this book and its essays, you should leave this course with a basic understanding of each of the principal kinds of television criticism, you should have seen each kind at work, and you should understand the range of meanings television produces in Americans about American society.

> The uncle, rank-and-file worker in Kazakhstan,
>   old Communist,
>   fled from the Whites in '18, took a
> German wife, built a sauna, burned it down
>   while drunk, and died.
>
> The sons went to sea, one
>   stabbed a first engineer in Stockholm
>   and is still doing time, the other
> went mad in the Azores, started swimming to Finland,
>   has not arrived.
>
> The daughter, last seen at the Finnish Hall
>   in Fitchburg, with her seven kids; her husband,
>   Hunting Wolf, had put on warpaint,
>   robbed a whisky train and now dwells
> with Manitou. (Rossi, 1965/1992, p. 147)

Perspectives on tragedy, Finnish style, can be spun out so long as the poet has the energy to find more examples of tragicomedic Finns to write about. Perspectives on television programs also will multiply so long as the networks, cable companies, and independent producers find new ways to visualize human experience of the world. It is time for you to get started writing about your experiences.

NOTES

1. Williams had offered a similar analysis of newspapers in his earlier book, *Communications* (1962/1976).
2. That same year Horace Newcomb brought out his anthology, *Television: A Critical View* (1976). It, too, was organized by different kinds of shows and different approaches to them—20 essays in all. The critical-approaches pattern was formally recognized as such by Arthur Asa Berger in 1982 and fully developed into textbook form by Robert C. Allen in 1987.

REFERENCES

Adler, R. (Ed.). (1975). *Television as a social force.* Aspen series on communications and society. New York: Praeger.

Adler, R. (Ed.). (1976). *Television as a cultural force.* Aspen series on communications and society. New York: Praeger.

Allen, R. C. (1987). *Channels of discourse: Television and contemporary criticism.* Chapel Hill: University of North Carolina Press.

Berger, A. A. (1982). *Media analysis techniques.* Beverly Hills, CA: Sage.

Burke, K. (1945/1982). *A grammar of motives.* Englewood Cliffs, NJ: Prentice-Hall.

Gronbeck, B. E. (1988, August). The academic practice of television criticism. *Quarterly Journal of Speech, 74,* 334–347.

Newcomb, H. (1974). *TV, the most popular art.* Garden City, NY: Doubleday/Anchor.

Newcomb, H. (1976). *Television: The critical view.* New York: Oxford University Press.

Rossi, M. (1965/1992). Tragedy, Finnish style. K. Bosley (Trans.). *A way to measure time: Contemporary Finnish literature* (pp. 147–148). Helsinki: Finnish Literature Society.

Williams, R. (1962/1976). *Communications.* Middlesex, England: Penguin.

Williams, R. (1974/1975). *Television: Technology and cultural form.* New York: Schocken Books.

4

Just Doing It: Writing Television Criticism

Although serious scholarly television criticism may generate a limited profit when it is published in a book or anthology, its primary purpose is rarely financial gain. Rather, it seeks to teach both the writer and the reader, to stimulate further critical insights about television, and to enhance our understanding of television as a social and cultural form and force.

Stages of Critical Analyses

This may surprise you a bit, but criticism doesn't begin when you sit down with a pen in hand to begin to write your critical essay. Criticism actually begins somewhere in the uncharted chambers of your mind. In fact, criticism is a three-stage communication activity that begins with a personal critical reaction or a critical question. This stage, in turn, eventually leads to the sharing of your critical insights, for example, by writing a critical essay. And the third stage is the response of other readers (your teacher, your classmates, roommates, fellow television fans)—feedback on your critical observations.

Stage One: Thinking About Television

Gronbeck (1984) calls the first stage *cerebration* (from the word *cerebral*, meaning "involving the brain or intellect"). It is at this stage that you select the text(s) you are going to analyze and the critical question you want to answer. In general, there are two ways we can go about this selection.

Aha! Reactions.   Sometimes the idea for a critical essay comes about through a sudden critical reaction as we are reflecting on a particular program or group of programs. Gronbeck (1984) compares this critical reaction to Archimedes' "Eureka!" formulation of the principle of specific gravity. For example, an "Aha!" reaction was the first step when Projansky wrote her critical essay on *Dr. Quinn: Medicine Woman*. As she explains in that essay, during the series' third season Jessica Bowman replaced Erika Flores as the actor playing the role of Colleen, Dr. Mike's adopted daughter. Projansky noticed that not only was there a marked difference in terms of the physical appearance of the two Colleens (Flores's body was sexually mature while Bowman's was that of a child-like prepubescent teen), but there was also a noticeable change in the character. As she continued to watch, Projansky's response to the change in Colleen from a brash, energetic, determined career-oriented teenager (Flores's character) to a quiet, timid, hearth-and-home family-oriented teenager was "Aha!" The change, she concluded, helped the series downplay the contradictions in Dr. Quinn's character between feminism and femininity. This insight convinced Projansky to undertake a feminist analysis of the cast and character changes in Colleen; you can read her conclusions about the implications of these changes for viewers' understanding of the series' depiction of idealized womanhood in Chapter 9.

Categorical Searches.   A second way that critical essays can come about is through systematic searches for critical methods or concepts that can help explain and interpret a television text. For example, Wenner went searching for a concept that would help him explain what he saw as a complex relationship among commercialism, nationalism, and sports in the 1992 "Dream Team" ads. After considering several different approaches, Wenner decided that the insights he gained from viewing these ads could best be organized and explained by combining a critical method called *reader-oriented criticism* with media scholar John Hartley's concept of "dirt." In Chapter 7 you can read the critical essay that resulted.

Another kind of categorical search resulted in Banks and Tankel's study of the focus on sex in television talk shows. They started with the impression that they had seen sex featured frequently on recent talk shows. This perception led them to posit several critical questions about how and why the discussion of sexuality on television talk shows might contribute to viewers' understanding of mainstream and alternative notions of sexuality. Their next step was to conduct a categorical search of a month's episodes of the three top daytime talk shows. You can read the critical interpretations that they arrived at in their Chapter 6 essay.

Stage Two: Communicating Critical Insights

Criticism is the process whereby we communicate thoughtful, considered interpretations about the meanings of television texts with other people. It is not, as we explained in Chapter 2, merely opinion. Serious criticism involves using critical methods and concepts to explain and justify your critical responses and insights about television texts to others. When this communication is done in writing, these creative insights are packaged in essays that more or less follow certain writing conventions. As we noted in Chapter 1, one of these conventions is that, at a minimum, all critical analyses must include three elements: (1) a clear thesis that states a critical interpretation, (2) well-developed arguments that explain how the critic arrived at this interpretation, and (3) specific supporting evidence—so readers can decide for themselves if the critic's interpretation seems reasonable, valid, and insightful. If the critic is writing a critical analysis for publication in a scholarly journal, the analysis needs some other elements as well—including a clear discussion of the critical method (or critical/theoretical concepts) that enabled the critic to arrive at this interpretation and a brief review (generally no more than one to two sentences each) of other relevant critical analyses that have looked at the same (or similar) television texts and/or have used this particular critical method or concept.

The central critical proposition (the main idea or thesis) of a serious television criticism essay may be framed as either an interpretive statement or a question. Gronbeck (1984) distinguishes between two styles of serious criticism essays—a deductive style (which begins with a critical proposition in the form of a statement) and an inductive style (which begins with a question). Hundley's essay, for example, illustrates a deductive approach, for she begins with the critical proposition that *Cheers*, a series set in a Boston bar, legitimized (or "naturalized") beer drinking by presenting it as a normal, acceptable everyday activity. She then goes on to discuss three strategies through which the series accomplishes this. Banks and Tankel's essay, on the other hand, illustrates an inductive style; it begins with a series of questions to which they develop answers after a categorical search and analysis of many program episodes. (Hundley's essay is in Chapter 8 of this text; Banks and Tankel's essay appears in Chapter 6.)

In both cases, however, after the introduction, which conveys the paper's central idea—in question or statement form, the essay should move on to discuss the assumptions implied in the statement or question. Next, it should provide an introduction to the critical constructs or method the critic uses to analyze the television program. The body of the essay should then walk the reader through this analysis using well-organized and amply supported arguments and should arrive at an interpretive, evaluative conclusion. This conclusion must follow logically from the analysis and should either answer the initial question or remind the reader of the initial interpretation or assertion.

In fact, if we removed the specific content from most television criticism essays and left only the skeletal frame, we would find that the underlying structure of most criticism essays is built along the following pattern:

I. Introduction

  A. Interest-arousing opening paragraph.

    Most essays begin with an interest-arousing quotation, authoritative fact, anecdote, or description. These elements are designed to capture the reader's interest so she or he will continue to read the rest of the essay.

  B. Rationale for writing (and reading) the essay.

    The introduction of an essay needs to provide a justification for writing—and reading—this essay on this program or topic. Some common rationales include the following:

    1. The uniqueness or importance of the text or issue being analyzed (e.g., the first prime-time television series featuring an Asian-American female star and an almost all Asian-American cast).

    2. The significance of the critical or theoretical insights produced by this analysis (e.g., the identification of the thematic and stylistic features that typify Aaron Spelling's television productions and define him as an auteur.

    3. The usefulness of the particular method or critical construct(s) used in this critical analysis for explaining other television texts (e.g., how a feminist method that demonstrates how the apparently progressive depiction of the character Murphy Brown really denigrates and scapegoats feminism can be used to analyze the ways in which other television series undercut portrayals of strong, independent female characters).

  C. Preview the critical approach or constructs that the critic used to explain and organize her or his critical interpretation of the television text(s).

  D. Review other relevant criticism essays (identified through a literature search). If you are writing criticism essays for publication, you need to mention other critical essays that have analyzed the same series. If you are writing for academic conference presentations or scholarly journals, you also need to reference critical essays that have used this critical approach in order to explain why this critical essay is unique.

  E. Briefly forecast the major points of the essay in the order in which they are presented in the body of the essay. (These road maps help readers follow the development of the argument the body of the

The Museum of Television & Radio in Beverly Hills, California

Founded by William S. Paley in 1975, The Museum of Television & Radio has a collection of over 75,000 radio and television program episodes and advertisements available for individual viewing at the museum's two locations—New York City and Beverly Hills (pictured here). The museum also organizes live satellite seminars for students that feature interviews and round-table discussions (and chances for telephone call-in questions) with writers, producers, directors, actors, and others in broadcast programming.   (AP Photo/Museum of Television & Radio.)

essay presents; they show readers how you arrived at your critical interpretation or insight—the paper's thesis.)

II. Body of the Criticism Essay

    A. Explain and define the critical method or constructs you are using to analyze the television text(s) in sufficient detail for the intelligent but uninformed reader to understand and use in his or her own critique.

    As we noted earlier, if the particular audience for whom you are writing this critical essay is an audience of academic television critics and/or other scholars, you may need to review other academic critical essays that have looked at the same television text(s) and perhaps also some critical essays that have used the same method or critical concepts to analyze other texts.

B. Analyze the text(s) by developing the ideas (arguments) embedded in the essay's thesis or central critical proposition/question.

C. Provide a sufficient amount of appropriate supporting material for this analysis.

   1. There is no rule for what is sufficient, but the general guideline is to provide enough proof so that an intelligent, skeptical, but reasonable reader will agree that your interpretation is *a* (*not* the) valid interpretation.

   2. The supporting material that you use to develop and support your argument should include several of the following:

      a. concrete, specific examples and/or dialogue from programs

      b. concrete, detailed description of specific plots, scenes, lighting, music, camera angles, mise en scènes,[1] etc., from specific program episodes (that's why it is a good idea to videotape the text[s] you are going to analyze)

      c. quotations from or references to relevant theoretical or critical scholarly sources

      d. quotations from other relevant sources (e.g., newspaper articles, reviews, etc.)

      e. attributed facts from authoritative sources (polls, census bureau, Nielsen ratings, etc.)

III. Conclusion

   A. Reiterate the initial critical interpretation (thesis or question).

   B. Summarize briefly the conclusions you arrived at as a result of the ideas, arguments, and evidence presented in the analysis.

   C. Discuss briefly the implications of the analysis for one or more of the following:

      1. Understanding of this program/text or subject.

      2. Future critical analysis of television texts using this method or construct(s).

      3. The television viewing public, the television industry, and/or society generally.

      4. The advancement of our understanding of television criticism, critical theory, and television studies.

There also should be a separate page of references on which you provide the complete sources (alphabetically by the author's last name) of the methodological essays you consulted, any other relevant critical essays about the same text that you cited in the essay as part of your review of other criticism of this text, and the source of any factual information you cited. The reference page usually also should contain a videography (which includes reference citations to the series' episodes you discussed, listing the title of the episode, date aired, writer, producer, director, and production company).

Stage Three: Responses and Feedback

Because serious television criticism is written primarily for those interested in viewing and studying television as a form of popular art, television criticism essays appear primarily—though not exclusively—in academic journals published by scholarly associations (e.g., *Critical Studies in Mass Communication, Western Journal of Communication, Journal of Popular Film and Television*), and in books and anthologies of television criticism. Readers of scholarly journals and criticism books do not usually write back to the authors of criticism essays they read in journals, though this has happened occasionally to the editors of this book. Most often, however, critical responses come as a result of other writers' citations of our essays when they are reviewing the published critical studies that are relevant to their own analyses.

For the critical essays you will be assigned to write for your classes, feedback will certainly come from your instructor and perhaps from the other students in the class. If you ask your roommate, significant other, or a friend in the class to read your essay, you can also receive valuable critical responses to your interpretation. These readers can also tell you if you have explained the critical method or concept you used well enough so that these readers can understand it and could apply it in their viewing of other programs. One audience we sometimes tell our own students to write for is the intelligent, curious, generally well-informed, and educated readers of *The New Yorker* and members of the Television Critics Association. Essays aimed at this audience should be literate and fairly sophisticated, but not filled with jargon. You will need to clearly explain and define the critical concepts and methodological tools you use because you cannot assume that your readers are thoroughly familiar with them. However, if these readers find your essay accessible, informative, and insightful, you will have made an important contribution to "education in the larger sense." This is, of course, one of the major goals of criticism that we discussed in Chapter 1.

The goal of critical essays is to stimulate a critical dialogue about the particular text and about television generally—to take television and critical thinking and writing about television seriously. Indeed, the worst fate a critic can imagine is to be ignored. As Gronbeck (1984) reminds us, "criticism's worth is measured by the degree to which it causes others to reflect upon, interpret, and evaluate their own experiences with the [television] object in question" (p. 11).

FYI: *Murphy Brown* original cast members Eldon, Jim, Murphy, Frank, Corky, and Miles

Now in its 10th season, Murphy Brown *remains among TV's top 20-rated programs. One explanation for this, Dow argues in her Chapter 9 essay, is that the series both celebrates and critiques Murphy Brown's liberal feminist lifestyle—enabling the series to provide (contradictory) pleasures to viewers with very different views about feminism and femininity.*

A Few Other Considerations in Writing Critical Essays

Timeliness.   For serious television criticism essays, timeliness is far less of a consideration than it is in the television section of the daily paper. The reason for this difference is that serious television criticism is not written to provide advice for upcoming viewing but rather to share an insightful interpretation of a television text. As a result, television critics can analyze historical, eso-teric, and unusual programs and episodes that journalistic writers, whose job is to advise a broad audience interested in "what is on television today that I might want to watch," cannot.

Vocabulary.   Criticism vocabularies consist of specialized terms such as *genre, discourse,* and *mise en scène,* which are tools that television (and film, literature, and theater) critics use not to make the subject or the critics interpretations inaccessible, but rather to efficiently convey the assumptions and constructs that underlie the critics analysis. Serious television criticism either relies on established critical theories, methods, or constructs—for example, fantasy-theme analysis (Bormann, 1972, 1982), genre theory (Altman, 1986), structural analysis (Fiske, 1984; Fiske & Hartley, 1978)—or creates a unique critical-analysis tool by adapting or combining existing theoretical or critical concepts—for example, Rushing and Frentz's (1978) social values model of narrative analysis, Vande Berg's television dramedy genre (1989), or Gumpert and Fish's (1990) concept of mediated therapeutic communication. When critics do create a unique approach, they are always careful to provide clear contextual or stipulative definitions for critical terms that may be unfamiliar to some of their readers. Critics also are careful to explain criticism terms whose everyday use differs from the way these terms or concepts are used in critical studies. For example, in everyday conversation we use the term *discourse* to mean "talk"; however, in television criticism, *discourse* means "a language or system of representation that has developed socially in order to make and circulate a coherent set of meanings about an important topic area" (Fiske, 1987, p. 14).

Length.   Critical analyses of television vary in length, but most are between 10 and 20 pages (double-spaced). Although 10 to 20 pages may seem long, remember that you need to introduce your critical idea, provide a brief summary of what the series or episode is about, describe the critical approach or concepts that you used as tools to conduct the analysis, and then explain and develop your critical interpretation as well as provide several supporting examples. Once you have written all of this, you will be amazed at how quickly you have written 8 to 12 pages. Length is not a goal in itself; it is simply that thorough discussion and adequate proof take a fair amount of space.

Proofs.   In serious television criticism essays, the critic must support the interpretive proposition (thesis) or answer the critical question posed as the essay's thesis by elaborating on the ideas or arguments implied in the thesis or question and by providing confirming, corroborating evidence for these arguments. This supporting evidence typically includes specific details and descriptions of exemplary scenes, dialogue, lighting and/or camera work, or citations from other television criticism essays, theories, and/or facts from reputable sources. Sometimes—in the case of institution-centered, auteur-centered, or audience-centered critiques, the proofs may include quotations from interviews conducted by the critics (see, for example, Halualani and Vande Berg's essay in Chapter 10).

Looking Ahead

As we explained in Chapter 3, critics can use many different approaches or tools to organize and explain their insights or answer their questions about television texts. In Chapters 5 through 10, we explain a number of these methods and provide sample essays to illustrate how some critics have used these methods to examine television.

NOTES

1. Mise en scène, as film critic Andrew Sarris (1977) has cogently explained, "includes all of the means available to a director to express his [sic] attitude toward his subject. This takes in cutting, camera movement, pacing, the direction of players and their placement in the decor, the angle and distance of the camera, and even the content of the shot" (pp. 52–53).

REFERENCES

Altman, R. (1986). A semantic/syntactic approach to film genre. In B. K. Grant (Ed.), *Film genre reader* (pp. 26–40). Austin: University of Texas Press.

Bormann, E. G. (1972). Fantasy and rhetorical vision: The rhetorical criticism of social reality. *Quarterly Journal of Speech, 58,* 396–407.

Bormann, E. G. (1982). A fantasy theme analysis of the television coverage of the hostage release and the Reagan inaugural. *Quarterly Journal of Speech, 68,* 133–145.

Fiske, J. (1984). Popularity and ideology: A structuralist reading of *Dr. Who.* In W. K. Rowland & B. Watkins (eds.), Interpreting television: Current research perspectives (pp. 165–197). Beverly Hills: Sage.

Fiske, J. (1987). *Television culture.* London/New York: Methuen.

Fiske, J., & Hartley, J. (1978). *Reading television.* London/New York: Methuen.

Gronbeck, B. E. (1984). *Writing television criticism.* (Modules in mass communication series.) Chicago: Science Research Associates.

Gumpert, G., & Fish, S. (Eds.). (1990). *Talking to strangers: Mediated therapeutic communication.* Norwood, NJ: Ablex.

Rushing, J. H., & Frentz, T. S. (1978). The rhetoric of *Rocky:* A social-value model of criticism. *Western Journal of Speech Communication, 41,* 63–71.

Sarris, A. (1977, July/August). The auteur theory revisited. *American Film,* 49–53.

PART II

METHODS OF TELEVISION CRITICISM

Auteur-Centered Approaches to Television Criticism

Auteur-centered approaches to television criticism originated in the 1950s with a group of French New Wave film director–critics writing criticism and film theory for the French cinema journal *Cahiers du Cinéma*.

Basic Assumptions and Unique Features of Auteur-Centered Criticism

Auteur is a French term for the artist whose vision and personality is "written" into a text—the "author." Auteur-centered criticism is based on the view of art as "the expression of the emotions, experience and 'worldview' of an individual artist" (Caughie, 1981, pp. 9–10) and on the romantic view of artists as creatively obsessed individuals who manage, despite the collective nature of film production and the commercial/industrial context within which films are produced and distributed, to put their stamp on their films. André Bazin (1957/1966) once described auteur-centered criticism as a critical approach that involves "choosing in the artistic creation the personal factor as a criterion of reference, and then postulating its permanence and even its progress from one work to the next" (p. 14).

In the earliest auteur criticism articles, these underlying assumptions led some critics to an excessive reliance on biographical interviews in their analysis of an auteur's works (see, for example, Sarris, 1968, p. 30); later auteur-structuralist critiques put the auteur's name in quotation marks to indicate their distinction between the flesh-and-blood director and the auteur as the critical construct that they saw written into the works (see Nowell-Smith, 1967; Wollen, 1969). Over time as more critics have written auteur-centered criticism and also have written metacritical and theoretical articles about auteur-centered criticism, this approach has developed into an insightful alternative to both biographical and genre criticism.

Although an auteur critique may use information gleaned in interviews as well as other biographical information about the potential auteur, such information is secondary to the analysis of the thematic and stylistic features of the auteur's productions. In contrast, biographical criticism sees an author's work (using *author* here for writer, director, producer, company, or actor) as fundamentally explicable through biographical information—either directly via the author's history or symbolically via Freudian psychoanalytical criticism of events in the author's life that have been condensed, inverted, or fragmented in the form in which they appear in the film or television production.

Likewise, although auteur-centered criticism includes some discussion of the genre (and industry) constraints that the auteur surmounted in order to place her or his uniquely consistent artistic signature on her or his works, auteur-centered criticism does not regard genre conventions as the most powerful shaping influence on the form and content of an auteur's work.

As you can see, auteur-centered criticism generally takes into account biographical information, genre conventions, and industry constraints (the commercial and organizational constraints of production, distribution, promotion). Although auteur-centered critiques differ in the emphasis they give to the challenges the auteur must overcome, the foci of all auteur-centered critiques are the stylistic and thematic features common across the entire body of the individual's work—including all the television, film, and video works that the auteur wrote for (alone or as a staff writer), produced, or directed. Specifically, auteur-centered critiques involve a close visual and textual examination of two aspects of the auteur's work—(1) the mise en scène (see page 61 for the definition) and (2) the pattern of thematic motifs occurring across the entire body of an author's work—those "defining characteristics of an author's work [that] are not necessarily those which are the most readily apparent" (Wollen, 1972, p. 532). As Wollen (1972) explains, auteur analyses must examine both the redundancies and the system of differences and oppositions in an auteur's works. In fact, Wollen argues that the real test of an excellent auteur analysis is not in the ability to explain what he calls "the orthodox canon of a director's works, where resemblances are clustered," but rather in the auteur critic's ability to identify these repeated motifs and oppositions in works "which at first sight may seen eccentricities" (1981, p. 139).

One of the strengths of auteur criticism is that, because auteur-centered critiques focus on mise en scène, they provide the critic with a way of "accounting for the text as pleasurable, pointing to its fascination as well as its meaning" (Caughie, 1981, p. 13). Indeed, French director–auteur critic Fereydoun Hoveyda once wrote, "If one insists on thinking that *Party Girl* is rubbish, then I proclaim: Long live this rubbish which so pleases my eyes, fascinates my heart, and gives me a glimpse of the kingdom of heaven" (pp. 13–23).

A Brief Overview of the History of Auteur-Centered Criticism

Although the notion of *auteurism* certainly existed in the 1940s, many film critics date auteurism as a unique critical perspective from the publication of a 1954 article in *Cahiers du Cinéma* written by French film director and critic François Truffaut (Caughie, 1981. pp. 15, 35–38). Truffaut's article attacked the then-dominant critical view that the writer was the central creative force behind a film and the director merely a translator who realized the writer's creative vision. Instead, Truffaut insisted that the real creative force in film was the director. However, he argued that not all directors were equal and that critics needed to distinguish between those directors who merely did a competent job of transferring the writers' work to the screen and those directors who turned the scripts into their own unique, artistic visual expression through the mise en scene (i.e., the disposition of the scene in front of the camera).

Les politiques des auteurs, as Truffaut called this critical perspective, did not emerge initially as a fully developed auteur theory. Rather, it grew up haphazardly through the criticism articles written in the French film journal *Cahiers du Cinéma,* the British journal *Movie,* and the writings of Andrew Sarris and others in the American journals *Film Culture* and *Film Quarterly.* Concomitantly, these film critics, many of whom were film directors as well, began to re-examine films of many directors. Among the directors whose films were looked at anew were expatriate European directors now working in Hollywood (such as Alfred Hitchcock) and American directors whom previous European film makers and critics had snubbed as too commercial.

This re-examination came about when these film aficionados again began to screen new films after World War II. Prior to the war, European film directors, film patrons, and literati—writers, artists, poets, and film directors—had gathered regularly in fairly luxuriously appointed film salons. At these ciné clubs they sat around tables and sipped espresso and wine while they screened films and then spent hours discussing them. World War II put a damper on this activity. As Peter Wollen (1972) points out, during World War II—from the late 1930s through the mid-1940s—American films were banned from France. Furthermore, in Europe little filmmaking besides propaganda films went on during the war. Thus, when the war finally ended and the

European film industry was beginning to recover, Hollywood films were among the few new films available for screening in French film clubs.

At the time, many European film aficionados were not particularly excited about Hollywood films, which they regarded as primitive, factory-produced, commercial fare. Part of the reason was that prior to World War II, most European films were written and directed by independent film makers (like American film makers Woody Allen and Spike Lee today). These directors oversaw every aspect of their films and were regarded as being totally responsible for them. The films of these European directors were viewed as the individual visions of their creators—like the individual art works of novelists; in contrast, the films of American Hollywood directors of this era were viewed by many Europeans as mass-produced, industrial products and not the reflection of identifiable creators' visions.

Indeed, during the height of the American Hollywood studio-system era of the 1930s and 1940s, the star was the most visible and highly touted creative force. The American public went to see films because of the stars, not because of the directors (Stacey, 1994, pp. 105–107). The Hollywood director of that era generally was viewed as part of the invisible production crew; the director was told to produce a given type of film (e.g., romantic comedy) with the script, the cast, and almost everything else already decided. All the director had to do was assemble these raw materials into a coherent film. As a result, as Wollen explains, "directors who built their reputations in Europe were dismissed after they crossed the Atlantic, reduced to anonymity. American Hitchcock was contrasted unfavorably with English Hitchcock" (1972, p. 532).

Given their views of Hollywood film, it is easy to understand why French film makers and other French film aficionados sitting around their salon tables after World War II were astonished to discover some Hollywood auteurs among those responsible for the Hollywood flicks the French critics previously had viewed as primitive, factory-produced, commercial fare. That is, they were astounded that some Hollywood directors had managed, in spite of the Hollywood studio-system constraints, to place their unique stylistic and thematic signatures on their films. This realization led to a renewed interest in American and European film directors' works. Indeed, Wollen (1972) asserts that from its inception, *Cahiers du Cinéma* published critiques by Truffaut and others who argued that Hollywood directors like Welles, Ford, and Lang, no less than European "art" cinema directors, had transformed their film material into personal artistic statements.

Over time, this polemical approach to film (called *les politiques des auteurs*) developed into the auteur-structuralist critical approach that film critics use today. Today auteur criticism is a method of analyzing film texts that combines elements from structuralist, aesthetic/stylistic, and historical/cultural methods. Its goal is to discover whether, behind the superficial contrasts of subject matter, there exist stylistic and thematic patterns in the whole body of a director's films that constitute his or her artistic signature. As Peter Wollen

(1972) explains, it is "the pattern formed by these motifs . . . [that] gives an author's work its particular structure, both defining it internally and distinguishing one body of work from another" (p. 532). What makes one director an auteur in contrast to just a competent journeyman or journeywoman director is the ability to establish and communicate his or her artistic vision within the constraints of the film production system and the culture in which the director is working.

Auteur-Centered Television Criticism

Auteur-centered film criticism did not develop until film had been around as an art/entertainment form for more than 50 years, so it should not be surprising to discover that auteur-centered television criticism is just emerging as an approach to the study of television. Television, after all, only recently arrived at the first half-century anniversary of its public demonstration at the 1939 New York World's Fair, and it wasn't until August 1948 that 7-day-a-week, four-network broadcasting[1] began in New York (McNeil, 1991).

Like film auteurism, auteur-centered television criticism assumes that television can be an art form and that some television creators deserve to be regarded as auteurs. Also like film, auteur-centered television criticism values the inscription of the auteur's personal signature into television texts precisely because of the barriers (genre, industry, sociocultural) to individual creative expression by the collective nature of the Hollywood production and distribution industry. Finally, like film auteurism, auteur-centered television criticism assumes that by using this approach, which combines structural, aesthetic, genre, and historical analyses, a television critic can uncover—behind the superficial contrasts of subject, actor, and genre—the recurring stylistic and thematic motifs that signify the creative presence of the auteur in and on these texts.

However, despite these similarities, there are also noteworthy differences between film and television auteur-centered criticism. One difference is the person regarded as the most influential creative force—that is, who is the most probable auteur. Film has focused almost exclusively on the director as the auteur (though there are some biographies of film companies and executives that could be regarded as auteur-centered). The reason for this is because in film the director is the individual with the greatest legal and financial responsibility over the final artistic product—the director is in charge of hiring and firing members of the production crew, establishing the creative vision, viewing the "dailies," keeping the production on budget, and keeping the cast and crew cooperative. In television, the executive producer has these powers and responsibilities: primary responsibility for the above-the-line and below-the-line production decisions and budgets and also for the overall continuity and quality of the final program. The importance of the executive producer is the reason that Horace Newcomb and Robert S. Alley (1983) argue that television is "the producer's medium." It also explains why almost all auteur-centered television criticism identifies the (executive) producer as the auteur.

For example, in one of the earliest essays on television auteurs, David Marc (1981) mentions four television candidates whom he thinks deserve the honor of auteur—producers Paul Henning (*The Beverly Hillbillies, Petticoat Junction, Green Acres*), Norman Lear (*All in the Family, Sanford and Son, Maude, Good Times, The Jeffersons*), Garry Marshall (*The Odd Couple, Happy Days, Laverne and Shirley, Mork & Mindy*), Aaron Spelling (*The Mod Squad, The Rookies, Starsky & Hutch, Charlie's Angels, Hart to Hart, Hotel, Dynasty, Beverly Hills 90210, Melrose Place*).[2] Don Davis's (1984) essay provides another short argument for two of these producers as auteurs—Norman Lear and Garry Marshall.

However, there are other possible television auteurs, including writers, writer-producers, directors, production companies, and even television executives. David Marc and Bob Thompson's (1992) *Prime Time, Prime Movers* book provides essays and videographies (lists of all the writing, directing, producing, and acting credits for books, films, plays, and television) of more than 24 producers as auteurs (including Susan Harris, Diane English, Marcy Carsey, Tom Werner, Steven Bochco, Quinn Martin, and Stephen Cannell, to name just a few). Additionally, Marc and Thompson argue that among those television writers who deserve recognition as auteurs are Paddy Chayefsky, Reginald Rose, Rod Serling, soaps writer/producers Irna Phillips and Agnes Nixon, and documentarist Ken Burns.

Another noteworthy early television auteur study is Jane Feuer, Paul Kerr, and Tise Vahimagi's (1984) book on the Mary Tyler Moore Company, titled *MTM 'Quality' Television*. In it they provide a convincing argument for regarding MTM as a corporate auteur whose works are immediately recognizable for their unique stylistic and thematic features, characteristics that made MTM programs quality television.

Still other as yet unexplored potential auteurs include network television executives such as Fred Silverman and Grant Tinker, both of whom clearly placed unique stamps on their television network's programming, and television directors such as Jay Sandrich, Gregory Hoblit, Gene Reynolds, Jackie Cooper, Bruce Paltrow, Georg Stanford Brown, Randa Haines, and David Anspaugh.

Discovering "authors" in any form of industrialized cultural production, like the television industry, is not an easy task, for it requires hundred of people to produce that finished half-hour of *Home Improvement* or *Seinfeld*. In fact, the difficulty of identifying the precise contribution and signature of particular individuals is exactly what Robert Thompson's auteur analysis of *St. Elsewhere* (the sample auteur essay included in this chapter) illustrates. However, despite the multiple authorial signatures that can be identified in television, film, and many other popular culture texts, someone eventually assumes the final decision-making responsibility for a television text. As Marc and Thompson (1992) note:

> The elements of personal style that emerge from such choices remain beyond the purview of what can be accomplished by interoffice memos, programmable machines of generic inertia. . . . Despite all odds, the necessity—as well as the mystique—of the individual artist has survived the late industrial age. By some measures it is resurgent. The growing desire of marketers to slap "designer labels" on every kind of mass-produced product from evening gowns to ice cream cones provides evidence of an increasing public awareness that the mass-culture apparatus is not some kind of self-sustaining engine but, rather, a distribution system for the products of a new class of designers and artists. Though there can be no doubt that the relationship of artist to audience has been altered by the nature of mass-distributed culture, it has not been destroyed. Surely if we can attribute the cut of our blue jeans to authorial influences, we can do at least as much for the substance of our national drama—television. (p. 4)

Auteur criticism typically has tried to avoid the *intentionalist fallacy* (i.e., second-guessing the author and asserting what an author—and a text—"really mean" to say) in two ways. First, by focusing on tracing the stylistic and thematic characteristics that chain throughout a body of creative works rather than by focusing on the intended meaning of the text, auteur criticism avoids the intentionalist fallacy through illustrating recurring features that constitute the creative fingerprint of a particular person (or group of persons) who assumes responsibility—and credit—for these works. Second, auteur criticism seeks to avoid the intentionalist fallacy by viewing the author as a textual construct—a collection of visual, verbal, musical, and narrative strategies—and not as a real person. Even so, as we discuss in Chapters 6, 8, and 9, television-studies scholars increasingly have argued that the ultimate authors of a text are really the audience members who take the raw material of a television program and create meanings through their interactions with it.

Thompson's essay on *St. Elsewhere* in this chapter offers a third strategy for avoiding making unwarranted and ultimately unsupportable claims about the intentions of texts' authors: acknowledging the multiple authors of a television series and exploring—through both textual analyses (of multiple texts with which the various contributing authors have been involved) and interviews—these authors' multiple intersecting contributions to television series.

Writing an Auteur-Centered Critical Analysis

Of all the types of television criticism discussed in this book, auteur-centered criticism is probably the most difficult for students to do as a class paper, primarily because of the difficulty in locating samples of the auteur's work to analyze. However, with the help of cable television's syndicated program archives and the use of some of the sources listed at the end of this chapter, a number of our students have done thorough and insightful auteur studies during the course of a term.[3]

Obviously the first step in writing an auteur-centered analysis is to select the auteur whose work you want to study. Suppose, for example, you decided to do your auteur study on Aaron Spelling. Your next step would be to compile his biography and his videography. For the biography, of course, you would go to the usual sources (e.g., *Celebrity Bios, Dictionary of American Biography, Who's Who in America, Who's Who in Television and Cable*). To compile the videography, you will need to go to a number of sources. The reference and resource section at the end of this chapter lists a number of general television program credit sources that you can consult (e.g., Brooks & Marsh, 1988; Eisner & Krinsky, 1984; Gianakos, 1978, 1980, 1981, 1983; Marill, 1984; Marc & Thompson, 1992; Newcomb, 1997; Newcomb & Alley, 1983; Perry, 1983; Ravage, 1978; Wicking & Vahimagi, 1979; Terrance, 1986, 1991). Of course, since these books are already in print, they won't cover the most recent television seasons. To update them you will need to check sources like Gale Research Inc.'s *Contemporary Theatre, Film & Television*, as well as indexes like *Reader's Guide to Periodicals* (which indexes *TV Guide*) and *Guide to Business Periodicals* (which indexes articles in trade magazines such as *Broadcasting, Electronic Media, Entertainment Weekly, Variety*) under the auteur's name. These sources will point you to articles about the auteur (e.g., Aaron Spelling) and recent television and movie productions with which he or she was involved that have appeared in such popular periodicals as *TV Guide* (the fall preview issue is especially useful), *Variety, Entertainment Weekly*, and *Broadcasting.*

The next step is the most difficult one—you need to locate sample episodes of all or almost all of the television series and films by the auteur. Possible sources of sample episodes. in addition to those programs you manage to record from cable television, include your instructor, the media library at your university, and video rental stores (e.g., Blockbuster Video). Some sources useful for this stage of your research are listed at the end of this chapter (see, e.g., Balkansky, 1980; Black, 1990; Culbert, 1984; Godfrey, 1983; Mehr, 1977; and Rouse & Loughney, 1989). Additionally, the Library of Congress in Washington, D.C., has more than 15,000 programs; the Academy of Television Arts and Sciences (ATAS)/UCLA Television Archives has more than 20,000 titles; and the Museums of Broadcasting in New York City and the Museums of Television & Radio in New York City and Beverly Hills have representative copies of more than 17,000 radio and television broadcasts. Most of these archives do not make copies of series' episodes for you, so you need to travel to them to view the sample episodes (one factor limiting the amount of auteur-centered criticism). However, in the case of the Library of Congress National Archives, you can request that a limited number of episodes be sent to a presidential library or one of its 13 regional archives where you can go to view the tapes (see Adams & Schreibman, 1978, p. 99).

Once you've located samples of the auteur's television series, you need to examine them for recurring stylistic features and thematic motifs (and, of course, take careful notes while you are doing so). In the case of Aaron Spelling, this process would involve analyzing sample episodes from the six television series on which he served as a staff writer, sample episodes from the 50-plus television series he has produced, and a representative sample (about one-quarter of the total) of his 150-plus television and feature films. In the case of a prolific television creator such as Aaron Spelling, the amount of screening time is another constraint you face in doing auteur-centered analyses.

Stylistic features analyzed in auteur critiques include the use of lighting (e.g., flat or chiaroscuro) and sound (including the use of dialogue, diegetic sound—that is, sound within the scene that the characters hear, and extradiegetic sound—including the musical soundtrack or the laugh track). Recurring stylistic features also can include the types of actors or specific actors used in multiple series (e.g., Steven Bochco has used James Sikking, Dennis Franz, and Barbara Bosson in several series), the camera work (including pans, zooms, dollies, soft focus), types of edits between scenes, length of takes, shooting on film or video, and the mise en scène. *Mise en scène,* as Andrew Sarris (1977) cogently explains, "includes all of the means available to a director [or producer] to express his attitude toward his subject. This takes in cutting, camera movement, pacing, the direction of players and their placement in the decor, the angle and distance of the camera, and even the content of the shot" (pp. 52–53).

In the case of Aaron Spelling, for example, an auteur-centered critique of his stylistic authorial signature would include a discussion of his recurring use of lavish, glamorous sets that emphasize wealth, class, and conspicuous consumption; heavily orchestrated musical themes; ritual introductory sequences that serve to introduce the regular cast members, the series' settings, and the various plot lines to be explored in that week's episode (a convention later borrowed by many other producers); heavy use of high-key lighting and a stylized symmetrical use of closeups, two shots, three shots, and long shots; the gratuitous display of nearly naked, Anglo bodies (more often women's rather than men's bodies); and the continuation of these features from action-adventure/romantic dramas of the 1970s to prime-time serial dramas of the 1980s and 1990s.

Analysis of Spelling's series would lead the auteur critic to discuss some of the following recurring themes (or thematic motifs): social relevance (e.g., in the 1960s this included the youth rebellion, the rehabilitation of these errant youths or criminals, and their subsequent incorporation into law enforcement or the justice system; in the 1990s relevance included problems of yuppie teens and ambitious middle-class young adults); valorization of wealth and capitalism—affirmation of the altruistic capitalism myth that one can be both economically and morally successful (e.g., *Charlie's Angels, Hart to Hart, Matt Houston, Vega$, Hotel, Fantasy Island*); the myth of the caring company (e.g., *Hotel, Love Boat*); the maxim that money can't buy love (e.g., *Dynasty, The Colbys, Beverly Hills 90210*); the myth that the grass always looks greener but rarely is (e.g., *Beverly Hills 90210, Melrose Place*), and the myth that good eventually triumphs over evil (e.g., *Mod Squad, The Rookies, Charlie's Angels, Dynasty, Hotel, Hart to Hart*).

Once these steps are accomplished and you can summarize the distinctive signature of your auteur, you are ready to follow (more or less) the outline suggested in Chapter 4. In other words, you are ready to share your auteur-centered critique with your fellow television viewers. Obviously, there are variations from one auteur critique to another, but this essay was written to give you a general sense of how to go about doing auteur-centered criticism. This background essay, coupled with the following example of an auteur analysis, should provide a solid foundation for your efforts at writing an auteur-centered critical analysis.

Looking Ahead

Now that you've learned something about the origins of auteur critical theory and about how critics go about doing auteur-centered television criticism, you can critically evaluate the following example of auteur-centered criticism.

Robert Thompson's auteur-centered analysis explores the multiple auteurial signatures identifiable in the television series *St. Elsewhere*. After his introduction of the series, Thompson briefly explores the confluence of unique thematic and stylistic contributions that television auteurs Joshua Brand, John Falsey, Bruce Paltrow, John Masius, Tom Fontana, MTM—the corporate auteur—Mark Tinker, and Stephen Bochco made to the series. Thompson goes on to describe the truly unique thematic and stylistic features of *St. Elsewhere*, focusing on the extraordinary artistry of the self-reflexivity and intertextuality of the series, while also illustrating its origins in these auteurs' shared experiences at "MTM U."

Thompson's critical essay included several direct communications with the television auteurs who produced this series, along with the historical research and close textual analysis of the television series. Although such direct communiques certainly add interesting insights to these critiques, you can write thorough, insightful auteur analyses simply by combining the historical/biographical information you located through library research with your close textual analyses of multiple examples of the auteur(s)' texts (i.e., the television series, plays, and/or movies she or he has written for, produced, and/or directed). In many cases you can locate through library research published media interviews with television auteurs and include these auteur comments in your essay.

In addition to the auteurs whose work is analyzed by Thompson, the work of a plethora of other potential television auteurs has yet to be studied using auteur-centered criticism—Steven Bochco, Aaron Spelling, Diane English, Gary David Goldberg, Quinn Martin, Glen Larson, James L. Brooks, Garry Marshall, Marcy Carsey and Tom Werner, and Norman Lear, to name only a few.

NOTES

1. These were NBC, ABC, CBS, and Dumont (which lasted from 1946 to 1955).
2. However, Marc (1981) acknowledges that comedic geniuses Ernie Kovacs and Jackie Gleason should also be considered as potential auteurs.
3. For example, our television criticism students have done auteur analyses of David Lynch; Steven Bochco; Gary David Goldberg; Glen and Les Charles; and Edward Zwick and Marshall Kerskovitz.

REFERENCES AND RESOURCES

Adams, W., & Schreibman, F. (Eds.). (1978). *Television network news: Issues in content research.* Washington, DC: George Washington University School of Public and International Affairs.

Adler, R. P. (Ed.). (1979). *All in the family: A critical appraisal.* New York: Praeger.

Balkansky, A. (1980). Through the electronic looking glass: Television programs in the Library of Congress. *Quarterly Journal of the Library of Congress, 37,* 458–475.

Bazin, A. (1957/1966). De la politique des auteurs. *Cahiers du Cinéma, 70,* 2–11. [English Ed. & Trans in 1966 by P. Graham, *The new wave.* London: Secker & Warburg.]

Black, S. (1990). *Thesaurus of subject headings for television: A vocabulary for indexing script collections.* Phoenix: Oryx Press.

Black, S., & Moersh, E. S. (Eds.). (1990). *Index to the Annenberg television script archives* (Vol. 1: 1976–1977). Phoenix: Oryx Press.

Brooks, T., & Marsh, E. (1988). *The complete directory to prime-time network tv shows, 1946–present.* (4th ed.). New York: Ballantine.

Campbell, R., & Reeves, J. (1990). Television authors: The case of Hugh Wilson. In R. J. Thompson & G. Burns (Eds.), *Making television: Authorship and the production process* (pp. 3–18). New York: Praeger.

Caughie, J. (Ed.). (1981). *Theories of authorship.* London: Routledge & Kegan Paul.

Culbert, D. (1984). Television archives. *Critical Studies in Mass Communication, 1,* 88–92.

Davis, D. (1984). Auteur film criticism as a vehicle for television criticism. *Feedback, 26,* 14–18.

Eisner, J., & Krinsky, D., (1984). *Television comedy series—An episode guide to 153 TV sitcoms in syndication.* Jefferson, NC: McFarland.

Feuer, J., Kerr, P., & Vahimagi, T. (1984). *MTM 'quality' television.* London: British Film Institute.

Gianakos, L. J. (1978). *Television drama series programming: A comprehensive chronicle (Vol. 2: 1959–1975).* Metuchen, NJ: Scarecrow.

Gianakos, L. J. (1980). *Television drama series programming: A comprehensive chronicle (Vol. 1: 1947–1959).* Metuchen, NJ: Scarecrow.

Gianakos, L. J. (1981). *Television drama series programming: A comprehensive chronicle (Vol. 3: 1975–1980).* Metuchen, NJ: Scarecrow.

Gianakos, L. J. (1983). *Television drama series programming: A comprehensive chronicle (Vol. 4: 1980–1982).* Metuchen, NJ: Scarecrow.

Godfrey, D. G. (Comp.). (1983). *A directory of broadcast archives.* Washington, DC: Broadcast Education Association.

Hoveyda, F. (1960). La réponse de Nicholas Ray. *Cahiers du Cinéma, 107,* 13–23. In B. Nichols (Ed.), (1976). *Movies and methods.* Berkeley: University of California Press.

Levinson, R., & Link, W., (1986). *Off camera: Conversations with the makers of prime-time television.* New York: Plume/New American Library.

Marc, D., (1981, November). TV auteurism. *American Film, 52–55, 65, 81.*

Marc, D., & Thompson, R. J. (1992). *Prime time, prime movers.* Boston: Little, Brown.

Marill, A. H. (1984). *Movies made for television—the telefeature and the miniseries 1964–1984.* New York: Zoetrope.

McNeil, A. (1991). *Total television—A comprehensive guide to programming from 1948 to the present.* New York: Penguin.

Mehr, L. (Ed.). (1977). *Motion pictures, television and radio: A union catalogue of manuscript and special collections in the western United States.* Boston: Hall.

Newcomb, H. (Ed.). (1997). *Encyclopedia of television.* Chicago: Fitzroy Dearborn.

Newcomb, H., & Alley, R. S. (1983). *The producer's medium: Conversations with creators of American TV.* New York: Oxford University Press.

Nowell-Smith, G. (1967). *Visconti.* London: Secker & Warburg (Cinema One).

Parish, J. R. (1973). *Actor's television credits 1950–1972.* Metuchen, NJ: Scarecrow.

Parish, J. R. (1978). *Actor's television credits, Supplement I, 1973–1976.* Metuchen, NJ: Scarecrow.

Parish, J. R. (1982). *Actor's television credits, Supplement II, 1977–1981.* Metuchen, NJ: Scarecrow.

Perry, J. (1983). *Universal television—The studio and its programs, 1950–1980.* Metuchen, NJ: Scarecrow.

Perry, J. (1991). *Screen gems: A history of Columbia Pictures Television.* Metuchen, NJ: Scarecrow.

Ravage, J. W. (1978). *Television: The director's viewpoint.* Boulder, CO: Westview.

Rouse, S., & Loughney, K. (Comp.). (1989). *3 decades of television: A catalog of television programs acquired by the Library of Congress 1949–1979.* Washington, DC: Library of Congress, Motion Picture, Broadcasting, & Recorded Sound Division.

Rowan, B. G. (1980). *Scholars' guide to Washington, D.C. film and video collections.* Washington, DC: Smithsonian Institution Press.

Sarris, A. (1968). *The American cinema.* New York: Dutton.

Sarris, A. (1977, July/August). The auteur theory revisited. *American Film,* 49–53.

Schatz, T. (1984). Film archives. *Critical Studies in Mass Communication, 1,* 83–88.

Schreibman, F. (1983). *Broadcast television: A research guide.* Los Angeles: American Film Institute.

Shapiro, M. E. (1989). *Television network prime-time programming, 1948–1988,* Jefferson, NC: McFarland.

Shapiro, M. E. (1990). *Television network daytime and late-night programming, 1959–1989.* Jefferson, NC: McFarland.

Slide, A., Hanson, P. K., & Hanson, S. L. (Comp.). (1988). *Sourcebook for the performing arts: A directory of collections, resources, scholars, and critics in theatre, film, and television.* Westport, CT: Greenwood Press.

Stacey, J. (1994). *Star gazing: Hollywood cinema and female spectatorship.* New York: Routledge.

Terrace, V. (1986). *Encyclopedia of television: Series, pilots, and specials.* (3 vols.). New York: Zoetrope.

Terrace, V. (1991). *Fifty years of television: A guide to series and pilots, 1937–1988.* New York: Cornwall.

Thompson, R. J. (1985). Capturing the ephemeral texts: Reference literature on American television programs. *Feedback, 27,* 37–41.

Thompson, R. J. (1989). Stephen J. Cannell: An auteur analysis of adventure/action. In L. Vande Berg & L. Wenner (Eds.), *Television criticism: Approaches and applications* (pp. 112–128). White Plains, NY: Longman.

Thompson, R. J. (1990). *Adventures on prime time: The television programs of Stephen J. Cannell.* New York: Praeger.

Thompson, R., & Burns, G. (Eds.). (1990). *Making television: Authorship and the production process.* New York: Praeger.

Truffaut, F. (1954). Une certaine tendance du cinéma français. *Cahiers du Cinéma, 31,* 15–28. [English translation in B. Nichols (Ed.), *Movies and methods.* Berkeley: University of California Press.]

Vande Berg, L. R. (1989). Dramedy: *Moonlighting* as an emergent generic hybrid. *Communication Studies, 40,* 13–28.

Wicking, C., & Vahimagi, T. (1979). *The American vein–Directors and directions in television.* New York: E.P. Dutton.

Wollen, P. (1969). The auteur theory. In *Signs and meaning in the cinema* (3rd ed., pp. 530–541). London: Secker & Warburg.

Wollen, P. (1972). The auteur theory. In *Signs and meaning in the cinema* (4th ed., pp. 530–541). London: Secker & Warburg.

Wollen, P. (1981). The auteur theory (extract). In J. Caughie (Ed.), *Theories of authorship* (pp. 138–151). London & New York: Routledge.

Woolley, L., Malsbary, R. W., & Strange, R. G. (1985). *Warner Brothers Television: Every show of the fifties and sixties—episode by episode.* Jefferson, NC: McFarland.

Too Many Cooks Don't Always Spoil the Broth: An Authorship Study of *St. Elsewhere*

ROBERT THOMPSON

Great art, we are told, is created by great artists. It is the result of inspired individuals doggedly staying true to their visions in the face of temptations offered by the marketplace and other worldly influences. Vincent Van Gogh's uncompromising dedication to his personal vision, for example, guaranteed both his immortality and his poverty. His lone struggle against selling out is the romantic stuff of legend.

Most people, of course, now recognize that this notion is a little old fashioned. Art isn't created in a vacuum. But most people also still like to attach a single name to the works they read, hear, or see: Jane Austen's *Pride and Prejudice*, Handel's *Messiah*, even Orson Welles' *Citizen Kane*. Even today, it's hard to take seriously works that aren't associated with a single person about whom we can do research and around whom we can organize a college syllabus.

One of the reasons that popular art has had such a hard time gaining acceptance by the educational and artistic establishments is that so much of it tends to be, if not anonymous, then authorially ambiguous. Who wrote the jingle that you can't get out of your head? Who painted that velvet Elvis? Not surprisingly, the movies began to make inroads in the university curriculum only after the auteur theory was developed. By suggesting that a film, in spite of those long lists of names that appear before and after it, is the creation of *a single individual,* the director, auteurism allowed us to organize the study of film around the same principles by which we organize the study of other art forms. More recently, a small group of scholars have adapted the auteurist approach to television. Identifying the creator-producer as the small screen auteur, several studies have begun to examine the stylistic signatures of some TV artists.[1]

As first steps toward understanding the dynamics of the creative process in television, these studies have been invaluable, and many more of them will need to be done before we have a complete sense of who the people are who make the TV we watch. The next step, however, is to come to grips with the fact that television programs are made not by single individuals but by large authorial crowds. Although strong creator-producers may guarantee an identifiable brand-name style, programs may also be significantly influenced by staff writers, directors, and actors—even by studio and network executives. Creation in television is creation by committee and compromise. And, believe it or not, that isn't always a bad thing.

I would be hard pressed to identify a single auteur to whom credit should be given for the show I will examine in the following essay. In fact, no fewer than ten people played a major role in making the show what it was. Many of the features of the program that were most celebrated emerged from the fact that so many people were involved in its creative process.

Indeed, a truly thorough auteurist examination of a television series would need to identify which thematic and stylistic features came from which of the many people who worked on the series. That degree of detail would require an entire book, however. In this essay I'll simply identify the multiple authorial influences at work in a specific series and briefly describe some of the unique signature elements that spring from this horde.

St. Elsewhere

Just off Wilshire Boulevard between Beverly Hills and downtown Los Angeles lie the La Brea tar pits, where, 35,000 years ago, giant sloths and woolly mammoths became mired in nature. Right beside them is the L.A. County Museum of Art where, today, modern men and women of taste can become mired in culture. Here, on a chilly night in early March of 1993, a growing crowd formed a line that extended halfway around one of the complex's five buildings. Within the hour they were all seated in the Leo S. Bing Theatre, filling it to capacity.

As one might expect at a major art museum function, the crowd was sober and polite. Jackets, ties, and dresses seemed to be the order of the evening. As they waited for the event to begin, many talked about books, several perused them, and one seated near me appeared to be writing one. Well-groomed and well-read, 600 of the country's Great Washed had made plans, ordered and paid for $15 tickets, negotiated the traffic, and arrived at the museum with time to spare.

But these people weren't here to see the exhibits of Japanese paintings, pre-Columbian Mexican art, or the costumes and textiles collection, for all of which the museum is known and admired. They were here to watch a TV show, and to celebrate, explicate, and discuss it with the people who made it. Five years after it had been canceled by NBC, *St. Elsewhere* had achieved the status of a museum piece.

When, under the rigorous conditions of network commercial television, a series comes along that is lauded by viewers, critics, and industry functionaries alike, it is an event to be marveled at. From a dramatic and literary standpoint, *St. Elsewhere* (NBC, 1982–88) stacked up nicely not only against other TV shows, but against other contemporary drama on film and on the stage. Literate and stylized, the show boasted some of the best writing, directing, and acting ever seen on TV and was a darling of critics and industry insiders alike. It racked up 63 Emmy nominations and 13 wins, a Peabody, a Humanitas Prize, a Television Critics Association award, and an assortment of other honors. Furthermore, it remained on the air for a full six seasons, a distinction that fewer than 150 other series have ever topped.

Set in a decaying hospital in a decaying Boston neighborhood, *St. Elsewhere*'s serialized stories concerned the personal and professional problems of that hospital's doctors, administrators, interns, nurses, staff, and patients. Along with *Hill Street Blues* (NBC, 1981–87), *Moonlighting* (ABC, 1985–89), *thirtysomething* (ABC, 1987–91), *China Beach* (ABC, 1988–91), *Twin Peaks* (ABC, 1990–91), and a few others, *St. Elsewhere* was one of the principal shows in television's second "Golden Age," the result of the networks' attempt to compete in the age of cable penetration and channel surfing. Losing audiences target by target—teenagers to MTV, men to ESPN, kids to Nickelodeon—NBC started a trend in the early 1980s by trying to lure the most lucrative audiences (young, upscale, well-educated viewers) back to their living rooms with "quality TV." That is, when nothing else seemed to be working, the networks briefly experimented with the idea that critical acclaim might be the quickest way to commercial success.

The Cooks

In an effort to trace *St. Elsewhere*'s authorial pedigree, a look at Joshua Brand is as good a place to start as any. Brand was working on the writing staff of *The White Shadow* (CBS, 1978–81) when his ex-college roommate, Lance Luria, began calling him and telling him about his experiences as an intern at the Cleveland Clinic (Luria, personal communication, March 30, 1993). Urged on by these conversations, Brand began to concoct an idea for a medical drama that would take place in a teaching hospital like the one at which Luria was working.[2] Brand took the idea to Grant Tinker, the head of MTM Enterprises, where *The White Shadow* was being produced. MTM was still best known for its classy hit sitcoms like *The Mary Tyler Moore Show* (CBS, 1970–77), *The Bob Newhart Show* (CBS, 1972–78) and *Rhoda* (CBS, 1974–78), but the company was about to become a major supplier of hour-long dramas as well. When Brand told Tinker about his doctor show idea, Tinker thought immediately of *Hill Street Blues,* the innovative new cop show that MTM was supplying to NBC. Tinker encouraged Brand to develop the show in the same style (Turow, 1989, p. 240). Brand in turn went to John Falsey, his *White Shadow* writing partner, for help with the project.

By April of 1981, *The White Shadow* was history, NBC had agreed to buy 13 episodes of an undesignated new series from MTM, and Grant Tinker had put most of *The White Shadow*'s creative staff to work on the development of Brand and Falsey's project, *St. Elsewhere.* As executive producer, Bruce Paltrow was the boss, as he had been on *The White Shadow.* With a made-for-TV movie, a few pilots, and a reasonably successful series under his belt, Paltrow was considered a bankable and dependable producer, and NBC had made it a condition of the deal that he oversee the series (Paltrow, personal communication, April 26, 1993). Under him were four writer-producers with classy credentials and not a lot of TV experience. Brand had graduated magna cum laude from the City College of New York in 1972 with Phi Beta Kappa honors and a B.A. in English literature. He continued his studies on a fellowship at Columbia, where he earned a master's degree with honors in 1974, and he was just beginning to gain some notoriety as a playwright when he took the job on *The White Shadow.* Falsey had also been an English major, a 1975 graduate of Hampshire College who went on to get a Master of Fine Arts degree in creative writing from the renowned University of Iowa Writer's Workshop and who had written for the *New Yorker.* John Masius also got his first job in television on *The White Shadow.* Prior to that he had been an aspiring playwright with a B.A. in economics from the University of Pennsylvania and an M.B.A. from U.C.L.A. Of the four, Mark Tinker, a graduate of Syracuse University's television, radio, and film department, was the only one with experience in the medium that went beyond *The White Shadow.* He'd been directing and producing on various MTM shows since 1975, and his directing of *St. Elsewhere* would provide the show with its unique visual identity.

In addition to these four producers, Paltrow hired a writer who, along with John Masius, would provide the narrative heart and soul of *St. Elsewhere* by its second season. Tom Fontana had not been part of *The White Shadow* team. In fact, he'd never been part of any television team. A theater-arts major from Buffalo State University, he had been a playwright in residence at the Williamstown Theater Festival in Western Massachusetts when Paltrow met him and invited him to write a script for the new series (Fontana, personal communication, March 19, 1993).

That the *St. Elsewhere* team had comparatively little television experience was a fact that greatly affected the nature of the series as well as its critical success. The show was celebrated for being different than past doctor shows like *Ben Casey* (ABC, 1961–66), *Dr. Kildare* (NBC, 1961–66), *Marcus Welby* (ABC, 1969–76), and *Trapper John* (CBS, 1979–86). As neophytes in the medium, many of *St. Elsewhere*'s principal staff may have found it easier to break rules of the medium and of the genre that they had never really known very well in the first place.

While the production staff was being assembled, Falsey and Brand were off at the Cleveland Clinic doing research. There they developed a strong desire to create a series that would be as realistic as possible, presenting life in a big city hospital, warts and all (M. Tinker, personal communication, April 19, 1993). They also discovered Samuel Shem's *The House of God*, a 1978 novel that all the residents were talking about. *The House of God* gave Falsey and Brand inspiration, a title (characters in the book referred to any run-down hospital as "Mt. St. Elsewhere"), and a religious subtext that would run throughout the series and the rest of their television work. While *St. Elsewhere* wasn't based on *The House of God*, the book, set in a major teaching hospital in an Eastern city that sounds a lot like Boston, nevertheless had a significant influence on the first season of the series.

For a film auteurist who likes to give credit to a single individual, *St. Elsewhere*'s creative lineage already appears impossibly messy. Dr. Luria comes up with the original idea, Brand and Falsey develop the concept, Shem's novel fills in some dramatic holes, and Paltrow, Tinker, Masius, and Fontana throw in a lot more than their two cents. But it gets worse.

For starters, there was MTM. Set up in 1970 by Mary Tyler Moore, her then-husband Grant Tinker, and her manager Arthur Price, MTM Enterprises was part of a new era in television when the independent production companies would make significant inroads on the major studios like Universal, Warner Brothers, and Paramount. MTM wasn't a slave to the traditional rules of television, and each of the company's series broke a few more of them. Shows in the MTM style included a large ensemble cast, a workplace family, a self-reflexive attitude (*The Mary Tyler Moore Show* had been a TV show about a TV show, after all), and the theme of first-rate characters working in second-rate environments. The creative staff at *The White Shadow* was, of course, part of this corporate aesthetic, and the new medical show they were developing clearly reflected it.[3]

The authorial impact of NBC also cannot be discounted. During the gestation period of *St. Elsewhere*, programming chief Brandon Tartikoff, under network president Fred Silverman, had already seen NBC through some lean, third-place years, and there were going to be more before he would preside over his legendary string of number one seasons. When the final ratings were in for the 1981–82 season, the year before *St. Elsewhere*'s debut, NBC didn't appear once in the Nielsen top twenty. This had never happened before in the history of the network. *Hill Street Blues* was one of the few bright spots on Tartikoff's losing schedule. It had debuted to dismally low ratings in January of 1981, but that fall it won a record-breaking eight Emmy Awards and its ratings began to climb. The show was also bringing in lots of upscale, urban 18- to 34-year-olds, a heavy-consuming group over which the advertisers were drooling and for whom they were willing to pay premium rates. The good public relations that came with the critical adoration didn't hurt either. In the cruel months before *The A-Team* (NBC, 1983–87) and *The Cosby Show* (NBC, 1984–92), *Hill Street Blues* was one of the few tricks up NBC's empty sleeve. So, of course, they were anxious to do it again.

But the notion that *St. Elsewhere* evolved out of *Hill Street* is an oversimplified one. Both NBC and MTM had in fact come up with the basic idea that would become *St. Elsewhere* before they started toying with the concept that would become *Hill Street*. In 1979, Silverman had ordered a pilot from MTM called *Operating Room*, which followed the professional and personal lives of three doctors who worked in a Los Angeles hospital. With its large cast, its "realistic" feel, and its facile blending of comedy and drama, *Operating Room* began experimenting with some of the characteristics that *Hill Street* would later employ so much more effectively. Two of the show's actors, in fact, would become members of the *Hill Street* cast. The pilot was produced by Mark Tinker and directed by Bruce Paltrow, both of whom would go on to make *St. Elsewhere*, and it was co-written by Paltrow and Steven Bochco. Silverman ultimately decided not to order a series based on *Operating Room*, claiming that the audience wouldn't accept such an irreverent portrayal of doctors. "Let's try it as a cop show first," he suggested, "and if it works we'll do it with doctors" (Turow, 1989, p. 239). Less than a year after co-writing *Operating Room*, Bochco began developing *Hill Street*. In his autobiography, Tartikoff claimed that "*St. Elsewhere* was our second and much more successful attempt to execute *Operating Room*, a pilot that . . . was actually the predecessor to *Hill Street*" (Tartikoff and Leerhsen, 1992, p. 166). At some basic level, then, *St. Elsewhere* wasn't so much "*Hill Street* in a hospital" as *Hill Street* was "*Operating Room* in a police station."

Calling *St. Elsewhere* "*Hill Street Blues* in a hospital" wasn't totally inaccurate, however. Early in *St. Elsewhere*'s development, Grant Tinker had told Joshua Brand to watch *Hill Street* and had emphasized that the new show should contain, just as *Hill Street* did, humor, a large ensemble cast, a serialized format, and a "real" and gritty look (G. Tinker, personal communication, June 2, 1993). Furthermore, *Hill Street*'s ratings also provided an environment at NBC that nurtured the new project along. Without *Hill Street Blues*, it is unlikely that *St. Elsewhere* would ever have been made.

So all the ducks were in the pond. A harried medical resident working on-call in a Cleveland clinic; a young TV writer on the make for a career-enhancing idea; a Rabelaisian novel about life in a teaching hospital; a hit cop show with a huge cast and a mantelpiece-full of Emmys; a third-place network panting for a repeat of the *Hill Street* dream; an independent studio with a reputation for quality, an established style, and a crowd of talented writer-producers working on a series about to go off the air, plus a guy from Buffalo who'd never worked in television a day in his life. Surely this was a recipe for success.

By the time *St. Elsewhere* made it to the air, Grant Tinker had left MTM to replace Silverman as the president of NBC. Several episodes had been ordered without a pilot, and when they began to air, the news was bad. The ratings were occasionally the lowest of the week. NBC executives insisted that the show was too depressing and needed to be "lightened up" (Brustin, 1983). Most of the show's staff agreed. But Falsey and Brand, who had come to be known as "Dr. Death and Mr. Depression" to their colleagues, insisted on retaining the grim realism of the show that they had based on their experiences at the Cleveland Clinic (Turow, p. 243). Two camps developed, with Falsey and Brand in one, and Masius, Tinker, and Fontana in the other (M. Tinker, personal communication, April 19, 1993). Relations between the two camps became increasingly strained until Falsey and Brand left the show at the end of the first season.

Falsey and Brand may have been so obsessed with the darker side of things that they eventually were forced to leave the show, but their insistence on that "reality" was crucial to the show's early development. What they created was a lot easier for Masius, Fontana, and Tinker to lighten up a little, than it would have been to darken and thicken an overtested pilot that may have come out looking like *Trapper John, M.D.* "Dr. Death and Mr. Depression's" jealous protection of the first season may well have been necessary to make this show what it would become. They took it far enough in an untraditional direction that it had negotiating space to go back a little without becoming just another doctor show.

Given its low ratings, everyone at MTM assumed the series would be canceled at the end of the season, and by the spring, most of the staff had dispersed. In what would become an annual ritual, however, they were wrong. Unlike most of the patients in St. Eligius hospital, this program wasn't going to die so easily. *St. Elsewhere* proved to be one of the first beneficiaries of the kinder, more patient new Tinker regime. For five years in a row, *St. Elsewhere* brought in ratings numbers that under normal circumstances would have been considered uncompetitive; yet each time the show was renewed. Ironically, when the series finally did leave the air after its sixth season, just as it was starting to win its time slot, it was at the decision of MTM (G. Tinker, personal communication, June 2, 1993). Changes were in the wind in the television industry in the late 1980s, and MTM could no longer afford to make the show on what NBC was paying them. With syndication prices at an all-time low for hour-long series, and with 137 episodes already in the can, the company finally made the decision to pull the plug.

The Broth

So what was so great about *St. Elsewhere?* What came out of this mob of auteurs, some of whom were at cross purposes with others? Three features of the program stand out as the most obvious results of this collection of creators: its "forbidden" content, its self-reflexive in-jokes, and its strikingly intricate level of narrative detail.

Though it may have been inspired by the innovations of *Hill Street Blues, St. Elsewhere* often strayed even further from traditional television conventions than its predecessor had. In its quieter, more anonymous way—the show never made the cover of *TV Guide—St. Elsewhere* did some truly shocking things. It was the first prime-time drama to tell a story about an AIDS patient, for example, which it did in December 1983. In the 1987–88 season, six years before the debut of *NYPD Blue*, network TV's first full moon shot was launched on *St. Elsewhere* when Dr. Westphall (Ed Flanders) dropped his trousers in front of his supervisor just before he resigned from the hospital.

In the areas of sex, scatology, and forbidden language, all trademarks of *Hill Street Blues, St. Elsewhere* was seldom outdone. NBC Standards and Practices executive Ralph Daniels claimed that *Hill Street's* Bochco and *St. Elsewhere's* Paltrow actually competed to see who could slip the most outrageous stuff past the "censors" who worked in Daniels' office (Daniels, personal communication, March 21, 1993). Given the nature of a hospital, with its ample narrative opportunities to feature a whole catalog of bodily fluids and functions, Paltrow had a distinct advantage in this competition. From testicular cancer to excessive flatulence, the writers of *St. Elsewhere* used the guise of clinical jargon to talk about parts and dysfunctions of the human body that could never have gotten by the standards department in any other context. Sometimes these stories were very serious, but often they were irreverently funny, employed in an effort to obey the NBC mandate to "lighten up" the show while at the same time maintaining the appearance that the show was realistic and ground-breaking.

Some of the dirtiest jokes ever told on television resulted from this delicate balance. The content of these jokes might have been bawdy and obvious, but their form was extremely subtle. Often only the most discerning viewer could even catch them. In one episode, for example, a semi-regular patient has come in for an inflatable penile prosthesis that he needs after prostate surgery has left him impotent. In one scene, we hear the patient behind the curtain of his hospital bed trying out the device for the first time. After a good deal of progressively more excited pumping, we hear a loud pop, followed by the patient's "Oh-oh." In the following scene, the carefully listening viewer could have heard someone being paged over the hospital intercom system: "Paging Mr. Rise, Mr. Peter Rise." In another episode, Dr. Craig (William Daniels) is dictating his novel to his assistant: "Chapter 10. . . . She came into the garden, cheeks flushed, arms filled with flowers. I sat playing my Worlitzer. She asked, 'Where would you like these?' I smiled. 'Put the roses on the piano and the tulips on my organ.' " Having slipped a reference to one variety of oral sex into a network TV show, the writers went for two in the same scene. Stumped on a plot point in his novel, Dr. Craig asks his assistant to help him "think about what happens to Constance, the daughter, after the Lingus family reunion." In yet another episode, a doctor who learns, in an exchange that is barely audible above the din of the hospital hallway, that one of his patients has "acute angina," responds, "A good thing. She's got ugly legs."

There were hundreds of these jokes, some much filthier and more graphic than the examples above and nearly all of which required very close attention to catch. Too disguised to offend the general public, dedicated fans of the show derived great pleasure and pride from decoding and identifying these dirty little secrets. "I have a tremendous respect for my audience," Paltrow said when describing the "just for sport" nature of these games. "[T]hey are so hip and bright. The people who get it aren't offended" (M. Gendel, 1985, p. 1).

St. Elsewhere was at its hippest, however, when it was making sly references to itself and other popular entertainments. Whereas the "in-joke" is told with tiresome frequency on television today, it was quite uncommon only a dozen years ago. *Hill Street*'s writers seldom indulged in the practice, but after *St. Elsewhere* these self-conscious narrative devices became one of the calling cards of "quality" television. In her 1984 essay on the history of MTM, Jane Feuer told us why, and the reason was similar to the one that explained the profusion of dirty jokes as well:

> "Intertextuality," a literary term, refers in its broadest sense to the ways in which texts incorporate previous texts. Sometimes this takes the form of "self-reflexivity," when a text refers in self-conscious fashion back to itself. . . . It has been argued that these self-conscious strategies distinguish "high-art" from the unself-conscious popular arts—such as TV series. . . . Intertextuality and self-reflexivity operate . . . as a way of distinguishing the "quality" from the everyday product. (Feuer, 1984, p. 44)

MTM's writers and producers had been playing intertextual games since 1970, but in *St. Elsewhere* they went crazy.

After the unexpected renewal at the end of the first season, NBC's Brandon Tartikoff and Grant Tinker had met with Paltrow and told him that they expected a cheerier atmosphere to go along with the intense drama in the subsequent season. Tinker specifically asked if the hospital could be made a "lighter, brighter place" (Turow, p. 247). On the first episode of the second season, there was an immediate sign of the production team's good intentions on both fronts. In an early scene in the first act, Dr. Chandler (Denzel Washington) asks Dr. Westphall (Ed Flanders) why the hospital halls are filled with scaffolding. Westphall responds that a new paint job is under way as "a gift from the Chairman of the Board" who "thinks brighter walls will let our patients live longer." This scene reveals that not only had the *St. Elsewhere* staff acceded to Grant Tinker's dictum by physically lightening the place up, they'd also initiated a new comic philosophy. The fact that only a limited number of viewers would ever catch this knavish dig at what they thought was "Chairman" Tinker's obsession with "lighter and brighter" was part of the fun and added to the show's air of exclusivity. Though these kinds of jokes had been present a little during the first season, the new, more humorous *St. Elsewhere* would now rely much more heavily upon them as a major source of comic material. From the obvious to the obscure, self-conscious stabs at television and at *St. Elsewhere* itself soon punctuated nearly every script.

Truly "successful" viewing of *St. Elsewhere* often depended upon how many of the obscure media references one could find in each episode. The best and the brightest of the TV generation delighted in explicating examples like the following to less scholarly viewers:

> ***In one episode, a trio of hospital staffers named Charles, Burrows, and Charles are offhandedly mentioned by a nurse as having reserved a meeting room. (Glen Charles, James Burrows, and Les Charles were the executive producers of *Cheers*.) In another, Dr. Craig takes attendance in a gathering of new residents, calling out the names "Weinberger, Brooks, Allan, and Burns." (Ed Weinberger, James Brooks, and Allan Burns were all writers on MTM's first series, *The Mary Tyler Moore Show*.)

> ***Throughout the series, quick off-the-cuff lines laced with hidden media references were commonly made in St. Eligius's morgue. Once a doctor mentions that "the Douglas family wants to see [the body of] their Uncle Bub." (Uncle Bub was the crusty pre-Uncle Charlie mother-substitute to the Douglases in *My Three Sons*.) In another morgue scene a request is made for the report on "the Hasselhoff car wreck." (David Hasselhoff was currently starring in *Knight Rider*, an NBC action-adventure about a futuristic car whose voice was supplied by William Daniels, one of *St. Elsewhere*'s stars.) Casual mentions were made of autopsy reports on patients named "Spelling," "Sagansky," and "Nielsen." (Aaron Spelling presided over *Hart to Hart*, *Dynasty*, and *Hotel*, all of which were series that at one time had aired on ABC during *St. Elsewhere*'s time slot, and all of which trounced *St. Elsewhere* in the ratings. Jeff Sagansky had been a programming chief at NBC during much of *St. Elsewhere*'s run. In the last example, the entire Nielsen family had apparently died while watching TV.)

***In the one-hundredth episode, a patient named Cindy Kayshun is reported to still be going strong after a hundred episodes of angina. (An industry rule of thumb at the time was that a series needed a hundred episodes to ensure a lucrative syndication deal. Of Cindy's prognosis, a doctor says he "hopes she lives forever.")

Never delivered with rim shots or knowing glances at the camera, these jokes were always intricately woven into the narrative, often as part of very serious and emotional scenes.

The in-jokes considerably lightened the tone of the series. *New York Daily News* TV critic David Bianculli, one of *St. Elsewhere*'s major boosters and the one who coined the term "teleliteracy" in his 1992 book of the same title, once said that "hunting for the in-jokes, hidden references, and bad puns within each episode of *St. Elsewhere* is one of the least known, but most enjoyable, spectator sports in America" (Bianculli, personal communication, June 19, 1995). In a story in *People*, Howie Mandel called the series a "drama-game show" (S. Haller, 1988, p. 40). Whereas shows like *Jeopardy* required knowledge of traditional subjects like history and politics, scoring big on *St. Elsewhere* required one to be literate in the fields most of its viewers knew best: sports, movies, rock 'n' roll, and, most of all, television. To a great extent, *St. Elsewhere* was made by and for the segment of the baby boom generation that columnist Bob Greene dubbed the "yuppies," a group whose collective knowledge of these subjects was extraordinary.[4] These in-jokes, one of *St. Elsewhere*'s most distinctive features, were the productive result of a clash between a network mandate and a set of TV generation writer-producers.

Intertextuality and self-reflexivity had, of course, been used in television before. As early as the 1950s, for example, episodes of *The George Burns and Gracie Allen Show* (CBS, 1950–58) would occasionally feature George retiring to his room to watch his personal TV set to see how the very episode we were watching would turn out. Years later, *Burns and Allen* alumni Al Simon and Paul Henning brought out *Green Acres* (CBS, 1965–71), an at-times surrealistic sitcom that often referred to its own soundtrack and production credits.[5] But it was MTM Enterprises that took these devices to a new level of sophistication.

The fun and games reached meltdown in the *St. Elsewhere* episode that aired on November 20, 1985.[6] In it a recurring character has been admitted yet again to St. Eligius's psychiatric ward because he has no memory of who he is. Referred to by the staff as "John Doe #6" (Oliver Clark), he makes valiant but unsuccessful attempts to work with the doctors who try to help him reestablish his identity. Unable to remember his own "reality," he eventually turns to television to adopt a new one. A confirmed couch potato, much of what comes out of John's mouth was originally written for TV. He strings together jingles from commercials, lines from classic series episodes, and trademark sign-offs of well-known news anchors. While most of the patients in the hospital are getting physical nourishment from an I.V. tube, John Doe #6 gets spiritual nourishment from a T.V. tube. Near the beginning of the episode, he watches the end of an installment of *The Mary Tyler Moore Show* and becomes convinced that he has finally discovered his true identity—he is Mary Richards.

From here on, the episode's intertextuality slowly achieves critical mass, as it becomes a serio-comic homage to the history of MTM Enterprises and of prime time television itself. The interplay between different levels of fictional "reality" is staggering. Consider the following:

—Oliver Clark plays John Doe #6 playing Mary Tyler Moore playing Mary Richards.

—Also in the psych ward is Jack Riley playing Mr. Carlin, the same neurotic character he played in MTM's *The Bob Newhart Show,* but Clark/Doe/Moore/Richards instead recognizes him as Rhoda (Valerie Harper), Mary's best friend on *The Mary Tyler Moore Show* and the subject of her own spin-off series. So Jack Riley is playing Mr. Carlin who is being mistaken for Valerie Harper playing Rhoda Morgenstern.

—Betty White also has a role in this episode as a U.S. Navy doctor. John Doe #6, of course, recognizes her as "Happy Homemaker" Sue Ann Nivens, the character Betty White played in *The Mary Tyler Moore Show,* but she doesn't know what he's talking about, because she's now in a different role. Betty White's character is not, however, completely out of the TV loop. She refers to her boss at NASA as Commander Healy, whom we can assume was once NASA's Major Healy on *I Dream of Jeannie,* a character played by Bill Daly, who also starred in *The Bob Newhart Show* in which Mr. Carlin was a character but who John Doe #6 recognizes as a character from another MTM series, *Rhoda,* even though Jack Riley *is,* unlike Betty White, playing his original MTM role in this episode, complete with Mr. Carlin's old red cardigan sweater. The presence in the episode of Mr. Carlin and the mention by a sane character of Commander Healy imply that the world of *The Bob Newhart Show* and the world of *I Dream of Jeannie* are both part of *St. Elsewhere*'s "real" world, which would mean that Bill Daly exists simultaneously as both Commander Healy *and* Howard Borden from *The Bob Newhart Show.* Furthermore, if Healy exists as the boss of Betty White's character, that implies that Jeannie herself also exists. Another reference is made to *I Dream of Jeannie* in this episode when a born-again astronaut refuses to obey Commander Healy's orders, saying, "You can't serve two masters."

—Oliver Clark also appeared on *The Bob Newhart Show* as one of Dr. Bob Hartley's patients, the insecure salesperson Mr. Herd. Teleliterate viewers could, therefore, solve John Doe #6's identity problem, but Mr. Carlin doesn't recognize this fellow group therapy patient of Dr. Hartley's. To complicate matters further, Oliver Clark also played Dr. Charles Webner, one of the principal characters on *Operating Room,* the early prototype for *St. Elsewhere.*

—The wall of John Doe #6's room is covered with a jumble of letters of the alphabet. Compare this to the solid, single "M" that appeared in Mary Richard's apartment. Mary knew who she was and her "M" showed it; John Doe #6's only hope of getting the right personalized initial on his wall is to use the entire alphabet.

—Warren Coollidge (Byron Stewart), who was a student of Carver High in *The White Shadow,* is now an orderly at St. Eligius and wears a Carver High T-shirt. Though Coollidge's presence in *St. Elsewhere* implies that the world portrayed in *The White Shadow* was "real," not just a TV show, an episode of *The White*

Shadow is viewed on a hospital TV set by John Doe #6 in this episode of *St. Elsewhere,* implying that the show and therefore Coolidge are fictional. As he watches *The White Shadow* with John, Mr. Carlin suggests that whoever came up with the program was "a real smoothy."

—Actual episodes of MTM shows play during this episode, with commentary by John Doe #6 and Mr. Carlin. We see the recognizable MTM kitty logo meow at the end of them. We'll also see it meow at the end of the episode we're watching.

—John Doe #6 throws a party in the psych ward and begins to quote dialogue directly from old *Mary Tyler Moore* episodes. At the end of the episode he tosses his Mary Richards-like hat into the air, just as Mary does at the end of the opening credits of her show, and, quoting from the *Mary Tyler Moore* theme song, he states that he's "gonna make it after all."

—John Doe #6 might remind the truly teleliterate of "Number 6," the only name ever given to Patrick McGoohan's character on *The Prisoner.*

—When commenting in this episode on names for babies, an ob/gyn doctor asks, "Whatever happened to good old-fashioned names like Bruce, John, Mark, or Tom?" *St. Elsewhere*'s writer-producers are *Bruce* Paltrow, *Mark* and *John* Tinker, *John* Masius, and *Tom* Fontana.

On one level, *St. Elsewhere*'s intertextual in-jokes were just that: amusing little nods to the minutiae and effluvia of TV culture. But they were more than that. They announced that there *is* a television tradition and they helped position *St. Elsewhere* within that tradition.

The John Doe #6 episode also illustrates how densely packed *St. Elsewhere*'s episodes were. More than any other series in the history of American television, *St. Elsewhere* rewarded the attentive viewer. The show's narrative consistency and attention to the tiniest of details was astonishing compared to other television programs before and even since, and it gave the series a literary value that extended beyond the mere playing of intertextual games. Examples of this are difficult to give without long and somewhat arduous descriptions like the one that follows.

In the pilot episode, victims of an explosion that went off in a bank are brought to St. Eligius. Over the next few episodes we get to know the ruthless terrorist (pre-*Player* Tim Robbins), who was himself injured when he set off the bomb, and the husband of one of the comatose victims, Mr. McAllister (Jack Bannon). Mild-mannered and excessively polite, McAllister faithfully stands vigil over his wife night and day. When she finally dies in the fourth episode, he goes to Dr. Westphall's office to make arrangements to have her body flown home to Minnesota. Mr. McAllister is examining a framed poster on the office wall which inspires him, as soon as Westphall arrives, to launch into a Proustian reverie about the day he fell in love with his now-dead wife:

MR. MCALLISTER: Dr. Westphall. I was just noticing your native plant poster.
DR. WESTPHALL: My daughter Elizabeth gave me that. She thinks my office is too stark.
MR. MCALLISTER: You garden?
DR. WESTPHALL: I try. Every year I try.

MR. MCALLISTER: (pointing to a plant on the poster): Viola tricolor.

DR. WESTPHALL: No, I think that's johnny jump-up, isn't it?

MR. MCALLISTER (looking more carefully):   Footsteps-of-spring, that's what it is.

DR. WESTPHALL: You got it.

MR. MCALLISTER: My wife Catherine and I went to college in New Hampshire. There was a section of campus where we used to play touch football that was bordered by footsteps-of-spring. Hundreds of them. I remember this one Sunday we were playing—Catherine was the quarterback on the other team. And as she faded back, I came in from the right, from the blind side, and she didn't see me. She looked so hopeful—scanning the field, looking for someone to throw to. I almost didn't want to disturb her but it was a once-in-a-lifetime shot and I took it. Caught her just below the hip, and we both went flying into the footsteps-of-spring.

The metaphors of flowers, football, and spring were effective in fleshing out the relationship of two characters who have been given only a few minutes of screentime and one of whom is in a coma. Then the episode ends, quite shockingly, when the grief-stricken Mr. McAllister shoots and kills the terrorist as he's being moved to the prison ward.

That episode played on November 23, 1982, and it was the last we'd hear of Mr. McAllister for nearly three and a half years. Then, in an episode aired in March of 1986, Dr. Jack Morrison (David Morse) is performing community service work in a local prison when he encounters McAllister doing time for the murder of the terrorist. McAllister has fallen in with a bad element, and during a prison uprising he helps hold Jack down while another prisoner rapes him. In the next episode we learn in a meeting of hospital administrators that Jack has gone to his hometown of Seattle to recover from the attack. In the very next scene, Dr. Phil Chandler is buying flowers in the hospital giftshop as a peace offering to his once-girlfriend Dr. Roxanne Turner (Alfre Woodard). As he purchases them, he tells a fellow doctor: "Roxanne loves johnny jump-ups," to which the other doctor replies, "Too bad, those are footsteps-of-spring." In this one line we are asked to remember the gentle innocence of Mr. McAllister's monologue from three seasons back and to link it to his recent role in Jack's rape. Only the most zealous fans, of course, ever made the connection.

Whenever one did happen to catch one of these details—and they were quite common to the show—one realized that this program was unlike any other. Never before had a television series maintained this level of intricacy and consciousness of its own history across seasonal lines. This degree of narrative consistency is unusual, partly because there is a great deal of turnover among the writing and producing staffs of most series from year to year. "I think it comes mostly from the fact that we were so inside the show," writer-producer Tom Fontana speculated. "It was so much a part of our reality that I knew as much about these characters' history as I did about my own" (Fontana, personal communication, May 27, 1993). For much of *St. Elsewhere*'s time on the air, every script, no matter who wrote it, took a final trip through the typewriters of Fontana and John Masius.[7] "It was important for us to do that in order to keep the consistency of the show," Fontana recalls. "We'd put something in a script in show number three that we knew would pay off in show number fifteen" (Fontana, personal communication, May 27, 1993). Unlike most successful producers, most of the people who worked on *St. Elsewhere* were working on no other programs for most of the run of the series. This dedication to a single series often isn't the best career move, but it certainly makes for good television.

*   *   *

It is clearly impossible to attach a single name to *St. Elsewhere*. It was, in fact, the cooperative nature of commercial television that made the show as good as it was. The ideas and input of network and studio executives, the original concept from a real medical doctor with experience in a teaching hospital, and the sometimes combative relationship between the writers and producers were all necessary in shaping the program.

Even network input, so often seen as the enemy of "quality," also played some important positive roles during the run of the series. *St. Elsewhere* came to NBC during a period when the network was consistently in last place in the ratings race. The experimentation made possible by the fact that the company had little to lose resulted in a rich string of critically acclaimed shows. Network executives played a significant role in the conception of the show and, more importantly, in keeping it on the air against all conventional wisdom. This allowed the show six full years to improve, evolve, and ultimately reach an aesthetic completion. Also by insisting the show be "lightened up," NBC helped the transformation of *St. Elsewhere* into a more comic program that opened the door for the self-reflexive and dirty jokes discussed above.

More importantly, *St. Elsewhere* launched a number of significant careers[8] and, along with *Hill Street Blues*, the new genre of "quality drama." Within a few years, *Newsday*'s TV critic Marvin Kitman remarked that "There are more creators/writers of *St. Elsewhere* floating around these days than people who came over on the Mayflower. [They], along with writers for *Cosby* and *M*A*S*H*, are the three leading cash crops in Southern California" (D. Paisner, 1992, p. 52). At the start of the 1992–93 season, Falsey and Brand had a critically acclaimed show on each of the three major networks: *Northern Exposure* (CBS), *I'll Fly Away* (NBC), and *Going to Extremes* (ABC). Other members of the *St. Elsewhere* staff went on to produce the series *Moonlighting*, *China Beach*, *L.A. Law* (NBC, 1986–94), and *Civil Wars* (ABC, 1991–93).

By the fall of 1995, attitudes about the quality of television were dramatically improving. Responding to new series like *Homicide: Life on the Street* (NBC, 1993–), *NYPD Blue* (ABC, 1993–), *ER* (NBC, 1994–), *Chicago Hope* (CBS, 1994–), and *Murder One* (ABC, 1995–1997), critics and journalists were starting to talk about television as though it had really come of age. Blazened across the cover of the October 20 issue of *Entertainment Weekly* was the announcement, "10 Reasons Why TV Is Better Than the Movies" (B. Fretts, 1995); two days later the *New York Times Magazine* carried a cover story entitled, "Want Literature? Stay Tuned. More Than Movies, Plays, and Even in Some Ways Novels, Television Drama Is Making Art Out of Real Life" (C. McGrath, 1995); the following week *Time* magazine ran a TV story claiming "The Real Golden Age Is Now" (B. Handy, 1995).

Many of the dramatic shows celebrated in these articles owe a lot to the *St. Elsewhere* style. The writers of *ER*, for example, regularly lift story ideas directly from the earlier medical series. Many of these shows are in fact being produced by *St. Elsewhere* alumni. Tom Fontana executive produces *Homicide: Life on the Street* with Baltimore film auteur Barry Levinson, and Mark Tinker is executive producer and occasional director of *NYPD Blue*. John Tinker and Lydia Woodward, writers who joined the *St. Elsewhere* team later in its run, produce *Chicago Hope* and *ER*, respectively.

St. *Elsewhere* served as a training ground for some of the most important creators working in television drama today. A true understanding of the critically acclaimed dramas that have appeared in the last few years depends upon further studies tracing the various lines of authorial influence that flow from *St. Elsewhere*.

NOTES

1. For a discussion of these studies, read the introduction to this chapter.
2. Dr. Luria now practices medicine in the upstate New York town of Middleburgh. His life as a doctor in this beautiful but remote place later inspired yet another of Brand's series, his biggest hit, *Northern Exposure* (Luria, personal communication, March 30, 1993).
3. *The White Shadow* also boasts an extraordinary alumni list: Steven Bochco (*Hill Street, L.A. Law*) and Marshall Herskovitz (*thirtysomething*) each wrote a script for the series, and future film directors Kevin Hooks and Thomas Carter were in the cast.
4. An excellent discussion of the "yuppie" audience can be found in Feuer (1995), pp. 25–41.
5. Tom Fontana, one of *St. Elsewhere*'s two principal writers, claims to have been a big fan of *Green Acres* and many references to the show can be found in *St. Elsewhere* (Tom Fontana, personal interview with the author, April 1995).
6. This episode has been discussed at some length by S. R. Olson (1987, pp. 288–289), A. Nehamas (1990, pp. 169–172), and D. Bianculli (1992, pp. 150–152).
7. This was the case only from the last episode of the first season through the end of the fifth season.
8. Falsey and Brand stayed with the medical genre when they created *Northern Exposure* (CBS, 1990–95) and *Going to Extremes* (ABC, 1992); Mark Tinker took his seamless directing style to *Civil Wars* (ABC, 1992), *L.A. Law* (NBC, 1986–1994), and *NYPD Blue* (ABC, 1993–), among others; and Tom Fontana went on to write complex, serio-comic scripts for *Homicide: Life On the Streets* (NBC, 1993–). Bruce Paltrow seemed to distance himself most from the show by returning to the half-hour form with *Nick and Hillary* (NBC, 1989, a sitcom retooled from his short-lived drama, *Tattingers*), and *Home Fires* (NBC, 1993), neither of which survived a season. The consensus among many critics and scholars, however, is that none of this work rivaled the overall quality of *St. Elsewhere*.

REFERENCES

Bianculli, D. (1992). *Teleliteracy: Taking television seriously*. New York: Continuum.

Brustin, M. (1983, May). *St. Elsewhere: Creative changes through re-examination*. Paper presented at the Third International Conference on Television Drama, East Lansing, Michigan.

Feuer, J. (1984). The MTM style. In J. Feuer, P. Kerr, and T. Vahimagi (Eds.), *MTM: 'Quality television'* (pp. 32–60). London: The British Film Institute.

Feuer, J. (1995). *Seeing through the eighties: Television and Reaganism.* Durham, NC: Duke University Press.

Fretts, B. (1995, October 20). TV saves the world! *Entertainment Weekly,* 22–30.

Gendel, M. (1985, September 4). The battle for the living rooms of America: Three producers who regularly push at tv's boundaries. *Los Angeles Times,* Part 6, p. 1.

Haller, S. (1988, May 23). Good night *St. Elsewhere. People,* 40.

Handy, B. (1995, October 30). The real golden age is now. *Time,* 84–90.

McGrath, C. (1995, October 22). The triumph of the prime-time novel. *New York Times Magazine,* 52–59, 68, 76, 86).

Nehamas, A. (1990, winter). Seriously watching. *South Atlantic Quarterly,* 157–179.

Olson, S. R. (1987). Meta-televison: Popular postmodernism. *Critical Studies in Mass Communication, 4,* 284–300.

Paisner, D. (1992). *Horizontal hold: The making and breaking of a network television pilot.* New York: Birch Lane Press.

Shem, S. (1978). *The house of God.* New York: Putnam.

Tartikoff, B., & Leerhsen, C. (1992). *The last great ride.* New York: Turtle Bay Books.

Turow, J. (1989). *Playing doctor: Television, storytelling, and medical power.* New York: Oxford University Press.

Text-Centered Approaches
to Television Criticism

Writing about the televised coverage of the 1972 Olympics, Raymond Williams argued that the events were not so much sport as politics:

> [N]obody could have been watching and not seen the conventional politics. Of the nation state, above all: the flags, the delegations, the *chefs de mission.* Everybody says that the medals table between states is unofficial and virtually everyone compiles and broadcasts or prints it. The victory ceremonies are submilitary, with national anthems and the raising of flags. At the official opening, in and through the marching columns, there was often a pleasant lightness of touch: people waving and smiling: the dancing and the pigeons. . . . All the time, in fact, behind these marvellous young men and women were the posses of appointed and self-appointed people who derive a right to control them (O'Connor, 1989, pp. 22–23).

Such an analysis of a sporting event raises many questions—about sports and nationalism and about television's penchant for presenting the dramatic in ever more dramatic terms. It also raises a bedeviling question for the critic: *What is "the text" of television programs?* Obviously, Williams thought the text of the 1972 Olympics was political—especially that olympiad, perhaps, where seventeen people, including eleven members of the Israeli Olympic team, were shot to death by members of the Black September guerilla group. Television was showing parades of athletes, competitions, and celebratory moments, but Williams was seeing nothing but political actions whereby one country was seeking advantage and power, even in murderous ways, at the expense of others. To Williams, during the 1972 Olympics, "an arranged version of what the world is like was invaded by an element of what several parts of the world are actually like" (ibid., p. 24).

The Ambiguous Status of the Text

What *is* the text? Such a simple question, but such a difficult answer because the answer depends upon how you look at the question. The idea of the text is actually an ambiguous concept in three ways:

Stability-instability. A common understanding of the word *text* is a written composition with a beginning, a middle, and an end—a sort of Aristotelian understanding of a literary work; yet technically the word means almost the opposite. The Greek word *techne* refers to an art or a craft, a technique for doing something. More specifically, we get our word *text* from the Latin verb *texere,* to weave. In a classical sense, therefore, a text is something—something verbal—being made: not already made, but being constructed, being textualized. The word comes into general use after 1953, when the French literary and social critic Roland Barthes contrasts a *text* with a *work* (*oeuvre*): to Barthes, a *work* is a complete, closed or finished *object* while a *text* is an open, even infinite *process* of meaning-making and remaking (Johnson, 1990, esp. p. 40).

Barthes's work-versus-process tension suggests that a text is both stable, as a work, and yet never stable, even instable, because it always is in process, always being remade. To Barthes, the tension that can exist between a particular *signifer* (e.g., a word or a picture) and a mental image (i.e., an idea) is simultaneously stable because the word or picture is, but also unstable because ideas can vary from time to time or situation to situation, even from an awake state to a dream. Signifiers may be stable, but *signifieds* can be variable—in process—because meanings change across time and setting. So *The Man from U.N.C.L.E.* was viewed as a television adventure story in the 1960s, but now would be understood better as a cold war fantasy. The signifiers are the same, but the signifieds, the meanings we attach to those signifiers, have changed.

Production-reception. A text is ambiguous because its meaning depends in part upon who's doing the weaving, the constructing of meanings. "Texts are the sites of conflict," argues John Fiske, "between their forces of production and modes of reception" (1987b, p. 14). What the makers of a television program may have intended and what the viewers of that program actually saw can be wildly divergent, and, further, different sets of viewers may "see" quite different shows. Many white viewers thought they were getting an inside view of black America in *The*

Cosby Show, while many African American viewers thought the show was a sellout by a gifted set of actors to white America. Some people see in NFL football exciting games that showcase the best in stereotypically male values (teamwork, physical perfection, personal commitment to self-development), while others see in those Sunday games some of the worst of presumably masculine values (celebration of the physical over the spiritual, ruthless competitiveness, revenge based on absolutist standards, rule-governed rather than creative interaction). Texts are ambiguous because people who read and see them tend to re-make whatever they've read and witnessed in terms of their personal and social situations.

Multiple codes. Particularly in the case of multimediated works such as television programs, the question, What is the text? becomes particularly difficult to answer because so many codes are operative. From among the array of codes with which we are presented, out of what materials do we as viewers construct the meanings of TV programs? the written script? the performed action framed in a decorated set? the speeches of actors and the other aural codes such as sound effects and mood music? That is, are television's texts verbal, visual, or acoustic, or all three (Figure 6.1)? As O'Sullivan et al. (1994, pp. 317–318) argue, "A text, then, consists of a network of codes working on a number of levels. . . . It is thus problematic and demands analysis." The notion of the text, therefore, is ambiguous because you must specify the codes with which you are working and the level (manifest or hidden, mundane or transcendent) on which you are attempting to read or interpret the text.

The idea of textuality, in summary, is an ambiguous concept because of problems of instability of meanings, variability in what people actually hear and see when they encounter a TV program, and multiplicity of codes comprising a televisual message. Yet in spite of—even because of—such problems, text-centered television criticism is popular and productive of vibrant critical television studies.

Assumptions Grounding Text-Centered Television Criticism

Taking some of the ideas just encountered, we can formulate three primary assumptions underlying most text-centered TV criticism in our era.

1. *Texts are constructed out of sequences of signs arrayed in codes and capable of being experienced or interpreted in common ways by members of a society.* One of the key words in this assumption is *sign,* something accessible to your senses, for example, the spoken word *tree* (sound), the written word *tree* or a drawing of one (sight), the odor of burning wood (smell), a piece of wood carved into a duck (touch and sight). A *sign* is something with which meanings are

---

FIGURE 6.1   The multiple codes of televisual communication

Verbal Codes: Linguistic Units

Naming: how are people (girl, Ms., Joan, Dr. Maxwell) identified?

Attitudinal language: what words are used to express positive or negative judgments?

Valuative language: what values—sociological, psychological, legal, moral, religious, and aesthetic—are encoded in dialogue?

Metaphorical language: with what kinds of metaphors are people, events, places, and ideas talked about?

Ideological language: are examples of ideological language—*democratic, heathen, scientifically proven*—used in arguments and advice-giving talk?

Verbal Codes: Communication Acts

Grammatical orientation: who asks questions? who give orders? who asserts something as a fact? do different characters use different kinds of grammar as signs of class, education, race, or status?

Verbal orientation (perspective taking): what perspectives or viewpoints are assumed in a character's speech? ("As your father, I think. . . . ," "You ladies always are. . . . ," "Nine out of ten doctors recommend. . . .")

Narrative orientation: what stories are told so as to emphasize what sorts of thoughts or actions?

Argumentative orientation: what kinds of arguments for or against some idea or action are offered?

Visual Codes: Orientation

Color: do particular colors in a shot carry special meanings?

Framing: are important people or objects centered or marginalized in key shots?

Light-dark: how does lighting control visual orientation?

Simplicity-complexity: are objects or people isolated in some shots (simplicity) or put into a multilayered picture (complexity)? (For example, many televised

---

associated. In the language of semiotics, a sign is a *signifier* or vehicle, while that which is associated with it, what we usually call "meaning," is *signified*. Taken together, a signifier plus a signified constitute a process of *signification*. A coherent series of signs—a string of words, for example, "Jack jumped over the candlestick"—makes up a *communication act*. Even a sequence of pictures can form a communication act, as when someone shows you a sunrise, then a picture of the sun overhead at noon, and finally a sunset, so as to suggest the passage of time through a day. A whole field of signs—the words in a language or recog-

plays isolate characters giving soliloquies, whereas a show such as *ER* often shows you activities in several areas at once to connote dynamism and excitement.)

Foreground-background relationships: what person or object is made the focus of a shot, and what people, objects, or scenes are made the context for the person or object in the foreground?

Conventionalized objects (icons): what icons—a flag, an identifiable kind of clothing, a way of standing or looking, a picture of a sunset—are used to convey particular meanings recognized across a society?

Visual Codes: Complex Meaning Systems

Emotionality: how are feelings coded into shots or sequences of shots?

Quotation: what characteristics of a particular shot or sequence evoke memories of similar shots or sequences from other visual artifacts?

Interaction with other codes: how do the verbal and acoustic codes affect the meaning of visualized people, places, things, or actions?

Acoustic Codes

Auditory signs: what sounds—a train whistle, a howling wolf, the sound of frying bacon—are used to convey particular meanings understood by members of a society?

Paralinguistic cues: what tones of voice—soothing, pleading, rasping, slurring, or whispering—are used to characterize physical or emotional states, relationships between people, and personality types?

Spatial organization: how is sound used to organize space (e.g., changing the sound of a train to signal its approach, arrival, and departure; two or three different auditory levels to indicate that some people are central, some farther away, and some still farther away, as in a busy shot in the emergency ward)?

Auditory echoes: what uses of sound trigger memories of one's previous experience with media (e.g., the theme song from a childhood cartoon) or important life or world experiences (e.g., "The Wedding March")?

Interaction with other codes: how is the meaning of sounds affected by what is said or what is shown?

nizable clothing from particular countries—is called a *code*. Television, we already have noted, is experienced through verbal, visual, and acoustic codes.

2. *Texts are capable of multiple kinds and levels of interpretation.* The second key concept from the definition of text is "experienced or interpreted." For something to be a text, the codes must be understood. If I'm in Finland and don't know that the word *puu* is a sign Finns use when talking about a tree, that sign is not significant to me—it's not a sign I can experience in the way Finns do. When we defined texts in terms of "common ways," we were sug-

gesting that unless people's understandings of signifiers and signifieds are similar, communication—the sharing of meaning—cannot occur.

This is not to suggest, however, that signs mean the same thing to all people, even of a society or region. Because meaning is grounded as much in personal experience as in common or shared experience, meanings are slippery and variable. Two people can and do construct different meanings from the same text for several reasons:

Social situation. The TV program *Homicide* might be watched in one way by a rich person worried about crime in his neighborhood and in another way by a poor person who has been hassled by cops on his block. Males and females often look at sports programs in different ways. Your social situation and status can affect how you understand what you see on TV. Stuart Hall (1980) argued that you can decode or read television in three ways: a *dominant reading* understands the signs pretty much as the producer did, a *negotiated reading* adjusts some of the meanings, and an *oppositional reading* reverses them. A dominant reading of a televised political convention produces meanings consonant with the ones the party wants you to comprehend, whereas an oppositional reading might cause you to laugh at the serious parts and boo the party's ideological statements. Women might do a negotiated reading, as when they understand the political sentiments but note the lack of female candidates on the platform.

Open and closed texts. Some texts invite you to make your own meanings; they are comparatively open. For example, weather programs often include outdoor shots over which a list of temperatures is scrolling. Those shots of the beach or wheat fields or mountains are open texts; you are invited to let your mind roam, to think of your own experiences or fantasies. The weather map, however, is a comparatively closed text; the list of specific places with particular geographic relationships to each other, and their temperatures, is strongly oriented to the communication of specific information in unambiguous signs. The relative degree of openness of a text affects your ability to participate in or even take over the meaning-making process. (See Eco, 1979; cf. Barthes on "readerly" and "writerly" texts, 1975.)

Polyvalence. Celeste Condit (1989) also suggests that people's value orientations affect how they experience televised scenes of abortions. Pro-Life and Pro-Choice students interpreted an episode of *L.A. Law* dealing with abortion in very different ways; they assessed the soundness of arguments made in the courtroom through their own values. Essentially, the Pro-Life and Pro-Choice students made different texts out of the episode.

Recoding and poaching. The example of *The Man from U.N.C.L.E.* mentioned earlier illustrates another interpretive process. Especially across time, viewers can look at shows in wholly different ways. Michael Real (1989) calls this process *recoding,* seeing a show in a totally alternative way, as many viewers of the channel Nickelodeon do when watching 1950s and 1960s reruns. They view the shows as illustrations of those decades rather than, say, as a sitcom or adventure show. Henry Jenkins (1992) suggests that viewers can go even farther than that. With the help of a remote control and a VCR, they can build their own programs out of bits and pieces of material from multiple channels; or they can invent whole lives for characters, as the *Star Trek* fans, the Trekkies, have done. Both of these activities are examples of what Jenkins calls poaching.[1] Meaning-making thus can be almost wholly in control of the viewers, not the producers.

Overall, then, although texts are arrays of signs that have to a large extent been precoded, that is to say, come with shared meanings associated with them, viewers have a series of interpretive strategies available, thanks to their social situations, the openness of codes, and their own desires, and can use those strategies to adjust or even remake meanings according to their own experiences and interests.

3. *What texts mean, therefore, varies with person, times, place, and context: with variations in language or code users, the times or styles of an epoch, and the specific situations in which the texts are consumed.* This is a fact with which people—and their critics—must live. Human communication is never perfectly efficient; misunderstandings and alternative understandings are part of the human condition. Recognition of this fact of life could cause you to quit the business of criticism, but that's too radical a response. We suggest another. We propose to handle "the problem of the text" in an arbitrary but serviceable way. We offer separate chapters on users (audience-centered criticism) and situations (context-centered criticism) so that we can reserve text-centered criticism for kinds of analyses that focus on *encoding processes,* that is, on text-making. Our focus is on *textuality*—how communication signs and acts are assembled, in our case by television producers, for the education and pleasure of viewers. This chapter features ways to analyze and interpret the arrays of signs that we call texts.

Some Types of Textual Criticism

Generally speaking, most criticism focused on texts per se falls into one of four categories: semiotic-structural, generic, rhetorical, and narrative.

Semiotic-Structural Analysis

Some critics are interested in the fine details of meaning-making, in the careful (often called "close") analysis of particular aspects of encoding. So, Ellen Seiter (1987) did a shot-by-shot analysis of the opening credits (1985–1986 version) of *The Cosby Show*. She charted the visual, verbal, and acoustic codes, talking about the kinds of shots, their sequence, their analogies to other shows in television history, and the overall impression left by the credits:

> *The Cosby Show* is itself a utopian representation of the family: money is no object; love and harmony is the rule; play abounds as a means of solving discipline problems; marriage is sexy; gender equality is the stated goal; parents and children enjoy stimulating, satisfying situations at work and in school; childcare and housework are either invisible or enjoyable. Like a musical, *The Cosby Show* presents the world not as it really is, but as it should be (p. 38).

Such a study takes us squarely into the operations of codes on television. Seiter not only uses the shots, title cards, and musical style to ground her conclusions, but also looks at dress, stereotyped reactions to other characters, icons of wealth, and the dance steps of each character. Visual coding is broken down into subcodes so that she can assemble multiple kinds of semiotic evidence to back her claims.[2]

Closely related to semiotics, structuralist studies of discourses ferret out the mechanisms and concepts we use to organize our life world—more especially, the ways we organize competing forces in life. All human beings presumably are aware of the oppositions between good and evil, the individual and society, justice and injustice, masculine and feminine, optimism and despair, and life and death. We deal with such binary oppositions in our literatures (e.g., *The Agony and the Ecstasy*), rituals (e.g., funeral ceremonies), myths (e.g., the Faust story), children's stories (e.g., *The Little Mermaid*), and yes, our television programs. To study the ways in which we use texts to structure the life world so as to better understand it and to more forcibly act in it is the primary goal of structural criticism.

In 1986 Robert Hodge and David Tripp did a semiotic-structural analysis of the children's cartoon *Fangface*. At the center of the program they found tensions between nature and culture, as well as, of course (this is a werewolf cartoon!), between animalness and humanness. Both halves of these oppositions were explored and shown in positive ways, and thus, they argued: "The result is not a single consistent message about the relations between the two. Sometimes nature is seen as threatening, sometimes as compatible with culture. Fangface is the focus of both ambiguity and ambivalence" (p. 28). Seiter (1994) shows that a similar analysis can be made of *Teenage Mutant Ninja Turtles*. This sort of analysis is typical of structuralism, which, as John Hartley notes (O'Sullivan et al., 1994, pp. 304–305), "shares with other twentieth-century enterprises—in physics and astronomy especially—attention to relations and systems as the framework for explanation." (See also John Fiske's structural analyses: 1983, 1984, 1987b.)

For most beginning students of television criticism, <u>semiotic studies of signs, the elements of a code, are the easier sorts of semiotic-structural analysis to perform.</u> More subtle and more difficult are analyses of what we earlier called the communication act—the structure of a sentence, a scene, an episode, or a program. As the example we've just mentioned suggests, the structure of most sorts of texts can be fruitfully examined in two ways: via *syntagmatic analysis* and *paradigmatic analysis*.

Syntagms are coherent sequences of signs. A sentence ("Jack jumped over the candlestick") is a syntagm, with the three primary signs—"Jack" (an agent), "jumped" (an action of the agent in some environment), and "candlestick" (an object defining that environment)—that, when taken together, provide a set of signifieds that most users of English would understand. Most students of texts are interested in larger syntagms—whole stories, even whole TV programs (e.g., the changes in *M*A*S*H* or *The Mary Tyler Moore Show* over time).[3] For example, whole types of programs can be defined by the sequencing of actions. A situation comedy was defined by Newcomb (1974), for example, as a sequence of four actions: setting a situation, complicating it, turning the world upside down in an episode of "uproar," and then resolving the situation (the *denouement*).

At the scenic level, what sort of acts precede a police officer's shooting of a presumed criminal? The shooting will signify different motivations if it's been preceded by the criminal (a) harming a member of the cop's family, (b) holding a hostage when cornered, (c) shooting at the police officer first, (d) running away from the scene of a capital crime, or (e) having repented and joined a monastery. Similarly, if a story about your state's financial crisis is followed by another on money the governor is spending on renovating his residence at state expense, the association of these two events almost demands that you question the governor's expenditures. Syntagmatically, one event can provide a context for our understandings of other events. Or if events tend to follow each other in predictable ways—as in the American Western (Cawelti, 1970, pp. 34–45, argued that there are only seven narrative plots for all of them)—then syntagmatic analysis is helping us define basic forms for discourse.

Paradigmatic analysis is not so concerned with sequences of signs as with their substitutability or general resemblances to each other. A paradigm, in this sense, is a group of signs that, though different, are so related to each other that they either (a) can stand for general ideas or principles or (b) can be exchanged for each other. O'Sullivan et al. (1994, p. 216) define *paradigm* as a "set of units from which one may be chosen to combine with units from other paradigms to form a syntagm (that is a combination of units into a signifying whole)." For example, "a Coke," "a soda," "a cup of well water [or spring water]," "a glass of iced tea," "a lemonade," "a beer," or "a cold one" signify, technically, different chilled liquids, yet paradigmatically are all closely related: each belongs to the family of liquids that is considered in Western thought to soothe, to refresh, to change bodily pain into physical pleasure. Similarly, the sentence "Your day of reckoning is here," the emergence of a Clint Eastwood or Charles Bronson out of the shadows and into the vision of an evil-doer, and/or particular kinds of music used in Eastwood or Bronson films all participate in a paradigm we could call signs of vengeance.

One more point about paradigms: as these examples suggest, the family resemblances among signs means that, once those resemblances are understood, individual signs can be used to evoke the whole family. For example, John Fiske (1984) argued that particular characters in the British serial *Dr Who* by their stereotypical behavior come to represent oppositions between democracy and totalitarianism, freedom and slavery, peace and violence, plenty and scarcity, freedom and captivity, life and death, truth and lies, and good and evil. He suggested that some characters in that show—Dr. Who, Taris, Romana, and K9—line up with the ideologically positive values, whereas Adrasta, Palace, Karela, and Wolfweeds signify the binary opposites. Such arguments—and those from Hodge and Tripp (1986)—depend upon paradigmatic analysis.

Semiotic analysis is the basis for many kinds of criticism because of its focus on codes. When paired with structuralist interest in syntagms and paradigms, that is, in sequences and oppositions among acts within the life world, semiotics helps us understand much of the dynamic, dialectical themes that engage television audiences.

Generic Criticism

Whenever you divide types of television programs into such categories as sitcoms, sports shows, dramatic shows, adventure shows, game shows, news, documentaries, and parodies, you're recognizing the underlying tenet of generic criticism: that different types of discourse have recognizable, even defining, characteristics—they form paradigms. Or from the viewpoint of human beings, some uses of languages are repeated often enough so that we can identify them and form expectations as to how languages *should* be used. *Genre* is roughly the French word for "type," and generic criticism features questions about type of discourse at various levels.

Television critics ask many different questions about genres:

Metagenres: how many different types of programs are there?

Generic evolution: how have sitcoms changed from the 1950s to the present?

Generic hybrids: what are the defining characteristics of the prime-time soap opera or the docudrama?

History of genres: why did the Western peak in the late 1950s and early 1960s and then all but disappear from television?

Generic criticism allows critics to talk sensibly about whole groups of programs, helping us map our viewing experiences in familiar ways. Generic analysis can also be a first step for other sorts of studies. So in one of the essays that follows, Gronbeck first defines *news* as a genre before doing a rhetorical analysis.

Rhetorical Criticism

Generally speaking, the study of rhetoric is the study of the force or power of discourse—of the ways in which texts affect the beliefs, attitudes, values, perceptual orientations, and behaviors of their consumers. Rhetoricians have most thoroughly studied political television (see Gronbeck, 1990, for a review of studies). They have also examined fiction programs: Robert Schrag et al. (1981) examined the "new humane collectivity," the caring circle of friends and associates that appeared in television sitcoms of the 1980s; Karen Foss and Stephen Littlejohn (1986) probed the rhetorical vision of the made-for-television movie, *The Day After;* Charles Larson and Christine Oravec (1987) examined the sort of community viewers and listeners were invited to fantasize about in *A Prairie Home Companion* radio and television programs; Jane Connelly Loeb (1990) found the ideological conservatism of *thirtysomething* remarkable for its time, though Bonnie Dow (1990) was not at all surprised to find the social-political limitations on the growth allowed Mary Tyler Moore on the program that bore her name.

Rhetorical analysis always builds the argument that even prime-time TV programs reach outside of their fictional universes to affect the real lives of real people. The orientations we see, the beliefs and values we hear articulated, and the behaviors we see exhibited on television can, to a greater or lesser degree, be absorbed by people watching television. Rhetorical analysis usually focuses on the televisual texts that are the vehicles for such kinds of changes.

Narrative Criticism

Most television programs, of course, are stories, so it is little wonder that many critics have studied the structure of those stories. Shlomith Rimmon-Kenan has defined a *story* as "a series of events arranged in chronological order," and an *event* as "a change from one state of affairs to another" (1983, p. 15, quoted in Kozloff, 1987). Critics are particularly interested in (a) what events are included in stories and what has been left out; (b) what events become pivotal in a story; (c) how characters are arranged into the action of a story; and (d) what sorts of lessons or morals of the stories we're asked to take away from an encounter with a story.

You might want to examine evening new stories with an interest in noticing how a labor strike is covered: who gets to speak? who gets to tell his or her story and who doesn't? is the story told from economic, political, and personal-social perspectives? and what's been made pivotal: a lockout by management, the grievances of labor, or the success/failure of a governmental arbitrator? In other words, what's this version of the story about? Character studies likewise could be done. How are the strikers dressed when we see them, and what are they doing? negotiating? drinking beer? hollering at management? And what's the moral of this story: uncaring management, radical labor, long-suffering families and destroyed communities, or governmental effectiveness or ineffectiveness?

Narrative analyses of events, their importance, the characters who make them go, and the lessons we are asked to draw from the stories all make narrative criticism a highly valued kind of textual study. In looking at programs ranging from *Men Behaving Badly* to *Rescue 911* to an ad for Draino, you'll find that stories are the lifeblood of American television and textualize an amazing range of beliefs, values, characterological virtues and vices, and lessons about life to be taken away after viewing experiences.

As this introduction indicates, text-centered television criticism comprises a full range of more particular approaches. That variety should not be surprising, as rhetorical and literary criticism always has been centered on the texts of speeches, newspapers, poems, plays, and novels. Film and television criticism likewise has adapted to those traditions.

Writing Text-Centered Critical Essays

What sort of writing challenges face the text-centered critic? The primary talents needed are those of the so-called close textual analyst, that is, talents in breaking down texts into discrete units that in turn can be profitably interpreted or evaluated generically, rhetorically, narratively, and so on. Two talents are paramount: the ability to decode verbal, visual, and acoustic signs and the ability to work interpretively across multiple codes.

Decoding Verbal, Visual, and Acoustic Signs

In a sense, all text-centered criticism begins with one sort or another of semiotic analysis—taking apart texts, isolating specific units of meaning that can be interpreted or evaluated. Unfortunately, there really aren't generally accepted, foolproof ways of decoding the verbal, visual, and acoustic signs that comprise a TV program. Figure 6.1 suggests some dimensions of those sign systems that might be explored.

The particular ways you'll decode texts will vary with your purpose. Suppose you're interested in male–female relationships in *Friends.* You'll probably want to focus on the valuative language employed by the males and the females (e.g., do they habitually emphasize different values?), and even their grammatical orientation (e.g., do males or females give more orders?). Argumentative orientation might be usefully examined to see if gender affects conflict and its resolution. If you're examining an advertisement for Crest toothpaste, however, ideological language would be important (e.g., what sorts of authorities are cited?), as is narrative orientation: what kinds of stories—based on fear or joy?—are told in Crest ads?

Similarly, in thinking about visual and acoustic codes, your analysis of *Friends* may well be sensitive to how characters are arranged in the shots: who's in the foreground and who's in the background? who's centered and who's not? who's lit and who's in the shadows? are particular clothing styles associated with each character, and is that style important in his or her relationships to other characters? Regarding acoustic codes, do males and females paralinguistically signal something about their power within the group? Or in looking at the Crest ads, how are the narrators dressed? How are fear at the possibility of tooth decay and joy when no decay is found conveyed acoustically?

Obviously, you can ask many more questions about verbal, visual, and acoustic coding in both *Friends* and toothpaste ads, depending upon your purposes. However you proceed, always let your critical purposes guide your decoding practices.

Sample Text-Centered Critical Essays

The essays in this chapter illustrate several different approaches to textual matters. We open with Jane Banks and Jonathan Tankel's genre study of talk shows (*Donahue, Oprah,* and *Sally Jessy Raphael*) and sexuality. They're interested in TV genres understood as mechanisms of ideological control—in this study, of control of viewers' understandings of sexuality. Heterosexual or "mainstream" gender relationships are seen as approved of, and various "marginal" sexualities are found to be shown but censored. By having examined twenty episodes of each of those talk shows systematically, Banks and Tankel are able to provide a welter of evidence from dialogue and production techniques for their claims.

Next is Bruce Gronbeck's rhetorical study of local news programs. Even though several other essays in this book (e.g., those by Geiser-Getz, Schrag, Ono, Scott, Dow, and Owen and Ehrenhaus) have strongly rhetorical contours, we include Gronbeck's essay in this section because it is grounded in close textual analysis. He explores two consecutive nights of ten o'clock local newscasts for a middle-market-size station in Iowa. With the help of Kenneth

Burke's distinction between the psychologies of form and information, he examines the ways in which news stories and the weather segments encode both traditional community standards for understanding the world and innovative, technologically enhanced ways for seeing the everyday world in new ways. Local news is depicted as a synthesis between the old and the new, the changing and the changeless; in that synthesis, Gronbeck argues, is to be found its power to frame listeners' perceptions of the world.

A text-based study of a television narrative is offered next. Michael Porter designed a tool for systematic analyses of shows' plots, characters, and settings or locations. Porter's study is a formalist study, that is, an examination of how particular actions, people, and places function to drive a story from beginning to end. The study is a social analysis of why television dramas focus so intently on character as the connection between the stories and those who watch them. An episode from the initial season of *ER* allows the reader to examine a close, technical analysis of plots, characters, and places performing particular meaning-making functions.

As an example of the ways in which contemporary critics do semiotic-structural analysis, there's probably no better theorist-critic to read than John Fiske. His mid-80s critical essay on the British TV program *Dr Who* (1984) is a dated but superb example. In it he spends much time explaining how to do semiotic-structural analyses, showing us how to build structural charts of thematic relationships between characters, how to read a range of verbal and visual codes in scenes from the program, and also demonstrating the relationships between semiotic-structuralist codes and the socially situated readers (viewers) of the program. As we noted earlier, semiotic analysis is the basis for many kinds of criticism. Chapter 8 discusses another type of critical analysis—discourse analysis—which builds on basic semiotic concepts to examine the relationship between television texts and their ideological contexts.

Some Final Thoughts

As you prepare to read and then write your own text-centered critiques, consider the limitations of and yet the promise offered by such approaches. In taking apart texts carefully and closely, you might be conceding too much power to languages or codes. Are not political acts, economic realities, and daily social practices more influential on our lives than *Friends* or *Frasier*? Maybe, maybe not. However you answer that question, though, you do need to remind yourself that text-centered criticism, like all other kinds, must be justified or defended by the person arguing for its importance.

A second problem that can arise is that by emphasizing their texts (their messages), we might be tempted to forget about the text-makers (the message-makers). As has been noted in the auteur chapter, producers should be studied more systematically, as should the authors of the political statements that are broadcast during political events. If textual study keeps us from studying the people who craft those texts, then they are distracting us from serious social-political-economic inquiry. Finally, textual studies can become so focused on such microscopic dimensions of codes as to actually obscure that which is presumably being studied. To analyze every single shot in a TV ad is possible, but you might be examining such particularized aspects of signs that you cannot say anything about meaning—which, after all, is your job.

But if textual critics might be tempted to avoid questions of real power, personalized motives, and the levels of consciousness at which meanings reside, they also face many rewards. When well done by sensible people, text-centered television criticism reinforces the truism that meaning-making is a process and that meanings are struggled with again and again, as text-makers and viewers vie for supremacy. The best textual critics allow us to see clearly that the human world is inscribed in the languages by which we communicate with each other.

Textual studies also can become the bases for explicitly evaluative or judgment sorts of criticism. In tearing apart *CBS Evening News with Dan Rather, The Wide World of Sports, Law and Order,* and the like, critics lay bare the ways in which our beliefs are manipulated in discourse, the two-valued thinking in news that so often forces us to see the world in terms only of good and evil, the springs of our socialization that form our social understanding of gender roles and racial attitudes, and the ways in which our perceptions of the world are filtered by the TV program that frames it for us.

Textuality may be an ugly word, yet it's a powerful one, for it signals that systems of meaning are organized for citizens of a country in verbal, visual, acoustic, and behavioral texts that stand between those citizens and the direct experience of life. An important mission for all television critics, for all critics, is to penetrate and seize control of texts so as to comprehend and critique their hold on our personal and social existence. That certainly was Raymond Williams's goal when he sought to understand the textualizations he witnessed in TV coverage of the 1972 Olympics.

NOTES

1. Jenkins acquires the term *poaching* from deCerteau (1984).
2. Semiotic analysis is often combined with other kinds of criticism. For example, Cathy Schwichtenberg (1983) combined it with psychoanalysis and ideological analysis in her study of the prime-time soap *Dynasty.*
3. The primary inspiration of syntagmatic study was Vladmir Propp's *The Morphology of the Folk Tale* (1968), actually a study from the 1920s. He studied hundreds of fairy tales, looking for the component parts of tales and the relationships among those parts as they gave meaning to tales as a whole. The basic unit of meaning he focused on was a cluster of signs that he called a *function* and that he defined as "an act of a

character, defined from the point of view of its significance for the course of action" (p. 21). Among the functions that he identified are initial situation, absentation, interdiction, violation, reconnaissance, delivery, trickery, lack and/or villainy, mediation, counteraction, departure, donor, reaction, struggle, liquidation, pursuit, rescue, and transfiguration/punishment. These were generated by looking at what happened in folktales, though the list could be easily adapted to other kinds of texts. Propp's formal-analytical techniques can be used to define recurrent literary structures, to interpret whole narratives by how their conclusions are put together (see Picarillo, 1986; White, 1981), or to disassemble a program (see Porter's essay following this chapter).

REFERENCES

Barthes, R. (1975). *The pleasures of the text.* New York: Hill & Wang.

Cawelti, J. (1970). *The six-gun mystique.* Bowling Green, OH: Bowling Green State University Press.

Condit, C. M. (1989). The rhetorical limits of polysemy. *Critical Studies in Mass Communication, 6,* 103–122.

deCerteau, M. (1984). *The practice of everyday life.* Berkeley: University of California Press.

Dow, B. J. (1990). Hegemony, feminist criticism and *The Mary Tyler Moore Show. Critical Studies in Mass Communication, 7,* 261–274.

Eco, U. (1979). *The role of the reader: Explorations in the semiotics of texts.* Bloomington: Indiana University Press.

Fiske, J. (1983). The discourses of TV quiz shows or school + luck = success + sex. *Communication Studies, 34,* 139–150.

Fiske, J. (1984). Popularity and ideology: A structuralist reading of *Dr Who.* In W. Roland & B. Watkins (Eds.), *Interpreting television: Current research perspectives* (pp. 165–198). Newbury, CA: Sage.

Fiske, J. (1987a). *Cagney and Lacey*: Reading character structurally and politically. *Communication, 9,* 399–426.

Fiske, J. (1987b). *Television culture.* New York: Methuen.

Foss, K. A., & Littlejohn, S. W. (1986). *The Day After:* Rhetorical vision in an ironic frame. *Critical Studies in Mass Communication, 3,* 317–336.

Gronbeck, B. E. (1990). Popular culture, media, and political communication. In D. Nimmo and D. Swanson (Eds.), *New directions in political communication* (pp. 185–222). Beverly Hills: Sage.

Hall, S. (1980). Encoding/decoding. In S. Hall, D. Hobson, A. Lowe, and P. Willis (Eds.), *Culture, media, language* (pp. 128–139). London: Hutchinson.

Hartley, J. (1994). Structuralism. In T. O'Sullivan, J. Hartley, D. Saunders, M. Montgomery, and J. Fiske (Eds.), *Key concepts in communication and cultural studies* (2nd ed., pp. 302–305). New York: Routledge.

Hodge, R., & Tripp, D. (1986). *Children and television: A semiotic approach.* Stanford: Stanford University Press.

Jenkins, H. (1992). *Textual poachers: Television fans and participatory culture.* New York: Routledge.

Johnson, B. (1990). Writing. In F. Lentricchia and T. McLaughlin (Eds.), *Critical terms for literary study* (pp. 39–49). Chicago: University of Chicago Press.

Kozloff, S. R. (1987). Narrative theory and television. In R. C. Allen (Ed.), *Channels of discourse: Television and contemporary criticism* (pp. 42–73). Chapel Hill, NC: University of North Carolina Press.

Larson, C. U., & Oravec, C. (1987). *A Prairie Home Companion* and the fabrication of community. *Critical Studies in Mass Communication, 4,* 221–244.

Loeb, J. C. (1990). Rhetorical and ideological conservatism in *thirtysomething. Critical Studies in Mass Communication, 7,* 249–260.

Newcomb, H. (1974). *TV, the most popular art.* Garden City, NY: Anchor Books.

O'Connor, A. (Ed.). (1989). *Raymond Williams on television.* New York: Routledge.

O'Sullivan, T., Hartley, J., Saunders, D., Montgomery, M., & Fiske, J. (1994). *Key concepts in communication and cultural studies.* (2nd ed.). New York: Routledge.

Picarillo, M. S. (1986). On the authenticity of televisual experience: A critical exploration of para-social closure. *Critical Studies in Mass Communication, 3,* 337–355.

Propp, V. (1968). *Morphology of the folk tale* (2nd ed.). Austin: University of Texas Press.

Real, M. (1989). *Super media: A cultural studies approach.* Newbury Park, CA: Sage.

Rimmon-Kenan, S. (1983). *Narrative fiction: Contemporary poetics.* London: Metheun.

Schrag, R. L., Hudson, R. A., & Bernabo, L. M. (1981). Television's new humane collectivity. *Communication Studies, 45,* 1–12.

Schwichtenberg, C. (1983). *Dynasty:* The dialectic of feminine power. *Communication Studies, 34,* 151–161.

Seiter, E. (1987). Semiotics and television. In R. C. Allen (Ed.), *Channels of discourse: Television and contemporary criticism* (pp. 17–41). Chapel Hill: University of North Carolina Press.

Seiter, E. (1992). Semiotics, structuralism, and television. In R. C. Allen (Ed.), *Channels of discourse, reassembled: Television and contemporary criticism* (2nd ed., pp. 31–66). Chapel Hill: University of North Carolina Press.

White, H. (1981). The narrativization of real events. In W. J. T. Mitchell (Ed.), *On narrative* (pp. 249–254). Chicago: University of Chicago Press.

Setting the Margins: Television Talk Shows and the Genrefication of Sexuality

JANE BANKS
JONATHAN DAVID TANKEL

A number of characteristics inherent to the genre make the television talk show an important site for examining cultural constructions of sexuality. The television talk show as a genre is particularly relevant to intimate topics such as sexuality because of its unique intervention into the fabric of everyday life and social relations. Increasingly, communication functions formerly fulfilled in physical spaces such as libraries, kitchens, barbershops, cafes, and pubs have moved onto the small screens in our living rooms, defining interactional space electronically rather than physically. Audiences, confronted with the need to revise some previously space-dependent concepts such as interaction, intimacy, relationships, and community, have learned to fulfill some of their interpersonal requirements through mass communication (Meyrowitz, 1985; Gumpert, 1989). If we want to hear the sound of another human voice, for example, all we need to do is turn on television. If we want to transcend the limitations of our particular part of the world and learn about something foreign or different, the television offers that as well. Television offers both public and interpersonal interactions, simultaneously fulfilling both kinds of needs for their audiences, who respond to the technology as if to human interaction.[1] Offering closeness across the miles and discussing private matters in a public forum, television meets seemingly contradictory needs for viewers. This is never more evident than in the "talk show" genre whose very title, referring as it does to interpersonal interaction, belies its public nature with signifiers of intimacy.

In their public function, television talk shows provide a forum for the discussion of important cultural and social issues. They serve, for instance, as an agenda-setter in the larger culture, helping to determine what subjects should and do occupy the public mind (McCombs & Shaw, 1972; Newcomb & Hirsch, 1984). In their interpersonal function, television talk shows allow audience members to eavesdrop on intimate discussions of these issues, with studio audience members acting as ordinary viewers' surrogates, asking questions and offering opinions (Banks, 1990). The intimacy of the entertainment talk show genre lends itself particularly well to discussions of issues that are more social and cultural (defining forms and modes of interaction, determining appropriate norms and practices) than overtly political (discussing formal political issues in the arena of deliberative decision making). Although there is certainly some overlap, "political" talk shows such as *Nightline, The Larry King Show,* and the Sunday morning roundup tend to focus on the political, while "entertainment" talk shows such as *Donahue* and *Oprah* deal primarily with the social. Entertainment talk shows not only blur the distinction between public and private by integrating the trappings of personal interaction and discussion into the very public arena of mass communications, but they also focus on sexuality as a central topic of importance for their audience. Why do talk shows seem to be mostly about sex? Conventional wisdom says that producers use sex as bait in the quest for ratings, but contemporary philosophers and cultural theorists would argue that this focus also reflects the central position of sexuality in late 20th century society (Foucault, 1980, 1985; Sedgewick, 1990). Some feminist critics have argued that sexuality in its social-interpersonal aspect traditionally has been seen as the purview of women, who constitute the primary audience for these shows (Banks, 1990; Rapping, 1991; White, 1992). Generally, commerce (providing the largest possible audience of consumers to advertisers) intersects with culture (positioning sexuality as women's work), dominating topic selection by talk show producers who commodify the visual and aural representation of sex and sexual practice as a means of attracting a desirable (consuming) audience to deliver to advertisers.

In her essay on feminism and sexuality, Gayle Rubin (1983) observed a "sexual hierarchy of value in American society where sexual practices and practitioners were differentially evaluated, rewarded, and punished." Rubin argued that "we never encounter the body unmediated by the meanings that cultures give to it" (pp. 276–267). Similarly, Foucault (1980) argues that attitudes about sexuality and even sexual desires themselves are socially constructed through discursive practice. Sexuality is indirectly regulated through social structures of "power-knowledge" that delineate who is allowed to speak with authority about sexual matters. Sexual vocabularies and categories develop through these structures and are gradually naturalized within the culture. That is, we arrive at *names* to describe what we regard as a like group of particular practices; for example, "sexual intercourse" refers to any of several activities that involve penile insertion. These names highlight some aspects of the phenomena they describe and de-emphasize others. Names develop at higher levels of abstraction, enabling their users to refer to more and more phenomena with a single label that foregrounds whatever these phenomena have in common while their differences disappear into the background.

This linguistic development allows for two opposing possibilities: regulation and oppression on one hand, and liberation and revolution on the other. The term "homosexual," for instance, refers to a group of individuals who relate sexually to members of their own sex or who might engage in any of a group of particular practices. The existence, use, and naturalization of this term transforms individuals into a group available for systematic (and efficient) regulation, diagnosis, and punishment. Simultaneously, a single label unifying a group of individuals also has the potential for establishing a community with political cohesion, solidarity, and resistance through affiliation and group identity. Naturalization occurs when societies forget the arbitrary nature of the names that phenomena are given and instead elevate the status of names ontologically. At that point, a name is no longer just what we happen to call someone or something but instead becomes its essence—a thing's name is what it *is*. If we agree that social attitudes toward sexuality are developed and naturalized through these kinds of discursive practices, then the talk show, with its mediated intimacy and its agenda-setting power, should be a central source for researchers on sexuality.

Studying media constructions of sexuality is important because we can look at the relations between sexual practice and social privilege that are manifested so often and so centrally in our culture. The instances of individuals being rewarded or (more often) punished for their sexual choices are legion.[2] Judith Butler (1990, 1991, 1993) addresses the issue of sexual oppression with her performative theory of gender. Like Foucault, she approaches the issue from the phenomenological perspective that knowledge is not something that people discover, but is instead socially constituted. Butler also agrees with Foucault that particular political interests are served by our sexual category system. To protect those interests, Butler says that the division between the sexes must be absolutely clear and distinct—our categories of female and male must be polar opposites. To this end, we are taught to "perform" our gender as if it were natural, but far from being natural, gender is not something one *is* but something one *does* in imitation of a cultural ideal. For Butler, gender and other sexual categories such as homosexuality and heterosexuality not only are socially constructed but are instruments for social control. Butler sees gender performance as a strategy of social regulation. Failing to perform one's gender correctly is what Butler refers to as "gender insubordination" and has punitive consequences—not the biological consequences of successful or unsuccessful mating, but public and social consequences like not being able to get or keep a job.

Part of the performance of gender is the performance of our sexuality. We commonly think of "sexual performance" as the ability of the male in heterosexual intercourse to achieve and maintain an erection. In that sense, the question of "performance" concerns private rather than public acts. From our perspective in this essay, sexual "performance" would be just the opposite—the *public* display or acting out of our sexuality according to a particular and narrow ideal. Deviation from this ideal, that is, sexual insubordination, has consequences for the insubordinate that are both dire and public. For adult heterosexuals, the public display of sexuality is sanctioned and even encouraged by the culture, but sexual minorities of any kind are required to remain sexually invisible. A pink triangle on a lapel, for instance, is seen as an indiscreet revelation about what one likes to do in bed, while a wedding ring on the third finger of the left hand is seen as a model of restraint and probity.

The United States is a country where many states still have anti-sodomy laws, and gays are threatened with violence, homelessness, and unemployment because of their sexual preference. In light of our society's tendency to punish sexual differences of any kind, an examination of the processes by which difference is defined, constructed, displayed, and sanctioned for the public contributes to our understanding of the relations between sexuality and the general social hierarchy. In television talk shows, sexual insubordination and its consequences are endlessly re-enacted and brought into our homes as an object lesson for audiences.

It is the purpose of this essay (a) to look at some ways in which television talk shows as a genre contribute to the placement of sexualities (and individuals) from the mainstream to the margin in larger cultural structures of privilege and (b) to look at the ways in which that genre allows the possibility of dismantling those structures of privilege and subverting sexual hierarchies based on particular patterns of speech and silence. In this essay we will argue that talk shows send a conservative message on sexual issues by presenting sexual minorities as spectacle for a curious and voyeuristic audience and providing opportunities for conservative audience members to spread intolerance and vilification against sexual difference. This conservative move is countered by the fact that talk shows provide a platform for the discussion of sexual issues and bring sexual minorities from virtual invisibility to the media mainstream. Moreover, the talk show form itself deconstructs our hierarchies of power-knowledge about sex by featuring the talk of outsiders (the guests, callers, and studio audience members) and marginalizing the talk of those in power who are either absent from the show entirely or on in a marginal role as "experts."

Genre Criticism

Thus far in the essay we have discussed the nature of the talk show genre in general and its focus on sexuality. We have presented sexuality as a socially constructed performance which is differentially rewarded or punished depending upon the extent to which it conforms to a cultural ideal or is insubordinate to it. The result of this move—that performance of insubordinate sexualities is punished—is for sexual minorities to seek invisibility. Where the public display and performance of sexuality is sanctioned for the sexual majority, it is dangerous for the sexual minority. Finally, we also have claimed that although certain characteristics of the talk show produce a conservative view of sexual issues, competing characteristics may override that conservative discourse with a progressive one. We would further contend that the multivocal nature of the sexual discourse on talk shows is a unique feature of the genre itself.

Genre criticism comes to mass media from literary studies, where works of literature were classified by type or kind with the idea that understanding the genre would help the critic understand the particular work better. The genres in literature were primarily theoretical—that is, they were post hoc classifications by readers and critics rather than formulae or literary templates according to which authors produced works of art. In the popular arts, commercial considerations were more important, and reproducibility meant that the culture industry could guarantee future commercial successes. To that end, genres were developed before the fact and artists were encouraged to make their products according to previously tested formulae. Formula fiction, for instance, was an early example of mass-produced and -consumed cultural products with the advent of the dime novels of the 1840s. These were written according to strict formulae so that their working-class readers could be assured of meeting their expectations after parting with their money. Indeed, according to some genre critics, it is familiarity itself that is one of the primary pleasures of genre-produced cultural artifacts. Genres such as these, arising from the culture industries and directing cultural production, are termed "historical," and are predominant in popular media such as television and film.

Feuer (1992) argues that there are three positions critics can take with regard to genre. The *aesthetic* approach looks at a genre's elements as they provide opportunities for artistic expression. The *ritual* approach sees genre from the perspective of the culture industries where genre functions as an agreement between the industry and its audience as these parties negotiate shared beliefs and values. The *ideological* approach views genre as a means of social control. At the level of the television industry that means honoring certain conventions in order to deliver consistent audiences to advertisers. At the textual level genre works to reproduce the dominant ideology by offering spectator positions that naturalize dominant ideals. Altman (1984) contends that genre operates both ritualistically and ideologically. The ideological function of genre reproduces dominant power relations while its ritualistic function effaces a genre's ideology by featuring its entertainment value.

Specific television genres in the United States have developed within the economic constraints of the commercial broadcast industry, which has shaped their nature and their evolution. For instance, "reality" television shows such as *Cops* and *Rescue 911* appear on television not just because they are popular but because they are inexpensive to produce. Genres also develop and evolve in response to changing audience tastes and demands. The generic hybrid "dramedy" was a fusion of dramatic and comedic elements designed to capture the attention of televiewers who wanted a more complex text (Vande Berg, 1989). The daytime television talk show moved from a focus on witty chat between a host and a celebrity guest or guests to an increasingly sensationalized examination of social and cultural (often sexual) issues with discussion among lay guests and studio audience members mediated by the host (the moment examined in this essay). This evolutionary moment of the talk show continues, but the most recent trend is a focus on interpersonal confrontation among family members, friends, and lovers in a free-for-all of emotional display encouraged by the host (see Munson, 1993, for a history and critique of the entire talk show genre).

Method

At this point in the essay it is time to turn our attention to the specific elements of the talk show as a genre and illustrate the relations between the genre's ritualistic and ideological functions as the talk show presents multivocal discourses on sexuality. We are examining a particular cultural moment in the evolution of the talk show genre where the interplay among guests, host, experts, studio audience members, and callers flows freely around a particular sexual topic. For the purposes of this paper we conducted a close textual analysis of specific talk show segments on sexuality taped from February 3 through February 28 in 1992, which roughly corresponded to the February 1992 ratings sweeps period. Our sample included all segments of *The Oprah Winfrey Show*, *Donahue*, and *Sally Jessy Raphael*, which were the top three daytime talk shows during the sampling period.

The use of the ratings sweeps period to define the limits of the data operates with the assumption that the programming strategies for that period were intended to secure the highest possible ratings. In other words, although the sample of program topics might be considered skewed when compared to the non-sweeps programs, the skew favors the inclusion of topics that titillate the audience (Head, 1989). For a study of sexuality in talk shows, the sweeps programs are ideal in that they should represent the greatest concentration of sexually oriented programs. Moreover, the intensified quest for ratings that is characteristic of sweeps periods provides the researcher with a more striking example of the interrelation between ritualistic and ideological functions of the genre.

In our close analysis of talk show segments, we were interested in the unique combination of capabilities and constraints, practices and participants, authenticity and performance, originality and intertextuality, hyperreality and fantasy that shed light on the relations between sexuality and culture. The defining elements of the television talk show genre include: (a) a traditional proscenium stage, (b) multiple-camera video production with the standard vocabulary of shots, (c) a live studio audience (some of whom may have been selected to appear on a particular program), (d) callers to the show who are carefully screened before they are put on the air, (e) a host, (f) one or more guests who speak about a sexual topic from personal experience, (g) an "expert" who speaks with the authority of some kind of academic credential (this element appears on some but not all talk shows), (h) videographic capability, (i) lighting, (j) costumes and makeup, and (d) set decor.

For this close analysis, we examine the ways in which the television talk shows in our sample presented mainstream and alternative sexualities with the following questions in mind: How do the generic capabilities of the television talk show contribute to the performance of sexuality and the reward and punishment of that performance? What does it signify for a television talk show to feature alternative sexualities? What is the stance of the show (as represented by its host, for example) vis-à-vis these sexualities? What is the role of the studio and call-in audience in constructing sexual hierarchies of value? Are alternative and mainstream sexualities portrayed differently in terms of how interaction with the audience is managed, how the guests themselves are presented through camera angles, lighting, placement on the set, order of speaking, costumes, makeup, and the presence or absence of an "expert" to interpret and evaluate guests' discussions? How do talk shows constrain discussions of sexuality in order to satisfy networks' standards and practices? What could be missing from these frank discussions of sexuality? In general, we asked how television talk shows offer discourses on sexuality that contribute to the social construction (or deconstruction) of sexual hierarchies in American culture.

Textual Analysis

For this study, all segments of the three top-rated daytime syndicated talk shows were taped from February 3 through February 28, 1992 (3.5 weeks within the ratings sweeps period). The sample offered twenty episodes of each program, which were informally coded for "sexual content" using broad inclusive criteria: shows that focused on sex (excluding sex crimes and public health issues such as AIDS) as their primary topic. The figures indicate a greater percentage of sexually oriented programs than during non-sweeps periods for *Donahue* (13/20: 65%) and *Sally Jessy Raphael* (9/20: 45%). For *The Oprah Winfrey Show,* sexuality seemed to be of lesser importance during sweeps (4/20: 20%). Overall, we saw a distinct increase in sexually oriented topics during sweeps.

Beyond the programming strategies for the sweeps, a closer analysis of individual programs reveals the extent to which mainstream and alternative sexualities are differentially portrayed and valued. An episode of *Donahue* provides our first example. This show featured supporters and detractors of a gay rights bill being considered in a small California community just outside of San Francisco. Typically, host Phil Donahue takes a position of support or at least tolerance toward alternative sexualities, especially on topics having to do with gay issues, and this show was no exception. Certainly the show provides a platform for the men who appeared in support of this gay rights bill. As we will see, however, this manifest content is undermined by contradictory messages which indicate to the larger audience that there are consequences to sexual differences. Phil Donahue's liberal message in support of gay civil rights is subverted by competing discourses emerging from a variety of sources, including Donahue himself.

A local minister, opposing what he referred to as the "homosexual agenda," prepared and distributed a videotape juxtaposing shots of families, churches, Cub Scout troops, etc., with some of the more outrageous moments of the San Francisco Gay Pride parade. One shot in the video showed completely nude male dancers on floats (necessitating a censor's patch covering the men's genitals); another showed a gay couple explicitly simulating anal intercourse. Donahue contributed to the shock value of the tape by telling the audience what the network wouldn't let them see for themselves, "these guys are buck naked, ladies and gentlemen!" Although Donahue later argued forcefully on the side of the gay activists that the videotape was unfair, unrepresentative, and inflammatory, the offending segment was shown over and over, reifying it as visual evidence in favor of the minister's argument. Donahue's own commentary on the videotape emphasized its scandalous nature, undermining his subsequent argument that the images on the tape were inflammatory and atypical. The visual impact of the videotape offered an alternative message to audience members who did not share Donahue's tolerance on gay issues. Contradictory discourses such as these ensure that the program meets its commercial requirements; the show engages the broadest possible audience by clearing an ideological space for viewers of all political (and sexual) persuasions.

Another instance in the same show where manifest content is undermined with contradictory signals is found in a graphic image used to reintroduce the show after a commercial break. One of the guests booked on the show was a man who appeared dressed flamboyantly in drag. The image showed two still shots from the previous segment of the show, slightly overlapping on the corners. The lower left hand photo shows the man in drag; the upper right hand photo shows a handsome young man from the studio audience whom we are (generally) meant to see as both straight and innocent. The microphone the young man holds upright suggests "normal" sexuality (to some) and the graphic as a whole represents the tension and contrast between mainstream and marginalized sexualities, firmly characterizing gay men as different and other. Simultaneously, the inner corners of the still images overlap, which suggests the "contamination" of straight with gay sexuality that could ensue if the latter should be "normalized" by measures ensuring gay civil rights. On this show there were several gay men who looked quite ordinary and could have been shown on this graphic, but the producers chose to polarize the gays and straights visually. At the same time, the gay activists (with Donahue in support) argued for a law that sought to mainstream the position of gays in this small community. Although Donahue himself often defends the rights of sexual minorities, this is not a univocal statement of his show. Indeed, the image itself operates on two levels since the picture of the young man holding the decidedly phallic microphone can also be seen as homoerotic, suggesting gay sexual practice to some audience members.

In this example, the guests on the show who supported the gay rights bill were what Butler might call sexual insubordinates, not so much because they were gay but because they insisted on talking about it. The show provided opportunities to punish their violation of this "don't ask, don't tell" policy through a variety of means. The repeated showing of the gay pride parade videotape worked by juxtaposing men who have chosen to look, dress, and act fairly conventionally with men who have made quite a different choice, suggesting a commonality that the former might not enthusiastically support. The presence of the minister and his allies fighting against the bill invited studio audience members to share their opposition to the bill and concomitant rejection of gay men. The appearance of the man dressed in a flamboyant drag costume (who was not involved in promoting the gay rights bill) invited comparison with the other gay men on the show who had to argue for their acceptance into the community as a "normal" component of it in the face of very extreme representations of themselves. The gay activists on the show were given a platform that was undermined and contested by their opponents and by the studio audience. The show brought gay sexual preference to the center of discussion while making it seem ridiculous or dangerous with extreme images. Contradictory discourses such as these ensure that the show meets its commercial requirements; the show engages the broadest possible audience by clearing an ideological space for viewers of all political (and sexual) persuasions.

Insubordinate performance of sexuality is a crime of representation. The display of one's sexual proclivities is only all right if one's sexuality is of the "unmarked" variety. The linguistic concept of "marking" refers to the way in which people make assumptions about gender roles (Tannen, 1994). If a term is "unmarked" by a modifier indicating gender, it is generally assumed that the term refers to a man. Thus, a doctor is assumed to be male unless the term is marked by a modifier indicating another gender, as in "woman doctor." Just as the unmarked gender is male, the unmarked sexuality is mainstream heterosexual. We assume that a man or woman is heterosexual unless we receive specific information to the contrary, but that information is often unwelcome. It is not so much the existence but the *performance* of sexual difference (even in its most abstract forms) that is unacceptable. In the following example, we see the intensified disapproval shown to those who exhibit sexual differences other than ordinary homosexuality. The sanctions against this version of sexual insubordination are even greater than the ones given gays, indicating a lower position on the sexual hierarchy of values for these individuals. While Donahue generally tries to negotiate the tensions between the guests representing alternative sexualities and the studio audience representing "normal" (unmarked) sexual behavior, the show in general uses techniques of visual signification to assign each group to its place on the hierarchy.

On a show about swingers, for example, two of the three couples who were guests asked to have their appearances altered for the segment. That this alteration was the result of the couples' own requests was made clear at the outset (they had no one to blame but themselves). Not surprisingly, the disguises were both obvious and unflattering—wigs that looked false, oversized glasses or sunglasses, harsh colors that clashed with skin tones, large false noses, and prominent false teeth. This aspect of the production works in at least two ways: The fact of disguise itself acts as a tiny morality tale to the audience, emphasizing as it does the terrible dangers of displaying and owning up to sexual difference. This is further underscored by the ugliness of the disguises, which say, in effect, that the social consequences of being a sexual minority are so dreadful and dire that even looking extremely unattractive on television in front of millions of people is preferable. Moreover, since Americans tend to associate sex with physical beauty, making these individuals unattractive works against any erotic allure they might otherwise have for the audience.

Other visual capabilities of the talk show function in the construction of marginal versus mainstream sexualities as well, suggesting particular interpretations of what the audience sees. On a segment of *The Oprah Winfrey Show*, for instance, a woman who married her own stepfather appeared together with her husband and her mother. The two women were seated on either side of the man who was their husband (and former stepfather) and ex-husband. Winfrey's questioning revealed that the relationship between the man and his stepdaughter had begun while he was still married to her mother and when the young woman was only fifteen. Although the terms "child abuse" and "incest" had not been mentioned up to that point, the latter term was suggested visually by the appearance of the two women. While not exhibiting a strong family resemblance in general, the women had been made up to look alike, with identical cupid's bow mouths painted on in dark red lipstick. Eventually, the discussion turned to whether the relationship in question was incestuous or not, but the suggestion that it was had already been made visually to the audience through the manufactured resemblance between the two women. In this instance, the expressive capabilities of make-up suggest a judgment to the audience visually well in advance of the verbal evaluation that eventually emerges on the show.

Although talk shows offer guests a platform to speak about sex, they do not reject outside authority altogether. Often "experts" are asked on the shows and given the last word, generally undermining whatever authority a guest might have when speaking about sex. Whether guests are allowed to be the sole interpreter of themselves and the sole definer of their sexuality, or whether the show provides an "expert" to speak for them is a significant sign of approval or disapproval from talk show producers. Experts on talk shows dealing with sexuality fall into one of two categories, and which kind appears on the show is a clue to the status of the guests. Sometimes the expert is literally a defender, an attorney for the guests, on the show to present arguments on behalf of the client. This frames the guest as falsely accused and wronged, aligning him or her with the studio audience and the host as part of the general citizenry whose civil rights deserve protection.

An example of this was a *Donahue* show that featured "people who have been fired for something they did off the job." This show is included in our sample because in every case, the "something" that resulted in the guests' being fired was sexual. In this instance, an attorney for a man who was fired because someone at work found an invitation to a "safe sex party" he gave argued that unless the person directly involves the company in the behavior, what an individual does off the job is irrelevant to his or her continued employment. The attorney functions as an equalizer between guest and audience, underscoring the mutual right of both parties to a professional defense. The presence of attorneys signals a general approval of the guests, and other signs of approval usually appear as well. For instance, several of the guests of the show mentioned above were fired because they posed for suggestive pictures, but no one of these pictures was shown to the television or studio audience. One of the guests (a former investment banker) performed an abbreviated strip act on a segment, but even that downplayed differences between him and the studio audience. His avowed heterosexuality, the approval from the female studio audience members, and his professional background in the mainstream of American business life all contributed to the establishment of common ground between the guest and the audience. The performance was framed as "good clean fun" and the bosses who fired the man were described as prudes and killjoys by the studio audience and by Donahue himself. The attorney's presence ensures that fundamental American freedoms and values are invoked in the guests' defense and that differences between the guests and the audience are effaced.

In contrast to the defender is the definer; the presence of a psychiatrist, psychologist, therapist, or counselor removes the guest from the mainstream of American culture into the isolated land of the sick. The therapist is allowed the final word on whatever behavior is being discussed, and his or her very presence makes a compelling statement about how sexual difference is to be construed. For instance, when *Donahue* featured professional dominatrixes and their masochist clients, a clinical psychologist was also on the show, there to define this sexual behavior scientifically. In this instance, the psychologist was not nearly as condemning and judgmental as the studio audience, arguing, for example, that there are widely varying degrees of masochistic practice and that this preference is not necessarily harmful. In this show, the doctor tried to present a moderate perspective on this issue in the face of vehement opposition from the studio audience. In spite of his efforts, though, his very presence signified a pathology and framed the guests as "sick," a label that no amount of argument on their part or on his could unstick. Interestingly, while those appearing on the show (either host, expert, or guest) occasionally remonstrate with the audience for intolerant or retrograde attitudes, the show is never unequivocally "against" the audience. As we shall see later, conservative audience attitudes fulfill an important function on talk shows.

The contrast between the guest who is on the show because of his or her sexual difference and the therapist who is on the show to interpret, define, and evaluate that difference is particularly marked if there is a significant distinction in social class as well. This was especially evident in a segment of *Sally Jessy Raphael* that aired during the sweeps period. This show was a rerun shown during the sweeps because of Raphael's absence from taping due to the death of her daughter. The guests were a 44-year-old woman and her 14-year-old husband. On this segment, the two were attired in matching torn jeans and Levi's jackets inscribed with various symbols and messages, including a swastika on the jeans of the boy. The woman's bad bleach job and harsh eyeliner contributed to this discourse of class, as did the boy's admission when questioned by Raphael that he didn't really know what the swastika meant; he just thought it was cool. Raphael's questioning further revealed the boy's functional illiteracy, the couple's unemployment, and their extreme poverty.

Adding to this unspoken focus on class was the therapist, who explained the dynamics of the relationship to the audience and predicted to the woman that her youthful husband would eventually leave her. The therapist's and audience's discussion contrasted sharply with the guests' in a variety of ways, all of which suggest differences in class. The therapist made long speeches in contrast to the brevity of the couple's responses, especially those from the young boy. The therapist's discourse was grammatically and syntactically correct and fairly formal in style. The couple's speech was full of grammatical errors and imprecise. Even though they had both appeared on talk shows before (they were favorite guests on a variety of shows because of their unusual marriage) they were not good at meeting the talk show's requirements for brevity, precision, and restricted language codes. For instance, in answer to the common accusation that his wife serves as a mother figure to him, the boy said:

I ain't lookin' for another mother. If I was I'd go to God for one.

In response to a family member's suggestion that the boy be put in a home, he said that he would just run away, and concluded:

If I had to, I'd probably gut somebody. [Raphael indicated that she didn't understand his meaning.] I'd probably stab somebody on the way out, too.

In response to a suggestion from the audience that he go back to school, the boy said:

I've been in school for the last four years. I say f—- school.

And finally:

I'm not a damn kid.

The boy's responses indicate both his lack of education and his inability to respond to the restricted codes of television talk that are well known to most television audience members. Together with his appearance, the boy's verbal behavior presents a strong message of alienation from middle class norms and values. The discourse of social class that emerges in this segment spills over into its sexual discourse. This connects low social and economic status with sexual difference and further reinforces the therapist's authority and diagnostic voice. Low social status and therapeutic interpretations work together in this segment to place intergenerational sex (at least in this instance where the woman is the older partner) lower on the sexual hierarchy of value.

The couple in the last example are certainly sexual insubordinates and have made something of a career out of displaying that fact on talk shows where they are cross-examined, criticized, and vilified. In the face of such negative sanctions, why do they persist in their insubordinate performance? Why do any of the talk show guests that I have described go on the air and discuss their sexuality before an audience of millions, particularly in the face of the punishments that have been discussed in this essay? The answer to this question helps us understand the progressive elements of the talk show genre. First, being on television is inherently rewarding (Priest, 1995). Whether the talk show host or studio audience approves of a guest's lifestyle is not relevant to the importance our culture gives to appearing on television. In addition, whatever may happen during the show with critical audience members, experts, or other guests, everyone who appears on a talk show is given the opportunity to speak out. Although some talk show guests have felt that they did not get to express themselves fully or completely, many more were grateful for the chance to tell their stories to the television audience.

Popular conceptualizations to the contrary, television talk shows do not univocally work to normalize marginal sexualities. Rather, a variety of ideological positions are presented from which individual audience members may choose as they like. In this way, the shows represent the broadest of broadcasting, meeting the commercial needs of the industry by attracting the largest possible audience. It is worth noting, for instance, that these shows never present any sense of closure on sexual topics. On *Donahue*, for instance, the discussion continues at the end of the show as the credits roll over the participants. This open ending allows the show to return to the topic again and again, since the final word is never delivered. This lack of closure also underscores Donahue's manifest presentation of a pluralistic sexuality, since no one is permitted a last pronouncement.

The studio audience and its interaction with guests, host, experts, and the larger audience also plays an important part in the show's dynamic. For example, Donahue once referred to his studio audience as "ladies and gentlemen of the jury," describing their function quite neatly. Donahue often signals to his audience what he wants them to be at any given moment by asking leading questions to the studio audience: "Now none of *you* have ever thought of doing this, have you?" he asked on a program on extramarital affairs.

In addition, the audience will say what Donahue will not. For instance, on a show about men who masquerade as women on the job, someone called in and said: "It's like a bunch of freaks sitting up there . . . line 'em all up and get rid of 'em." Donahue responded jovially, "This is getting you too upset. You shouldn't watch the show anymore." Donahue's good-natured disavowal notwithstanding, audience members like this one fulfill an important function of the show, enabling it to present a strongly conservative discourse on sexuality without Donahue himself having to "own" it.

As television talk shows raise questions of sexual definition, the audience participates in this voyeuristic game, taking responsibility for the probing questions about specific sexual preferences and practices. Audience members ask about everything from the precise anatomy of pre- and post-surgical transsexuals to the exact point in their relationship an intergenerational couple first made love. On the *Donahue* segment about men masquerading as females on the job, one audience member asked a guest if his breasts were real. The camera colluded with this individual's curiosity, pulling back from an extreme to a medium close-up, showing the guest's chest area so that the home audience could examine the parts in question. Wholesale probing into sexual details is a hallmark of the television talk show, and another instance where the transgression of sexual insubordination is shown to have punitive consequences. The talk show guests do not simply reveal what they choose, but must submit to the curiosity of all the other participants as they expose their sexual difference.

The collusion between audience and camera in uncovering sexual difference is further demonstrated in a *Donahue* show about dominance and masochism. On this show, the guests who were masochists wore leather masks, and again, the camera made inquiries in the same probing way that the audience did. In this instance, the camera zoomed in for an extreme close-up in three-quarters profile—a highly unusual move in three-camera video production—allowing the home audience an opportunity to peek inside the mask at the eye hole to catch a glimpse of the person within. Ironically, at the same time as the television camera framed its subjects with this voyeuristic and penetrating look, the studio and call-in audience roundly condemned the guests' fetishistic sexuality. This sequence also empirically demonstrates the polysemic nature of the television talk show. For like-minded viewers, the show provides uncommon attention to their preference, allowing individuals with a particular sexual interest to see others who share their desires thus establishing a temporary media community. Some audience members are likely to find sexual gratification in the fetishistic way in which this sequence's guests are shot. For curious viewers, the text serves as spectacle, allowing them to look their fill and probe for details. And for its conservative audience, the talk show functions as a public pillory where miscreants display their shame and deviance.

Conclusions

In general, the extent of sexually oriented topics varied widely from show to show with *Donahue* the clear winner, *Sally Jessy Raphael* a fairly close second, and *Oprah* a poor third in the sexual sweepstakes. The nature of the sexually oriented topics differed also from show to show with some clear distinctions in approach. *Donahue* had the most issue-oriented shows: one on conjugal visits in jail, one about people who were fired for off-the-job sexual behavior, one about homophobia, and one on gays achieving legal minority status. In addition, Donahue himself tends to frame many sexual issues politically, as happened on several other of his shows. *Sally Jessy Raphael* tended to focus on sexual topics that provided an opportunity for displays of skin (Sexy Stripper Sisters, Women Who Work in the Buff, Sally's Fantasy Female Beauty Pageant) or to stage family battles over sexual issues (44-year-old woman married to a 14-year-old boy and their disapproving families, teenage girls who dress like sluts and their disapproving mothers, wives who want their husbands to shut up about sex, and sex fantasies that come true for women with controlling husbands). *The Oprah Winfrey Show* had too few sexual topics to come up with a single clear approach, although family battles and on-air confrontations seemed to predominate.

To what extent and with what resources do these shows present judgments of their guests? The talk shows use the conventions of television and specifically of the genre to present ideological discourses on sex. Cameras zoom in or out, tilt up or down at a subject, or pan laterally across one or more individuals, include background in long or medium shots, present intense focus in extreme close-ups, and imitate the eyes of curious onlookers. Television producers juxtapose distant images, include the disembodied voices of callers in the discussion, reinforce or break through the proscenium separating audience and performers. Makeup artists can make people look attractive or unattractive, alike or different, old or young. These and other acts of televisual legerdemain are available as vocabulary for sexual pronouncements. In the previous section, we have seen some examples of how the capabilities of the medium are used to reward and punish, approve or disapprove.

The talk show genre with its call-in and studio audience format joins with the technological capabilities of television to offer multivocal evaluations of sexual behavior. The selection of guests, presence or absence of a therapist or attorney, screening of callers to the show, and the presentation of the host can all present latent but compelling arguments about a sexual issue. The studio audience and callers can produce a multiplicity of opinions or univocal approval or disapproval of an individual or a practice. Again, we have seen examples in the previous section of how these capabilities can be used to suggest judgments.

In order to attract the maximum number of viewers, people from all kinds of backgrounds and sexual orientations must be accommodated by the television talk show. The various capabilities of the television medium and the talk show genre allow it to present a variety of different and even conflicting discourses simultaneously so that most people watching can find some position on the show that agrees with theirs. The television talk show is constructed with the ability to subvert manifest discourses of tolerance and acceptance with latent messages of condemnation and disapproval. These multiple discourses of sexuality do not operate in a simple progressive-regressive dialectic, but rather in a more postmodern circulation of ideologies. Sexual minority members are given a platform and an audience of millions and are tried and condemned on that platform for their sexual transgressions. Alternative sexualities are moved from the margins of the culture to the center of public attention and are then subject to minute examination and vilification by outraged audience members. Talk show guests subvert mainstream sexualities with insubordinate sexual performances and are criticized for being shameless by the same people who probe for the smallest detail in their questions.

On the television talk show, every chance to condemn and vilify sexual insubordination is countered by other opportunities afforded by the genre to accept, tolerate, or even propagate alternative discourses on sexuality. The talk show displays the punitive consequences of sexual transgression again and again, but simultaneously moves the transgressors to the forefront of the public's sexual agenda. Finally, whichever competing discourse wins out over the others, the sound of univocal sexual authority has been irrevocably drowned out by the postmodern cacophony of talk show voices.

NOTES

1. Stanford communication researchers Byron Reeves and Clifford Nass have found that subjects repeat human interaction patterns in response to television and computer and communication in a variety of situations. Ellen K. Coughlin, "The Human Side of Technology," *The Chronicle of Higher Education*, March 15, 1996, p. A12, A17.
2. For a comprehensive history of the regulation and punishment of sexual practice in the United States, see J. D'Emilio & Freedman (1988).

REFERENCES

Altman, R. (1984). A semantic/syntactic approach to film genres. *Cinema Journal, 23(3)* 14–15.

Banks, J. (1990). Listening to Dr. Ruth: The new sexual primer. In Gary Gumpert & Sandra Fish. Eds. *Talking to strangers: Mediated therapeutical communication* (pp. 140–168). Norwood, NJ: Ablex.

Butler, J. (1990). *Gender trouble: Feminism and the subversion of identity.* New York: Routledge.

Butler, J. (1991). Imitation and gender insubordination. In D. Fuss (Ed.), *Inside/out: Lesbian theories, gay theories* (pp. 131–151). New York: Routledge.

Butler, J. (1993). *Bodies that matter: On the discursive limits of "sex."* New York: Routledge.

Coughlin, E. (1996). The human side of technology. *The Chronicle of Higher Education*, March 15, A12+.

D'Emilio, J., and E. Freedman (1988). *Intimate matters: A history of sexuality in America.* New York: Harper & Row.

Feuer, J. (1992). Genre study and television. In R. C. Allen (Ed.), *Channels of discourse, reassembled: Television and contemporary criticism* (pp. 138–160). Chapel Hill: University of North Carolina Press.

Foucault, M. (1980). *The history of sexuality, Vol. I: An introduction.* R. Hurley (Trans.). New York: Vintage Books.

Foucault, M. (1985). *The history of sexuality, Vol. II: The uses of pleasure.* R. Hurley (Trans.). New York: Vintage Books.

Gumpert, G. (1989). *Talking tombstones and other tales of the media age.* New York: Oxford University Press.

Head, S. (1989). A framework for programming strategies. In S. Eastman, S. Head, & L. Klein. (Eds.), *Broadcast/cable programming.* (3rd ed.). Belmont, CA: Wadsworth Publishing Company.

McCombs, M., & Shaw, D. (1972). The agenda-setting function of mass media. *Public Opinion Quarterly, 36,* (176–184).

Meyrowitz, J. (1985). *No sense of place.* New York: Oxford University Press.

Munson, W. (1993). *All talk: The talkshow in media culture.* Philadelphia, PA: Temple University Press.

Newcomb, H., & Hirsch, P. (1984). Television as a cultural forum: Implications for research. In W. R. Rowland, Jr. and B. Watkins (Eds.), *Interpreting television: Current research perspectives* (pp. 58–73). Newbury Park, CA: Sage.

Priest, P. (1995). *Public intimacies: Talk show participants and tell-all tv.* Creskill, NY: Hampton Press.

Rapping, E. (1991). Daytime inquiries. *The Progressive.* October 1991, 36–38.

Rubin, G. (1983). Thinking sex: Notes for a radical theory of the politics of sexuality. In C. Vance (Ed.), *Pleasure and danger: Exploring female sexuality* (pp. 267–319). Boston: Routledge & Kegan Paul.

Sedgwick, E. K. (1990). *Epistemology of the closet.* Berkeley: University of California Press.

Tannen, D. (1994). *Talking from 9 to 5: How women's and men's conversational styles affect who gets heard, who gets credit, and what gets done at work.* New York: William Morrow.

Vande Berg, L. (1991). Dramedy: *Moonlighting* as an emergent generic hybrid. *Communications Studies, 40,* 13–28.

White, M. (1992). *Tele-advising: Therapeutic discourse in American television.* Chapel Hill: University of North Carolina Press.

Tradition and Technology in Local Newscasts[1]

BRUCE E. GRONBECK

One of the most interesting discussions in Kenneth Burke's *Counter-Statement* (1931) concerned the psychology of information and the psychology of form. To Burke, the scientific and psychoanalytic perspectives on the world in the 1920s had misdirected much reading of literature by putting a premium on subject-oriented information rather than audience-oriented form. Critics, thought Burke, too often approached literature as a laboratory in which to study human life or to psychoanalyze the age. Such purposes even "led the artist . . . to lay his emphasis on the giving of information—with the result," said Burke, "that art tends more and more to substitute the psychology of the hero (the subject) for the psychology of the audience" (p. 32). The emphasis on subject matter, he suggested, draws our attention away from the audience's experiences that are engaged in the reading process and even amalgamated into the interpretive process. "Truth in art," Burke argued, "is not the discovery of facts, not an addition to human knowledge in the scientific sense of the word. It is, rather, the exercise of human propriety, the formulation of symbols" (p. 42).

With his usual circumflex prose style, Burke did not get much more clear than this. Yet, his attempt to describe how it is that meaning-making is grounded in the form rather than the content of literature is significant. Burke was not merely repeating traditional pieties on the separation of form and content. Because he defined form as "the creation of an appetite in the mind of the auditor, and the adequate satisfying of the appetite" (p. 31), he rather was redefining meaning: meaning is not to be understood as information contained "in" texts but rather as kinds of understanding that are possible because of what audiences bring to those texts.

To Burke, the individualized datum, the fact, is made significant to human beings and hence capable of being shared only when cast into social frameworks that people can bring to their encounter with that datum. To the Burke of *Counter-Statement*, those frameworks are the sources of what he called "eloquence" in that they permit meaning to transcend the word-by-word text of literature. Two-thirds of a century ago, Burke was on to something very important.

Perhaps the best test of the utility of Burke's thoughts is in the study of news. News is, presumably, important public information. That which is "newsworthy," most of us assume, is information gathered from our local, national, and international environments and presented to us in written, verbal, and visual forms: as newspaper stories with accompanying pictures, as radio programs filled with oral speech and background sound, as television reports etched in speech and video segments. Surely in the presentation of news we have texts, paralleling the "literature" Burke studied, that permit us to explore and even extend Burke's thinking on the psychology of information and form.

We need to begin by considering what kind of information news is. I suggest that *news is relevant, formalized, public information.*

* "Relevant" information has social-institutional implications. That which is relevant has been constructed and structured so as to be linked to the lives of the people to whom it is presented. Unless some datum can be linked to my country, region, government, bank, church, family, health and wellbeing, or livelihood, I likely will care little about it.

   * "Formalized" information has been structured and unitized in some socially understandable way. Most news is structured narratively, as stories about people doing something to some effect, that is, as coherent series of events with beginnings, middles, and endings enacted by particular people with purposes. News also, however, can be structured as an announcement (a recitation of coherent facts about some present or future event), a conversation (two or more voices related to each other topically or attitudinally), or an anecdote (a humorous, heartwarming, or angering story about someone's trials or triumphs in life).[2] And, we can distinguish, along with Iyengar (1991), episodic from thematic news stories, i.e., those stories that report concrete events in terms of particular people and events vs. those that offer more abstract background on or generalized (thematic) views of those events.

   * "Public" information is made up of data that are worthy of communal sharing. Even a newscast's final anecdote, which often seems like trivial information, can be thought about as important public information. That story about a feisty grandmother who wards off burglars with a broom or a farmer who runs his tractor on chicken manure has a social dimension; at the least it is a bonding device, one that demonstrates human aspirations and foibles that many of us share. And certainly most news stories—70–85 percent of which involve governmental-institutional actors (Gans 1979)—are clearly narratives of general, shared, institutional interest, celebrating the accomplishments of cultural heroes or warning us of the dangerous actions of villains.

Now, if we accept the general proposition that news is relevant, formalized, public information—information valued for its timeliness, uniqueness, and sensitivity to controversy (Schwoch, White, & Reilly 1992)—then of course its form, as Burke under-stood that idea, is crucial to the ways we comprehend that information, for formaliza-tion is essential to the very definition of news. News is never composed of random or isolated data, but always put into forms that give it social relevance and justify its pub-licness.

But, Burke's definition of form as the arousal and fulfillment of appetite does not help us much in understanding the formative process itself: how does "form"—the psychology of form, more precisely—turn data into relevant, public information? That question, I think, draws us into rhetorical studies of public discourse.

Rhetorical Analysis and Television News

To examine news rhetorically is to explore relationships between news programs and their audiences. At least since Aristotle defined it as "the faculty of discovering in any given case the available means of persuasion" (1954), rhetoric has been focused on conceptions and theories of persuasion: on how to build persuasive messages, how to analyze situations and audiences so as to change people's beliefs, attitudes, values, and behaviors via symbols, and how it is that message-makers can gain and maintain power over message-receivers. For well over two millennia, Western world philoso-phers and critics of discourse have explored rhetoric as "the art of verbal influence" (Brummett 1991, p. xi).

Relationships between texts and audiences are inevitably complex. On the one hand, communicators attempt to get you to understand ideas, assume attitudes, and act upon values you don't presently hold, and yet, on the other, communicators can achieve those goals only by referencing ideas you do understand, attitudes you can comprehend, and values with which you are familiar. That is, communication can oc-cur only when language and some set of beliefs, attitudes, and values are shared be-tween rhetor and audience; persuasive messages, perhaps paradoxically, can change you only by working from some things you already believe and value. Furthermore, because you might have been terrified by a dog when you were young while I always had slobbering, friendly dogs around the house, the use of even a simple word such as "dog" can produce sharply different reactions in us; personal experience is always the foundation of meaning, so there is no neutral language, no stable set of universally un-derstood meanings, available for communicating ideas between people.

The rhetorical critic's job, then, is to explore how it is that people use codes—not only words, but also sounds and pictures—to influence the thoughts and actions of each other. Those codes are communal resources; that is, they are instruments more or less shared by people, even if meanings always vary somewhat from person to per-son—instruments constructed so that I in fact can influence you with something other than force.

To see the importance of these simple ideas for our lives, I propose to look at news rhetorically. In asking the questions, how do news organizations go about the business of presenting me with "the news" and how does the news work persuasively? we are driven to probe the psychology of form as Burke suggested we should. To begin to an-swer the questions, we will examine local news, for it is easier to discuss news-audi-ence relationships with local than with national news. We will examine an exceedingly small data set: two broadcasts (23–24 March 1993) of the ten o'clock news from a middle-market, middle-America television news operation at KCRG-TV in Waterloo-Cedar Rapids, Iowa.

I will argue that what Burke calls the psychology of form is schizophrenic: two psychologies of form are operative in televised news, and they compete with each other. The tension existing between *the psychology of technological form* and *the psychology of social (conventionalized) form* produces two kinds of persuasion in local news: one a force to separate us from our comfortable lived experiences, and the other, a force to envelop us in shared community. The significance of this tension between newness and oldness, change and permanence, will be explored in the concluding section of this paper.

The Competing Presentational Forms in Local News

In exploring competing forms for the public information we call news, I am examining what are often referred to as *frames* for information. By frames I mean the perspectives from which we are presented or asked to understand information. Such a definition calls up the old story of the two Jesuits arguing about whether praying and smoking can be done at the same time. They each wrote to the pope for an opinion. The first Jesuit asked, "Is it proper, holy father, for a man to smoke while praying?" The pope replied, "Of course not, for prayer is a time for intimate relationships between God and man, and should not include any distractions whatsoever." The second Jesuit rephrased the question: "Is it permissible, holy father, for a man to pray while smoking?" to which the pope replied, "Of course, my son, for a man may pray anytime and in any circumstances."[3]

Framing is a sociocognitive process whereby some viewpoint is taken, in Burke's language (1945/1954), to be the "container," and some object is taken to be the "thing contained." And, of course, as the two Jesuits discovered, what is asserted to be the container for what containments can be of determinative importance. As Iyengar (1991, p. 11) puts it, "The manner in which a problem of choice is 'framed' is a contextual cue that may profoundly influence decision outcomes." Our frames are in part individualized, cobbled together out of our personal experiences in the world. More interestingly and more importantly, however, our frames for viewing sensate environments are social and institutional, given to us by institutions and learned both formally and informally; in so many ways, you have been told by parents, church, government, peer groups, and television programs what to look at and how to see or understand it.

"Social situations," in Joshua Meyrowitz's words (1985, p. 23), "form the hidden ground for our figures of speech and action." That is, social situations and our experiences in them are the containers, the points-from-where-we-look, when we encounter strange or unknown ideas or experiences. Those containers are never neutral shells or merely places from which we comprehend the world; given their social origin, they come with habituated ways of understanding and evaluating occurrences. They include what Parenti (1992, p. 23) called "opinion visibility"—"perceptual limits around which our opinions take shape." Social-institutional frames, therefore, are perspectives with attitudes. And so, I suggest, when television news frames information, forms it in ways to make it comprehensible, it casts the news makers and the news viewers into particular social roles.[4]

News as Items of Communal Interest

Consider first the opening—the presumably most newsworthy—stories from the KCRG-TV ten p.m. newscast. The lead story on Tuesday, March 23, 1993, concerned the danger of flooding in Cedar Rapids. With a "LIVE" logo and a digital clock in the upper left-hand corner assuring us that we were witnessing news as it happened, reporter Alicia Richards was on the scene at the Cedar River, "preparing for the meltdown"—a word of unease and ambiguity, given the nearby Payloe nuclear plant. It was dark, but we were treated to live shots of the high water and, from another location, pictures of city workers filling sandbags. We were told that citizens could get fifteen sandbags free, and then saw footage from earlier in the day, when one Pam Harris had been interviewed. She had been flooded out six weeks' previous and was sandbagging her property this time around. Alicia Richards assured us that "The best thing to do is be prepared" and that "Being ready really helps—that was Pam's trouble last time." This story was presented twelve days before the Cedar River actually crested above floodstage (for the first time of many in this, the spring and summer of the great Midwest floods of 1993). It thus was a community-service story, oddly, a lead story. The news department decided that the most newsworthy information of the day related to preparing the citizenry for rampaging nature.

The community theme continued in the next two stories that evening, both trials. The second story began "A Linn County jury has decided that Joseph Hughes Jr. will spend the rest of his life in prison," opening a story on a first-degree murder conviction. The third story opened similarly, with "The fate of a Norwalk, Iowa, woman accused of killing her infant son will soon be in the hands of the jury." Both stories thus were framed as events wherein citizens were enforcing community standards; both stories were framed as jury actions, not criminal actions.

Wednesday evening again opened with Alicia Richards on the road "LIVE"—this time, at an Alburnett, Iowa, high school that had been robbed. The story was about the twenty-three rural schools burglarized over the previous eight weeks. Precisely why Richards was live in Alburnett was unclear, as the previous evening's burglaries occurred in other communities, two of which had been featured in earlier newscasts that day. Perhaps Alburnett's proximity to Cedar Rapids made it the easier site for a live report that evening.

Whatever the rationale for putting Richards in Alburnett, she reprised her pattern of the previous night, giving us good advice about being prepared and, this evening, assuring her viewers that she would "continue to look in on this situation." She exuded the same confidence that Sheriff Popenhagen did when he guaranteed on camera that the burglars would be caught "in a matter of time," especially if citizens would be on the lookout for suspicious vehicles around their communities' schools.

These lead stories from mid-week March 1993 are interesting not only because they frame newsworthy information in social-institutional ways, but also because they reinforce or reaffirm particular values, and therein lies their essential rhetorical edge. That is, these stories all had *communitarian force.* The Cedar Rapids Department of Streets and Channel 9 were keeping citizens safe from natural disaster; the Sheriff's

Department in cooperation with Channel 9 were making the school break-ins a top priority so as to protect the youth of eastern Iowa. Pam Harris was a repentant citizen who knew enough to prepare for the second onslaught by the river, and citizen-juries saw that justice was served and the public was protected from evil-doers. These stories provided valuative orientations that clearly suggested what aspects of news items were to be assessed positively and what, negatively. Personal and civic responsibility were combining to save Cedar Rapids from the swollen river, juries were judging fairly (one person guilty and another, innocent, as we found out the next night), and conscientious law enforcement together with citizen vigilance in watching for the all-important license plate numbers of suspicious vehicles offered viewers values worth admiring and emulating. Even as viewers were given information within particular social frames, those frames themselves were legitimated by their very use in information-giving processes employed by KCRG-TV, itself a well-known and significant community institution.

Such tendencies toward social-institutional and even communitarian orientations were visible in different but equally powerful ways in the other half of the ten o'clock evening news in middle America. Of the twenty-one or so minutes of actual news time, only ten or eleven minutes are devoted to what we usually think of as "news." The rest of the local newscast is occupied with weather and sports in almost equal proportion. While weather forecasts undoubtedly help farmers and golfers decide on next-day activities and while local sports help mollify the citizens of school districts who grumble about the high cost of K-12 education, weather and sport segments do more than that rhetorically. They, too, are powerfully communitarian in their force. In both segments, we consistently find a *roll call of community interests.* In reeling off basketball or wrestling scores, sportscasters identify discursively the towns of the viewing area, circumscribing the viewing area as a social place—here, "eastern Iowa," which was labeled as such and is composed of a series of locales that regularly have their names mentioned.

The weather forecaster went even farther. Denny Frary of KCRG-TV not only mentioned and showed on a map the communities of eastern Iowa, but even named particular people who were KCRG-TV's "weather spotters." So, on 23 March 1993, Frary did an eleven-segment spot for his main four-minute appearance as follows:

1. Weather video of a rural mail carrier driving through snow and mud as a community servant living out the cliché of "Neither snow nor ice. . . .";

2. A look at the temperatures in the main cities of eastern Iowa;

3. Looks at Iowa City, Cedar Rapids, Waterloo, and Dubuque through a high-tower camera ("The Hawkeye"), showing the viewers exactly what those places looked like "live";

4. An "almanac" review of the highs and lows around eastern Iowa, including mentions of some of Frary's weather spotters: Bob Steika in Iowa City, Gene Kuhl in Prairiesburg, Sidney Hibsion in Bellevue, "Mrs. Eckhardt in Waukon, back from vacation," Boyd Larew in Manchester, and Bud Steich in Sigourney;

5. Some computer graphics with more Iowa temperatures;

6. A national weather map with temperatures from around the country;

7. Satellite time-lapse photos of moving clouds over an animated map;

8. A colorized shot of national radar;

9. The close-up computer map of the southeastern United States, showing moving clouds;

10. A jump-cut to a close-up computerized map of the central United States, with clouds moving across Iowa;

11. Finally, a five-day weather forecast, followed by Frary returning to the anchor desk.

Notice that Segment 1 celebrated the commitment of a public servant; Segment 2 offered the first roundup of viewing-area communities, by name; Segment 3 featured the four main cities of the viewing area through the "Hawkeye" camera, a piece of technology humanized with the nickname of the state. Personification, whereby communities are materialized through references to some of their actual citizens, induced a sense of community via geographical representatives in the by-now communal process of weather-watching in Segment 4. Segments 5–9 presented a dazzling machined display under the seeming control of weather wizard Frary—weatherman as shaman. Segment 10 united the geographical with the technological, as the communal lands were framed in iconic representations of their weather. And Segment 11 added the dimension of time to the already-present dimension of space, thus fully situating the people of eastern Iowa in the two positional orientations to life (Hall 1959).

Local weather is a virtuoso televisual performance by old pros like Denny Frary, full of wisdom and lore about weather patterns coupled with what undoubtedly are the most expensive graphics the station puts out. Through technological framing, geographical roll-calling, and temporal progress from past (today's weather) to present (current conditions) to future (the forecast), the weather person works communal magic, not only scientifically predicting the weather but also articulating the lived conditions of a people. The sportscaster does much the same things; the graphics are different—a few video clips and scores on the character generator—but dominating, and the roll-calls, especially during reports of end-of-the-week sporting contests in eastern Iowa high schools, are community-building discourses.

In these ways, the sports and weather segments of the ten o'clock news in middle America spatially construct the viewing area as a bounded community, one that shares symbolic relationships through the roll-calls of towns. In sum, the information offered during local newscasts is framed socially-institutionally and communally. Interpretive frames are provided so that information becomes relevant in particular ways; roll-calling permits sports and weather segments—fully half of the ten p.m. show— to construct the geographical-symbolic boundaries around those institutions and communities.[5]

News as Technologically Innovative

Before we wax too romantic about the prairie ideology re-presented nightly in Cedar Rapids, Iowa, however, let us examine the technological framing a bit more closely. With technological innovations such as ENG (electronic news gathering via mini-cams and microwave transmissions), satellite relays (delivery of voice and pictures via uplinks, downlinks, and satellite transponders), color radar (mapping of atmospheric conditions locally and nationally, time-lapse satellite weather photos, and a feeling of three-dimensional pictures of clouds), and other color graphics (e.g., computerized graphic reproductions of such events as the bombing of sites in the Gulf War of 1991, unfolding economic graphs, computer-enhanced pictures), electronic forms also organize information in significant ways. No longer is news a matter of having put radio's newscast on a TV set; no longer does news consist of talking heads. Three innovations in particular over the last twenty years are of special importance:

1. The visual has taken on increasing importance among the communication channels. There is more to see. Stories are written to emphasize the visual. Especially with international news, the stories *must* follow the pictures because there often are no other depictions available; notice how often you see "ITN" (International Television News, a British video service) on the corner of international stories—a sign that the station has accepted video from a distributor of pictures and then fit the story to those pictures. The visual has become the dominant sense in the Western world (Levin, 1993; Jenks, 1995). Television's ability to deliver and even enhance the visual has not gone unnoticed among news departments.

2. "Live" and "action" news formats, featuring live reports in real time from some scene, are presented primarily because they convey a sense of the vital and the anxious as they are present in lived experience. They add excitement and dynamism to local news. Additionally, of course, if a station has purchased a truck and microwave transmitter, the technology must be used if the investment is to pay for itself.

3. Improvements in electronic animation have given stations new specialities. Not only are the show openings and closings much more pleasing[6] because of animation, but better visuals are constructed: moving line graphs, rotating objects, time-lapse segments, mixtures of black-and-white and color, figures inserted from one setting into another, colorization and recolorization, removal of unwanted images from pictures. The computerized animation technology can remake brute reality or reframe it in consciously aesthetic or even ideological ways.

Overall, thus, televised local news is visually focused, temporally oriented to the present, and susceptible to electronic elaboration or reformation. Technological form differs in significant ways from social or conventional form.

Furthermore, the psychology of technological forms makes certain sorts of data or information more newsworthy than other kinds. The hi-tech world is here and now, and the hi-tech arena of television news also is visual-aural. Stories with visual attractiveness and action and with commanding sound, those with a sense of nowness rather than thenness, and those that use the wonder-working technologies (computerized animation, moving graphics, multiple-location interactions) are more likely to be seen than stories that are simply read by the folks at the anchor desk. Stories that visualize agony (Bosnian massacres, dragging the Cedar River for bodies), forbidden pleasure (wet T-shirt contests, raids on houses of prostitution), and children (the search for "Campbell Soup Kids" shown on KCRG-TV on March 24) are more likely to be broadcast than a serious discussion of health care costs or the economy. Yesterday's hero drops out of the lineup in favor of today's new discovery. And, a story such as the one on rural high school break-ins, where the reporter can interact as a professional with the newsmaker, will get on whether or not it has much genuine community urgency and interest.

The point I have been driving toward is this: the technological formalisms of the kind we've been discussing often exist in dialectical tension with the sociocultural formalisms I noted when examining the lead stories from March 23 and 24. The visual-presentist aesthetics of technologically shaped information is largely decontextual-ized, often de-socialized; and it certainly is de-familiarizing because of its unnatural-ness, its very unreality. News technology even may sever or at least de-emphasize sociality and lived experience. Verbalized stories recall past experience, while comput-erized animations re-present them; the technological formalisms stress the visualiz-able present, while the social formalisms put a premium on the verbalized and recol-lected past. The lure of specularized here-and-now, with its aesthetic and ideological pleasures, serves as temptation for viewers to think less (or not at all) about the ver-bally evoked past of social truths and commitments. The technological spectacle is a form that can compete with the framing *doxa* or generally received (doxastic) opinions of the collectivity.[7]

Within recent memory, the news coverage from Baghdad during the Gulf War shellings is an excellent example of these ideas. We learned much about the reporters' lives in hotels without amenities and about tracer-shells making patterns in the eerie green-tint video on which the night sky was captured, but little about the lives of city dwellers subjected to the bombardment. Even when covering American warriors, re-porters spent more time on military hardware than the human side of soldiering. My favorite local story during the Gulf War came from another Waterloo-Cedar Rapids sta-tion, KWWL-TV, which ran a four-minute story on 21 January 1991 on the technology involved in getting reports from Saudi Arabia to Iowa; that technology was depicted as heroically as the sons and daughters of the Heartland stationed there. The technology was often the news in the Gulf War. Televised news's favoring of the interesting visual, the larger-than-life technology, and the Nintendo-like war waged with "smart bombs" and "Scuds" rather than human bodies demonstrate various ways in which the very defamiliarized (and hence interesting), technologically enhanced aspects of life and the familiar (and hence less interesting), socially sanctioned dimensions of living can do battle to frame viewers' understandings and interpretations of the world.[8]

Secondary Orality as an Epistemological Battleground

We now have ventured into territory that belongs to what Walter Ong calls "secondary orality." Because television allows us to share common experiences in ways analogous to how they are distributed in pre-literate societies, Ong believes that contemporary society is strongly oral in its orientation. In his words (1982, p. 136), "This new orality has striking resemblances to the old in its participatory mystique, its fostering of a communal sense, its concentration on the present moment, and even its use of formu-las." Yet, because the literate age followed the oral age and because electronic tech-nologies have intruded forcibly into our lives, that orality is "secondary"—marked and redirected by both literacy and technological apparatuses.

In positing a dualistic psychology that can be seen in contrasts between socially and technologically formative forces, we may have yet another way to talk about sec-ondary orality in contemporary life. If technological forms are not simply facilitators of sociality—i.e., conduits connecting people—but competitors with more traditional oral mechanisms for social connection, then we may have found an important way of looking at current worries over mass media and mass society. Critics who dislike and distrust the mass media may have missed some important facets of the contests over human understanding being waged in our time.

Media-bashing is popular sport these days. Some attacks follow in the curmudgeonly footsteps of Neil Postman, whose book *Technopoly* (1992) is subtitled *The Surrender of Culture to Technology.* He does not appreciate living in a society dominated by various technologies and their reformation of life experiences: medicine focused on machines rather than the laying-on of hands, omnipresent computers and computerese, technologically driven ideologies (the politics of the possible), and an overarching scientism that flows from such thinking. All such manifestations of a technological mind-set Postman views as anti-individualistic and anti-libertarian; his solutions to such problems feature a kind of liberal arts education treating the valuative and ethical complexities of what it means to be a human being. Normative criticism is the only way to hold back the craven New World.

Other attacks follow the more self-centered concerns of French social critic Jacques Ellul. His *The Humiliation of the Word* (1985) is a more theologically or philosophically oriented treatise on the destruction of the interior life, of subjectivity. In the word, says Ellul (p. 23), we find "discussion, paradox, and mystery." In such processes dwell insight and the secrets of human life, which are eliminated by technology and scientism. We live in societies, argues Ellul in 1973, dominated by *la technique:* a technological environment that desacralizes and de-individuates human beings.

Perhaps the strongest attack on electronic media comes from the French poststructuralists, most notably Jean Baudrillard (e.g., 1983, 1988). He argues that we are not surrounded simply by deceptive signs (vehicles for mistaken meaning), but in fact empty signs—a mass-mediated language and package of icons that mean nothing. We live in a technologically driven simulacrum, a world of seemingness, a world of ecstasy without joy, of mass appeal without cultural effect on individuals. To another of the postmoderns, Guy Debord (1990), material social relations, exemplified in the idea of being able to actually touch others, have been replaced by visualized ones. Such conceptions of simulacra, which of course can be traced back to Plato's Allegory of the Cave, of life shadows and appearances as mistaken for reality, have been much written about since World War II. Theodor Adorno and Max Horkheimer's critique of mass culture in the late 1940s as well as Dwight Macdonald's essays on mass culture and alienation in the 1950s belong to the tradition now being featured in postmodernist thought (Aronowitz, 1993, p. 79). As Gilles Deleuze (1990) summarizes these views, thanks to technology everything we experience is a copy of a copy.

What are we to make of such assaults on technology, the (presumably) resulting changes in social structures, and even the cultural redefinitions that appear to flow from technological innovation, particularly in public communication? While it is undoubtedly true that the New Technologies have altered social processes in determinative ways, must we wring our hands in despair over cultural surrender, humiliation, and simulation as Postman, Ellul, and Baudrillard have done? I think not.

All of the critics of electronically mediated communication media that we have reviewed have different arguments yet one assumption in common: *they assume that the electronic media have brought with them cataclysmic changes in communication, culture, and consciousness.* Postman assumes that television destroys the rational bases of public deliberation and our sense of social obligations (see esp. Postman, 1986). Ellul (along with Postman) assumes that literate language—and hence controlled, discursive inquiry—is humiliated and hence human beings lose their ability to consider social change reasonably as well as their sense of self-sufficiency, i.e., their capability for independent cognitive activity. And, Baudrillard (1988) alleges that media technology creates desires to consume rather than to make goods, hence making social relations into economic encounters and refashioning individuals into "a multitude of identical miniaturized egos" (p. 40). Such arguments for *new* modes of communication, culture, and consciousness simply must be premised on the cataclysmic change thesis to be rational.

The assumption of the cataclysmic change thesis, however, is easily challenged. As Ong has noted, for example, the electronic media seemingly recoup traditional experiences that characterized oral societies thousands of years ago by recovering a sense of oral (aural) connections through broadcast talk, by allowing large segments of wired cultures such as that of the U.S. to share experiences simultaneously, and by creating a sense of face-to-face co-presence, which makes *ethos* or character so important to televised discourses.

Those aspects of KCRG-TV news that we examined, I think, provide compelling evidence for Ong's analyses of secondary orality. The social forms of the stories we reviewed—the arousal and satisfaction of social expectations, in Burke's terms—were traditional forms wherein community interests and values framed the new information being presented in the lead and follow-up stories from those evening in March of 1993. Alicia Richards, the anchors, Denny Frary—these human beings had a kind of presence, even a sense of character (*ethos*), in their televised presentations; they freely used the first-person singular so as to manifest and work from their professional personae. Their presentations combined professionalized credibility based on their training and expertise with their sensitivities to the collective bases of popular knowledge—references to Pam Harris's learning from experience, to juries of peers making determinations of guilt or innocence, to the weather spotters who could materialize various communities' existence and climatological activities.

Now, of course, the social connections between the citizens of eastern Iowa were fabricated electronically those mid-week nights in March of 1993. And Patterson and McClure (1976, p. 90) offer us more than a grain of truth when they argue that "Since the nightly news is too brief to treat fully the complexity of modern politics, too visual to present effectively most events, and too entertainment-minded to tell viewers much worth knowing, most network [and local?] newscasts are neither very educational nor very powerful communicators." But yet, such views, in a sense, are based on what Burke long ago identified as a psychology of information or what Lazega (1992) called the technical conception of information control. The psychology of social form, however, reconceptualizes our understanding of the kind of information we get from the ten o'clock news; "messages need legitimation," as Lazega (p. 31) suggests, "to be considered as informative," and that is a truism borne out by our look at KCRG-TV news.

The electronic fabrication of the temporal and spatial dimensions of social relationships, however, was also visible in those newscasts. The viewers of the 23 March 1993 evening news program found themselves immediately in three places at once: at home, at the KCRG-TV studios in Waterloo, Iowa, and on location with Alicia Richards along the Cedar River in Cedar Rapids, Iowa. Being in three different places at once electronically, viewers were active simultaneously in three different social relationships: in (presumably) familial and familiar relationships at home, in parasocial relationships (Horton & Wohl, 1986) with news anchors and a weather forecaster they had come to feel they know personally over the years, and in institutional relationships with expert news-gatherers or truth-finders such as Alicia Richards. Richards' live reports were presented to the anchors, who in turn positively sanctioned them and passed them on to the viewers. Three sorts of relationships with three types of people in three different locations could not be assembled without technology.

If the television technology can remake space, it also can rescore our sense of time. "File footage," i.e., videotape of past events, can be made a part of now, as it was in the story about high school break-ins. The past thus is retextualized into the present.[9] Time-lapse photography of the kind Frary used to show us twenty-four hours of cloud movement in a matter of microseconds telescopes time, elongating the present by pulling both past (yesterday's satellite photos) and future (tomorrow's predicted air flow) into our sense of nowness. Thanks especially to its visuality and its ability to manipulate the "realisticness" (Fiske, 1987) of its icons and images, televised news can create a sense of an enduring present, an unfolding here-and-now that represents nothing less than a remanufacture of cultural orientation, that is, our understanding of our positions in time and space.

And yes, we have come to expect both social form (tradition) and electronic form (technology) to energize our lives every evening at ten p.m. in middle America via a discursive structure—live report, other news stories, weather, sports, signoff anecdote—that is created through repeated use and that is productive of a sense of collective well-being. Eastern Iowans can go to bed in a quiescent state, assured that they have surveyed the socially important events of the day, packaged in collectively sanctioned frameworks, and have been treated to a technological display of retooled time and space that defamiliarizes the environment enough to create kinds of information impossible to make present to them in any other way.

And so, the virtues of past social relations so mourned by Postman, Ellul, and the French poststructuralists have not been lost but are maintained even as they are reconstructed. In the era of secondary orality, we come to know our world and its boundaries through an amalgamation of two psychologies of form that bond tradition with innovation, the familiar with the defamiliarized, the heard and the seen—the *gnosis* that is traditional (historically specific) knowledge with the *episteme* that is demonstrated (decontextualized) knowledge.

Parting Thoughts

In 1931, Kenneth Burke (p. 31) was worried about "the disorders of the social system," even the "disorders of culture and taste" that would follow in the wake of too tight a focus on information and too little attention to doxastic processes for bringing collectively valued and socially integrative frames of analysis to bear on literature. Burke saw the enemy of literature—of the examined life, of the eloquent aesthetic experience that in its transcendence could help us understand lived experience—to be information. To him, information was the enemy, not because having factual or scientific knowledge was bad, but because such information was a special kind of knowledge: a knowledge of things without their contexts, without a sense of the social weighting and of the significance of its import.

Information, in this sense, was what resulted from the Enlightenment revolution, when truth and ideas were thought of not in human terms (the doxastic way) but in reportive terms (the scientist way): "This great Source, of most of the *Ideas* we have," averred John Locke (1700/1975, p. 105), "depending wholly upon our Senses, and de-rived by them to the Understanding, I call SENSATIONS." To Locke, ideas were the mind's reports from the human being's sensory equipment of what the outside world was like, and they could be checked and rechecked for accuracy by repeated observa-tions. But to Burke, if that's all ideas were, then disorder or even anarchy was all we could expect to see in collectivities, for there would be no way of bonding one person's ideas (sensory experiences) with another's. We might be able to share information per se with each other, but without social-valuative frames in common, we could not un-derstand its force in our collective lives. And so Burke distinguished between the psy-chology of information and the psychology of form, denigrating the one mind-set and celebrating the other.

In this brief look at a small piece of local newscasts in the Midwest, I hope we have both made good use of Burke's musings and yet extended them in useful ways. In kinds of public communication that include not only the verbiage of literature but also the visual and acoustic codes of television signals, the information-form distinction is important but in a different manner than Burke suggested. While I agree that the psy-chologies of information and of form exist in tension to each other—as traditional sta-bility in understandings does to innovative, technologically driven destabilizations—I suggest that we not think of them in disjunctive terms. Either-or ways of thinking can be destructive; such thinking, I am convinced, has led the likes of Postman, Ellul, and Baudrillard down very crooked paths. Disjunctive thought almost inevitably leads to attempts to eliminate—at least to decry—one of the alternatives, usually the innova-tive one. Television destroys politics! Television destroys literacy! Television destroys meaning! Down with television! Such interjections enervate analysis and contempla-tion, as they seek to erase a part of experience, our experience with communication technologies, rather than forcing us to deal thoughtfully with that experience.

A rhetorical analysis of the type offered in this essay, I would hope, demonstrates that (1) the preachments of the anti-technology critics misdirect our attention away from rather than into the meaning-making mechanisms that are at work in mass-mediated communication enterprises; (2) the messages of such enterprises are com-posed of multiple discourses that arise because of the co-presence of social (collec-tivized) and technical (remanufactured) knowledge; and (3) the consumers of such messages, the viewers of nightly news in this case, are treated to meaning-systems grounded in the socially sanctioned and familiar frames of (doxastic) interpretation and yet extended in the deculturing and defamiliarizing frames of technological innovations. The roll calls of places and people, together with the social framing of stories, construct a psychology of social form that is a force for stability, a sense of enduring time and place. Yet, the technological transportation across space and ma-nipulation of time within an elongated sense of here-and-now is a force for innova-tion, for reframing our life experiences by pulling us into other realities and other perspectives on those realities.

Thus, for the viewers, the psychologies of tradition and technology are jointly op-erative, making the viewing even of the news in eastern Iowa a complex psychocultural experience. The rhetoric of local news—that is, the power of what we have defined as relevant, formalized, public information—goes well beyond its narrative structures, its electronic spectacle, and its encapsulation of new information. The rhetorical power of local news resides in its ability to reconcile structure, spectacle, and informational content in forms that arouse and then satisfy a full range of human interests in the old and the new, the stable and the destabilizing. The rhetorical power of local news lies in its ability to discursively anneal multiple times and places—multiple experiences—into a seemingly unitary one.

Our experience with television, Hart (1994, p. 12) coos, is "unanticipated and, yet, curiously anticipatable." The curiosity Hart expresses arises, I am convinced, from the dual psychologies at work in viewing, the dual rhetorics through which we make meaning from what we see on the tube. That's why a large percentage of eastern Iowans turn over to channels 2 (KGAN-TV), 7 (KWWL-TV), or 9 (KCRG-TV) at ten o'clock on weekday evenings: to discover what Richard Campbell (1994, p. 327) sees as the psychological coherence, experiential sense of continuity, and social assurance that comes from viewing television news programs.

NOTES

1. An earlier version of the paper was presented at the Midwest Sociological Society convention in Chicago, 1993. I thank the University of Iowa's Center for Advanced Studies for providing the expansive environment that encourages the sort of speculative thought comprising this paper; special thanks to its director Jay Semel and administrator Lorna Olson. Thanks as well to A. Susan Owen and manuscript readers for *Sociological Quarterly* for their insightful critiques as this study was prepared in somewhat different form for its Winter 1997 publication.
2. I draw these distinctions from Ekdom (1981).
3. Thanks to Postman (1992) for remembering this story.
4. Interestingly, the classical theory of *topoi*—of "topics" or "places" where ideas acceptable in some society can be found—is also a kind of geographical or spatial notion. That there is a "topography" of accepted beliefs and values in every collectivity is an enduring belief. See Enos (1996), s.v. "topics."
5. I am dealing with the social sides of this process. It also is possible, of course, to understand community-building and maintaining as political-economic moves, as what Lance Bennett calls "[k]eying information delivery to American life-styles through marketing research" (1988, p. 7). I agree, but that in no way lessens the importance of the social processes at work.
6. And, we must remember, pleasure is not innocent in social situations. With the pleasures of the socially shared can come reinforcement of social standards; laughter can critique the socially deviant, while public, positive enjoyment is a sign of collective acceptance. Pleasure in this sense is what Roland Barthes talked about as *plaisir*. See Fiske 1987, esp. chap. 12.
7. I don't have room to develop this idea, but, as already suggested, the history of rhetorical thought contains interesting tensions between the heard and the seen. The heard is associated with *doxa*, with generally received opinion or cultural wisdom, especially as it passed from generation to generation in oral or oral-dominated societies—via such vehicles as nursery rhymes, fables, the read-

ing aloud of sacred scriptures, and other oral, shared discourses. The seen is associated with the descriptive, even with the deceptively alluring and decorative. Rhetorically, the heard is associated with *inventio*, with the ideas granted status by a collectivity, while the seen is associated with *elocutio* or style, the verbal ornamentation of ideas. It is not an accident that Yahweh's name could not be uttered in the Old Testament or that in the gospel according to John, Jesus became *logos*, the word as it is heard. Historically, the social has been dominatingly oral, strongly oriented toward tradition. The attack upon the oral (and not just the written) in the ocularcentric age of television is significant. I extend these ideas in Gronbeck, 1993.

8. The familiar, of course, certainly was shown on local TV, especially during the Gulf War: reports of high schools following their graduates at various stations in the Gulf area, of local youth killed in action, of flag-and-yellow-ribbon parades (see the KWWL-TV 1/21/91 newscast). The war itself, however, was seldom depicted as death and destruction, except for national news shots of Marines firing over town walls at unseen enemies and long-distance pictures of tanks shelling targets in the night. The only sights of human suffering came from reports out of Baghdad and Israel, and those were always framed in U.S. commentary on the heinousness of Saddam Hussein for causing civilian pain. The almost daily footage of war machines and computerized animation (maps with moving symbols, diagrams of bombings) were the more usual fare. See Jeffords & Rabinovitz, 1994.

9. The very word "text" comes from the same Latin root as "textile"—both having to do with weaving. To textualize the past, thus, is to weave it into a discourse, making it a part of now.

REFERENCES

Aristotle. (1954). *Rhetoric.* W. R. Roberts (Trans.). New York: Random House.

Aronowitz, S. (1993). *Roll over Beethoven: The return of cultural strife.* Hanover, NH: Wesleyan University Press.

Baudrillard, J. (1983). *In the shadow of the silent majorities, or, The end of the social and other essays.* P. Foss, J. Johnston, and P. Patton (Trans.) New York: Semiotext(e).

Baudrillard, J. (1988). *The ecstasy of communication.* B. and C. Schutze (Trans.) S. Lotringer (Ed.). New York: Semiotext(e).

Bennett, W. L. (1988). *News: The politics of illusion* (2nd ed.). New York: Longman.

Brummett, B. (1991). *Rhetorical dimensions of popular culture.* Tuscaloosa, AL: University of Alabama Press.

Burke, K. (1931). *Counter-statement.* Los Altos, CA: Hermes Publications.

Burke, K. (1945, 1950/1954). *A grammar of motives; A rhetoric of motives.* New York: Meridian Books.

Campbell, R. (1994). Securing the middle ground: Reporter formulas in *60 minutes.* In H. Newcomb (Ed.), *Television: The critical view* (pp. 303–331). (5th ed.). New York: Oxford University Press.

Debord, G. (1990). *Comments on the society of the spectacle.* M. Imrie (Trans.). New York: Verso.

Deleuze, G. (1990). *The logic of sense.* New York: Columbia University Press.

Ekdom, L. R. (1981). An interpretive study of the news: An analysis of news forms. Ph.D. dissertation, University of Iowa.

Ellul, J. (1973). *Propaganda: The formation of men's attitudes.* New York: Vintage Books.

Ellul, J. (1985). *The humiliation of the word.* J. M. Hanks (Trans.). Grand Rapids, MI: William B. Eerdmans.

Enos, T. (1996). *Encyclopedia of rhetoric and composition: Communication from ancient times to the information age.* New York: Garland Publishing.

Fiske, J. (1987). *Television culture.* New York: Methuen.

Gans, H. (1979). *Deciding what's news.* New York: Pantheon Books.

Gronbeck, B. E. (1993). The spoken and the seen: The phonocentric and ocularcentric dimensions of rhetorical discourse. In John Frederick Reynolds (Ed.), *Rhetorical memory and delivery: Classical concepts for contemporary composition and communication* (pp. 141–157). Hillsdale, NJ: Lawrence Earlbaum Associates.

Hall, E. (1959). *The silent language.* Garden City, NJ: Doubleday.

Hart, R. P. (1994). *Seducing America: How television charms the modern voter.* New York: Oxford University Press.

Horton, D., & Wohl, R. (1986). Mass communication and para-social interaction: Observation on intimacy at a distance. In G. Gumpert and R. Cathcart (Eds.), *Inter/media: Interpersonal communication in a media world* (pp. 185–206). New York: Oxford University Press.

Iyengar, S. (1991). *Is anyone responsible? How television frames political issues.* Chicago: University of Chicago Press.

Jeffords, S., & Rabinovitz, L. (1994). *Seeing through the media: The Persian gulf war.* New Brunswick, NJ: Rutgers University Press.

Jenks, C. (1995). (Ed.). *Visual culture.* New York: Routledge.

Lazega, E. (1992). *Micropolitics of knowledge: Communication and indirect control in workgroups.* Hawthorne, NY: Aldine de Gruyter.

Levin, D. M. (1993). *Modernity and the hegemony of vision.* Berkeley: University of California Press.

Locke, J. (1700/1975). *An essay concerning human understanding.* P. H. Nidditch (Ed.). Oxford: Clarendon Press.

Meyrowitz, J. (1985). *No sense of place: The impact of electronic media on social behavior.* New York: Oxford University Press.

Ong, W. J. (1982). *Orality and literacy: The technologizing of the word.* New York: Methuen.

Parenti, M. (1993). *Inventing reality: The politics of news media.* New York: St. Martin's.

Patterson, T., & McClure, R. (1976). *The unseeing eye: The myth of television power in national elections.* New York: G. P. Putnam.

Postman, N. (1985). *Amusing ourselves to death: Public discourse in the age of show business.* New York: Penguin Books.

Postman, N. (1992). *Technopoly: The surrender of culture to technology.* New York: Alfred A. Knopf.

Schwoch, J., White, M., & Reilly, S. (1992). (Eds.). *Media knowledge: Readings in popular culture, pedagogy, and critical citizenship.* Albany: State University of New York Press.

The Structure of Television Narratives

MICHAEL J. PORTER

Television narratives are unique. They do not follow the traditional linear model of mass consumption narratives common to literary, theatrical, and film narratives. Unlike its narrative cousins, television uses the same characters, week after week, to tell its stories. We tune in because we want to see our favorite characters in action—fighting against corruption, sparring with their friends, or saving a life. What they do is not as important as the fact that we have "connected" with them and these characters are an important part of our lives. In television narratives character is as important, if not more important, than plot; indeed, for some programs, character *is* the story.

Most viewers are unaware of the structure of a television narrative. In fact, the structure of the narrative they are watching is one of the last things on their minds as they become engaged in a taut thriller or laugh at the implausible situations on their favorite sitcom. On one level, narrative analysis examines how a "story" is presented. On another level, however, it focuses on how a culture presents the myths of a society to the members of that society. Fiske and Hartley (1978) maintain that television has replaced the oral and written traditions of narrative and has become the "bard" of modern culture. If so, then it is important to analyze how this medium tells us stories so that we can better understand both the culture from which the stories come and the people for whom the stories are told. The goal of any examination of a television text is greater awareness and understanding of the text itself. Ultimately, such analysis will lead to a greater understanding of the potential impact of the text as a discursive voice in the culture. This study presents an analytical tool designed to help one better understand the function of the scenes in television narratives.

Narrative Theory and the Primacy of Character

Narrative theory exists to answer the question: How are stories told? Classical narrative theory states that narrative has two components: the story and the discourse. Simply put, "the story is the *what* in a narrative that is depicted, discourse the *how*" (Chatman, 1978, p. 19). In other words, the story is "what happens to whom," and the discourse is "how the story is told."

The classical narrative model includes such characteristics as exposition, disturbance, obstacles, crisis, climax, and resolution—all elements of the story. Gustav Freytag, expanding on Aristotle's delineation of the plots of tragedies, introduced the concept of the "dramatic triangle" wherein each play begins with exposition, rising through various complications to the climax and ending with resolution (1968; cited in Kozloff, 1992, p. 70). These concepts are useful in describing most theatrical, cinematic, and written narratives. Television's episodic series and serials, however, are significantly different from cinema in a number of aspects. Feuer (1986) notes that television is not very well described by narrative models based on linearity and resolution. While these linear narrative models help us understand narrative structure, they are not sufficient to completely describe what happens in each scene. While most films, for example, are self-contained, it is difficult to say where most television stories end. We see the same characters each week. For some, the problem introduced one week will be developed in the next. It appears as if resolution and closure are not important in many of today's television programs. More series are using story arcs, wherein a story is introduced one week, and develops over several episodes before it comes to a conclusion, comparable to the ongoing story lines found in daytime soap operas. In some series resolution is only implied and is not necessarily presented (see Moeder, 1994, for a complete discussion of implied resolution).

Chatman (1978, p. 113) writes that "The contemplation of character is the predominate pleasure in modern art narrative." Feuer (1987) notes that the paradigmatic growth of characters is a defining characteristic of television series and serials. Kozloff (1992) quotes Robert Allen, who states: "television stories generally displace audience interest from the syntagmatic axis to the paradigmatic—that is, from the flow of events per se [the syntagmatic axis] to the revelation and development of existents [characters, and the paradigmatic axis]" (p. 75). In other words, we, the television audience, are more concerned with character than we are with the story. We remember from week to week what our favorite characters are experiencing. We tune in to see what adventures they will encounter. Our history with the characters is both personal and cumulative, and the more time we spend watching them, the stronger our ties. This is the luxury of television narrative, which allows for the growth and maturation of television characters—slowly, and over time. Hence, any analysis of the structure of a television narrative must provide for a way to focus on character growth as well as on the syntagmatic and linear development of the story line.

The Narrative Analysis Tool

The narrative analysis tool presented here lists discrete scene functions. The tool has evolved over time and is useful because it tries to provide a common language for describing the function of any particular scene in a television narrative. It has been applied to daytime serials, primetime serials, situation comedies, and hour-long television dramas. The tool is designed to answer these questions:

- What does the scene tell us about the story?
- What does the scene tell us about character?
- What does the scene tell us about setting?
- What would happen if this scene wasn't here? Could I still understand the story?[1]

According to Chatman's narrative theory (1978) each narrative contains exactly three *signifieds*—event, character, and detail of setting. The *signifiers* are "those elements in the narrative statement (whatever the medium) that can stand for one of these three, thus any kind of physical or mental action for the first, any person (or, indeed, any entity that can be personalized) for the second, and any evocation of place for the third" (p. 25). Even though all three are present in any scene, for the sake of analysis it is valuable to look for the *primary,* or most important, function per scene.

For the benefit of this analysis, a modified definition of scene is used. Technically speaking, according to Christian Metz (1974), a scene contains two or more shots and shows action that is spatially and temporally continuous. Previous research (Porter, 1983) has shown that the scene is the most frequently used unit in television dramas. To simplify the process of analysis I use "scene" to describe all units held together by continuity of time or place, or parallel action in separate locations, or a sequence of shots unified thematically.[2]

Plot Function

The plot functions used in this tool are based on traditional narrative elements. They can be found in any theatrical script analysis textbook. (See, for example, Smiley, 1971; Kirk and Bellas, 1985). Terms commonly used to describe narratives—such as exposition, conflict, resolution, dramatic question, and climax—are the basis for the plot functions. In developing this tool some new terms evolved that could describe more distinctly the function of a particular scene found in a television narrative, such as "plan revealed," "clarification," and "conflict continues."

The specific plot functions follow. For the sake of coding, each plot function is numbered and is preceded by the letter P. (Character functions are preceded by the letter C, and the "setting" function is labeled S.) While there are more specific functions that identify plot elements (15) than character function (7), do not assume that there is greater emphasis in the tool for describing plot rather than character. It is simply that within our culture, the focus in traditional narrative analysis has rested primarily on helping to unravel the events, or the plot of the story. Hence, our culture has more specific language to describe particular functions found in these plot-oriented scenes.

Plot Scene Functions

Scene Code	Principle Function	Description
P-1: **Exposition**	Presents background information that happened before the narrative begins (back story)	Primary purpose is to inform the audience of relevant facts we need to know to follow the story.
P-2: **Disturbance**	Reveals the initiating event that upsets the balanced life of the lead character and leads to the ensuing action of the story.	Presents the disruption Establishes the nature of the conflict May occur off-camera and be revealed only through dialogue.
P-3: **Dramatic Question**	Raises basic question the story will answer.	Relates to conflict of the story Look for question answered at the climax to determine when the dramatic question was introduced; e.g., how will they resolve the dilemma?

P-4: **Obstacle**	Introduces an obstacle; an opposing force; reveals the antagonist.	Answers the question: who (or what) is standing in the way of the hero achieving his/her goal?
P-5: **Plan Revealed**	Presents the hero's goal for eliminating the disturbance.	What must the hero do to achieve his/her goal (to restore balance)? Shows character searching for a solution.
P-6: **Plan in Action**	Shows characters as they carry out their plan.	Most "in-transit" scenes serve this function. Characters accomplishing daily tasks related to their plan Shows characters trying to accomplish their goal.
P-7: **Complication**	Reveals a change in the course of the action; it "complicates" the situation.	Introduces a new angle to existing complication Develops a *new* opposing force Complications can include character, circumstances or events, mistake, misunderstanding, discovery
P-8: **Clarification**	Solidifies the dramatic question of the story, clarifies the basic conflict.	The "a-Ha" scene Presents *new* information about the conflict Only now do we understand ramifications of the conflict.
P-9: **Conflict Continues**	Keeps audience aware of the basic conflict of the story	Heightens suspense, anticipation, tension Introduces "minor" revelations in the conflict "Teases" the audience; draws out the story. "Chase" scenes are good examples of this
P-10: **Confrontation**	When the hero confronts an obstacle.	Can occur in the same scene as complication (P-7)
P-11: **Crisis**	When the opposing forces are in conflict and the outcome is uncertain. This is the decisive confrontation for the story.	Term is used synonymously with climax. The turning point in the action
P-12: **Resolution**	Balance is restored.	The results of the crisis are revealed.

		Always follows crisis scene, may take place in the same scene
		Occurs at end of episode
P-13: **Theme**	Sole function is to underscore the theme of the story.	The "Mallet" scene (you are hit over the head with the "theme" of the story if you haven't gotten it by now). Can explain "why" the hero has his/her goals May explain a character's behavior or attitude Will usually reflect cultural or social issues, values, commonly held beliefs.
P-14: **Foreshadowing**	Foreshadows a later event.	Gives later events more significance Creates anticipation for future conflict May reveal character traits that factor into the story later on Establishes credibility needed later
P-15: **Relief**	Provides a release for the audience, a diversion from preceding story	Provides relief from the emotional intensity found in the preceding scene Comic relief Focus may be on secondary characters.

Character Function

The next seven functions describe scenes which focus primarily on character instead of plot or setting. Some television series focus as much attention on character as they do story. *These scene functions are useful when the scene does not further the linear story.* Most scenes will reveal something about character given the nature of storytelling; however, we, the audience, tend to focus more on plot than character. That, in fact, is what a story is all about. We expect a story to go somewhere; we expect it to end. Consequently, in the retelling of a story, we will focus on the linear narrative and minimize the role of the character in the story. One of the unique elements of television series' narratives, compared to films, for example, is that we come to our viewing already familiar with the central characters. They are the major drawing cards for the series and, just like good friends, we want to know more about them. This leads to scenes that focus on character; scenes that reveal more information about the characters' backgrounds, their relationships, their views toward various issues; or scenes that simply show the characters performing their normal, daily routines.

Character Scene Functions

Scene Code	Principle Function	Description
C-1: **Introduction**	Introduces a new character or set of characters.	May be similar to P-4, if introducing the "obstacle" or antagonist.
C-2: **Development**	Reveals background information we did not know before.	Information revealed through dialogue, action, or first-person accounts focus on providing back story to make characters more familiar
C-3: **Revelation**	Focus on or reveals new information which explains a character's actions or attitude.	Makes the character more familiar to the audience. Reveals information about a character's state of mind.
C-4: **Relationships**	Focus on the interaction between or among characters.	Characters may talk about incidental events or personal events unrelated to main story May reveal new information about characters in the relationship Characters show supportive action of one another
C-5: **Affirmation**	Reminds us of the nature of the relationship between or among characters.	Found in daytime serials, when purpose is to keep the story alive. Little new development or change in relationship is revealed.
C-6: **Action**	Focus on the character performing tasks, job related.	Shows character doing routine tasks Could emphasize a character's level of competence and particular skills (or lack thereof)
C-7: **Ambiance**	Serves to intensify our emotional response to the story.	Designed to draw the audience into the story at an emotional level. Adds dimension to the character by revealing character's emotional response to an event or another character. Usually related to the theme of story. "Emotional" scenes do little to further the story.

Setting Function

Although rare, some television series use the convention of providing a scene whose sole purpose is to identify the setting for the action that is about to take place. In some cases, we have called such scenes "establishing shots" when the scene is composed of a single shot, often an exterior shot of the building wherein the ensuing action will take place. Such scenes are more common today in "made-for-television" movies. Such a function is usually absent from daytime serials and situation comedies. While each new scene will tell the audience about setting, this scene function should be used only when none of the other functions is appropriate. If the primary and sole function of a scene is to identify the time of day and the location, or to place a character in a new setting, then that scene serves this function. What follows is an application of the scene function tool to an episode of a television series, *ER*.

The Television Series *ER:* An Example

The surprise hit of the 1994 fall season was the emergency room drama, *ER*, created by Michael Crichton and produced by Steven Spielberg and John Wells. *ER* has been called "the MTV version of medical care in America" (Rapping, 1995, p. 36). The series is set in the emergency room of a Chicago hospital; the "background is urban chaos and violence, of social and family disintegration" (ibid.). From a narrative perspective, the series focuses on both the public and private lives of a disparate group of surgeons, interns, residents, nurses, and medical students working as a team to save the lives of those under their care. A highly trained staff of efficient nurses, technicians, and clerks assists them.

In any episode several continuing story lines (story arcs) are played out over a series of episodes. Most hour-long television narratives include two primary stories (often referred to as the A and the B story), which typically will be thematically related. There is often a third story, independent of the two main stories, that focuses on one of the other central characters. (In a large ensemble series there is always the need for additional story lines both to fill out the episode and to keep the central characters in the story.) In this episode entitled "House of Cards," which aired during the first season, there were five stories:

The "House of Cards" Episode

	Story	Number of Scenes
A	Dr. Mark Green: 　A1: Public Story 　A2: Personal Story 　　A2a: Confidence Crisis 　　A2b: Family Crisis	13
B	Medical Student Story: 　B1: Deb Chen Story	12

	B2: John Carter Story	
C	Dr. Doug Ross:	8
	C1: Public Story	
	C2: Personal Story	
D	Dr. Peter Benton and his mother story	3
E	Dr. Susan Lewis and her sister story	2

The main stories are the A and B stories, which are thematically related; the C story focuses on character; the D story is the conclusion of a major story arc; and the E story is the beginning of a new story arc. What follows is a brief description of what I consider to be salient points describing the narrative structure of each of the five stories. To facilitate the discussion, specific scenes will be identified (see the Composite Scene Analysis Table on pages 152–156). The method of describing scenes will include two sets of numbers, such as 2:3. The first identifies the act, and the second, the scene within the act, numbered sequentially beginning with 1. In *ER*, a tease or a prelude precedes the first act, which will be numbered as "0." As is typical of hour-long dramas, there are four acts, each separated by a series of commercials.

As is typical of this series, the primary story—the Mark Green story—is two-pronged. The public Dr. Green story focuses on his interactions with a patient, Mrs. Salazaar, and his ability to persuade her to bring her family in for treatment because they have all been exposed to tuberculosis. This is a relatively minor story, found in only four scenes (1:3, 1:41, 2:1, 4:10). The private Dr. Green story is also two-pronged. Both are extensions of his life stories developed in previous episodes, and both focus on his inability to cope with difficult situations. One of them, the larger story arc (which means that the story has been "evolving" for a longer period of time), involves his relationship with his wife, a lawyer who moved to Milwaukee to further her law career, taking their young daughter with her. This story line is the focus for only two scenes (4:3, 4:7). (This is one way for the writers to keep the story thread alive in the minds of the audience.) The more immediate cause of Dr. Green's angst is his reaction to the death of his patient, who died while under his care in the preceding episode. He must deal with this experience of profound failure, and during the first half of this episode, his response to his patient's death affects his ability to care for this week's patients. In this episode he is asked to "present" the case to a seminar of physicians and medical students. Due to the great interest in the case the seminar was moved to the auditorium (2:7, 3:1). The questions posed demanded frank answers and Dr. Green does a masterful job of presenting the facts of the case and a rationale for the decisions which led to the woman's death. Green is presented as competent though flawed. This story, found in seven scenes, serves as the focal point of the episode: how does one experience such profound failure and continue on with one's career?

This theme is presented in direct contrast with story B—the Medical Student story. One of the central characters of the series is John Carter, medical student. We see the world of medicine through his naive and youthful vantage point. In this episode, John serves as a thematic foil to another medical student, Deb Chen. Each approaches the study of medicine from different perspectives: John is interested in the person behind the patient (as is Dr. Green), while Deb Chen seems more concerned with the science of medicine. In this episode Carter is presented as an imperfect medical student (in contrast to the more experienced and mature Dr. Green). Three of the scenes (1:7, 1:10, and 2:2) exist solely to show us Carter in action (C-6) or to reveal something new about the character (C-3). These scenes remind us of Carter's perspective on medicine which contrasts sharply with Deb's.

Of the five stories in this episode, it is this story (B) that most conforms to the traditional presentation of a plot line. Below is a listing of the scene functions for this story:

0:2	P-2	Disturbance
1:1	P-3	Dramatic Question
2:6	P-5	Plan Revealed
3:4	P-5	Plan Revealed
3:5	P-6	Plan in Action
3:7	P-7	Complication
3:8	P-11	Crisis
4:1	P-9	Conflict Continues
4:9	P-12	Resolution

The Disturbance (P-2) is introduced early in the episode. Dr. Peter Benton informs both Chen and Carter that their procedure books are due by seven that evening. Both Chen and Carter are surprised by this apparent change in scheduling. Chen's problem is that she has not completed as many procedures as Carter and fears that she will fail as a medical student unless she can perform more procedures.

The first scene of Act I is a classic Emergency Trauma Room scene. A burn patient is rushed in and Carter is allowed to perform a central line procedure (a risky procedure which involves placing a tube directly into the heart. Enough of the guide wire must remain exposed so it can be recovered). Deb Chen delivers some X-rays, sees Carter performing this procedure, and is envious of his good fortune. The scene ends with a close-up shot of Chen, looking both upset and jealous. The scene serves the function of revealing something about the character (C-3) and raising the dramatic questions for the story: Will Chen do something to jeopardize her chances of success? Will Chen be able to complete enough procedures in time?

In the next scene of this story (2:6) Chen is allowed to go to the operating room (OR) with Dr. Benton. She was chosen over Carter because he had just made a rather serious mistake. In a previous scene (1:7) he gave water to a woman who was due to have gall bladder surgery; her operation must now wait. This scene serves the function of P-5: Plan Revealed. In this case, Chen, the heroine, is eliminating the disturbance—the need to acquire additional procedures for her book—by assisting Benton in the OR.

The same scene function (P-5: Plan Revealed) takes place in scene 3:4. Chen hands a nurse a list of procedures she still needs, and asks her to pass them her way if any come in. She even bribes her by offering to get her some coffee. The nurse accepts the coffee and tells her: "You can start by helping Wendy get an I-V going on our junkie friend in Two." Chen reminds her that finding an I-V is not one of the procedures on the list she still needs to complete. The nurse replies: "It is now."

The next scene serves as the Plan in action (P-6) scene. Both Chen and Wendy are desperately searching for a usable vein so they can start an I-V in the patient. None seems available. They concur that he will need a central line.

In scene 3:7, Chen, on her own initiative and without supervision, performs the "central line" procedure. When the nurse, Wendy, re-enters the room and sees what Chen is doing, she yells: "Are you crazy? You aren't allowed to do a central line." Chen replies: "I was just going to get it started, but then it seemed so easy." In the process, Chen loses the guide wire, an action that we know from Scene 1:1 is dangerous. This is the complication (P-7) scene for this story.

In the following scene, (P-11, Crisis), several doctors are able to retrieve the guide wire; the patient is saved, although the doctors mention that the hospital could be sued. Chen runs out of the room and Carter chases after her. Although the patient will live, this scene is not the resolution of the story, because the hero of the story is not the patient. Instead this is Deb Chen's story and we are interested in how this action will influence her.

The first scene of Act IV takes place around the nurse's station and serves as a P-9 (Conflict Continues) scene. Head nurse Carol asks Carter if he found Deb. He says he has not and tells Carol that he feels responsible. Carol replies: "Why? You aren't the one who nearly killed a patient." Benton comes in and tells Carter that he must find Deb because the head of ER wants to see her.

The story ends near the end of Act IV. The scene serves as the resolution (P-12) of the Chen story. The scene takes place that evening at Chen's parents' home. They are celebrating their anniversary and the large, beautifully decorated rooms are filled with glamorous and richly attired individuals; white-jacketed waiters are serving champagne and hors d'oeuvres. As Carter walks by one of the servers he helps himself to some of the food. He sees Deb Chen, casually dressed, walking down an elegant staircase. Carter and Chen retreat to the kitchen where they can speak in private. She tells John that she is quitting. She elaborates by saying: "I didn't care about the patient, I just wanted the procedure." Carter objects, but she stands firm. She tells him: "I don't like it. That's not true; I like the science of it. But the patients, the sickness, sometimes it almost scares me." Chen concludes by saying: "You think about treating the patients. You care." Carter replies: "Thanks." End of scene, and the end of the Deb Chen, Medical Student story.

This story parallels the A story, the Dr. Mark Green story. Dr. Green experienced failure but was determined to go on. He overcame the obstacles that were in his way—negative evaluations from some of the medical staff and his own personal sorrow over the tragic outcome of his actions (the woman's death)—and eventually was able to call on his years of experience and training to successfully direct an emergency procedure (3:3). Deb Chen experienced failure and quits. Chen is a capable and intelligent young Asian-American woman who has probably never experienced defeat or failure in her life. When she does, she does not know how to respond; she is incapable of digging down into her well of personal strength to find the courage to continue with her medical career. Her story is a tragedy for her career goals are ruined.

The third story line, the Dr. Doug Ross story, can be divided in two—the public Dr. Ross and the private Dr. Ross. A total of eight scenes, found primarily in Acts I and IV, tell his story. The Doug Ross "personal" story includes very little "story." None of the scenes serves a "plot-line" function; all of them serve the "character" scene function. Four of the eight scenes (0:1, 3:2, 4:2, 4:5) focus on Doug's relatively new relationship with Diana, the mother of a ten-year-old boy who is enamored with Dr. Ross (both the boy and his mother were introduced in previous episodes). Diana, a staff member of the hospital, seems pleased with the developing relationship. There is no conflict; there is only an evolving relationship that looks, for the moment, hopeful. Hence these four scenes that focus on the "relationship-story" are categorized as character scenes and not plot scenes.

The Dr. Doug Ross, professional doctor, story is played out in four scenes (1:2, 1:5, 1:8, 4:4). The scenes serve the sole purpose of showing us that Dr. Ross is a good and noble doctor; he is a caring, compassionate, competent diagnostician who keeps his cool under the crisis of an emergency (Scenes 1:5, 4:4). Hence, all of these scenes were categorized as C-6 (Action).

The Dr. Doug Ross "story" exists to keep the character in the foreground; he is an important member of the ensemble cast. In previous episodes he had experienced various forms of personal rejection all due to his inabilities to maintain successful, long-term personal relationships. (On the other hand, Dr. Ross, the professional, is presented as being superior in his ability to handle his patients and their needs.) He exhibits many of the characteristics of a contemporary playboy, successfully using his charm and good looks to win his way into many women's hearts. His "stories" have many of the trappings of a primetime soap opera.

Story D is the conclusion of a lengthy story arc, the Dr. Peter Benton and his mother story. His elderly mother, who had been living with Peter's sister, fell down the stairs and was hospitalized. It was determined that she needed more extensive care than her daughter could provide. In this episode, she is told she will be moved to a nursing home. This story is concluded in three scenes:

0:4	P-10: Confrontation	Peter informs his mother that she must move to a nursing home.
2:4	P-11: Crisis	Peter waits with his mother outside for the ambulance to arrive to move her to the nursing home. She is sullen and Peter appears anxious. There is little interaction, but we are unsure of the outcome of this exchange.
4:6	P-12: Resolution	In Mrs. Benton's new room, that evening. The mother appears satisfied, even pleased with her new living arrangement. Peter appears grateful.

It is conceivable that this story arc is finished, although the mother could resurface again in later episodes.

The other truncated story, Story E, is the Dr. Susan Lewis and her Sister story which only begins near the end of Act IV.

| 4:8 | P-2: Disturbance | Susan find Chloe waiting for her arrival at her apartment. |
| 4:11 | P-3: Dramatic Question | Susan tends to Chloe's needs by feeding her, comforting her, and telling her that everything will be all right. |

Chloe, Susan's estranged sister, returns to Susan's for comfort and support. She is pregnant and alone. Scene 4:8 introduces Chloe as the disturbance, and the concluding scene for the episode (4:11) raises a series of dramatic questions to be answered in future episodes: How much will Chloe disturb her sister's life? Will the baby be born healthy or will her abusive lifestyle interfere? Will Dr. Lewis be so drawn into Chloe's life as a new mother that she will be unable to perform her own tasks? The questions are limitless. It is obvious that this will become a major story line in future episodes, and will remain until Chloe and her child leave both Chicago and Susan's life. Notice that each of these two stories conforms very tightly to the sequential plot functions as outlined above; the Benton story has obviously concluded, and the Lewis story is just beginning.

ER is known for its heart-stopping, adrenaline thumping emergency trauma room procedures, and an analysis of the narrative elements of this series cannot end without a brief discussion of these emotionally charged scenes. In this episode there were four emergencies (scenes: 1:1, 1:5, 3:3, 3:6, 4:4). In none of the scenes were the patients significant to any of the story lines. We never heard of them again. What is the function of these scenes? They reveal how members of the staff operate under stress. The characters often must overcome personal crisis while directing others in the emergency trauma room procedures. The scenes typically reveal controlled chaos, one or two of the residents barking orders, everyone speaking a shortened form of medical jargon, the sounds of life-saving equipment beeping with the pulsating musical background intensifying our reactions to the scene. The focus is not on the patient. It is on how the physicians, residents, and nurses are able to survive another heart-stopping emergency. We see needles being stuck into fleshy sides, tubes being forced down patients' noses, and gushing blood ("It's a pumper"). The scenes are exciting, filled with moving cameras shooting close-up shots of the medical staff and close-up shots of the various body parts being pricked, prodded, and X-rayed.

In the four trauma procedures in this episode (the Act 3 procedure was divided between two scenes), we never heard from the patient again. The first emergency (1:1) focused on the competence of the staff and Carter's chance to do a central line procedure, and Chen's disappointment that she was not the one so chosen; the second emergency (1:5) shows us how proficient Dr. Ross can be in an emergency. The focus of the third emergency (3:3 and 3:5) was on Dr. Green's proficiency, especially after he underwent the seminar grilling in scene 3:1. He came back with full control of his talents and skills as a diagnostician and physician. The fourth emergency (4:4) focuses again on Dr. Ross and his emergency room skills.

Three of the scenes (1:4B, 1:6, 2:3) were not assigned to any of the described "stories" but instead are listed as ER. In these scenes the focus is on the unusual cases that come to the ER for help. The cases are always interesting because of their uniqueness. In this episode, scenes 1:4B and 1:6 focus on two elderly women who were in a car accident due to the driver's poor vision; 2:3 focuses on a woman who carries an arsenal of weapons in her purse, hears voices, and acknowledges that she suffers from paranoid psychosis. In both of these cases the patients are cared for by Dr. Susan Lewis and a member of the nursing staff. These scenes are unrelated to the primary narratives of the episode and consequently are identified as "relief" (P-15) scenes, for they do provide relief from the angst and trauma the medical staff is experiencing. Consider these scenes as *anecdotes*, memorable stories that would be told by the staff at a later time.

They remind us, the viewers, of where we are and reveal something about the uniqueness of the setting itself.

Conclusion

This tool for narrative analysis is designed as an analytical aid. For it to work, intelligent interpretation from the user is required. Often these interpretations can be open to considerable negotiation. The application of this tool will become more precise after you become more familiar with the different categories and their meanings. One's specific interpretation of a scene function should remain open for discussion. For some scenes, you may not be able to tell what the function of that scene is until you have viewed more of the story. In other words, the exact function of some scenes may not jump out at you immediately. Don't become distraught if everything doesn't seem to fit together immediately. While I prefer that there be agreement among the users of this tool, the tool can accommodate differences of opinion. In other words, the reason for using this tool is not to locate the "correct" scene function. Instead the tool is to be used to help one to come to a clearer understanding of how television narratives are structured (and there will undoubtedly be some differences of opinion over that). I also should point out that there will be occasions when a scene serves more than one primary function. This is acceptable and can often explain the complexity and richness found in some television narratives.

I encourage the reader to analyze the narrative structure of a television series and notice the richness that can emerge from such an exercise. You should emerge with a clearer understanding of the structure of the story and a greater awareness of the thematic richness, if present. If not, then narrative weaknesses will emerge and you will begin to recognize *why* a series seems so flawed and incomplete. In either case, the scene function tool can help users to increase their awareness of the possible complexity and richness found in television's narratives.

Composite Scene Analysis Table

Story Lines

A: The Dr. Mark Green Story
   A1) Public story
   A2) Personal story
      A2a: Confidence crisis story
      A2b: Marital problems story
B: Medical Student Story
   B1) Deb Chen story
   B2) John Carter story

C: Dr. Doug Ross Story
   C1) Public story
   C2) Personal story

D: Dr. Peter Benton Story
   D1) Peter and his mother story
E: Dr. Susan Lewis
   E1) Susan and her sister story

Act Scene Number	Story Line	Characters	Location	Scene Function
0:1	C-2: Doug Ross	Doug Diana Jason (son)	Diana's Apartment	C-3: Revelation
0:2	B-1: Deb Chen	Chen Carter Benton	Hallway	P-2: Disturbance
0:3	A-2a: Mark Green	Green Lewis	Exam Room	C-6 Action
0:4	D-1 Peter Benton	Benton Jackie (sister) Mrs. Benton	Mrs. Benton's Hospital Room	P-10 Confrontation
		Commercial Break ACT I		
1:1	B-1 Deb Chen	Chen Carter, Green Lewis, Benton others	Emergency Trauma Room	P-3 Dramatic Question
1:2	C-1 Ross	Ross Mrs. Ryan Jeanette	Exam Room	C-6 Action
1:3	A-1 Green	Green Mrs. Salazaar Carter	Exam Room	C-6: Action
1:4A	A-1: Green	Green Carter, Lydia	Hallway/ Nurse Station	P-6: Plan in action
1:4B	ER	Lewis, Carol Shirley, Saree	Exam Room	P-15: Relief
1:5	C-1 Ross	Ross Lydia, Jeanette Mrs. Ryan	Emergency Trauma Room	P-11: Crisis C-6: Action
1:6	ER	Lewis, Carol Shirley, Saree	Exam Room	P-15: Relief

Act Scene Number	Story Line	Characters	Location	Scene Function
1:7	B-2 Carter	Carter, Woman	Exam Room	C-6: Action
1:8	C-1 Ross	Ross Mrs. Ryan	Hallway	C-6: Action
1:9	A-2a Green	Green, Lewis, Lydia	Hallway	P-7 Complication
1:10	B-2 Carter	Carter, Patient	Exam Room	C-3: Revelation
1:11	A-2a Green	Green, Dr. Swift	Hallway	P-7: Complication
Commercial Break ACT II				
2:1	A-1 Green	Green, Carter Salazaar	Exam Room	P-10: Confrontation
2:2	B-2 Carter	Ross Carter Baby	Exam Room	C-3: Revelation
2:3	ER	Lewis, Woman	Exam Room	P-15: Relief
2:4	D-1 Peter Benton	Peter, Mother	EXT:	P-11: Crisis
2:5	A-2a Green	Green, Ross	Hall	C-4: Relationship P-11: Crisis
2:6	B-1 Chen	Carter, Chen, Benton	Nurse's Station	P-5 Plan Revealed
2:7	A-2a Green	Green	Auditorium	S-1: Scene P-14: Foreshadow-ing
Commercial Break ACT III				
3:1	A-2a Green	Green et al.	Auditorium	P-10 Confrontation

Act Scene Number	Story Line	Characters	Location	Scene Function
3:2	C-2 Ross	Doug, Diana Jason	EXT: Hospital	C-4: Relationship
3:3	A-2 Green	Green, others	ER Trauma Room	C-6: Action
3:4	B-1 Chen	Chen, Nurse	Nurse's Station	P-5: Plan Revealed
3:5	B-1 Chen	Chen, Nurse, Patient	Exam Room	P-6: Plan in Action
3:6	ER	Emergency Room	ER Trauma Room	C-6: Action
3:7	B-1 Chen	Chen, Nurse, Patient	Exam Room	P-7: Complication
3:8	B-1 Chen	Benton, Swift, Chen, Carter	Exam Room	P-11: Crisis
		Commercial Break ACT IV		
4:1	B-1 Chen	Carter, Carol	Nurse's Station	P-9: Conflict Continues
4:2	C-2 Ross	Ross, Diana	Hallway	C-5: Affirmation
4:3	A-1b Green	Green, Lewis	Diner	P-5: Plan Revealed
4:4	C-1 Ross	Ross, others	ER Trauma Room	C-6: Action P-11: Crisis
4:5	C-2 Ross	Ross, Diana	Hallway	C-4: Relationships
4:6	D-1 Peter Benton	Peter, Mother	Mrs. Benton's New Room	P-12: Resolution
4:7	A-1a Green	Green	Doctor's Lounge	P-9: Conflict Continues
4:8	E-1 Susan Lewis	Lewis, Chloe	Apartment Hallway	P-2: Disturbance
4:9	B-1 Chen	Chen, Carter	Chen's House	P-12: Resolution

Act Scene Number	Story Line	Characters	Location	Scene Function
4:10	A-1 Mark Green	Green, Nurse Mrs. Salazaar	Doctor's Lounge	P-12: Resolution
4:11	E-1 Susan Lewis	Susan, Chloe	Susan's Apt.	P-3: Dramatic Question

NOTES

1. In fact, it is not uncommon for a scene to be omitted or considerably trimmed during postproduction editing because of length restrictions or technical problems which cannot be fixed. In addition, directors will sometimes override the writer's vision and flip-flop the linear position of scenes which the director believes will make the story play better. Sometimes scenes are edited when series go into syndication to make room for more commercials.
2. An example would be a sequence of shots showing different characters in various locations getting ready for a wedding. There may be background music which is heard in each location and which ties the locations together. While this may more accurately be defined as a sequence, for the sake of simplicity, the disparate shots *function* as a whole and therefore would be coded as a "scene."

REFERENCES

Chatman, S. (1978). *Story and discourse: Narrative structure in fiction and film.* Ithaca: Cornell University Press.

Feuer, J. (1986). Narrative form in American network television. In C. MacCabe (Ed.), *High theory/low culture* (pp. 101–114). New York: St. Martin's.

Fiske, J., & Hartley, J. (1978). *Reading television.* London: Methuen.

Freytag, G. (1968). *Technique of the drama: An exposition of dramatic composition and art.* E. MacEwan (Trans.). New York: Benjamin Blom.

Kirk, J. W., & Bellas, R. A. (1985). *The art of directing.* Belmont, CA: Wadsworth.

Kozloff, S. (1992). Narrative theory and television. In R. C. Allen (Ed.). *Channels of discourse, reassembled* (pp. 67–100). Chapel Hill: University of North Carolina Press.

Marc, D. (1984). *Demographic vistas: Television in American culture.* Philadelphia: University of Pennsylvania Press.

Metz, C. (1974). *Film language: A semiotics of the cinema.* Michael Taylor (Trans.). New York: Oxford.

Moeder, M. (1994). *A comparative analysis of narrative structure in the prime-time television situation comedy.* Unpublished doctoral dissertation, University of Missouri, Columbia.

Porter, M. J. (1983). Applying semiotics to the study of selected prime time television programs. *Journal of Broadcasting, 27,* 69–75.

Rapping, E. (1995). Bad medicine. *The Progressive, 59,* p. 36.

Smiley, S. (1971). *Playwriting: The structure of action.* Englewood Cliffs, NJ: Prentice Hall.

7

Audience-Centered Approaches to Television Criticism

Much criticism of television in the popular press focuses on how bad programs on bad television may be doing bad things to good people. More than other popular art forms, television comes under scrutiny for what it may be doing to the hearts, minds, and souls of its audience. Recurring fears about television sex and violence drive the preponderance of this criticism, but this is not all we worry about. We worry about television news affecting our political beliefs and actions. We worry about gender and race portrayals affecting our children. We worry about commercials selling us things that we shouldn't want, can't afford, and don't need.

Why are we so worried about television? Relative to the doing of television criticism, it is safe to say we wouldn't be worried about television if it didn't have an audience. After all, "bad" television programs without an audience wouldn't garner much attention. Indeed, they might be theorized by some as problematic. However, without audiences, we are looking at the philosophical question of what happens when a tree falls in the forest with no one around to hear it. In television's forest there are many people.

So just as we need to know about the industry and auteurs that create television texts, we need to understand the audiences that they wish to reach. Similarly, our efforts to understand the television text in context are incomplete without consideration of the audience. Thus, other forms of "centered" criticism can take account of the audience. Audience-centered criticism merely uses the concept of the audience, and the experiences and positioning of its members as readers, as a central point of departure.

Television, Audience, and Criticism

When television came on the scene, the notion of the *invisible mass* and its perceived vulnerability seemingly precluded thinking about television's audience in dynamic terms. With its large audience, the realism of its pictures, and dependence on a few big networks for programming, fears over the propagandizing effects of television were amplified. The apparent anonymity of the television audience and its seeming inability to effectively influence either the sender of the message or the message itself were sources of added concern. These concerns fueled a new mass society/popular culture debate (see Chapter 2). However, this debate largely avoided useful distinctions about the audience. The debate was over content, over types of art and their merits: popular versus mass versus folk versus elite. The debate was over our well-being. Audiences were often seen as masses to be reached or "taste" publics whose opinion could be molded.

Approaching the Audience

A quick look in the mirror argues against the invisible mass. Looking in the mirror, most people see someone largely unaffected by television, whereas they often see others unduly influenced by its workings. How can we make generalizations about the invisible mass when our own experiences as part of it belie our generalizations? Simply put, our notion of audience shifts based on our perspective; in this case the shifts depend on whether we see ourselves as in the audience or apart from it. Effective critics need to recognize that perspectives of the audience may be variant and elusive.

The Elusive Audience.   Defining *audience* is not so simple as defining an inert substance. What exactly is the television audience? As Moores (1993, pp. 1–2) points out, this question is difficult to answer because "there is no stable entity which we can isolate and identify as the media audience, no single object that is unproblematically 'there' for us to observe and analyze." Are we thinking of faceless millions out there watching television? Are we thinking of potential purchasers of products advertised on television? Are we thinking about loyal fans of our favorite show? Are we thinking about our families and ourselves sitting at home in our living rooms? Are we thinking about dupes or couch potatoes ready to be bowled over by advertisers? Or are we thinking about our rational and resilient selves who talk back to our sets and see through the ploys of corporate allure, and place our own meanings on their missives? In thinking about the audience, we may be thinking about many different things. Critics need to be clear about their vantage point on the audience and represent this to readers.

Vantage Points.   The critic's vantage point on the audience tends to align with one's view of the human being and human condition. For example, a deterministic vantage point would tend to see the audience as having little control over the workings of television. One type of determinism, *textual determinism,* might see the television message as having the upper hand and the audience member's fate being determined largely by the text itself. Another type of determinism, *structural determinism,* would see the audience member's alternatives determined largely by any one or combination of economic, class, gender, race, and other cultural or contextual issues. Alternatively, one may view audience members' actions as essentially *rational* and purposeful. This rationalist vantage point sees the audience with a work ethic and the power to rationally pursue goals and interests in watching television. Other critics might see the audience as similarly active but focused on *pleasure.* Here the audience creatively plays with television as experienced and reappropriates meanings to gain pleasure in ways that make rationality immaterial. Another vantage point sees the audience as particularly *resilient.* This view focuses on audience self-protection, resistance, and opposition to the dominant meanings of the television text. The resilience-oriented critic tends to see the human being and the world in political and ideological terms. Here the audience is in constant struggle over meaning in television as part of the daily politics of life.

Priorities.   Beyond the vantage point from which he or she views the audience, the critic needs to assess priorities of concern with the television audience. Critics are usually concerned with the television audience for some larger purpose, its interaction with something else. Pose this concern clearly and state what your issue or problem really is. One simple way to assess priorities with the television audience is to construct your focus as an equation that equals a multiplicative product. For example, some critics might be most concerned with the characterization of the audience by the television text; thus Characterization = Audiences $\times$ Texts. The priorities of this type of critic would not be on real audiences out there, but instead focus on what the television text says about the audience and what it does to encourage certain reading positions. A critic interested in the pleasures that actual readers get from a specific text might frame priorities as Pleasures = Texts $\times$ Readers. Critics interested in the culture of fans of a particular show or genre of shows might frame priorities as Fans = Genres $\times$ Cultures. A feminist culture-centered critic might be concerned with the political implications of audiences consuming television. Here the equation Politics = Interpretation $\times$ Ideology might state a priority. In this case the critic might seek to assess the real political function of the interaction between interpretive processes on the part of the audience and the ideological implications of the text for a feminist perspective on politics and power.

Audience and Critical Context

Critical work on the television audience is situated relative to *institutional* and *behavioralist* perspectives. The institutional perspective assumes rational behavior and focuses on the "audience-as-market" (Ang, 1991). Primary interest is in the size and sociodemographic quality of the audience. While there is interest in audience tastes in programming, larger goals dominate: to establish brand identity, to increase market share, to retain product loyalty, and ultimately to increase profits. In contrast, the behavioralist perspective sees television as a social problem with its effects on the audience being textually and structurally determinable. Early on, behavioralists used a "hypodermic needle" model and empirical social science methods to study the effects of television on political and violent behavior. Encountering mixed results, behavioralists came to see the television audience as active. They found a wide range of uses made by the audience that might modify effects. Still, the behavioralists' methods limited their ability to explain the dynamics behind television uses. Much simply could not be measured. Some behavioralist research programs, such as cultivation analysis, clearly suggested that a "powerful ideological agency" was at work (Morgan, 1989; Lewis, 1991). Evidence pointed to the political "mainstreaming" of heavy TV viewers, but little was known about the interpretive processes in television viewing. Here was an area in which audience-centered television criticism could make a real contribution.

While some behavioral audience researchers were discovering the need for critical audience study, a group of critical researchers in literary and cultural studies were discovering the audience. Here, some scholars were finding that traditional concerns about the text and its powers had hit a dead end. In literary studies, reactions against the textual determinism of the New Criticism in the late 1950s brought varied calls to understand the role of the audience, both in the text and relative to it. In cultural studies, efforts to understand and to prove the hegemonizing effects of media through demonstrations of strategic encoding of texts needed systematic study of the audience to corroborate whether "preferred" readings were indeed "dominant" with the audience (see Jensen, 1991).

Although these relatively late discoveries of the audience by literary and cultural studies have some key differences that will be discussed later, there are some striking similarities. Both recognize that *audience* can be seen as essential in the construction of the text and in the reception and interpretation of it. Both are concerned with the dynamics, strategies, and meanings of the audience. Both are equipped for methodological diversity. Both audience-oriented approaches are characterized by a *centeredness* on the audience that reaches out to other critical approaches as appropriate, guided by the particular critical question. Finally, both the literary and cultural studies perspectives share an understanding of the audience that has an allegiance to the etymology of the term.

Implications in the Origin of Audience.   Radway (1988) traces the etymology of the word *audience* to the face-to-face communication situation. Here one would *give an audience* to another person. This notion moved to the audience for public speeches, to theater and film audiences, and to radio and television audiences. Framed in a rhetorical communication model, we give an audience to someone, *the rhetor,* and to the text of that person's message, *the rhetoric.* Conversely, the rhetor gives to the audience by taking note of the audience in the delivery and framing of the message.

Audience Power and Interpretation. For the television critic, this audience-oriented approach to the communication process has some very important ideas. In giving an audience, a "hearing" of ideas is "granted." There is implicit recognition that the person providing the ideas has some standing, but that the standing may be influenced by the audience. This delicate tension recognizes a relationship between the audience and rhetor, of a giving back to the rhetor, and consequently to the rhetorical message or text likely to be fashioned by the rhetor. It is important to recognize that this notion points to the power of the audience. Not only does the individual or group giving an audience garner power by granting a certain standing to the rhetor, but power is exercised by the ability to in some way activate or move the message through interpretation and reaction and thereby exercise some control over the rhetor. As Bennett (1982, p. 14) asserts, neither the audience nor the critic has a choice in this matter because "the text is never available for analysis except in the context of its activations." Audience-centered critics recognize this active tension and thus confront questions about the context and processes of interpretation by the television audience. As a result, audience-centered critics often focus on strategies used by real audience members and "lived experiences" with television.

Audience in the Text. Conversely, the rhetor gives standing to the audience through cues embedded in the message or text. Assumptions about and characterizations of the audience can be seen in a variety of ways in the television text itself. Sometimes the audience is seemingly on the screen. For example, your stand-in can be seen laughing in the live audience or asking a question. Other times, your stand-in can be seen buying products that an advertiser would like you to buy. The audience is recognized off screen as well. For example, you might be spoken to directly by a newscaster or sports announcer who makes assumptions about what you know or how you feel. The audience is recognized in other ways in constructing the television text. For example, redundancy in the television text recognizes the situation of the reader: at home, often simultaneously engaged in other activities and often missing earlier episodes or scenes. Similarly, gaps in the text recognize the reading abilities of the audience. Thus, a character can walk out of the house and in the next scene miraculously appear at work, without the audience being disoriented or concerned about the character's mode of transportation or events that happened en route. Reading position and a characterizing of the audience can also be seen through the camera's point of view. Seeing a scene from the point of view of our hero or heroine tells us something about where we ideally or sympathetically should be or what we know relative to the story that is unfolding. This notion of the reader in the text (and the reader relative to the text) argues against the notion of audience as something that is simply out there and apart from the text.

Making Your Approach.   Compared to the variety of text-based approaches to television criticism, audience-centered approaches have been the less traveled road. Audience-centered approaches pose special challenges. Finding the audience in the television text can often seem like looking for a needle in a haystack. Determining how the text attempts to manipulate the reading position can be even more problematic. And actually going out and qualitatively assessing audience experience by speaking to real viewers is a time-intensive task. However, because the audience-centered critic believes the meaning of a televised text cannot be adequately determined without considering the audience, these hurdles must be overcome. You will find that the twin issues of the embedded audience and audience power in interpretation define a fork in the road in doing audience-centered television criticism. You will need to decide on one issue as dominant over the other, and this choice will guide your critical approach. This decision will point you to either audience-oriented criticism or critical audience study.

> *Audience-Oriented Criticism.* Fundamental concerns with the text's characterizing of the reader and its attempts to control the reading act distinguish the literary studies approach to audience-oriented criticism. It is a deductive approach: the critic deduces key issues about readers and reading from the text itself. As such, audience-oriented criticism is largely concerned with "potential" as opposed to "actualized" meanings of the text to an audience (Jensen, 1991, p. 137). Only occasionally will audience-oriented critics corroborate their analyses with real readers; such efforts tend to fall in the province of critical audience study.

> *Critical Audience Study.* In contrast to literary studies approaches to audience-oriented criticism, critical audience study, as inspired by cultural

studies, endeavors to understand the reading processes and sense making strategies of real people consuming television in the context of their everyday lived experiences and relations with other people and things. As such, critical audience study can be seen as an inductive approach that uses qualitative and ethnographic methods to understand meanings attributed to the text by people as a result of their everyday lives. In contrast to audience-oriented criticism, critical audience study is concerned with meanings that are actualized by audiences in reference to their experiences with televised texts.

Audience-Oriented Criticism

In what might be taken as the case of the "missing reader," literary critics embarked on a variety of paths to understand the roles of the reader and the reading act. Reader-oriented criticism gained steam in the 1970s. This increased interest was in part a reaction to the autonomy of texts—texts seemingly without readers—as framed in New Criticism. However, some parts of this "new" reader-oriented criticism were not really new. This "return of the reader" (Freund, 1987) was partly a return to a historically framed sociology of literature (Holub, 1984) and partly a return to thinking about literature as a rhetorical communication act in which reader and the reading act play central roles (Richards, 1929).

Audience-oriented criticism does not represent a unified critical position (cf., Freund, 1987; Holub, 1984; Suleiman & Crosman, 1980; Tompkins, 1980). Its development can be seen in the wide-ranging work of literary critics who use the terms *"reader, the reading process,* and *response* to mark out an area for investigation" (Tompkins, 1980, p. ix). The approach is often called *reception theory* (or reception aesthetics) when framed in terms of the work of German critics (Gadamer, 1975; Ingarden, 1973; Iser, 1974, 1978; Jauss, 1982a, 1982b). In its more contemporary American castings, the approach is likely to be called *reader-response criticism.* Here, the influential works of Wayne Booth (1961, 1974), Jonathan Culler (1981), Norman Holland (1968), and Stanley Fish (1980) are often cited. Although the approach has developed largely in reference to the reading of literature, its merits in terms of understanding the reading of film and television can be seen in the work of Roland Barthes (1973), Umberto Eco (1977), and Robert Allen (1987, 1992). The approach is characterized by diverse voices, differences in theoretical starting points, a multiplicity of methodological strategies, and ideological fissures. As a result, critics using this approach to study television center their criticism in a way that best fits their concerns.

The possibilities for audience-centered television criticism go well beyond the many overlapping centers that Sulieman (1980) and others (Crosman, 1980; Freund, 1987) have identified as variants in reader-oriented literary criticism. *Rhetorical* approaches focus on the communication situation, the meanings of the communicative transaction, its ideological significance and persuasive powers. *Semiotic* and *structuralist* approaches focus on the codes and conventions that affect the process of reading, the text's readability, and ultimately how meaning is made possible. *Phenomenological* approaches move questions about the reading act as a sense-making activity to the foreground and seek "to describe and account for the mental processes that occur as a reader advances through a text and derives from it—or imposes on it—a pattern" (Sulieman, 1980, p. 22). *Psychoanalytic* and otherwise subjective approaches look beyond a generalizable phenomenon of reading and focus on the rights and reading experiences of ordinary readers; such an approach is most interested in how the personality of the reader contributes to reading strategies and interpretation. *Sociological* and *historical* approaches focus on the social and cultural context of the reading of specific works, genres, or bodies of works by collective reading publics at a particular point in time. Sociohistorical approaches vary according to how the relationship between the work and the public is viewed by the critic. Accordingly, a variety of context- and culture-centered underpinnings (see Chapters 7 and 8) can shape perspectives on the social and historical situation of reading. Finally, *hermeneutic* approaches offer the possibility of bringing together a variety of critical approaches and tools to understand the deeper structures by which texts inscribe social meaning. Perhaps because the focus of hermeneutic criticism is on "the nature and possibilities of reading and interpretation as such" and deeper "unapparent" meanings, the approach is the most self-conscious, turning to "reflect on its own intentions, assumptions, and positions" (Sulieman, 1980, p. 38). As a result, hermeneutic analysis is likely to "deconstruct" audience experience with television (Derrida, 1976) by questioning textual authority and to be guided by diverse concerns. For example, one study might blend feminism, Marxist ideology, psychoanalysis, and mythic study in hermeneutic analysis. As you approach your first effort in audience-oriented criticism, be aware of the many approaches but focus on the larger issues discussed in the next section.

Doing Audience-Oriented Criticism

Audience-oriented television criticism begins with finding a television text or texts you are concerned about. As your primary focus will be on how the text characterizes its audience and attempts to control the reading act, it is best to limit your analysis to a specific program or series. Next, articulate your vantage point on the audience. How exactly do you see the audience? Is its fate structurally determined, and if so, by what? Or is the audience ultimately rational, creative, or resilient? You will have to assess the priorities of the audience and also your priorities in doing a particular study. Are you most concerned with the characterization of the audience by the text? Or are you more concerned with the process and pleasures of reading? Or are you concerned with the text's ideological thrust and its workings to position readers relative to it? It is most important to understand your underlying priorities to limit and focus your analysis. Beyond this, understanding your priorities can also help you identify a variant of audience-oriented criticism (e.g., rhetorical, semiotic/structural, phenomenological, sociological) that can help you with your methodological approach. After deciding on these preliminary issues, you are ready to start. To begin the analysis, you will need to clarify your vision of viewers as implied by the television text and your understandings of the interpretive communities of these viewers.

Implied Viewers.   Narrative forms such as the novel are stories told by someone, a narrator who has a certain character. Similarly, stories in novels are told for the benefit and enjoyment of someone, who also has a certain character. Authors necessarily have to think about the readers for whom their work is intended. The same is true for television. Producers don't just make television, they make a television text for certain kinds of viewers intended for a certain text. Thus, MTV was not intended for your grandparents. Football telecasts are not intended for people who know nothing about football. Television speaks to viewers with implied characteristics. That which is spoken in the text tells the audience-oriented critic about the ideal or model viewer the producer had in mind—a viewer who is likely to garner the same meanings intended by the producer. Different reader-oriented critics have used the terms of *implied, intended, ideal,* and *model readers,* as well as others such as *superreader* and *fictive reader,* to refer to the reader who is desired by the construction of the text. Here we use the term *implied viewer* as a composite term of assumptions about the reader seen in a television text.

By looking carefully at the television text, you can find out what the implied viewer is supposed to know or is likely to believe. Knowledge may be about the program and its history or about the world pertinent to the program. Beliefs and attitudes may be about other groups of people, about entities such as government or democracy, or simply about what's cool or not. The audience-oriented critic needs to assess which textual, lexical, cultural, and ideological codes the text presumes are shared with viewers to understand its casting of the implied viewer. The implied viewer is somewhere relative to every shot in a television text. Thus, the implied viewer may be continuously cast throughout a program in reception: at one moment the viewer may be cast as appreciative, at others smart, offended or scared. The text may in one instance imply that the viewer needs redundant information and in another pose that the viewer is able to fill in gaps of information not directly presented.

Interpretive Communities.   Television programs are not made for one implied viewer. Regular viewers of particular programs or certain kinds of programs (i.e., national news, exercise fitness shows) develop a commonality of understandings and beliefs relative to that programming. In the parlance of reader-oriented criticism, such groups are often thought of as *interpretive communities*. These interpretive communities can be conceptualized to be synonymous with tightly knit fan communities such as the loyal followers of *Star Trek*, a particular soap opera, or a professional football team. Alternatively, interpretive communities can be conceptualized broadly as fans of televised science fiction, daytime soap operas, or football.

The notion of interpretive communities, as postulated by Fish (1980), attempted to overcome reliance on self-realized individual identity themes read into texts independently by reader-oriented critics. For Fish, the reader is a social product, constructed from a system of beliefs shared by communities of readers. From this perspective, the reading of television necessarily occurs within the situated contexts of interpretive communities. These situated contexts may be historically differentiated such as 1950s viewers taking first runs of *Dragnet* episodes seriously in postwar America, those watching the umpteenth rerun of the show as 1990s camp, or those watching reruns today in India in a yet different context. Alternatively, interpretive communities may coexist at a given time, drawn by differences in gender, race, class, citizenship, or ideology. The audience-oriented television critic needs to identify the character of interpretive communities for texts of interest, looking for ways that the sensibilities of these communities interact with each other and with textual representations of the implied viewer.

Having outlined your understandings of the implied viewer and having characterized the relevant interpretive communities to your analysis, you can move on to look at some specific elements that will help you understand the transaction between the text and the audience and its implications. Here you will need to consider the role of the addresser, the characterization of viewers, and the nature of the reading act.

The Addresser. Just as television texts are told to implied viewers as *addressees* in interpretive communities, they are told *by an addresser*. The *addresser* may be an unseen omniscient auteur fashioning a television drama or may be seen clearly on screen as a narrator, host, or character. Just as important as who the addresser is is the mode of address. Allen (1987, 1992) distinguishes between two modes of address developed by television. The *cinematic mode of address*, used in television dramas and some situation comedies, mirrors the Hollywood feature film and "engages its viewers covertly, making them unseen observers of a world that always appears fully formed and autonomous" (Allen, 1992, p. 117). Here the addresser is an unidentified storyteller who is not part of the story. Still, as the story is told, the addresser continually puts us somewhere relative to the action, attempting to control reading by positioning implied viewers as flies on the wall in preferred places for the desired interpretation.[1] Thus, we may be appropriately scared, scornful, or sympathetic as the story proceeds. The story may be told from the point of view of one of the characters, but most important, the characters do not directly address the viewer.

Television's *rhetorical mode of address* simulates face-to-face communication, not only recognizing but also directly addressing the viewer. This form is typically seen in television news programs, talk shows, game shows, religious programs, educational programs (e.g., cooking, fitness, home repair), home shopping, standup comedy, variety programming, and in many commercials. The addresser plays a variety of characterized roles, such as news anchorperson, reporter, host, guest, moderator, contestant, music video vee-jay, or live audience member. Each role uses different conventions in addressing the viewer. For example, consider the different treatment viewers receive from Dan Rather and David Letterman. Rather and Letterman not only present themselves differently but also relate to and acknowledge viewers in very different ways. In each instance, the pose of the addresser tells us of assumptions about the implied viewer and the way the text should ideally be read. Whereas the rhetorical mode of address provides insistent reminders that *you* are the one being spoken to, both the rhetorical and cinematic modes of address attempt to engage and characterize the viewer. The audience-oriented critic needs to assess these strategies carefully in conjunction with characterizations of the viewer that can be seen on screen.

Characterized Viewers.   The off-screen viewer is most clearly characterized when directly addressed by someone on-screen. The cinematic mode of address also characterizes the viewer by placing the viewer somewhere relative to the action, thus indicating what the viewer should know or feel. However, as Allen (1992, p. 121) points out, television goes one step further by regularly providing us "with on-screen characterized viewer–textual surrogates who do what real viewers cannot: interact with other performers and respond (usually in an ideal fashion) to the appeals, demands, and urgings of the addresser." Television makes use of two types of textual surrogates.

The nonfictional characterized viewer can be seen in the form of the live-audience viewer on the television set, the game show contestant, or the "average person" who shows up as a guest on a talk show such as *Donohue* or *Oprah*. Here we find living, breathing, exemplary viewers who not only stand in for us, but act the way we would if we were there. This nonfictional characterization of us is often capitalized on by others such as announcers, newscasters, and talk show hosts as they employ the "fictional we" (Stam, 1983) to join our group as exemplary viewers. Thus, the talk show host roaming the audience can frame *our* questions (e.g., "what we really want to know is . . .") or the news reporter can join *us* (e.g., "we'll take a closer look at . . .").

The fictional characterized viewer is more clearly not a real person (that is, someone playing one's self) standing in for *you*. The fictional characterized viewer is an actor who is playing a role that characterizes you as you should ideally play your role. This approach is most frequently used in commercials as people like you (played by actors) act out your idealized responses for you in your role as a consumer. However, unlike your real-life response, your textual surrogate always buys the advertised product.

Over the years, television producers have crafted ways of diversifying textual surrogates so that there is something (and somebody) to identify with for everyone. This is seen in the multicultural world of commercials such as those used by Coca-Cola or AT&T, in the audiences of daytime talk shows, and in dramatic programs and soap operas that feature large ensemble casts. Somewhere in these television texts, you will find one or more characterizations of *you*. Audience-oriented television critics assess how these characterizations affect reading and interact with the casting of the implied viewer, who is supposedly watching television and taking all this in.

The Reading Act.   Reader-oriented literary criticism is particularly concerned with the process of reading. Beyond modes of address and textual surrogates, television uses a variety of strategies to control the reading act. In confronting television texts, viewers encounter a skeletal structure of meaning. Viewers necessarily encounter this schemata piecemeal as they watch something on television. As a result, viewers progress through television texts with what Iser (1978) calls a "wandering viewpoint" from somewhere inside the schemata. An artifact of viewing television is that a program can never be experienced in its entirety while it is being viewed. However, along the way, television texts make demands on viewers, encouraging them to read the texts in a desired or ideal way. Audience-oriented critics need to assess these structural demands of the text on the readers in terms of what they say about implied readers and their interpretive communities.

The *camera's position* relative to the action is one of the most obvious ways the viewer is placed for a correct reading. The camera's vantage point often characterizes the interests, knowledge, allegiances, and sympathies of the implied viewer. *Redundancy* in the television text can also say a number of things to and about the viewer. Redundancy can simply say that viewers are forgetful or need a reminder of something important. Alternatively, it might be a demand for a reading position, saying "here is something so important that we are reminding you of it again so that you will get these next things right." What appears to be needless redundancy may be restatement commanding the viewer to see how different characters in a drama react to the same information; such retraining is necessary to read developments in a crime drama or soap opera.

Redundancy aids *retention*. Borrowing from Iser (1978), Allen (1992, p. 106) points out that the viewing process is "an alternation between *protension* (expectation or anticipation) and *retention* (our knowledge of the text to that point)" because each shot in a television text "both answers questions and asks new ones." Answers to new questions are posed to the viewer either sequentially (syntagmatic organization) or by association (paradigmatic organization). Because of the call of protension, *strategic juxtaposition* of shots and scenes feeds on expectation and directs the reader to make desired syntagmatic connections, to stay with the text in the intended order. Still, strategic juxtaposition of disparate scenes regularly leaves gaps that need to be filled in by the viewer. Such strategic gaps force the viewer to make paradigmatic connections between the familiar and unfamiliar in the television text. Strategic gaps occur not only between scenes but also within programs.

Perhaps the most strategic gaps in the televisual text are created for and by commercial interruptions. The commercial gap is one form of strategic interruption that aims to control the viewer. Thus, television programs often break for commercial with a cliffhanger, or put another way, heightened protension. The gap brought about by strategic interruption aims to have the viewer reflect on the situation and want to see how it is resolved, and in the process, stay put for the commercial messages. Gaps are also naturally found between episodes of programs; a strategic interruption at the close of one episode aims to call the viewer back next week after some reflective enjoyment in the gap that has been posed.

Writing Audience-Oriented Criticism.   Writing an audience-oriented analysis does not follow one set pattern. Most critics start with a television text that is problematic in terms of what it thrusts before the audience or of what it says about the audience. Swirling texts such as music videos or commercials may pose seemingly complex challenges to the viewer. Sports programs or soap operas may imply gendered sensibilities in their audiences. Game shows may make assumptions about the value of consumerism for their fans. The problems that the television text poses will often be introduced in conjunction with what the writer knows to be true about the audience. Here the critic may focus on a broad group of fans for particular programming such as soap operas or sports coverage or may focus on a subset of viewers whose relationship with the material may be complex, unusual, or disturbing.

Once material is chosen for analysis and audience focus is specified, the critic generally begins by looking at who the text implies are viewers and the assumptions that are made of their interpretive communities. Beyond this starting point, the critic may be more interested in some things than others. Certain critics may be more concerned with understanding the addresser and the mode of address being used to approach the viewer. Others may be more concerned with how viewers are characterized, both off screen and as textual surrogates. Still other critics may focus on the nature of the reading act and the ways in which production strategies work to manipulate the viewer and encourage certain meanings. Regardless of the areas examined, the general goal of this section of the essay is description, to describe and provide examples of how the text works to establish relations with the audience.

Many critics reserve the latter part of the essay to discuss the implications of the text's relationship to the audience in terms of the problems outlined early in the essay. For example, a critic might be concerned with certain programming that builds on sexist or racist assumptions of its audience. Others may be concerned that a text is preaching to an audience cast as remarkably stupid or materialistic. Critics can use this discussion phase of the essay to identify and deconstruct a finite number of themes that characterize the audience and its relation to the televised material. Linking these themes to larger social dynamics and the problem focus of the essay in convincing fashion is often the overriding goal of audience-oriented criticism.

Strengths and Limitations.   The major strength of audience-oriented television criticism is its ability to discern how the text characterizes and attempts to engage the viewer. By determining how the viewer is addressed, how the viewer's textual surrogates are characterized, and how the text attempts to strategically control the reading act, audience-oriented criticism can illuminate in a unique way. The approach's special strengths lie in providing tools for analyzing those forms of television where the viewer is directly addressed and has readily apparent textual surrogates. As a result, audience-oriented critiques of talk shows, game shows, news programs, sports broadcasts, home shopping, and specialty educational or hobby shows (e.g., gardening, exercise, car repair) should be enlightening. Similarly, audience-oriented critiques of commercials for certain product groups (e.g., beer, luxury cars, dishwashing detergent) or commercials aimed at audiences for particular kinds of shows (e.g., news, self-help talk, sports) hold much promise.

Audience-oriented approaches to television narratives are more difficult. Since opportunities to explore the characterized reader through mode of address and textual surrogates are limited in the television narrative, the analysis must focus on the text's role in reading, and unless there is considerable knowledge about the interpretive communities, the analysis might best be subjectively derived from the critic's own reading experiences. Herein lies the most severe limitation of audience-oriented television criticism. It is dependent on deducing the reading act, and based on the critic's own experiences, largely theorizes the reader. One can never be sure that the television text is being read as the text suggests or as your knowledge of an interpretive community might lead you to believe. Critical audience study attempts to resolve these issues by looking at the reading processes and interpretation of real television viewers.

Critical Audience Study

Critical audience study informed by British cultural studies (Turner, 1990) has debated the merits of a deductive versus an inductive approach to the audience. Ang (1991) has characterized this debate as a drawing of lines between looking at the audience as a "discursive construct" versus "the social world of actual audiences." Whereas some (Hartley, 1987) have argued that the audience is a fictional construct and there is no real audience beyond its discursive construction, many more culturally oriented critics are interested in understanding television viewing in the context of the lived experiences of actual viewers. Such critical audience study contrasts with audience-oriented criticism in being concerned with actualized meanings of real viewers, as opposed to potential meanings of implied viewers. Critical audience studies also move beyond theorized conceptions of interpretive communities seen in audience-oriented criticism to experiences materialized through actual practices of viewers.

Just as audience-oriented criticism was a reaction to the case of the "missing reader," where criticism routinely avoided considering reading experience, critical audience study was partly a reaction to the analysis of the audience and its subject position as theorized in a tradition seen in the British journal *Screen* in the 1970s. The *Screen* theory posited that the spectator's "subject position" was naturalized through a "gaze" manufactured by the view of the camera. The implications of the enforced spectator position were interpreted through complementary concerns of Althusian Marxism and Lacanian psychoanalytical theory. Althusser (1984) saw mass media as one of the key institutions (called "ideological state apparatuses" or ISAs) that work to sustain inequalities in industrial economies. Althusser saw ideology as a representation that hails (or "interpellates") individuals as spectators. Lacan (1977) was similarly concerned with the "hailing" effects of discourses on the "de-centering" of subject or spectator position. For Lacan, the gaze of movie spectators works to confuse film language with reality. As Moores (1993, p. 13) has put it, "like speakers who misrecognize the relationship they have to language, spectators come to feel as though they are the source of 'the look.'" Unfortunately, *Screen* theory constructed a spectator with few options other than to align with the meanings as made by the film. The fact that this kind of textual determinism was ahistorical, avoiding both the cultural situation of texts and the relation of discourses to broader social structures, caused cultural studies to rethink their approach to understanding spectators and the audience.

Cultural Studies and Critical Audience Study

Formative work done during the 1970s by the Media Group at Birmingham University's Centre for Contemporary Cultural Studies (CCCS) reframed critical audience study. The CCCS focus on the relationship between human agency and ideology can be seen as a response not only to mainstream (behavioral) media studies but also to *Screen* theory and to reader-oriented literary theory. Focused on historically situated struggles over meaning construction, the CCCS approach looked at the wielding and imbalances of power.

There was particular interest in the processes by which popular media played a hegemonizing role (Gramsci, 1971). *Hegemony* was the exercise of power by creating conditions that would have the dominant set of social relations willingly accepted by those who did not benefit by that set of relations. The critical audience study that emerged from the CCCS was part of a larger effort to theorize cultural power and social relations. Thus, audience activity was seen as "a network of ongoing cultural practices and relationships" that were "related to social and political structures and processes" (Ang, 1989, p. 101).

At the heart of the CCCS approach was an encoding/decoding model that blended sociological and semiotic concerns in viewing the communication process as a whole. The approach saw the media industries largely as an Althusian ISA. Television producers, working within the confines of the norms and routines of professional practice, tended to encode preferred messages that were in line with goals of the industrial economy. However, even though encoded texts structured with semiotic meaning were put out there, the texts were necessarily interpreted by viewers engaged in their own semiotic labor. As a result of differences in reading, distinctions between dominant, negotiated, and oppositional reading positions were drawn. Viewers who interpreted within the preferences of the dominant codes read the preferred meaning. *Negotiated readings* are made by viewers who grant legitimacy to the hegemonic set of social relations but take issue with specific assumptions or assertions in the dominant coding of the message. *Oppositional readings* are made by viewers who question fundamental assumptions in the dominant set of social relations. The oppositional position reads against the grain, bringing different contextual understandings to the fore, thus challenging the dominant text by reappropriating its meaning.

As characterization of the three reading positions suggests, different degrees of symmetry occur between the encoded text and meaning as decoded by the viewer. In its reading, the text is seen as *polysemic,* that is, open to variant readings.[2] However, as Hall (1973, p. 13) has suggested, polysemy should not be confused with pluralism, and a "structure of dominance" remains that needs to be contended with in reading texts. Still, there can be much room to maneuver. In reading, the social semiotics of audiences can reform the dominant text and dialogically contest its meaning. As a result, the CCCS approach focused on the diversity of reading practices. It sought to locate "significant clusters" of meaning and to chart those to a "cultural map" of the audience drawn by social and discursive positions of readers (Morley, 1986, p. 12). As a result, there was a focus on understanding subcultures as actualized, interpretive communities of viewers. Key ideological differences in reading were seen to be anchored in the power disparities coming out of class and gender differences in reading communities.

The Research Agenda.   The cultural studies approach to critical audience study begins with the selection and analysis of a television text, genre, or context of viewing that is of social concern. If the text or genre is the starting point, the text is usually deconstructed by the researcher using the tools of semiotics, although alternative methods of analyzing the text may be used to set a critical baseline. Then the researcher goes into the field, using qualitative methods and an ethnographic approach, to understand the culture, sensibilities, strategies, and sense making of the audience. It is important to understand what is going on in a context defined by viewers and to understand meaning production according to the terms and conditions they see. The researcher attempts to discover patterns, or sets of rules, that govern viewers' experiences and to relate these experiences to the workings of the text and to power in the larger set of social relations. Over the years, the cultural studies agenda with television has moved from concerns with decoding and ideology to gendered genres and fans to the largely domestic contexts of consumption, and most recently, to television consumption within the larger context of other communication technologies.

Archetypal of studies focusing on the interaction between decoding and ideology is Morley's (1980) study of the audience for the British news program *Nationwide.* Morley explored the ways in which the program's preferred reading was received by viewing groups from different socioeconomic classes. He painted a cultural map that ranked the groups' decodings within a grid that characterized dominant, negotiated, and oppositional readings. Although there was evidence linking ideological workings with reading position, more evidence argued against this kind of sociological reductionism, especially the predominant reliance on class to distinguish meaning. The results from the *Nationwide* study and other studies (Dahlgren, 1988; Lewis, 1985) that looked at differential interpretation strategies pointed to two needs: (1) to focus on the viewing of people who normally watched certain programs, and (2) to focus on understanding the dynamics of viewing within the context that viewing normally took place. As a result, the research moved to look, on one hand, at genres and fans, and on the other, at television viewing within broader contexts.

Brunsdon (1981) and other studies focused on female fans and their viewing of soap operas, open-ended texts with multiple layers that implied a feminine viewer. Studies such as Hobson's (1982) study of *Crossroads* and Ang's (1985) study of *Dallas* focused on the pleasures of viewing for female fans. They used concepts such as *emotional realism* and the *melodramatic imagination* to characterize negotiations viewers had as they engaged both the soap opera and the larger patriarchal relations of power. Female viewers brought gendered cultural competencies, a focus on their everyday lives, and experience with domestic labor to interpretations of the soap opera and the gaining of escape and compensatory pleasures. These studies and others of fan cultures (see Lewis, 1992) pointed to often contradictory dynamics of viewing; readers' meanings were not only "multiply determined" (Radway, 1987, p. 7) but also simultaneously resistant and compliant. This gendered nature of television viewing was seen to interact with power relations within the family viewing context. Key studies by Lull (1980, 1990) and Morley (1986) examined the "relational" aspects of viewing as a "social event" situated in the family as a system. By focusing on the politics and power of the "sitting room," these studies show how differences in orientations to domestic space for wives and husbands lead to disparities in freely viewing television and to gaps between masculine and feminine styles of viewing. By examining television viewing in the larger context of family life, these studies pointed to the need to examine television viewing in still larger and comparative contexts. Consequently, important efforts have been made in critical audience study to understand television viewing within the context of using other communications technologies in the household (Silverstone, 1991) and to understand how television viewing differs across national cultures (Liebes & Katz, 1990; Lull, 1988). Collectively, the diversity of critical audience studies has pointed to the complex dynamics of television viewing, meaning, and power and to the richness of the ethnographic method.

Doing Critical Audience Study

Critical audience study is driven by an ethnographic "impulse" (Allen, 1992, p. 129). Although often not applying the elaborated protocols of ethnography as might be used by anthropologists or sociologists, the critical television ethnographer shares some of their fundamental concerns and practices. The goal is to understand cultural practices and sense making in the natural context, and from the point of view, of people living their everyday lives. The researcher, using commonsense knowledge and methods, becomes the primary "research instrument" (Hammersley & Atkinson, 1983, p. 18). Rather than eliminating the effects of the researcher, an attempt is made to understand them. As a result, interpretation and self-reflexivity are integral to the researcher's task. Theory, while being revealed to the researcher, does not come from the researcher. Rather, theory is inductively derived from lived experiences and their grounding in the realities and logic of people's lives (see Geertz, 1973; Trujillo, 1983).

Method and Approach.   Doing critical audience study means going into the field. Researchers often spend considerable time observing television viewing in the natural setting. Failing extended observation, and often in addition to it, the researcher will need to find other ways to somehow approach viewers about their experiences. In any case the researcher should not create a special event in the lives of viewers. The aim should be to understand the characteristics of everyday viewing rather than to ferret out aberrant events. The researcher's engagement with the viewer should be on the viewer's terms. Thus, the basic approach should be unobtrusive and nonjudgmental. Establishing good rapport and building trust with viewers is essential in getting candid, honest pictures of viewing and the viewing context. The researcher should use the pose of naiveté as a tool to approach the viewing context as anthropologically strange, as it might be seen in first stepping on the planet. Consequently, everyday happenings should not be discounted as merely normal or natural and thus without meaning. The researcher needs to work to truly hear stories and listen for the context and meaning as set out by the viewer. The researcher focuses on getting thick descriptions of viewing experience from which a set of rules governing action can be derived (Lull, 1990). These largely implicit rules will reveal patterns in viewing and the logic behind them. Experiences of different viewers will undoubtedly reveal multiple realities that fuel differences in understanding or applying rules. *Theorizing* the audience means not only seeing these different patterns of meaning but also seeing their interrelationships and framing them in struggles over power as they relate to the lives of viewers.

It is often observed that ethnography has no standard method and is not any one method. Indeed, ethnography is usually approached using more than one method. Although extended unstructured observation and in-depth interviews are key features of most ethnographically inspired studies, so too is a triangulation of methods. *Triangulation* is the use of multiple methods. Using multiple methods protects the researcher from the biases or idiosyncracies that arise from using a single methodology or measurement technique. Various forms of methodological triangulation exist. In critical audience study, triangulation is commonly achieved by analyzing the text, observing television viewing, and then cross-checking observation with extensive interviews.

Just as texts may be analyzed in a wide variety of ways (see Chapter 6), observation and interview methods vary. The term *participant-observation* is itself very often thought to mean the blending or combination of methods used in ethnographic inquiry (Jankowski & Wester, 1991). At the very least participant-observation methods involve some amount of genuine social interaction in the field with television viewers, some direct observation viewing and the viewing situation, and a goodly amount of informal interviewing. There is some controversy over how much participant-observation must be done, but it is safe to say that more is better than less (see Lull, 1988). Extensive observation of television viewing may be difficult. Gaining access to the home, and further, gaining access to private parts of the home where more and more television viewing takes place, may be perceived as intrusive. As a result, much critical audience study relies on the interview.

The general style of the initial qualitative interview should be open and loosely structured. It is more useful to think of interviews as conversation rather than as directed information gathering. Allow interviewees to move in their own directions, to compose their own definitions, and to explain their own interpretive frameworks. Ask interviewees to tell you about what happens in a certain situation, to retell a story, or reconstruct a meaningful event. This approach allows you to hear experiences on the viewers' terms and allows you to be naturally curious and to ask for further explanation. Don't get impatient when interviewees go off-track because the track they are on is, for them, the right one in terms of the topic. Later in the interview, or in successive interviews, a more structured or closed approach will allow you to focus on issues you would like to compare among viewers. While one-on-one interviews will allow you to focus on individual interpretations in some detail, and these can be compared, group interviews are also often used. Interviewing a family group or small group of friends who share their fanship will often stimulate insights and reveal better contextualization of common understandings. Interviewing a less intimately acquainted, and often larger, focus group of people who share some demographic or cultural attribute will give you yet a different assessment, often telling you about what is publicly acceptable in reacting to television. Regardless of your research goals, triangulating interviews by interviewing in various settings or interviewing at successive points in the study will allow you to understand sense making about television at a deeper level.

Triangulation of methods may be approached in a variety of other ways in critical audience study. The researcher may choose to analyze documents, such as family albums, clothing, or memorabilia, and to do corresponding interviews with viewers about how these items relate to the meanings made from viewing. For example, a child's room decorations might serve as a good point of departure to contextualize his or her television viewing. Researchers such as Morley and Silverstone (1990) have also used time-use diaries and mental-mapping exercises to triangulate observational and interview data. Light may be shed on the different realities of family members by comparing their mapping of household geography, program characters, or themes. Triangulation may also be achieved through the use of institutional data such as program ratings, broken out by demography, or other market research data. Finally, it is important not to overlook that triangulation may be achieved by validating viewers' responses at different points in time or by comparing accounts of different participants in a setting. In short, the ethnographic enterprise in critical audience study may be enhanced by triangulation of the "time, space, and analytical level in which information is obtained" (Jankowski & Wester, 1991, p. 62).

Writing the Critical Audience Study. The amount of qualitative data collected in critical audience study can be overwhelming. Strategies on how to analyze data and write a useful report vary considerably. Lofland (1971, p. 5) proposes that four overarching tenets guide the report: (1) it is close to the data and based on substantial inquiry and observation, (2) it is written in good faith and aims to be truthful, (3) it uses much description and relies on illustrative quotations from those studied, and (4) it states explicit procedures for analyzing data. In terms of writing style, Agar (1980) has suggested that the report be accessible to the group studied so that it may be useful in their lives. The "story" in the critical audience report is often crafted as either a "realist" or "confessional" tale (van Mannen, 1988). The more common realist tale is told from the vantage point of those studied; liberal quotations are used and the story is framed in terms of everyday life. The less common confessional tale stresses the critic–fieldworker's vantage point. Here the critic's activities, intentions, and perceptions are featured in clear relation to the data. Although there has been much discussion about the merits of either "writing in" or "writing out" of the identity of the writer–researcher (Ang, 1989, 1991; Lull, 1990; Moores, 1993), there is no question that the writer is part of the story and that some revealing of identity can help the reader. However, regardless of the type of tale being fashioned, writing the critical audience study relies on art as much as science. Consequently, literary techniques such as the use of metaphor and analogy are key features of ethnographic writing.

Beyond style, the critic's analysis will need to (1) reduce a tremendous amount of qualitative data, (2) display those data in an organized and illustrative way, and (3) use articulated procedures to draw conclusions (Miles & Huberman, 1984). Systematically taken field notes will need to be organized by person, topic, and theme and then reduced to a set of topics emerging as most significant in the context of viewers' lives. Instead of reducing data by topic, descriptive case studies of individuals or groups may be chosen to characterize overarching patterns of experience. Conclusions may be drawn through the use of either analytic induction or grounded theory. Analytic induction works from the researcher's initial assumptions to systematically examine cases or situations to find whether a goodness of fit occurs and causal generalizations hold. In the absence of goodness of fit, then either the description is modified so that the case or situation is excluded from analysis or the researcher's hypotheses are revised. Experiences with analytic induction inspired the use of grounded theory to guide conclusions. *Grounded theories* arise from the data, and thus should be relevant and fit the context under study (Glaser & Strauss, 1967). Wester (1987) sees four phases in developing grounded theory. First, the exploratory phase aims to identify "sensitizing concepts" from the material that has been collected. Second, the defining phase aims at constructing "variables" based on the concepts. Third, the reduction phase aims to provide the contours of workable theory. Fourth, the integration phase relates the concepts to one another and these relationships are tested on the data. Conclusions drawn at each stage are iteratively reviewed through each phase until the data have exhausted theoretical formulation.

Strengths and Limitations.   Critical audience study's main strengths come from the depth of its description and the fact that it depends on understanding meanings about television on the viewers' terms. The primary weaknesses are its built-in limits to generalize the experiences of the viewers under study to those of the larger culture. Further, although meaning is approached on the terms of viewers, the larger cultural significance is necessarily seen through the interpretive eyes of the researcher. Facing this issue head-on is the key to successful critical audience study. The researcher must acknowledge the power of the critical researcher. One should be self-reflexive about one's own biases, about incompleteness in data gathering, and even about gaps that can be seen when data were gathered. The pull toward self-indulgence on the part of a critic using the style of the confessional tale can be considerable. Although there should be no fear in unmasking the researcher in a postmodern approach, overly subjective and self-reflexive exercises in psychoanalysis can pose new problems. When the experiences of the researcher overshadow those lived experiences of real viewers, the grounding of meaning, and consequently the critical method, has been changed.

Looking Ahead

What follows are some case studies in both audience-oriented criticism and critical audience study. Using a reader-oriented approach to the characterized fictional reader of commercials shown during the Olympic games, Wenner offers a good example of audience-oriented criticism. His analysis starts with a look at how the myths and values of sport are communicated as "dirt" used in the context of selling. The analysis that follows examines how commercials attempt to control the reading act by characterizing and positioning the viewer. The critique's conclusion examines commonalities in advertisers' attempts to place viewers in a special social world.

The next two essays come from the tradition of critical audience study. These studies both used ethnographically inspired methods to examine real audience experience with different kinds of televisual texts. Geiser-Getz examines audience experience with the reality-based program *COPS*. His assessment links a reality-intended text to some revealing and often surprisingly humorous tertiary texts that tell us a great deal about the range of audience pleasures and the variant interpretations that are little evident at first glance. As an interesting contrast to the Geiser-Getz analysis, Halualani and Vande Berg examine some of the serious sides to polyvalence in the situation comedy text of *All-American Girl*. Their ethnographically based inquiry is set in the political-economic context of multiculturalism and inferential racism. While their findings show the remarkable range of critical sensibilities brought by viewers with different backgrounds as they attempt to negotiate and deconstruct a text that has the experiences of a typical young Asian-American woman as its centerpiece, they present telling arguments about why these audience experiences still very much cast a colonialist shadow.

NOTES

1. This is called the "fourth-wall" convention.
2. See the discussion of polysemy and polyvalence on pp. 229–231.

REFERENCES

Agar, M. (1980). *The professional stranger: An informal introduction to ethnography.* New York: Academic Press.

Allen, R. C. (1987). Reader-oriented criticism and television. In *Channels of discourse: Television and contemporary criticism* (pp. 74–112). Chapel Hill: University of North Carolina Press.

Allen, R. C. (1992). Audience-oriented criticism and television. In *Channels of discourse, reassembled: Television and contemporary criticism* (2nd ed.). (pp. 101–137).

Althusser, L. (1984). *Essays on ideology.* London: Verso.

Ang, I. (1985). *Watching 'Dallas': Soap opera and the melodramatic imagination.* London: Methuen.

Ang, I. (1989). Wanted: Audiences, on the politics of empirical audience studies. In E. Seiter, H. Borchers, G. Kreutzener, & E-M Warth (Eds.), *Remote control: Television, audiences, and cultural power* (pp. 96–115). London: Routledge.

Ang, I. (1991). *Desperately seeking the audience.* London: Routledge.

Barthes, R. (1973). *Mythologies.* London: Paladin.

Bennett, T. (1982). Text and social process: The case of James Bond. *Screen Eduction, 41,* 3–15.

Booth, W. (1961). *The rhetoric of fiction.* Chicago: University of Chicago Press.

Booth, W. (1974). *The rhetoric of irony.* Chicago: University of Chicago Press.

Brunsdon, C. (1981). 'Crossroads': Notes on soap opera. *Screen 22(4),* 32–37.

Crosman, I. (1980). Annotated bibliography of audience-oriented criticism. In S. Suleiman & I. Crosman (Eds.), *The reader in the text: Essays on audience and interpretation* (pp. 401–424). Princeton, NJ: Princeton University Press.

Culler, J. (1981). *The pursuit of signs: Semiotics, literature, and deconstruction.* London: Routledge & Kegan Paul.

Dahlgren, P. (1988). What's the meaning of this? Viewers' plural sense-making of TV news. *Media, Culture, & Society, 10(3),* 285–301.

Derrida, J. (1976). *Of grammatology.* Baltimore, MD: Johns Hopkins University Press.

Eco, U. (1977). *The role of the reader.* Bloomington: Indiana University Press.

Fish, S. (1980). *Is there a text in this class? The authority of interpretive communities.* Cambridge, MA: Harvard University Press.

Freund, E. (1987). *The return of the reader: Reader-response criticism.* New York: Methuen.

Gadmader, H-G. (1975). *Truth and method.* New York: Seabury Press.

Geertz, C. (1973). *The interpretation of cultures.* New York: Basic Books.

Glaser, B. G., & Strauss, A. L. (1967). *The discovery of grounded theory: Strategies for qualitative research.* Chicago: Aldine.

Gramsci, A. (1971). *Selections from the prison notebooks.* New York: International Publishers.

Hall, S. (1973). Encoding and decoding in the television discourse. CCCS Stenciled Paper 7, University of Birmingham. [Reprinted in I. Graddel & O.B. Barrett (Eds.), *Media texts: Authors and readers.* (1994). London: Milton Keynes: Open University Press and Multi Lingual Matters. See also "The television discourse: Encoding and decoding." In A. Gray & J. McGuigan (Eds.), *Studying Culture* (1993, pp. 28–34). London: Edward Arnold.]

Hammersley, M., & Atkinson, P. (1983). *Ethnography: Principles and practice.* London: Tavistock.

Hartley, J. (1987). Invisible fictions: Television audiences, paedocracy, pleasure. *Textual Practice, 1*(2), 121–138.

Hobson, R. (1982). *Crossroads: The drama of a soap opera.* London: Methuen.

Holland, N. N. (1968). *The dynamics of literary response.* New York: Oxford University Press.

Holub, R. C. (1984). *Reception theory: A critical introduction.* New York: Methuen.

Iser, W. (1974). *The implied reader: Patterns of reading in prose fiction from Bunyan to Beckett.* Baltimore, MD: Johns Hopkins University Press.

Iser, W. (1978). *The act of reading: A theory of aesthetic response.* Baltimore: Johns Hopkins University Press.

Ingarden, R. (1973). *The literary work of art: An investigation of the borderlines of ontology, logic, and theory of literature.* Evanston: Northwestern University Press.

Jankowski, N. W., & Wester, F. (1991). The qualitative tradition in social science inquiry: Contributions to mass communication research. In K. B. Jensen & N. W. Jankowski (Eds.), *A handbook of qualitative methodologies for mass communication research* (pp. 44–74). London: Routledge.

Jauss, H. R. (1982a). *Aesthetic experience and literary hermeneutics.* Minneapolis: University of Minnesota Press.

Jauss, H. R. (1982b). *Toward an aesthetic of reception.* Minneapolis: University of Minnesota Press.

Jensen, K. B. (1991). When is meaning? Communication theory, pragmatism, and mass media reception. In J. Anderson (Ed.), *Communication Yearbook* (Vol. 14). Newbury Park, CA: Sage.

Lacan, J. (1977). *Ecrits: A selection.* London: Tavistock.

Lewis, J. (1985). Decoding television news. In P. Drummond & R. Paterson (Eds.), *Television in transition: Papers from the first international television studies conference* (pp. 205–234). London: British Film Institute.

Lewis, J. (1991). *The ideological octopus: An exploration of television and its audience.* New York: Routledge.

Lewis, L. A. (Ed.). (1992). *The adoring audience: Fan culture and popular media.* New York: Routledge.

Liebes, T., & Katz, E. (1990). *The export of meaning: Cross-cultural readings of 'Dallas.'* New York: Oxford University Press.

Lofland, L. (1971). *Analyzing social settings: A guide to qualitative observation and analysis* (2nd rev. ed.). Belmont, CA: Wadsworth.

Lull, J. (1980). The social uses of television. *Human Communication Research, 6,* 197–209.

Lull, J. (Ed.). (1988). *World families watch television.* Newbury Park, CA: Sage.

Lull, J. (1990). *Inside family viewing: Ethnographic research on television's audiences.* London: Routledge.

Mannen, J. Van (1988). *Tales of the field: On writing ethnography.* Chicago: University of Chicago Press.

Miles, M. B., & Huberman, A. M. (1984). Qualitative data analysis: A sourcebook of new methods. London: Sage.

Moores, S. (1993). *Interpreting audiences: The ethnography of media consumption.* London: Sage.

Morgan, M. (1989). Television and democracy. In I. Angus & S. Jhally (Eds.), *Cultural politics and contemporary America* (pp. 162–184). New York: Routledge.

Morley, D. (1980). *The Nationwide audience.* London: British Film Institute.

Morley, D. (1986). *Family television.* London: Comedia.

Morley, D., & Silverstone, R. (1990). Domestic communication: Technologies and meanings. *Media, Culture, and Society, 12*(1), 31–55.

Radway, J. (1987). *Reading the romance: Women, patriarchy, and popular literature.* London: Verso.

Radway, J. (1988). Reception study: Ethnography and the problems of dispersed audiences and nomadic subjects. *Cultural Studies, 2*(3), 359–376.

Richards, I. A. (1929). *Practical criticism.* New York: Harcourt Brace Jovanovich.

Rosengren, K. E., Wenner, L. A., & Palmgreen. *Media gratifications research: Current perspectives.* Beverly Hills, CA: Sage.

Silverstone, R. (1991). From audiences to consumers: The household and the consumption of information and communication technologies. *European Journal of Communication, 6*(2), 135–154.

Stam, R. (1983). Television news and its spectators. In E. A. Kaplan (Ed.), *Regarding television—Critical approaches: An anthology* (pp. 23–43). Frederick, MD: University Publications of America.

Sulieman, S. R. (1980). Introduction: Varieties of audience-oriented criticism. In S. Suleiman & I. Crosman (Eds.), *The reader in the text: Essays on audience and interpretation* (pp. 3–45). Princeton, NJ: Princeton University Press.

Suleiman, S. R., & Crosman, I. (Eds.). (1980). *The reader in the text: Essays on audience and interpretation.* Princeton, NJ: Princeton University Press.

Tomkins, J. P. (Ed.). (1980). *Reader-response criticism: From formalism to post-structuralism.* Baltimore, MD: Johns Hopkins University Press.

Trujillo, N. (1993). Interpreting November 22: A critical ethnography of an assassination site. *Quarterly Journal of Speech, 79,* 447–466.

Turner, G. (1990). *British cultural studies: An introduction.* Boston: Unwin Hyman.

Wester, F. P. (1987). *Strategies for qualitative research.* Muiderberg: Coutinho.

The Dream Team, Communicative Dirt, and the Marketing of Synergy: USA Basketball and Cross-Merchandising in Television Commercials

Lawrence A. Wenner

By the time all was said and done in the 1992 Olympic Games, USA basketball's bringing home the gold rang to many as tin. Novelist Stephen King called the Dream Team a horror show following a new Olympic motto: "Make Sure You're Going to Win, Then Go Ahead and Do It." What purity was left in the amateur ideals of the Olympics had been put to rest. USA basketball's team was populated by the superstars of NBA basketball. They were bigger than life. Bigger than the Olympics. They stayed in fancy hotels. They played golf as if they were on vacation. Magic was back for a victory lap, AIDS and all. Never was the outcome of the basketball competition in doubt.

It is not surprising what took center stage under such conditions. Along the way to the medal stand, we found the Dream Team quibbling with the various Olympic committees over who has what rights in the pursuit of commercialism. The issues were seemingly trivial. Charles Barkley was to be paid to write a column for *USA Today*. The International Olympic Committee (IOC) said no. Athletes may write only for their hometown paper. Michael Jordan, claiming loyalty to his Nike®contract, refused to wear a Reebok®outfit on the medal stand. The U.S. Olympic Committee said athletes not wearing Reebok would not be allowed on the medal stand.

In the latter dispute, international diplomacy yielded to the commercial code. Olympism recognized a new world order where new loyalties—endorsement contracts—reign. Jordan and other Dream Teamers in the Nike stable hit the medal stand, their jacket flaps consciously covering anything Reebok. In what might be taken as a perversion of Barthes's (1973) "ex-nomination" process, these athletes nominated Nike.

The struggle over commercialism, endorsement contracts, and consumer loyalties in the modern Olympic Games is a competition with stakes far greater than those between athletes. This is because Olympism is an idealized premium product. In that idealized form, the Games celebrate the virtues of amateurism, sportsmanship, international goodwill, and "healthy" nationalism, all in the context of heroic athleticism. And because of its 4-year cycle, the product's potency has built-in curbs against market fatigue.

The commercial value of the Olympics is great to sponsors and advertisers attempting to get a "cultural rub" from values associated with the Games. The growth of cross-merchandising and "synergy" as a marketing strategy among products recognizes this (Hewitt, 1991). The IOC allows only 12 worldwide Olympic sponsors. The tariff is high. It is estimated that Coca-Cola®spent $33 million to become the "official" soft drink of the 1992 Games. Visa®International spent $20 million to be the Olympic credit card (Beckett, 1992). NBC spent $402 million for the television rights to the 1992 Summer Games, more than double what ABC paid in 1984 (Elliott, 1992).

With such large figures at stake, the purity of Olympic ideals is necessarily compromised. *New York Times* television critic John J. O'Connor (1992) noted that it was such a big business undertaking leading to possible future payoffs for the athletes that the word hype was utterly inadequate. With so many jumping on the Olympic marketing bandwagon, some advertising executives feared that this amount of hype would backfire into consumer backlash as the event became archetypal of overcommercialization (Marinucci, 1992, p. E1).

Yet for most advertisers there was not enough of a good thing to go around. If they could not get in the front door, they would get in another way. A growing group of "ambush marketers" including Pepsi®, Fuji®, American Express®, and Converse® developed ads that suggested an "Olympic rub" without actually mentioning the Games. "Ambush" ads were placed in close proximity to those of official Olympic sponsors. John Krimsky, Deputy Secretary General of the U.S. Olympic Committee, angrily called the strategy "parasitic marketing" (Beckett, 1992, p. B1).

The rush to get a commercial "rub" from the Olympic Games recognizes the strong communicative power of sports "dirt" in an "interpretive community" of sports fans (Wenner, 1991). It is ironic to hear Olympic officials single out "ambush" marketers as parasitic. Official Olympic sponsors are parasitic as well; they just pay for it. Perhaps that is the difference between a sponsor and a parasite.

The sponsorship and advertising of the Olympic Games is by necessity a "dirty" one, parasitic if you will. As it is used here, the term "dirt" has no inherent negative connotation. Rather, the term refers "to the cultural borrowing that allows one cultural entity to adopt the logic of another" (Wenner, 1991, p. 392). Hartley (1984) suggests that television texts are necessarily contaminated by seepages from other parts of culture. For example, dominant ideologies expressed in sports values (nationalism, patriotism, authoritarianism) are couched in the celebration of heroism, equality, commitment, and pride in the television sports text (Wenner, 1989). Beer commercials use sports dirt—the logic and values of sport—to infuse alcohol consumption with athleticism (Wenner, 1991). Nike commercials use nostalgic dirt from the Beatles' song "Revolution" to empower their shoes (Howell, 1991).

The power of dirt ascends with its cultural primacy. At the apex of Olympic commercialism, Dream Team dirt was powerful. Through a reader-oriented analysis of the workings of dirt in commercials featuring the Dream Team, this study examines how we are characterized and positioned as readers through the use of sports dirt. Eleven commercials appearing during NBC's broadcasts of two games—USA versus Cuba's game 1 in the Tournament of the Americas and USA versus Angola's game 1 of the 1992 Olympics—are analyzed. These 11 ads were the only ones in these games that relied on Dream Team dirt as a primary strategy.

A reader-oriented approach is central to understanding the advertiser's agenda in sports. Attempts to position the reader are made easier because fans have many of the characteristics of an interpretive community (Fish, 1980; Wenner 1990, 1991). Such group membership often contributes to a shared sense of place and cultural identity (Wenner, 1990). The resultant group cohesiveness allows sports fans exposed to commercials featuring Dream Team dirt to be more easily identified as "characterized fictional readers" (Allen, 1987, 1992). Advertisers characterize the interpretive community when fans are directly addressed. We often see on-screen characterized fans as "textual surrogates who do what real viewers cannot: interact with other performers and respond (usually in an ideal fashion) to the appeals, demands, and urgings of the addresser" (Allen, 1992, p. 121).

The structuralist version of reader-oriented criticism focuses on how the text attempts to control the reading act (Suleiman, 1980). Television ads, in particular, attempt to position the viewer " 'some place' relative to the action in every shot" (Allen, 1987, p. 90). The positioning strategy attempts to blur distinctions between the characterized addressee on the screen, the implied addressee viewing at home, and the addresser. The overriding goal in this attempt is to elicit a positive answer to the addresser's question "Will you buy?" (Allen, 1987, 1992).

The reader-oriented analysis that follows focuses on the reader in the text; the Dream Team fan who is the characterized fictional reader of these commercials. It is assumed that the fan as implied reader and the advertiser as addresser both bring dirt from sport to their constructed meanings of these commercials. Because dirt from sport is highly valued by the sports fan, a position is taken that negotiated readings of these commercials will be far more dominant than oppositional (Hall, 1980). Although the study focuses on how sports dirt encourages preferred readings through characterizing the reader, it is recognized that texts are interpreted in the context of a range of "activations" (Bennett, 1982). Thus, given indications of consumer "backlash" to the "overhype" of the Olympics, likely oppositional readings from within the interpretive community are also explored.

The World of Dream Team Dirt

All 11 of the commercials that build on connections to the Dream Team fall into the category of being explicitly contaminated by sports dirt (Wenner, 1991). An earlier study (Wenner, 1991) suggests three variants of explicit sports contamination in commercials:

1. *Active sports dirt* focuses on portraying characterized fictional fans actively engaged in sports activities.

2. *Implied sports dirt* focuses on portraying fictional fans in situations that imply sports activity or demonstrate empathy for sports activities (that is, engagement in fan activities).

3. *Idealized sports dirt* focuses on constructing narratives that idealize activities culminating in professional sports success.

The 11 commercials featured in the two USA basketball games often blurred the genres of active, implied, and idealized sports dirt. Given the sophistication of modern merchandising, this structural "polysemy" should not be surprising. Still, a telling categorical scheme can be devised by asking, where is the locus of the sports dirt's power in the commercial? What central logics about sports and culture empower the connection to the product? By answering these questions, the 11 commercials can be organized into three types:

1. *Nationalistic sports dirt* focuses on sport as a tool for promoting nationalism and the metaphor of the team as soldiers.

2. *Youth sports dream dirt* focuses on the idealized notion in the sports world that if one works hard enough, one's sports dreams can be realized.

3. *Sports hero dirt* focuses on the ideal of the sports hero as a role model and the power of the "reflected glory" that comes from identifying with the hero.

The analysis that follows considers the workings of dirt and the characterizing of the reader in each of these categories.

Nationalistic Sports Dirt

Support the Troops (Team) and Salute the Flag (Uniform)

Champion® athletic clothes chose to rely on the notion of teamwork in the context of nationalism to smear sports dirt on its product. The 30-second ad relies on a simple, unhurried, but patriotic narration:

> This summer in Barcelona, 12 of our best men will be bound by a common path, a common goal, and a common thread. Champion is proud to be chosen to make the uniform for America's team. Because we understand teams. It takes a little more to make a Champion.

The narration directly addresses the characterized reader as powerful by assuming the reader's participation in collective ownership of the team. The "bound" men are positioned in our service. Derivative of this, the reader is characterized as agreeing to the commonality of "path, goal, and thread." This positioning has entailments, used in service of characterizing the reader. The reader is a patriot, supportive of America's dream, team, uniform, and flag. Implicit is the reader's support of commonality among the variant threads of America's melting pot. Implicit is support for our team as if its members are troops. And the last logical leap makes the last and most important dirty connection. In our supporting our team, we take "pride" in the uniform our troops wear, and, as we see time and time again in the visuals, the uniform in red, white, and blue is a flag made by Champion.

Complex video imagery uses 61 shots to amplify these connections and position the reader. There are many visual juxtapositions of the USA basketball team competing and the Champion uniform being sewn. The direct address of the narrator positions us to accept the logic of this juxtaposition. As we root for our team, we root for the uniform being sewn. As we root for our powerful USA team's ball to go through the basket (5 shots), we root for the Champion's powerful needle to penetrate red, white, and blue fabric (8 shots). When the narration positions us to take "pride" in "America's team," we must take in the red, white, and blue of the uniforms. When we are positioned as having the knowledge to "understand teams," we are positioned visually to equate that understanding with a consumer sweatshirt made by Champion. In the end, the "little more" that it takes "to make a Champion" amplifies the reader's position that nationalism makes sports a little better. Supporting Champion means supporting that dirty but potent mix.

Fairy Tales of U.S. Domination

Converse athletic shoes chose to rely on a fairy tale about the power of the Dream Team as a parable for the power of its "magical shoes." In one of what is known as the

"Larry Johnson's grandmother" ads, we see a grandmother sitting in a rocking chair reading a fairy tale to a multicultural group of young children. Quickly, we find sports dirt. The grandmother is a large Black mustachioed man with a gold tooth who is dressed in a prim flowered dress and high-top basketball shoes. The grandmother says,

> This is a story about two of the baddest men that ever put on little short pants. One day they were surrounded by the Russians and the dreaded Italians! Arghh! They quick put on their magical shoes from Converse and ditched them all big time! And snatched up all the gold and brought it home to Grandmama.

As the story unfolds, we find out who the "baddest men" are by seeing storybook pictures of Larry Bird and Magic Johnson. The grandmother is animated, excitedly telling the story. We see that the children are nervous and scared as the story unfolds. When the story's problem is resolved by putting on "magical shoes from Converse" we see storybook pictures of the Bird and Magic Converse shoes. We see the children pleased as the story is resolved as Bird and Magic "snatched up all the gold." In the end, a small Black boy is incredulous, asking, "Is that true, Grandmama?" The grandmother provides reassurance: "It will be, child, it will be" as we see a closing graphic of "Converse—Official Shoe of USA Basketball."

Closing the ad with the questioning of the veracity of the story formalizes dual reading positions for the characterized readers. For the adult reader, it is clear from the start that this ad is a put-on. The reader is positioned outside the scene to appreciate the pictured children being taken in. For the child, the reading position is perched delicately on the edge of plausibility. This could be a fairy tale, and this could be a grandmother. Their on-screen textual surrogates are shown to be largely suspending disbelief.

Nationalistic dirt works on both reading positions in concert with sports hero dirt. As our "bad" men are surrounded by the Russians and the "dreaded Italians," nationalism is invoked. To the child reader, "foreigners" are scary. For the adult reader, the Dream Team is an invincible national force and a foreign challenge laughable. The child is positioned to interpret Bird and Magic as mythlike, something the adults are already positioned to bring to their interpretation. The child is positioned as well to interpret Bird's and Magic's shoes as mythlike. For the adult reader, such positioning is unlikely. More likely, the ad works to position the adult to accept and expect the child's interpretation of the shoe as inheriting mythlike qualities. Thus the reading position of the adult specifies two roles. First, the adult is positioned as parent or prospective parent, who feels good about the myth the child may value. Second, the adult is positioned as adult-child, who can play along with the fairy tale and its assumptions. In either case, dirt works in a fairly straightforward way. Bird and Magic are America's team, they will win, they will wear Converse, and you should wear Converse if you want to support America and win.

Youth Sports Dream Dirt

Lifelong Friendship as an Olympic Value

Archetypal of the youth sports dream dirt commercials was AT&T's 30-second spot that featured a narrator telling an idealized flashback story about young Scottie

Pippen and his childhood friend Ronnie Martin. The narrator speaks to us as implied readers who embrace Olympic ideals and hard work leading to athletic success. The narrator tells us that "long before Scottie Pippen was chosen for the USA Basketball team, he knew he could count on his friend Ronnie Martin." Meanwhile, we see a romanticized scene set in a warmly lit gym in Hamsburg, Arkansas, in 1976. Young Pippen and Martin take on the challenge from an older, bigger, threatening boy named Big Harold. We see young Pippen and Martin work a play together to beat Big Harold. Here, the narrator tells us "AT&T salutes all of our Olympic hopefuls and everyone that helped them get this far." We enter the present by panning up an "official" team jacket arm with signage "Pippen" and the USA basketball logo. We see Ronnie Martin asking Scottie Pippen whether "those guys in the Olympics gonna be tough?" Pippen asks, "Why? Did they sign Big Harold?" as the two laugh. Theme music comes up as we see the USA Olympic logo that transforms itself into the AT&T logo while a graphic proclaims AT&T as "Proud Sponsor of the 1992 Olympic Team."

This ad works to position the reader in three interrelated places. In direct address, the narrator positions the reader as a USA basketball fan who can be counted on in joining AT&T in "saluting" (as one would the flag) our "hopefuls." Second, we are cast as voyeurs of nostalgia, appreciative of a Horatio Alger story with a little bit of Tom Sawyer and Huckleberry Finn thrown in for good measure. Third, we are cast as privileged spectators of a private friendship, about which we share their private history. Throughout, sports dirt helps position the reader. As sports fans we are receptive to rooting for the underdog, sympathetic to the idea that hard work leads to sport success, seeing teamwork as an ideal in life, and interpreting sports histories as the culmination of these ideals. In today's sports world, we are treated to many tales of athletic prima donnas; thus the painting of Pippen as one who remains an Everyman who is true to a lifelong friend rings the bell of sports fans who likely hope that they too would remain unchanged with sports success. In short, we feel good about sport dreams, about friendship, and about AT&T. As dirt, these sport myths merely add power to a preexisting crafted connection between friendship and AT&T, amplifying both "reach out" and institutional "feel good" campaigns.

A Champion of a Young Boy's Dreams

A second Champion athletic clothes spot is more forthright in waxing poetic about a young boy's dreams of competing in the Olympics. We see a young boy alone in a gym through nostalgic soft focus and lighting. We see him fantasize playing with the Dream Team as he tells himself,

> It's Barcelona. Cautious, he came down. He brings the ball up, Drexler's open on the wing. Great pass from Malone. USA needs a basket to win. Magic goes to the hoop. Yeah!

We see the boy hit the winning basket. He jumps in celebration. The boy's hand hits a "high five" with a fantasized man's Black hand. The boy, surprised by the fantasy crossing into reality, looks at his hand and looks around. As he seemingly questions whether his dream has come true, we hear the narrator: "When USA basketball plays for the dream they'll wear the uniform Champion proudly earned the right to make."

The visuals connect the Champion uniform and consumer products to the dream. As the boy leaves the gym, we see the shadowy outline of four of his Dream Teammates that remains as the narrator tells us "It takes a little more to make a Champion."

The reader's position in this ad is as spectator to the dream, a voyeur who appreciates well-worn fantasies of young children who dream to play with their heroes. The positioning relies on the notion of the fan as one who played sports and entertained those same dreams. Specifying the Dream Team as the dirt that fuels the fantasy allows Champion to not only be equated with the best but to contribute to all of our fantasies of being the best.

If I Could Be Like Mike

One of Gatorade®'s generic "Be Like Mike" ads appeared during the Tournament of the Americas game. We hear singing:

> Sometimes I dream. The key is me. You've got to see that's how I dream to be. I dream I move. I dream I grew. Like Mike. If I could be like Mike. I'm gonna be, gonna be like Mike. Like Mike. If I could be like Mike. Be like Mike. If I could be like Mike.

The visuals intercut Dream Teamer Michael Jordan playing NBA basketball, multicultural girls and boys playing playground ball, and Jordan playing with the kids. The lyrics pose youthful sports dream as the driving dirty force that is energized by association with Jordan as sports hero. A variety of basketball-playing textual surrogates are seen: a teenaged Black boy (seen with Jordanesque tongue hanging), a teenaged White girl, a 5-year-old White boy, and a 10-year-old Black girl. A multicultural group of textual surrogates drinking Gatorade join Jordan as he goes to the playground. Other shots place the reader in a familiar spectator role, joining a crowd cheering Jordan as he slays the NBA. From any angle, and any age, readers are shown to like Mike and like being his friend. Only a step away is dreaming his dream and to do so is to "be like Mike." In that dream, we are those good textual surrogates shown to drink Gatorade "like Mike."

McDonald's® Olympic Dream

McDonald's youth sports dream spot relies on heavy doses of nationalistic dirt and sports hero dirt to round out the dream. The narration draws a bridge between nationalism and youth sports dreams:

> The 1992 Olympic Summer Games. The year basketball trades NBA colors for red, white, and blue. For everyone who's longed to see America send nothing than their very best. For every family whose hearts still beat faster when they hear the national anthem. For the young who dream that someday they too may soar so high. For every one of us. McDonald's is proud to sponsor the 1992 USA basketball team. To help Olympic dreams come true.

Quite simply, the commercial is dedicated to the implied reader. We are patriotic citizens. We are traditional families. We hold great hopes for our children. We share sports dreams with our children.

The visuals position us as well in the role of spectator. At the start, we see the Olympic flame and a montage of Dream Teamers on the NBA court. Our first textual surrogate is a middle-aged middle-American White couple with hands over hearts as the national anthem plays to start a game. The dreams "we" have for our young to "soar so high" are characterized by our appreciative reactions to the Dream Teamers in action. Our children with youth sports dreams are characterized by a young Black boy seen first in a stadium crowd watching action and later cheering as a championship is won.

Interestingly, the sealing of the championship for "every one of us" is accomplished by a Larry Bird shot. This ushers in McDonald's "being proud" to "sponsor the 1992 USA basketball team" as we see the McDonald's arches blend with Olympic rings encased in red, white, and blue ribbon. As spectators, McDonald's has taken the time to position us to appreciate White heroism as a Black boy looks on from the sidelines. Admittedly, this is fleeting, but from the reading position established, it is the Black boy who needs help in making "Olympic Dreams Come True." The net result is a very paternalistic, traditional reading position that embraces sport as an agency for social mobility.

Sports Hero Dirt

Almost all of the commercials discussed previously placed benefit substantially from sports hero dirt. The five commercials discussed in the sports hero dirt category deemphasize nationalism and youth dreams. Rather, these commercials rely more directly on the importance of the sports hero as a public figure, the ideal of the sports hero, and the power of the "reflected glory" of identifying with the hero.

Visa as Player on the All-Defensive Team

The Visa credit card relies on the collective strength and power of the Dream Team to make its dirty link between the strong Dream Team defense and Visa as defense against merchants who "don't take American Express." The audio pulses as the narrator introduces individual members of the Dream Team, saying "They've been called the greatest team in Olympic history." Implied readers are positioned as spectators seeing on-court exploits of the Dream Teamers. In mid-commercial, with the lead "Olympic basketball may never be the same," the narrator queries the reader, "But if you think they're tough, wait until you see the guys at the ticket window, if you don't have your Visa card." We see tough-guy shots of Dream Teamers followed by a shot of a surly ticket seller. A textual surrogate saves the day: placing a Visa card on an elegant table emblazoned with the familiar dirty Olympic rings and telling us Visa is "worldwide sponsor, 1992 Olympic Games." When we are told that "the Olympics don't take American Express" a montage of Dream Teamers blocking shots is followed by another textual surrogate whipping out the Visa card and then a Dream Teamer getting off a tough shot. The ball goes into the basket as the narrator closes "Visa, it's everywhere you want to be."

Again, we have three main reading positions. First, we are spectators of the Dream Team. Second, we are tormented textual surrogates caught without our Visa. Third, we are elegant textual surrogates playing the Dream Team game with our forceful defense—our Visa card. We are shown to appreciate the attributes of the Dream Team, and we are characterized on-screen using the desired behavioral path to demonstrate those attributes in our consumer lives.

The Magical Ambush of Pepsi

Pepsi drew much criticism from Olympic worldwide sponsor Coca-Cola for its "ambush" ads featuring HIV-positive Dream Teamer Magic Johnson (Marinucci, 1992). Placed in the first games of the Olympics, the ad does not mention the Games. The ad is simple. It opens with inspirational classical music over the graphic "We Believe in Magic." A soft-focus shot of Magic dribbling to the basket is faded in. Dreamlike shots of Magic are intercut with a montage of shots showing a multicultural world of individuals and groups supporting him. We see Little Leaguers, a teenaged girl, a father and son, an Asian restaurant chef, a young White woman at a picnic, a Black garbage man, commercial fishermen on a boat, Pepsi employees in front of a Pepsi truck, young children in a multicultural classroom, and parochial school girls in uniform. Groups and individuals are shouting variously "Go for it, Magic! Go Magic! Go get 'em, Magic! Good luck, Magic! Magic!" And from the young woman at the picnic, "We love you, Magic!" This outburst of affection from our many textual surrogates is contextualized mid-spot by a narrator who provides a contextual "from all of us at Pepsi" to allow Pepsi to join in our fanship group and, in a sense, take ownership of it and responsibility for it. Pepsi and Magic become rallying points for our fanship group in supporting an AIDS-infected athlete in the Olympic games, although neither AIDS nor the Olympic Games need be "nominated" (Barthes, 1973).

Herein lies the inherent "ambush" problem in Olympic dirtied ads. The Olympics has reached such a point of collective excess that the need to "nominate" it only presents risks in marginalizing its marketing impact. To not mention the Olympics may be far more powerful dirt than "announcing" that the dirt was purchased for the purposes of fulfilling marketing goals. If Barthes (1973) is right, "ex-nomination" is far more powerful, and the IOC really has something to worry about with these ambushes. AIDS, on the other hand, remains ex-nominated for more complex reasons. To name it, Pepsi would be patting itself on the back for being politically correct. Without doing so, it may have made a stronger statement in that Pepsi signifies that *they* know *we* know the story of Magic, thereby legitimizing their role as organizers in the interpretive community.

The Magic of Skybox® Cards

The shadow of AIDS remains in the interpretive background of the Skybox trading card commercials featuring Magic Johnson and his young son Andre. The opening drumbeat beckons excitement. The first visual features the official USA basketball logo and the statement "The Greatest Team Ever Assembled." Magic and Andre are excitedly dealing Dream Team player cards. Magic trades Jordan and Barkley to Andre for Ewing and Mullin. We are privileged spectators to this interaction. We see them fantasize game play. Magic claims he won. Andre disagrees, coyly posing a last-minute trade: John Stockton for Magic. Magic protests. Andre playfully explains he would sit Magic on the bench and bring in Stockton. Magic mocks being upset, gets up, and comes at Andre. The drum beats, and we see a store display of cards as the narrator announces "USA Basketball collector cards, from Skybox." The last frame shows the graphic: "Skybox, The Magic of Cards."

With regard to our spectator reading position, it is implied that we like Magic, have a preexisting relationship with him, and have sympathy for him as he struggles for a normal life as the world's most famous HIV-infected individual. For the implied child reader, the AIDS question is out of the picture. The child fan learns more insider information about what Magic really likes to do, and his role model legitimizes card trading as a worthwhile and fun activity. In both cases of implied readership, the dirt comes into play as Magic stands in for us, the characterized textual surrogate who enjoys the fantasies of card trading.

Be Like Dave

Kellogg®poured Dream Team dirt on its Corn Flakes®by featuring star player David Robinson in a spot aimed at promoting a "commemorative USA Olympic jacket" that was available for a couple of box tops and $4.99. The primary implied reader is a child with sports interest. A secondary implied reader might be a parent interested in fueling sports interest in a child. An announcer cues the ad: "Kellogg's Corn Flakes presents the basketball stars from the Olympic Games. Center David Robinson." We see Robinson enter, dribbling a basketball. Robinson wears basketball shorts and a tuxedo top. A comedy of errors is signaled. "Hey Dave, wrong jacket," cries the announcer. Comedic sound effects punctuate Robinson's perplexed discovery. Robinson appears back on screen wearing a red sport shirt and green plaid sport coat. The announcer cries, "No, not that jacket! This jacket, featuring you, Malone, Stockton, Bird, and Mullin." We see the stars on the jacket as the announcer makes the pitch "for you to get into the action of this basketball first." We see the jacket modeled, first by father and son cheering at a basketball game, and then by Robinson as super-surrogate. As the camera comes close to examine the jacket, the dirt of USA Olympic logo is clearly seen. The ad closes on a comedic note, with the announcer making a quip about Robinson's plaid Bermuda shorts.

The self-reflexive comedy of the sports hero works to soften the blow of an explicitly Dream Team-dirtied pitch by Kellogg. The deliberate casting of a Dream Team giant as a mere mortal who takes his frequent mistakes with good humor puts the child reader "in the know," in an "insiders" community of readers that knows something special about David Robinson. We know Dave. We like Dave. Be like Dave. Buy the Corn Flakes to get the jacket.

Be Like Mike, Part 2

The last commercial featuring sports hero dirt focused on a discussion between Michael Jordan and his father over the attributes of Hanes®underwear. An opening graphic reads "Hanes. Fashion Underwear." Uptempo music accompanies Michael Jordan's entrance, shooting a basketball into an empty chair next to a man reading a newspaper. Another graphic reads "Michael Jordan & His Dad. After the Game." Jordan sits down. We see his dad pick up a pair of red underwear sitting on the floor atop blue and white underwear. Dad asks, "Michael, are these your Hanes?" Jordan smilingly nods. His dad continues, "Son, is there a reason you wear 'em?" Jordan's wife comes into the scene, hugging, then kissing Jordan, and answering the question with a fond "Definitely."

Holding the underwear up, Jordan's dad quizzes Mike, "Think Mom would like me in these?" Jordan responds, "Maybe." A graphic responds, "Definitely." Music comes up as we see a montage of shots of red, white, and blue underwear. A chorus is heard singing "Just wait'll we get our Hanes on you" while Jordan smiles and a graphic reinforces the chorus's line.

The implied reader is a privileged spectator of a drama about a superstar who can do it all. For the male spectator, the textual surrogate is likely embraced by Jordan's dad, who wonders how the Jordan-empowered underwear might work for him. For the female spectator, a textual surrogate is found in Jordan's wife. She testifies to the power of the red, white, and blue underwear. The focus of the dirtiness in this "Be Like Mike" ad is very different from the Gatorade ad. However, the workings of the dirt are similar. The power of the sports hero is transferred to the product and to the use of the product by the textual surrogate and implied reader. Both the Gatorade and the Hanes underwear make a great Jordan better, just as they could for you. Only in the Gatorade case it is fairly clean dirt. With the Hanes underwear, there is a layer of dirty dirt that commodifies and potentially reinforces cultural myths of sport and the Black male's sexual prowess (Majors, 1990). As in the case of the ex-nomination of the Olympics connection and AIDS, the nomination of the stereotype would have worked against the cultural power of the ad and made placement of the implied reader that much more difficult.

Making Sense of Dream Team Dirt

This analysis of commercials featuring the Dream Team points out that advertisers have a strong working knowledge of cultural anthropologist Edmund Leach's (1976) observation "that power is located in dirt" (p. 62). The collection of Dream Team commercials is rich with the workings of sports dirt. A triad of nationalism, youth sports dreams, and sports heroism interact in most of the texts to characterize or position the reader.

Nationalism, of course, is a long-standing centerpiece of the American sports creed (Edwards, 1973). As we can see from these commercials, the characterization of the Dream Team as troops fighting the Russians and "dreaded Italians" and as emblematic of the strong personal defense we need in using credit cards in foreign countries, play off of idealized connections between sport and national character. Implied readers and characterized textual surrogates are shown as patriots, waving flags, supporting the team as troops going to battle, embracing them as our team, and celebrating team members expectantly, as foregone (competitive) war heroes.

Youth sport dreams encapsulate the widespread social belief that there is a strong correspondence between sport participation and social mobility. This, of course, is a finding that is highly questioned in the sociology of sport literature (see Braddock, 1981; Nixon, 1984). Yet the four commercials placed in this analytic category explicitly position the reader as accepting the basic tenets of this belief. Other ads, such as Converse's fairy tale and Skybox's "Magic of Cards" also employ logics derivative of this assumption. These commercials play a role in positioning the reader to embrace a cultural belief that is at odds with what seems to be actually happening. Because marketing plays on cultural desires rather than perplexing fact, this should come as no great surprise.

The last category of commercials relies on the dirty power of the sports hero to function as a positive role model. The cultural power of sports heroes is derivative of the notion that sports builds character and that those who succeed in sports are those with the most desirable traits. Related to the myth of sport and social mobility, this notion also flies in the face of most research in sport sociology. The character that is built in sport, with its increasing focus on winning, may often be dysfunctional (see Sage, 1988). Much of the positive light that is cast on sports heroes comes from the "halo effect," extrapolating from the athletes' sport success that they are more broad-based heroes (Coakley, 1990).

In the case of these commercials, all of Klapp's (1962) five categories of heroes are enlisted. Both directly addressed implied readers and textual surrogates are cast as appreciative of sports heroes as winners, splendid performers, heroes of social acceptability, independent spirits, and group servants. Using Dream Teamers as winners, splendid performers, and independent spirits provides the core dirt in all the ads. That this is assumed by the reader also establishes our baseline reading position.

In that all of the featured heroes in the ads—Magic Johnson, Michael Jordan, Scottie Pippen, and David Robinson—are Black, they are necessarily being used as heroes of social acceptability. In a society with so few Black role models outside the sports world, characterized White readers can be more easily positioned to accept these cases as extraordinary success stories of people who have heroically fought the odds. Thus these heroes can be read as legitimate purveyors of social acceptability for Whites as well as for the minority community. Thus readers can be comfortable with these athletes breaking small but critical social acceptability rules in these commercials. The heroic David Robinson can don clownish clothes in a pitch to children, Michael Jordan can go public about the "definite" reasons for his red, white, and blue underwear, and Magic Johnson can be a role model for adults who wish to engage in the fantasies of trading cards.

Finally, it is important to recognize the positioning of the Dream Team members and the team itself as group servants. Very likely lurking beneath all of the readings of the Dream Team is the notion of the reader being aware of the team's Olympic effort being altruistic public service. It is well known to the reader that these are well-paid professionals who do not have to play in the Olympic Games for fame or fortune. Knowing this, it is likely that the reader grants some indenture for this service.

Nationalistic sports dirt, youth sports dream dirt, and sports hero dirt are all pervasive in the interpretive structures that readers bring to both the Dream Team and the commercials featuring its members. Most typically, given the sympathies of the sports fan, they may be enlisted in preferred readings. Occasionally, oppositional readings may be seized by readers attempting to make sense of intrusions into the Dream Team world. Thus knowledge about Magic Johnson's HIV infection or Michael Jordan's bouts with gambling may affect the ability of advertisers to position readers. Even with such opportunities, it can be seen that three types of Dream Team dirt interact in ways to answer questions about how the reader is cast in the wider world of sports dirt.

Where Is the Reader in the Sport Dirtied Text?

Most cultural studies theorists argue for the inherent openness or "polysemic" nature of the television text (Fiske, 1987). Savvy scholars demand that texts be seen in terms of all of their "activations" (Bennett, 1982). This reader-oriented analysis of Dream Team dirt suggests that the reader is routinely characterized in a variety of ways. If one cannot be the child in reading the Converse fairy tale ad, one can be the parent. If one is uncomfortable with being cast in the AT&T Scottie Pippen spot as patriot, we are offered alternative reading positions as voyeurs of nostalgia or privileged spectators of private friendship. The variant ways one can "be like Mike" is itself an open text.

Similarly, there are a myriad of textual surrogates offered in these Dream Team ads. Pepsi's "We Believe in Magic" spot and Gatorade's "Be Like Mike" spot offer literally hundreds of textual surrogates as opportunities to see ourselves and take comfort in the implied reading positions. Most important, the variety of textual surrogates provides opportunities for readers to see themselves in social roles in relation to these products. Of course, it is this relationship that works ultimately to contain the preferred reading position to consumer roles.

It is important to not mix up options with any inherent openness of these texts. Options, as to reading position or to one's textual surrogate, should not be confused with fuel for oppositional readings. Whereas options may facilitate multiple reading positions, the strategies employed do not cultivate oppositional reading positions. The offering of multiple reader positions does not rule out oppositional readings but, rather, reduces the likelihood of having to resort to seeking them out. If the green grass is in the near proximity, one need not go to an unfamiliar field where there is work to be done in establishing a position for interpretation. This is the inherent pleasure of sports dirt, and sports fans revel in rolling around in it (Wenner, 1990, 1991). With its archetypes of heroism in a rational world where hard work makes for success, the reader who has engaged in mediated sport as pleasure is far more likely to choose a reading position offered from the advertiser's pleasing but limited menu than to impose a special order on the sports chef.

Still, one can reach outside and off the menu. To what degree this is done cannot be answered by this study. People have variant defenses to commercials. And intertextuality with other social texts affects reading position. Advertiser try to avoid this by limiting our options. We must nominate AIDS in the interpretation of Magic Johnson, Pepsi, and Skybox. We must nominate gambling in our making sense of "Be Like Mike." How, and to what extent, this is done is beyond the purview of this study. Ethnographic study of the reading process can complement the foundational understandings about the positioning of the reader suggested in this analysis.

What Kind of Society Does the Characterized Reader Live In?

In Dream Team dirtied commercials, the implied reader and the characterized textual surrogate live in a multicultural but nationalistic society. Nationalism is explicit in the reader's characterized world not only in the two ads featuring nationalistic dirt but in three of the four youth sports dream ads that feature explicit nationalistic positioning. Only in Gatorade's generic "Be Like Mike" ad is nationalism not part of the reading position. All of the sports hero dirtied ads offer nationalism as a context for reading. It is most dominant in the Visa, Pepsi, and Kellogg's Corn Flakes ads, but it can even be seen as the interpretive frame for Michael Jordan's red, white, and blue Hanes underwear.

Multiculturalism in the reader's domain is a slightly more tricky issue. Stereotypically, multiculturalism is evoked in ads offering a wide variety of textual surrogates. Here the wide world of support for Magic by Pepsi and the "we" we see in Gatorade's "Be Like Mike" are archetypal. Converse similarly positions a multicultural audience of children for its fairy tale of U.S. domination. Ads such as these, featuring cheerfully coexisting multicultural faces in the crowd, risk calling attention to themselves with their sprinkling of self-conscious but politically correct multiculturalism. So contrived are they and so at odds are they with the prejudices and segregation of American society that they risk disruption of the suspension of disbelief necessary for the ad to work. The incredulity may evoke a resistant reading to the advertiser's advance. Still, the cultural ideal rings true, even though the construction of it may not.

Some advertisers, such as McDonald's, belly flop with multiculturalism in other ways not likely to be as evident to the reader. In McDonald's multicultural America, "we" are the patriotic middle-aged middle-class White family. Blacks are players, like Dream Teamer Malone, who mirror our characterized patriotism. Our characterized hero, however, is Larry Bird, whose shot brings the championship basket. Youth sports dreams are seen for the young Black boy, who McDonald's positions as needing help to make his "Olympic Dreams Come True." This paternalistic stance, under the guise of multiculturalism, reinforces some very problematic stereotypes. Beyond the stereotyping of the White hero, the more serious issues lie with the subtext of throwing money at the "Black problem" and reifying the dysfunctional path of sports as an efficient agency of social mobility for Blacks.

The issue of race causes interactions with reading position in other ways. Cultural myths of the Black male's sexual prowess (Majors, 1990) interact with the implied reading position in the Michael Jordan Hanes underwear ad and are added to the frame of AIDS infection in making sense of the spots featuring Magic Johnson. These issues are not nominated in these ads. AIDS is thoroughly avoided. Sexual prowess, while suggested in the Hanes ad, attempts to nominate the underwear more than the individual wearing them. Race-related dirt also interacts with the reading position in Kellogg's David Robinson spot. The casting of Robinson as comedic buffoon is perched on the edge of a backward-looking stereotype and a forward-looking humor that recognizes the stereotype by daring to go beyond it in an equal opportunity kind of way. The way the issue is raised gives the reader much room to maneuver.

The self-conscious nomination of multiculturalism and race helps mask the way gender interacts with reading position. In six of the ads, women are absent. Here, the texts ex-nominate men as having power in the natural order of sport. To read but not oppose these ads implicates such a worldview. In the AT&T/Pippen, Champion, and McDonald's youth sport dream ads, the dream is projected for a young boy. Women populate the multicultural mix of Pepsi's "Believe in Magic" ad and Gatorade's "Be Like Mike" ad. In the Pepsi ad, women as textual surrogates are merely supportive. In the Gatorade ad, women are actually shown competing successfully against men on the court. Even though completely in the shadow of Mike, this is as active as women get in this series of ads. In Converse's fairy tale, young girls are the most scared by the story of U.S. domination. In the McDonald's ad, the woman's role is a patriotic and traditionally supportive wife. In the Hanes underwear ad, the men talk about the powers of underwear (sex), with women positioned as goals to be scored. On a positive note, the woman's textual surrogate is actively complicit in the sexual transaction, even though the transaction is defined by men.

How Does Sport Fit into the Characterized Reader's Society?

Last, these Dream Team commercials help answer questions about how sport fits into the characterized reader's society. The categories of youth sports dream dirt and sports hero dirt address this question most directly. Here we get a very steady picture of the characterized reader. Both through directly addressing the implied reader and characterizing the textual surrogate, the reading position entails that sport promotes social mobility, that individualism and teamwork are both to be valued, that athletes provide good role models, that the power of the athletic hero or team may be transmitted through a product, and that sport is best seen as a spectacle.

As considered earlier, the sport and social mobility nexus dominates the reading position of the youth sports dream ads and is implied in most others. The emphasis in this nexus is on individualism—on transcendence through winning to become a star. This serves to give teamwork a more limited range as a value in characterized reading positions. Teamwork most dominates the reading position when we see the Dream Team members as soldiers on "our" team. Thus the two nationalism ads and the Visa ad, where the team functions as an emblem of Visa's strong defense, include us on the team. Here, teamwork is inclusive for the reader, and we are implored to take on the values of the team. In less nationalistic settings, teamwork is seen in a different light. In Champion's youth sports dream, the team helps the young boy become the hero who scores the winning basket. In the Pippen AT&T youth dream, teamwork is more personal, transformed into lifelong friendship. In the "Magic of Skybox" ad, teamwork is merely a necessary function of team sports, where teams are composed of individuals who can be freely traded in an open market.

The reader is further positioned to appreciate the power of individualism by assuming the value of athletes as positive role models. As suggested earlier, the wide range of Klapp's (1962) five types of heroes can be seen in this limited sample of Dream Team commercials. This naturalization of such multifaceted heroism is what allows the transference of power from athlete to a wide range of products. Only in the institutional identity ads by AT&T, McDonald's, and Pepsi are there no attempts to make this transfer specifically to their products in the telecommunications, fast food, or soft drink marketplaces. Yet in all these commercials the characterized reader is positioned to accept the transfer of power. It may be close to sport, such as athletic clothing, shoes, sports drinks, or trading cards, or more far flung, bringing power to credit cards or underwear, or it may be the power to relax and feel good about a multinational corporation. In a society where heroes are decidedly hard to find, a wide range of power has been fabricated and granted to sports dirt. In these ads, reading positions are characterized as accepting that broad range of power.

The final lesson about reading position that can be extracted from these Dream Team commercials concerns the naturalization of seeing sport as spectacle.

Commercials, of course, have no life apart from being spectacles. They are there to bring products to spectators. To use Stone's (1955) notion about sport, they are there to put products on "dis-play." It is not surprising in such an environment that the reader's essential interpretive frame for sport in its modern commercialized, televised forms depends on seeing it as spectacle. In the specific case, the Dream Team was the spectacle that overtook the Olympic spectacle. As DeFord (1992, p. 27) put it, the Summer Olympics were presented to us as

MICHAEL JORDAN
LARRY BIRD
MAGIC JOHNSON
in
THE DREAM TEAM GOES
TO BARCELONA
Also starring
Track and Field
Swimming
Boxing
Boris Becker and
Some Other Foreigners[1]

With this as a backdrop for the reader's interpretive frame, it is difficult not to see sport as spectacle. The Dream Teamers were megastars. They were already winners and champions before they graced the Olympics. They had transcended outcome, a key element in commercialized sport as it moves to spectacle (Coakley, 1990). The Dream Team commercials reinforce this. The individual exploits and team traits are cast to be in our service. Because the athletes don't need to be there for the fame and fortune, we feel good about them. Our textual surrogates cheer them. Our children are shown as wanting to be like them. Even corporations are shown cheering their presence by facilitating more Olympic dreams. Our reading positions entail all of this. But in reality, much of how we got there is based on dirty connections to sport, social mobility, and the wide range of power we have granted to sports heroes. But isn't that really what sport is all about?

NOTES

1. From *Newsweek,* (July 6). © 1992, Newsweek, Inc. All rights reserved. Printed with permission.

REFERENCES

Allen, R. C. (1987). Reader-oriented criticism and television. In *Channels of discourse: Television and contemporary criticism* (pp. 74–112). Chapel Hill: University of North Carolina Press.

Allen, R. C. (1992). Audience-oriented criticism and television. In *Channels of discourse, reassembled: Television and contemporary criticism* (2nd ed., pp. 101–137). Chapel Hill: University of North Carolina Press.

Barthes, R. (1973). *Mythologies*. London: Paladin.

Beckett, J. (1992, July 15). Struggle over Olympic ads heats up. *San Francisco Chronicle*, pp. B1, B3.

Bennett, T. (1982). Text and social process: The case of James Bond. *Screen Education, 41*, 3–15.

Braddock, J. H. (1981). Race, athletics, and educational attainment. *Youth & Society, 12*, 335–350.

Coakley, J. J. (1990). *Sport in society: Issues and controversies* (4th ed.). St. Louis: Times-Mirror/Mosby.

DeFord, F. (1992, July 6). Team of dreams. *Newsweek, 26–28*.

Edwards, H. (1973). *Sociology of sport*. Homewood, IL: Dorsey Press.

Elliott, S. (1992, August 6). A top event: NBC's dash for the ads. *The New York Times*, p. C1.

Fish, S. (1980). *Is there a text in this class? The authority of interpretive communities*. Cambridge, MA: Harvard University Press.

Fiske, J. (1987). *Television culture*. London: Methuen.

Hall, S. (1980). Encoding/decoding. In S. Hall, D. Hobson, A. Lowe, & P. Willis (Eds.), *Culture, media, language* (pp. 128–138). London: Hutchinson.

Hartley, J. (1984). Encouraging signs: TV and the power of dirt, speech, and scandalous categories. In W. Rowland & B. Watkins (Eds.), *Interpreting television: Current research perspectives* (pp. 119–141). Beverly Hills, CA: Sage.

Hewitt, J. (1992). Building media empires. In A. A. Berger (Ed.), *Media USA* (2nd ed., pp. 395–403). New York: Longman.

Howell, J. (1991). "A revolution in motion": Advertising and the politics of nostalgia. *Sociology of Sport Journal, 8*, 258–271.

King, S. (1992, August 9). Dream team: Just another horror show. *The New York Times*, Sec. 1, p. 29.

Klapp, O. E. (1962). *Heroes, villains, and fools*. Englewood Cliffs, NJ: Prentice-Hall.

Leach, E. (1976). *Culture and communication*. Cambridge, England: Cambridge University Press.

Majors, R. (1990). Cool pose: Black masculinity and sports. In M. A. Messner & D. F. Sabo (Eds.), *Sport, men and the gender order: Critical feminist perspectives* (pp. 109–114). Champaign, IL: Human Kinetics.

Marinucci, C. (1992, July 26). Olympics: Pinnacle of hype, hard-sell. *San Francisco Examiner*, pp. E1, E4.

Nixon, H. L. (1984). *Sport and the American dream*. Champaign, IL: Leisure Press.

O'Connor, J. J. (1992, February 13). These Olympic Games are brought to you by . . . . *The News York Times*, pp. B1, B6.

Sage, G. H. (1988). Sports participation as a builder of character? *The World & I, 3*, 629–641.

Stone, G. (1955). American sports: Play and display. *Chicago Review, 9*, 83–100.

Suleiman, S. (1980). Introduction: Varieties of audience-oriented criticism. In S. Suleiman & I. Crosman (Eds.), *The reader in the text* (pp. 3–45). Princeton, NJ: Princeton University Press.

Wenner, L. A. (1989). The Super Bowl pregame show: Cultural fantasies and political subtext. In L. A. Wenner (Ed.), *Media, sports, and society* (pp. 157–179). Newbury Park, CA: Sage.

Wenner, L. A. (1990). Therapeutic engagement in mediated sports. In G. Gumpert & S. L. Fish (Eds.), *Talking to strangers: Mediated therapeutic communication* (pp. 221–242). Norwood, NJ: Ablex.

Wenner, L. A. (1991). One part alcohol, one part sport, one part dirt, stir gently: Beer commercials and television sports. In L. R. Vande Berg & L. A. Wenner (Eds.), *Television criticism: Approaches and applications* (pp. 388–407). New York: Longman.

COPS and the Comic Frame: Humor and Meaning-Making in Reality-Based Television

Glenn C. Geiser-Getz

Although many critics have rebuked reality-based television programming as exploitive, cheap, tasteless, sensationalistic, tabloid television ("Cheers 'n' Jeers," 1992, p. 6; Saynor, 1990, p. 46; Waters, 1992, p. 60), many viewers appear to receive pleasure from this form of vernacular culture. Reality-based programming is defined here as television stories based on the characters, conflict, and drama of actual events. This definition references a variety of television programs, including the nightly newscast and news magazines such as *60 Minutes*. In this essay I focus on reality-based shows that explore relationships between police, publics, criminals, and victims, such as *America's Most Wanted*, *COPS*, and *I Witness Video*. The ratings received by these and other shows, as well as their recurring presence in television schedules, demonstrate that a great many viewers watch such programs (Getz, 1994). Although "Why is a program popular?" is not the only important question to ask, it is a useful starting point for exploring audience pleasures and interpretations. The puzzles of meaning and pleasure prompt scholars to consider how diverse audiences enjoy and understand popular media texts in different ways, bringing various experiences, perspectives, intertexts, and socioeconomic positions to bear in the creative viewing process.

In this study I use ethnographic methods to better understand how a college fan audience of the reality-based television program *COPS* experiences the text, receives pleasure from that experience, and interprets messages about the police, the public, and the city. Although this is not intended as a widely generalizable effort, as a case study it will be useful in theorizing how other fan audiences might respond to the texts of popular culture. The most important data for this project are what have been called tertiary texts. Fiske explains that these are discourses constructed by viewers in response to primary and secondary texts:

> These are the texts that the viewers make themselves out of their responses, which circulate orally or in letters to the press, and which work to form a collective rather than an individual response. (1987, p. 124)

Tertiary texts can include published letters, opinion polls, conversation, gossip, and multiple other forms of private or public communication.

The collective character of the tertiary text is important to consider because such texts express a group's rather than an individual's response to experience. Tertiary texts are social. In studying the tertiary, then, we can improve our grasp of an audience's group identity and culture. Audiences are social groups that interact with cultural environments to construct identities and satisfy needs and desires through the creation of meaning. Quoting Pollock in his *Nationwide* study, Morley maintains that tertiary texts are a social phenomenon:

> [It is a mistake] to think of every individual as a monad, whose opinions crystallize and take on permanent existence in isolation, in a vacuum as it were. Realistic opinion research [has] to come as close as possible in its methods of research to those conditions in which actual opinions are formed, held and modified. (Pollock, 1976, p. 229)

From this perspective, focusing on individuals "divorced from their social context" is an inappropriate way to engage responses to television because people interpret media texts through a highly social and discursive process that involves, among other things, conflict, disagreement, and argument. Due in part to the cultural character of the tertiary text, then, ethnographic studies increase our understanding of how communities of viewers read and circulate primary and secondary texts and through that collective process construct meaning in unique—and uniquely social—ways (Fiske, 1987, p. 124). Many significant studies of television have examined the audiences of television by analyzing tertiary texts, including Ang's study of letters written by *Dallas* fans (1985), Morley's study of interviews with *Nationwide* viewers (1980), and Jenkins' study of stories produced by *Star Trek* fans in fanzines (1988). The general approach (of which these three are diverse representatives) is discussed more fully elsewhere in this book, so I will now turn to the specific study in question.

Method

To prepare for this study I first conducted a series of pilot studies in which groups of 10 to 15 undergraduate college students completed surveys, viewed episodes of reality-based programs, and responded to discussion questions. Although the surveys were helpful in gathering basic demographic details, I found them most useful as stimuli for discussion; subjects began to contemplate their favorite shows, viewing habits, and attitudes toward reality-based television as a result of the surveys. The pilot studies demonstrated that studying reality-based television fans would be more productive than examining more general groups of television viewers. The more inclusive viewing groups inevitably included students who either had never watched reality-based programs or had no opinion about them. Fan audiences, on the other hand, engaged the texts of reality-based television with great creativity, thought, and planning. They also—as a group—had more to say in response to questions concerning their reception of the shows than the more general viewing groups.

After processing the pilot studies, I interviewed three groups of eight or nine undergraduate students at a large midwestern state university. As mostly communication majors, these students were highly aware of the encoding techniques used by television producers and advertisers. Some of the students had worked in the television news industry. All had volunteered for the study and reported in advance that they were fans or regular viewers of reality-based television. Although data on the audiences of reality-based programming are limited, such shows are popular among younger demographic groups, people who have not completed a college education (Times Mirror, 1993). Although they may not be the largest audience, undergraduates represent a significant viewing group for reality-based programming.

Each of the groups met for a two-hour interview in which I first stated the purpose of the study—to better understand a group of television programs that focuses on images of emergencies, crime, and law enforcement using videotape of actual and re-enacted events—then distributed a questionnaire to gather information on demographics, television viewing habits, and preferences for reality-based and non-reality-based television programs. After administering the surveys I answered their questions about the research and asked a few pre-viewing questions to get them to focus on the topic of the study. This pre-viewing discussion took approximately fifteen minutes. I showed each group a 30-minute videotape of an episode of *COPS* broadcast March 5, 1994, on Fox affiliate KOCR (Cedar Rapids, IA) from 8:00 to 8:30 p.m. EST.

I chose this particular reality-based program because of its popularity, prominence, basic themes, documentary format, and openness. It is one of the most successful and longest running of the reality-based programs, especially of the video vérité subgenre noted by viewers in the pilot studies. At the time of the study, *COPS* was not only shown weekly on a major network during prime time, but was also in syndication, opening up additional time slots in station schedules across the country. The show was broadcast on Fox twice each Saturday night at 8:00 and 8:30 EST. *COPS* deals exclusively with justice themes that constitute the primary subject matter of reality-based television programming. The images of *COPS* are strikingly similar to documentary and news footage. Grainy videotape, low light levels, shaky hand-held camerawork, quick pans and zooms, blurry images, and heavy use of ambient sound make for a confusing but powerful news-like mix. The show lacks a host, narration, and the obvious presence of camera operators or other creators. Like the documentaries of Frederick Wiseman, *COPS* hides the means of its own production. This makes the program especially critical for analysis because viewers may ascribe a greater degree of realism to the text.

COPS also lacks many of the framing devices of other reality-based programs; there are no celebrity hosts providing omnipotent narration, no ethos-charged anchor desks, no re-enactments, no melodramatic musical score, etc. Although there are certainly other framing devices in *COPS*, such as the dialogue of the officers involved, compared to other examples of the genre this show seems a more open text. As such, it may be the most useful for examining diverse viewer pleasures and interpretations because the narrative structures are more "producerly," more flexible to multiple readings (Fiske, 1987, p. 95). Curious about the intertextual influence of advertisements and public service announcements that were part of the recording, I chose not to edit the *COPS* videotape when I played it for the subjects in the study.

Episode

Due to the narrative consistency of *COPS*, almost any episode is appropriate for examination. Each of the 2–3 segments that comprise a half-hour episode begins with an officer commenting on police work and ends with the same officer discussing events that have just occurred. Each of the segments takes place after sunset in the poorer sections of a metropolitan U.S. city. Although some of the starring officers are Hispanic and some are female, most are white males. Most of the suspects who are arrested in *COPS*, on the other hand, are minorities (African Americans and Hispanics). The crimes covered are blue-collar, occur at night, and usually involve damage to property or person, such as burglary and assault.

The first segment of the episode I chose begins with an Hispanic officer in his patrol car talking about the city's teenage paint inhalation problem. Teens have been purchasing cans of gold or silver paint to get high by inhaling the fumes after spraying it on a sock or rag. The officer's monologue is interrupted by a radio call, and from the perspective of the patrol car one can see a drugstore's broken front window. At least two other police officers are led by the first officer into the store. A police dog, brought to locate the suspect among the many aisles of shampoo, batteries, pain killers, electronic equipment, and other products quickly finds a teenage Hispanic male hiding under a bench.

The officer, speaking alternately to the boy in Spanish and English, handcuffs the boy and begins to question him. The inarticulate, mumbling boy denies having inhaled paint, even after the officer points with the beam from his flashlight to silver stains on the boy's nose, mouth, and hands. The officer also points to cuts on the youth's hands and arms, suggesting that the suspect had broken the window to enter the store. When the boy finally admits having inhaled, he claims it the first time he has done so. Two other officers find a white garbage bag full of products that the boy may have collected after breaking into the building. The segment ends with two of the police (one of them the officer I described earlier) walking away from the drugstore and talking about how inhaling paint makes young people not care about pain or anything else. As is common in *COPS*, the story ends with officers talking and the show's logo, which spells out the title of the show.

After a fade to black and a sequence of commercials, the second segment begins, again with the logo and an officer's voice. As the image fades in, one can see two officers on their nightly patrol discussing the liabilities involved in law enforcement. One of the officers complains about the great care he must exercise when applying handcuffs so as to avoid police brutality suits. The other officer nods in agreement when their conversation is ended abruptly by a call from the dispatcher. We do not hear the entire call and the officer who is driving explains that there is a gang fight in a nearby alley where people are attacking each other with knives and bats.

The officers turn into an apartment complex, get out of their car, and run toward a group of officers and civilians. Most of this segment involves police attempting to extract an explanation from a large, intoxicated male Caucasian with a heavy southern accent and a torn shirt. The man is out of breath and has a large cut on his nose that, as he later explains, resulted from another man hitting him in the face with a shovel. After searching the injured man and convincing him (with some difficulty) to press charges, the police knock on a nearby apartment door, arrest the Hispanic man who admits having committed the assault, and deposit him in a waiting patrol car. After the arrest, officers talk with the injured man and two other people, a young man and woman, and ask that they please call the police before getting involved in any future fights. The injured man, stuttering and repeating himself, points to his nose and complains about the shovel attack, then tells the police he plans to buy a gun to protect his "little girl." He points to a female companion, whose voice can be heard but whose face has been blurred from view by the program's producers, indicating she has not signed the release that allows her face to be broadcast. The episode ends with the two (now amused) officers noting that the complainant (the injured man) was intoxicated, belligerent, and probably deserved what he got. Still, they advise, one must not go over the edge when defending oneself.

The third segment of the show begins in a similar fashion. An officer driving in a patrol car explains that someone has called to report an assault and that he is currently looking for the address. Normally, according to the officer, such complaints are rarely answered because the caller does not show up to meet with police. Several people along the street wave down the patrol car and the officer gives their address to the dispatcher. An Hispanic woman, her husband, and their three children (two male, one female) explain to the officers that they have been attacked by the landlords while trying to get into their apartment. The officers clean and bandage several cuts on the man and woman, then speak with a female witness who supports the story.

When two of the officers confront the landlord with the family's accusations, he claims he was defending his wife against their unprovoked attacks. Both groups decide to press charges, so the police officers arrest all the adults involved and decide to take the children to the Human Services Department for care until their parents are released. The three children watch with great alarm as their mother and father are handcuffed and placed in police cars. All the children cry and scream, even as police attempt to calm them and explain the situation. This final segment ends with two officers complaining about how the kids will always have a bad impression of the police because of this incident. Closing credits follow.

Surveys

The three groups were surprisingly consistent, with similar statements made about the program in each case, so I will analyze just one group here. It included one woman (age 27) and eight men (ages 19, 19, 20, 21, 22, 22, 22, and 23). Although the responses of this viewing group may not be representative of the entire reality-based television audience, they can provide critical insights into how groups of fan viewers experience and interpret television. Before analyzing the interview results, however, a brief examination of the pre-viewing surveys will complete my description of this fan audience.

The surveys contained surprisingly detailed responses about viewers' previous contacts with and opinions on reality-based television. *COPS* was a special favorite for these viewers. It appeared twice in lists of students' favorite television shows of all time; no other reality-based shows appeared in such lists. Of the seven viewers (out of nine) who named it as their favorite reality-based program, five reported watching four to six times each month, and two reported watching seven to nine times each month. The only female viewer in the group named *Unsolved Mysteries* as her favorite reality show, and one of the male viewers named *Highway Patrol.*

COPS was described in the surveys as a "grittier" reality-based show, partly because of the absence of re-enactments. Students wrote that they appreciated the realism of the program in particular. One viewer highlighted the realistic violence in his response:

Viewer 9: It shows live, taped footage. We can see actual crimes and cut through all the fake Hollywood portrayal of law enforcement. If I see blood, for example, it "hits home" more and causes some sensitive reaction, because I know it's real blood, not just special effects.

The distinction that this viewer makes between the "fake Hollywood portrayal" and the "real" portrayals of *COPS* becomes significant later in the interviews. For most of these viewers, the realistic violence of *COPS* has a greater emotional impact than that of a film such as *Lethal Weapon* (several subjects used this film for comparisons). In other references to realism, viewers report that they enjoy stories about real people who "struggle to survive" and indicate that they think *COPS* "shows the real aspects behind the police force." Another viewer writes he is interested in "seeing police work in action" because he has relatives in law enforcement and feels a special connection with the officers of *COPS*.

The ability of *COPS* to inform or educate arises in several survey responses. Viewers claim they watch this "informative" program because it shows how police officers treat suspects, illustrates "what not to do" in criminal situations, and communicates important legal data:

Viewer 2: A better knowledge of some commonly broken laws and what my rights are as a citizen. It also shows real reaction to cops, and what kinds of crooks are really out there.

Another viewer, employed as a camera operator for a local news station, learns from the camera work in the show:

Viewer 5: I have done some on-scene camera work similar to this. I can relate to the police officers and the victims. I like to watch for production values, also to maybe improve my skills.

Humor was one of the most significant pleasures represented in viewer comments about *COPS*. One viewer responds in the survey that he liked seeing "how stupid the people are getting arrested." He explains there is humor in "the criminals' mistakes and watching them trying to get out of their trash by lying." Another viewer uses the phrase "comic relief" to describe *COPS*. This viewer seems to concur with that interpretation:

Viewer 5: I think that the camera work and how "real" or poor it is, has an impact on why I watch. It's also humorous to see people get busted and their reaction. The slanted view, i.e., the cops always gets some sort of victory, no matter what.

COPS also seems to satisfy "some kind of natural curiosity about criminals and criminal activity," according to the viewers. One student wrote it was "interesting to see the behavior of people in extreme situations" while another indicated the show "gives the viewer an artificial adrenaline rush." The pleasure of voyeurism, of seeing without being seen, is highlighted in the following comment from another student viewer:

Viewer 7: I think it's very interesting to see how we deal with the horror that occurs on city streets. The police have **really** tough jobs and I enjoy watching what they do . . . especially when I am in no danger.

The surveys helped stimulate thought about reality-based television among the subjects prior to viewing, but they also helped identify themes that developed further in the group interviews.

Interviews

Following the viewing of the videotape, I led a 30-minute discussion that focused on the episode specifically, although the relatively open conversations sometimes moved to discussion of other shows and reality-based programming in general. I designed a schedule of questions for the group interview but did not use all or even most of them (see Appendix I). Asking "What did you think?" often triggered a chain of responses that did not necessitate my use of additional questions. The subjects were extremely active in their discussion of the *COPS* episode and almost without exception had firm opinions about it and other reality-based shows. Sometimes the interview lost focus and I had to guide the conversation back to issues identified in my schedule of questions. I began the post-viewing discussion by asking for general reactions to the episode; most group members interpreted this as inquiring about their liking or disliking of the episode. After a few comments from the group, I progressed from more general, open-ended queries to specific questions in several areas.

I audio-recorded both pre- and post-viewing discussions and took handwritten notes during both interviews, later typing the notes and transcribing the audiotapes. These notes and transcripts became the tertiary texts for analysis. Because of the frequency of interruptions during the group discussion, I sometimes had difficulty transcribing brief moments of overlapping discussion. Subjects regularly completed each other's sentences and often communicated statements of disagreement or (more often) agreement while others were talking. It seems important to note that these interruptions existed, because they indicated the group was communicating with great energy and spontaneity. For the most part I interpreted the interruptions as indicating a group bonding or collective agreement in response to various aspects of the *COPS* episode. Another example of this phenomenon is that group members who agreed strongly with something often seemed unwilling to wait to state their agreement and instead blurted out their thoughts in the moment. Although this agreement may have been due to a concern for the liking of peers, a more reasonable explanation could be what reader-response critics such as Stanley Fish argue, that interpretations are formed in communities of viewers who use communication to reach agreement about their perceptions (Fish, 1980). Interestingly, the college student fans seemed intent on eventual agreement. Although they disagreed often, the subjects dealt with those disagreements in subtle ways, either by expressing disagreement while simultaneously complimenting what a previous viewer had said or by stating a disagreement as if it were a statement of agreement, sometimes accompanied by regular and rapid nodding.

The dominance of males in the viewing group may have influenced the results. While information on viewers of reality-based programming is scarce, generally such shows are thought to be more popular among males. Programs that focus on crimes (such as *COPS* and *America's Most Wanted*) are particularly popular for this audience. Female viewers seem to prefer re-enactment programs such as *Unsolved Mysteries*, which in addition to NBC play is also aired on Lifetime, a cable network that caters to a largely female market. These factors may help to explain why women interviewed for the study were generally less familiar with *COPS*, while men interviewed were very familiar with the show, a few even describing themselves as "diehard fans."

As Ang notes in her analysis of fan letters about *Dallas,* drawing conclusions from viewer responses is not simply a matter of reporting audience documents at face value. Viewers are unaccustomed to discussing how they receive pleasure from televisual texts or what kinds of interpretations they create in their viewing. Ang explains:

> [T]he ideas of each of the letter-writers . . . cannot be regarded as a direct expression of their "motives" or "reasons" for watching *Dallas*. They can at most be regarded as indications or symptoms of deeper psychological incentives and orientations. (1985, p. 26)

This, Ang argues, necessitates that the critic analyze viewer responses and subject them to a "symptomatic reading," done in her study to identify "the pleasure of *Dallas* that rises above the individual level" (1985, p. 26). Similarly, in my examination of reality-based television I look at audience responses as a text. The import and meaning of this text, like any text, become clearer as I uncover patterns and "look behind" audience comments about their television viewing.

Analysis

I analyze the responses of the viewing group with two principal questions in mind: (1) What pleasures do viewers receive through their viewing of the program? and (2) What interpretations do viewers construct from the program? I first look at terms and concepts that surface repeatedly in the audience responses, examining those that viewers defined in similar and in different ways. For example, I examine references to humor in their responses to better understand their common meaning for humor and their pleasures gained from it. I also investigate the interaction as argument, studying how audience members made claims, offered evidence, asked for the support of other viewers, and employed argumentative strategies (e.g., argument by example and argument by analogy). As Fiske notes, tertiary texts not only represent an audience's response to a program, but also influence meaning construction in future viewing. The responses are "read back into" (Fiske, 1987, p. 125) a given program and activate meanings in specific ways. The argumentative aspects of the discussion seem especially important in this regard, because viewers sometimes attempt to persuade others to accept or reject particular interpretations or valuations. Viewing groups can also use discussion as a form of argument to decide upon a particular interpretation. By making claims, considering the claims of others, and debating about evidence, the group can form a collective response to a particular show that then stays with each of the individuals as he or she experiences future television texts.

Ingredients of a "Good Story"

In this tertiary analysis I examine several categories of viewing group responses that occurred throughout the interviews. Although a complete analysis of these tertiary texts will not be possible here, I will shed some light on the reality-based television phenomenon and the practices of fan audiences by examining one aspect of the interviews: the many references to comedy and humor made by fan viewers.

Although one can learn much from a study of the preferred meanings of a televisual text such as *COPS*, the popularity question always depends upon how viewers interpret a program. One surprising conclusion here is that the audience experienced the ostensibly dire text of *COPS* as a comedy. The college viewers found something laughable in this violent, dark, serious reality program.

When I asked the viewers why they watched *COPS*, their first few comments contained references to humor:

> *Viewer 1:* I find it humorous sometimes. See how stupid some of these criminals are. I mean, there's one where, uh, some guy called the police on this girl. No, a girl called the police on this guy because he didn't give her her money back from buying drugs. And she told the cops that. They're like, "Well, you're under arrest too." She couldn't understand why . . . it was just like, "you're pretty stupid."
>
> *Viewer 2:* To see the reaction of people and in kind of extreme situations 'cause sometimes you don't necessarily automatically side with the cops. I mean, they can be jerks, they can be hassling someone. It depends on the situation and it's humorous and it's just interesting to see the way people will react to kind of extreme events.
>
> *Viewer 5:* I find it humorous to see people busted and see the reaction.

One of the primary pleasures in viewing *COPS*, claimed many of the viewers, was that it was humorous in some way. It made them laugh.

While watching the *COPS* episode, the nine viewers often laughed and smiled at similar points in the narrative. The opening credit sequence, which often previews the stories covered on a particular episode, contained a brief shot of the boy crawling out from his hiding place under the drugstore bench. This prompted a great deal of laughter from the college viewers. Similarly, the police dog used to sniff out the hiding intruder prompted comments like "Look, the dog is going right for the dog food." They laughed at the obvious lie told by the silver-lipped Hispanic boy who denied inhaling paint in the first segment. The intoxicated man hit by the shovel in the second segment of the episode prompted a variety of comments amidst much viewer laughter. One subject, upon observing the man's strange behavior, commented that perhaps the man had been hit too hard. Another suggested he "get some psychiatric help." When the drunk man asked the officer if he needed to do anything to press charges, one viewer said he should "drink some coffee." The man's often repeated line—"the guy hit me in the face with a shovel"—also inspired laughter in the group.

One possible explanation for the laughter could be that college students in group situations perform for each other, creating humor as a result of the context rather than as a characteristic of the text. However, I found strong consistency between the comments on the pre-viewing survey and the comments during the group discussion. Also, through pilot interviews with individual viewers, I found similar references to the humor in *COPS*. It seems unlikely, in this light, that all or even most of the laughter was due to situational factors.

Although most of the viewers found humor in observing the suspects, victims, and bystanders in *COPS*, occasionally the police officers were also subjects of humor. One viewer explained that although *COPS* implies officers are always engaged in exciting pursuits, often they are "driving around doing nothing," to which another viewer responded that they were probably "chewin' on doughnuts." One viewer found the overwhelmingly positive portrayals of the police humorous:

> *Viewer 5:* You gotta love it, every time the cop pulls somebody over you know, even if it's like for a simple speeding ticket you know they find five bags of cocaine in the back and it was their intuition you know and the guy's bumblin' drunk and they gotta beat him up you know and they always win. No matter what. Even when one guy gets away they'll get two. "Well, we'll get him later when we interrogate these guys." It's always, I find it humorous that they always, always win.

The humorous pleasures of the audience would seem to contradict the preferred meaning of *COPS*, which is quite dark. The dominant world of this narrative is a dangerous one in which, as Newcomb says of the mystery story, "men of very limited power clear up individual difficulties" (1974, p. 89). Viewers generally agreed that the show is supposed to be serious, perhaps even depressing, but nevertheless found much to laugh about in its content. One viewer admitted that laughter as a response may violate producer expectations: "I don't think it's intended to be funny, but I think it really is."

Humor functions in many different ways, of course. People sometimes use humor to distance themselves from something that is undesirable or that makes them feel uncomfortable. The humor fans find in *COPS*, then, could be a nervous reaction to the preferred meaning of the text, namely, that our world is a sick place and that we need police officers to protect us from all sorts of degenerates. However, the responses I obtained indicate that something else is probably happening. Viewers hardly seem to be hiding a nagging grief with humor when they laugh repeatedly at the "shovel boy" or the cop who "combs it over." They seem to have constructed something new from the text. They are particularly pleased with the fake explanations constructed by suspects (the more creative the better) and often laugh at such explanations. Fan viewers know that suspects will always be arrested in *COPS* and that the stories never fool the police. These viewers, then, are in a privileged position; like audiences familiar with the conventions and slapstick antics of early stage performers, these viewers are already in on the joke and can enjoy that position of power with the knowledge of what is coming next. They can anticipate the final click of the handcuffs that indicates the suspect story's failure.

Two broad categories of theories of humor may increase our understanding of this phenomenon: psychological and formal (Holland, 1982). Psychological theories of humor, from Freud and others, address the comic response as a function of tension and guilt. People laugh, according to this view, when they feel both attracted to and repulsed by some socially questionable subject. They also laugh as an expression of nervousness when violating (or observing the violation of) social norms of behavior. Fan audiences of *COPS* and similar shows may feel themselves attracted to images of violence, sex, and otherness while simultaneously repulsed by those same things and repulsed by their own attraction. Suspects in *COPS*, usually the target of fan laughter, often break middle class norms of hygiene, dress, behavior, and communication. Finally, fan audiences may laugh in a complicated reaction to simultaneous feelings of sympathy for suspects caught in compromising situations, relief at being distant from the sources of danger involved, and cruel criticism of the suspects as representatives of "difference."

Formal theories of humor, largely derived from studies of literature and the comic, note that laughter is a response to perceived incongruities: (1) within a text, (2) between two or more texts, and (3) between a text and the world of experience. Humor can also, according to this perspective, result from observing a similarity between two things that normally are considered quite different. These ideas can certainly be seen in the study of *COPS*. Within the text, there is an extreme difference or incongruity between portrayals of the police and portrayals of suspects. The fan viewers find suspects humorous in light of this stark contrast. Fan experiences with police officers, crime, and the construction of television news programing (such as Viewer #5, who works at a television station) also mediate perceptions of incongruity that sometimes result in humor. The realism of the text *COPS* breaks down at this point and is revealed as a melodramatic pro-police construction, an obvious fiction aimed at increasing public trust in law enforcement.

Paradoxically, for the college viewers humor functions to simultaneously support and resist the text's preferred meaning. Much of the humor is directed at suspects in *COPS*, who are portrayed as clownish and bizarre. Suspects speak unclearly, are caught on camera in heightened emotional states, are inarticulate, and carry on in various states of filth and undress. If the preferred meaning of the program is to define the police as competent crime-fighters, then these cartoonish portrayals of suspects effectively fit within that purpose. Officers are camera-sensitive, articulate, and gentle when dealing with suspects. The suspects, often caught in uncomfortable or frightening situations, seem ignorant of the camera. They are like simpletons in contrast to the men and women in blue. *COPS* may raise public fears of crime and criminals, but it also seems to dissipate such fears by presenting suspects as incompetent and by promoting the police as the best answer to the dangers brought by undesirable people.

Strangely, however, humor also functions for these viewers as a tool for resisting that same message. Police officers in the program are almost as often the butt of viewer jokes as are suspects. The comic perspective adopted by fan viewers involves an active searching for humor within the text as well as a creative spinning out of humorous stories from without the text. The police are viewed from within this frame as obviously acting for the camera, as pretending to be people they are not. Their politeness is seen by viewers as exaggerated, as a kind of hyperbole that betrays the intentions of the police. Humor, then, not only functions to support the text's preferred messages about crime, but also to resist them by poking fun at the representatives of the status quo, namely, the police.

Conclusions

This analysis helps answer in part the popularity question raised earlier by identifying a significant source of viewer pleasure in reading the *COPS* text as a comedy. Audience pleasures in this study ranged from those that were expected based upon the text's preferred reading (voyeurism, positive portrayals of police, the news-like power of the vérité form) to those that were more unexpected (such as the humorous elements). The comic reading of *COPS* becomes a critical frame through which viewers interpret characters and evaluate those characters' actions, searching for irony, hyperbole, weakness, and error.

Significantly, tertiary texts such as the comments made by this viewing group not only tell us about audience pleasures in and interpretations of media texts. The responses are, as Fiske argues, "read back into the program as a textual activator" (1987, p. 124). The process of constructing meaning is an inherently social phenomenon. It involves interaction, group dynamics, even argument. Comments made by fans during and after viewing function as another intertextual force by privileging certain meanings and dismissing others. This process deserves far more study, but a few additional comments about both tertiary influence and reality-based television seem warranted.

Viewing groups engage in arguments that may have an important influence on the meaning-making processes of individual viewers. Usually the viewers involved in this study sought to maintain harmony by expressing agreement verbally and nonverbally, by telling parallel stories and making similar comments, and by laughing together. These common activities seemingly help people develop a stronger group identity, which then makes the social process of reading even more critical, for as the group becomes stronger these tertiary texts may have a greater impact on the group's interpretive work.

The arguments of the college viewers were restrained, subtle, and brief. These viewers exercised great caution in a group made up largely of strangers. Their arguments drifted into comparing experiences—with the police, with other reality-based television shows, and with television news. One viewer, employed as a camera operator for a local news station, expressed great disgust at the directions taken by news programming toward the techniques typical of reality-based television. Other viewers engaged him in an argument over the relative worth of various journalistic production techniques that ultimately brought their own experiences of television news into the conversation.

Both of these examples illustrate how tertiary texts can have an important impact on the meaning-making processes of viewers. When confronting each other with diverse thoughts and experiences in conversation before, during, and after viewing, audience members attempt to influence each other in a way similar to how producers and reviewers attempt to influence their audiences. Argumentative style may be more significant than one would initially think. These college viewers maintained stable argumentative positions, although at times they seemed to disguise disagreement as agreement, perhaps for the sake of politeness or group cohesion. Other viewing groups, however, might argue differently, and this difference in argumentative style might have an important influence on the meaning-making process. Such differences, for example, could have a considerable impact on how tertiary texts are read into interpretations in distinct ways for older and younger viewers of reality-based programming. Group dynamics could be usefully integrated into this type of study to better understand how variables such as leadership style and gender influence interpersonal argument and the reading process.

Above and beyond other interpretive factors, in this study social and communication forces, such as agreement, commentary, argument, joking, and group laughter, seemed to have the greatest impact on what viewers perceived as important, entertaining, and meaningful in reality-based television programming. Viewing television became more than an act of passive spectatorship that would suggest scholars primarily examine program elements to understand televisual meaning. Viewing television became simultaneously an active performance, one in which fans took in and interpreted images and sounds from the television set, collected the responses of other viewers in the community, and at the same time added their own verbal and nonverbal responses for the benefit of others in the room. Comedy entered this meaning-construction process from various places, including the programs themselves, the interpretations of individual viewers, and the verbal and nonverbal reactions of other viewers in the room over time. The pleasure of television humor here works in a way similar to most jokes; there is pleasure both in the listening and in the telling, both in the reception of comedy and in its performance. Scholars who seek to understand the experiences and interpretations of the diverse viewing groups of American television are likely to miss critical forces if they neglect the power of communication and the social involved in watching television.

While this study has provided a useful examination of the activity of fan audiences when engaging reality-based television texts, much work remains to be done. To begin to grasp the nature of the negotiation process between audiences, cultural texts, and social contexts in the construction of meaning, other audiences need to be included as subjects of study. One larger audience of reality-based programming, for example, are viewers who are low-income, low-education, and non-white. Police officers and inmates constitute other audiences of programs such as *COPS*. Each of these groups arrives at responses to *COPS* and similar reality shows based on very different social environments. By examining each of the groups ethnographically, we can better understand not only this particular text, but the nature of the tertiary and social construction of meaning for the different subcultures that make up television's American audience.

Appendix I

Post-Viewing Questions for Group Interviews

Do you have any general reactions? What did you think?

Did you enjoy the show? Why or why not?

What was the show about?

What are the show's creators trying to accomplish?

Is this a typical episode of *COPS?* Why or why not?

Is this a good example of the show? Why?

What does a "good" *COPS* consist of?

What do you get from it?

How do other shows of this type compare to *COPS?*

How do shows that use re-enactment footage compare with shows that use live footage?

How does this show compare to news programming?

Does this show seem more depressing or more uplifting?

Does this show seem realistic? Why or why not?

What do you think about the portrayals of the police officers/suspects/ victims/bystanders?

Is this how these people act in real life?

Is the show more complimentary or more critical of the police/suspects?

REFERENCES

Ang, I. (1985). *Watching Dallas: Soap opera and the melodramatic imagination.* London: Routledge.

Brummett, B., & Duncan, M. C. (1990). Theorizing without totalizing: Specularity and televised sports. *Quarterly Journal of Speech, 76,* 227–246.

Cheers 'n' Jeers. (1992, March 6). *TV Guide,* 14–20.

De Certeau, M. (1984). *The practice of everyday life.* Berkeley: University of California Press.

Fish, S. (1980). *Is there a text in this class?: The authority of interpretive communities.* Cambridge, MA: Harvard University Press.

Fiske, J. (1987). *Television culture.* London: Routledge.

Getz, G. (1994). The rhetoric of the real: Audience responses to reality-based television. Unpublished doctoral dissertation, University of Iowa.

Holland, N. (1982). *Laughing: A psychology of humor.* Ithaca, NY: Cornell University Press.

Jenkins, H. (1988). *Star Trek* rerun, reread, rewritten: Fan writing as textual poaching. *Critical Studies in Mass Communication, 5,* 85–107.

Jenkins, H. (1992). *Textual poachers: Television fans and participatory culture.* New York: Routledge.

Lacan, J. (1977). *Ecrits* (A. Sheridan, Trans.). New York: Basic.

Morley, D. (1980). *The Nationwide audience: Structure and decoding.* London: British Film Institute.

Newcomb, H. (1974). *TV: The most popular art.* Garden City, NY: Anchor Press.

Pollock, F. (1976). Empirical research into public opinion. In P. Connerton (Ed.), *Critical sociology.* Harmondsworth, Eng: Penguin.

Saynor, J. (1990, February 11). Stop making sense. *The Listener* 46.

Singer, L. (1990). Eye/mind/screen: Toward a phenomenology of cinematic scopophilia. *Quarterly Review of Film and Video, 12* (3), 51–67.

TV violence more objectionable in entertainment than in newscasts. (1993, March 24). *Times Mirror Media Monitor,* pp. 1–30.

Waters, H. (1992, June 15). America's ugliest home videos. *Newsweek,* 59–60.

"Asian or American": Meanings In, Through, and Around *All-American Girl*

RONA TAMIKO HALUALANI AND LEAH R. VANDE BERG

The opening credits of the television series *All-American Girl* provide a fitting visual metaphor for the diverse meanings of this "ethnicom." The opening credits featured a white backdrop against which alternating thin and thick royal blue stripes lay atop a red stripe—all waving and rippling as if a gust of wind has just passed. Accompanied by a jumpy musical beat, the words "All-American Girl" slowly glide across the stripes. The moving landscape of the series credits metonymically signifies both the American flag and the imposed "fixed" cultural terrain of meaning that is played out *in, through,* and *around* the ABC/Disney 1994 *All-American Girl* sitcom text: the opposition between "American" and "non-American" or "Asian."

The dualism set up between "American" and "Asian" is not new. For at least six decades, Asians and Asian Americans have been constructed as "foreign" and "Oriental"; both dangerous invaders and inferior subjects from the East (Choy, 1978; Farquhar & Doi, 1978; Fung, 1994; Hamamoto, 1994; Kim, 1986; Paik, 1971).[1] Asians and Asian Americans have been constructed as the antitheses of everything "American." In this way, the racist "American" ideological system of a purely "Anglo Saxon monoculture" can be strategically preserved (Hamamoto, 1994).

Asian Americans, who are both born in this country and of Asian descent, are often forced to choose between "American" and "Asian." Either way, both extremes— an "American" identity stripped of any racial and ethnic significance, or that of an unassimilable "Asian" alien—ultimately point to the superiority of a "white," Anglo American-dominated social system. Inevitably, any attempt to shape a fluid, multicultural identity of being both Asian and American is constrained. Thus, the dichotomous terrain of "American" versus "Asian" that is continually reproduced in public discourse serves as a hegemonic vehicle to perpetuate an entrenched color-caste system of inequalities (see Hamamoto, 1994; Kim, 1986).

This essay argues that meanings *in, through,* and *around All-American Girl* move between the dualistic poles of "American" and "Asian," thereby reflecting a discourse "tightly organized around [white American] social power" (Fiske, 1990, p. 126). *In, through,* and *around* refers to the many different "voices" that take part in a dialogic struggle for meaning about *All-American Girl*. For instance, the meanings *in* refers to the divergent readings of the televisual text by the two differently situated critic authors. The meanings *through* represent diverse Asian and Asian American viewers' responses to the sitcom. Meanings *around* pertain to texts from the production context (e.g., press interviews with *All-American Girl* actors and creators, journalistic comments about the show) and from Asian/Asian American activists, journalists, and scholars. The participating voices either affirm an "American" position or demand more of an "Asian" perspective. Although a few reject such a dualism, the majority are confined within a socially created framework of racial identity that secures status quo (Anglo American) power arrangements.

We decided to study *All-American Girl* because, for television critics, "firsts" are interesting and important to study and this series was a first—the first time that an American prime time television series starring an Asian female and featuring an almost entirely Asian American cast had aired on network television. However, as we began to watch episodes together, we increasingly became convinced that it was important for us to study together the multiple meanings various audience members created in viewing the series.

To do this we use an approach we term a critical multicultural studies ethnography. In this essay, we explain briefly some of the assumptions and processes involved in using this method of critical analysis. Next, we summarize some of the textual interpretations or meanings created *in, through,* and *around All-American Girl* by various Asian American viewers of the series, television series' producers and actors, Asian American journalists, and Asian American scholar activists. We support our critical analysis with descriptions of scenes and story lines, transcripts of interviews with viewers, and commentary from producers, actors, journalists, and activists. We conclude with an assessment of the efficacy of this approach for studying the case of *All-American Girl.*

A Critical Multicultural Ethnographic Approach

This approach to audience-centered research has developed from the assumption made by cultural studies that textual meaning is the result *both* of the preferred meanings encoded into a text and of interpretations created by audience members as a result of their viewing positions. As Stevenson (1995) and other scholars have explained, "This does not mean, however, that the audience is able to read any meaning into the text." Rather, it means that "the text acts as a structured polysemy" which is open to the creation of a number of possible meanings, depending upon the audience members' cultural identity or position (Stevenson, 1995, p. 79). Gender, ethnicity or race, social class, religion, and nationality all affect the reading strategies and meanings that are created.

Critics often have been guilty of what Pierre Bourdieu (1990) has labeled the "scholastic fallacy": the assumption of critics that everyday readers create the same meanings from texts that the critics do. One way of avoiding the scholastic fallacy is to use audience-centered approaches in which critics present their personal interpretations of the text in conjunction with those created by audience members. In doing so, critics must talk with audience members about the television text, learn about their reading positions, and understand their sense-making processes.

In this essay we explore the meanings and interpretations created by viewers who come to the text from multiple, diverse cultural positions. These "spectator positions" include those of an Anglo-American upper middle-class feminist critic (the second author), a Japanese American/Hawaiian/English graduate student/feminist critic (the first author), and a diverse group of 20 Asian and Asian American viewers, females and males ranging in age from their mid-teens to their late 50s, with different cultural backgrounds (e.g., Korean, Korean American, Chinese, Chinese American, Japanese American, Pilipina American, Hawaiian, Indonesian).[2]

Microlevel cultural studies ethnographies frequently avoid addressing the political economic context (see Beezer & Barker, 1992; Kellner, 1995; Philo, 1995). We attempt to address this weakness by providing some description of the social and political economic context within which *All-American Girl* was produced and by reflecting on commentary about the ideological import of the meanings constructed *in, through,* and *around* the series.

The Political/Economic Context of *All-American Girl*

Kellner (1995) has observed that "the system of production often determines what sort of artifacts will be produced, what structural limits there will be as to what can and cannot be said and shown and what sort of audience effects the text may generate" (p. 9). *All-American Girl* is located within a multidimensional context that is constituted by political and economic factors. Debuting in fall 1994 on ABC, the sitcom arose from a sociopolitical scene of neoconservative leanings and overtly racist sentiments (Marin & Lee, 1994; Zoglin, 1994). Rising racial tensions could clearly be seen in the anti-Mexican/anti-"foreigner" legislation and strong attacks on affirmative action programs. Beneath such measures, the ideological message was clear: minorities would not be tolerated in a "reinvigorated," xenophobic America. Many—led by Anglo-American males—felt this threat to the existing power structure needed to be contained (Marin & Lee, 1994; Zoglin, 1994).

Economically, the mainstream comedy *All-American Girl* represented a product of the profit-oriented Disney Touchstone Television, a major player in a Hollywood culture industry increasingly driving the American economic engine. Disney is a multinational entertainment conglomerate with a legacy of materially entwining entertainment and political ideology ever since its inception.[3]

In the Hollywood entertainment industry environment that produced *All-American Girl,* the norm for film, literary, and televisual representations of Asians has been what Edward Said (1978) has called the "Orientalized" other. These "Orientalist" depictions have included such stereotypes as the dangerous Asian invader (historically the samurai warrior and more recently the ruthless, wealthy Japanese banker/real estate invader), the mysterious and cryptic Charlie Chan, the simultaneously subservient and hypersexualized "Oriental Butterfly" woman, and the Kung Fu master of powers seen and unseen. As various media critics have noted, these images have consistently represented Asians, and by extension Asian Americans, as subordinate "Oriental" subjects justifiably dominated by the superior Anglo West (Choy, 1978; Farquhar & Doi, 1978; Fung, 1994; Hamamoto, 1994; Kim, 1986; Paik, 1971; Said, 1978; Salvador-Burris, 1978; Tajima, 1989).

However, the 1990s have been labeled the "Asian American decade" because of the influx of progressive "Asian chic" Hollywood films which revolved around Asia-Pacific themes (Corliss, 1992, p. 14; Hagedorn, 1994, p. 76; Simon, 1993). This view has been countered by others who see these newer Hollywood images of Asians in films such as *Rising Sun* and *Heaven and Earth* merely as updated versions of Oriental stereotypes (Cacas, 1995).[4] Some, like playwright Kan Gotanda, have taken the argument further and have suggested that the effects of decades of mediated stereotypes of Asians are evident "in acts of anti-Asian hate violence, as well as sophisticated forms of racism evinced in how Asian Pacific American actors are cast" (p. 14). It was against this background, then, that *All-American Girl* premiered in fall 1994.

Based on comedienne Margaret Cho's stand-up comedy material, *All-American Girl* was a thirty-minute prime time situation comedy whose story lines centered around Margaret Cho's character, Margaret Kim, her two-generational Korean American family, and her friends. The Kim family, who owned, ran, and lived above a bookstore in San Francisco, included brash, valley girl-talking twentysomethingish college student Margaret, her high-achieving brother Stuart—a medical resident—her fifth grade brother Eric, her grandmother, and her parents, Ben and Katherine. According to the series' central actor, Margaret Cho, the anticipated goal of the series was to bring "Asians and Asian Americans in focus and to bring their traditions and attitudes into national view" (Shields, 1995, p. 23). Further, ABC promotion touted *All-American Girl* as the "first situation comedy in television history based on the trials and tribulations of an Asian American family" (Mendez, 1994, p. 28).

That the series was produced by Hollywood giant Disney and aired on ABC is somewhat surprising in a media culture industry whose history has been dominated by the oppressive Asian/Asian American images. In light of this, the series would seem to be quite progressive. However, close analysis of the text indicates that the progressiveness hoped for in this television "first" was undercut by the series' actual content. Our interpretive analysis of the text led us to conclude that the series' cultural insensitivity toward the diversity of Asian American cultural identities and its privileging of "American" over "Asian" identities in an ongoing theme of cultural dualism merely perpetuated the hegemony of the Anglo-American monoculture.

Meanings In, Through, and Around *All-American Girl*

The text does not determine . . . meaning so much as delimit the arena of the struggle for that meaning by marking the terrain within which its variety of readings can be negotiated. (Fiske, 1992, p. 303)

The dichotomy of "American" versus "Asian" is a floating public text that historically has helped to secure the Anglo American political, economic, and cultural power structure (see e.g., Radhakrishnan, 1994). Popular representations of Asians/Asian Americans in the media have repeatedly oversimplified Asian American identities as binary terms: as "conflicts between those who identify closely with the immigrant or nationalist positions versus those who are more Americanized and assimilated" (Lowe, 1991, p. 32; Osajima, 1995, p. 81). This categorization hegemonically mirrors white nationalist power in that "nation" is privileged over "ethnicity" (see e.g., Radhakrishnan, 1994). To be "American" is to both disavow one's Asian ancestry, history, and cultural background(s) and uphold a colonialist social system. To choose on the side of "Asian" is to comply with the dominant construction of the invading, foreign, and "homogenized" Asian. For Asian Pacific Americans, being "forced" to "choose" between these poles restrains the defining of their own richly dynamic subjectivities. Asian Americans are therefore deprived of discursive space which represents their varied identities and experiences while "American" versus "Asian" dualism is continually reproduced in public discourse (including this television series). That is why, despite the apparent progressiveness signaled by a prime time series featuring an almost all Asian American cast, many viewers argue that *All-American Girl* merely perpetuates an entrenched color-caste ideology of inequalities (see e.g., Hamamoto, 1994; Kim, 1986).

The master narrative pitting American (nation) over Asian (ethnicity) moves *in*, *through*, and *around All-American Girl*.[5] Such a cultural text is not determinate nor completely polysemous (Condit, 1989; Fiske, 1992). Instead, the television sitcom, like most mainstream televisual texts, delineates an area of containment for meaning. Scholarly critics, television viewers, journalists, and production participants are drawn into dichotomies which help shape their meanings of the text. Indeed, the very terms of the struggle between "American-ness" and "Asian-ness" legitimizes an (Anglo) American capitalistic system undergirded by static oppositions and racialized/genderized inequalities.

In this struggle, the critics' readings of *All-American Girl*, the production texts (e.g., actors' comments, publicity, journalistic accounts, press interviews of cast), the readings of Asian/Asian American activists and scholars, and the Asian/Asian American viewers' responses do not lie in a textual hierarchy, but rather move intertextually.[6] Fiske (1990) explains intertextuality as the way in which texts are read in the context of other texts in order to create meanings. The meanings of *All-American Girl* are shaped by a variety of texts: the sitcom text itself, past mediated Asian images, previous roles of the actors, social discourses, and personal experiences. Because intertextuality connotes a sense of movement among meanings, the circulation of meanings for *All-American Girl* are best presented in a collage of participating voices.

De-Orientalized and "American": One Critical Reading of All-American Girl

Many audience members—viewers, journalists, reviewers, and one of the critics authoring this essay—interpreted *All-American Girl* as a progressive text that showcased positive, "deorientalized" portrayals of Asians as "Americans." Specifically, these viewers of *All-American Girl* "read" the show as depicting the Kims as real people and Asian women as strong, independent females. Some of these readers lauded the sitcom primarily for bringing Asian Americans to network television as a symbol of movement away from the invisibility of Asians in mainstream culture.

Asian/Asian Americans as "Real." Some viewers celebrated *All-American Girl*'s portrayal of the Kim family as a "universal" family as opposed to Asian American. They saw the sitcom as breaking away from Asian stereotypes to portray Asian Americans as "normal" people with the same pleasure, pains, fears, and hopes as other Americans. In effect, they saw *All-American Girl* as doing for Asian Americans what *The Cosby Show* did for African Americans. For instance, the series' executive producer and co-creator Gary Jacobs explained that the show's "stories will demonstrate how many of their [Kims'] experiences are universal and immediately comprehensible to all" (Mendez, 1994, p. 28). Production members such as lead actor Margaret Cho emphasized the Kims' universal appeal in her statement that, "aside from their cultural uniqueness, the Kims are also an identifiable, individual family as well, with the same problems, communication barriers, and the same love" (Mendez, 1994, p. 28). Cho hailed her show as successfully "taking away some of the mystery about Asian Americans and demonstrat[ing] that we're like everybody else" (Mendez, 1994, p. 28).

Two Japanese American male college students shared this view:

> Viewer A: For once, we see Asians—the Kims—as just like everybody else. No different from other people in this society. We are not odd, not freaks, just normal people who go about life.
>
> Viewer B: Yeah, you see that family as a typical American family. You know, just like other families around us. They fight, laugh, and come together when they have to. But, those kids and the star. They want to break away from their parents. You know, just like how normal teenagers do. And sometimes they do not always want to be together. Like the time, the father wants a family night and grandma runs away. You see, Asian families aren't always tight-locked, you know. They are just normal people.

Another viewer, a Pilipina American mother, located the source of her positive response in the series' "human" portrayals of Korean Americans:

> I really like the treatment of the Korean characters as real people, as humans. They are not speaking in Confucian lingo or appearing in tight silk sams. The Asian is not made into such a big spectacle—they are just real. They are Americans here. You don't see that much, do you?

These positive responses to the show's portrayal of Asian Americans as "universal," "normal people," "just like everybody else," "real," and "typical" reflect the series' broad appeal for audience members desiring a "normalizing" first. That the show de-ethnicizes and obscures the unique aspects of Korean American culture is, for these viewers, progressive and laudatory.

The appeal of an "Asian-stripped" *All-American Girl* for Asian American audience members is understandable within the context of past stereotyped images of Asian and Asian Americans as ruthless, threatening infidels, as mysterious and inscrutable other, and as "Oriental Butterflies." For these audience members, replacement of the symbolic annihilation[7] of Asian Americans with normalizing albeit "whitened" representations is seen as positive.

A critical, multicultural studies perspective requires that we ask what is ignored, eclipsed, or marginalized in and through audience perceptions of these homogenized images. When these audience members describe the Kims as Americans and "typical American family," what they are missing are descriptions of these characters as "real" Asian American people. Here the show is being embraced for its "white" American portrayals of Asian/Asian Americans, and as Toni Morrison (1992) explains, "American means white" (p. 47).

A whitened/colorless *All-American Girl* is a marketable media product providing some measure of acceptance and relief from a history of racist stereotypes. That for once Asian characters are not dehumanized or demonized, for these readers, represents a victory of great magnitude. Alternatively, however, producer Jacobs' (1995) hopes that "people will stop seeing" the Kims as "Asian Americans" (p. F3) can be viewed as merely another socially sanctioned strategy for denying race and ethnicity and the accompanying racial biases that are the foundation of the dominant American social/political, ideological order.

"American Asian" Women as Independent. Other audience members read the series as positive because they interpreted it as a decolonialist presentation of independent "American" Asian woman. One of the authors of this article saw in several of the narratives a counter to the subservient "Oriental Butterfly" stereotype of the exotic and hypersexualized yet "quiet, unassuming, and non-threatening doll" whose submissiveness reaffirms traditional Asian and American patriarchal authority (see Halualani, 1995; Lai, 1988). For this critic/audience member textual analysis revealed episodes which modeled feminist awakening and provided empowering anti-"Oriental Butterfly" images. To illustrate, this critic points to the episode in which Stuart and his Asian American girlfriend Amy announce their engagement and Margaret is pressed into taking her new sister-in-law-to-be out with her friends for a female celebration. This critic argues that the change depicted in Amy (and Stuart) over the course of the half-hour—from Amy's initial identity as a submissive, self-effacing traditional "Oriental" female to her evolution into a modern, independent female—is a positive, feminist, and counterstereotypical depiction of Asian American womanhood.

In this episode, when we first meet Amy she is self-effacing, enthusiastically subservient, old-fashioned, wholesome, and demure, despite being well-educated and economically well-to-do. She wears modest, dowdy, ankle-length, old-fashioned floral dresses. She sits demurely on the couch next to Stuart, her hands folded on her lap. She allows Stuart to answer questions directed to her, and nods in delight when Stuart announces their engagement. These narrative details constitute Amy as an "Oriental Butterfly."

However, this stereotype is shattered after Margaret takes Amy out with Margaret's friends for a final "girl's night out," and Amy accepts Margaret's advice to take control of her life and be "free" to be her own person. At the bar, Margaret, dressed in her usual black miniskirt and leather jacket, advises Amy, "Don't start every sentence with 'Stuart and I.' " Margaret chastises Amy about her clothes and doormat-like behavior. Amy comes to realize that she has subsumed her identity to Stuart's, and that she has never explored who Amy is. Exchanging her traditional dowdy dresses for new mini-skirted leather attire, Amy rebels against Stuart's kindly but patriarchal treatment of her and demands "to be treated as an equal." By the end of the episode, Amy "sees" how disempowered she was, and learns that she does not have to "settle for less" than she wants. She learns that she does not have to pretend to be "decorative, invisible, or one-dimensional" (Hagedorn, 1994, p. 79). This feminist narrative of Amy's empowerment debunks American and Asian patriarchal stereotypes and enacts a feminist image of an empowered American Asian female not content to be merely an appendage.

A mixed Chinese/Japanese American female audience member, who shared this critic's view, liked the show because of its "strong Asian women":

> TV does not place minority women, especially Asians, in seats of power. They are just tools for a greater end. *All-American Girl* captures a sense of autonomy among the women. Margaret Cho is both independent and entertaining. She does not have to hide her wild side and she doesn't take crap as a strong American woman. That is good to see.

While these audience members lauded the images of "strong" Asian women as progressive, an alternative (critical multicultural) interpretation of the show needs to note that the strength, power, and independence of this portrayal is derived largely through the character's choice of an "American" over an "Asian" female identity. In fact, both the critic's and viewer's readings of the text highlighted the series' feminist counter-"Oriental Butterfly" images and identified these as essentially "American." The dualism of identity is again brought forth by "the positive equals American" readings, reaffirming the dominance and superiority of an American liberal democratic ideology. However, such a reading foregrounds the national/ethnicity opposition over the contemporary/traditional opposition.

Presence as Positive: Countering Symbolic Annihilation. As we discussed earlier, many positive readings were based on the show's mere existence in mainstream television. One Korean male viewer, for instance, saw the show as a landmark because it "shows our faces":

> My children grow up watching white faces. Here I saw one time it had our faces and I immediately loved it. It is a first. You know how important that is?

Throughout his interview, this reader did not describe any of the episodes or characters that struck him as particularly important. In fact, it came out later that he saw the show only once at the beginning of the season. His interpretation revolved around placing the show in juxtaposition to past oppressive Asian stereotypes. For him, *All-American Girl* symbolized an "upturn." That he "immediately" loved the sitcom's presentation of Asians suggests that the show provides a mark of Asian empowerment and presence in society.

Two Chinese American professionals, one male and the other female, also viewed the series as a "breakthrough" for Asian Americans:

> Viewer C: It was refreshing to see Asian images in mainstream TV. American television. Now that's a switch. I am surprised it even happened.
>
> Viewer D: It finally happened. That is the point. For decades, we have been excluded from the screen. And such politics of exclusion is damaging because people do not see Asians/Asian Americans as complex individuals. The show is actually pretty stupid. The characters, story lines, everything is based on silly stuff. But it is good in the sense that it made its way to TV. That is what we should recognize.
>
> Viewer C (nodding head): The Asian Pacific community should look at the show in that way—as gaining major ground in an industry that we are purposefully kept out of. Although *All-American Girl* is no winner of quality material, the fact that it is here is extremely important.

Here even audience members who disliked the sitcom's content looked beyond the substance of the show to its ground-breaking role. These viewers created positive interpretations of the text because they saw the series as strategically important as a reversal of the ethnically exclusionary history of American media. Production members, Asian/Asian American activists, and scholars also interpreted the mere fact that the show existed on prime time as positive and significant for Asian American viewers. For example, cast member B. D. Wong (Stuart Kim) explained that he felt that the show's presentation of Asians was progressive because: "When I was little, whenever there was an Asian person on television, everyone in the family had to stop what they were doing and come see. That's how unusual it was" (Mendez, 1994, p. 28). Guy Aoki, the president of the Media Action Network for Asian Americans, shared the sentiment that the sitcom "is positive because it is the first television series to feature an Asian American family" and countered Asian American criticism of the show by focusing on how "Seeing ourselves on television gives validity to our existence" (Price, 1994, p. 129).

For these culturally situated Asian American readers, the fact that *All-American Girl* brought Asian faces to the television screen outweighed all other aspects of the show, including the quality of the representations. Yet from a critical multicultural interpretation, these portrayals are isolated exceptions. From this vantage point, until we see substantial numbers of Asian American actors cast in all sorts of roles, not just ethnic roles, such depictions remain tokens that reaffirm the dominance and the moral legitimacy of the Anglo-American dominated political economic order.

"Bleaching Asian-ness": The Americanization of **All-American Girl**

In contrast to these audience members' interpretations, other viewers "read" the series more negatively. A number of interpretations characterized the series as erasing Asianness. These viewers interpreted the series' portrayals as assimilating ("Americanizing") or "bleaching" the Korean American family to make them resemble white (Anglo) Americans. For these audience members. *All-American Girl* signified not a turning point but rather a confirmation of "Oriental" stereotypes and the subtle ways the Anglo-American status quo is preserved and authentic representations of Asian American-ness are denied.

All-American Girl *as an "Orientalized" Text: A Different Critical Reading*

Long Live the American Dream. For example, one of the authors of this chapter read the program as an attempt to encourage seeing Asian/Asian Americans as a homogenized mass of assimilated "American" citizens. For this viewer, the Kims were symbolic devices celebrating the dominant American capitalist order and distracting from the racialized, genderized, and sexualized inequalities of American institutions. This critic points to several episodes which confirmed the "Oriental" stereotypes of the "model minority," the "Oriental Butterfly," and the American liberal democratic myth of "Individual Freedom" (i.e., the myth that all citizens are free to be whoever/whatever they want to be).

All-American Girl's confirmation of Asian Americans as a "model minority" can be seen in an episode in which a commercial bookstore franchise offered to buy out the Kims' bookstore. The narrative here overtly reinforced the American Dream myth (and work ethic) that holds that in America those who work hard, obey the law, and are committed to education will succeed economically.

FATHER: Your mother and I came to this country with nothing. That bookstore represents everything we've become.

MARGARET: Dad, this is the American Dream. I mean, this is why you worked so hard for thirty years. You've built something of value and now you can cash in.

This scene affirms the efficacy of the American myth that impoverished immigrants who come to America and work hard can achieve economic success. Absent from this episode are references to the difficulties caused by prejudices ethnic minorities have experienced in establishing their own businesses in America, an omission that implies that all immigrants can succeed through determination, commitment, and a solid family environment. From this critic's critical multicultural perspective, this omission obfuscates the inequalities due to prejudice that ethnic immigrants face and uses them to confirm the working of the current ideological system. They become, as Hamamoto (1992) points out, an

> example to other ethnic minorities of how a formally disadvantaged group can overcome limited life chances, social discrimination, and economic hardship through self-reliance, personal discipline, and mutual assistance, all within the opportunity structure afforded by a liberal democracy. (p. 36)

The sitcom text suggests that if ethnic groups like Korean Americans can succeed, the American system of individualistic capitalism truly works for everyone. As Nakayama (1988) argues, "Asian American success affirms the workability of American social institutions" and that the problems of "minority groups are a result of their own neglect." Hence, race and the intersecting of race/gender are constructed as *not* impeding the pursuit for mobility and status (p. 70). According to this interpretation, *All-American Girl* participates in legitimizing a hegemonic social order under attack by ethnic, women's, and gay and lesbian civil rights groups since the 1960s.

Interactions between the parents, Katherine and Ben Kim, and their son, Stuart, further reinscribe the Model Minority stereotype. Stuart, the mid-twentyish obedient son and hard-working medical resident, represents the quintessential Model Minority figure as do his hard-working parents who hold high educational aspirations for their son. In one episode, Katherine boasts to Stuart, "I am so proud of you. Today ranking resident, tomorrow chief resident. And someday, the cover of the *New England Journal of Medicine.*" In this episode, because of pressure to achieve from his parents, Stuart nearly collapses trying to keep up his grueling resident physician work schedule. As he explains, "You can't make chief resident by slacking off." Pained by the emotional pressure that she sees Stuart is feeling to be the perfect "model minority" son, Margaret has the following conversation with her mother:

MARGARET: Mom, you're starting to do to Eric exactly what you did with Stuart.
MOM: What? Motivate him toward excellence? I hope so.
MARGARET: It's just too much pressure. Look at Stuart. When he screws up, his whole world crumbles.
MOM: Well, you are the ones who took him to Skid Row when he was six, pointed to a bunch of winos and said, "That's what happens when you get an A minus in phonics."

Later in this episode, an exhausted Stuart, who has been working literally night and day to please his parents by becoming chief resident, mixes up two files. When he is temporarily suspended because of a mishap, Stuart explains to Margaret his fear of the "look" he gets from their parents, "a look reserved for the eldest son who has gravely disappointed his parents." With Margaret's encouragement, Stuart sheds the debilitating burden of being the "model minority" his parents want him to be by singing "Yankee Doodle Dandy" and thereby exorcises the haunting memory of a childhood recital in which he flatly sang "Yankee Doodle Dandy" and disappointed his parents. However, Stuart's defiantly singing the refrain, "I am that Yankee Doodle Boy" ironically corroborates rather than debunks the Asian Model Minority myth. Here again, "Yankee Doodle Dandy" symbolically links Stuart's newfound feeling of autonomy to the American tenets of independence/freedom and justice in opposition to his parents' "old country" expectations of the eldest son. Again, then, American (nation) and contemporary are opposed to ethnicity (Asian) and traditional, and the former are preferred while the latter are rejected.

This interpretation views *All-American Girl* as ironically affirming the Oriental Butterfly myth as well. This occurs in an episode in which Margaret's mother finally succeeds in persuading Margaret to date an eligible young Asian professional listed in Mrs. Kim's "Marriage" computer file. Margaret's date, Raymond Han, is a successful Korean American doctor from a traditional family. Margaret forgoes her usual black leather punk attire and dresses in conservative, demure clothing when she is with Raymond. However, when Margaret begins to giggle with her hand over her mouth and softly respond, "Whatever you say, Raymond," in her conversations with him, her Anglo friends Ruthie and Gloria confront her:

MARGARET: He treats me great. . . . So, if in return, he wants me to be a little bit. . . .
GLORIA: Subservient.
RUTHIE: Doormatish.
MARGARET: Demure, then it's my business.

After several dates, Raymond invites Margaret to dine with his family. To prepare her for this, Margaret's mother and brother Stuart spend several days coaching her on traditional Korean etiquette. At the dinner, she is "looked over" by Raymond's parents who eventually indicate that they agree she would be a suitable wife when they deliver a traditional, patriarchal toast:

MRS. HAN: May you have the joy that comes from selfless devotion to your husband!
MR. HAN: May you swell with the bounty of many masculine children!

Once they return to Margaret's house a horrified Margaret tells Raymond that this relationship will never work. As she explains to him, because "I like you. I wanted it to work out so I tried to become the person you wanted me to be." When Raymond asks what Margaret is really like, she answers, "I'm really opinionated and I say exactly what I think. And frankly, I have no immediate plans to swell with the bounty of any children, masculine or otherwise." Having heard this, Raymond then admits that he could never live with the "real" Margaret (or any American girl who would just say what she thought), and they part ways.

This episode reflects the continued vitality of the subservient Oriental Butterfly myth. This episode, as well as the earlier episode which depicted Amy's evolution from subservient Butterfly to empowered modern woman (and the concomitant efforts of Stuart to develop a more feminist, egalitarian relationship with her), reaffirmed traditional Asian culture as oppressively patriarchal in contrast to the democratic, egalitarian, even feminist American culture. For example, in the Margaret/Raymond episode Raymond negatively contrasted traditional, demure Asian girls (which he thinks Margaret is) who keep their opinions to themselves with "American girls who are going to say what's on their minds" and Margaret tartly reminded him that she was "American." Here again, the "Oriental Butterfly" stereotype reinscribes Asian/Asian American culture as sexist and thus, legitimates the superiority of the contrasting "American" way of life.

Another way in which *All-American Girl* reflected the essentializing dichotomy of American (nation) over Asian (ethnicity) was in its casting of the series. Although the series claimed to focus on the lives of the members of a Korean American family in the 1990s, Margaret Cho was the only member of the cast who was actually Korean. Cho's older brother on the show was played by B.D. Wong who is actually Chinese, and her grandmother was played by Amy Hill, who is Japanese-Finnish (Marin, 1994). Apparently Disney-Touchstone and ABC felt that most Americans wouldn't notice this. Such collapsing and essentializing of multiple Asian and American ethnic identities into a singular "Asian American" identity is a version of the racist stereotype that all _____ (fill in the ethnic minority group—here Asians) look alike. The series' casting, thus, reflects the dominant American culture's homogenization of diverse Asian cultures and contributes to the difficulty Asian Americans face in establishing their own truly multicultural identities.

Many Asian/Asian American viewers objected to the "model minority" and Oriental Butterfly stereotypes depicted in *All-American Girl*. One Pilipino male said:

> *All-American Girl* is totally a sell-out. The question is—Where are the Asians? Where are the Asian Americans? You see none of it. It's all bleached white. I saw the film episode, when Margaret Cho is in the film class and the teacher gives her a "D" cuz he had different expectations for someone like her. Let me spell it out for you—M O D E L   M I N O R I T Y. Model minority, plain and simple. Of course, the Asian American student is held up to a different standard than all the others. Even a "D" student is placed with those kinds of stereotypical expectations. I mean, come on.

To illustrate the source of his interpretation he referred to an episode in which Margaret's (Anglo male) writing teacher told her that because she had great potential he would be judging her work by a "different standard." The outraged viewer interpreted this as unequal treatment based on the "Model Minority." His critical reading of the episode was that the performance of Asian American students was being measured by a racist standard couched in the socially laudable form of the overachieving "Model Minority."

Another Korean American male viewer also saw the series' depictions as "extremely insulting":

Asian American men and women are jokes in the show. All that stuff about the Korean guy she is set up with and Stuart. And they are supposed to be these incredibly domineering men. What is communicated is that all Asian men, Asian American men, especially Korean American men, are oppressive. This is so incredibly misleading. All my life, people have either expected that from me or told me that was how I should be. I grew up in a household where my father split the child-rearing/home duties. Where the sons and daughters were both expected to treat each other with respect and love. I respect all of those around me. My significant other is my best friend. She is not this object who I speak for. My mother is a college professor and my father is a civil engineer who endured stereotypes like this.

Even the Asian women are portrayed as ridiculous. The mother is completely devoted to her family. While this is true in many Asian families, this is not always the case. But Margaret is supposed to be this really radical woman who rebels against oppressive Asian men and does not want to be like her mother. If that isn't adding credence to stereotypes, I don't know what is.

This reader used personal experiences to interpret representations in the series as stereotypical constructions of oppressive Asian/Asian American men and acquiescent Asian women. This viewer felt such stereotypes had affected his life and he critiqued Margaret Cho's seemingly "radical stance" as an "insulting" attempt to reinforce "Orientalized" images. Equally critical of the series was a female Vietnamese viewer who rejected the series' privileging of national/American over ethnic cultural/Asian identities:

I knew I would never watch the show when I saw it that one night. When the mother tells Margaret how much she hated her making fun of them in public, Margaret said something like this isn't Korea, it is America and I have freedom of speech. Just slap Asians in the face, why don't you? The creation of comments like that are negative for Asians. It makes America seem like this great, redeeming place that allows minorities to speak their mind. And we know that isn't so. We are muted in the media, in politics, in colleges. The show made a lot of those digs into Asian culture. So much so that at the end all you see is an assimilated, Americanized, white family with "black hair."

This viewer denounced the text's oppositional contrasts between an old world, repressive Korea and an American nation of boundless freedom. She interpreted the show as an assimilationist effort that effaced Asian race and ethnicity, except for the Kims' black hair as a signifier of racial difference. She "read" the series' promotion of American ideals in the narrative content as reinforcing Anglo superiority and a non-threatening Asian inferiority (see Fiske, 1992, pp. 287–288).

A mixed Japanese/African American male viewer concurred and pointed to the title of the sitcom and the grandma character as signs of the series' affirmation of "Americanization" and rejection of Asian identity:

The title explains much: *All-American Girl*. Not *All-Asian-American-Girl*. Or *Asian Girl*. Or *Asian-American Girl*. But, *All-American Girl*. Meaning all and completely, totally American and not at all Asian. I think that says much about the show.

When the show first came out, all my friends raved that this would be a new fo-cus. *All-American Girl* would look at Asian American stories. Now, we come to find out that there is an extremity being taken. Total Americanization is the ploy, the catch. And the grandma falls into this ploy. No one notices this. You may have? She watches TV all the time. American TV. Day and night. She lives within that tube. Everybody laughs but it's such a ploy. That grandma is the most despi-cable evidence of complete assimilation to American culture.

This audience member deconstructed the show's title, which he saw as a reflection of the text's assimilationist ideology. He explained that his oppositional reading was based on the implication that the word "All-American" meant "all and completely and totally American and not at all Asian." He interpreted the show's "Americanization" as a manipulative effort to embrace assimilation to American culture as a most desir-able choice for Asian Americans because it wouldn't threaten Anglo Americans.

All of these viewers critically interrogated the sitcom's presentation of admirable Asians/Asian Americans as those who embrace only the "American" portion of their identity. Without explicitly using the critical vocabulary that critics use, both the Viet-namese female and the Japanese/African American male viewer argued that the series naturalized the characters' assimilationist actions and, thus, were examples of hege-mony in action (e.g., Gray, 1995).

Commentary about the series in the popular media reflected tensions between production members who positively interpreted *All-American Girl* as affirming "Amer-ican-ness" and Asian American journalists and activists who attacked the sitcom for its totalizing emphasis on American ideals and its rejection of Asian cultural values. For example, one preview of *All-American Girl* featured a picture of Margaret Cho wearing an American flag as an apron and holding up an apple pie. The caption read "Miss Ko-rean-American Pie." Although this caption specified "Korean-American," it was con-tradicted by the picture of an Asian American woman adorned in the quintessential emblem of American-ness—the flag. The potential for representing Asian American-ness was further defused by the hyphenated term "Korean-American," which repro-duced "a metaphor that highlights the boundary between minority Americans and white Americans" (Chen, 1994, p. 9). Margaret Cho's comment that if her show is re-newed, "then I think that we have arrived at hot dog-baseball-American cheese sta-tus" reiterated this focus (Chin, 1994, p. A12). For Asian American journalists and activists, the emphasis on American rather than Asian symbols in these production texts implied *All-American Girl* was designed to represent and encourage the assimila-tion of Asians into the homogenized Anglo-American culture, not to endorse the inclu-sion of Asian culture as part of the national (American) culture.

The meanings constructed by Asian American journalists and activists contra-dicted the preferred readings proffered by the sitcom text and its surrounding produc-tion texts. For example, *Asian Week* columnist Bill Wong (1994) condemned the show as "ethnically inauthentic" and proof that "Asian Americans can be part of banal, unin-spired entertainment. Equal Opportunity mediocrity" (p. 9). According to Wong, the show's featuring of a generic "American" shell inferiorized Asian/Asian American voices under the rubric of "Equal Opportunity." Wong also attacked the series' "ethnic inauthenticity" and raised the question, "What is a true Asian/Asian American experi-ence(s)?" Wong's interpretation suggested that essentializing ethnic identity is prob-lematic because it encourages using a standardized criterion for affirming or negating cultural identity and experience. In so doing, individual identity construction is denied. Furthermore, tensions among various Asian/Asian American groups are fostered by attempts to determine authentic Asian American experience and identity.

Asian American activist/journalist Cacas (1994) attacked the sitcom because in a multicultural San Francisco setting the character Margaret Kim interacted predominantly with only Anglo Americans:

> Will the non-Asian Pacific American persons she has contact with eventually include Latino Americans, African Americans, Native Americans, Gays and Lesbians? Or will they continue to be European Americans exclusively? Only time will tell just how All-American "All-American Girl" will be. (p. 23)

Cacas ironically retitled the show, "All European American in Margaret Kim's World" (p. 23), to illustrate his criticism of the series' limiting Margaret's interactions primarily to Anglo Americans (e.g., Ruthie, Gloria, Casey, Margaret's mostly Anglo American male dates and roommates, and Eric's little Anglo American female friend). His comparison of the show's ethnic landscape with the flourishing multicultural Bay Area population underscores the disparity between the series' representation and Asian American social reality. Cacas' reading reveals an interpretive strategy used by a number of viewers who feel that if images do not fit actual experience(s), they should be discarded and branded as (whitened) "Americanized."

Many audience members left their encounter with the series deeply resentful of what they interpreted as "bleaching" (i.e., Anglo "Americanization") of its Asian American representations. Like Hamamoto (1989), they saw *All-American Girl* as typical of commercial television in its "packag[ing]," "market[ing]," and reproducing the "affirmative aspects" of American liberal democratic ideology: freedom, equality, and social and economic opportunity (pp. 2, 4). From these Asian American viewers' perspectives, "true" Asian/Asian American experience was subverted by the sitcom's binary framework of "American" versus "Asian," the concomitant essentialization of Asian/Asian American identities, and the privileging of American over Asian.

Ironically, despite the diversity among the meanings viewers created *in, through,* and *around All-American Girl,* all shared the view that the series was a politically charged program. These Asian American cultural readers felt there was little choice in identity or reading position—either one had to affirm the dominance of the Anglo American socioeconomic order and subordinate one's Asian ethnicity or accept perpetual alien status in the country of one's birth. Either they must hail *All-American Girl's* portrayals as "real" and "American" or denounce the text's erasure of Asian ethnicity and hardship as an American televisual assimilationist effort to elevate "colorblind" or rather "bleached white" American-ness over "yellow" Asian-ness.

Chow (1990) has explained that ethnic identity in America is not "voluntary," but rather "a matter of history" (p. 45). The history of political, economic, and social subordination of Asian Americans and their "Orientalist" media representations have propagated a social marginality and dualism that is actively reflected in the meanings many viewers constructed from *All-American Girl.* However, affirmation of Asian American experiences as cultural hybrids also was articulated by some viewers (e.g., Lowe, 1991; Osajima, 1995). Indeed, some viewers, including this Korean American female viewer and avid Margaret Cho fan, rejected this dualism and called instead for articulating and representing the diverse, hybrid experiences of Asian Americans:

> I was disappointed with the show. It did not capture the real complexities in being a Korean American, or an Asian Pacific American. The terms—Asian, American—become useless at some point. Sometimes I do not always feel just Asian or American or just half of each. It is always both at the same time. Does that make sense? You can't even describe it. I have watched all of Margaret Cho's comedy specials; saw her perform in the city once and ABC should have just filmed her routines; that is where she gets at the complexities of being diversely Asian American.

This reader stressed that the multiple identities that she experiences as an Asian American led her to resist *All-American Girl*'s dichotomized and preferred "American" versus "Asian" identity. That is, her lived cultural position led her to reject the situation comedy's preferred reading and to affirm instead Cho's stand-up comedy routines because in the latter Cho mocks this dichotomy and affirms a multicultural Asian American identity. This viewer recalled this portion of Cho's stand-up comedy routine in which Cho explained to the audience her frustration with being constantly cast as a "forever foreign" Asian:

> I was supposed to go on the show and tell jokes. What was I supposed to do. (She speaks with an exaggerated accent): "My husband is so fat that when he sits around the hopaku, he really sit around hopaku! Gong!"

This excerpt reflected the viewer's frustration with the series, a frustration generated not only from the content of the series or published commentary about the series but from the viewing self she brought to the series. Like all viewers of *All-American Girl*—including the authors of this essay—this viewer brought to her viewing of the series her previous experiences with literary texts and her knowledge of other texts, her social self, her life experiences, and her self-identity. And in consequence, she constructed a reading of the text which disrupted the "American" versus "Asian" identity framework.

Final Observations

Condit's (1989) concept of polyvalence describes one of the major findings in this critical ethnographic study of the meanings of *All-American Girl*. Condit's (1989) essay critiqued Fiske's (1986) concept of polysemy and posited the concept of polyvalence as a corrective. Fiske's concept of polysemy posited that popular texts are constructed in ways that enable audience members—especially members of gender, ethnic, cultural, political, and economic minorities—to use the "openings" or ambiguity in texts to resist the text's expressions of dominant ideology and to negotiate alternative, pleasurable, and empowering interpretations of the text. Condit (1989) offered another explanation for negotiated readings; she argued that perhaps the empowering process of audience interpretation has less to do with attributing entirely new meanings to textual signifiers than it does with audience members choosing to evaluate the meanings differently. Thus, she advanced the notion that audiences indeed may recognize the preferred meanings encoded in texts and may simply differ in the positive or negative valence they give these meanings.

Condit's notion of polyvalence seems to describe our finding that although all the audience members whose interpretations are discussed in this study—the Asian American critic, the Anglo American critic, and the Asian and Asian American audience members—acknowledged at some level that the series privileged (Anglo) American (national) over Asian (ethnic) representations, values, and norms, these viewers differed greatly in their interpretation of this as positive/empowering or racist/constraining. Some viewers—including a number of Asian American audience members and the Dutch American author of this essay—saw *All-American Girl* largely as positive, a progressive first through which past overtly racist Asian and Asian American stereotypes were rejected. These audience members gave the series a positive valence for its legitimization of images of Asians as normal, regular albeit Americanized humans, and for its strong, feminist Asian female protagonist. Other viewers—including the Japanese Hawaiian American author of this essay and a number of Asian American audience members—interpreted the same text as yet another neocolonialist text whose inferential racism subtly affirmed the dominant Anglo cultural ideology in which Asian Americans are forever viewed as foreign "others" despite rejection of their Asian identity and attempts to assimilate into Anglo American society.

Cloud's (1992) essay, like Stuart Hall's (1981/1990) essay "The Whites of Their Eyes," points out that polyvalent readings of ambi-valent stereotypes are not necessarily subversive of the dominant ideology. In contrast to Fiske's (1986) focus on the subversive pleasures that viewers can find in popular texts, Cloud cautions critics and cultural studies ethnographers, "that we cannot simply assume that ambivalent or contradictory articulations of racial difference are in and of themselves subversive" of the dominant social structure and ideology. Indeed, Cloud argues that "the playful discovery in popular texts of moments of contradiction and opposition" (such as some viewers found in *All-American Girl*), "is perhaps not as vital a critical task as coming to an understanding of how a carefully structured cultural variance can work in support of an oppressive society" (p. 322).[8]

This is Stuart Hall's (1981/1991) point as well. Hall argues that as critics, we need to think about "the way[s] in which the media—sometimes deliberately, sometimes unconsciously—define and construct the question of race in such a way as to reproduce the ideologies of racism" (p. 8). In doing so, he reminds us, we must remember that "ideologies 'work' by constructing for their subjects (individual and collective) positions of identification and knowledge which allow them to 'utter' ideological truths as if they were their authentic authors" (p. 9).

Cloud's (1992) essay reminds us that our obligation in audience-centered criticism, as critical ethnographers, is to step back and recontextualize texts and viewers' interpretations of texts—to read them against the backdrop of the sociopolitical and economic context in which they were produced. From such a perspective, then, we can conclude that the Orientalist colonialist stereotype is still alive and well in *All-American Girl*. As Bhabha (1983) has explained, "The colonial stereotype is a complex, ambivalent, contradictory mode of representation . . . [whose] predominant strategic function is the creation of a space for a "subject peoples" through the production of knowledges in terms of which surveillance is exercised and a complex form of pleasure/unpleasure is incited" (pp. 22–23).

One important way this is accomplished, as Hall (1981) explains, is through media "representations of the social world, images, descriptions, explanations and frames for understanding how the world is and why it works as it is said and shown to work" (p. 11). And some of these are "apparently naturalized representations of events and situations relating to race, whether 'factual' or 'fictional,' which have racist premises and propositions inscribed in them as a set of unquestioned assumptions . . . [and which therefore] enable racist statements to be formulated without ever bringing into awareness the racist predicates on which the statements are grounded" (p. 13). Hall terms this *inferential racism,* and he cautions that it is both widespread and insidious (p. 13) and also that "neither a unifiedly conspiratorial media nor indeed a unified racist 'ruling class' exist in anything like that simple way" (p. 12). For example, our textual analysis of *All-American Girl* revealed a number of examples of such inferential racism, including the series title "All-American Girl," the casting of only one Korean American actor in this situation comedy about a Korean American family, Stuart Kim's singing of "I'm a Yankee Doodle Dandy" as his song of liberation from conformity to his parents' expectations, and Margaret's assertion to Raymond Han that "I am an American girl."

Clearly, the evaluations audience members attached to these representations were polyvalent. Despite the series' apparent opposition to Orientalist or colonialist stereotypes, close textual analysis revealed the insidious and largely invisible presence of the series' racist premises. Some audience members resoundingly rejected the series when their own readings of it revealed this unapparent inferential racism. However, other viewers who also recognized the underlying racist premises and assumptions, attached a positive valence to the series' recoding of Orientalist stereotypes. For these viewers the series, however imperfect, was nonetheless a positive and empowering step—a revolutionary first—in combating racist ideological assumptions about Asian Americans. And indeed, as Hall (1981/1990) has observed, "the argument that *only* 'deconstructivist' texts are truly revolutionary is as one-sided a view as that which suggests that forms have no effect" (p. 21).

We agree with Hall (1981/1990) that one of the most difficult problems cultural theorists and critics face is that of finding effective strategies and tactics to use in challenging "media construction of race, so as to undermine, deconstruct and question the unquestioned racist assumptions on which so much of media practice is located" (p. 8). The two critics authoring this chapter disagree about the overall efficacy of this series as an anti-racist strategy. Our ethnographic analysis, however, suggests this is not solely the result of occupying different subject positions. One author is a third generation Dutch American middle class heterosexual woman for whom her university education was an intellectually, emotionally, and ideologically liberating experience, and as a scholar and professor she strives to create a climate which can enable all of her students and her readers to have similarly empowering experiences. The other author is an ethnically mixed fourth generation (yonsei) Japanese American/Hawaiian/English female graduate student who strives to work for the social emancipation of the silenced and the suppressed. Like many of the audience members we interviewed, we "read" the series differently. Using Cloud's (1992) term, we attached different valences to its representations. We both agree, however, that critical readership studies such as this encourage all viewers—Asian Pacific/Asian Pacific American, African American, Latina/Latino American, Chicana/Chicano, and Anglo American—to recognize and challenge inferiorizing representations that appropriate and marginalize dynamic, multicultural social identities.

NOTES

1. We struggled with the identifying terms and labels we use throughout this essay. We recognize the problems and limitations in our linguistic choices; however, despite our sincere attempts we were not able to find a satisfactory linguistic means of communicating our awareness that identity is a multifaceted construct that certainly is not simply or solely a function of national origin, ethnicity, and culture. We acknowledge that throughout this essay the distinction between "Asian" and "Asian American" is oftentimes blurred. Broadly speaking, in this chapter, "Asian" refers to those of Asian descent from different parts of the world while "Asian American" refers to those of Asian descent who are born in the United States. Used mostly as a mobilizing device, "Asian American" is a problematic "essentializing" term in that it both fails to represent the ever-present diversity in and among Asian cultures and excludes a large population of Asians who live in other parts of the world (e.g., Canada). Thus, in this essay, the "Asian American" term is used as a strategic discursive device to disrupt the dichotomy of "American" versus "Asian" and represent multiple, heterogeneous Asian subjectivities.

2. Open-ended single person and group ethnographic interviews were conducted with 20 diverse Asian and Asian American viewers. Participants represented various ages (e.g., from the mid-teens to late fifties) and different Asian cultural groups (e.g., Korean, Korean American, Chinese, Chinese American, Japanese American, Pilipina American, Hawaiian, Indonesian), and included both females and males. Each interview averaged forty minutes in length and were audiotaped with the permission of the interviewees. Participants had the option of watching the 14 analyzed episodes before the interviews. Interviewees authorized the inclusion of interview excerpts in this paper.

3. Disney's founder, Walt Disney, served as FBI informant (Eliot, 1993) and accepted federal government underwriting of military training films, propaganda cartoons, and shorts designed to sway public and government opinion in favor of strategic bombing during World War II (Holliss and Sibley, 1988; Jewett and Lawrence, 1977). Subsequently, while overseeing his growing entertainment empire, Walt Disney served as a U.S. State Department goodwill ambassador to South America and produced a series of films related to this which were intended to "show the truth about the American way [and] carry a message of democracy and friendship below the Rio Grande" (Burton, 1992, p. 55). In addition to Disneyland, Disney World, and EuroDisney, the corporate Disney also owns Childcraft, an educational toy company (Bell, Hass, & Sells, 1995). Recently, Disney opened a new enterprise also explicitly designed to combine education (ideology) and entertainment—The Disney Institute in Lake Buena Vista, Florida. At the Disney Institute's vacation campus guests can choose to take courses from 80 different programs (including story arts, television broadcasting, lifestyles, environment, etc.) as well as enjoy the recreational offerings of Walt Disney World (Clarke, 1996), and purchased the ABC television network. Clearly, Disney is intimately involved in the commercial combining of entertainment and educational experiences.

4. In the 1990s, several mainstream films that portrayed Asians were released. Some of these were *Dragon* (1994), *Golden Gate* (1993), *Farewell, My Concubine* (1994), *Rising Sun* (1992), *The Joy Luck Club* (1993), *Heaven and Earth* (1993) and *M. Butterfly* (1994). However, most of these re-inscribed "Orientalist" stereotypes of the past, creating

one-dimensional, "foreign" Asian characters. Cacas (1995) documents the panel meeting of Asian Pacific American scholars, playwrights, and artists who concluded that "Charlie Chan," "taken as a collective conscious of all the negative images of Asians in this country," is still alive and well (p. 14). This designation of an Asian male stereotype to represent all Asian images unjustly glosses over the degradation of Asian female images. Tragically, in film and television, Asian women have been appropriated as "mirrors" of Anglo American male supremacy (Halualani, 1995). The tendency to protest some stereotypes over others is just as oppressive as the negative images themselves. A glaring example lies in Hamamoto's (1994) misguided attack on Asian woman as enjoying "favorable exposure" in the media in their frequent pairings with Anglo males.

5. Seventeen episodes of *All-American Girl* were aired during 1994–1995. Of these, we managed to acquire 14 for textual analysis, thanks to the gracious assistance of Guy Aoki, co-founder and president of the Media Action Network for Asian Americans (MANAA).

6. Fiske (1990) describes cultural studies analysis of a text as involving three levels: primary (i.e., reading of the text on screen), secondary (i.e., reading fan gossip, publicity, journalistic comments, feature articles), and tertiary (i.e., reading audience talk about the show). Fiske's terminology hierarchically privileges the meanings drawn from the primary text and oversimplifies the complex task of analyzing the ways cultural readers (and critics) move among these different but interrelated levels to activate meanings. In addition, texts from grassroot-based ethnic communities (outside the production context) are not considered in Fiske's discussion; however, such texts are also integral to the creation of meaning for some viewers.

7. The concept of *symbolic annihilation* was used by sociologist Gaye Tuchman (1978) to describe the way in which women are marginalized and kept in their proper place—by their absence—neither seen nor heard. This strategy also describes the way in which television has symbolically annihilated minorities and reaffirmed the normal, natural dominance of Anglo American society—by simply excluding images of minorities from the television screen.

REFERENCES

Allen, R. C. (1992). Audience-oriented criticism and television. In R. C. Allen (Ed.), *Channels of discourse, reassembled* (pp. 101–137). Chapel Hill: University of North Carolina Press.

Bell, E., Hass, L., & Sells, L. (Eds.). (1995). *From mouse to mermaid: The politics of film, gender and culture.* Bloomington: Indiana University Press.

Bhabha, H. (1983). The other question: The stereotype and colonial discourse. *Screen, 24*(6), 18–36.

Bordieu, P. (1990). *In other words: Essays toward a reflexive sociology.* Cambridge, MA: Polity Press.

Burton, J. (1992). Don (Juanito) Duck and the imperial-patriarchal unconscious: Disney studios, the good neighbor policy, and the packaging of Latin America. In A. Parker, M. Russo, D. Sommer, & P. Yaeger, (Eds.), *Nationalism and sexualities* (pp. 21–41). New York: Routledge.

Cacas, S. (1994, September 23). How all-American is *All-American Girl? Asianweek, 12,* 23.

Cacas, S. (1995, November 10). Charlie Chan is alive and well. *Asianweek, 17*(12), 14–15

Chen, V. (1994). (De)hyphenated identity: The double voice in *The Woman Warrior.* In A. Gonzalez, M. Houston, V. Chen (Eds.), *Our voices: Essays in culture, ethnicity, and communication* (pp. 3–11). Los Angeles: Roxbury.

Chin, C. (1994, Sept. 11). Asian American goes prime time. *San Francisco Examiner,* B2.

Chow, R. (1990). Politics and pedagogy of Asian literatures in American universities. *differences, 2*(3), 29–51.

Choy, C. (1978). Images of Asian-Americans in films and television. In R. M. Miller (Ed.), *Ethnic images in American film and television* (pp. 145–155). Philadelphia: The Balch Institute.

Clark, J. (1996, February 25). Disney Institute breaks new ground: Learning and fun combine at Florida "vacation campus." *Sacramento Bee,* travel sec., pp. 1, 5.

Condit, C. M. (1989). The rhetorical limits of polysemy. *Critical Studies in Mass Communication, 6,* 103–122.

Corliss, R. (1992, October 4). Betrayal in Beijing. *Time,* 14.

During, S. (1993). Introduction. In S. During (Ed.), The *cultural studies reader* (pp. 1–25). London: Routledge.

Eliot, M. (1993). *Walt Disney, Hollywood's dark prince: A biography.* Secaucus, NJ: Carol/Birch Lane Press.

Farquhar, J., & Doi, M. L. (1978, Fall). Bruce Lee vs. Fu Manchu: Kung fu films and Asian American stereotypes in America. *Bridge: An Asian American Perspective,* 23–32.

Fiske, J. (1990). *Television culture.* London: Routledge.

Fiske, J. (1992). British cultural studies and television. In R. C. Allen (Ed.), *Channels of discourse, reassembled* (pp. 101–137). Chapel Hill: University of North Carolina Press.

Fung, R. (1994). Seeing yellow: Asian identities in film and video. In K. Aguilar-San Juan (Ed.), *The state of Asian American: Activism and resistance in the 1990's* (pp. 161–172). Boston, MA: South End Press.

Gray, H. (1995). Television, black Americans, and the American dream. In G. Dines & J. M. Hunez (Eds.), *Gender, race and class in media: A text-reader* (pp. 430–437). Thousand Oaks, CA: Sage.

Hagedorn, J. (1994, January/February). Asian women in film: No joy, no luck. *Ms.,* 10–12.

Hall, S. (1980/1993). Encoding/decoding. In S. During (Ed.), *The cultural studies reader* (pp. 90–103). London: Routledge, 1993. [Originally published in S. Hall et al. (Eds.), *Culture, media, language* (pp. 128–138). London: Hutchinson.]

Hall, S. (1981/1990). The whites of their eyes: Racist ideologies and the media. In M. Alvarado & J. O. Thompson (Eds.), *The media reader* (pp. 7–23). London: British Film Institute. [Originally published in G. Bridges & R. Brunt (Eds.), *Silver linings* (pp. 28–52). London: Lawrence and Wishart.]

Halualani, R. T. (1995a). *Hollywood film's construction of "Asian femininity."* Unpublished master's thesis, California State University, Sacramento, Sacramento, CA.

Halualani, R. T. (1995b). The intersecting hegemonic discourses of an Asian mail-order bride catalog: Pilipina "Oriental Butterfly" dolls for sale. *Women's Studies in Communication, 18,* 45–64.

Hamamoto, D. Y. (1989). *Nervous laughter: Television situation comedy and liberal democratic ideology.* New York: Praeger.

Hamamoto, D. Y. (1992). Kindred spirits: The contemporary Asian American family on television. *Amerasia Journal, 18*(2), 35–53.

Hamamoto, D. Y. (1994). *Monitored peril: Asian Americans and the politics of tv representation.* Minneapolis: University of Minnesota Press.

Holliss, R., & Sibley, B. (1988). *The Disney studio story.* New York: Crown.

Jacobs, G. (1995, March 20). In defense of the *All-American Girl. Los Angeles Times,* F3.

Jewett, R., & Lawrence, J. S. (1977). *The American monomyth.* Garden City, NY: Anchor Press/Doubleday.

Kellner, D. (1995). Cultural studies, multiculturalism and media culture. In G. Dines & J. M. Humez (Eds.), *Gender, race and class in media* (pp. 5–17). Thousand Oaks, CA: Sage.

Kim, E. H. (1986). Asian Americans and American popular culture. In H. C. Kim (Ed.), *Dictionary of Asian American history* (pp. 99–113). New York: Greenwood Press.

Lai, T. (1988). Asian American women: Not for sale. In J. Cochran, D. Langston, & C. Woodward (Eds.), *Changing our power: An introduction to women's studies* (pp. 163–171). Dubuque, IA: Kendall-Hunt.

Lowe, L. (1991). Heterogeneity, hybridity, multiplicity: Marking Asian American differences. *Diaspora, 1*(1), 24–44.

Mendez, C. (1994, August 26). Margaret Cho ushers in a new era for "All-American" television sitcoms. *Asianweek, 16*(1), 28.

Morrison, T. (1992). *Play in the dark: Whiteness and literary imagination.* Cambridge, MA: Harvard University Press.

Nakayama, T. K. (1988). "Model Minority" and the media: Discourse on Asian America. *Journal of Communication Inquiry, 12*(1), 65–73.

Osajima, K. (1995). Postmodern possibilities: Theoretical and political directions for Asian American studies. *Amerasia Journal, 21*(1 & 2), 79–87.

Paik, I. (1971). That oriental feeling: A look at the caricatures of the Asians as sketched by American movies. In A. Tachiki, E. Won, F. Odo, & B. Wong (Eds.), *Roots: An Asian American reader* (pp. 30–36). Los Angeles: University of California Press.

Price, D. L. (1994). *All-American Girl* and the American dream. *Critical Mass, 2*(1), 129–146.

Radhakrishnan, R. (1994). Is the ethnic "authentic" in the diaspora? In K. Aguilar-San Juan (Ed.), *The state of Asian America: Activism and resistance in the 1990s* (pp. 219–233). Boston: South End Press.

Said, E. W. (1978). *Orientalism.* New York: Vintage Books.

Salvador-Burris, J. (1978, Spring). Changing Asian American stereotypes. *Bridge: An Asian American Perspective,* 29–40.

Shields, M. (1995, May 14). Margaret Cho returns to her roots in stand-up. *Sacramento Bee,* encore sec., pp. 23–24.

Simon, J. (1993, November 15). Chinoiserie. *National Review,* 61–62.

Stevenson, N. (1995). *Understanding media cultures: Social theory and mass communication.* London: Sage.

Tajima, R. E. (1989). Lotus blossoms don't bleed: Images of Asian women. In Asian Women United of California (Eds.), *Making waves: An anthology of writings by and about Asian American women* (pp. 308–317). Boston: Beacon Press.

Tuchman, G. (1978). The symbolic annihilation of women. In G. Tuchman, A. K. Daniels, & J. Benet (Eds.), *Hearth and home: Images of women in the mass media* (pp. 3–38). New York: Oxford University Press.

Wong, B. (1994, September 23). Column. *Asianweek, 12,* 9.

(Con)Text-Centered Approaches to Television Criticism

> Text always includes context. Texts occur only within a culture, a system with subsystems and multiple layers of meaning. Textual interpretation takes "text" as the center of meaning, but of meaning that is social and historical as well as personal.
>
> —Real, 1989, p. 57

Michael Real's observation highlights the focus of context-centered critical analysis: the study of the ways in which forces outside of television discourse structure or constrain meaning-making processes. What is involved in context-centered criticism is bringing both textual and social knowledge and experience to bear upon a television text (or set of texts) in order to understand how that text is constructed and read in terms of lived social experiences.

One classic example of outside forces shaping and being shaped by television discourse is the Super Bowl, America's preeminent annual sports event. More people watched the 1974 Super Bowl than watched the first person walk on the moon (Real, 1977, p. 92). Indeed, we are as likely to speak of football season and Super Bowl Sunday as we are fall and Thanksgiving Thursday. The Super Bowl is the most widely viewed (and the most lucrative) annual spectacle in American mass culture because, as Real (1977) explains, it is the perfect marriage between the ideology and dominant institutional structures of television and American culture:

> The Super Bowl combines electronic media and spectator sports. . . . The structural values of the Super Bowl can be summarized succinctly: American football is an aggressive, strictly regulated team game fought between males who use violence and technology to win monopoly control of property for the economic gain of individuals within a nationalistic, entertainment context. . . . In other words, the Super Bowl serves as a mythic prototype of American ideology collectively celebrated. (Real, 1977, pp. 92, 115)

To understand the meanings and popularity of the Super Bowl, Real explains, we must analyze the relationship between the Super Bowl and American culture: both focus on the physical (sports, and especially football, is very physical)—on the body and on dramatic action; both valorize acquisition, territoriality, and immediate and violent responses to challenges; both have clearly delineated occupational and social roles that reflect the sexual, racial, and organizational hierarchy of American power structure and the institutional organization of American business. Both are shared cultural experiences. In short, Real argues that the Super Bowl functions as a mythic spectacle that "structurally reveals specific cultural values proper to American institutions and ideology" (1977, p. 92).

As this Super Bowl example illustrates, understanding the contexts—institutional, historical, and sociocultural—within which television narratives are created, distributed, and received helps explain why some kinds of shows appear and then disappear and helps explain the resonance between social values and institutions and television texts.

Because contexts can be understood either ideationally (meaning can be understood as centered in empowered ideas) or structurally (meaning can be understood as positively sanctioned in social structures), we can divide context-centered criticism into two general types of approaches–ideological and sociocultural.[1]

Understanding (Con)Texts Ideologically

Ideology is a structure of beliefs, principles, and practices that define, organize, and interpret reality. Ideology is not the hidden message in a television program; rather, it is the systematic representation of ideas and beliefs that members of a society regard as the normal or natural way things are. As Stuart Hall (1993) explains, in an important sense one can never be "outside" ideology: "When we contrast ideology to experience, or illusion to authentic truth, we are failing to recognize that there is no way of experiencing the 'real relations' of a particular society outside of its cultural and ideological categories" (p. 105).

Classical Marxist Theory

Most contemporary ideological criticism is rooted in Marxist economic theory and as such is based on the assumption that television—and other cultural texts—are produced within specific historical, social-economic contexts by specific social groups for other social groups. Ideological criticism defines ideology as "meaning in the service of power," and it investigates the ways in which "meaning mobilized by symbolic forms" (Thompson, 1990, p. 7) serves "the vested interests of the prevalent power structure and its privileged beneficiaries" (Real, 1989, p. 53).

Although classical Marxism has gone the way of the Model T car, subsequent reconceptualizations and extensions of aspects of Marxist economic theory have shaped much of contemporary ideological and cultural studies criticism. Classical Marxism (sometimes called vulgar Marxism) is an economic theory that argued that the system of economic relationships in a society (the base) was the most powerful and fundamental shaper of all other social structures and institutions (superstructure) within a society. Those individuals who controlled/owned the means of production (the bourgeoisie) become the ruling class. The rest of us, who own relatively little, are part of the proletariat or working class. In this theory, moreover, because economic relations shape and constrain other social institutions (the educational system, the legal system, etc.), the bourgeoisie or power elite control not only the economy and economic institutions but also the ideas in a society. As Marx (1964) put it,

> The ideas of the ruling class are, in every age, the ruling ideas: i.e., the class which is the dominant material force in society is at the same time its dominant intellectual force. The class which has the means of material production at its disposal, has control at the same time over the means of mental production. (p. 78)

Classical Marxism views ideology as "false consciousness." In the case of television, this view means that we would expect television, as part of the media industry owned by wealthy individuals and corporations, to reflect ideas, beliefs, and values that serve the interests of the economic elite, which at bottom is maintaining its current power—the status quo. Classical Marxist theory sees television viewers who adopt these beliefs and values as their own as participating in their own oppression—they are, in short, dupes of the dominant ideology.

Neo-Marxist Critical Theory

Critical or neo-Marxist theory developed in the United States when a group of German intellectuals were forced to leave the Institute for Social Research (called the Frankfurt School because of its location in Frankfurt, Germany) in the 1930s. They fled Germany and emigrated to the United States where they continued their reconceptualizations of classical Marxism. The theoretical and critical work of members of the Frankfort School (including Theodor W. Adorno, Herbert Marcuse, Max Horkheimer, Erich Fromm, and Walter Benjamin) was heavily shaped by their own experiences. They sought to explain the rise of fascism, the dearth of worker revolutions, and the role of the mass media (or the "culture industry" as they called it), which they argued "performed a highly manipulative role in advanced capitalist societies, serving to contain and subvert forms of oppositional or critical consciousness on behalf of the dominant capitalist class" (O'Sullivan, Hartley, Saunders, Montgomery, & Fiske, 1994, pp. 123–124). Their efforts, which came to be known as *critical theory,* helped focus scholarly attention on the role of the mass media in modern societies (Thompson, 1990, pp. 75–76) and provided the foundation for ideological criticism.

The Frankfurt School and other critics of classical Marxism noted that classical Marxism had neglected to acknowledge and account for modes of domination other than class[2] (e.g., it ignored race and gender), failed to explain why people did not simply rise up in protest, and failed to explain how people might derive pleasure from cultural productions such as television. Thus, although classical Marxism provided an explanation for the alienation felt by the working class members of a society, the classical Marxist view has been subject to critique and revision because it "(1) reduces the superstructure to a reflection of the base; (2) abstracts from historical processes; (3) characterizes human needs as economic rather than social; and (4) isolates cultural questions from issues related to economic organization" (Stevenson, 1995, p. 16).

The reformulations of the Frankfurt School and later neo-Marxist critical theorists explained that the power of the ruling elite is maintained not through force but through ideology (dominant discourses). It is exerted through establishing the ideas, values, and practices that serve the interests of the ruling class as the normal, natural, common sense of the society. No longer viewed as false consciousness, ideology was re-theorized as "the means by which ruling economic classes generalize and extend their supremacy across the whole range of social activity and naturalize it in the process, so that their rule is accepted as natural and inevitable; and therefore legitimate and binding" (O'Sullivan et al., 1994, p. 141).

Althusser's Theory of Overdetermination

Louis Althusser, a French neo-Marxist philosopher, further refined classical Marxist theory by replacing the base/superstructure theory with a theory of overdetermination. In contrast to the classical Marxist view of the economic base of society as controlling the superstructure—the cultural, social, and political institutions, activities, and practices of the society, Althusser's (1970) neo-Marxist theory argued that the superstructure is related to, yet relatively autonomous from, the economic base. Althusser proposed that we think of society as a social formation that consists of ideological and institutional social practices (ideological state apparatuses, or ISAs) that reproduce the dominant ideology (and economic relationships) through systems of representation.

Geras (1987) illustrates this reconceptualized relationship between the base (economy) and the superstructure (cultural and political institutions) with an analogy. Imagine the classical Marxist base and superstructure model as a person chained to a post. The chain doesn't prevent the person from watching television or playing the violin, but it does prevent the person from going to a concert or going shopping. The similarity, then, is that just as the person chained to the post has a relative autonomy, so too does the superstructure have relative autonomy from the economic base.

Althusser's (1970) reformulation also offered a more elaborated explanation of how ideology works to position us as social subjects within a particular economic system. Ideology, he explained, is a system of representation that functions through interpellation, that is, through social practices and structures that address or hail us as individuals and construct social identities for us. Althusser emphasized the role that ideological discourses play in letting us think that we are independent, autonomous agents when, in fact, we are passive social subjects of ideology whose social identities have been formed through the ideological discourses of social institutions. According to Althusser, in capitalist societies this process occurs constantly, smoothly—indeed, virtually invisibly—because the ideology of the dominant class in a society is conveyed not through coercion but through ISAs—and among the most powerful of these social institutions are the media.[3]

Following Althusser, Stuart Hall (1977), one of the founding members of the Birmingham Centre for Contemporary Studies, argued that the mass media are the main ideological institutions of contemporary capitalist societies. However, as John Fiske (1994a) has noted, where ideological theory differs both from other forms of Marxist theory such as political economy theory and from cultural studies is "in the emphasis of one social force over all others" (p. 197). At the center of ideology theory is class domination. Althusser brought psychoanalysis into ideology theory, which enabled him to explain the relationship among capitalist institutions, the dominant ideology, and individuals' subjective consciousness of their own identities. Cultural studies scholars agree that Althusser's reformulation is an important theoretical evolution in exploring the relationship between contexts, texts, and meanings. However, cultural studies finds Althusserian-type ideology theory too deterministic and reductionist because, according to Fiske (1994a), "in both ideology and psychoanalytic theories, texts became agents of domination" (p. 197).

Cultural theory, as developed by Hall, Fiske (1994a), and others, shares with ideological theory the view that "texts always carry the interests of the dominant classes, for those interests have developed the conditions of production, and the conditions of production are necessarily inscribed in the product" (p. 197). However, cultural theory is less concerned with describing how the macro-level structural strategies of domination (ideology) work through texts and more concerned with revealing sites and strategies of resistance. Describing how powerful forces are at work in texts—commodification, capitalist ideology, and patriarchy—is the focus of ideological criticism. However, as Fiske has noted, "describing those forces does not describe the totality of ways in which texts can be put to work" (p. 197). That is the task of culture-centered criticism, which we discuss in Chapter 9.

Both context-centered criticism and culture-centered criticism can and do use discourse analysis. However, the emphasis in each is slightly different. As Fiske (1994a) explains:

> In ideology theory, subjectivity plays the role that the commodity does in political economy. Capitalism reproduces itself, in this account, in the way that the dominant ideology makes all who live under it into "subjects-in-ideology." This concept implies that the overridingly effective part of our consciousness, of our ways of understanding our identities, social relations, and social experiences, is a totally pervasive ideology. This ideology and its ways of working is [sic] institutionalized into the "ideological state apparatuses"—the law, education, the media, the political system, and so on—and in the ways they go about their daily operations; it is internalized in the consciousness, or rather subconsciousness, of the individuals who live within that society and its institutions. (p. 197)

Ideological Analyses

Practically speaking, television critics doing ideological criticism seek to examine the ways in which television series present ideological conflicts and the messages about social reality conveyed through these representations and their resolutions. In the next sections, we discuss two approaches television critics can use to analyze the ideological meanings and conflicts generated by television programs—discourse analysis and metaphor analysis.

Discourse Analysis

One approach television critics have used to analyze the relationship between television texts and their sociocultural and institutional contexts is discourse analysis. As Fiske (1994b) explains, "Critics do discourse analysis in order to make sense of the relationship between texts and the social world. . . . [and] to make sense of the world is to exert power over it" (p. 3).

At its simplest, discourse is a "system of representation that has developed socially in order to make and circulate a coherent set of meanings about an important topic area. These meanings serve the interests of that section of society within which the discourse originates and which works ideologically to naturalize those meanings into common sense" (Fiske, 1987, p. 14). Discourses can promote the dominant ideology and serve the dominant interests, as the legitimated, naturalized discourse of patriarchy does. Discourses also can oppose the dominant ideology, as, for example, the emergent, marginalized discourse of feminism does (O'Sullivan et al., 1994, p. 94). In each case, however, discourse is "politicized, power-bearing language employed to extend or defend the interests of its discursive community" (Fiske, 1994b, p. 3).

Discourse, as Fiske (1994b) notes, always has three dimensions: "a topic or area of social experience to which its sensemaking is applied; a social position from which this sense is made and whose interests it promotes; and a repertoire of words, images and practices by which meanings are circulated and power applied" (p. 3). Discourses, then, can be thought of as ideological codes that link texts, producers, and readers. Whereas social discourses enable readers to make sense of texts, in turn, texts reinforce social discourses through a kind of mutual validation and sense making.

As we noted in the discussions about Althusser and Hall, the media's social circulation of discourses plays a crucial role in the reproduction and maintenance of the dominant ideology. According to Fiske (1991a):

> Ideology works to naturalize the means of the social world that serve the interest of the dominant; it works to create common sense out of the dominant sense . . . and it has to work constantly in order to establish and maintain this common sense against the social experiences of the subordinate which consistently contradict it. One of the most important agents in this ideological work is discourse. Discourse is an ideological way of thinking about and representing an important topic area in social experience. Insofar as much of this experience contradicts the meanings given it by ideology, discourse is a site of struggle, so reading a text becomes a struggle for meaning that reproduces the social struggle. (pp. 446–447)

Although we can identify the institutions and discourses that structure and attempt to shape the meanings we construct from television programs, our analysis cannot identify the discourses viewers will use to read these programs. Indeed, as we discussed in Chapter 6, Stuart Hall (1993) has explained that individuals can respond to a text's interpellations by adopting one of three reading positions: the preferred reading position, a negotiated reading position, or an oppositional position.[4] Multiple ways of reading a text are possible because television texts are *polysemic* (i.e., open to multiple interpretations or meanings). Indeed, Fiske argues that television texts have to be polysemic because they simultaneously "have to serve the economic interests of their producers and distributors, and, as these are capitalist institutions, their economic interests must be aligned with capitalist (and patriarchal ideology)" and have to give pleasure to viewers who "are subordinated in one way or another by patriarchal capitalism" (p. 446). In other words, as Fiske explains, "to be popular, mass cultural texts must not only reproduce the dominant ideological meanings, but they must also offer opportunities to contest them, to negotiate with or to modify them" (1991a, p. 447).[5]

Discourse analysis is one approach available to critics who wish to study the interconnection between television texts and their social and ideological contexts. To do discourse analysis, you begin by looking for the pattern of binary oppositions in the text. Next, you identify the topic that organizes the ideological relationship between them. Then you could explore the relationship between the discourses out of which the text is constructed and the social discourses that viewers may use to create meanings from the text. In doing so, you ask (and try to answer) such questions as these:

- Whose/what point of view, feelings, and experiences are viewers invited to identify with in this television text by virtue of the camera angles, editing, narrative structure, and conclusion (i.e., in what subject position do the discursive and dramatic narrative elements place the viewer)?
- Who is the ideal viewer who is hailed or addressed by the text?
- What does the text invite that ideal viewer to regard as normal, natural, and/or enjoyable?
- Through what formal and technical strategies and codes is this point of view conveyed?
- Do the roles, values, actions, images, and words in this text maintain, deconstruct, or reconstruct dominant cultural discourses on this topic?
- What oppositional positions, if any, does the text encourage?

Ultimately, discourse analysis is a tool that television critics can use to discover the ways in which television texts produce and/or question struggles over ideological meanings and to relate the ideological conflicts in television texts to those in our social experience. As Fiske (1991a) reminds us, using discourse analysis to study television texts "can reveal much not only about television, but also about our society" (p. 446).

Metaphoric Ideological Analysis

A second approach media critics have taken to analyzing the intersection between television texts and their social context is to examine the metaphoric language used in the telling (in the case of news, talk, sports, and other non-fictional programs) and in the enactment (in the case of comedic and dramatic programs) of the ideological conflicts, issues, and perspectives conveyed in television programs (see, for example, Aden, 1995; Mumby & Spitzack, 1991). This approach combines key concepts from rhetorical and narrative criticism and theories of ideology to examine the ideological positions organized by the metaphors in a text.

At its simplest, a *metaphor* is the juxtaposition of two terms usually regarded as very different. By juxtaposing these terms, the structure of the metaphor (and the ideas evoked or entailed by the metaphor) argues for a particular understanding of the terms. This understanding occurs because "In allowing us to focus on one aspect of a concept . . . a metaphorical concept can keep us from focusing on other aspects of the concept that are inconsistent with the metaphor" (Lakoff & Johnson, 1980, p. 10).

Analyzing the verbal metaphors used by speakers, news reporters, or actors in television dramas and comedies as well as the visual metaphors created by camera work, lighting, music, and other technical/production codes in a television text enables us to see the ideological positions that are foregrounded and affirmed through the text and those that are being hidden or absorbed. For example, in their analysis of television news stories, Dennis Mumby and Carole Spitzack (1991) showed how using different metaphors to describe politics radically alters our sense of what political activity is; what political behaviors are natural, normal, and right; and what the outcome of political conflicts should be. They noted, for instance, that the metaphor *politics is war* invites a radically different understanding (and evokes different expectations) of political activities and outcomes than do the metaphors *politics is a dance, politics is dramatic performance,* or *politics is a game*. These different understandings occur because each metaphor includes a system of subsidiary, related concepts called *entailments,* which together create an ideological framework.

As Mumby and Spitzack (1991) have pointed out, the metaphor *politics is war,* for example, entails these concepts: war involves two or more enemies; war involves strategies, attacks, use of weapons, conflict, violence, a struggle for domination; war has leaders; war is dangerous; war usually ends in victory or defeat. The notion of politics here, then, is one in which aggression, violence, danger, and negativity are highlighted as normal and natural while opposing views of politics—as cooperation in democratic governing, mutual understanding, and shared social goals are de-emphasized (pp. 324–325). In contrast, the metaphor *politics is a game* entails such related concepts as play, role playing, cooperation with teammates, friendly competition, strategy, use of skill, spectators, and rules. As Mumby and Spitzack explain, the ideological framework structured by this game metaphor, then, suggests that politics is play—neither serious work nor war—and, therefore, is a friendly diversion rather than a serious commitment; that the outcomes of political contests are a reflection of the strategic skills of the participating political teams and not necessarily their inner qualities; and that political activity is something that we can watch—as game spectators—without becoming actively involved in it.

These examples illustrate how metaphors structure our perceptions and the meanings of texts by highlighting some aspects of a topic or issue and by hiding or de-emphasizing others. Metaphoric analysis, then, enables critics to see the taken-for-granted ideological assumptions conveyed in television texts through verbal and visual metaphors.

Practically speaking, as Foss (1996) explains, metaphor analysis usually involves several steps. First, you need to examine the text carefully and identify the principal metaphors used to structure the text. In doing so, you need to pay careful attention to the context (to see if the metaphors are used ironically, comedically, seriously, etc.).

If you identify many metaphors, you need to sort these metaphors into clusters that share *entailments* (those subsidiary, related metaphoric concepts). Next, you analyze the clusters of metaphors to determine what Lakoff and Johnson (1980) call *external systematicity*—the common perceptions created when the principal metaphors share entailments. Finally, you need to explore how these metaphors ideologically structure viewers' attitudes toward the characters, actions, and issues in the text. As a critic, then, you ask (and answer) these questions:

- Which ideological positions are highlighted and—equally importantly—which are hidden by the use of these metaphors?
- What view of social reality is constructed, affirmed, interrogated, or rejected by foregrounding these metaphoric understandings and obscuring others?
- In what ways does this text reinforce, question, or critique the dominant ideology?
- What alternative ideological perspectives (if any) does it present or consider?
- What insights does this analysis provide about television's hegemonic function? about its empowering function?

Verbal and visual metaphors are two devices that television texts use to shape the meanings viewers are invited to create from their viewing experiences. Metaphor analysis, then, is another tool that critics can use to uncover and examine the hegemonic qualities of television texts and explore the connection between television texts and their ideological contexts.

Sociocultural Analyses

As we explained at the beginning of this chapter, contexts can be understood either ideationally (meaning understood as centered in empowered ideas) or structurally (meaning understood as positively sanctioned in social structures). Again, there are a variety of ways in which to examine the structural contexts that shape the form and content of television texts. Chapter 10 discusses several approaches to understanding how institutional structures shape the meanings of television texts. Another approach, which we discuss in the remainder of this chapter, is to explore how the social formations reflected in television texts reaffirm and reinscribe viewers into the dominant ideology of the society. We call this approach to the study of the interrelationships between television texts and their social context *sociocultural criticism*.

Sociocultural criticism focuses on the ways in which television programs and television viewing reflect the structured patterns and organizations of social life. This critical method offers interpretations of the ways people use television and the ways in which television viewing may function for individuals, groups, or societies as a whole.

One of the fundamental assumptions underlying sociocultural analysis is that television is an important social and cultural force because its stories offer lessons about rules and roles that portray idealistic and realistic visions of society, social organizations, social norms, and social experiences. This assumption is based on Albert Bandura's (1986, 1994) social cognitive theory, which argues that human beings learn social roles, rules, norms, and values both directly (i.e., through personal experience) and also indirectly (i.e., through observing others) in real life and in/on the media. Applied to television, then, social cognitive theory leads critics to assume that viewers can learn social roles and rules—can be socialized—through watching the actions (and the results of the actions) of people in newscasts and characters in entertainment programs. Thus, sociocultural critics look at the same kinds of social phenomena that sociologists and cultural anthropologists do—the roles social actors play in various settings, the norms and values represented by sequences of characters' actions, and the social rules and advice being communicated through the negative and positive outcomes in these portrayals.

Sociocultural criticism assumes that television is a social institution and set of practices that both reflects and shapes the ideological context within which viewers make sense of their world. That is, sociocultural analyses of television texts regard television as the context within which viewers see particular views of social, occupational, and sexual roles, social class, deviance and conformity, and race and ethnicity affirmed and disconfirmed.

Sociocultural criticism takes existing sociological, anthropological, and cultural concepts and uses them to examine television texts in order to understand television program portrayals of the social, mythic, and ideological worlds and then to make inferences about the potential implications of these representations for individuals and groups in societies. Although in the 1970s sociocultural criticism used such terms as *prosocial* and *antisocial* (see, for example, Smith, 1976, 1980) to describe television program content's relationship to its social context, today's sociocultural critics tend to use vocabularies inflected by semiotics; they tend, therefore, to speak of the relationship of the content of television programs to viewers and society in such terms as *empowering* and *hegemonic*. The shift reflects the realization of critics over the past two decades that to speak of television's power as a social and cultural force is to acknowledge its ideological nature.

Some Central Concepts in Sociocultural Criticism

Some sociocultural constructs used by television critics to analyze the ways in which television texts communicate ideology through the social structures it displays and enacts are roles, stereotypes, values, sex and gender, race and ethnicity, and social class.

Roles. Roles are "socially defined positions and patterns of behavior which are characterized by specific sets of rules, norms, and expectations which serve to orientate and regulate the interaction, conduct, and practices of individuals in social situations" (O'Sullivan et al., 1994, p. 270). We all have many different roles, each connected to different contexts. For example, there are social roles (e.g., citizen, neighbor, friend), occupational roles (teacher, doctor, lawyer), and family roles (parent, spouse, sibling, child). We learn sets of expectations related to these roles and their proper performance; we are socialized (i.e., we learn about these roles) through various institutions—the family, the school, religious institutions, and the media. Sociocultural analysis explores television's depiction of roles and analyzes the meanings conveyed through them about power, status, and identity.

Stereotypes. Stereotypes are implicitly or explicitly judgmental ways of categorizing particular individuals and groups based on oversimplified and overgeneralized features or signs. Stereotypes can be positive (e.g., Officer Friendly, the policewoman, or the kind, dedicated family physician) or negative (the crooked politician or the dumb jock), and they can be based on racial, occupational, sex, or gender characteristics. Their intensity and perniciousness may vary, but they "generally represent underlying power relations, tensions or conflicts. . . . encourage an intuitive belief in their own underlying assumptions, and play a central role in organizing common sense discourse [ideology] (O'Sullivan et al., 1994, pp. 299–301).

Values. In sociocultural studies, values are attitudes we have about what behaviors and goals are desirable and undesirable, good and bad, and about the means of obtaining them. According to Milton Rokeach (1980) values are "shared prescriptive or proscriptive beliefs about ideal modes of behavior and end states of existence that are activated by, yet transcend object and situation" (p. 262). Values, then, are social or cultural, not strictly personal. Rokeach (1973) distinguishes between terminal (or "ends") values, such as freedom, security, and salvation, and instrumental (or "means") values, such as honesty, courage, and ambition. Robin Williams (1970) also has described a set of fifteen major clusters of value orientations that, he argues, have long been salient in American society. These include achievement and success, activity and work, morality, humanitarianism, efficiency and practicality, progress, material comfort, equality, freedom, external conformity, science and secular rationality, nationalism, democracy, individual personality, and group superiority. In studying the depiction and enactment of values in television narratives, Suzanne Williams (1991) explains that we need to look at three things: what characters say their values are, what characters' actions imply their values are, and which characters and which values are affirmed in the narrative's conclusion. Suzanne Williams used this approach to analyze values in children's television and film cartoons. John Fiske (1991b) studied how quiz shows use the discourses of education, capitalist economics, gambling, and sex to naturalize and legitimatize the dominant ideology and its attendant value structure.

Sex and gender. Sex is a bio/physiological term, based on primary and secondary biological and reproductive differences, which differentiate females from males. Gender is a cultural term that includes social concepts of the traits, roles, and behaviors deemed typical and desirable for females and males. Sociocultural analysis examines how discourses and other textual devices such as language, character, settings, narrative structure, camera work, laugh tracks, and musical soundtracks construct gender ideologies that reflect, maintain, or challenge dominant cultural notions of gender and sex roles (see Kervin, 1991).

Race and ethnicity. Race is "a social category of people who are supposedly distinguished by inherited and invariable characteristics" while ethnicity "assumes the further addition of cultural characteristics for a group of people" (O'Sullivan et al., 1994, pp. 255–257). However, the concept of race "carries a hidden ideological agenda" about the nature of racial stereotyping. (See Hall's [1990] and Fiske's [1994b] discussions of racist ideologies and the media.)

Social class. Social classes "are those distinct social formations made up of groups of people who have a similar relationship to the means of production in a society and, as a result, a common social and cultural position within an unequal system of property ownership, power and material words . . . the term refers to the fundamental determinant of social stratification within modern industrial societies" (O'Sullivan et al., 1994, pp. 39–42). As we noted in the discussion of classical and neo-Marxist ideology theory, the major social division is between the class of owners and the class of workers or producers. According to Marxist theory, social classes can be distinguished by the ideologies or forms of consciousness they characteristically possess as a function of their position in the socioeconomic system. However, even Marx recognized other class divisions and that classes often are divided and at odds (e.g., conflicts between skilled and unskilled workers). The key is that different class positions "confer what Weber called different 'life chances' upon individuals" because they "govern access to a wide variety of scarce and valued products and services in society" (p. 41). Sociocultural ideological analysis examines the strategies through which class conflicts and inequities inherent in the dominant ideology and social institutions are naturalized and legitimized.

Among the kinds of questions critics using sociocultural analyses to explore the contexts shaping the meaning of television programs ask (and seek to answer through analyses of the content and structure of television programs) are these:

- In what kinds of roles (social, occupational, familial, sex) are the characters in this text portrayed?
- What attributes, attitudes, and behaviors do they display in these roles?
- Which of these roles are portrayed as psychologically, emotionally, socially, economically, or spiritually rewarding?
- What social rules and lessons are explicitly and indirectly communicated through the characters' words and actions and the narrative outcomes?

Sample Context-Centered Essays

The sample critical essays in this chapter illustrate both ideological and structural approaches to understanding the ways that contexts shape the meanings of television texts.

Robert Schrag's essay explores social roles and social identities through an analysis of the evolution of the character of Margaret Houlihan in *M*A*S*H*. He describes three phases of Margaret's growth in self-esteem, self-identity, and consciousness raising during the series' eleven years of episodes and concludes with an analysis of Margaret's final career choice. As Schrag explains, this narrative conclusion reflects Margaret's gradual recognition and ultimate rejection of her subordinate position as a subject in the patriarchal gender ideology of her family and the army. Schrag argues that Margaret provides viewers, especially young female viewers like his daughters, with a positive female social role model. Margaret's depiction illustrates the ways social, familial, societal, and organizational structures shape our consciousness and also that it is possible to recognize and resist ideological domination.

Heather Hundley's essay examines the ways in which the discourse of beer in the television series *Cheers* was naturalized through its characters, dialogue, actions, consequences, settings, and the narrative strategies of humor, camaraderie, and detoxification. Taking as her focus the final year of the series' eleven-year prime-time run, Hundley explains how the discourse of excessive consumption of beer was made to seem a normal, natural social practice. She presents extratextual information that supports her argument that the series' entertaining endorsement of excessive beer drinking served the economic interests of the beer producers at the expense of beer consumers, who were invited to learn from the series that there were no negative consequences and several positive consequences—sociability and relaxation—

associated with excessive beer drinking. Her analysis illustrates quite clearly the ideological work of television in the service of the ruling class and the dominant ideology.

Similarly, Kent Ono's study of the popular children's program *Mighty Morphin Power Rangers* explores the social and ideological contexts within which this program functions to legitimize the combination of militarism, vigilante actions, and neo-racist and neo-sexist attitudes that reflect a neocolonial ideology. Ono begins by explaining how he (and other critics) might go about doing an ideological critique of neocolonialism. Next, he briefly explains a construct of neocolonialism before discussing how television has aided in justifying and legitimating neocolonialist relations and practices both within the United States and between the United States and other countries. Following this introduction, Ono examines one episode of the *Mighty Morphin Power Rangers* in detail to show how colonialist relations and beliefs about race, gender, sexuality, and class function in this program (and by extension in other similar children's television series).

As we explained at the beginning of this chapter, context-centered criticism explores how texts are created and read in terms of social contexts—social knowledge and experience. Because contexts can be understood either ideationally (meaning can be understood as centered in empowered ideas) or structurally (meaning can be understood as positively sanctioned in social structures), we divided this chapter on context-centered criticism into two general types of approaches—ideological and sociocultural. The essays that follow illustrate several approaches that critics use to analyze ideological meanings of television texts and the relationship between television and its ideological and institutional contexts within which television programs are produced and viewed.

NOTES

1. As we explained in Chapter 3, we use the label *centered* to describe various clusters of critical approaches because using a critical method to analyze television texts is not like using a cookie cutter to make gingerbread cookies. Critical methods are not neat, narrow, clean tools. Indeed, in practice, most critical analyses combine elements of several approaches, especially those approaches we include in this chapter on context-centered criticism and those in the following chapter on culture-centered criticism. Arguably, many of the approaches discussed in Chapters 8 and 9 could fit within either chapter; however, we believe the concept of centeredness helps explain both the similarities and the different emphases between these clusters of approaches.

2. *Class* here is defined as a category or group of individuals based on their economic resources, the social and cultural resources that their economic situation gives rise to, and their concomitant assumed positionality within the social system. Indeed, in Great Britain, for example, there can be Lords who are poorer than merchant class

people; hence the concept of the nouveau riche ("new rich"). It is really only in the United States that class is defined in primarily economic terms.

3. Althusser's critical focus, as Stevenson (1995) cogently explains, was on the ways in which "the cultural transmission of traditions through institutions, like mass communications and the education system, helps form a dominant consensus in contemporary society . . . [and the ways in which] hegemonic modes of dominance are also dependent upon formations within civilized society" (p. 17). *Formations*, here, mean "certain conscious movements and tendencies (like literary movements) that largely work within dominant meanings and values" (p. 17).

4. A viewer adopting such a *dominant reading,* for example, would most likely come away from watching *Cheers* episodes like those described in Hundley's essay in this chapter thinking what a great thing it would be to have a neighborhood bar in which one could drop into and share a pleasant evening sipping beer with drinking buddies like Norm, Cliff, and Frasier while listening to the wisecracks of Carla, Rebecca, Sam, and Woody. On the other hand, Hall argues that audiences can also read texts from a negotiated position in which they accept the general ideological position of the text that they are invited to assume (through narrative structure, musical soundtrack, laugh track, and other codes) but resist or contest some of the text's meanings.

A *negotiated* reading of *Cheers,* for example, might lead a female viewer to come away from watching the series thinking that it sure would be nice if Cheers were a friendly neighborhood bar in which women as well as men could quench their thirst and engage in pleasant, friendly conversation as just people—not as sex objects. Adopting such a reading position would entail accepting the series' overarching ideology of naturalizing alcohol while not accepting the series' sex stereotyping of bars as masculine enclaves in which women either serve men drinks or serve as voyeuristic sexual objects.

Viewers reading texts *oppositionally* refuse to accept the preferred ideological position encoded into the text. Such an oppositional reading of the series *Cheers* might interpret the series as yet another ploy by television and its major advertisers—beer producers—to persuade the public to vicariously share "the good life" of the lower middle class, racially segregated, male-dominated patrons—all of whose names you know—portrayed in *Cheers* by spending their evening in front of the television set drinking beer, laughing at Sam's sexual predations, and of course, never getting drunk or experiencing any ill effects.

5. Of course, Fiske also recognizes that texts are polysemic because of the inherent instability of language thanks to irony, metaphor, jokes, contradiction, and excess (see, for example, Chapter 6 in his 1987 book, *Television Culture*).

6. This step requires that you look outside the television text at other cultural documents and artifacts (e.g., popular periodicals, books, magazines, polls, etc.).

REFERENCES

Aden, R. C. (1994). Back to the garden: Therapeutic place metaphor in *Field of Dreams. Southern Communication Journal, 59,* 307–317.

Aden, R. C. (1995) Nostalgic communication as temporal escape: When it was a game's reconstruction of a baseball/work community. *Western Journal of Communication, 59,* 20–38.

Althusser, L. (1970). *For Marx.* (B. Brewster, Trans.). New York: Vintage.

Bandura, A. (1986). *Social foundations of thought and action: A social cognitive theory.* Englewood Cliffs, NJ: Prentice-Hall.

Bandura, A. (1994). *Social cognitive theory of mass communication.* In J. Bryant and D. Zillman (Eds.), *Media effects: Advances in theory and research* (pp. 61–90). Hillsdale, NJ: Lawrence Erlbaum.

Brown, M. E. (1994). *Soap opera and women's talk: The pleasure of resistance.*

Fiske, J. (1984). Popularity and ideology: A structuralist reading of *Dr Who.* In W. Rowland & B. Watkins (Eds.). *Interpreting television: Current research perspectives* (pp. 165–197) 1984, Beverly Hills: Sage.

Fiske, J. (1987). *Television culture.* London: Methuen.

Fiske, J. (1991a). Methodological preface [to "The discourses of tv quiz shows, or school + luck = success + sex"]. In L. Vande Berg & L. Wenner (Eds.), *Television criticism: Approaches and applications* (pp. 445–447). White Plains, NY: Longman.

Fiske, J. (1991b). The discourses of tv quiz shows, or school + luck = success + sex. In L. Vande Berg & L. Wenner (Eds.), *Television criticism: Approaches and applications* (pp. 445–462). White Plains, NY: Longman.

Fiske, J. (1994a). Audiencing: Cultural practice and cultural studies. In N. K. Denzin & Y. S. Lincoln (Eds.), *Handbook of qualitative research* (pp. 189–198). Thousand Oaks, CA: Sage.

Fiske, J. (1994b). *Media matters: Everyday culture and political change.* Minneapolis: University of Minnesota Press.

Foss, S. K. (1996). *Rhetorical criticism: Exploration & practice.* (2nd ed.). Prospect Heights, IL: Waveland.

Geras, N. (1987, May–June). Post-Marxism? *New Left Review, 163,* 40–82.

Gramsci, A. (1971). *Selections from the Prison Notebooks.* (Q. Hoare & G. Nowell–Smith, Eds. & Trans.). New York: International.

Hall, S. (1977). Culture, the media and ideological effect. In J. Curran, M. Gurevitch, & J. Woollacott (Eds.), *Mass communication and society* (pp. 315–348). London: Open University/Edward Arnold.

Hall, S. (1990). The whites of their eyes: Racist ideologies and the media. In M. Alvarado & J. O. Thompson (Eds.), *The media reader* (pp. 7–23). London: British Film Institute.

Hall, S. (1993). *Encoding, decoding.* In S. During (Ed.), The cultural studies reader (p. 90–103). London: Routledge. [Edited and reprinted from *Encoding and decoding in television discourse,* CCCS Occasional Paper, by S. Hall, 1973, Birmingham].

Kervin, D. (1991). Gender ideology in television commercials. In L. Vande Berg & L. Wenner (Eds.), *Television criticism: Approaches & applications* (pp. 235–253). White Plains, NY: Longman.

Kohlberg, L. (1968). *Moral development. International encyclopedia of the social sciences* (pp. 489–494). New York: Crowell, Collier, & Macmillan.

Lakoff, G., & Johnson, M. (1980). *Metaphors we live by.* Chicago: University of Chicago Press.

Marx, K. (1964). *Selected writings in sociology and social philosophy.* (T. B. Bottomore & M. Rubel, Eds.; T. B. Bottomore, Trans.). New York: McGraw-Hill.

Mumby, D. K., & Spitzack, C. (1991). Ideology and television news: A metaphoric analysis of political stories. In L. Vande Berg & L. Wenner (Eds.), *Television criticism: Approaches and applications* (pp. 313–330). White Plains, NY: Longman.

O'Sullivan, T., Hartley, J., Saunders, D., Montgomery, M., & Fiske, J. (1994). *Key concepts in communication and cultural studies* (2nd ed.). London: Routledge.

Real, M. (1977). *Mass-mediated culture.* Englewood Cliffs, NJ: Prentice-Hall.

Real, M. (1989). Structuralist analysis 1: Bill Cosby and recoding ethnicity. In *Super media: A cultural studies approach* (pp. 106–131). Newbury Park, CA: Sage.

Real, M. (1996). *Exploring media culture: A guide.* Thousand Oaks, CA: Sage.

Rokeach, M. (1973). *The nature of human values.* New York: Free Press.

Rokeach, M. (1980). Some unresolved issues in theories of beliefs, attitudes, and values. In H. E. Howe, Jr. and M. M. Page (Eds.), *Nebraska Symposium on Motivation 1979* (pp. 261–304). Lincoln: University of Nebraska Press.

Ryan, K. (1976). Television as a moral educator. In R. Adler & D. Cater (Eds.), *Television as a cultural force* (pp. 111–128). New York: Praeger.

Smith, R. R. (1976). Social effects and the criticism of broadcasting. In *Beyond the wasteland: The criticism of broadcasting* (pp. 80–94). Falls Church, VA: Speech Communication Association/ERIC Clearinghouse on Reading and Communication Skills.

Smith R. R. (1980). Social effects and the criticism of broadcasting. In *Beyond the wasteland: The criticism of broadcasting* (Rev. ed., pp. 88–102). Falls Church, VA: Speech Communication Association/ERIC Clearinghouse on Reading and Communication Skills.

Stevenson, N. (1995). *Understanding media cultures: Social theory and mass communication.* London: Sage.

Thompson, J. B. (1990). *Ideology and modern culture: Critical social theory in the era of mass communication.* Stanford, CA: Stanford University Press.

White, H. (1981). The narrativization of real events. In W. J. T. Mitchell (Ed.), *On narrative* (pp. 249–254). Chicago: University of Chicago Press.

Williams, R. (1970). *American society: A sociological interpretation.* (3rd ed.). New York: Alfred Knopf.

Williams R. (1979). *Marxism and literature.* Oxford: Oxford University Press.

Williams, S. (1991). Bugs Bunny meets He-Man: A historical comparison of values in animated cartoons. In L. Vande Berg & L. Wenner (Eds.), *Television criticism: Approaches and applications* (pp. 201–219). White Plains, NY: Longman.

"Hotlips" No More: Margaret Houlihan's Personal Voyage

Robert Schrag

Once upon a time, in a monarchy far away, there lived the lovely young princess Snow White and her stepmother the evil Queen—well, maybe not evil but one who had been socialized to equate physical attractiveness and self-worth. Every morning the non–self-actualizing Queen would stand before her magic mirror and ask "Mirror, mirror on the wall, Who's the fairest of them all?" The mirror would, of course, respond with information that would overtly confirm the Queen's beauty and therefore her feelings of worth and acceptability in her society. Covertly, however, the Queen's dependence on the response of mirror continued to affirm that she really felt that she had no true worth beyond her appearance.

My two daughters have a magic mirror in the corner of the living room, with remote control and a VCR. They, too, consult their reflection in the mirror with daily regularity, and I am concerned with the image they see reflected there. My concern stems from the fact that they see not only an image of themselves but an image of the world—a constructed symbolic and social reality that will have a significant impact on how they behave, relate, and communicate in, and to, the world around them.

What models exist in that mirror that are worthy of emulation? For most of 1984 our elder daughter was entranced with the congresswoman from New York and would come running into the kitchen to tell us, "Mommy, Daddy come quick, it's Geraldine Ferraro!" While that particular role model quickly faded from view, television since 1984 has done better with admirable rejections of women in its magic mirror. The women of *L.A. Law, St. Elsewhere, Hill Street Blues, The Days and Nights of Molly Dodd, The Trials of Rosie O'Neal, Civil Wars, Murphy Brown, Northern Exposure,* and so forth, have begun to add a competence and variety to the images of women on television that were previously all too absent.

Yet these new women did not spring full-blown from some network head. Rather they are all, in one way or another, the daughters of an earlier television woman, a woman who is laudable and worthy of emulation, not because she came to her final self-actualization through some bionic implant or superpowers, but rather through the painful process of suffering, maturation, and growth. And it is that woman I am saving for my daughters on videotape so that they can see for themselves the progress this one female character made over the course of one television series. She is, of course, Major Margaret "Hotlips" Houlihan of *M*A*S*H*.

Before explaining further why I have selected this particular model, I will first discuss why I felt it was necessary to select any model. The "why" centers on a relationship between television and viewer that has had a myriad of labels hung on it. The chaining out of a rhetorical vision (Bormann, 1972), the construction of social reality (Bormann, 1972; Bantz, 1975; Schrag, Hudson, & Bernabo, 1981), the clawing back of a message to the center of a culture's consciousness (Fiske & Hartley, 1978), the creation of symbolic environments (Bernabo, 1984a), and so on, all address the central issue of concern: the myths, meanings, messages, and models of the mass media are the stuff that contemporary dreams are made of. And, as always, we are tempted to live our dreams.

The problem, as my colleagues and fellow critics, both female and male, have pointed out in conversation and publication, is that even with television's "new women," the dream material provided for little girls fails to measure up to the most meager standards of acceptability. In the early years of M*A*S*H Margaret Houlihan was no exception.

But how do we go about assessing where the flaws appear in this particular dream? As Margaret herself says (Alda et al., 1984, p. 114), "I have always looked to my father for guidance." So have I. My father is a sociologist, and as a child I was subjected to one final question from my father, after the usual queries regarding homework, play practice, etc. My father's closing question was always, "And what are the sociological implications of what you have done today, Robby?"

Given my history, can it be any wonder that the elements that have come to define sociocultural criticism permeate my work in general and this analysis in particular? I am concerned with issues of socialization; for example, how did Margaret's childhood and adolescence help create the worldview Margaret accepted? How did the assumptions and the assertions of the world in which she lived come to define her perceptions of an appropriate set of behaviors for her—how did they define her social role? And how did that role and her perception of the reality of the world come together to define her internalized view of herself—her identity? Finally, what is the dynamic that moves this identity out into the world as a "mirror, mirror on the wall" that will in turn become a step in the socialization process of other girls and young women?

Margaret's M*A*S*H identity is not a constant one. Bernabo (1984b, p. 4) argues that the history of M*A*S*H can be critically divided into three distinct periods: Stage 1: 1972–1977, the traditional situation comedy stage; Stage 2: 1977–1981, the development of the program into the archetypal representative of the human collectivity (Schrag, Hudson, & Bernabo, 1981); and Stage 3: 1981–1983, the regression of M*A*S*H to a more traditional situation comedy. Although one might argue that Bernabo's third stage results from a failure to expand the concepts of the collectivity as opposed to a stagnation of the program, his divisions provide an insightful framework for the examination of Margaret's evolution.

Margaret, too, passes through a series of three stages. In the first stage Margaret accepts a very traditional and sexist view of herself as an "army brat" who is worthy of little respect in the military world, and can increase her worth only by becoming the lover of a powerful military male. In the second stage Margaret is empowered by her identity as the wife of a man respected in the world she values. While this allows her to see herself as almost worthy of personal and professional respect, it is still worthiness conveyed by another. However, in the third stage, a liberated Margaret finally claims her identity as a strong yet caring, self-actualized person who gives and receives respect from both men and women.

Stage 1: Boot Camp Margaret

In stage 1 Margaret is "Hotlips." The name derives from a scene from the original Altman film in which Hawkeye and Trapper slip the camp's public address system microphone into a tent where Margaret and Frank Burns are sharing a particularly torrid interlude. Frank tells Margaret, and the listening camp, that her lips are hot, and the moniker sticks. Unfortunately, that isn't all that stuck—the one-dimensional, mostly unlikeable characterization also followed Margaret into the television program.

The fact that it is almost impossible to think of stage one Margaret without also thinking of Frank Burns is one clear indication that Margaret allows herself to be defined to a great extent by the men she chooses to have around her. In stage 1 she could not have made poorer choices, as the men she welcomes into her life serve only to bring out the worst in her.

What parents would want their daughter to identify with a woman who actually worries that the horrors of war might cease and separate her from her seemingly lobotomized lover, as in the episode "Cease-fire" from the series' debut season? In this episode one of the repeating rumors of a cease-fire sweeps the camp. Everyone is aflame with hope that hostilities will cease and they can return to the world they left behind. Everyone except Margaret. Margaret is *afraid* the rumors are true, *afraid* that the hostilities will cease and she will have to leave Frank Burns, who she sees as her link to both personal and military respectability.

Although it is true that Margaret occasionally becomes exasperated with old "ferret face," even to the point of requesting a transfer ("Hotlips and Empty Arms," second season), she always seems to return to him and the limited self-identity he represents. Always, that is, until the very end of stage 1 when she marries the "real army" Col. Donald Penobscot. ("Margaret's Engagement," "Margaret's Marriage," fifth season).

Stage 2: Empowered Margaret

Margaret's marriage, which ran from the last few episodes of the fifth season through the middle of the seventh season before ending in divorce, bridges stage 1 and stage 2 of the series. Margaret's personal evolution in this second stage of the program again can be assessed in terms of her relationships with men. Her husband, even though a traditional military straight arrow, is a liberating influence on Margaret. That assertion may seem strange to those of you familiar with the series, but consider this perspective: Margaret will never cease to be "Hotlips" until she is freed from Frank Burns; and it is her marriage that allows her to finally break off her affair with Burns. Furthermore, since her husband is not stationed at the 4077th, Margaret remains relatively free from his direct dominance and is suddenly placed in a situation that simultaneously satisfies her longings for permanence and commitment and allows her to begin to explore relationships with more potential for mutual growth and development.

Margaret's relational opportunities on *M*A*S*H* had actually been evolving prior to stage 2. Trapper John and Col. Blake had both disappeared by the end of the third season, replaced by the more complex and sympathetic characters of BJ Hunnicutt and Col. Potter. It was, however, the presence of Frank Burns, defined by Bernabo as the personification of ritualized incompetence (1984a, pp. 11–14), that most constrained the evolution of the series. His departure and subsequent replacement with Charles Emerson Winchester III at the beginning of the sixth season marked the final liberation of the series, for Margaret and for the other protagonists who often were ranged against her and Burns, seemingly at times for the simple lack of any more-challenging targets. Winchester provided that more challenging target for BJ and Hawkeye as he gave articulate voice to a new perspective on the world of *M*A*S*H;* and, in doing so, helped to create a freer environment for Margaret.

Margaret blossomed in this new environment, growing swiftly to fill a space beside the program's other dominant protagonists. She began to establish more realistic, compassionate relationships with Hawkeye and BJ, particularly during the fifth and sixth seasons. The pivotal episode is "Comrade-in-Arms," a two-part episode which aired during the fifteenth and sixteenth weeks of the program's sixth season. In this episode the friendly relationship that had been evolving between Margaret and Hawkeye turns passionate. They become lovers while perilously stranded near the front. Subsequent episodes gave little or no indication (with the possible exception of their record-breaking kiss in the final episode) that they maintained any physical relationship after that one night. However, a genuine caring relationship remained and grew throughout the rest of the series. Hawkeye became the respected colleague to whom Margaret would turn for advice, and Margaret became the woman who would always tell Hawkeye the truth. They provided a wonderful model of a relationship that moves beyond passion to compassion.

Margaret also entered into a combative, yet mutually respectful, friendship with Winchester. His Bostonian arrogance and her military reserve prevented it from ever leaving a very formal plane, yet it was nonetheless a relationship. Perhaps this relationship was best evidenced in his gift to her of a book of Browning's sonnets, something that could never have been possible in the days of Frank Burns.

Stage 3: Liberated Margaret

Is Margaret Houlihan a product of the men in her life? The initial two stages of the series would seem to argue that she was—Frank Burns shaped her character in the first sitcom stage of the series and her liberation from Frank in the second stage of the series, while a positive step, still seemed to lead her only to new relationships with men who continued to define her dreams and aspirations. Yet an examination of the last several years of the series, and particularly the final episode, "Goodbye, Farewell and Amen," provides evidence that such an interpretation is flawed, that a search for meaning, not a search for men, lies at the center of Margaret Houlihan's personal odyssey.

Before examining this final stage of the series, let us again remember why we are trying to walk around in Margaret's boots in the first place. The underlying assumption is this: TV provides potent role models. Breen and Corcoran (1982) even assert that television can function mythically to "create exemplary models for a whole society . . . thereby setting up patterns for imitation" (p. 129). One major concern about these potent role models revolves around the system of beliefs, attitudes, and values upon which the model is based. To what extent is this system in accord with the value system held collectively and individually by audience members? Is it a system worthy of general emulation? And, in this case, is it a value system our daughters should imitate?

In the first two stages of the program's development, Margaret hardly provides a desirable role model as she moves from silly to sympathetic and evidences only brief flashes of admirable behavior. In the final stage of the program, however, Margaret becomes an exemplary model as she discovers the importance of individualized meaning in her life. By "individualized meaning" I do not mean the self-indulgent "you-are-a-child-of-the-universe-don't-invade-my-space" individuality so cherished by the "me generation." I refer, rather, to the search for meaning and awareness as defined in Vicktor Frankl's discussions of logotherapy (Frankl, 1963).

Frankl asserts that the striving to find meaning in one's life is humanity's primary motivational force. He feels that our search for meaning supersedes both the will to pleasure that anchors Freudian analysis and the will to power that is a central concept in Adlerian psychology. In Frankl's model, our search for meaning is unique and specific in that it must and can be fulfilled by the individual alone. It is only after embarking on this individual journey that we come to realize the significance of our existence that will satisfy our individual will to meaning (Frankl, 1963, pp. 154–57).

Margaret, throughout most of the series, looked for meaning outside of herself. Initially she found relevance only in her relationships with the Army and Frank Burns. Personal value was conferred upon her by others. The rewards and privileges of rank were vital to her because, in the final analysis, she had nothing else. She certainly did not have, as previously mentioned, fulfilling relationships with men. Indeed, Margaret's relationships with men obviously deserve special attention.

Frank Burns, a ritualized incompetent, is literally without redeeming characteristics. Why then does Margaret remain with him? Because he is, if nothing else, a human being. Someone besides the Army who legitimizes her existence. Yet, eventually Margaret realizes that the relationship with the very-married Burns is a dead end and personally unfulfilling. This realization drives Margaret to a succession of relationships of varying degrees of intimacy and value. What characterizes these relationships? If we were to proceed from a Freudian perspective, we could have a field day with the notion that Margaret is spending her life taking surrogate fathers to bed trying desperately to please an unpleasable father. Frankl's model suggests an interpretation that provides a better fit with Margaret's behavior—particularly in the highly significant final episode.

In addition to finding meaning in our existence, Frankl also argues that our meaning structure must find a relatively pure expression in our lifework (Frankl, 1963, pp. 162–63). It stands to reason, then, that if we are truly moving toward a personal notion of meaning in our lives, we are also coming to a clearer understanding of how meaning is being manifested in our lifework. Margaret seeks to understand the lifework into which she has plunged herself. As she explains it to an old friend in the episode "Temporary Duty" (sixth season), she had to make the transition from "just Margaret" to "Major Houlihan, Head Nurse" literally overnight. She then found herself in a lifework situation in which all of the power was held by men.

Furthermore, her relationships with the women around her were severely constrained by the fact that she was the officer to whom all those women reported. This reality, combined with her fealty to the military model, naturally forced Margaret into reproducing male dominated relationships simply because there are no accessible dominant females in her work world to model. Her error, in pursuit of those relationships, was to assume that those relationships must follow traditional male/female, romantic/sexual models. The significant evolution for Margaret's character unfolds with the gradual realization that the legitimacy of organizational truth must be tested by individual reflection and that significant relationships transcend sexuality.

Bernabo's examination of Margaret's transition into the human collectivity's notion of personhood reveals a portion of this evolution (1984b, p. 31). Margaret, again during the paradoxical liberation of her marriage, establishes a growing number of same-sex and cross-sex asexual relationships. ("Margaret's Marriage," fifth season; "Fade Out, Fade In," and "What's Up Doc," sixth season). These relationships create firmer, deeper ties than any of her earlier, more frantic relationships. This is evidenced when her friends unite to protect her as she regroups emotionally after her divorce in "Major Ego" during the seventh season. This new solidarity with her coworkers allows Margaret to reconcile more smoothly the dictates of her beliefs and values with the obligations and demands of her work. This sense of unity between work and meaning also allows Margaret to demonstrate, in the final seasons of the series, a growing sense of comfort with her competence and her position of command.

It is, however, the final episode of the series "Goodbye, Farewell and Amen," that establishes once and for all Margaret's legitimacy as an exemplary role model. As the episode opens, we have ample cause to fear that Margaret may well end the series as still her father's pawn, sacrificing her personal dreams and aspirations on the altar of her military career. But the unfolding of the episode reveals that Margaret, perhaps more than any other character in the program, has learned Frankl's lesson: one's psychic well-being, while often group supported, is ultimately dependent upon a clear individual notion of life purpose (Frankl, 1963, pp. 160–63, 173–76).

"Goodbye, Farewell and Amen" spends most of its time and energy addressing the central characters' abilities, or lack of abilities, to cope with the forced dissolution of the supportive M*A*S*H group and the resultant confrontation with the characters' new individual life orientations (Schrag, 1984, p. 8).

The personal growth reflected in Margaret's behaviors is most obvious when compared with the choices made by the program's most dominant protagonist—Hawkeye. Hawkeye's choices are regressive. Throughout the eleven-year program, Hawkeye's medical proficiency and interpersonal insights have anchored his own feelings of competence. Yet, his inability to deal with his perceived responsibility for the death of a child on the bus and the resultant anxiety when he finally does return to surgery— "Yesterday I spent a year in the operating room. I was up to my ankles in panic. I'm a little out of control, Sidney. Surgery used to be like falling off a log. Now it's more like falling off a cliff" (Alda et al., 1984, p. 113)—clearly indicate that it is the confrontation of combined personal and professional vulnerability that unravels Hawkeye's world. His choices—to get out of the medical fast track, to retreat to Crabapple Cove—are regressive because they need to be. Frankl implies that a clearly focused hierarchy of beliefs, attitudes, and values manifested in a lifework that is consistent with that hierarchy forms a solid basis from which one continuously pursues meaning (pp. 160–164). Hawkeye's technical skills have outstripped the spiritual core that is necessary to guide their application; hence, Hawkeye panics and feels a need to regroup in the relative tranquillity of Crabapple Cove.

In contrast, Margaret evidences choices that reflect her final synthesis of value system and lifework. Margaret, as mentioned earlier, is confronted with two choices that her father has created for her. One involves an administrative post in Tokyo that will take her out of nursing but that is, according to Papa Houlihan, "the best way to get promoted" (Alda et al., 1984, p. 11). The other is a chance to be assigned to NATO headquarters in Belgium. Both are in conflict with Margaret's own stated desire to "get back to the States and work in a real hospital" (Alda et al., 1984, p. 8). In considering those options Margaret directly confronts the issue of unifying her lifework and her values. She must decide whether to continue to accept externally presented definitions of meaning, as represented by her father and the army, or to make a decision based on her own, internally defined, search for meaning. The dialogue in which she reveals her decision is significant enough to be quoted in its entirety. At the company's farewell dinner Margaret stands to address the group. She states that after finishing her obligations in Korea, she intends to take a little furlough and begin her next assignment-

POTTER: Tokyo, right?

KLINGER: Wrong. Belgium.

MARGARET: You're both wrong, I've always looked to my father for guidance. When he makes up his mind to do something, he does it, no matter what anybody says. That's what I'm going to do. What I wanted all along, to work in a hospital in the States. I guess there's a lot of my father in me. It was never his way to tell people how he felt about them. So maybe that's why I've never told my nursing staff what I've told other people about you. It's been an honor and a privilege to have worked with you. And I'm very, very proud to have known you. (Alda et al., 1984, p. 114)

This speech may well be the most significant bit of dialogue spoken by Margaret Houlihan in eleven years of *M*A*S*H*. It reveals that an extraordinary amount of change has taken place in the woman we met in the clutches of Frank Burns during stage one of the series. It reveals a woman who has gained the wisdom necessary to effectively integrate the value structure of the organization in which she works with her own, now clearer, value structure. It reveals a woman now able to resist the pressures of a male dominated power structure and to acknowledge the contributions made by those most responsible for her own success—the women who work for her. It reveals a woman at peace with herself, her values, and her lifework. It reveals a woman I would like my little girls to see in their "mirror, mirror, on the wall."

An Afterword on Criticism and Learning

Although this analysis examined the development of Margaret's selfhood, tracing her evolution from an initial stage characterized by low self-esteem and self-identity and a desire to please men to a final stage in which she is a self-respecting, self-actualizing grown-up woman, this essay is probably not feminist criticism. It is however, criticism that grows out of a deep concern for women, their options, and their images in society and in the media. Furthermore, it is an expression of personally motivated concern— the critical impulse for writing this essay stems from a father's concern for his daughters. And what do I hope my daughters, other daughters, and you, the reader, learn from watching Margaret's evolution? A variety of things:

- That personal identity is most admirable when it moves to a selflessness that is grounded in a clear understanding of self.
- That women and men are equal partners in the complex process of making a life.
- That doing for others is more satisfying than doing to others.

- That television can teach us meaningful things about our lives and our culture but that it rarely allows itself to.

REFERENCES

Alda, A., Metcalfe, B., Rappaport, J., Wilcox, D., Pollack, D., Davis, E., & Hall, K. (September 16, 1984). "Goodbye, farewell, and amen." *M*A*S*H.* New York: CBS Television.

Bantz, C. R. (1975). Television news: Reality and research. *Western Journal of Speech Communication, 39,* 123–130.

Bernabo, L. M. (1984a February). Rhetorical environments in television criticism: Ritual incompetence on *M*A*S*H* the "sitcom." Paper presented at the annual meeting of the Western Speech Communication Association, Seattle, WA.

Bernabo, L. M. (1984b November). Evolution to collectivity: *M*A*S*H* defines a symbolic reality. Paper presented at the annual meeting of the Speech Communication Association, Chicago, IL.

Bormann, E. G. (1972). Fantasy and rhetorical vision: The rhetorical criticism of social reality. *Quarterly Journal of Speech, 58,* 396–407.

Breen, M., and Corcoran, F. (1982). Myth in television discourse. *Communication Monographs, 49,* 127–136.

Fiske, J., & Hartley, J. (1978). *Reading television.* London: Methuen.

Frankl, V. E. (1963). *Man's search for meaning: An introduction to logotherapy.* New York: Washington Square Press.

Schrag, R. L. (1991). From yesterday to today: A case study of *M*A*S*H*'s Margaret Houlihan. *Communication Education, 40,* 112–115.

Schrag, R. L. (November 1984). After collectivity: A critical exploration of individual growth in "Goodbye, Farewell, and Amen." Paper presented at the annual meeting of the Speech Communication Association, Chicago, IL.

Schrag, R. L. (1985). Of butterflies and criticism. *Critical Studies in Mass Communication, 2,* 430–434.

Schrag, R. L., Hudson, R. A., & Bernabo, L. M. (1981). Television's new humane collectivity. *Western Journal of Speech Communication, 45,* 1–12.

Twain, M. (1884). *Adventures of Huckleberry Finn.* H. N. Smith (Ed.). (1958). Boston: Houghton Mifflin.

The Naturalization of Beer in *Cheers*

Heather L. Hundley

Alcohol consumption in the United States is related to a variety of safety and health risks.[1] Because of the problems associated with alcohol, it is important to examine how it is portrayed in the media. Of particular concern to many health and safety officials is the portrayal of beer consumption since 1) drinkers underestimate the negative consequences of beer consumption, and 2) beer consumption is an integral part of the socialization routines of young drinkers (Strate, 1992).

Cultivation theory posits that repeated exposure to consistent media portrayals and themes may influence viewers' perceptions so that they become congruent with media portrayals (Gerbner, Gross, Morgan, & Signorielli, 1980). Gross and Morgan (1985) explain that the more time one spends living in the world of television, the more likely one is to report conceptions of social reality that can be traced to television portrayals. Krugman and Hartley (1970) concur, arguing that "the mass media have taught our society what it needs to know in order to have attitudes on a thousand serious matters" (p. 189). Similarly, Bandura's (1977) social learning theory holds that viewers can learn a variety of attitudes and behaviors by observing behaviors and then modeling the observed behavior. Both of these theories suggest that over its eleven television seasons, *Cheers* may have "cultivated" some of its millions of viewers to accept the perception that excessive beer drinking is an unproblematic activity.

Critical Approach

The structural method used in this analysis is the application of the construct of discourse. Fiske defines discourse as "both a topic and a coded set of signs through which that topic is organized, understood, and made expressible" (1984, p. 169). Later, Fiske (1991) elaborates on the utility of examining discourse within texts because it is "an ideological way of thinking about and representing an important topic area in social experience" (p. 447). This study examines the discourse of beer in the television series, *Cheers*. The approach is well suited to the purpose of the study because, as Fiske (1987) argues, "to understand both the production of the programs and the production of meaning from them, we need to understand the workings of discourse" (p. 14). Discourse works ideologically to naturalize particular meanings on social topics within a text. The discourse of beer, then, is used by viewers not only in making sense of *Cheers*, but also in making sense of their social experiences (Fiske, 1987).

This method and this analysis stem from Fiske's theoretical development. To analyze various television programs and genres, Fiske (1984; 1986; 1987) uses such semiotic constructs as discourse and codes. Fiske has studied a variety of discourses such as sex, politics, and education, among others. For him, codes are conventionally shared meanings in a culture for a system of signs. In his television analyses he examines (1) social codes of appearance, dress, speech, (2) representation codes of camera, lighting, narrative character, and (3) ideological codes such as individualism, sex, and alcohol (Fiske, 1987).

Fiske's (1986) study notes that in order for television programs to be popular (like *Cheers*), they have to be open to multiple readings; the dominant ideology of the culture will be structured in both popular texts and the social system. The structure of meanings in a text is much like the structure of subcultures in society, that is, as Fiske argues, "both exist in a network of power relations, and the textual struggle for meaning is the precise equivalent of the social struggle for power" (p. 392).

Although a text must be open to different readings, Fiske explains that "the text can appeal to this variety of audiences only if there is a common ideological frame that all recognize and use, even if many are opposed to it" (p. 399). The identification of this common ideological frame is the focus of this study of the portrayal of beer drinking in *Cheers*.

While Fiske notes that there is a seemingly endless array of discourses that a reader can bring to a text, he explains that there are limits to a text's polysemy. Fiske's (1986) metacritical essay elaborates on the relationship between popularity and the semiotic construct of polysemy, which he first notes in his (1984) analysis of *Dr. Who*. Fiske's (1984) essay greatly contributes to this work in that connections are drawn between the symbolic television world and the social world, as I attempt to explain how the naturalization of beer on television stereotypes reality's concept of masculinity. Additionally within the *Dr. Who* essay is a definition of discourse, a discussion on polysemy, and an understanding of popularity. Specifically regarding popularity, Fiske believes that in order to be popular, a television program's textual signs must evoke social or ideological meanings which resonate with a wide diversity of audience members, all of whom must find the program appealing. While I acknowledge the polysemic possibilities presented by the *Cheers* text, I concentrate the analysis on the dominant reading encoded in the text's narrative structures (Fiske, 1984; 1986).

The Television Text

Cheers was an eleven-year-long prime time situation comedy set in a Boston bar named Cheers. It was television's longest-running situation comedy, having first appeared on September 30, 1982, and ended on May 20, 1993, totaling 275 episodes. During the 1989-1990 season, *Cheers* was among the top ten most watched prime-time shows in the United States, and in the 1990-1991 season it was "the top-rated show of the year" (*Facts on File*, 1991). *Cheers* received more Emmy nominations than any series, 111, and received 28 total Emmys.

During its last season (1992-1993), *Cheers* featured seven regular characters (four employees and three patrons); the bar in this season was co-owned by Sam Malone (a recovering alcoholic) and Rebecca Howe. *Cheers'* only cocktail waitress was Carla LeBec. Working as *Cheers'* bartender, Woody Boyd served regular bar patrons Norm Peterson, Cliff Clavin, and Frasier Crane. Norm was known for his outstanding bar tab, his non-existent relationship with his wife, and his frequent unemployment. Cliff was a letter carrier known for sticking his foot in his mouth and for his penchant for trivia—both factual and fictional. Frasier, a well-known, respected psychiatrist, was the "brains" of the *Cheers* group.

As of December 1994, 170 individual stations ran *Cheers* in syndication. The November 1993 sweeps showed that *Cheers*, in syndication, earned a 5.6 rating in 168 markets, and in its continuing popularity, "the show's license price [had risen] from $1.3 million to roughly $2.3 million in its second cycle" (Tobenkin, 1994, p. 18). *Cheers'* immense popularity has earned the greatest revenue in Paramount's history, more than any other television product (Chagollan, 1993). *Cheers* is one of the few television series that has kept the interest of a diverse audience for over a decade with few character and setting changes (Galloway, 1990). Because of the show's popularity, the Bull and Finch (the real bar in Boston after which *Cheers* was designed) made at least $7 million a year selling *Cheers* t-shirts, ashtrays, Bloody Mary mix, etc. (Gliatto, 1990).

Numerous content analytic studies have pointed to the excessive consumption of beer on television (Cafiso, Goodstadt, Garlington, & Sheppard, 1982; DeFoe, Breed, & Breed, 1983; Fernandez-Collado, Greenberg, Korzenny, & Atkin, 1978; Signorielli,

1987; Wallack, Breed, & Cruz, 1987; Wallack, Grube, Madden, & Breed, 1990). Interestingly, without *Cheers* the situation comedy genre would move from second highest to lowest in the portrayal of alcohol consumption. These studies afford documented evidence of *Cheers'* alcohol-related content and hence underscore the suitability of *Cheers* for purposes of this critical investigation.

This essay argues that over its eleven seasons *Cheers* naturalized beer drinking, presenting it as a normal, natural everyday activity. To explore the naturalization of beer in the last season of *Cheers*, 23 half-hour episodes and one hour-long episode, plus the one and one-half-hour-long finale are analyzed. The last season was chosen because the final season of any series is the last opportunity for the producers to change or alter the presentation of characters and/or topics before the show's end, and leaves the audience with a sense of closure regarding the characters' behaviors, traits, and motives (Piccirillo, 1986).

Naturalization is, as Fiske (1987) explains, the self-disguising process of "exonomination." A "naturalized" subject "present[s] itself as common sense, as an objective, innocent reflection of the real" (p. 42). Thus, "the only views that need no explanation or defense are those that have been naturalized or exonominated into common sense" (p. 134).

Even casual viewers should have been able to recognize at a glance that alcohol is an important and essential element of *Cheers*, since the setting for their sitcom is a neighborhood bar. However, a more critical examination suggests that beer, unlike other alcohol in the bar, is naturalized. Characters sit for hours and swill beer, seemingly without feeling any effects, in contrast to characters who drink wine, champagne, scotch, and other types of alcohol. In short, beer drinking is presented as a normal, acceptable behavior, naturalized through the use of three narrative devices: humor, camaraderie, and detoxification.

Strate (1992) points out that "often, beer is shown to be a product that is natural and pure, implying that its consumption is not harmful, and perhaps even healthy" (p. 83). I agree and argue in the remainder of this essay that *Cheers* naturalizes beer in that viewers are encouraged to think of beer not as a potentially harmful alcoholic beverage, but rather as a beverage no more dangerous than soda pop or water.

Humor as a Naturalization Strategy

Berger's (1987) psychoanalytic approach to humor suggests that jokes pertaining to alcohol, for example, "make possible the satisfaction of an instinct in the face of an obstacle that stands in its way" (p. 101). The logic of humor includes laughing at obstacles that stand in the way of masked desires which are ridiculously presented in excess. While excessive beer drinking is not an instinctive need of most people, it is presented as a virtually instinctive, pervasive, and apparently satisfying activity of most of the *Cheers* characters. However, the human body cannot tolerate the quantity of beer Norm consumed. "Such excesses," Palmer (1989) argues, "are implausible because excesses pursued more modestly are normal" (p. 151).

Norm provides the most exemplary portrayal of the use of this strategy to naturalize beer. In the 10/8/92 episode, for instance, Norm participated in a beer taste test and critique. After sampling beers A, B, and C, and critiquing them, Norm then asked to be really challenged. The marketing representative responded by offering him samples D through V. Beer, apparently, had little effect on this seasoned drinker and after tasting 22 beers, Norm went to *Cheers* to "hoist a few" as his lunch.

This portrayal of Norm's drinking implies that beer could be consumed in excessive amounts. Furthermore, the equivalence with which other characters respond to Norm's drinking in general and his drinking while describing his beer testing strongly affirms beer drinking as a normal, natural, and acceptable activity.

Overindulgence which allows the audience to laugh at the (non)consequential effects of excessive beer drinking as well as the characters' apparent inability to learn lessons from overindulgence were, for example, in the 4/29/93 episode. After a night of drinking too much hard liquor, Norm returned to the bar and Rebecca asked, "How are you doing?" Norm responded, "Terrible, I've got a splitting headache and I think I might be sick. Can I have a beer Sammy?" At this point the laugh track sounded, positioning the viewers to regard drinking beer as the "natural" thing to do, despite having a hangover and being nauseous. Berger (1987) explains that while characters "may often be 'low' and motivated by relatively trivial concerns, the function of humor is not trivial by any means" (p. 14). Applying Berger to the above example then, we see that one seriously important function of this vignette is the naturalization of beer drinking, regardless of one's health.

Another humorous device used to naturalize beer in this comedy is the use of quick one-liners strewn throughout each episode regarding beer drinking. For example, in the 10/1/92 episode Norm and Cliff were sent to retrieve Carla who was temporarily employed at Mr. Pubb's while *Cheers* was being rebuilt after a fire. The two were amazed at the vast selection of beers from every country, so before returning to *Cheers*, Norm suggested a "trip around the world." The laugh track and Cliff's approval suggest that consuming a great amount of beer, which is physically impossible, is humorous. In the 3/18/93 episode, Rebecca remarked that Norm had been making green beer for three hours to prepare for the St. Patrick's Day celebration, to which Norm responded, "And I'm prepared to work on it all night long if I have to because, damn it, I care!" The laugh track again indicates that Norm's affixation to beer is humorous. Both of these examples reflect the acceptability of beer drinking by using humor as a strategic device.

Camaraderie as a Naturalization Strategy

Cheers centers on the relationships of characters in a bar. Strate's (1992) study of beer commercials describes the typical bar setting which closely resembles the *Cheers* bar:

> It is generally portrayed as a relaxed and comfortable context for male socializing, as well as a place where a man can find entertainment and excitement. The bars are immaculate and smokeless, and the waitresses and bartenders are always friendly; thus, bars are the ideal male leisure environment. (p. 84)

This male camaraderie both enables male viewers to parasocially relate to *Cheers'* characters and functions as another narrative strategy by which beer drinking is naturalized.

People are brought together within this "boys club" to fraternize, to share the joys and sorrows, and to drink. In the Cheers bar, where "everybody knows your name," beer is the common link among patrons and employees who are quite diverse in age, education, and socioeconomic status. For example, Frasier, who is an educated, white collar patron, befriended Norm, an unemployed accountant/painter. While it might seem that the two have little in common, they drink beer together at Cheers and in the rare occasions they meet outside the bar, beer is still present. Strate (1992) explains the role of beer as a medium of male bonding and as a facilitator of group solidarity. Both of these aspects are quite clear and present in *Cheers*.

That this (primarily male bonding) process evolves while tippling beer together is illustrated over several episodes, it cumulatively naturalizes beer drinking as a positive social activity. For example, Frasier at first drank Manhattans and was not welcomed as part of the Cheers gang. However, over time as he began quaffing drafts, he became increasingly accepted as part of the Cheers "family." Indeed, by the final season, when he and his wife, Lilith, separated, the Cheers gang gave him a surprise divorce party at the bar. Later they went to his house (Norm brought beer) to keep him from feeling lonely and depressed.

Montgomery (1989), DeFoe & Breed (1986), and Strate (1992) note that heavy drinking on television is a macho activity and, in fact, often a requirement for proving oneself as a man, and gaining membership into one's social environment. Woody illustrated this rite of passage to join the membership and camaraderie of the "boys club" in the 2/11/93 episode. Specifically, Al (a minor character) saw Woody serving himself a beer and queried Woody about his drinking. Wood's response, "Why not? I'm a grown man. I'm an adult. I can handle my alcohol," suggests that drinking beer is a normal, natural indicator of male adulthood. Furthermore, the rest of Woody's explanation, "Plus, we're out of chocolate milk," suggests that his decision to drink beer is a conscious attempt to prove that he is an adult, a "manly man." Subsequently, though, we saw that Woody's attempts to gain the respect of others by drinking like the men only resulted in his passing out, as affirmed later by Cliff's comment, "He's still out cold. Should we wake him?" Norm, Sam, and Frasier join Cliff in looking at Woody who had passed out on a bar table, and responded by shaking their heads no, and smiled indulgently at the "kid's" inability to hold his liquor. However, while Woody's attempt to drink beer like the other men in the bar failed, nonetheless, his beer drinking is positively acknowledged by the other patrons as an effort to join the beer brotherhood and share the camaraderie since "beer functions as a symbol of initiation and group membership" (Strate, 1992, p. 85).

This "boys club" is the crux of naturalizing beer in *Cheers*. Drinking beer is the socializing agent which bring together a diverse group of people, primarily men. Beer drinking is the "secret code" that indicates to the audience which members of the club are "cool" and serve as role models.

Detoxification as a Naturalization Strategy

A third strategy through which beer is naturalized in *Cheers* is by the paradigmatic opposition of its harmlessness with the strong effects of other alcoholic beverages, a strategy which in essence detoxifies beer. By repeatedly portraying characters who drink beer all day without showing any signs of drunkenness, *Cheers* exnominates and naturalizes beer's alcoholic content.

Norm arrives when the bar opens and shortly thereafter Cliff stops in. Both patrons usually do not leave the bar until closing time. Sam often has to tell them to go home because he must close the bar for the evening. During this daily ritual Cliff and Norm always have a beer with them indicating that they spent the entire day at Cheers drinking beer.

Frasier increasingly spent more time at the bar in the final *Cheers* seasons and he too would be drinking beer throughout the day and night. These characters do not show any signs of drunkenness after the day-long beer drinking ritual and thus allow the audience to understand beer to be a relatively harmless beverage.

Cheers further naturalizes beer by contrasting its harmlessness with the debilitating effects of other types of alcoholic beverages such as wine, champagne, scotch, and mixed drinks. An example of this strategy occurred in the 4/29/93 episode. In it Carla was left in charge of the bar and proceeded to make everyone a drink called "I Know My Redeemer Liveth." This Long-Island-Iced-Tea-like drink came from a recipe that Carla had learned from her grandfather. Everyone enthusiastically tried it, and Norm asked Carla to "make mine a double." Subsequently, however, everyone who drank Carla's grandfather's concoction became drunk and suffered a hangover the next morning.

In addition to this depiction of the negative effects of alcohol other than beer, several episodes feature characters becoming drunk after consuming other alcoholic drinks while their beer drinking companions apparently are unaffected. For example, although Frasier became intoxicated from drinking scotch, his beer drinking bar companions, Norm and Cliff, appeared to suffer no ill effects (11/5/92).

Indirect contrasts between beer and other alcoholic drinks are provided in episodes in which Frasier drank too much champagne at his divorce party (2/11/93), and when Rebecca drank too much wine at Mr. Gaines' home (5/6/93), while the guys drinking beer back at Cheers had no such problems (5/6/93). Indeed, the only character whoever was shown suffering any unpleasant consequences from drinking too much beer was Woody who was passed out at the bar (2/11/93).

As evident in these examples *Cheers* detoxifies beer and highly toxifies other alcoholic beverages; by doing so it naturalizes beer and presents it as if it were water. In sum, beer is naturalized in *Cheers* by contrasting its non-effects with the powerful effects of other alcohol.

Conclusions

"Television is a subtle, continuous source for learning about the rules of life and society" (Huston, 1992 pp. 57–58) and popular shows like *Cheers* can educate the masses. *Cheers'* final season presented a humorous, tolerantly acceptive attitude toward beer that was amplified by *Cheers'* failure to depict any serious economic, social, or emotional consequences due to regular or excessive beer consumption. The absence of beer-related deaths, accidents, D.U.I.s, alcoholism, or other body dysfunctions and diseases invites viewers to disassociate the possible consequences of beer consumption from drinking and encourages them to instead associate only sociability and relaxation with beer drinking.

Such portrayals of beer are certainly those endorsed by the beer industry. Approximately $839.6 million is spent each year on beer advertising (*Advertising Age*, 1992) which celebrate friendship and good times (e.g., "Proud to be your bud, Budweiser," and "Here's to good friends, tonight is kind of special . . . Michelob"). Strate (1992) notes that like *Cheers*, "the emphasis on the group in beer commercials plays on the common misconception that drinking, when it is done socially and publicly, cannot be harmful" (p. 88). The conclusions in his analysis of beer commercials are quite similar to the findings in this study, thus acknowledging that naturalizing strategies can be found in other forms of media. Strate (1992) argues that beer commercials stereotype masculinity, and in order to prove oneself as a man, one must drink beer. Consequently, beer commercials and *Cheers*, which support the American male myth, promote masculinity which, in turn, promotes alcoholism.

Television plays an important role in American lives. It is pervasive; it accounts for an average of 28.5 hours of human (in)activity per week (Kubey & Csikzentmihaly, 1990). And for many Americans, viewing *Cheers'* naturalization of beer is part of this weekly activity. In the case of *Cheers*, the dominant ideological position affirmed throughout the series and in the final season is that beer drinking is normal, natural, and harmless. No matter what quantity of beer consumed, there are few risks and intoxication is rare.

Noted, Cheers is very much a man's haven. Even though Rebecca is very much part of the bar, she is not included in the antics of the male patrons and employees. Carla asserts herself as part of the male camaraderie, but nonetheless, her sole purpose in Cheers is to serve the men. As found in beer commercials, the same is true for *Cheers* in that "women tend to be passive, not participating but merely watching as men perform" (Strate, 1992, p. 91).

Drinking beer is not only presented as a man's activity, but stereotypes masculinity and upholds the male working class. For example, unlike Rebecca, Lilith, and Diane, Carla is more accepted as part of the group because she is more like the working class males. Strate's (1992) study explains the types of occupational roles that are shown in beer commercials which includes cowboys, construction workers, and lumberjacks. At the end of a hard day's work, these laborers are rewarded with beer. Although Cheers patrons are not all from the working class, representing a variety of occupational roles, the common thread of the portrayal of beer drinking is their maleness. Drinking beer supports masculinity which, according to Strate (1992), favors the working class; however, it cannot be determined whether beer drinking stereotypes the working class like it certainly stereotypes masculinity. This is especially apparent since women are also part of the working class force.

Even though *Cheers* is polysemic, the dominant reading is from a white, male, working class perspective. In fact, the majority of audience members consist of males 18 to 34 years old. The humor is primarily directed toward women, homosexuality, white collar workers, and non-beer drinkers. Gender, race, and class are definitely underscored in the *Cheers* narratives.

This analysis discussed three strategies—humor, camaraderie, and detoxification—through which "layers of encoded meaning were constructed into [the] television program" *Cheers* (Fiske, 1987, p. 6). Fiske (1987) explains that television uses a variety of social and technical codes, including camera work, lighting, editing, music, casting, setting, costume, make-up, action, dialogue, and ideology, to create realistic representations. He also notes that television "shows have to serve the economic interests of their producers and distributors, and, as these are capitalistic institutions, their economic interests must be aligned with capitalistic (and patriarchal) ideology" (1991, p. 445). *Cheers'* "drink and make merry" message certainly parallels and serves the economic and ideological interests of the beer producers and the television networks who profit from beer advertising time purchased.

It is important and valuable for critics to understand how audiences read texts, and a variety of methods must be employed to do so. Because survey research such as uses and gratifications, as well as audience effects research, have been scrutinized for their constrained and simplistic responses, more innovative research methods need to be employed to further develop this study. Focus groups that consist of die hard *Cheers* fans could provide great insight on their experience of watching *Cheers*. The naturalization strategies identified in this work can be "tested" in such focus group discussions to determine whether or not audiences identify the same or other strategies. Contrasting the responses from groups of males to those of groups of females may reveal further evidence to support the naturalization strategy of camaraderie via the male bonding process found in this research. Shaefer and Avery's (1993) essay is one such example of how focus groups can be implemented in research. While the focus groups added depth and revealed insight into their understanding of the talk show *Late Night with David Letterman*, the same can be accomplished with *Cheers* and other television programs. Along with focus groups, audience ethnographies (see, e.g., Ang, 1985; Morley, 1980, Radway, 1985) would also be an appropriate methodology with which to explore audience understandings of the portrayals of beer drinking in the media.

NOTES

1. Alcohol consumption in the United States is related to 2,000,000 deaths per year, which accounts for 10% of the annual mortality rate ("Message From," 1992). Driving under the influence arrests have increased over time (U.S. Department of Commerce, 1992). Long and short term abuse of alcohol affect virtually all body systems ("Message From," 1992).

REFERENCES

Advertising Age. (1992, September 23). [CD ROM]. *World almanac and book of facts.* Crain Communications, Inc.

Ang, I. (1985). *Watching Dallas: Soap opera and melodramatic imagination.* New York: Methuen.

Bandura, A. (1977). *Social learning theory.* Englewood Cliffs, NJ: Prentice Hall.

Berger, A. A. (1987). Humor: An introduction. *American Behavioral Scientist, 30*(1), 6–15.

Cafiso, J., Goodstadt, M. S., Garlington, W. K., & Sheppard, M. A. (1982). Television portrayal of alcohol and other beverages. *Journal of Studies on Alcohol, 43,* 1232–1242.

Chagollan, S. (1993, May 17). Audiences say goodbye to old friends at "Cheers." *Broadcasting and Electronic Media,* p. 1.

DeFoe, J. R. & Breed, W. (1986). The family, research, and prime-time television in alcohol education. *International Quarterly of Community Health and Education, 7*(1), 33–40.

DeFoe, J. R., Breed, W., & Breed, L. A. (1983). Drinking on television: A five year study. *Journal of Drug Education, 13*(1), 25–38.

Facts on file. (1991). New York: Facts on file.

Fernandez-Collado, C. F., Greenberg, B. S., Korzenny, F., & Atkin, C. K. (1978). Sexual intimacy and drug use in TV series. *Journal of Communication, 28*(3), 30–37.

Fiske, J. (1984). Popularity and ideology: A structuralist reading of *Dr. Who*. In W. D. Rowland Jr. & B. Watkins (Eds.), *Interpreting television: Current research perspectives* (pp. 165–198). Beverly Hills: Sage.

Fiske, J. (1986). Television: Polysemy and popularity. *Critical Studies in Mass Communication, 3*, 391–408.

Fiske, J. (1987). *Television culture*. London: Methuen.

Fiske, J. (1991). The discourses of TV quiz shows, or school + luck = success + sex. In L. R. Vande Berg & L. A. Wenner (Eds.), *Television criticism: Approaches and applications* (pp. 445–462). White Plains, NY: Longman.

Galloway, S. (1990, November 3–9). The gang at *Cheers* toast their most memorable moments. *TV Guide*, pp. 20–25.

Gerbner, G., Gross, L., Morgan, M., & Signorielli, N. (1980). The "mainstreaming" of America: Violence profile no. 11. *Journal of Communication, 30*(3), 10–27.

Gliatto, T. (1990, November 12). The taproom that inspired *Cheers* tries to change its name, until barflies cry, "Bull— & Finch!" *People Weekly*, pp. 81–82.

Gross, L., & Morgan, M. (1985). Television and enculturation. In J. Dominick & J. Fletcher (Eds.), *Broadcasting research methods* (pp. 221–234). Boston: Allyn & Bacon.

Huston, A. C., et al. (1992). *Big world, small screen: The role of television in American society*. Lincoln, NE: University of Nebraska Press.

Krugman, H. E., & Hartley, E. L. (1970). Passive learning from television. *Public Opinion Quarterly, 34*, 184–190.

Kubey, R. W., & Csikzentmihaly, M. (1990). *Television and the quality of life*. Hillsdale, NJ: L. Earlbaum Associates.

Message from the president. (1992, July). Summary of health consequences of alcohol and other drug use, pp. 1–2. [Available from CSUS Division of Student Affairs and Alumni Insurance Agency—Seymour Canter, C.L.U. 6000 J Street, Sacramento, CA.]

Montgomery, K. C. (1989). The Hollywood lobbyists. In K. C. Montgomery (Ed.), *Target: Prime-time* (pp. 174–256). New York: Oxford University Press.

Morley, D. (1980). *The nationwide audience: Structure and decoding*. London: British Film Institute.

Palmer, J. (1989). Enunciation and comedy: "Kind Hearts and Coronets." *Screen, 30*, 144–158.

Piccirillo, M. S. (1986). On the authenticity of televisual experience: A critical exploration of parasocial closure. *Critical Studies in Mass Communication, 3*, 337–355.

Radway, J. (1985). Interpretive communities and variable literacies: The functions of romance reading. In M. Gurevitch & M. Levy (Eds.), *Mass communication yearbook, Vol. 5* (pp. 337–361). Beverly Hills: Sage.

Schaefer, R. J., & Avery, R. K. (1993). Audience conceptualizations of *Late Night with David Letterman. Journal of Broadcasting & Electronic Media, 37*, 253–273.

Signorielli, N. (1987). Drinking, sex, and violence on television: The cultural indicators perspective. *Journal of Drug Education, 17*, 245–260.

Strate, L. (1992). Beer commercials: A manual on masculinity. In S. Craig (Ed.), *Men, masculinity, and the media* (pp. 78–92). Newbury Park, CA: Sage.

Tobenkin, D., (1994, April 4). Sitcoms: On a laugh track to profitability. *Broadcasting and Cable*, pp. 15, 18.

U. S. Department of Commerce, Bureau of the Census. (1992). *Statistical Abstract of the United States*. Washington, DC: U.S. Government Printing Office.

Wallack, L., Breed, W., & Cruz, J. (1987). Alcohol on prime-time television. *Journal of Studies on Alcohol, 48,* 33–38.

Wallack, L., Grube, J. W., Madden, P. D., & Breed, W. (1990). Portrayals of alcoholism on prime-time television. *Journal of Studies on Alcohol, 51,* 428–437.

Power Rangers: An Ideological Critique of Neocolonialism

Kent A. Ono

Like the unrest in Watts nearly 25 years before, the 1992 Los Angeles urban uprising (Gooding-Williams, 1993) or "Saigu," as it is called within Korean American and other Asian American communities (Choy, Kim, and Kim-Gibson, 1993), tells us at minimum that social conditions and racial relations continue to remain at a low point in the United States. Nevertheless, nearly one year after the Los Angeles urban uprising, many two- to eleven-year-olds and curious adults began watching a new science-fantasy television show: *The Mighty Morphin Power Rangers* (*MMPR*). Perhaps they attributed a calmer 1993 Los Angeles to the appearance of five (and now six) ordinary teenagers who become superheroes and fight the menacing evildoers who wreak havoc each episode on their city named—you guessed it—"Angel Grove."

MMPR is a syndicated children's television series primarily but not exclusively directed at young boys. Its overarching narrative offers hopes of equality, understanding, happiness, and success to future generations. Despite its idealism, *MMPR* glorifies militarism through its heroes: a uniformed unit of socially attractive vigilante youths (the "power rangers") who fight with their bodies, weapons, "zords," and "megazords" against those who threaten the town of Angel Grove *and win.* Originally on the series, Rita Repulsa, a thinly veiled stand-in for the wicked witch of the West in *The Wizard of Oz* who is even sometimes known to ride a broom,[1] and later her masculine but more powerful counterpart, Lord Zedd, plot to destroy Angel Grove. Lord Zedd, who faintly resembles Darth Vader from *Star Wars* (voice played by James Earl Jones), and Repulsa recently got married and now appear together in most episodes in order to interrupt the power rangers' fun. To help them counter this evil, the power rangers have a command center and a benevolent father figure, named Zordon, who lives there. Zordon, a powerful being who resembles the "Wizard of Oz," appears only as a holographic face and voice, doomed to a bodiless existence by the evil Repulsa.

By juxtaposing these two seemingly unrelated events—the summer 1992 L.A. uprising and the blockbuster childrens' show *MMPR* that burst onto the television scene in fall 1993—I hope to illustrate the disjuncture yet important interrelationship between the social world and television. Though the L.A. uprising does not have any necessary logical connection to *MMPR,* they both play a role in the history of racial antagonism and oppression *on television.* Despite terrible living conditions and rampant social injustices for many people in South Central Los Angeles during and after the L.A. rebellion, news reports tended to villainize people of color and to portray African Americans in particular as violent and out of control. In contrast, *MMPR* narrates the story of a military unit whose duty is to protect Angel Grove from "the dark forces" who want to destroy the city. The power rangers fight on behalf of their Caucasian patriarch Zordon and the people of Angel Grove and appear as reasonable people trying to destroy evil in order to restore peace and justice.

Television both draws from and covers over the social world. The first season of *MMPR* may help Los Angelians and others to forget the destruction caused by the rebellion through its representation of military superheroes. The dichotomy of military "good" and dark "evil" illustrates this process. My purpose here is to show how racial relations among members of the power rangers team contribute to the overall racial and gendered dynamics of the series as a whole. I will accomplish this through a textual analysis of one *MMPR* episode that effectively illustrates this connection.

Ideological Criticism of Neocolonialism

The approach I will take to this analysis of the *MMPR* can loosely be called a critique of neocolonialism, which is a form of ideology critique. Ideology critique seeks to understand the ideas, beliefs, attitudes, and values underlying what we see and hear on television. The critic using this approach searches beyond what television *says* it shows us, for the *system* of ideas, beliefs, attitudes, and values the audience actually receives and sometimes believes. Ideology critique attempts to expose the disjuncture between the social world and the world of television. Thus, the main function of ideology critique is to explain consistent patterns of what critics call "representation" across multiple popular cultural texts.

A critic of ideology realizes that television does not always, if ever, fully represent what humans experience in the everyday world beyond television. Representations *stand in for* reality; they are illusions or fictions of what could be, not evidence of what actually exists. Thus, critics who study what television shows us about rich and poor people (i.e., an ideology critique focused on social class) often note that television tends to overrepresent—or present over and over in exaggerated numbers—the experiences of bourgeois, upper-middle- and upper-class families (e.g., Fiske, 1987; Kellner, 1995). An ideology critique of gender representations might study the complex way television depicts relationships between women and women, men and men, and men and women in support of a patriarchal system of power. The primary function of an ideology critique of neocolonialism is to explain multiple levels of oppression (race, gender, class, sexuality) and their connectedness, or "webbed-ness," as historically produced within the United States. As Lorde (1984) writes:

> *Racism, the belief in the inherent superiority of one race over all others and thereby the right to dominance. Sexism, the belief in the inherent superiority of one sex over the other and thereby the right to dominance. Ageism. Heterosexism. Elitism. Classism.* It is a lifetime pursuit for each one of us to extract these distortions from our living at the same time as we recognize, reclaim, and define those differences upon which they are imposed. (p. 115)

Neocolonialism is akin to what Balibar (1991) calls "neo-racism." Balibar asks about the 1980s and 1990s, "On the one hand, are we seeing a new historical upsurge of racist movements and policies which might be explained by a crisis conjuncture or by other causes? On the other hand, in its themes and its social significance, is what we are seeing only a *new* racism, irreducible to earlier 'models,' or is it a mere tactical adaptation?" (p. 17). Balibar ends up arguing that neo-racism, in fact, exists in and through human practices, discourses, and representations—in what we do, say, and see. As Balibar states:

> Racism—a true "total social phenomenon"—inscribes itself in practices (forms of violence, contempt, intolerance, humiliation and exploitation), in discourses and representations which are so many intellectual elaborations of the phantasm of prophylaxis or segregation (the need to purify the social body, to preserve "one's own" or "our" identity from all forms of mixing, interbreeding, or invasion) and which are articulated around stigmata of otherness (name, skin color, religious practices). (pp. 17–18)

Neo-racism partly explains neocolonialism; however, neocolonialism has other characteristics. First, neocolonialism addresses coordinated aspects of multiple levels of oppression (gender, class, sexuality, *and* race) as they have been historically handed down to those of us living in the United States from generation to generation. That is, a critique of colonialist ideology begins with the realization that in the United States colonialism was never eliminated; it merely changed form, transmogrifying into the shape in which it now appears. Colonialism changed and adapted to each new historical era. So today colonialism has changed so many times that we no longer recognize it as colonialism. Neocolonialism, then, is a construct that describes the way racism, together with allied forms of oppression, form a contemporary U.S. national identity. Examining neocolonialism acknowledges that racism is not only similar to sexism, classism, and homophobia, but that it could not exist in its current form without them. Racism is part of a network of oppressive relationships irreducibly connected to various forms of oppression as they currently exist.

Neocolonialism, itself, which relies heavily on a history of colonization, is the newly fashioned belief system that maintains colonialist relationships as its primary purpose in order to justify and legitimate forms of power that tend toward the denigration, brutalization, and oppression of people defined as less important, less worthy of humane treatment, less civil, less rational, and ultimately less human than those wielding such power. Unlike colonialism, neocolonialism takes the ownership of land as something that is god-given or willed. Unlike colonialism in which colonialists used brute force to conquer others who had desired possessions, neocolonialism, in which colonizers already possess the baubles of warfare, maintains the current state of power via representational means, utilizing such forces as television to justify present proprietary relations.

Recent social events like the L.A. uprising are not surprising, given U.S. history. This nation began when colonists took land away from indigenous peoples and slaughtered them in the process. Before and after these colonists created, recognized, and established a government, they enslaved African peoples by the millions and lynched, raped, and disembodied them physically. Once a "democratic" government was established, "the nation" legalized exploitation of cheap labor—new European immigrants and people of color—to till fields, build railroads, do domestic labor (often the most difficult, painful, degrading, and physically demanding work available) for

little money. All of this was part of a system of colonization: the successful procure-
ment of property through the annihilation and subjugation of anyone or anything
standing in the way of colonialist expansion.

The beliefs about superiority and inferiority which inspired this colonial history
are not behind us. Indeed, while legal slavery is over and white women and people
of color now can vote, the colonialist relations, relationships between colonizers and
those they saw as inferior to them, remain. Why would they have changed? Unlike
many civilizations, colonialist relations were never thrown off in the United States.
No indigenous political movement was ever strong enough to throw the colonizers
out of the Americas. Unlike "post" colonial India, the Philippines, and Algeria, U.S.
colonization, while protested, nonetheless succeeded in maintaining its domi/na-
tion over colonized people. Colonialism is more deeply rooted in U.S. culture than
in places like Algeria and India (Said, 1993, p. 282), which indicates that the manifestations of colonialist domination are exceedingly difficult to challenge and transform.

As is the case with any critique of ideology, critics who undertake a critique of
neocolonialism do so with the hope that their analysis may have an effect on the present neocolonialist condition by altering discourse and practice. That is, by acknowledging that colonial relations exist, and by criticizing those relations where we see
them, we as critics invite a conversation that may, in fact, challenge and help uproot
those relationships. A critical analysis of neocolonialism examines the relationship
among narrative roles (e.g., those of hero, victim, villain, leader, follower, insider, and
outsider) of characters and their sex/gender, race/ethnicity, sexuality, and social class
to see recurring patterns that help support the underlying racist, sexist, heterosexist,
classist ideology the series reproduces.

A critique of neocolonialism assumes narratives produced within U.S. society
tend to reinforce a belief system that deems that colonists rightfully took what was
theirs. U.S. ideological beliefs in "manifest destiny," "only the strong survive," the
"right to own land and property," and beliefs about inherent racial superiority
grounded in Darwinism tend to support such a system. Discourse that reproduces or
relies upon current colonialist relations should be exposed and criticized through a critique of neocolonialism.

Neocolonialism and Television

Television can be a very powerful and persuasive civilizing instrument, for television lets us know what actions, behaviors, and beliefs are and are not acceptable to
others. It has played no small part in justifying and legitimating colonialism. One of
the most obvious ways television has contributed to neocolonialist relations is by
aiding the U.S. government in demonizing people of color worldwide, such as
Saddam Hussein, Moammar Kadafi, Manuel Noriega, the Ayatollah Khomeini, and
Fidel Castro. Whenever the U.S. government and military want to justify a military
intervention to reestablish their domination over economically, technologically, and
militarily less powerful peoples, they manufacture a demonic view of someone, almost always a swarthy male, as a psychopathic, uncontrollable, irrational, and
fascistic leader (Said, 1988; Kellner, 1992). Having created such a "devil," the govern-

ment justifies actions that would normally be considered inappropriate, or even illegal. Take, for example, the planned invasion of the sovereign nation of Cuba, which broke international law.

In addition to the more obvious ways in which television representations help maintain colonialist relations and practices, television also creates and reproduces degrading images of people of color within the U.S. Television does so through codes or cues that make clear distinctions between heroes and villains; television encourages viewers through these codes to root for one side over another. As Stuart Hall (1980) writes, "These codes are the means by which power and ideology are made to signify in particular discourses. They refer signs to the 'maps of meaning' into which any culture is classified; and those 'maps of social reality' have the whole range of social meanings, practices, and usages, power and interest 'written in' to them" (p. 134). These codes, in context, encourage viewers to judge actions as moral and immoral.

In this study, I carefully examine one episode of the *MMPR* television series in order to show how colonialist relations and beliefs about race, gender, sexuality, and class function in the context of children's entertainment. This kind of analysis is important because it reminds us that neocolonialism is not just a political system; it also consists of an ideological system into which we all enter as children. It helps us to see how television teaches children (and adults) either to ignore social reality taking place beyond the living room or to understand social events metaphorically through the struggles and victories of the power rangers and the enemies they fight.

Cultural critics of all kinds analyze specific episodes of television shows in order to explicate television's continued representation of the "naturalization" of oppression. As Byars and Dell (1992) point out, "[S]ome cultural studies scholars take on the task of textual analysis, explicating the power relationships that determine reading" (p. 191). After viewing most episodes from the first two seasons of *MMPR*, I selected one episode, "The Wanna-Be Ranger," because it provides, in its depiction of Zack, an especially powerful visual example of the racist dimension of the series' neocolonialist ideology. Through the analysis of this episode, I will illustrate how the series as a whole, television in general, and representations within U.S. society operate to inscribe a neocolonialist ideology. Although I am examining one representative episode to show what it reveals, I am not privileging this particular episode over others; rather, I am merely using it as more exemplary of the neocolonialist matrix than other episodes. In the case of *MMPR*, as analysis of this episode demonstrates, television did not sufficiently hide the ideological system that structures the dynamics of the show (indeed, some might argue it flaunts it). While the series as a whole codes race in ways that maintain a neocolonialist system, analyzing one selected episode of *MMPR* demonstrates the complexity of the mechanisms through which television affirms a neocolonialist system that justifies oppression of those who are different.

Mighty Morphin Power Rangers

To understand both the ordinariness and the excessiveness of the neocolonialism in "The Wanna-Be Ranger" as compared to *MMPR* as a whole, it is useful to examine the show's standard narrative. Each episode usually begins at school, in the park, or at the command center. As regular students of Angel Grove High School, the power rangers are usually depicted in plain clothes, drinking soda pop, playing touch football, or doing something else generically "high-school-like." Immediately, Repulsa or Zedd interrupts the fun and acquires an object (a suit, a purse, or a guitar) or something less directly related to the story (flowers, a scorpion, or a fish), and creates a monster from this object. Then, they announce their intention to take over the world, the Earth, the power rangers, and/or Zordon, the power rangers' paternal, sympathetic, but dismebodied adviser/mentor. In the process, they often try to convert one of the heroes or one of their friends into becoming part of the "dark" purpose.

This opening sequence is usually followed by a transitional clip from Fox Children's Television Network and a slew of commercials for toys, movies, food, or more *MMPR* paraphernalia; you know, kid stuff. After the commercial break, another Fox clip announces the show's return, and *MMPR* comes back to explain how Zedd has to create a diversion with the Putty Patrol: black-faced, lanky, clay golems in light gray suits, with large Zs on their chests that, when hit, make them break apart and disappear. When needed to fulfill Zedd or Repulsa's dastardly plan, the Putties are called upon by Goldar, their obsequious commander, to frighten and distract the power rangers. Once the Putties have diverted the rangers, the Putties or Goldar seize the object Zedd has magically empowered to do evil and place it someplace (e.g., on the "dark planet") where Zedd can shoot a lightning bolt out of his gold stave (with a Z on top) in order to transform it into a monster. Once he has created the monster, Zedd usually speculates with Goldar on how successful he ultimately will be. Of course, viewers know from watching other episodes or reading the popular discourse that Zedd will fail and the power rangers will win.

Usually after the first sign of trouble (e.g., a fight with the Putties, the capture of a ranger or a friend of the rangers, or an unsuccessful encounter with Zedd's new monster), the power rangers return to the command center. There, with Alpha 4 (a computer resembling R2D2 from *Star Wars*) and Zordon, the power rangers plan their rescue of the object-person. As part of the rescue, the power rangers morph—they magically don their color-coded suits and fight with renewed superhuman strength and martial arts skills. They attack the monster, and when it has been temporarily disabled, Zedd makes it bigger. In response to this overwhelming threat, the power rangers call up mechanical dinosaurs that, when united, create the Thunder Megazord. In later episodes, Tommy, the sixth ranger, calls on his animated knife, Saba, to create the Tigerzord. These larger and more powerful creatures, often together, fight Zedd's enlarged monster. Either the Thunder Megazord or the Tigerzord inevitably falls down from a blow by the monster, and either a boost in energy by Zordon, or the use of the power saber allows one of the Zords to defeat the monster. Episodes, sometimes shown in multiple parts, ultimately end on happy notes, usually with the rangers at the juice bar or in some other part of the high school, where they laugh at something stupid Bulk and Skull have done. This shared laughter allows the rangers to reestablish their friendships and reaffirm their ideology as the preferred one. An unrelated moral follows some episodes, in which kids and power rangers are explicitly advised to reject immorality, unproductive aggression, laziness, or illusion.

The Wanna-Be Ranger: A Narrative Summary of the Episode

The particular episode I examine differs little from the generic episode just described. "The Wanna-Be Ranger" opens with the power rangers, sans Zack, playing basketball and listening to rap music. During three slow motion sequences, we see Tommy, Billy, and then Jason each dunk the ball; Kimberly and Trini feed the ball to them. After she passes the ball to one of the boys, Kimberly is startled by a touch on her shoulder from behind. She turns around to face a human-sized white gorilla and jumps back in fright. When the gorilla takes off its head and reveals African American ranger Zack under the mask, Kimberly caustically says, "Very funny, Zack!" Jason tells Zack to get out of his suit so he can play basketball, but as Zack takes off his suit, Zordon summons the other rangers, who transport back to the command center. The final shot before showing the rangers at the command center shows Zack, alone, dropping the suit on the ground next to the outdoor basketball court.

At the command center, Zordon tells the rangers he must temporarily "deionize" because of the change in atmosphere. Since this means that while deionized he will lack his usual powers, Zordon charges Alpha, alone, with monitoring Angel Grove with Zordon's surveillance equipment (akin to a crystal ball). Before leaving him alone in the center, Jason tells Alpha to contact the rangers should a problem arise that Alpha cannot handle himself.

The next scene features Lord Zedd who says he will send the Putties to scare the rangers and create "Primator" to destroy the rangers. After a commercial break, we return to the same scene. Lord Zedd taps his three gold fingers with talons on his chair arm, then fires his sword at the white gorilla suit. The suit turns into a monster, "Primator," an oversized gorilla with large white, sharp teeth, yellow hair, a white tail, red eyes, and a blue face, breast, stomach, shoulders, feet, and hands.

In the next scene, Alpha, alone in the command center, looks at the viewscreen and sees a little boy, who has lost his mother, crying in the park. Alpha decides to solve the problem himself. He leaves the command center and transports down to help the little boy when suddenly Primator appears. A scene in which Zedd announces that, with Alpha away from his post, this is the perfect time to destroy Zordon, is followed by a return to the park scene in which Primator, who pretends to be Billy, approaches Alpha and the boy. When Alpha sees Primator behind the mask, Primator knocks Alpha unconscious and takes the boy.

Zedd orders Primator to leave Alpha alone and transport to the power center. Primator goes, but not before transforming himself into the image of Zack. Unlike his behavior when he impersonates Billy, Primator, disguised as Zack, swaggers like an ape, smiles broadly to display his white teeth, crouches down low, and smirks when others are not looking. As Zack, Primator returns to the high school, sits at the juice bar, and says in an aside to the camera how much he likes banana shakes. Once there, Zack-Primator runs into Kimberly and Trini, who are waiting for Tommy. He smiles as he tells them that Tommy is in the park and turns to face the camera so they cannot see the smirk he displays to the audience. Although Kimberly and Trini find his story unbelievable and ask him a lot of questions, Kimberly eventually says, "Oh, no!" and decides to go to the park, while Zack-Primator remains behind and, with museful laughter, drinks his banana shake.

The next shot shows Zedd at his headquarters proclaiming, "Now is the perfect time for my Putties to eliminate the pink and yellow rangers." On these words, the scene shifts to Kimberly and Trini alone in the park. As they cross a walking bridge, the Putties suddenly appear. Dressed in plain clothes, Trini and Kimberly fight them. Kimberly knocks one Putty over the rail which makes it disintegrate. Trini says, "Hiya!" and rolls on the ground to avoid being hit by one of the Putties. At one point Kimberly stands facing the camera with her back to a Putty. The Putty comes up from behind her, grabs her breast, then her stomach. She struggles to get away, runs toward a tree, does a back flip, and kicks the Putty in the chest, making it disintegrate.

After a commercial, the scene shifts to school where we see Tommy doing kicks by himself during a demonstration. Kimberly and Trini approach, and Kimberly almost gets hit by one of his feet as she approaches him and asks if he is okay. Tommy tells her he is fine and says he was not in the park. When Kimberly accuses Zack of playing another practical joke, Jason tells Kimberly that Zack was with him and Billy at the lab the entire time. To solve this contradiction, Kimberly and Trini suggest calling Alpha. When they cannot contact him, Jason orders the rangers back to the command center. Once there, Zordon, who has mysteriously been revived to save Alpha, tells the rangers that they are going to have to destroy Primator who "has the power to disguise himself as any one of you." Hearing this, Kimberly apologizes to Zack for having suspected him of foul play. Zack responds, "It's solid."

In the next scene, the rangers fight Primator in the park when two identical yellow rangers appear. Zack and Tommy agree that they cannot tell the two apart. Jason challenges them both to a fight. When one says she cannot fight a friend and the other pulls out a knife and attacks Jason, the other rangers shoot the attacking yellow ranger, who then turns into Primator. In a series of identity switches, Primator takes the shape of each of the rangers, although he assumes the image of the pink ranger only briefly. In the form of all but the pink ranger, Primator pretends to be the real ranger by mimicking his or her actions. For example, when Primator becomes Jason, Jason challenges his alter-ego to a duel. As Jason, Primator fires on them through its helmet. Then Primator laughs, jumps, and beats its chest.

An intercut to the command center shows Zordon unable to maintain his semi-corporeal state. Zordon tells the rangers that a mirror will expose Primator's facade. In response, Kimberly produces a mirror from her boot and says, "I never leave home without one."

The next scene takes place on a dock, where five rangers meet up with the green ranger (Tommy), who says he is losing power. When the green ranger suggests that the power rangers give up, Jason kicks the green ranger and claims he is a fake. When Tommy's facade melts to reveal Primator, Kimberly flashes her mirror in Primator's face. Primator sees itself in it and throws the mirror down, which shatters the glass.

At this point, Zedd sends a ball to make Primator bigger, and the rangers become the Thunder and Tiger zords. In the ensuing confrontation, the Thunderzord uses its sword to slay the giant white ape. As Thunderzord returns its sword to its sheath, the scene shifts to Alpha, who is about to self-destruct. Zordon orders the rangers to rescue Alpha. They morph but really are carefully coded back into "regular" high school kids and arrive just before Alpha self-destructs. Billy pushes what appears to be the computer-scientific services buttons on Alpha's chest randomly (to us), in sequence (to him). This deactivates the self-destruct mode and revives Alpha. Meanwhile, the mother returns to the scene to find her lost boy and thanks the power rangers for finding and protecting him. The show ends with Zordon instructing Alpha to act responsibly and to stay at his station in the future.

Analysis

While there are many indications of the neocolonialist dynamics in this episode, for the sake of brevity and clarity, I will discuss only two—the construction of patriarchy and the reconstruction of the myth of the black rapist. I will then examine their relationship to each other in order to emphasize the interconnection of gender, race, and sexuality in neocolonialism.

We can begin analyzing this episode's construction of patriarchal power by focusing on the last scene. Here, Zordon, upset with Alpha for abandoning his post to aid the lost boy, chides him for being irresponsible and reminds him to obey commands more rigorously in the future. Because Alpha abandoned his post, even while acting in a beneficent manner, he failed his duty to "man" the station. This is particularly problematic to Zordon, because Alpha's absence corresponds to the threat posed to Zordon's existence. Concomitantly, the punishment Zordon metes out to Alpha is the very punishment patriarchy applies to women who leave the domestic space of the home either to work on their own accord or in defiance of masculine control over their decisions and actions: one that produces guilt and self-consciousness in the subject. The show defines Alpha, despite his male voice, as feminine.

Nevertheless, *MMPR* portrays Alpha as a complex mixture of the feminine servant and the masculine centurion. Not only is Alpha expected to be Zordon's constant companion, confidante, attendant, and the power rangers' cheerleader—all traditionally feminine roles, he also must be "a man" who stays at his post, takes responsibility, and obeys orders. Had the rangers not returned to the command center, Zedd might have been able to obliterate Zordon. When, in the end, Zordon's power is restored, he uses his power to chastise Alpha who in Zordon's absence momentarily forgets his rightful place.

Alpha—Zordon's servant, body, and sometimes mind—understandably seeks control over his own body and a sense of autonomy. Like the child, Alpha admires the power rangers as heroes, implicitly instructing the audience to do the same. But, as a robot whose thoughts, feelings, and rights are necessarily "inhuman," he is denied the freedoms afforded his human counterparts. As a result, Alpha is the perfect slave, unable to attain his humanity and always acquiescing to humans who have power over him. His position in life is fully determined—he is of a certain lot—and he accepts this position without resentment, bitterness, or anger.

Zordon and Zedd are excellent markers of the conception of power employed by the show. According to the show, Zordon exemplifies good power, friendly power, and trustworthy power, while Zedd symbolizes bad power, evil power, and power of which one should be skeptical and frightened. Zordon and Zedd signify two faces of patriarchal power—one light, floating, and airy; the other dark, heavy, and stable. Zordon punishes responsibly; Zedd punishes immorally. Not surprisingly, Alpha and Goldar, too, are paradigmatic opposites. On the receiving end of orders, advice, instruction, and sometimes punishment, while Alpha is prone to making mistakes without Zordon or the rangers' guidance, he also works efficiently, intelligently, and with sincere obedience. Goldar, on the other hand, though skillful and physically strong, appears obsequious and incompetent as a result of his failures.

Despite these differences, however, both Zordon and Zedd represent a similar kind of threat. Both command their subjects to act, and both punish their subjects when they deviate from their roles as loyal, effective followers. While the power rangers are spared the ignominy Alpha experiences, they nonetheless, like him, are bound to follow Zordon's orders. While Zordon thanks, praises, and rewards the rangers for successful performances, he also expects absolute obedience, trust, and faithfulness. No wonder the rangers let loose kicks and screams whenever they leave "the command center."[2]

That Zordon represents "goodness" and Zedd evil "darkness" is no mere coincidence. The depiction of darkness as evil is replete throughout the episode and the series. In the depiction of Zack as an ape we find this equation again, albeit in a different form. In other contexts, the depiction of an African American man as an ape is considered to be gratuitous racism. However, such a depiction in this episode appears without criticism. The racist implication of this representation derives from an ideology based on Darwin's nineteenth-century theory that humans evolved from apes. Racist rhetoric within the United States relied heavily on Darwin's precepts in order to argue that those who looked least like apes were more intelligent, more civilized, and therefore were biologically superior and deserving of higher status. Concomitantly, this racist ideology argued that African Americans and other people of color looked like apes and therefore were not as advanced (a species) as their non-ape-like (Anglo) counterparts. Likening African Americans to apes has racist overtones within our culture precisely because racist ideology appeared materially in discourse that compared human beings to animals (En Vogue, 1992).[3] Racist people throughout history pointed to physical similarities between people of color and animals in order to demean and subjugate people of color (e.g., Japanese and Jews look like rats) (Keen, 1986) and to make themselves look superior.

"The Wanna-Be Ranger" shows Kimberly being startled by Zack and attacked by Putties. Thus, the dark skinned characters on the show present a physical, arguably sexual, threat to Kimberly, the central Caucasian woman in the episode. MMPR defuses the rape threat Zack poses to Kimberly with humor, ironically making Zack subject to suspicion for his pranks because of the "real" physical threat he ostensibly poses to Kimberly. In equating Zack with the white ape, the episode reconstructs "the myth of black rapist"—the false myth Angela Davis (1983) argues was constructed post-slavery to justify lynching African American men accused of raping white women (1983). What at first may appear to be a self-reflective critique of that myth ends up being a complex reconstruction of it. Even while Primator (a name etymologically evocative of the term "primitive") can masquerade as any of the rangers, Zack is the original wearer of the ape suit and Primator dons the appearance of Zack more often than any character on the episode. By depicting Zack as most like an ape, the episode implies African American men, generally, because of their biological race, are primitive, animalistic, and worst of all, a sexual rape threat to white women.

Moreover, except for Billy's very brief appearance as the ape, like Primator, Zack is the only character who appears outside of his ranger suit as the ape. He plays the ape the longest of any character in the show, and arguably crouches lower and mimics the swagger of an ape more than any of the rest of the characters. Walter Jones, who plays Zack, gives a strong performance here that matches the ideological message the editing, narrative, and mise en scene convey in the show, that "black people and apes really are similar." By taking this (ideo)logic further, we realize the show thinks Zack's "color doesn't matter," that "he acts just like white kids even though he's black." The logic that prevails in the series is akin to statements commonly made to people of color: "I don't think of you as _____(racial other). You're just one of us." Thus, the ironic, though not humorous, racial logic of this episode is that Zack is like a white gorilla.

As a result of this logic, Zack is always questionable, always potentially culpable, and therefore untrustworthy. Despite Kimberly's eventual apology to Zack and regardless of whether the other rangers see him themselves "as just another member of the team," the possibility remains that Zack may, at some point in time, represent a sexual threat to Kimberly. This latent threat is enough to permanently imbue Zack's character with the status of "potential threat." Moreover, the racist logic of the myth of the black rapist relies on the belief that African American men have an uncontrollable biologically driven, primitive, animalistic obsession with possessing white women. Within this mythic logic, then, even though Zack may not want to do harm, his body, depicted as beyond his control under the forces of Zedd, poses a threat, despite himself. For example, the Putties wear a light gray, almost white outfit but have black faces. Coupled with the Putty's attack on Kimberly, and within a context in which racist ideology is at work, Zack is to Primator as Primator is to Putty. All three pose a threat, especially to the white woman on the show; that threat is sexual in nature, and all are bound by forces beyond their individual control, namely, a lack of civility.

The show's construction of patriarchal power and the myth of the black rapist work hand in hand. The punishment Zordon applies to Alpha and the distrust evoked by the racist depiction of Zack as ape-like function together to code black as evil and to reestablish Anglo-masculine power over femininity and people of color. Zordon punishes Alpha for abandoning his post because of the threat Zedd's "dark" patriarchy poses. By illustrating the "dark" threat Zack poses, the show lets us know what patriarchy can never allow: unpatrolled relations between white women and African American men. The episode demonstrates that miscegenation and disruption of white masculine power and authority must be fought at all costs. This may be why, following this episode and "Bloom of Doom," in which Trini's greater popularity among girls at school poses a social threat to Kimberly who cannot get people to join her club, Zack and Trini become minor characters. They fade into the background and ultimately disappear during the beginning of the second season. The closer each comes to inhabiting the racial subjectivities they signify, the closer to extermination they are.

Conclusion

Besides changes in technology and television production, little differentiates the ideology of today's "Power Rangers" from that of the superhero show from my childhood, *The Lone Ranger*. Not unlike Tonto, Zack, Trini, and then Aisha, Rocky, and Adam, play sidekicks to the main, white superheroes on the show. The ideology of race relations remans the same; little has changed, though the number of sidekicks has multiplied.

This series, as does most of television, serves a pedagogical function as well as provides pleasure to its viewers. While the show stresses themes of cooperation among all rangers, that cooperation has more to do with the sort of coordination required for corporate task completion than it does with mutually validating humane social relationships in which people voluntarily join together to address social problems and improve living conditions. In so doing, *MMPR* distracts the viewer's attention away from social conditions, social relations, and ultimately social responsibility. Moreover, the show gives greater responsibilities to Jason and Tommy, who represent white male privilege, than to the other rangers. Both are depicted as having more talent, leadership skills, *ethos,* attractiveness, and a heightened sense of duty to preserving the Angel Grove social system responsible for conferring greater status and power upon them than on their white female and non-Anglo counterparts.

When coupled with popular discourse, the show de-emphasizes racial relations while relying on a complex set of racial conventions, and requiring the audience's own conventional knowledge and acceptance, hence *normalization,* of those race relations. The show teaches viewers how to avoid social differences, how to repress them, and how to appear as if those social differences do not really matter after all. Racial relations are to be considered only insofar as they contribute to leisure and entertainment and so long as they can be dismissed later as irrelevant markers of a world outside of suburban experience. While Zack's race as an African American is never overtly discussed, Zack is presented as an expert shadow and break dancer and, in the introduction to each episode, dances as he fights. Similarly, while Trini's Vietnamese American race-ethnicity is never narratively foregrounded, she is represented as being handy with electronics, having expert knowledge of Rita Repulsa's "dark" intentions, and, unlike the other rangers, is knowledgeable about Eastern philosophy behind martial arts. She is often shown doing "karate chops" and says "Hiya!" when she strikes. Concomitantly, *MMPR* depicts Rita Repulsa and regular villain Scorpina as Asian witches, or "dragon ladies"—beautiful, yet evil and sinister. The show relies on the conventional metaphorical relations between black and evil: the evil Putties' faces are black; evil Lord Zedd's chair is black; Lord Zedd controls the "dark planet" and recruits humans to become part of his "darkness."

The rangers' color coordinated morphing uniforms match their socially stereotypical categories: Zack in black, Trini in yellow, Kimberly in pink, Jason in red, and Billy in blue. Zack and Trini's colors correspond to the color equivalent generally supported in U.S. culture for the actor's race. While Kimberly is not the only woman on the show, that her Anglo character represents quintessential feminine behavior is indicated by her pink uniform, a color conventionally used to distinguish between boys and girls. While Trini, too, is a woman, only Kimberly's morphing outfit has a skirt over her tights. Kimberly loves to shop, carries around a large bulky mirror—proudly—is prone to emotional responses, and fawns over Tommy for most of the series. Jason is a "red-blooded" ranger. He gives orders, tends to downplay what girls say, shakes a lot of hands, and takes the lead in almost every circumstance. In the only episode in which the rangers rescue Jason, his capture is treated as a symbolic castration, and his rescue represents the return of the phallus. Finally, Billy's blue trimmed outfit signifies his gender and his stereotypically masculine-minded focus on science.

Tommy, first the green, then the white ranger reveals much of the series' attitude toward race. Having been recruited by Zedd to stand with him on the "dark side," the green ranger cannot be trusted. He has strength and intelligence, but he has been taken over by Zedd and, against his will, he uses both to do evil. After Tommy is freed from his enslavement by Zedd, Zordon knights Tommy as the "white" ranger, the new, all-powerful leader of the power rangers. As the white ranger, Tommy loses his earring and gains his own Zord, the Tigerzord, and a magical saber, which no other ranger possesses. As the white ranger, not only does Tommy get (phallic) cool toys, but he also "gets the girl." Kimberly and Tommy's romantic relationship plays a significant role on the series. Kimberly pines over Tommy's disappearance, and Tommy's vigilance in rescuing Kimberly when she is captured and or put in danger makes them the melodramatic center of the show. As a result of the dominance of the romantic narrative, the other characters are relegated to the margins.

As this analysis of "The Wanna-Be Ranger" in the larger context of *MMPR* indicates, while the show's discourse relies heavily on racial and gender dynamics, it rarely raises the issues of race and gender as specific points of identification for characters or as significant factors affecting either the way events evolve or the social relations among the characters. Instead, the series encourages us to have increased trust in policing agencies. The power rangers themselves wear uniforms, carry weapons, and their motto is to "bring justice to communities through group service." *MMPR* encourages increased legitimation of and sympathy for policing agents, first by normalizing the aggressive, violent, and apparently vigilante actions the power rangers take to serve "justice" and second by encouraging more tolerance of violence against those depicted as "demonic" and "abnormal."

Through the ritual reconstruction of the inherent logic of race, gender, class, and sexual differences, this series contributes to a society that, far from being post-colonial, merely reproduces latent colonialist relations. Without more criticism of neocolonialism on television, a more effective response to the kind of lessons television teaches us and the children who follow us will not be forthcoming.

NOTES

1. This is a bit of an inside racist joke, because in the *Wizard of Oz* the witch of the East is a good witch. But in *MMPR*, because Repulsa, a mighty "eastern" sorceress, is played by an Asian actor, whose voice in English is poorly dubbed onto the original Japanese film stock, thereby highlighting her Asian difference, she successfully portrays the evil witch.
2. Apparently, so do kids who watch *MMPR*. A study done on *MMPR* not long after it premiered showed that after watching only a few minutes of the power rangers, children were prone to breaking out into spontaneous bouts of kicking, screaming, and ultimately fighting with other kids (Franey 1994).
3. En Vogue's video "Free Your Mind" specifically criticizes visual depictions of African Americans as apes in Darwinist thinking.

REFERENCES

Balibar, E. (1991). Is there a "neo-racism"? In E. Balibar & E. Wallerstein, *Race, nation, class: Ambiguous identities* (pp. 17–27). London: Verso.

Byars, J. & Dell, C. (1992). Big differences on the small screen: Race, class, gender, feminine beauty, and the characters at *Frank's Place*. In L. F. Rakow (Ed.), *Women making meaning: New feminist directions in communication* (pp. 191–209). New York: Routledge.

Choy, C., Kim, E. H., & Kim-Gibson, D. S. (Prod.). (1993). *Sa-i-gu.* [Video.] D. S. Kim-Gibson (Dir., Writ., Narr.) San Francisco: CrossCurrents Media.

Davis, A. Y. (1983). Rape, racism and the myth of the black rapist. *Women, race and class* (pp. 172–201). New York: Vintage Books.

En Vogue (1992). *Free your mind.* [Music video.] M. Romanek (Dir.), Satellite Films (Prod.). Atco EastWest Records.

Fiske, J. (1987). *Television culture.* London: Methuen.

Franey, L. (1994, March 6). *Power Rangers* stirs aggression. *Los Angeles Times,* p. A25.

Gooding-Williams, R. (Ed.). (1993). *Reading Rodney King/reading urban uprising.* New York: Routledge.

Hall, S. (1980). Encoding/decoding. In S. Hall, D. Hobson, A. Lowe, & P. Willis (Eds.), *Culture, media, language* (pp. 128–138). London: Hutchinson/CCCS.

Keen, S. (1986). *Faces of the enemy: Reflections of the hostile imagination.* San Francisco: Harper and Row.

Kellner, D. (1992). *The Persian Gulf tv war.* Boulder: Westview.

Kellner, D. (1995). *Media culture: Cultural studies, identity and politics between the modern and the postmodern.* London: Routledge.

Lorde, A. (1984). *Sister outsider.* Freedom, CA: The Crossing Press.

Said, Edward. (September/October 1988). Identity, negation and violence. *New Left Review, 171,* 46–60.

Said, E. (1993). *Culture and imperialism.* New York: Alfred A. Knopf.

Culture-Centered Approaches to Television Criticism

[C]ulture [is] a pursuit of our total perfection by means of getting to know, on all the matters which most concern us, the best which has been thought and said in the world; and through this knowledge, turning a stream of fresh and free thought upon our stock notions and habits, which we now follow staunchly but mechanically, . . . [T]he culture we recommend is, above all, an inward operation.

—Arnold, 1869/1916, p. x

With this statement, British poet and essayist Matthew Arnold launched, so far as we know, the English-speaking world's first fully developed theory of culture. As can be seen in the quoted passage, that theory was strongly normative, that is to say, oriented to a proper critique of "our stock notions and habits, which we now follow staunchly but mechanically." His example of a people without such a proper critical attitude was the citizenry of the United States. Quoting a French critique of U.S. taste, Arnold noted:

The countries which, like the United States, have created a considerable popular instruction without any serious higher instruction, will long have to expiate this fault by their intellectual mediocrity, their vulgarity of manners, their superficial spirit, their lack of general intelligence. (Ibid., p. xxii)

Yet, Arnold recognized that others thought better of the young country across the Atlantic. In particular, the famous British political radical John Bright had praised all of the classes in the United States for being "sufficiently educated to be able to read, and to comprehend, and to think; and that, I [Bright] maintain, is the foundation of all subsequent progress" (ibid.). Bright's argument, Arnold noted, was built on a discussion of sociality and politics, not the spirituality of the best theology and the best art—by someone with no sense of "the harmonious perfection of our whole being, and what we call totality" (ibid., xxvii).

A theorizing of Bright's position came from the pen of an American sociologist, Yale University's William Graham Sumner. In 1906 he published *Folkways: A Study of the Sociological Importance of Usages, Manners, Customs, Mores, and Morals.* The proper study of character, he argued, arose from an examination of the everyday or ordinary beliefs and actions of people:

> [F]olkways are habits of the individual and customs of the society which arise from efforts to satisfy needs; they are intertwined with goblinism and demonism and primitive notions of luck ([see] sec. 6), and so they win traditional authority. Then they become regulative for succeeding generations and take on the character of a social force. . . . They can be modified, but only to a limited extent, by the purposeful efforts of men. In time they lose power, decline, and die, or are transformed. While they are in vigor they very largely control individual and social undertakings, and they produce and nourish ideas of world philosophy and life policy. (Sumner, 1906/1911, p. iv)

Here is a more descriptive and observationally based understanding of culture; in defining culture as "folkways," Sumner was tapping into conceptions of social life that were being developed in the new science of anthropology. In such a tradition, culture is what holds a society together—the beliefs, habits, values, and customary ways of acting collectively that distinguish Americans from Brits and both from the people of New Guinea.

Thus, coming into the intellectual world of the twentieth century were two conceptions of culture, the one normative and reformative, and the other, descriptive and preservational. Cultural studies as an academic practice today unites aspects of both of these traditions. Cultural studies today generally focuses on the everyday, on meaning-making processes that are practiced by portions or all of society, and yet has a normative edge as well, though one today having less to do with aesthetics than, as we shall see, with politics. The aesthetic domain of culture has been but sporadically attended to since the 1950s' and 1960s' debates between "hi brow" and "lo brow" art (see, e.g., Rosenberg & White, 1957) and has generally been replaced by worry about oppression and a people's role in its own subjugation to authority and societal institutions.[1]

Today, "Cultural Studies" as an academic discipline has gotten more complicated. Within the British intellectual tradition, Matthew Arnold's vision was last seen in the 1970s' television series *Civilization*, when Kenneth Clark took audiences through the magnificent, progressive evolution of British politics, society, architecture, and art. These days, British scholars of culture are much more interested, following the lead of the late Raymond Williams, in studying the manifestations of cultural rules and role relationships in texts. Using tools from psychoanalysis and Marxian thought about society and politics, together with an understanding of signs derived from semiotics, British media critics such as Stuart Hall (1980; 1982; Hall et al., 1978) and John Fiske (1987; 1994; Fiske & Hartley, 1978) offer a cultural studies that engages society's institutions but primarily through studies of their discourses. Television is one of the institutions studied by their mentor Williams (especially 1974) and by their students—Hall's, primarily from his days at the University of Birmingham's Centre for Contemporary Studies, and Fiske's, primarily from his teaching at Australian and American universities.

The French tradition of cultural studies has been dominated by anthropologist Claude Lévi-Strauss (especially 1958) and linguistic critic Roland Barthes (1968; 1973; 1977). They set the French on a language-focused kind of cultural study. Lévi-Strauss was the great structuralist who understood the cultural world as one we use to structure—organize, interpret—everyday life, whereas Barthes was the great critic who taught that all kinds of symbol systems (road signs, clothing, eating practices, sporting events) embodied significant aspects of popular culture. Their work has been supplemented by three later sorts of cultural studies: the anticultural (postmodern) critiques of the masses, sign systems, and politics (Debord, 1970; Baudrillard, e.g., 1983, 1988), the intensive scrutiny and detailed subjective interpretation of highly particularized pieces of social behavior (deCerteau, 1984), and, in an opposite move, the sweeping visions of societal shifts in practices of discoursing, knowledge making, and power over time (Foucault, e.g., 1972, 1977, 1980).

American cultural studies—particularly, the cultural study of mass communication practices—can be dated from 1938 (Park), though the master text of the Americanist view is Edward Hall's *The Silent Language* (1959). Here, we are shown that culture—social behavior—can be analyzed like a text, by breaking the behavior down into units that are much like words and that are organized into sets that are much like sentences. Hall identified every aspect of social life as part of a "primary message system," and in general argued that "Communication is culture and culture is communication," because (1) one can communicate with others only when one knows their culture, and yet (2) cultures are revealed or exhibited only in communicative behaviors. Human communication, in this view, is both ground for relationships and the process by which those relationships are maintained. Hall's views became the bases of social-scientific studies of cultures and subcultures (e.g., Smith, 1966) and of critical studies of popular novels and movies and of everyday social practice (e.g., many of the writings in the late 1960s volumes of *The Journal of Popular Culture* and the 1972 anthologies of media studies edited by Lewis and by Voelker & Voelker). The American tradition of cultural studies, therefore, was more descriptive and celebratory of democratic politics than its continental relatives, perhaps because of its scientist outlook in all aspects of academic practice and probably because American scholars were less concerned with critiquing and reforming social process than their trans-Atlantic counterparts.

But by the late 1970s and early 1980s, both the British and the French approaches to cultural studies (usually capitalized as Cultural Studies to signal the ideological or critical force of their particular theories) invaded mainland America. American cultural studies became interested in semiotics, institutional critique, and power relationships between people based on race, class, and gender, even getting caught up in the concern for political correctness and multiculturalism as agendas for social reform (see Aronowitz, 1993, for a telling of the story of the invasion). America once again has become a kind of melting pot, blending bits and pieces of European thought but adapting them to the particular personal-social-political climate of the new world. The following discussion of culture-centered television criticism will reflect the sort of intellectual homogenization that often happens in this country.

Culture-Centered Television Criticism

For our purposes, we can think of culture-centered television criticism as grounded in four assumptions:

1. *A culture is a social group's system of meanings.* Following Sumner, earlier anthropologists and social commentators thought of culture as particular behaviors and thought patterns possessed by a people, often broken down into the categories of habits, beliefs, and artifacts (e.g., Chase, 1948/1956, p. 64). Such a view is too confining, for it walls off some behavior as cultural and some as not. Today, culture is seen as the ways in which anything and everything shared by people in some temporal or spatial grouping is thought to be meaningful. *Meanings* and *meaningfulness* are socially derived understandings and accounts of things people take shared perspectives on: persons, places, things, ideas, routines, rituals, and strategic behavior (social action). Individuals generally are taught from infancy on to conform their understandings and their behaviors to social standards for meaning when communicating with others. Although context-centered criticism, as we discussed it in Chapter 8, tends to focus on ways that external institutions or practices shape discourse, culture-centered criticism generally focuses more directly on the discourses themselves and how it is that they give meaning to lived experience.

2. *To study culture is to study meaning systems both descriptively and normatively.* Descriptively, students of culture outline the meaning systems of societies or social groups, seeking to better comprehend the "webs of signification" that Geertz (1973, p. 6) says comprise our social relationships. Inventorying the meanings attached to objects and actions or, for our purposes, arrayed in a television show is the beginning of cultural studies. Additionally, the culturalist often goes a step further, exploring the ways in which meaning systems, whether understood institutionally or textually, control the perceptions, thoughts, or actions of people. So, descriptively, you might inventory the celebrities Larry King interviews on his show for a year, but then, normatively, you could talk with viewers to see how their understandings of the world seem to have been affected by the kind and range of guests he has featured. That second activity would allow you to argue that King's impact on the country is positive or negative according to some standard.

3. *Members of a society usually are complicitous in their own subjugation to meaning systems.* If you ask someone why he pays taxes, he's likely to say "Well, because I have to" or "Because that's the way the system works" or "That's just the way things go in this country." In recognizing social obligation ("I have to") or a general acceptance of social demands ("the way the system works"), people signal that they've internalized the demands of society. The phrase "That's the way things are done around here" is a signal that someone has adopted what is called "the natural attitude": social convention has been made to seem "natural" (see the final essay in Barthes, 1973, for a discussion of naturalization). Individuals' tolerance of institutional control over their lives—schools, banks, churches, places where you buy and sell goods—is amazing. That tolerance allows society to function—to keep us from killing each other or eating our young, and working together for mutual protection and growth. Few individuals (we call them revolutionaries or radicals) get disturbed enough to want to overhaul the system. Thus, although it is ridiculously easy to document personal, social, economic, and political injustices all over the country, most of us shrug our shoulders and get on with our lives. Cultural stability cannot really, for a very long time, be maintained by force; most of the people have to go along with social practices for them to continue. In our time, one of the mechanisms for encouraging people to go along, to get along, is television.

4. *The goal of most culture-centered criticism is critique.* Going along, getting along can lead to individual demoralization, social stagnation, economic inequality, and political injustice. The goal of most culture-centered critics, therefore, is change, change associated with such socially charged concepts as liberation, empowerment, and freedom. Almost all aspects of such change are tinged with politics. In an era when "the personal is political" (individual control of self-identity) and "the social is political" (the fights for the self-determination of people of varying racial, class, and gender backgrounds), it

is little wonder that the final paragraphs of cultural studies almost inevitably deal with power. "Power/knowledge," as Foucault (1980) conceived of that term, is to be found in two modes of critique:

a. *The critique of domination:* analyses that strip away the imprisoning institutional, social, and linguistic forms that control individual word and deed.

b. *The critique of freedom:* analyses that urge the individual on to a sense of empowerment, the courage to act constructively with and through others once liberated in a call for a new social awareness (see McKerrow, 1989).

Cultural studies, thus, often looks like many other kinds of socially oriented forms of critical study but differs from those other forms because it is completed, usually, in political assessment and exhortation. That assessment and exhortation can sound whiny, leading to what Robert Hughes (1993) called "the culture of complaint," in a book subtitled *The fraying of America.* Those critical activities are not understood as complaints, however, when done well. We take up this question at the end of the chapter.

Some Central Concepts in Cultural Studies

So far, we have talked about cultural studies without getting too far into the actual vocabulary used by culturalists. As you read and practice culture-centered criticism near the turn of the twenty-first century, you'll need to understand the concepts discussed next.

Textualization

Cultural studies arose in part out of a particular branch of literary studies (Raymond Williams taught literature at Cambridge). It is therefore little wonder that the idea of *text* is central to this scholarly activity. Thanks to literary theorists with strong social concerns, we have come to understand that television texts are sequences of verbal, visual, acoustic, or behavioral signs that can be understood or interpreted in multiple ways (see Chapter 6). Another implication is that many kinds of human activities or even natural events can be *turned into texts.*

So a person is walking down the street and drops a gum wrapper. You're likely to say, "What a thoughtless person," because you've textualized the event, that is, created a little story: "This person is walking down the street and deliberately throws down a gum wrapper because he just doesn't give a hoot about the environment and doesn't care what others think—what a loser. What a thoughtless person." You just textualized that person's act into a story with a character who has motives and morals of a particular type. A better example is one of the nature programs from the Discovery Channel where a narrator talks about a group of baboons. She talks about them as "a family," notes "the mother's love

and affection for her baby," worries whether "she'll be able to protect her innocent baby from the ravages of the predator," and concludes by saying "So love
triumphs, even among the citizens of the veldt." Here, a series of animal behaviors is socialized, that is, talked about in human terms and, again, turned into a
story—a text. Textualization produces interesting stories, but stories that critics
must examine closely for their implications and their control of our perceptions.

Rules–Roles

Cultural tenets often are expressed as rules or exhortations: "Don't drive over
fifty-five mph in this zone" (regulation of activity), "Children should be seen
and not heard" (regulation of behavior), "Neither a borrower nor a lender be"
(regulation of relationships with others)," "You better watch out, you better
not cry, you better not pout, I'm telling you why—Santa Claus is coming to
town" (regulation of thought and feelings). A cultural rule is a statement that
directs or constrains an individual's thoughts, words, and deeds. Television
programs—sitcoms such as *Seinfeld, Friends,* or *Coach* are especially full of cultural rules—present us with a rich array of rules for living.

Just as we learn about the rules of life from television, we also learn much
about roles and role identity: who we are and what people of our types think
and do. This is not to say that you learn how to behave by watching *Martin,
Boston Commons, One Life to Live,* or *Late Show with David Letterman.* But you
learn much about "types"—about what are called "social, cultural, and discursive *formations*" (Hayes, 1992, p. 361). Others around you (social connections), the rules for living (cultural tenets), and discourses (e.g., television
texts) have considerable power in forming you into various kinds of subjects,
that is, into a person or spectator with particular relationships to others.
Those formations are usefully thought of as roles, more particularly, roles you
play in relation (reciprocally) to others—a child to another's parental role, a
male vis-à-vis someone's femaleness, a friend to another's role as friend.

Bill Clinton's inaugural ceremony in 1993 contained music, walks,
speeches, and ceremonies of remembrance all designed to make you into a
particular kind of spectator: a citizen watching proudly from home. The
broadcast events were shot so that you as viewer were subjected to a stream of
visual, verbal, and acoustic messages that flowed in and through you, always
emphasizing your status as citizen. You were formed socially and culturally,
through texts or discourses, into that citizen. Role analysis is an important
part of the TV critic's attempt to explain the power of spectatorship.

Performance

The discussions of textualization and rules–roles both point to another concept important to cultural analysis: performance. Cultural rules, of course,

can often be framed in words: in aphorisms ("Birds of a feather flock to-gether"); in orders ("Buckle up!"); and in warnings ("All backpacks subject to search as you leave this store"). But if imitation of others is one of the potent forms of social learning in your life (Hall, 1959), then seeing your culture per-formed is terribly important. And, of course, you see culture performed every night on television. *Embodiment* is a process whereby ideas, attitudes, values, and social character are given corporeal existence in texts.

You see the presidency, and learn about its powers and responsibilities, in televised news conferences, international ceremonies, and speeches to Con-gress. *Home Improvement* exaggerates husband–wife gender talk so as to cri-tique the relationships existing between too many husbands and too many wives. In *Chicago Hope* you have illustrations of how the personal and the pro-fessional dimensions of life are actually inseparable. The *News Hour with Jim Lehrer* strives to embody the best of public deliberation over pressing issues. The virtues of positive regard for others are performed weekly on *Mighty Morphin Power Rangers*. Television has these cultural powers because of its narrative traditions and its multimediated ability to represent drama as life across the verbal, visual, and acoustic channels at its disposal.

Ideology

Televisual texts, along with so many others in your experience, naturalize (Barthes, 1973) the power of social, economic, educational, religious, and po-litical institutions. You matter-of-factly take those institutions as legitimate in-fluences, as institutions with the right, even obligation, to control significant aspects of your life. That power is expressed in ideologies, in systems of thought that embody social values and perceptual orientations to life, role re-lationships and the authority to enforce them, and the very rules of thinking themselves. For an extended discussion of ideology, see Chapter 8.

Hegemony

The term *hegemony* has been current since the ancient Greeks used it to iden-tify the conquering country/conquered country relationship. In this century, however, thanks to the Italian Marxist Antonio Gramsci, we have employed the term to explain the everyday mechanisms whereby an elite or dominant class or group exercises control over a lower or subordinate class or group. While the ancient Greeks backed their claims to power over others through force of arms, puppet governors, and control of economic resources, Gramsci noted that the force of hegemony is not so much coercive as social. An essen-tial aspect of a hegemonic relationship between peoples or classes is *complic-ity*—the acceptance of power relationships as normal, as the way things are done in a society. To Gramsci, hegemonic struggles are attempts to break that sense of normalcy by installing another wherein classes rework popular understandings of relationships. Thus, for Gramsci, revolutions don't begin with the first shot but earlier with the intelligentsia who exercise "moral and intellectual leadership" in the processes of redefinition (Aronowitz, 1993, especially pp. 103, 112). The idea of the "national-popular," to Gramsci (1971), is one wherein the state, the *civitas,* and the people, the *communitas,* are united in a revolution to break the old hegemonies by redefining and re-embodying hierarchies in the social and political-economic orders.

Yet, of course, the force of the idea of hegemony is less in how social change is produced than in how the existing social order is maintained: through voluntary compliance, through acceptance of one's place as normal or natural. In our time, one of the predominating tools for normalizing or naturalizing the existing social order is television. Day after day, you see the operations of government on the news, the importance of Wall Street on investment and stock-reporting shows, the happiness of traditional families and the unhappiness of families in divorce proceedings on the afternoon soaps, and the predominance of white Anglos in positions of power in most of the prime-time lineup of shows. Seeing is believing to a greater extent than we might like to recognize. Martin Heidegger went so far as to argue that "the fundamental event of the modern age is the conquest of the world as picture" (1938/1977). To see relationships is to be exhorted to live them, contentedly.

Television critics with avowedly cultural interests, therefore, often explore the ways in which social, economic, and political—which is to say, power—relationships are reinforced again and again in television programs.

Myth

Our word *myth* comes from the Greek *mythos,* which was Aristotle's word for plot or story. While we sometimes use the word to distinguish truth from falsehood, as when Edwin Black (1973) accused Richard Nixon in 1972 of trying to make his hometown, Whittier, California, into an environment characterized by rich, positive values—of mythifying that town—we usually think of myths as particular kinds of stories. Myths are stories often set in the past, wherein are recorded virtuous and villainous, larger-than-life characters whose actions have *morals,* that is, can teach us how to behave in our own world (this understanding of myth is grounded in Lévi-Strauss, 1958). Myths are set in the past, yet are endlessly translatable into present-day circumstances. Thus, the myth of Faust, the man who sold his soul to the devil for power only to regret it, was first recorded in a play by Thomas Kidd in the sixteenth century; it later appeared as a German drama in the eighteenth century by Goethe, a twentieth-century novel by German-American writer Thomas Mann, and even a 1978 episode of the cartoon *Thundarr the Barbarian.* Whether the Faust persona was a philosopher (Kidd), a scientist (Goethe), a musician (Mann), or a wizard (*Thundarr*) made no difference; each was a hero whose excessive desires to know and have power over others brought about his own downfall. The lesson in each case was the same: don't try to reach too far outside of your own circumstances or too far beyond the abilities of others. The Faust story is an excellent example of the socializing powers of myth.

Myths work at multiple levels: as localized accounts, say, of your own family, as regional or national stories about valued or despised actions and characters, or even as universal stories about struggles that all human beings face in making their way through life (see Gronbeck, 1989). As they become so large as to account for a people's understanding of life as a whole, their place in the universe, their origins, and their destinies, myths become what Earnest Bormann (1972, 1985) calls *rhetorical visions*—a people's way of seeing social life and using that way of seeing as an orientation to the world.

Mythic analysis represents an important kind of cultural criticism because myths can become constraints that work to prevent social change or rationales that drive people to act even violently against "the other." So, as television in most of the 1950s and 1960s domestic dramas and sitcoms showed white nuclear families raising their children lovingly and wisely, such programs constrained Americans' views of family life: we were not allowed to explore alternative family arrangements, the family life of nonwhites, or the conditions experienced by children being raised in less-than-loving environments. Furthermore, the myths that justify whites' sense of superiority to blacks, males' belief in their superiority over "the weaker sex," and America's destiny and mission to democratize in capitalistic ways the rest of the world often appear in television programs as the way things are, that is, as naturalized. On few programs are African Americans in leadership roles (*NYPD Blue* and *Homicide: Life on the Street* stand out as exceptions), are women stronger, wiser, and more adroit than men (*Ink* in 1996 was launched with that myth as its central premise), or are the poor shown as superior to the rich. One of the cultural critic's primary tasks, for many, is to problematize and strip away such myths.

Political communication via television often is rife with mythic allusions, whether to America's mission in the case of presidential messages or to the virtues of small-town origins in the case of campaign ads. Social myths often frame the action of prime-time shows. Saturday cartoons teach the myths of gender differences to the young. Game shows embody the myths for success: knowledge (*Jeopardy*), an understanding of everyday truisms (*Wheel of Fortune*), common sense (*Family Feud*). Mythic analysis helps you dig into the unarticulated assumptions about good and bad thinking and behavior undergirding so much of television programming.

Race/Class/Gender

A particular set of questions about ideology and myth has been raised in the last quarter century of American life. Recognizing that the social is political, the United States has lived through a series of revolutionizing movements that have critiqued the systematic domination of racial groups (civil rights), one gender group (women's rights), and America's underclasses (the right to social services regardless of ability to pay). Over the last forty years, especially, the United States has tried to make sense of the idea that racial, gendered, and class-based marks of one's social identities in fact are political matters. That idea has led to political action—protests, parades, rioting, martyrdom—and even to political process: the great civil rights bills and War on Poverty legislation of the mid-1960s, the groundbreaking legislation on affirmative action and women's rights of the 1970s, and in 1991 the Americans with Disabilities Act, which guaranteed rights and consideration to anyone "environmentally challenged"—a sweeping illustration of the politicalization of the social.

Because hierarchical power is always best witnessed materially, in the historical or temporospatial specificity of concrete actions in particular moments, television is a great weapon in the struggle to redefine racial, gender, and class relationships. One can study Madonna's MTV videos to see an assault on traditional gender roles or Phyllis Schlafly on *Larry King Live!* to see them reaffirmed. The very lack of racial commentary on *Friends* is as significant as its presence is on *NYPD Blue. COPS* almost always shows police officers chasing lower-class rather than middle- or upper-class perpetrators. The white, male, seemingly upper-class narrator still is the preferred presenter of television's fare. Insofar as the cultural critic critiques domination and freedom, to that extent is he or she bound to pursue matters of race/class/gender in our time. Questions of monoculturalism and multiculturalism, homogenization and diversity, political correctness and hate speech—all of these ugly matters lurk in the study of race/class/gender by television critics.

The concepts central to cultural studies, it should be clear, have been built to make possible the systematic description and evaluation of out-of-awareness relationships between individuals and peoples. Only in that way will the goals of both Sumner and Arnold be met in humane scholarship.

Writing Culture-Centered Television Criticism

The central challenge in writing culture-centered criticism, as you might guess, is to negotiate description and assessment, or, if you prefer, fact-based and value-based argument. Sumner and Arnold must be made to work together. Working only descriptively or only judgmentally makes for less-than-satisfying criticism.

Suppose you wanted to do a critical-cultural study of ABC news. Were you to work with the content only in a factual sort of way, you could describe each story in order, examining (a) the narrative structure; (b) the principal players assumed to be relevant to the story; (c) the location of the story (local, national, international); (d) people affected by the story but not mentioned in it; and (e) the placement of the story on the newscast. You might also wish to describe relationships between the reporters and the players as well between Peter Jennings and the reporters; the methods Jennings uses to control our interpretations of the story also would be of interest. A descriptive cultural study might leave you focusing on stories, their setting, and their principal characters mentioned and ignored, as well as the ways in which those stories are framed or interpreted by ABC.

Were you to work, instead, only in a valuative or judgmental way, you might focus on assessing the institutionalized ideology of ABC: the way that the network historically has had positive (or negative) relationships with government; the question of ownership (e.g., the significance of ABC's ownership by the Disney Corporation); its heavy focus on governmental spokespersons rather than other sorts of sources of information; and its cutback of international bureaus, forcing ABC to rely on others for much of its international pictures and reports. You then might launch a diatribe against the economic control of public information, that is, about ways in which ratings are worth money to national news operations and about the degree to which you think that ABC has sold out to big government and big business in its coverage.

Neither the descriptive nor the judgmental study of ABC is satisfying by itself. Merely describing cultural rules and roles, ideological orientations and hegemonic mechanisms, or the moves an institution makes in performing or acting out some perspective on life is not enough. In the face of mere description, readers cry out "So what?" "So what if Ted Koppel is polite to business representatives or if ABC never attacks the Disney empire?" On the other hand, a series of charged value judgements without evidence—"The national networks are among the biggest and most sales-conscious industries in the U.S." or "The quack, the charlatan, the jingo, and the terrorist can flourish only where the audience is deprived of independent access to information" (Lippmann, 1920, p. 55)—is alarming and engaging, but it is also merely exhortative: that is, a lot of advice on how to evaluate without proof that anything is really wrong.

As we noted in Chapter 4, for the good critic, descriptions of typical and/or usual action from programs become evidence both for generalizations about programs and for judgments about their beauties and ugliness, their force for justice or injustice, and their political force. Descriptions without judgments are sterile; judgments without descriptive evidence are mere expressions of taste or preference. Sumner's description of cultural practices together with Arnold's normative assessments of those practices comprise a complete piece of culture-centered criticism.

Writing culture-centered criticism, thus, calls for great discipline, bringing together both your analytical skills and your sense of injustice yet hope for the future.

Culture-Centered Critical Essays

The sample essays we include in this chapter begin with a study of American racial myths and the ways in which myth-based stereotypes can come to control our understandings of social-professional relationships. Ronald B. Scott takes us back to the 1991 televised coverage of Judge Clarence Thomas's Senate confirmation hearings, where rearticulation of myths about African Americans (their sexual prowess, uninhibited love of the discourse of sex, and social delinquency) overrode the real questions presumably at stake in the hearings—questions about sexual harassment, truth telling, and the politics of Supreme Court appointments. Not only does Scott offer us a mythic analysis, but he also demonstrates how racial studies can sensitize us to the power of cultural stereotyping.

Next come two feminist studies. Sarah Projansky is interested conceptually in relationships between feminist concerns (to unmask patriarchical structures and to empower women in society) and postfeminist concerns (to *normalize* relationships between men and women often, it would seem, to the detriment of the independent woman). She pursues that tension in Colleen, Michaela Quinn's adoptive teenage daughter on the series *Dr. Quinn, Medicine Woman*. Because the part of Colleen has been played by two quite different actresses, Erika Flores and Jessica Bowman, who not only behave differently but also possess very different bodies, Projansky is able to explore the tensions between feminist and postfeminist portrayals of Colleen that likewise are embodied in contrasting ways. In this study, she explores the ideological tensions that can arise from the material appearance and behavior of women in prime time.

Bonnie Dow's study of *Murphy Brown* moves in a similar direction. The liberal feminism espoused by Brown and illustrated by her life as a major news professional is not a threat to patriarchy, Dow argues, because the program defuses that threat. Murphy's masculine aggressiveness and physical presence, her lack of sensitivity and even ruthlessness, are critiqued in comedic ways in the show; the bottom line is that we are shown an unmarried woman without a romantic relationship, perennially unhappy with both her work and her personal life. Murphy's suffering reinforces some of the very stereotypes she is presumably countering as a successful working woman.

With A. Susan Owen and Peter Ehrenhaus's study of the 1993 miniseries, *Wild Palms*, we move into ideological territory. They explore a piece of postmodern television, a miniseries that was chopped into seemingly disconnected episodes, involving characters whose relationships were undefined, in plot lines that moved back and forth through time. But if *Wild Palms* seems to have been premised on a world of paradox, fragmentation, fatigue, and play, where social and political-economic institutions presumably have surrendered their governing roles to mass media and powerful secret societies, in fact the series, they argue, was perfectly conventional: a romantic myth treating the struggles between good and evil, where those who expressed faith in the dominant political and social institutions win because of that faith, where the white, middle-class family representatives triumph over those professing other values. Oliver Stone, an executive coproducer of the series, is shown to regularly reaffirm the American dream in spite of and through the vehicles of his seemingly unorthodox films.

We end this chapter with Robert Hanke's study of *Northern Exposure.* Hanke's task is to understand and then critique the multicultural world of Cicely, Alaska, the site of the program. He combs the program to discover a series of moments when gendered and raced differences in identity are recognized and commented upon. This study allows him to describe and then evaluate the sort of multicultural vision embodied in the program: to understand that when cultural difference is attributed to individuals rather than to groups or classes and when that difference is merely accepted by people in a society, then the more progressive dimensions of multicultural politics are muted and even safely contained. When difference is thusly contained, it becomes just another kind of cultural sameness, as freedom in an odd way turns into just another form of domination.

The Pain and Promise of Culture-Centered Critical Study

Among scholars of television criticism, culture-centered studies are tremendously popular. The critique of domination and the critique of freedom are heady enterprises. For some critics, of course, there is sheer pleasure to be had in blasting a politically and economically motivated network for its right-wing ideology. And for almost all culture-conscious analysts, the feeling that one is working on the side of angels in attempting to improve society through criticism is undeniable. Rooting out racism, sexism, classism, selfishness, ruthlessness, and megalomania seems today like a near-perfect justification for a career in television criticism; the joy one can feel in trying to ennoble the powerless in society justifies the long hours of analysis and composition.

There is a happiness to be found, too, in the very act of writing cultural criticism: the prose of such critics can be fearsomely rhetorical. As Michael Parenti (1994, p. 173) was completing his cultural study of connections between American politics and economic institutions, he wrote the following passage:

> In 1907, the sociologist E. A. Ross noted that as society develops so does sin. With commerce comes piracy and smuggling; with banking comes embezzlement and forgery. Many latter-day sins are impersonal. The victimizer is far removed by an elaborate organizational system from the victim. Rather than using the gun or bludgeon, as might the brigand, the impeccable gentlemen who preside over great business empires resort to bribery, false claims, safety violations, child labor, toxic dumping, war profiteering, and the like, causing material loss, physical injury, misery, and death to persons whom they never see. While their actions and decisions may harbor no malicious intent toward specific individuals, they are guilty of neglect, deception, illegality—and liability. Still, these estimable individuals never think of themselves as criminals, nor does the press or any other established

opinion-maker. On the contrary, the "systemic sinners" sit on the boards of foundations, museums, churches, and universities, are given honorary degrees, and are welcomed into the best clubs.

You can hear this passage in your mental ears. You can almost imagine a great pipe organ and chorus blasting out the concluding coda of a magnificent oratorio in these words. Parenti's sensitivity to pain, to the obliviousness of established opinion-makers, his rhythmic prose, his ironic references to foundations, museums, churches, and universities, and above all his devotion to the victims of politically and economically empowered victimizers make this passage "a good read." And he undoubtedly had a wonderful time writing it. His joyful state of mind shows in the words.

Parenti's *Land of Idols* illustrates many of the strengths and potential weaknesses of culture-centered criticism. For example, he wants to build the argument that, politically, black–white differences are less a matter of race than of class: America has a system of class power that privileges whites. To build that argument, he textualizes (see above) class differences by analyzing mortality rates between blacks and whites of all classes, by examining television depictions of stereotyped black fathers who refuse to pay child support, by looking at court decisions that talk exclusively about race and not class inequalities, and by quoting African-American leaders W. E. B. DuBois and Malcolm X on relationships between class and racism (1994, pp. 135–138).

What is visible in this section of Parenti's book is an example of *case building, not analysis.* That is, Parenti obviously looked for examples that would help him build a case for the idea that class, not race, is the key cultural factor dividing black and white; this argument is important to the overall argument of this book—that economics determines in many ways what our political and social relationships are all about. Looking at different dimensions of black–white relationships (where people sit or stand in public buildings, scores on "standardized" intelligence tests, gerrymandering or the construction of congressional districts), one could come to the opposite conclusion: that racism in social and political matters, regardless of class, is alive and well in America.

The point here is not to disparage Parenti's fascinating book, for it's very enlightening and yes, a good read. Rather, the point is that the best critics always start with the texts or textualizations and see where they take them, rather than starting with some judgments and then searching out evidence to support them. If a critic seems always to be case building, he or she certainly is writing a critical essay but is not really doing criticism as we defined it earlier in the book. Because culture-centered criticism ends in judgment, it's very tempting to start with the judgment and then work more or less backwards. Resist that temptation. As we have noted more than once, the promise of culture-centered analyses and assessments of television programs comes in the careful execution of both description, a la William Graham Sumner, and normative judgment, a la Matthew Arnold.

NOTES

1. Just as Horace Newcomb (see Chapter 3) asserted that television in fact does have an aesthetic, so have some critics continued to do aesthetic studies of television programming, for example, Thompson's study of *Love Boat* (1983), Gitlin's analysis of *Hill Street Blues* (1983), and Gronbeck's examination of *Family* (1985). Most normative studies of television programming, however, are much more concerned about social and political than aesthetic issues.

REFERENCES

Arnold, M. (1869/1916). *Culture & anarchy: An essay in political and social criticism.* New York: Macmillan.

Aronowitz, S. (1993). *Roll over Beethoven: The return of cultural strife.* Hanover, NH: University Press of New England.

Barthes, R. (1968). *Elements of semiology.* London: Cape.

Barthes, R. (1973). *Mythologies.* London: Paladin.

Barthes, R. (1977). *Image-music-text.* S. Heath (Ed. & Trans.). New York: Hill & Wang.

Baudrillard, J. (1983). *In the shadow of the silent majorities, Or, the end of the social, and other essays.* New York: Semiotext(e).

Baudrillard, J. (1988). *The ecstasy of communication.* New York: Semiotext(e).

Black, E. (1973). Electing time. *Quarterly Journal of Speech, 59,* 125–129.

Bormann, E. G. (1972). Fantasy and rhetorical vision: The rhetorical criticism of social reality. *Quarterly Journal of Speech, 58,* 396–407.

Bormann, E. G. (1985). *The force of fantasy: Restoring the American dream.* Carbondale: Southern Illinois University Press.

Chase, S. (1948/1956). *The proper study of mankind.* Rev. ed. New York: Harper & Row.

Debord, G. (1970). *The society of the spectacle.* Detroit: Black and Red.

deCerteau, M. (1984). *The practice of everyday life.* Berkeley: University of California Press.

Fiske, J. (1987). *Television culture.* London: Methuen.

Fiske, J. (1994). *Media matters: Everyday culture and political change.* Minneapolis: University of Minnesota Press.

Fiske, J., & Hartley, J. (1978). *Reading television.* London: Methuen.

Foucault, M. (1972). *The archeology of knowledge and the discourse on language.* (A. M. Sheridan Smith, Trans.). New York: Harper & Row.

Foucault, M. (1977). *The order of things.* London: Tavistock.

Foucault, M. (1980). *Power/knowledge: Selected interviews and other writings, 1972–1977.* (C. Gordon, Ed.). New York: Pantheon.

Geertz, C. (1973). *The interpretation of cultures.* New York: Basic Books.

Gitlin, T. (1983). *Hill Street Blues:* Make it look messy. *Inside prime time* (pp. 273–335). New York: Pantheon.

Gramsci, A. (1971). *Prison notebooks.* New York: International Publishers.

Gronbeck, B. E. (1985). Audience engagement in *Family*. In M. J. Medhurst & T. W. Benson (Eds.), *Rhetorical dimensions in media: A critical casebook* (pp. 4–32). Dubuque, IA: Kendall/Hunt.

Gronbeck, B. E. (1989). Mythic portraiture in the 1988 Iowa presidential caucus bioads. *American Behavioral Science, 32,* 351–364.

Hall, E. (1959). *The silent language.* New York: Doubleday.

Hall, S. (1980). Encoding/decoding. In S. Hall, D. Hobson, A. Lowe, & P. Willis (Eds.), *Culture, media, language* (pp. 128–139). London: Hutchinson.

Hall, S. (1982). The rediscovery of ideology: The return of the repressed in media studies. In M. Gurevitch, T. Bennett, J. Curran, & J. Woollacott (Eds.), *Culture, society, and media* (pp. 56–90). London: Methuen.

Hall, S., Critcher, C., Jefferson, T., Clark, J., & Roberts, B. (1978). *Policing the crisis: Mugging, the state, and law and order.* London: Macmillan.

Hayes, J. (1992). Afterword. In *Channels of discourse, reassembled: Television and contemporary criticism* (pp. 354–385). Chapel Hill: University of North Carolina Press.

Heidegger, M. (1938/1977). The age of the world picture. In *The question concerning technology and other essays.* New York: Harper & Row.

Hughes, R. (1993). *Culture of complaint: The fraying of America.* New York: Oxford University Press.

Lévi-Strauss, C. (1958). The structural study of myth. In T. A. Sebeok (Ed.), *Myth: A symposium* (pp. 81–106). Bloomington: Indiana University Press.

Lewis, G. E. (Ed.). (1972). *Side-saddle on the golden calf: Social structure and cultural character.* Pacific Palisades, CA: Goodyear.

Lippman, W. (1920). *Liberty and the news.* New York: Harcourt Brace Jovanovich.

McKerrow, R. E. (1989). Critical rhetoric: Theory and praxis. *Communication Monographs, 56,* 91–111.

Parenti, M. (1994). *Land of idols: Political mythology in America.* New York: St. Martin's Press.

Park, R. (1938). Reflections on communication and culture. *The American Journal of Socialism, 45,* 187–208.

Rosenberg, B., & White, D. M. (Eds.). (1957). *Mass culture: The popular arts in America.* New York: Free Press.

Smith, A. E. (Ed.). (1966). *Communication and culture.* Englewood Cliffs, NJ: Prentice-Hall.

Sumner, W. G. (1906/1911). *Folkways: A study of the sociological importance of usages, manner, customs, mores, and morals.* Boston: Ginn & Co.

Thompson, R. (1983). *Love Boat:* High art on the high seas. *Journal of American Culture, 6,* 59–65.

Voelker, F. H., & Voelker, L. A. (Eds.). (1972). *Mass media: Forces in our society.* (4th ed.). New York: Harcourt Brace Jovanovich.

Williams, R. (1974). *Television: Technology and cultural form.* London: Fontana.

The Rearticulation of Popular Myths and Stereotypes: The Hill-Thomas Hearings

Ronald B. Scott

Long-held cultural stereotypes and myths deeply ingrained in the American psyche surfaced during the Supreme Court confirmation hearings for Judge Clarence Thomas. These racial myths are so ingrained in American cultural mythology that they deflected much of the attention away from the issue of Judge Thomas's sexual harassment of attorney Anita Hill, which the hearings were intended to resolve. This essay focuses on the stereotypes and the racial myths suggested throughout the coverage of the Hill-Thomas hearings and how those stereotypes and mythic images, while advancing one cause (the awareness of sexual harassment), may have compromised another (equality in race relations).

The Significance of Racial Imagery in Media

To fully understand the depths of the problem presented by the overwhelmingly negative and mythic presentations of African Americans on television, one only has to consider the context and content of news coverage that deals with African Americans. If one scans the coverage of African Americans by the major networks on any given night, with the occasional rare exception, one will most likely be exposed to images of African Americans who, based on their looks and actions, pose a threat to the stability and well being of the larger white community. During the 1990s extensive media coverage of narratives such as the Charles Stuart case in Boston (an alleged murder of a pregnant white woman by a black male), the Central Park case in New York (a brutal assault and rape of a white female jogger by black youths), the Rodney King verdict in California (where law and order broke down in the aftermath of a verdict), the Mike Tyson case (a rape and assault of a black woman), the Susan Smith case (the accusation of an alleged kidnapping of white children by a black male), and the 1995 O. J. Simpson trial (a black male accused of killing a white male and female) has served to keep emotionally charged images and negative beliefs about race and racial relations, and hence African Americans, in the public consciousness. In isolation, these narratives probably would not pose much of a problem or undermine a positive perception of race in general or African Americans in particular. These negative narratives and images, however, are not isolated.

The barrage of images of African Americans being arrested and led away in handcuffs or chains for drug- and gang-related activities, charged with rape and assault, engaging in welfare fraud and abuse, steeped in destructive social and cultural practices, as the undeserved benefactors of quotas, and as the subjects of racial discrimination contributes to the perception that the honest efforts of the white population are being thwarted. When African Americans speak on television, especially as witnesses to a recent crime or political event, they are too often seen and portrayed as either highly emotional or barely able to form complete, intelligible sentences. What is even more frustrating yet indicative of a negative public perception is the image of African Americans seemingly selected for their "just got out of the shower or bed" look, with uncombed hair and disheveled clothing or wearing shower caps.

Given the predominantly one-dimensional portrayal and presentation of African Americans in the media and their even more limited appearances in news, Anita Hill and Clarence Thomas, at first glance, appear to be unlikely characters to be included in an analysis of ongoing negative characterizations of African Americans. In September 1991, prior to the beginning of Judge Thomas's confirmation hearings for the Supreme Court, when the charges of sexual harassment first emerged publicly, few would have perceived either Anita Hill or Clarence Thomas as vehicles for the perpetuation of negative stereotypes or myths about African Americans. On one side of the drama was Anita Hill, a law professor specializing in commercial law at the University of Oklahoma. On the other side was Clarence Thomas, a federal judge being considered for the highest judicial position in the country—that of Supreme Court Justice. Together the unlikely pair, both graduates from the Yale Law School, represented the highest levels of achievement within the African American community. Both were from less than privileged economic backgrounds yet each had gone through the system to emerge as credible, articulate examples of what many could say was the best the African American community had to offer. In addition to their complementary racial and cultural backgrounds, Hill and Thomas had both worked for the Department of Education (Office of Civil Rights) in 1981–1982 and the Equal Employment Opportunity Commission (EEOC) from 1982 through 1983 for Republican administrations.

Beginning in July 1991, Thomas's nomination to the Supreme Court by President George Bush was steeped in the political and social issues that exacerbate much of the racial tension in the country today. Thomas was chosen to replace the retiring Justice Thurgood Marshall, and claims of racial quotas or a black seat on the court were cynically denied by those in the White House. Claims of affirmative action may have been denied, but what is clear is that Thomas rose to the top of the list of possible nominees despite his limited experience and judicial qualifications. Consequently, regardless of any intent from the outset, the specter of race was an undercurrent of the process that would, once Hill's charges of sexual harassment were leveled in September, diffuse into discussions of racial and sexual myths that have hampered and negatively defined African Americans historically in this country.

Issues of Race and Sexual Harassment

From the moment the first cameras of the 21 hours of gavel to gavel nationally televised confirmation hearings began, it became clear that the extended coverage of the Anita Hill-Clarence Thomas testimony before the Senate Judiciary Committee would, at the very least, become both historic and historically controversial. In consort with the narratives on Susan Smith, Charles Stuart, the Central Park jogger, the Rodney King verdict aftermath, and the O. J. Simpson case, the Hill-Thomas hearings moved from base coverage of the events to a substantial staple on both daytime and evening programming. Like other sensationalized cases, the Hill-Thomas hearings preempted game shows, talk shows, and soap operas and became grist for nightly programming as well. Although the hearings preempted programming and caused some of the curious and interested to adjust their weekend plans and schedules, the nation was virtually transfixed by hearings to which few, regardless of the real significance of Thomas's confirmation to the court, had seriously attended to.

The public's attention was sustained in part because, like much of the daytime programming it preempted, the hearings incorporated the best elements of game shows, soap operas, talk shows, and drama. In effect, the hearings offered dramatic actions, appealing characters, and vicarious involvement in a realistic story line steeped in one of the most controversial issues of the day, sexual harassment. Maybe the nation was focused on the hearings because they satisfied the same morbid fascination that many Americans seem to have for viewing car wrecks or volatile human interactions on television. The hearings promised to have something for everyone: good and evil, clear-cut issues and those shaded in gray, blacks and whites, sinners and saints, heroes and villains, males and females, suspense and tension, and explicit but safe and erotic vicarious sex, all covered with few commercial interruptions. This scandal, with its discussion of male sexual prowess, elongated genitals, sexual props (such as Coke cans with pubic hair), mythic sexual stereotypes generally applied to blacks, and power and powerlessness in relationships and confrontations, plus the dramatically riveting elements of intense emotional pain conveyed convincingly by a cast of unknown but serious actors, may have been, in the end, nothing more than an X-rated popular spectacle. More was revealed about human nature and American character than about race relations or sexual harassment. Why else would a culture that claims high moral convictions tune in and irresistibly watch, on the same channels where commercials for AIDS and condoms are deemed too controversial and offensive to air, sit as if controlled by some irresistible force and watch events that many would describe later as repulsive and disgusting?

At the conclusion of the hearings, however, in spite of the hours of coverage and extensive media analysis generated at the local and national level, much was obscured and little seemed to change as a direct result of the confusing confrontations. For all the value the public discussion of sexual harassment generated across the country, the question "at whose expense?" has remained unexplored. While needed discussions and debate about the treatment of women in American society were momentarily elevated in the public consciousness, that elevation allowed for the equally important issue of race and racial relations in this country to become both subordinate and race specific. In a country that still remains bound by its own racial and racially motivated sexual mythology, the image of another highly successful black male being accused of a sexual crime or sexual harassment is historically striking and disturbing. Although the general benefits of discussing sexual harassment are clearly significant, grounding them in and with racial overtones obscures the issue the same way that talking about black males raping white women during slavery was used to obscure the equally real, and more prevalent, sexual behaviors practiced by white males against all women. The real problem, in essence, was not so much in the hearings themselves but in the stereotypical images of race that were utilized, articulated, and focused on during discussions about the harassment of women.

In recounting the historic moment of a full Senate vote on Thomas's judicial appointment, Bob Franken, one of CNN's Washington, D.C., correspondents, remarked during televised coverage of the vote that it was quite a day:

A couple of observations. First of all, rarely do you see all the senators in their seats, standing to vote in the way that they do it in movies. This is one of those rare occasions, but probably an appropriate one, given all the controversy and significance of this vote.

Following more than a hundred days of deliberation (105 to be exact) the Senate was about to vote not on an arms treaty or on aid to victims of manmade or natural disasters, or even on a bill that would directly address the economic crisis that gripped the nation. Instead, the senators were about to vote on the confirmation of Judge Clarence Thomas to the United States Supreme Court. The issue in the hearings, which amounted to a duel between Judge Clarence Thomas and black female law professor Anita Hill, was whether the judge had sexually harassed Professor Hill in the early 1980s when both worked at the Equal Employment Opportunity Commission. What was lost was an analysis of whether Judge Thomas was qualified to sit on the highest court of the land and whether he was a fitting replacement for the black associate justice Thurgood Marshall.

Though sharing the same racial heritage as Marshall, Thomas differed dramatically from Marshall in his political and judicial philosophies. Instead of possessing a proactive, liberal civil rights philosophy, Thomas expressed conservative revisionist views that threatened the sacred relationship and bond between the high court, civil rights groups (especially in the area of affirmative action and the rights of women), and the black community. Perhaps the most disturbing and telling element of Thomas's character was the fact that as a black male he had directly benefited from civil rights rulings, yet he publicly raised doubts about their fairness and necessity. In effect, President George Bush had found in his appointment of Thomas a black man who held promise for undermining the social, political, and cultural advances of various minority groups, especially blacks and women. In a political and social move that was consistent with the tenor of the conservative eighties and nineties, a white administration had found a black ally who would help curtail the social progress of his own race.

One year later the hearings were credited with directly raising the consciousness of black and white women, asking questions about the traditional political alliance between blacks and the Democratic party, and heightening the awareness and understanding of sexual harassment by bringing it into the forefront of the consciousness of the entire culture. In terms of direct actions the hearings were at least partially responsible for the record number of women who ran for the House of Representatives (113, up from the 70 who ran in 1990) and the United States Senate (11, up from the 8 who ran in 1990). The televised hearings and the extensive media coverage also were responsible for the clarification and redefinition of sexual harassment as both verbal and physical, and helped to establish the tragic breadth of the problem.

What was less clear one year after the hearings and confirmation vote was the real significance of the 52 to 48 vote for the confirmation of Judge Thomas. As former U.S. Representative Claudine Schneider suggested during an interview on CNN, the final vote was almost meaningless because it failed to reveal whether the senators were voting for or against Thomas, motivated by political concerns for not wanting to offend black voters (60% of surveyed blacks in one poll supported Thomas), or motivated by real concerns about women's issues, specifically abortion rights. What became clear several years later was the fact that Judge Thomas is a critical swing vote aligned with those on the court who seem set on undermining and eroding civil rights, affirmative action, and women's rights.

In the wake of the hearings one fact remains: the country remains divided on issues of both race and gender. While much of the subsequent public discussion and debate focused on the issue of sexual harassment, the intertwined issue of race and racism has received much less serious noncrisis attention. The significance of race in the hearings, however, was not lost on the African American community as a whole. During the hearings, debate about the Thomas nomination was extensive. In a Times Mirror poll for example, 43% of the black community indicated that they were following the hearings (compared to 26% of the white community). When asked if race was a factor influencing the all-white Senate panel that heard the initial charges, 45 percent of the blacks surveyed (compared to 20 percent of whites) believed that race was a factor, according to a poll conducted by the Joint Center for Political Studies, a black think tank (see Fiske, 1994).

Although the hearings themselves were steeped in emotionally charged racial references and sexual stereotypes that culminated in Thomas's characterizations of the hearings as a "high tech lynching," post hearing discussions have all but ignored the racial overtones and age-old concerns that were raised. Just as issues of sexual harassment have been elevated, concerns and questions about the double jeopardy (sexual and racial discrimination) faced by black women in this culture and questions of whether or not this was another case of a black male being abused (ironically by the same judicial system he wished to be part of) by the system, to the amusement of some whites, were and have been lost. Given the prevailing myths, stereotypes, and negative attitudes about interracial relationships, it was ironic that Thomas's marriage to a white woman was also virtually ignored.

Ignoring Thomas's personal choices may be the first positive sign that interracial relationships are less controversial than they have been traditionally. It is also positive that for once the serious issue of sexual harassment gained the attention of white and black males. What is disturbing, though, is the fact that an equally important discussion about long-held racial and sexual stereotypes, as specifically applied to blacks and raised by the dialogue of the hearings, has not received much attention.

To some extent, the failure to fully discuss the racial issues involved is historically grounded and fully understandable. By focusing on sexual harassment and ignoring the racial stereotypes embodied in the text of the hearings, white and black women could effectively be pitted rhetorically against men in general and black men in particular. At the same time the fragile alliances within the black community also could be undermined and once again black men and women could be further divided from themselves.

In conjunction with the other issues and problems raised, the hearings underscored the ahistorical penchant of Americans to focus on one issue at a time. In this instance, while sexual harassment and racism or racist stereotypes were both relevant issues, most attention in this case went to sexual harassment. Forgotten or left out of the public discussions was the connection between race and sex and the real role both have played in the continuing segregation of blacks from whites. In his book *An American Dilemma*, written over one-half century ago, Gunnar Myrdal (1944) suggested that fears over sex and race were tools used by whites to defend segregation. Myrdal noted the paternalistic insistence of white males to protect white women from black males as evidence supporting his theory. Although protecting white women from the onslaughts of black males was not a theme of the Hill-Thomas hearings, much of the public discussion of the specific sexual stereotypes long attributed to black males was a disturbing backdrop. At the same time, while the issue of sexual harassment clearly affects all women and is perpetuated by both black and white males, the visual argument presented by the televised hearings served to ground and focus the discussion in one hue. It is this electronic rearticulation of sexual myths and stereotypes that is of primary concern.

Myth, Race, and Media Images

As Gronbeck (1984) indicates, mythic criticism and its utilization in the analysis of television narratives and visuals have been interpreted in a number of ways. The perspective used in this essay is grounded in two variations. First, cultural myths, as suggested by Claude Lévi-Strauss (1958), are narratives (stories) that are constructed to help members of a given culture cope with the fundamental oppositions found in life: love and hate, life and death, and social status and acceptance. Accordingly, myths exist in society to help facilitate the understanding and solution of problems tied to the human condition and the struggle to ascend to a higher order of harmonic existence. In the specific case of race and racial relations in this country, mythic narratives play a significant role in our understanding of the origins, social duties or roles, and placement of African Americans within the social matrix of American culture.

This placement of African Americans in a social matrix leads to a second variation of myth. In this variation, as suggested by Hal Himmelstein (1984), myth is viewed as a construct of social vision. Consequently, myths are not just passive narratives texturized in literature; they are active, centrally located narratives directly influencing daily lives and perceptions. These perceptions are often, as in the case of race, articulated as negative stereotypes and are particularly relevant given the storytelling function (mythic function) of contemporary television.

Lawrence Reddick (1944) suggested that:

> It is an old generalization that equality and full democracy will never be achieved this side of basic changes in the objective conditions of life. To this old maxim must be added another: democracy in race relations will never be achieved until the minds of people are changed. The direct route to these minds is through the great agencies of mass communication.

Reddick's claim about mass communication's power and more specifically its potential impact on this country's race relations underscores the importance of critically examining media texts and the myths they disseminate. His view represents the optimism held by those who believe in the power of mass media to develop a positive social consciousness, particularly as it applies to those who are different. A brief description of the colonization of the new world illustrates this concept further.

There are three ways diverse groups were incorporated into the new cultures formed in the Americas. They were amalgamated, as was the case in Canada, where ethnic groups retained their independent identities while creating a new society; absorbed, as in Brazil, where factors such as intermarriage created new variations on old cultures; and assimilated, as in the United States, where immigrants shed their old cultures (to varying degrees) and were melted down into a new American alloy.

To a large extent, the way that white Americans think about the fusion of cultural differences is shaped by the prevailing myth of the American "melting pot." Although the belief in the "melting pot" may have been useful for laying the groundwork for the assimilation of European immigrants, who shared similar racial characteristics of what would become known as mainstream culture, it did not allow for the assimilation of indigenous peoples (Native Americans) or those who came to America under involuntary circumstances (African and Chinese Americans). These groups were not blended into the Euro-American stew because of visually identifiable racial characteristics, which were later incorporated into debilitating negative stereotypes. Therefore, as suggested by Wilson and Gutierrez (1985), the assimilation of those who are visually different has always been problematic because the melting pot was never designed for the assimilation of racial difference.

To protect the myth of inclusion, what grew up around racially different groups in America was a set of stereotypes that justified why they (Africans, Chinese, Native Americans, and later Hispanics) could not be assimilated into the Euro-American melting pot. To illustrate the specific case of Africans, Reddick (1944) published a list of the principal stereotypes of African Americans. The list, which reflects many of the problematic elements of news coverage previously discussed, included familiar characterizations of African Americans as superior athletes, vicious criminals, light-hearted entertainers, irresponsible citizens, and most important for this analysis, sexual supermen. The argument here is that these characterizations, prevalent in American mass media since their inception and reworked today in television comedy, drama, music videos, advertising, and, most important, news narratives and visuals, continue to argue against the assimilation or full inclusion of African Americans and all non-Europeans into mainstream culture. These stereotypes have taken on mythic proportions and become so powerful that, as Lippmann (1922) suggests, they shape our psychological sets and perceptions to the extent that the world we are presented through media becomes our reality.

Even though there is growing physical evidence and data in addition to a body of contemporary American rhetoric that acknowledges the need to recognize the demographic shift toward a more racially and culturally diverse majority, media messages about this growing (minority) population have, for the most part, remained negative and one dimensional.

One must recognize that media, particularly television, are among the most significant and prevailing forces of influence in American culture. If seeing is believing, one must question what stories, myths, and characterizations of other people viewers glean from a medium that, on one hand, is relegated to the background of cultural consciousness and yet, on the other, is central to the average American's information network.

Not only was Reddick (1944) concerned with the proliferation of negative stereotypes[1] directed toward blacks, he was sounding an alarm that called for more serious consideration of "anti-Negro propaganda which pollutes the minds of people through the major channels of ideas and information." In an age where electronic media provide instantaneous coverage of news events and the widespread dissemination of images, especially negative ones, his warnings are even more profound. Reddick's warnings are profound because the unquestioned and continued use of and reliance on negative stereotypes have directly hampered the application of democratic rights to the black community and served to reinforce old myths about blacks. In many respects this is most evident in the imagery of the Hill-Thomas hearings.

Sexual Supermen, Social Delinquents, and Uninhibited Expressionists

In their examination of the history of black rhetoric, Golden and Rieke (1971) raised a critical and relevant question for consideration in this analysis. Having examined 200 years of black rhetoric, they note:

> On balance, the failure of black Americans to achieve their intended goal [equality and freedom] through rhetoric seems puzzling. For the rhetorical documents and essays contained in this study tend to show that traditional variables of persuasion—message content and structure, credibility of source, and effective use of media—have been skillfully employed. Yet, a breakdown often has occurred when blacks communicate either with whites or members of their own race. What, then, are the causes of this failure? (p. 5)

One of the direct causes of that failure may be, as Reddick warned, the nature of the highly negative and persuasively powerful racial images contained in mass media like those that were all too clearly played out during the Hill-Thomas hearings.

In the final analysis it might not matter how eloquent African Americans are, or how convincing the arguments for black rights may have been or are. Although African Americans may have effectively used the media to bring their plight to the population on a limited basis, a white-controlled media, steeped in its own stereotypes and myths about black people and its extensive ongoing outreach, have trapped blacks and countered all efforts for their participation in the social, economic, and political benefits of the American dream.

In the critical analysis of the Hill-Thomas hearings, three of Reddick's mythic stereotypes will be considered: the sexual superman, the uninhibited expressionist, and the social delinquent.

The Sexual Superman

The most damaging image and most persistent myth presented during the hearings was the reference to Thomas's sexual prowess, specifically, and the prowess of black men in general. Validity claims aside, the image of black men with ever-ready elongated "tools" that send women into sexual bliss is historically one of the most enduring stereotypes and myths existing in this country. As presented within American culture, the myth revolves around both the alleged insatiable sexual proclivity (usually for white women) of black males and their elongated sexual organs. This mythic image was repeatedly expressed during the hearings in the persona of the black porn star and the ultimate sexual superman, Long Dong Silver. Throughout the hearings and the televised coverage the repeated references to Silver and pornographic films and to Thomas's alleged descriptions of his own size and sexual abilities became as central, if not more so, to the case as the major issue of sexual harassment. Even more disturbing was the extensive coverage that many so-called reality-based news programs (e.g., *A Current Affair*) extended to this issue. In the guise of investigative reporting, images of Long Dong and descriptions of his films were aired, in contrast to a virtual lack of discussion about the historic nature of the myth and stereotype itself. At issue here is the tenor and tone of the questions being asked and the apparent fascination the graphic descriptions held for Americans. It is almost as if the unanswered question was not whether Thomas said these things but whether he could literally measure up to the myth itself.

At the same time what was most disturbing was the failure of all involved to realize that they were, in fact, parties to and thus implicitly supporting a negative characterization of Thomas and all black men. Throughout the hearings and their aftermath, media coverage of the definitions of sexual harassment and ways in which it could and should be handled were prolific. But the damning myth of sexual prowess itself went unchallenged, almost as if there was a tacit national agreement that the mythic lore was true and therefore must be maintained. When the hearings ended, Thomas's guilt or innocence relative to the charges of sexual harassment was never definitively established, yet, because of his race, the taint of the myth remained. A discussion of Thomas's behavior and prowess as they related to the specific charges of sexual harassment was necessary, but the open discussion served to rearticulate the mythology of black males' sexual behavior and size.

The Uninhibited Expressionist

The uninhibited expressionist myth centers on the view that black people openly and without reservation express their emotions freely. While whites, the belief suggests, are capable of controlling emotion and the expression of it in public forums, blacks in contrast have and practice no such restraint. Uninhibited expressionists who are often portrayed as having a tendency to break into song, are depicted as individuals who "wear their emotions on their sleeves" and express that emotion without regard for the setting or circumstances at hand. With respect to Anita Hill, the stereotypes of the uninhibited expressionist and social delinquent were the most graphic images applied to her persona. According to Jack White (1991, p. 66):

> The lowest point on the first day of the hearings came when Pennsylvania Republican Arlen Specter implied that Hill had simply fantasized Thomas's asking for dates and his lurid remarks about pornography. . . . On Saturday the campaign to discredit Hill sank to even lower depths when Utah Republican Orrin Hatch suggested that she had fabricated her accusations, in cooperation with liberal interest groups, from such disparate sources as court cases and *The Exorcist*.

While the white male senators repeatedly phrased their questions behind a guise of modesty and personal moral outrage at having to ask offensive questions, Hill, in the context of testimony, was forced to articulate graphic descriptions of the outrageous verbal harassment she suffered at the hands of Thomas. Thus, while the white pillars of the community were able to blush and apologize for offending anyone who was watching, Hill was placed in the position of having to repeatedly describe in graphic detail the verbal harassment she endured in front of millions of viewers who, considering the racial factors involved here, were unable to detect the slightest blush.

It is the image of Hill repeating the charges under the relentless and cynical questioning that is most troublesome and problematic. For one to believe that she had fantasized or fabricated the charges and willingly appeared in a public forum suggests that one would also buy into the belief that blacks possess a low moral and social demeanor and practice uninhibited expressionism associated historically with the sexual morals of the black community. For those steeped in the negative and mythic beliefs that the morals of the black community are lower than those of the white community, Hill's supposed inability to blush and her seemingly unemotional testimony were nothing more than an affirmation of the myth. Her failure to request a closed-door session, where the graphic details could be discussed in more private and less embarrassing circumstances, played into images of the openly graphic and sexual communication allegedly occurring freely in the confines of the less inhibited black community and led to blatant disregard for her feelings or public image.

There are clearly larger implications of the Hill testimony for all women, but the implication that Hill would even listen to Thomas's graphic descriptions of his sexual prowess and pornographic films and to his snide comments about pubic hairs on Coke cans raised questions about her moral character.

At the same time, questions about Thomas's moral character and uninhibited nature were also implied and raised. The image of Thomas not only sitting in his office graphically discussing pornographic films but making secret sojourns out into the night to rent or purchase X-rated films was disturbing. Again, given the sexual myths associated with black males, the allegations themselves convey and underscore the belief that black men are sexually uninhibited. White (1991) notes:

> On the other hand, race played a role in the rush to judgment against Thomas. Given the stereotype of sexually rapacious black men, it was easy for many Americans, black and white, to conclude that Thomas was guilty even before they heard Hill's testimony. (p. 66)

Regardless of the defense Thomas offered,[2] he could not, and did not address the question of his personal moral character that hung over him because of his race.[3]

The Social Delinquent

Social delinquents are best characterized as individuals, blacks in this case, whose behavior is clearly outside the norms held by members of society in general. In effect social delinquents consistently, via their behavior and beliefs, violate all established moral codes and rules in society.

In tandem, Hill and Thomas were both unwitting players in a larger social game. The free flowing charges and graphic detail of the various testimonies served only to raise questions about the moral fabric of the black community itself. Although Hill and Thomas were able to effectively call upon positive images and the value of family to different degrees, neither was able to address the lingering myths of social delinquency and uninhibited expressionism that prevail in media and society. It really does not matter who one believes if one realizes that little was done to undermine a mythic and negative perception of black morality and behavior as being somehow different from that of white Americans, and the white senators who exemplified decency.

Conclusions

One can only speculate about the charges and the defenses offered during the hearings. What is clear, however, is that either Anita Hill or Judge Clarence Thomas is lying about the closed-door events that led to the hearings. What can also be stated with confidence is that up until this moment no evidence publicly exists that can convincingly verify the motives of either of the participants. Many may choose to speculate about the outcome of the hearings, applying various "what if" racial permutations; what remains, in the end, is the damage done to the image of the entire black community. Clarence Thomas and Anita Hill had in common an inability to overcome the realities of race and negative myths long associated with blacks in this country. Like pawns, both ended up simply underscoring long-held beliefs and negative attitudes that question the morality of the black community and restrict that community to the outskirts of larger society. Instead of providing insights and understanding of the real moral issue of sexual harassment, the hearings only served to fragment society further. As West (1994) indicates:

> [T]he debate evolved around glib formulations of a black "role model" based on mere pigmentation, an atavistic defense of blackness that mirrors the increasing xenophobia in American life, and circled around a silence about the ugly authoritarian practices in black America. . . . Hence a grand opportunity for substantive discussion and struggle over race and gender was missed in black America and the larger society. (pp. 47–48)

Although the media may not have had a conscious hand in presenting the age-old negative images that constrict the black community, their very lack of public acknowledgment of their role in perpetuating negative mythic images about blacks, and, in contrast, ignoring the very real issues that should have been raised is most damning and problematic. If, as West (1994) suggests,

> we confine discussions about race in America to the "problems" black people pose for whites, rather than consider what this way of viewing black people reveals about us as a nation (pp. 5–6)

then we as a society are destined to be restricted to a world of imagery that inhibits the equality and full democracy in racial relations necessary for this country to survive in the next century. As long as the narratives and visual images that occur in the news depict African Americans as problems and threats that need to be solved, no real understanding or progress toward inclusion in the myth of the "melting pot" in American culture can or will occur. Consequently, in spite of any rhetoric or programming content that may attempt to suggest otherwise, African Americans, and whites as well, will remain trapped in a world of narratives and images that are illusory and mythic. From this standpoint the problem with myths is that they restrict inclusion and prohibit real understanding. They no longer allow us to learn what we can become or how to deal with the subsequent and substantial issues of the day. Instead, myths limit our ability to transcend an us-versus-them mind-set and do no less than threaten this democracy.

As long as televised narratives and images of African Americans are largely restricted to negative stereotypes and myths, the growing fears and tensions between the races (and sexes) should not be surprising or unexpected. Charges that a black male murdered a pregnant white woman (Stuart) or kidnapped children from the back of a car (Smith), or that black people are responsible for the growing welfare rolls and crime, should not seem surprising in either the claim or the beliefs that follow from those claims. Similarly, when a public hearing on sexual harassment, as in the Hill-Thomas case, centers more on sexual and racial myths than on the moral realities confronting this country, one should not be surprised. One year after the hearings one only had to look at the new images of African Americans on prime time television to discover whether any lessons had been learned, whether the consciousness of producers and the networks that air their products had been raised, and whether the myths had diminished at all. As the images of Hill and Thomas fade, the legacy of newly rearticulated black characters continues. On the TV comedy *Martin*, the leading characters Gina and Martin openly discuss their sexual yearnings for each other over dinner and uninhibitedly express their carnal desires; they thus reinforce the old myths and stereotypes about the black community.

West (1994) points out that:

> In these downbeat times, . . . we must accent the best of each other even as we point out the vicious effects of our racial divide. . . . We simply cannot enter the twenty-first century at each other's throats, even as we acknowledge the weighty forces of racism, patriarchy, economic inequality, homophobia, and ecological abuse on our necks. We are at a crucial crossroad in the history of this nation—and we either hang together by combating these forces that divide and degrade us or we hang separately. (p. 159)

West's optimism that Americans can accept the best that each member of society has to offer is highly reminiscent of the views expressed by Reddick some fifty years earlier. This shared view of acceptance and participation in the democratic process is, however, severely limited and contradicted by the continued negative and one-dimensional presentation of African Americans on television. Though I believe that both scholars are correct in their assessment, the continued presentation of African Americans as the problem and the reliance on negative and mythic images in television programming may bind us to relive our mythic separate pasts.

NOTES

1. Here is the comprehensive list of stereotypes presented by Reddick in 1944 (p. 369): savage African; happy slave; devoted servant; corrupt politician; irresponsible citizen; petty thief; social delinquent; vicious criminal; sexual superman; superior athlete; unhappy non-white; natural-born cook; natural musician; perfect entertainer;

superstitious churchgoer; razor and knife "toter"; uninhibited expressionist; and mental inferior.

2. Ironically, Thomas evoked another historically powerful image, that of lynching, to defend himself against the charges. White (1991, p. 66) stated:

> After Hill's charges burst into print, Thomas and his supporters equated her claims with the lynching of thousands of black men [usually for rape or offensive sexual behavior]. "I will not provide the rope for my own lynching," Thomas declared at the start of the hearings; later he added that the broadcast of Hill's testimony was a "high-tech lynching" of an "uppity" black.

Thomas consequently utilized one stereotype, that of black men being lynched, to counter another, that of the sexual and moral behavior of black men.

3. Unlike Anita Hill, Thomas was not forced to describe in graphic detail any of the charges against him. A consequence of this is that Hill clearly was placed in a more compromising position morally than Thomas, who was free, perhaps because of gender, to take a higher moral stand. This is not meant to suggest that he was not, by virtue of race, painted with the same brush of low moral fiber.

REFERENCES

Bogle, D. (1994). *Toms, coons, mulattoes, mammies, and bucks: An interpretive history of blacks in American films.* (3rd ed.). New York: Continuum.

Brummet, B. (1994). *Rhetoric in popular culture.* New York: St. Martin's.

Dates, J. L., & Barlow, W. (Eds.). (1990). *Split image: African Americans in the mass media.* Washington, DC: Howard University Press.

Fiske, J. (1994). *Media matters: Everyday culture and political change.* Minneapolis: University of Minnesota Press.

Franken, R. (1991). *CNN's news coverage of confirmation hearings* (TV newscast), October 1991.

Golden, J. L., & Rieke, R. D. (1971). *The rhetoric of black Americans.* Columbus, OH: Charles E. Merrill.

Gronbeck, B. E. (1984). *Writing television criticism.* Chicago: SRA.

Hacker, A. (1992). *Two nations: Black and white, separate, hostile, unequal.* New York: Charles Scribner's Sons.

Himmelstein, H. (1984). *Television myth and the American mind.* New York: Praeger.

Lévi-Strauss, C. (1958). The structural study of myth. In T. A. Sebeok (Ed.), *Myth: A symposium* (pp. 81–106). Bloomington: Indiana University Press.

Myrdal, G. (1944). *An American dilemma.* New York: Harper and Brothers.

Reddick, L. (1944). Educational programs for the improvement of race relations: Motion pictures, radio, the press and libraries. *Journal of Negro Education, 13(3),* 367–389.

Wallace, M. (1992). *Black popular culture.* (G. Dent, Ed.). Seattle: Bay Press.

West, C. (1994). *Race matters.* New York: Vintage Books.

White, J. E. (1991, October). The stereotypes of race. *Time,* p. 66.

Wilson, C. C. II, & Gutiérrez, F. (1985). *Minorities and media: Diversity and the end of mass communication.* Beverly Hills, CA: Sage.

Shifting Bodies, Changing Texts: Representing Teenage Womanhood on *Dr. Quinn, Medicine Woman*

Sarah Projansky

It's just all going too fast.

—Erika Flores as Colleen

I'm all grown up now.

—Jessica Bowman as Colleen

I want to do more than get married and have babies.

—Erika Flores as Colleen

I want to have children. [Pause] That is, after I go to medical school.

—Jessica Bowman as Colleen

During the first two-and-one-half seasons of *Dr. Quinn, Medicine Woman*, Erika Flores portrays Colleen, Dr. Michaela Quinn's (Dr. Mike) teenage adoptive daughter. During this time, several episodes focus on Colleen's relationship to her quickly developing body, her fantasies about romance and sexuality, and her interest in education and medicine. In the middle of the third season, however, Jessica Bowman—a younger, or at least physically smaller, actor—replaces Flores. Flores's body is sexually mature; Bowman's body is childlike. Flores's Colleen is outspoken, brash, energetic, determined, intelligent, and generous; Bowman's Colleen is timid, quiet, sexually chaste, relatively uninterested in medicine, and selfish. What is the relationship between these descriptions of two different actors' bodies and the changes in the single character each actor portrays, consecutively? What danger does Flores's maturing body represent to the cohesiveness of the text? Why are both Flores's/Colleen's and Bowman's/Colleen's material and representational bodies inseparable from the shape of Colleen, the character?

This essay considers the implications for the televisual representation of teenage womanhood in this unexplained cast and subsequent character change. While *Dr. Quinn* focuses on one social issue after another each week (such as hate crimes against African Americans, women's suffrage, fear of Jews and Judaism, etc.), with Dr. Mike always representing the appropriate response (she is—or becomes in the space of one episode—race-blind, gender-blind, religion-blind, etc.), the issues raised by Flores, her body, and that body's relationship to the narrative ultimately escape the bounds of even this text's overdetermined liberalism. The show's celebration of tolerance, it seems, does not extend to tolerance for the undisciplined changes of a teenage woman's physical body. By insisting on blurring the fine line between actor's body and character's body, this chapter interrogates the costs—to the construction of women's bodies and to the cultural imagining of teenage women—of *Dr. Quinn, Medicine Woman*'s inability to contain Flores's Colleen.

Introducing Flores/Colleen in the Context/Shadow of *Dr. Quinn*/Dr. Mike

When we first see Flores/Colleen in the pilot episode, she is leaning against her mother, Charlotte Cooper, the only midwife and boardinghouse owner in the 1860s town of Colorado Springs. Colleen looks on silently while Charlotte talks to the newly arrived (and for the townspeople surprisingly female) Dr. Mike. Colleen's silence and stance might suggest a child-like and feminine passivity; however, the two adult professional women in this scene also introduce a recurring theme of the show: women deserve (because of their competence) but must fight for (because of men's prejudice and ignorance) their independence and right to engage actively in the public sphere. Thus, the scene juxtaposes Colleen with competent adult women. As the scene progresses, Colleen takes a chicken from her mother in order to finish plucking it and then asks Dr. Mike a direct question about her education as a doctor. Whereas Colleen's younger brother Brian asks Dr. Mike "You're a real doctor?," a question the men in town and male characters passing through town repeat week after week, Colleen asks a more specific question: "You went to college, and everything?" Brian wonders if Dr. Mike is qualified; Colleen wonders about the process of becoming qualified. Dr. Mike's first words to Colleen are "And everything."

This scene establishes three tenets germane to Colleen's gendered identity. First, Colleen is a loving person who draws support from and provides support to her family through physical contact. As she does in this first scene, Colleen often leans against other characters, including Dr. Mike; Sully, Dr. Mike's suitor (and now husband); Matthew, Colleen's older brother; and Grace, a former slave, the town's one cafe owner, and yet another entrepreneurial woman. Colleen sometimes clings to these characters when she is upset, but she also hugs them when she is happy. Furthermore, she provides Brian with a comforting body to cling to when he is upset. Thus, she oscillates easily between child-like care-needing and adult-like care-taking.

Second, this scene and the series as a whole further develop Colleen's adult and caring identity through her competence as a cook and a homemaker. In several early episodes, Brian, Colleen, and Matthew prefer Colleen's tasty cooking to Dr. Mike's unappetizing cooking, and both Dr. Mike and Colleen often state that Colleen is teaching Dr. Mike how to cook and keep house. Colleen's ability to manage the chicken her mother hands her in this particular scene initiates this theme. Because the series generally problematizes a traditional link between cooking and femininity by representing Dr. Mike as an extremely sexual and feminine woman who nonetheless is a terrible cook and homemaker, Colleen's skill at cooking is simultaneously a mark of her femininity (none of the men cooks regularly) and more generally a mark of her competence as an adult.

Third, the scene that introduces Colleen suggests that she is interested in education and women's independence and that that interest parallels Dr. Mike's. Colleen's question—"You went to college?"—evidences her curiosity about the possibility of achieving a higher degree. Her tag line—"and everything?"—draws attention both to the implications of the difficulties Dr. Mike faces as a woman doctor and to the difficulty Colleen faces as a bright intellectual young woman in a town decidedly suspicious of intellectual women. Dr. Mike's repetition of the line initiates the series's continuing analogy between Dr. Mike and Colleen vis-à-vis their intellectual ability as well as their sexuality and feminine identity. Colleen and Dr. Mike thus exchange adult feminine competencies as Colleen teaches Dr. Mike how to keep house and Dr. Mike teaches Colleen how to doctor.

The series's link between homemaking and femininity, which marks homemaking as an important and yet nonessential skill to competent femininity, and the series's links among medicine, independence, and femininity are all equally complex. The narrative structure of one *Dr. Quinn* episode after another ties feminine beauty and heterosexuality—represented by Dr. Mike—to intelligence, insightfuness, and competent and life-saving medical practice. As a whole, the series reworks the definition of feminine heterosexuality in relation to work both in the home and in the community, claiming the possibility of "having it all" (the "and everything") after using the threat of losing it all to develop the narrative trajectory. In short, *Dr. Quinn* celebrates the femininity of a feminist woman who forges new ground and insists on her right to be heard, to practice medicine, to race horses, to vote, to challenge General Custer and President Grant on their policies toward the Cheyenne and other Native Americans, and to run for public office—to name just a few of Dr. Mike's adventures.

As the "queen of mini-series" (Schindehette, Armstrong, and Healy, 1993), Jane Seymour's body and star persona make this feminine feminism possible. Her tiny waist, long strawberry blond hair, and previous highly sexually charged television roles coupled with her weekly exploits as the foremost feminist in the Colorado territory represent the ideal to which Flores/Colleen aspires—with her child-like softly round face, long strawberry blond hair, occasional exploits as a friend of the Cheyenne and Chinese, competence as a doctor's assistant and diagnostician, skill as a homemaker, and identity as an intellectual. Flores/Colleen functions as a currently mini-Dr. Quinn and a potential future and complete Dr. Quinn. As Colleen and Dr. Mike exchange skills and knowledge about homemaking, doctoring, and sexuality, they work together to become the perfect woman as *Dr. Quinn* defines her: feminine, intelligent, independent, and bound to romantic heterosexuality. This essay's critical focus on Colleen rather than Dr. Mike (the series' central character), then, both provides insight into the show's construction of femininity and further illuminates the *process* by which the show suggests (Dr. Quinn's) idealized femininity can be achieved.

This critical approach falls within the context of recent television criticism that addresses the representation of feminism on contemporary television. This criticism confronts the seemingly progressive representation of powerful and independent women in 1990s television and argues that these stars and narratives negotiate the relationship between traditional patriarchal definitions of women and feminist redefinitions of femininity. Some scholars offer primarily optimistic readings, suggesting that figures such as Madonna provide strategies for "simulat[ing] and deconstruct[ing] the 'truths' of sex and gender" (Schwichtenberg, 1992, p. 141). Janet Lee (1992) argues that while *Roseanne* operates in the "conventional format of the [heterosexual and white] family sitcom" (p. 97), Roseanne's humor in that context is a "strategy of resistance that subverts gender identities defining women as trivial, subordinate and marginalized" (p. 96). Other scholars see less resistant potential in similar contemporary representations of women. Bonnie Dow (1992), for example, argues that the humor in *Murphy Brown* serves to relieve patriarchal anxiety about feminism: "Murphy's function as a comedic character, whose extreme personality traits are often the source of humor, provides the relief necessary to keep her character appealing. The fact that Murphy 'suffers' for her success makes it easier to accept her rejection of traditional womanhood" (p. 152). Elspeth Probyn (1990) and Leah R. Vande Berg (1993) (among others) have named this ambivalent representation of feminism and feminist characters "postfeminist." In their studies of *thirtysomething* and *China Beach*, respectively, they argue that these shows celebrate feminism while simultaneously implying feminism is no longer necessary: hence the term *post*-feminist. More specifically, they argue that the shows represent women who freely "choose" to give up feminist independence to return home (Probyn) or represent women's "free choice" in order to recenter men and masculinity (Vande Berg). Vande Berg argues that in *China Beach* "women's presence in Vietnam is characterized . . . as the empowered choice of free individuals in contrast with that of many military men who are present under compulsion—and who, thus, are victims" (p. 356).

I have characterized these scholars as falling into two different categories–one that sees resistant potential in contemporary feminist narratives and the other that sees hegemonic recuperation in postfeminist narratives—however, each of these scholars also acknowledges the complexity of textual interpretation. Despite their different conclusions, each author insists on the importance of understanding the multiplicity of meanings in the text and acknowledges the possibility of alternative interpretations of, resistances to, and pleasures in the contemporary representation of powerful women. By looking at the process of developing femininity in Colleen's character across two different actors on *Dr. Quinn*, my own reading here acknowledges, in fact incites, this complexity. The series's development—over time—of Colleen's character and her relationship to Dr. Mike provide an opportunity to examine not only the representation of independent women but also the means by which television envisions achieving that version of femininity. From a feminist critical perspective, this process alone suggests both a resistance to traditional definitions of femininity and a reinscription of the norms of feminine beauty. Flores's, Bowman's, and Colleen's bodily transformations trouble the idealized white femininity offered by *Dr. Quinn* through the figure of Dr. Mike. By focusing on the links between narrative and bodily changes, I hope to illustrate both how the text struggles to recuperate feminist representations as examples of postfeminist tolerance and how the existence of a teenage woman's material body necessitates that that struggle be a continuing one. In short, as Flores's body changes, it makes explicit the process of textual representation and thus provides a wedge for the feminist critic.

The Trouble with Bodies for Narrative and Criticism

During the pilot episode discussed above, Flores/Colleen appears to be a cherubic child on the brink of adulthood. Her silky long strawberry blond hair and huge dark eyes promise a future beauty on the scale of Jane Seymour. However, as the first season ends and the second season develops, Flores's body begins to mature; she deviates from the adolescent ideal, gains weight, and develops large breasts. She grows from a small child to a full size adult who moves with some awkwardness in her new body. What is a television series to do when the body does not cooperate with the narrative?

On the one hand, the change in Colleen's material body is par for the course on television. Because television shows take place across time, often across years, bodies change and/or actors quit or are fired, and television is well equipped to respond. Sometimes shows work to maintain a static body; for example, when Ted Danson began wearing a hairpiece on *Cheers* so that Sam would not bald along with Danson; or when pregnant actors position pillows, furniture, or other props in front of their character's stomach in order to represent a nonpregnant body/character. But shows might just as easily deflect the disruptive and transformative power of bodily changes by replacing one character with a new, yet similar character, for example when Tiffani-Amber Thiessen/Valerie replaced Shannen Doherty/Brenda on *Beverly Hills, 90210*. Less often, shows explicitly acknowledge actors' physical changes by working them into the narrative, as did *Roseanne* with Roseanne's pregnancy and *Oprah* with Oprah's weight changes. In all these cases, television is prepared for the problem of bodily changes, and television audiences are used to adjusting to these substitutions.

Television's preparation and the frequency with which bodies change on television, however, do not place bodily changes outside of ideological meaning, and thus feminist television criticism must develop methods for analyzing these changes. Certainly, discussions in the popular press of the *Roseanne* (e.g., Birnbaum, 1995; "Blues of the birth," 1993) and *Oprah* (e.g., "Fit, not fat," 1994; Lyall, 1994; Randolph, 1993; Reynolds, 1995) body changes, for example, illustrate ideological negotiations over the representation of women's independence and identity. To offer one more example, Julie D'Acci (1994) argues that the cast changes between the pilot and then the first few episodes of *Cagney and Lacey* quite specifically illustrate the television industry's attempts to dictate a certain kind of femininity. For example, when Loretta Swit played Cagney during the pilot episode, ads emphasized her feminine sexuality. Swit was unavailable for the series, however, so Meg Foster replaced her. Foster, who portrayed Cagney in narratives that emphasize her toughness and independence, immediately developed a lesbian following and generated anxiety among the network executives. As a result, mid-first season, Sharon Gless replaced Foster, and simultaneously Cagney became richer, more conservative, thinner, and "softer" (in costume, hair, and character). As D'Acci argues, these complex cast and character changes reveal television negotiating the representation of independent femininity in ways that seek to contain independence within a sanctioned heterosexual feminine body. I would ask, then: How does *Dr. Quinn*, as a television narrative, respond to an uncooperative body, and how can a feminist television critic use criticism to negotiate that relationship between the material and representational body?

Dr. Quinn responds in two ways to Flores's/Colleen's body changes, first by attempting to address the materiality of the teenage body and then by abandoning this more contestatory representation, as did *Cagney and Lacey*, by replacing the troubling body with a more traditionally feminine body. The movement between these two responses highlights the ideological tension that surrounds televisual representations of the materiality of women's bodies.

Initially, when the show struggles to incorporate Flores's body into Colleen's identity, it develops stories that directly address her feelings about her body and sexuality, further supporting the romantically heterosexual intelligent woman as an ideal. For example, in the most explicit episode about Flores's/Colleen's changing body, all the boys at school are talking about Colleen's large breasts. One boy tries to persuade Colleen that he is interested in talking and studying with her, but then he tries to touch her breasts when she agrees to meet him after school. Colleen, who was excited about the possibility of dating a boy interested in her intelligence, is shocked and devastated by his behavior. Dr. Mike reassures Colleen and provides narrative closure by promising Colleen that she will eventually find a man who loves her mind as well as her body.

Episodes like this one acknowledge and begin to grapple with Flores's/Colleen's body in a way that suggests a future for Colleen like Dr. Mike's, but costuming throughout this section of the series also strenuously marks a divide between Dr. Mike and Colleen. While Dr. Mike's clothes are well groomed, always match, and show off her body, Colleen's clothes are ill-fitting, often clash, and hide her body. One of her most frequent costumes, for example, is a blue skirt, a pink top, and a loose bib that covers her growing breasts. Dr. Mike rarely wears the same clothes, but whatever she wears hugs her body and provides her a freedom of movement that Colleen's long blue skirt hinders. In this way, the series visually resists the very narrative parallels it draws between Flores/Colleen and Seymour/Dr. Mike. While the dialogue and narrative trajectory might point to links between Dr. Mike and Colleen as they struggle to combine their intelligence and independence with their feminine heterosexuality, their costumes promise us that Dr. Mike will be successful while Colleen will continue to struggle against the body in which she has found herself.

Inserting Bowman/Colleen into the Context/Shadow of *Dr. Quinn*/Dr. Mike

The series's second response to Flores's new body solves this ideological tension. In the middle of the third season, with no explanation, Jessica Bowman replaces Erika Flores as Colleen. Unlike Flores, Bowman is small, thin, and has small breasts that "need" no covering. The only physical characteristic the two actors share is long strawberry blond hair. And, while Bowman/Colleen does not wear fancy clothes as does Dr. Mike, her clothes more often match and show off her body than do Flores's/Colleen's clothes. For example, Bowman/Colleen often wears a tight-fitting soft-pink dress that hugs her body. She also frequently wears a green coat three sizes too large for her, emphasizing her waif-like body and suggesting the possibility that she will blossom into Seymour/Dr. Mike in a physical way that Flores/Colleen could not. While this oversized green coat ensures that Bowman/Colleen is not (yet) as beautiful as Seymour/Dr. Mike, it simultaneously promises that she might be eventually.

While I would not want to argue that Flores's growing body led directly to her exit from the series, either through her own decision or through dismissal, I would argue that the tension surrounding her body already in the series and the *particular* new body that replaced her together illustrate a troubling containment of teenage women's bodies. The trajectory from child-Flores to adult-Flores to Bowman in one character suggests that the shape of a woman's body must always strive to be like the shape of a child's body. While this backwards movement evokes links scholars have made between cultural representations and the problem of anorexia in both children and adults (e.g., Bordo, 1993; Urla and Swedlund, 1995; Chernin, 1981), in the context of *Dr. Quinn* Colleen's infantilization also informs the entire series's definition of the idealized feminine feminist. Because, when Colleen gets a new body, she also gets a new personality. While her basic character description does not change—she is smart, interested in medicine and medical school, a friend of the Cheyenne and the Chinese, an excellent homemaker, and concerned with heterosexual romance—the balance of her personality shifts toward the feminine, positioning her intelligence and independence behind heterosexuality and an attendant self-absorption.

As with Flores/Colleen, the first scene with Bowman/Colleen illustrates this shift nicely. When Bowman/Colleen appears, she is moving around inside the family's cabin, preparing dinner while Brian practices his Latin. The first shot of her shows her pausing in her work to correct Brian's pronunciation and to announce to the family that "Roman day" is coming up at school. When Sully asks Colleen what Roman day is, she responds: "We've been studying about Romans. We're going to spend a whole day doing things like the Romans do. We're going to give speeches in Latin and even wear togas."

As does the introduction of Flores/Colleen, this introduction of Bowman/Colleen emphasizes Colleen's interest in education. She not only is able to correct Brian's Latin, marking her as the smartest child, but she also is excited about the prospect of delivering a speech in Latin. Yet, unlike the introduction of Flores/Colleen, the introduction of Bowman/Colleen emphasizes Colleen's interest in costume and feminine roles as well. Thus while the end of Flores's/Colleen's opening line, "you went to college, *and everything?*" evokes a woman's struggle for education, the end of Bowman's/Colleen's opening line, "we're going to give speeches in Latin *and even wear togas,*" deemphasizes her interest in scholarship. As the scene develops, in fact, we learn that while Brian is excited about planning and building a catapult—doing things—Colleen asks Sully to build a chariot for her to ride in (as we see later, passively) during the father/daughter race. Bowman's Colleen wants to be looked at.

Also, similar to the Flores/Colleen introduction, this Bowman/Colleen introduction illustrates Colleen's loving relationship to her family. Yet if Flores/Colleen leans intimately against her mother and later shifts her attention to Dr. Mike, Bowman/Colleen is more interested in Sully as a father figure. When Sully and Dr. Mike ask the children if they would be willing to be legally adopted, Colleen expresses pleasure and rejects her biological father because "he doesn't care about us." Indeed she symbolically names Sully her father in this first episode by asking him to participate in the father/daughter race with her.

Finally, as does the earlier scene introducing Flores/Colleen, this scene establishes Bowman's/Colleen's status as an adult, in this case through Colleen's role as homemaker and Brian's educator. Nevertheless, in this case that skill leads Colleen not to a consideration of a future education and career as a doctor, but to the prospect of riding in a chariot pulled by her "father," Sully. Her status as "adult" is linked not to women's education and independence ("and everything"), but to pleasure in more traditionally heterosexual feminine activities: costume, chivalry, and attachment to a man. Later in this episode, as Colleen argues with her biological father who wants to take her away from her adoptive family, she says, "I'm all grown up now." The irony here is that Colleen's body has returned to a child-like state just at the moment when she declares her adulthood. While Flores/Colleen struggles against the speed with which her body takes her toward adulthood, Bowman/Colleen steps past the troubling materiality of her body's growth to insist that she is already completely adult. She makes a claim on adulthood in the process of insisting that she has a right to choose to remain a daughter to Dr. Mike and Sully.

This comparison of the introduction of the two versions of Colleen illustrates both that the themes of family affection, intelligence, and adulthood continue to be central to the character, and that Colleen relates to these issues in subtly new ways when a new actor takes over the role. Based at least on these two scenes, Bowman/Colleen is as intelligent and competent as Flores/Colleen, but Bowman/Colleen appears to be a less independent person. The new Colleen's femininity and role within the family move to the foreground, pushing her intellect and interest in medicine into the background. By looking more closely at three additional sets of episodes in which Flores/Colleen and Bowman/Colleen each face similar events, I will illustrate in more detail how *Dr. Quinn* contains Colleen's body and independence.

Falling Ill

The Flores/Colleen Version: Appropriate Romance

The first episode that focuses primarily on Flores/Colleen occurs toward the end of the first season. In this episode, Colleen discovers serial romance reading through her friends' subscription to a weekly. She immediately becomes overinvolved in the story, which the narrative represents metaphorically when Colleen absentmindedly leaves behind the stethoscope she ordered as a gift for Dr. Mike. Colleen literally tries to live out the romance story by putting herself in peril, but she develops frostbite in her hands while waiting for Sully to rescue her, and thus she finds her future career as a doctor threatened. Faced with this anxiety and Sully's disinterest in her as a romantic partner, Colleen begins to distance herself from the romantic texts. She helps a young man, Louis, use his microscope to identify worms in meat as the cause of a townperson's illness, recovers the use of her hands, gives the stethoscope that Louis returns to her to Dr. Mike, and then begins a romance with Louis.

The narrative trajectory of this episode moves Colleen through excessive romance reading to an inappropriate fixation on her father figure that endangers her future career. The narrative's conclusion resolves these threats (which an excessively passive feminine romance consumption produces) with Colleen's satisfactory child-like romance with a young man her age who shares her interest in science and scholarly books. As the episode begins, Colleen eagerly receives the package with the stethoscope for Dr. Mike, explaining to Louis, his uncle Horace, and three of her female friends that she has ordered the medical instrument as a gift. Framed alone or with Horace, Colleen is separated from both Louis, who is interested in both Colleen and her stethoscope, and from the three girls clustered together around their weekly. As Louis offers Colleen a chance to look through his microscope, something she responds to with excitement, Alice calls to her from off-screen, inviting her to read the weekly.

Torn between these two choices—masculine science or feminine romance—Colleen goes toward what she does not know (romance reading) rather than toward what she currently prefers (science). These choices do not remain opposites, however, because Louis's interest in Colleen offers the possibility of pairing science with romance. The last shot before Colleen makes her initial choice positions the three girls in the foreground, sitting on a bench and huddling around the weekly, with Colleen standing behind them listening and Louis behind Colleen, also listening and watching

Colleen. Thus, in this episode, Colleen has no choice but to engage in romance. The question is whether she will read about a traditional romance in the weekly or experience a romance with Louis during which she can continue to enact her active, inquiring, intellectual identity. When Alice offers Colleen a turn to read aloud, she steps forward and sits on the bench with the three girls, leaving Louis standing behind them alone. Although Colleen makes the "wrong" choice in this early scene, she learns through the narrative development what the "right" choice is.

It is ironic that the wrong choice is to consume serial romances, given that that is exactly what the regular viewer of *Dr. Quinn* does. This episode's insistence on women's ability to pair romance and independence, love and intellectualism, however, also justifies the viewer's process of consumption and thus presumably makes the irony pleasurable rather than painful. After all, the romance that *Dr. Quinn* viewers consume week after week is not about a silly, passive woman who needs constant rescuing by men named after a horse—"Colt" (the hero in the romance story Colleen reads)—but is instead about a frontier doctor who faces constant sexism with strength and determination. Dr. Mike rescues her lover, who respects and supports her independent ways, as often as he rescues her. This is the idealized romantic identity toward which this episode moves Colleen and which her excessive response to her maturing body/identity threatens.

The threat to Colleen's hands makes this idealized identity explicit by constructing a shocking outcome and representing a form of masochism in Colleen's enactment of romance. If Colleen loses her hands, her future career as a doctor will be over. Furthermore, Colleen, herself, is at fault for the threat to her hands. Colleen decides to spend a stormy winter night without gloves or a coat in an abandoned shack, expecting Sully to rescue her, as does the romance hero about whom she has read. Close-ups of dripping icicles and the collapse of the entrance to the shack emphasize Colleen's danger, as do close-ups of her red and swollen hands and her inability to use her damaged hands to dig her way out of the shack. Her excessive involvement in romance and her determination to play a passive victim threaten her intellectual identity and professional future. And, while Sully eventually does rescue her from the shack (with Dr. Mike's help), it is Dr. Mike who saves Colleen's hands by insisting on a "new" method of treating frostbite—very slow warming in tepid water—despite the town barber Jake's insistence that they warm Colleen's hands as quickly as possible. Dr. Mike (not Sully) ensures Colleen's ability to grow up to be a doctor, and thus Dr. Mike is Colleen's true hero.

During Colleen's recovery, she continues to be obsessed with Sully as a romantic figure, but she also begins to welcome Louis as a friend. The threat to her future, then, is enough to move her toward the other version of romance the episode offers. True to his identity as a romantic *and* intellectual hero, Louis brings Colleen flowers, chocolate, Dr. Mike's stethoscope, and his own microscope to share. While Colleen is unable to take the flowers because of her damaged hands, she still has the use of her eyes, and thus is able to look through the microscope. While the children set out to simply "play" with the microscope, when Myra brings Colleen a sample of the meat Hank eats before he get sick, Colleen and Louis use the microscope to discover the cause of Hank's illness and contribute to his cure. When Louis says, "I think I found something," Colleen, the more experienced medical practitioner, looks through the microscope and says, "You're right, Louis. We've got to tell Dr. Mike." Although Colleen has not yet shifted her romantic attention to Louis, she has returned to her role as an active, intellectual, independent woman rather than a passive victim. Immediately after confirming Louis's discovery, Colleen reaches out toward Dr. Mike's stethoscope (not the flowers or the chocolate, which are still sitting beside the stethoscope on her bedside table), realizes the feeling has returned to her hands, and runs to thank Dr. Mike for saving her (hands) and finally to deliver the gift she so anxiously awaited in the beginning of the episode.

At this stage of the narrative, although the threat to and subsequent recovery of her hands return Colleen to her active engagement in study rather than her passive engagement in consumption, she still has not shifted her romantic attachment from Sully to Louis. She is, however, on her way toward making the right choice by integrating romance with active intellectual pursuit rather than passive consumption and victimization. Under a tree in a scene similar to one earlier in the episode when Colleen read the story and daydreamed, Sully and Colleen enact the final episode of her personal romance serial. Although Colleen bases this ending on the one she has been reading, it ends differently than she would like.

C: You saved me. You're my hero, Sully. You'll always be.
S: Like Colt in the story? That's all this is: a story. Colleen, I don't want to be your hero, I just want to be your friend.

When Colleen does not answer him, Sully leaves the frame, and Colleen replaces him with the final chapter of the romance, the one she had hoped to live out. She reads: "Colt has come for her. I'm here my love, and I'm never leaving you again." By juxtaposing Sully's pragmatic response to Colleen with Colleen's tearful reading of the story, this scene emphasizes, again, the polarity between passive romance and active independent romance coupled with intellectual pursuits. While Colleen crumples the newspaper after reading this final line and continues to cry, the narrative resolves this tension by moving immediately forward in time to that evening as Colleen and her family have supper at Grace's Cafe. Positioned again at the edge of the group of people she is with, Colleen looks away from her family (and her child role) toward Louis, who sits alone at a separate table. Calling him a friend, she asks to be excused to talk to him as Dr. Mike and Sully smile at each other over her head. The adults both represent and sanction *this* version of romantic involvement. The final dialogue of the episode between Louis and Colleen is as follows:

L: [Sully] seems like a nice friend.
C: You're nice, too.
L: I am?
C: Yeah, and you're smart. [Pause, smile] I bet you could be a scientist.
L: You could be, too. There's this lady scientist. Rea Mitchell. She discovered a comet.
C: Like Halley's comet?
L: Yeah. You know, if I discovered a comet I would name it after you.

This dialogue explicitly connects romance and science as Louis both encourages Colleen to be a scientist (she could be a scientist like Rea Mitchell) and identifies his love for her with his own identity as a scientist (he will name the comet he discovers after her, rather than himself). The final shot of the series holds Colleen in a close-up as she smiles at Louis, possibly dreaming of her future when romance and scientific discovery merge in the figure of a comet named Colleen Cooper. That the reason for the imaginary comet's name is ambiguous, either the result of Colleen's scientific discovery or the result of Louis's love, emphasizes the version of romance the series (and this episode in particular) celebrates. Heterosexual romance for women is inevitable, but it must be paired with personal intellectual success. Colleen's illness, an illness that she causes herself as a result of her involvement in an inappropriate type of romance, leads her toward this idealized position.

The Bowman/Colleen Version: Appropriate Femininity

In contrast to this Flores/Colleen episode, the first episode in which Bowman/Colleen appears represents illness as leading toward family and independence rather than toward romance and independence. Thus the later episode offers a more child-like version of the independent Colleen. In this episode, Colleen's biological father, Ethan, returns to town to take her and Brian back to San Francisco with him. While the court awards custody to Ethan and orders the children to go to live with him, when he finally insists that it is time to leave town, the children run away. In an almost exact opposite trajectory of Flores's/Colleen's movement from passive romance reading to active romantic intellectualism, Bowman/Colleen moves from active self-determination within and against the family (running away) to passive illness from which she must be rescued and returned to a powerless child's position within the more appropriate family.

When Colleen and Brian first run away, Brian complains that he is tired, to which Colleen responds: "The sun's getting higher. It will be warmer now." She is the leader of the two, explaining to Brian that they cannot hide at Sully's lean-to because "that's the first place they'll look" and encouraging him when he wants to give up. After this initial scene, however, Brian and Colleen change places. When they come to a river, Brian immediately runs across a log serving as a bridge. The camera pans from a medium shot of him back to a long shot of Colleen, who looks nervous and lost. Brian encourages her to cross and she begins moving forward into a medium shot, but a cut to a long shot from the side emphasizes her smallness and precariousness (something the closer shot of Brian as he crosses does not suggest) and anticipates the fall she inevitably takes into the water. Thus, while Flores/Colleen learned in an earlier episode to control her fear and discomfort with her body by walking a *tightrope* dozens of feet above the ground in front of all the townspeople's watchful eyes, despite her fear, Bowman/Colleen is incapable of crossing a thick log her little brother easily runs across. Furthermore, as a result of this incompetence and her subsequent fall into the river, Colleen catches pneumonia. This illness teaches her not to return to independence, but to depend on others, including her younger brother, for direction. As night sets in, the following conversation between Colleen and Brian ensues:

c: I'm freezing. Did you light a fire?
b: No, they'll see the smoke. . . . Let's go back to Sully's lean-to. There's skins and
       blankets. We can get you warm.
c: They'll find us.
b: I bet they looked there already and went away.
c: What if they go back?
b: We won't stay long. Just until you feel better. Come on.

Not only does Brian take over the leadership role, answering questions rather than asking them, but he reasons away Colleen's earlier warning against the lean-to. When they arrive at the lean-to he continues his "doctoring" role, giving her water to drink and touching her neck to diagnose her fever. From this scene on, Colleen is trapped by her situation, first ill and delirious, then resigned to her new life with Ethan in San Francisco. Thus, while in Flores's episode Colleen's illness teaches her to respect her independence, in Bowman's episode Colleen's illness teaches her the inevitability of her lack of independence. The show reduces her character to a mere effect of family.

It is ironic that this is the episode in which Colleen tells her father "I'm all grown up now." This incongruity suggests that the struggles Flores/Colleen went through with her body and her own intellectualism are magically resolved when Bowman/Colleen replaces her. The process of growing up is simply replaced with the statement that she has grown up. This adult state, however, involves an intense identification with Dr. Mike and Sully, not with both as role models or even with Sully as an inappropriate lover, but with both as parents. While Flores/Colleen frequently refers to her own interest in medical school and education, defending banned books and constantly studying Dr. Mike at work, other characters simply talk *about* Bowman/Colleen in this way.

The final scene of this episode suggests the subtle shift that takes place when Bowman replaces Flores. As Dr. Mike gives final instructions to Colleen's "new" parents, Ethan and his wife, Lillian, she mentions two of the issues that have been central to Colleen's role on the show. To Ethan she says: "Colleen has her heart set on medical college. She has been studying and planning. I want you to make sure she goes to medical school," to which he replies, "I have no objection." That he does not object is completely out of character for the transitory male characters on *Dr. Quinn*. However, the lack of objection simply reinforces the "matter-of-fact" nature of Colleen's interest in medicine. While the show struggles to encourage and establish this interest when Flores plays Colleen, when Bowman plays Colleen the show marginalizes this interest by simply declaring its existence and then getting on to other issues—such as Colleen's feminine nature. To Lillian, Dr. Mike says, "Please help her with 'special questions.' "

In this final scene, Dr. Mike, in an unusual move, addresses Ethan and Lillian in traditionally gendered roles: Ethan is in charge of education and Lillian is in charge of femininity. In this episode, at least, Colleen, while still nominally interested in an untraditional career, has a much less contestatory and much more traditional relationship to femininity. The episode ends when Ethan changes his mind about taking the children. The last shot shows Colleen hugging her (appropriate) loving family. As the entire family watches Ethan and Lillian ride out of town alone, they also look back toward Colleen's (and Brian's) childhood rather than ahead either toward Colleen's future career and reproductive capacities, briefly alluded to through Dr. Mike's conversations with Ethan and Lillian, or toward the independent and intellectual romance illness initiates for Flores's Colleen.

Watching Women

Two additional episodes are particularly important to this discussion of the representation of teenage femininity on *Dr. Quinn* because they introduce teenage women as alter-egos for Colleen. These episodes contrast Colleen and visiting young women, in each case representing an exchange between the two that presumably leads to the betterment of both. Once again, however, a comparison of the two episodes illustrates how Flores/Colleen struggles with her body and achieves a level of personal power through her struggles, while Bowman/Colleen struggles with her asexual femininity only to achieve a more stable passivity as a result.

The Flores/Colleen Version: Competent Femininity on Display

When a traveling circus comes to town, Flores/Colleen meets Atlantis, a young woman who has an unusual physical anomaly: webbing between her fingers. While Atlantis is acutely uncomfortable with her hands, wearing gloves to cover them and eventually taking a knife to herself in an attempt to cut away the webbing, she is also an intensely independent and physically competent woman.

When the two-person circus (Atlantis and her adoptive mother, Heart) arrives, Heart immediately identifies all the main characters in the show by their dominant personality trait, giving them roles in her performance. Her identifications trouble the characters because they uncover what each likes to keep hidden or to pretend is not part of who they are. For example, she invites the Reverend to play a magician, thus insisting that he acknowledge the power he himself (rather than God) has. And of course Heart insists that Dr. Mike and Sully perform together. Heart knows they are capable of matching their physical patterns and predicting each other's moves well enough to perform on the trapeze. While each character initially resists Heart's suggestion only to be persuaded by her insistence, when Heart suggests that Colleen walk the high wire—metaphorically take the difficult path while displaying her body—Heart does not insist when Colleen refuses. Thus, the episode develops suspense around whether Colleen will learn to walk and then perform on the high wire or, metaphorically, whether she will be able to face the difficulties her changing body represents and thus achieve her future as an independent woman.

In the process of confronting this challenge, Colleen becomes friends with Atlantis. This is a friendship based on mutual admiration. For example, when Colleen shows Atlantis around the clinic, they have the following conversation:

C: And this is where we do our operations. Well, Dr. Mike does them. I assist.
A: You're so accomplished for someone of your age.
C: What about you? You're a performer. I don't know how you get up in front of all those people. It would scare me to death.
A: And I'm sure I'd faint if I had to see blood.

Colleen must learn to display her body rather than simply to practice medicine, but she also offers Atlantis a chance to observe a talented and committed woman practice medicine. She offers Atlantis a role model of independent feminine competence even as Colleen learns to display her own body. Furthermore, through its representation of the young women's friendship, this episode *problematizes* the audience's gaze. When Colleen first tries to cross the high wire, rather than the low wire Atlantis has set up for practice, she balks. A long shot holds on her as she climbs down the long ladder and runs away. Atlantis follows her and offers the following words of comfort: "I know how you feel. People staring at you. You never really get used to it." While Atlantis presumably is referring only to the act of performing, given the episode's focus on her anxiety about her webbed hands, her words have further resonance. They suggest that the staring is as much about performance of appropriate femininity as it is about competent performance.

Both Atlantis and Colleen must find a way to integrate their fierce independence into a version of femininity that elicits just the right amount of "staring." By the end of the episode, despite the fact that Colleen has declared that she will not perform, she does cross the high wire. After Dr. Mike reassures her that "there's nothing to be sorry about. If you make a decision that you truly believe is the right one for you at the time, then that's a good decision," Colleen realizes her refusal to perform was the wrong decision; thus she drops her wrap—to reveal the most tight-fitting costume Flores/Colleen ever wears—and then heads across the high wire. When Heart and Atlantis leave town at the end of the episode, Dr. Mike says: "We should all thank you for helping us see what we are capable of," and then she looks at Colleen. In this episode, Colleen and Atlantis move together toward the idealized femininity represented by Dr. Mike: the ability to perform competently through a feminine body (Colleen on the high wire, Atlantis's desire for "normal" hands) while simultaneously celebrating one's own independence and intellect (Colleen's identification with medicine, Atlantis's ability to teach and perform). Metaphorically, then, when Heart asks Colleen to walk the tightrope, she asks her to adjust to (displaying) her developing, "disfigured" body. As Colleen struggles to meet this challenge and Atlantis overcomes her disfigurement through self-inflicted plastic surgery, the episode offers a sustained representation of teenage women struggling toward and against feminine display. While the episode ends with successful bodily femininity for both Flores/Colleen and Atlantis, it does so only after problematizing, even temporarily rejecting, that desire.

The Bowman/Colleen Version: Competent Femininity in the Home

Bowman's/Colleen's encounter with a young woman just passing through town also provides an opportunity for the two women to learn from each other and exchange parts of themselves. However, in this episode, the young women fight rather than share admiration. When Belle Starr, a "real live outlaw," gets shot after robbing the saloon, Dr. Mike takes her in, hoping to reform her with a warm family environment. Dr. Mike is less than successful. Calling Colleen "Miss Priss," Belle constantly draws attention to distinctions between herself and Colleen. Belle makes fun of Colleen's interest in housekeeping, criticizes her ability to take care of Belle's injuries, swears on purpose to irritate her, treats her like a servant by constantly demanding more food and drink, makes fun of her dresses, and teases her for being afraid of horses. Thus while Flores/Colleen and Atlantis struggle together both to problematize and then to accept their bodies as objects on display, Bowman/Colleen and Belle struggle against each other, each settling more firmly into their feminine and anti-feminine personas.

This episode begins by drawing attention to Colleen's fear of horses, something that has never come up before. While Flores/Colleen rode a horse with abandon in order to collect medical supplies when her brother Matthew was trapped in a collapsed mine, Bowman/Colleen neither wants to ride nor can. Indeed, when her family's teasing forces her onto a horse in the opening scene, she falls off and refuses to get back on.

Colleen's clothing in this episode further highlights her identity as a feminine home-maker rather than a competent horse-rider. Throughout most of the episode she wears a soft pink dress that fits her body snugly. In particular, when Belle's identity as a "girl" is revealed (when Hank shot her in the back as she rode away from robbing the saloon he assumed she was a boy), Colleen—positioned directly in the middle of the frame—stands out in her soft pink dress, which contrasts sharply with the dark brown colors of all the other characters' clothing. Her attire, as does her incompetent horse-back-riding, emphasizes her femininity and draws a clear distinction between Colleen and Belle, who is easily mistaken for a boy.

Colleen's treatment of Belle contributes to this distinction. She insults Belle for not bathing, says she both eats and smells like a pig, and taunts her with the jail sentence she surely faces. Furthermore, in a particularly uncharacteristic moment (at least based on the two and one half seasons in which Flores played Colleen), Colleen allows her emotions to affect adversely her ability to perform her medical abilities. After Belle insults her ("I ain't some prim little ninny who takes baths everyday like you. I don't wear no ribbons in my hair either"), Colleen rubs Belle's head too hard with the cloth she is using to clean her face, causing Belle to swear at her again. Initially, then, the episode works to draw distinctions between the two young women, rather than to highlight the similarities as it does when Flores's Colleen meets Atlantis.

Dr. Mike tells Colleen that Belle is mean to her because she is jealous of her, and she urges Colleen to be patient. Unlike Atlantis, who admired (Flores's) Colleen's medical skills, Dr. Mike says that Belle is jealous of (Bowman) Colleen because she is "pretty and smart [and has] a family that loves [her]." Dr. Mike suggests that rather than admiring Colleen for what she can do, Belle hates Colleen for what she has. Interestingly, however, Belle's actions do not really support Dr. Mike's interpretation. Instead, Colleen and Belle eventually become friends when Belle is able to teach Colleen to overcome her fear of horses. Thus, the episode provides a tension between Belle's supposed desire to be pretty and live in a family (something she repeatedly rejects) and her interest in Colleen when she shifts toward horse-riding rather than homemaking. However, because this tension is never resolved, neither Colleen nor Belle learns to integrate femininity and independence as a result of their encounter, as do Colleen and Atlantis when they become friends. While Bowman/ Colleen spends a brief moment on a horse, during which she rescues Brian from Belle's gang and gains everyone's, including Belle's, respect as a result, the final shot of the episode returns her to her warm family environment, dressed in her feminine clothing and hoping Belle will reform someday. While Colleen may have (re)learned to ride a horse in this episode, the episode emphasizes her place within a warm and loving family, a place that positions her explicitly in the "homemaking" role.

Defining the (Same) Lover: Flores's/Colleen's and Bowman's/Colleen's (Different) Futures

The final set of episodes I would like to compare are particularly interesting because they represent a continuing story line that Flores/Colleen and Bowman/Colleen share. As a result, the contrast between the two versions of Colleen and her related responses to both her body and her femininity is particularly clear.

In the first episode of the third season, the railroad comes to town. Along with it comes Peter, a young Chinese man who is the adopted son of Mr. Tate, the white man who has the power to decide whether to send the railroad through Colorado Springs. In this episode, Peter and Flores/Colleen meet, become friends, and begin to fall in love. In the 18th episode of the third season (Bowman's third episode) Peter and Mr. Tate return to town during the process of building the railroad that eventually will go through Colorado Springs. Colleen and Peter continue their friendship, now talking abstractly about marriage and children. While a series of issues are consistent across the two episodes, including Colleen's unwillingness to be swayed by her friends' racism against Peter and Peter and Colleen's discussions about world travel, many issues are different in slight, but significant, ways.

For example, in the first episode Dr. Mike praises Flores/Colleen for making her first independent diagnosis; however, in the second episode Bowman/Colleen does little doctoring, serving only as Dr. Mike's helper as Dr. Mike deduces why the Chinese men who are working on the railroad are sick. In the first episode, Peter develops a high fever while Dr. Mike is away, and Colleen takes him into the clinic alone. A shot of a microscope pans up to show Colleen looking through the microscope, away to a book, and back through the microscope, thus emphasizing her serious study and her commitment to curing Peter. When Dr. Mike and Mr. Tate walk into this scene, Dr. Mike and Colleen discuss Peter's symptoms.

DR. M: What's the nature of the fever?
C: It seems to be a three stage fever [separate reaction shots of each adult] with high temperatures, then cold chills, then the sweats.
DR. M: Hum.
C: I remember from my reading that malaria's a three stage fever that comes from the swamps.
DR. M: That's correct.
C: And come look. It matches the picture in the book.

Later, when Dr. Mike has examined Peter, she says, "Congratulations Colleen, you've just made your first diagnosis." Not only does Colleen successfully work alone here, but the episode emphasizes the importance of her medical work.

In Bowman's episode, Colleen never works alone as she helps Dr. Mike to realize that "the Chang brothers" (they are never individually named) are sick because they ate biscuits accidentally laced with lead. Colleen helps by simply providing the information that Matthew and Peter drank milk while eating the same biscuits, but Dr. Mike engages in the deductive reasoning that leads her to realize that Matthew and Peter are not sick because the milk coated and thus protected their stomachs from the dangerous biscuits.

In addition to her pleasure in doctoring and true to her more excessive body and sexuality, Flores/Colleen is explicitly attracted to Peter on a physical level. The first time Colleen sees Peter after she first meets him, she happens upon him while he is bathing in a stream. The camera follows Colleen as she picks flowers and then looks up and stops. Then a long shot of Peter's naked back and long queue reveals Colleen's optical and emotional point of view and initiates a shot/countershot sequence. When Peter turns and notices Colleen watching him, a cut to a close-up of Colleen reveals her discomfort. In the next shot he ducks down to hide himself. The following shot is a close-up of Colleen saying "I'm sorry, I was . . . I was . . ." and then running off. The final shot of this scene holds Peter in a medium shot—his upper body still naked and visible for the viewer—looking after Colleen. This sequence eroticizes Peter's body and his race for the viewer and draws attention to Colleen's erotic and orientalizing pleasure. The audience and Colleen together are able to imagine (and experience) feminine desire.

Because it crosses racial boundaries, this desire is particularly dangerous both for Colleen within her racist hometown and for the text as it negotiates a tension between celebrating interracial harmony and perpetuating a disempowered representation of the Asian/Asian American man. This tension around the representation of Colleen's desire for the Other heightens a tension around the representation of Colleen's intellect. In fact, the eroticism is directly connected to Colleen's doctoring in her next scene when she again gets a good look at Peter's naked torso while nursing/doctoring him with a sponge bath during his illness. In this context, her gaze at his body is motivated by her role as a caretaker, but it also simultaneously refers back to her erotic and desiring gaze in the previous scene. Together, these two scenes in which Colleen gets to look allow her sexuality and her independent intellect to coexist.

Although Bowman/Colleen is also interested in Peter romantically, the dangerous erotic element of the relationship disappears. In the second episode, Peter never appears without his shirt, Colleen and Peter hardly touch, and Colleen rarely gazes at him directly. Whereas Flores/Colleen's attraction to and care of Peter signify her medical ability, Bowman's Colleen's attraction to and care of Peter signify her homemaking ability. In fact, almost every scene between Peter and Bowman/Colleen takes place after she delivers food to him and the other men repairing the railroad's mule. While Flores/Colleen's medical ability and knowledge justify her touch, her gaze, and her eroticism, Bowman's/Colleen's ability to serve justifies her flirtations with Peter.

The content of the flirtations between Peter and Colleen changes as the actor changes, as well. For instance, when Peter and Colleen meet in the first episode, they talk of traveling to China and think analytically about their names. Thus, when Peter gives Colleen a box of earth from China, she understands the seriousness of the gift.

C: What is it?
P: It's China. I brought it with me when I came over on the boat.
C: I can't take this.
P: You must. I want for you to have this little piece of my homeland until you can go there and walk upon it yourself.

The connection between Flores/Colleen and Peter, then, is based both on eroticism and a developing consciousness about immigrant identity and interracial relationships. But when Peter returns to town and asks Bowman/Colleen if she still has the earth he gave her, her response reveals a subtle shift in her attraction to Peter.

P: Do you still have the earth I gave you?
C: Of course. I keep it right next to the silver comb and brush my grandma gave me.
P: I was afraid that after time you might come to see it as only dirt.
C: Oh no. You gave it to me.

Although in Flores's episode Colleen understands the earth as part of Peter's identity as a Chinese immigrant, in Bowman's episode Colleen understands it only as part of Peter's identity as a potential suitor. By keeping the earth next to her silver comb and brush, gifts her adoptive grandmother gave Colleen when she began menstruating and that mark the feminine refinement the grandmother and her home in Boston represent, Bowman/Colleen associates Peter with her femininity. While, arguably, Flores's/Colleen's erotic interest in Peter also links him to her femininity, this version of femininity is active and desirous. Conversely, Bowman's/Colleen's version of femininity is a form of display represented by the fancy comb and brush to which Colleen refers.

Furthermore, rather than imagining traveling to China with Peter as does Flores/Colleen, Bowman/Colleen fantasizes about marriage and *worries* about Peter's desire to return to China.

C: Will you go back to China when your work is done here?
P: Only to find a wife.
C: Oh. [downcast]
P: That is if I could not find one here.
C: Oh. [pleased]
P: But I would live in this country, perhaps in San Francisco.
C: Oh, I hear there are lots of Chinese there.
P: I want to build a big house on one of the hills and have lots of children.
C: I want to have children, too. [Pause] That is, after I go to medical school.

For Colleen here, Peter's identity as Chinese is about her ability to marry him. While Flores/Colleen is interested in world travel and Peter's experiences, Bowman/Colleen is interested in children. By drawing attention to the Chinese population in San Francisco, in fact, Colleen encourages Peter to alter his relationship to China and his Chinese identity in order for them to continue their relationship. The big house on the hill for which he hopes, one that few if any Chinese or Chinese Americans had in the 1800s, fits Colleen's dreams of marriage rather than any particular element of Peter's identity as Chinese.

Conclusions

Colleen's line—"I want to have children, too. [Pause] That is, after I go to medical school"—marks most starkly the change in Colleen's character when Bowman replaces Flores. Compare it to the following exchange between Flores's Colleen and Dr. Mike about how hard it is to be a woman dissatisfied with limited feminine roles.

C: I wish I was a boy. Did you wish you were a boy?
DR. M: Yes, yes I did. Especially when I was your age. I was expected to learn needle-point and look pretty. All I ever wanted to do was see the world. The only ones who got to do that were the boys.
C: Boys get to do everything.

DR. M: No, not everything. I was a little older than you when I first assisted my father during a birth. It was a little girl. Her mother named her Julia. It was nothing short of a miracle, to create a life.

C: *I want to do more than get married and have babies.* (My emphasis)

DR. M: There are no rules, Colleen. Look at me. Never hide behind the fact that you're a girl, a woman. And don't give up your dreams just because you're afraid you won't achieve them in a man's world. You just have to fight even harder to make them come true.

While Flores's/Colleen's desire to do more than get married and have babies is at the forefront of her mind, Bowman/Colleen remembers she wants to go to medical school only after expressing her desire for marriage and a family. The complex link Dr. Mike articulates between women's independence and femininity here, the link that so many of the episodes in which Flores portrays Colleen develop, disappears by the time Bowman replaces Flores. When Dr. Mike tells Colleen boys do not get to do everything, she does not simply mention (some) women's biological ability to give birth, she highlights her fascination with that ability from a medical perspective. For Dr. Mike, and for Flores/Colleen who is learning to be like Dr. Mike, being a woman is irrevocably connected to being independent and intelligent and to fighting for a woman's rights.

This link between traditional categories of femininity and women's independence, represented by both Dr. Mike and Flores/Colleen, is one that I find both intriguing and troubling. On the one hand, *Dr. Quinn* works week after week to represent women's independent intellect as something to celebrate and emulate. The series' complex interweaving in Dr. Mike of two "poles" of women's identity into an inseparable whole provides a model of femininity that does not offer an either/or choice. And narratives about Flores's/Colleen's negotiation of this identity illustrate the process and possibility of embodying this complex feminine identity. On the other hand, Flores's/Colleen's changing body and erotic sexuality mark a fissure in Dr. Mike as a feminine ideal, drawing attention to versions of women's identity, body, and sexuality that cannot be contained by the televisual form. The materiality of Flores's teenage body forces the text to respond to a version of womanhood that it has not yet articulated, making the "completeness" of the ideal feminine identity highly suspect. The episodes that represent Flores's/Colleen's growing sexuality and eroticism work both to acknowledge the materiality of women's bodies and desires, and, simultaneously, to draw a distinction between Flores/Colleen and Seymour/Dr. Mike. While Colleen aspires to be Dr. Mike (in one episode, after Colleen saves Sully's life, Sully says: "I'm proud of you. You're becoming more and more like your ma everyday"), the excessiveness of her body makes her fulfillment of that role impossible.

When Flores leaves the series, *Dr. Quinn* replaces her with a body that no longer troubles the smooth representation of a link between traditional femininity and independent intellect. However, Bowman's small, child-like body does more than return Colleen to a careful balance between these two poles. Instead, Bowman/Colleen shifts ever-so-slightly toward a family-oriented, intelligent by default, frightened, feminine girl/woman. While Colleen declares her adulthood ("I'm all grown up now"), that adulthood is predicated on the erasure of bodily sexuality, competition between women rather than mutual admiration and love, marriage rather than world travel, and family rather than independence.

In comparison to Bowman/Colleen, Flores/Colleen marks an important ideological break in the representation of teenage womanhood as passive, isolated, and family-oriented. When examined through the materiality of the teenage woman's body, Erika Flores and her rendition of Colleen mark an ideological fissure that highlights the fragmentation and partiality in *Dr. Quinn*'s idealized feminist femininity. That fissure provides a place at which the feminist critic can both challenge the cohesive representation of the postfeminist woman and pause over the potential pleasures and resistances in the text's negotiation with the independent and desirous body of the teenage woman. Nevertheless, *Dr. Quinn* as televisual text cannot sustain that fissure. When it responds by filling the fissure with Bowman, I would argue, the critical and spectatorial tension around the material woman's body dissipates. As I hope my analysis here illustrates, I would not uncritically celebrate *Dr. Quinn*'s representation of Flores's/Colleen's body. Nevertheless, I would suggest that Flores's/Colleen's body offers a feminist potential that Bowman's/Colleen's body rescinds.

While this essay focuses exclusively on the first three seasons of *Dr. Quinn*, Bowman's teenage body will inevitably change over time—as does Flores's. What will be the result of those changes, in the context of the more passive and child-like yet nominally adult identity Bowman/Colleen now has? And in what way will that body change? Will Jessica Bowman face eating disorders, as so many teenage women stars have? Will she lose her job, whether by "amicabl[e]. . . 'mutual agreement' " as *TV Guide* ("Ask *TV Guide*," 1995) reported Flores's exit from the show, or by firing? What will happen to the narrative in response to the body? These questions, which address the intersection of the material body and the ideological narrative, are central to a careful understanding of the representation of teenage women on television and have the potential to remind us that our own material bodies and their various transformations are also embedded within ideological narratives.

REFERENCES

Ask *TV Guide*. (1995, March 4). *TV Guide*, 2.

Birnbaum, J. (1995, February 27). Seen and heard (Roseanne gets pregnant and Demi Moore does movie in the nude). *Time*, 77.

Blues of the birth. (1993, March 27). *TV Guide*, 20.

Bordo, S. (1993). *Unbearable weight: Feminism, western culture, and the body.* Berkeley: University of California Press.

Chernin, K. (1981). *The obsession: Reflections on the tyranny of slenderness.* New York: Harper & Row.

D'Acci, J. (1994). Women characters and "real world" femininity. In *Defining women: Television and the case of Cagney and Lacey* (pp. 10–62). Chapel Hill: University of North Carolina Press.

Dow, B. J. (1992). Femininity and feminism in *Murphy Brown. Southern Journal of Communication, 57*, 143–155.

Fit, not fat, at 40, talk show queen Oprah Winfrey runs the Marine Corps marathon. (1994, November 7). *People Weekly*, 44.

Lee, J. (1992). Subversive sitcoms: *Roseanne* as inspiration for feminist resistance. *Women's Studies, 21*, 87–101.

Lyall, S. (1994, June 8). A cookbook that's hot (*In the kitchen with Rosie*, Rosie Daley's Oprah diet cookbook). *New York Times.* pp. B2, C18.

Probyn, E. (1990). New traditionalism and post-feminism: TV does the home. *Screen, 31,* 147–159.

Randolph, L. B. (1993, October). Oprah opens up about her weight, her wedding and why she withheld the book. *Ebony,* 130.

Reynolds, G. (1995). The Oprah Winfrey plan. *Runner's World, 30* (3), 64.

Schindehette, S., Armstrong, L., & Healy, L. S. (1993, February 15). What's up, doc? With umpteen miniseries and three marriages behind her, Jane Seymour still thinks romance is good medicine. *People Weekly,* 74–80.

Schwichtenberg, C. (1992). Madonna's postmodern feminism: Bringing the margins to the center. *Southern Communication Journal, 57,* 120–131. [Reprinted in C. Schwichtenberg (Ed.), *The Madonna connection: Representational politics, subcultural identities, and cultural theory* (pp. 129–145). Boulder, CO: Westview Press.

Urla, J., & Swedlund, A. C. (1995). The anthropometry of Barbie: Unsettling ideals of the feminine body in popular culture. In J. Terry and J. Urla (Eds.), *Deviant bodies: Critical perspectives on difference in science and popular culture* (pp. 277–313). Bloomington: Indiana University Press.

Vande Berg, L. R. (1993). *China Beach,* prime time war in the postfeminist age: An example of patriarchy in a different voice. *Western Journal of Communication, 57,* 349–366.

Femininity and Feminism in *Murphy Brown*

Bonnie J. Dow

In the last two decades, feminist issues have become salient in the field of communication as scholars have made cogent cases for the inappropriate trivialization of women as communicators (see Campbell, 1985; Campbell, 1991; Carter & Spitzack, 1989; Foss & Foss, 1983; Spitzack & Carter, 1987). Among rhetorical critics, efforts to remedy neglect of women's communicative practices have emerged most visibly in analysis of texts produced by female rhetors in feminist movements (e.g., Campbell, 1973, 1980, 1986, 1989; Dow, 1991; Japp, 1985). This scholarship expands understanding of American public address, and provides a vocabulary with which to understand women's rhetorical practice. However, emphasis on this type of work inadvertently limits feminist rhetorical criticism primarily to *criticism of the rhetoric of feminists.*

I note this limitation not to devalue this work but to suggest the need for feminist rhetorical analysis of communication *about women.* To move forward, the feminist project in communication must explore how the patriarchy talks about women as well as how women talk about the patriarchy.[1] This focus has implications for the evaluative phase of feminist criticism. In past rhetorical analyses of women's communication, evaluation has been relatively uncomplicated, because one begins with the presumption that a feminist rhetor intends to affirm feminist goals and the major task is to explain how that goal is accomplished.

However, feminist evaluation of discourse *about* women is complicated by the growth of feminist theory and research in various disciplines, making it clear that there are *varieties* of feminism, including liberal feminism, radical feminism, socialist feminism, and feminism with an emphasis on race (Donovan, 1985; Jaggar, 1983; Lorde, 1984; Steeves, 1987). This diversity means that interpretations of affirmation or devaluation of women are not necessarily shared among acknowledged feminists, much less among men and women in general. I do not intend to resolve such conflicts, but simply to note that expansion of the range of artifacts for feminist analysis can also enrich the perspectives brought to bear on them.

In this essay, I focus on entertainment television as a pervasive and potent source for rhetoric *about* women. With television as artifact, traditional rhetorical approaches require adjustment. Because television programming is produced collaboratively and is inherently commercial, specific knowledge of rhetor, audience, and context is difficult to establish. Moreover, because entertainment television is dramatic and nondiscursive in form, its arguments are implicit, placing a greater burden of interpretation on both the audience and the critic.

Television influences others through symbols structured for persuasive effect, a process with varying levels of intentionality (see Chesebro, 1991; Hall, 1982). These structures/strategies function rhetorically by interacting with an audience's experiences, attitudes, and values to encourage a particular view of the reality of a situation, event, or person(s) (Burke, 1973, pp. 1–3). If we can regard "any work of critical or imaginative cast as the adopting of various strategies for the encompassing of situations," then all artistic work can be approached as "the *functioning* of a structure," designed to accomplish something (Burke, 1973, pp. 1, 74).

Thus, feminist rhetorical criticism of television asks what view of symbolic reality about women is encouraged by a television text and what function that view of reality might serve. Inherent in this perspective is the belief that television texts contain recurrent persuasive strategies, and that to argue for the potential articulation of such strategies by audiences is to begin to build a vocabulary with which to discuss the valuation of women in a variety of texts.[2]

As an example of such an approach, this analysis explores the rhetorical function of patriarchal definitions of feminism in the television situation comedy *Murphy Brown*. I argue that *Murphy Brown* exemplifies how popular conceptions of liberal feminism can be coopted and used as part of a rhetorical strategy to reaffirm patriarchal definitions of femininity and feminism. This analysis proceeds in three sections. First, I view *Murphy Brown* as an interpretation of liberal feminism, demonstrating why the program is likely to be perceived as such by its audience, and arguing that liberal feminism is subject to social control through the use of comic rhetorical strategies. Second, I analyze the rhetorical functions of the patriarchal representation of liberal feminist ideology enacted by *Murphy Brown*'s title character, including the character's function as a comic scapegoat. Finally, I offer conclusions and implications of this analysis for feminist rhetorical criticism.

Murphy Brown, **Liberal Feminism, and Comic Strategies**

Murphy Brown's status as one of prime-time television's most visible representations of liberal feminism is supported by the interpretive cues contained in media coverage of the sitcom, as well as by the program's reiteration of the major themes that have defined "feminism" on television in the past. However, *Murphy Brown*'s use of comic rhetorical strategies, particularly the scapegoating of its feminist title character, exemplify the possibilities for commercial television to incorporate and coopt popular notions of "feminism" for hegemonic purposes.

Television and Liberal Feminism

Media treatment of popular television shows provides potential viewers with powerful cues for interpretation that affect not only *if* a program is watched, but *how* it is viewed. From its debut in 1988 *Murphy Brown* was well publicized, and two major themes dominating publicity included the program's focus on a "strong" woman, and *Murphy Brown*'s relationship to another well-known situation comedy, *The Mary Tyler Moore Show (TMTMS)*.

Popular press coverage characterized *Murphy Brown* as a challenge to the typical portrayal of women on television and suggested that the series' title character, a successful, fortyish, female television journalist, was "different," an example of the "womanpower" taking hold in prime-time network television (Waters & Huck, 1989, p. 48). Critics highlighted certain qualities: her ambition and competitive drive (Elm, 1989; O'Connor, 1989; O'Reilly, 1989), her often harsh wit and sarcasm (Cavett, 1989; Wisehart, 1989), and her checkered past as an alumna of the Betty Ford Center (Panitt, 1989; Wisehart, 1989). In short, critics claimed that Murphy Brown represented "the very apothesis of the new video woman" (Waters & Huck, 1989, p. 49). Various adjectives used to describe her: "workaholic," "amazon," "highly competitive and confident," and "tough" gave potential viewers clues as to the original slant of the character (O'Connor, 1989, p. Y17; Panitt, 1989, p. 40; Wisehart, 1989, p. 39; Zehme, 1989, p. 1).

Excessive media treatment of *Murphy Brown* continually underscored its position at the forefront of progressive female representation on television. Candice Bergen, the actress who plays Murphy Brown, was featured (in character) on the cover of a *Newsweek* issue that trumpeted: "How Women Are Changing TV: New Power On and Off the Screen" (Waters & Huck, 1989). Murphy Brown's credibility as a representation of female status in the workplace was reinforced by a *TV Guide* story (again featuring Bergen on the cover) titled "TV's real newswomen give thumbs up to Murphy" (Elm, 1989). Essentially, it was not even necessary to watch the program to be aware of *Murphy Brown*'s implications for the status of women, both on television and in the "real" world.

A related theme among journalists' reactions to the show reflected on the similarities between *Murphy Brown* and *The Mary Tyler Moore Show (TMTMS)*, broadcast in prime time from 1970 to 1977. Like Mary Richards, the main character in *TMTMS*, Murphy Brown is a bright, single, attractive woman working in a television newsroom. However, the most important link between the two sitcoms is their perceived status as feminist artifacts. *TMTMS* was the first successful sitcom about a single, independent, working woman. When it debuted in 1970 it was perceived as a breakthrough show because of its feminist implications and its timing in relation to the women's liberation movement (see Alley & Brown, 1989; Dow, 1990).

Popular media have so thoroughly construed these programs as feminist artifacts that even a casual television viewer would be hard pressed to miss the point. For example, a recent CBS special focusing on the twentieth anniversary of *The Mary Tyler*

Moore Show was not only broadcast on a Monday evening (February 18, 1991) with *Murphy Brown* as its lead-in show, but the special was advertised as "An Evening with Murphy and Mary," clearly establishing a link between the two programs. More recently, the ABC news magazine show *Primetime Live* of July 25, 1991, introduced a feature on *Murphy Brown* by placing the show on a continuum of liberated woman sitcoms that included *That Girl* and *The Mary Tyler Moore Show*. Indeed, the producers of *Murphy Brown* claim that they "intend Murphy to be for the 90s what Mary Richards was for the 70s" (Horowitz, 1989, p. 1H), and a headline in *USA Today* described the sitcom as "Mary Tyler Moore Updated for the Eighties" (cited in Alley & Brown, 1990, p. 204).

The perceived progressivism of both *Murphy Brown* and *TMTMS* rests in their emphasis on the liberal feminist ideal of increasing women's access to the public sphere (Jaggar, 1983, p. 188). Generally, liberal feminism emphasizes evaluation of the position of women on the basis of their equality with men within dominant cultural systems. Liberal feminists compare women's economic, legal, and social positions with those of men and argue that women's rights and privileges be expanded to equal those of men. Key characteristics of this view are that it accepts as desirable the cultural standards established through male dominance and it focuses almost exclusively on women's equality in public life (Donovan, 1985; Jaggar, 1983; Steeves, 1987). Liberal feminist goals have dominated the mainstream feminist agenda, fueling reforms such as the woman suffrage movement and the Equal Rights Amendment. The result is that liberal feminism "is often thought to be the only feminism there is" by the general public and mass media (Jaggar, 1983, p. 197; see also Donovan, 1985; Steeves, 1987).

Programs like *Murphy Brown* and *TMTMS* that feature single, independent, working women who have chosen career over marriage and motherhood promote liberal feminist values by rejecting television's tradition of domestic women and by portraying female characters in roles formerly reserved for men. Indeed, characteristics that the press claims make *Murphy Brown* unique (e.g., "workaholic," "highly competitive," "tough") seem unusual only when applied to a female character rather than a male character. *TMTMS*'s and *Murphy Brown*'s embrace of the notion that progress for women requires rejection of domesticity (the feminine sphere) and pursuit of a career (the masculine sphere) has long been attached to liberal feminism reinforced by documents such as Betty Friedan's *The Feminine Mystique* and the battle over the ERA.

In short, television's approach to the demands of feminism has generally been to allow women the opportunity to act like men. The problems with such an approach reflect the general problems of liberal feminist ideology: uplifting women by placing them in formerly masculine roles undermines traditional female roles and further reifies the perceived incompatibility of the public (masculine) and private (feminine) spheres (Jaggar, 1983, pp. 187–189). Simply moving women into the public sphere does not correct oppressive role definitions. For example, *TMTMS* depicted Mary Richards as a domestic helpmate within the office environment, and the feminist premise of the program was undermined by the message that a woman at work is expected to do essentially the same tasks as a woman at home: nurturance, support, and relationship maintenance (Dow, 1990).

Murphy Brown offers yet another opportunity to examine television's hegemonic treatment of liberal feminism. I argue that the feminist character of Murphy Brown functions as a comic scapegoat ritually punished for inappropriate manifestation of patriarchal traits such as competitiveness, ambition, egoism, and interpersonal insensitivity. By sacrificing Murphy, the threat that feminism poses for the patriarchy is controlled, and the perceived dichotomy between masculine and feminine roles is maintained. Using the writings of Kenneth Burke and Hugh Duncan, I conclude that this process illustrates how comic strategies can function as social control.

Comic Strategies and Social Control

Rhetorical critics have noted the use of comic strategies to encourage progressive social change (Burke, 1959; Carlson, 1986; Duncan, 1962; Murphy, 1989); comic strategies, particularly humor, are often used to address troublesome issues in a nonthreatening manner. For example, situation comedy has served as a forum for exploration of controversial issues in American culture such as feminism (e.g., *TMTMS*), racism (e.g., *Good Times, The Jeffersons*) or the Vietnam war (e.g., *All in the Family, M*A*S*H*).

However, comic strategies do not always function progressively; they can also serve an opposite function by reducing challenges to the social order to a level at which they do not have to be taken seriously. For example, a rhetorical act may contain a comic scapegoat that represents a threat to the dominant social order (Duncan, 1962, p. 395). Functioning as a caricature of the values in contention, the scapegoat is comically sacrificed, through ridicule, embarrassment, or humiliation, and the social order is protected from the threat it represents (Duncan, 1962, pp. 401, 378).

Such a comic strategy ultimately is aimed at acceptance of the scapegoated character; however, that acceptance must come on the terms set by the dominant cultural group. As Duncan notes: "There is hostility in our laughter, but it is not the hostility of derisive laughter which ends in alienation and hate. . . . Such joking is really a form of instruction, a kind of social control, directed at those we intend to accept once they learn to behave properly" (1962, p. 389). This is the conservative function of comedy; it requires sacrifice of the scapegoat so that authority can be maintained (Duncan, 1962, p. 380).

In the case of *Murphy Brown*, the need to defuse the threat of a liberal feminist character through scapegoating is economic. Positive portrayal of a female character who successfully rejects patriarchal constructs of traditional womanhood undermines television's commercial basis. Women aged 18–49 (the preferred viewing group for *Murphy Brown*) are the most sought-after group of consumers by television sponsors, primarily because of the large amount of consumption attached to these women in their traditional roles as wives, mothers, and objects of heterosexual appeal (Kaplan, 1987; Nightingale, 1990). To offer a message that devalues those roles is not in the interest of commercial television.

However, such a concern must be balanced against the need for programming that reflects the changing interests of female viewers. The result is the creation of subtle rhetorical strategies which offer seemingly progressive female characters but limit the approval and success those characters receive. *Murphy Brown*'s manipulation of liberal feminist ideology is an example of such a strategy.

In *Murphy Brown*'s interpretation of liberal feminism, success in the male-dominated world of national television journalism requires surrender to the norms and values of the patriarchy. Murphy's enactment of patriarchal qualities enables her success as a professional, but conflicts with expectations for her as a woman. Resolution of such conflicts often is achieved through comic sacrifice of Murphy as the feminist scapegoat. This sacrifice is facilitated by the development of a dichotomy in *Murphy Brown* between feminism and femininity, illustrated by Murphy's juxtaposition with another female character who is successfully feminine, but less successful professionally.

Cooptation of Liberal Feminism in *Murphy Brown*

A description of Murphy Brown's character as a patriarchal representation of liberal feminism must be understood within the larger context of *Murphy Brown.* The regulars on *Murphy Brown* consist primarily of Murphy's colleagues at "FYI," the weekly prime-time news magazine show of which she is a co-anchor. The other primary anchor on "FYI" is Jim Dial, an older, experienced television newsman known for his rigid, uptight nature and his stiff, laconic style. Miles Silverberg, the executive producer of "FYI" and Murphy's boss, is less experienced and younger than Murphy, a situation that Murphy finds consistently irritating. Two other regulars are Frank Fontana and Corky Sherwood [Forrest], reporters for the program. Frank is an experienced investigative reporter and Murphy's closest friend in the group.

In contrast, Corky has little journalistic experience. She is an ex-Miss America who was hired at "FYI" for her beauty queen status. Corky is young, pretty, and perky, a softer character than Murphy, and she provides a traditionally feminine foil for Murphy's feminist character. Murphy's relation to Corky is competitive rather than cooperative. Corky's role on "FYI" is to produce "soft" news features (e.g., "Twelve Angry Women in Hairdresser Horror Stories," "Dinner with the Van Patten Family") that appeal to female viewers. Murphy does not see Corky as her professional equal, and a strong theme in their relationship is Murphy's disdain for Corky's journalistic ability. Two other regulars on *Murphy Brown* are not connected to "FYI." They are Murphy's ever-present housepainter, Eldin Bernecky, who appears in most of the scenes set in Murphy's home, and Phil, the owner of a bar frequented by the "FYI" staff.

This review of characters shows a kinship between *Murphy Brown* and *TMTMS.* Like Mary Richards, Murphy is surrounded by men, reinforcing the liberal feminist orientation of "a woman in a man's world." However, unlike Mary Richards, Murphy does not achieve success by playing a domestic role in the workplace; rather, she absorbs the characteristics of her environment, enacting a patriarchal interpretation of liberal feminism. Murphy's role as such is evident from an examination of her personal and professional characteristics and the contrast of her character with Corky's enactment of traditional femininity.

The fact that Murphy's professional competence is never an issue on *Murphy Brown* shows progress since *TMTMS.* Murphy is a media "star," a knowledgeable, driven investigative reporter who has won numerous awards. *Murphy Brown* implies that Murphy has achieved much success by acceding to the demands of the patriarchal professional world. When viewed by traditional standards, Murphy offers support for the claim of anti-feminists that women who compete in the public world are masculinized (Rowland, 1984).

Murphy's "masculinized" character can be discerned on several levels. Her name is not "feminine;" culturally, "Murphy" would be more likely to refer to a man than a woman. Moreover, while she is attractive, even a beautiful woman, her "look" is not traditionally feminine. Murphy's clothing is severely tailored, and she tends to wear high collars and boxy suits with straight lines. Even her less formal clothes have a masculine aura; when Murphy is relaxed, she often wears a baseball cap, tennis shoes, and baggy, man-tailored slacks. Reinforcing the idea that she and Corky are two extremes on a spectrum, Murphy's tendency toward black, brown, and strong colors are a clear contrast to Corky's frequent pastels, soft scarves, and bows. While Murphy often wears flats, Corky always wears high heels. Murphy's subdued make-up and hair are also striking in comparison to Corky's teased, bleached hair and bright lips. Corky's appearance is part of her general performance of femininity, while Murphy's style reflects the goal of gaining credibility in a male world.

Murphy's physical presence also is noteworthy in defining her character. Her stride is aggressive, her gestures strong, her manner of speaking forceful, and she commands primary attention. Murphy's physical and facial expressions are excessive; she often does double-takes, and her expressions of distaste, amazement, or triumph are exaggerated. Her strength and autonomy are underscored by the way in which camera angles often show her physically isolated from other characters in a scene.

Murphy's physical aura is reinforced by her aggressive communication style. She is supremely confident about her opinions and expresses them easily, often with little regard for others' feelings. For example, in "The Strike"[3] (1989), Murphy is disgusted by the way men around her handle a management/union dispute. She accuses them of being blinded by male pride, and comments, "just pull down your pants, I'll get a ruler, and we'll settle this once and for all." The insensitivity evident in Murphy's taste for such harsh sarcasm and her habit of hostile practical jokes are typically male-associated traits. When angry at her producer, for example, she has pizzas delivered to him every half hour all night long, later hiring a polka band to play outside his window. Upset with Corky, she sends religious missionaries to her house.

A clear message of *Murphy Brown* is that the personality traits alluded to above, such as aggression, competitiveness, and lack of interpersonal sensitivity, are key to Murphy's professional success in a patriarchal world. For example, in "The Unshrinkable Murphy Brown" (1989), Murphy so relentlessly interviews a subject that he suffers a heart attack and dies on the air. Guilt-stricken, Murphy vows to be a nicer person, and in subsequent scenes she is uncharacteristically polite and considerate. Her colleagues are shocked and dismayed at the change in her behavior, concerned that it will affect the quality of her work.

This episode is instructive, because it implies that Murphy's display of traditionally "nice," feminine qualities is not only shocking, but incompatible with her success as a journalist. In order to be successful she must be tough and competitive, and must reject behaviors that contradict such a persona. While other reporters on "FYI" are also capable and successful, notably Jim Dial and Frank Fontana, they do not behave as ruthlessly. To compete in a male culture, Murphy becomes an extreme caricature of the consequences of liberal feminism. Alison Jaggar notes that a typical liberal feminist argument is that "women are capable of participating in male culture and of living up to male values" (1983, p. 250). Murphy's success proves this argument; however, the negative consequences she suffers as a comic scapegoat illustrate the patriarchal subtext of *Murphy Brown*.

As the following extended example illustrates, a recurring theme in *Murphy Brown* is that Murphy's competitiveness and ambition are excessive. In "Devil with the Blue Dress On" (1988), Miles assigns Corky to assist Murphy on a difficult story, claiming that Corky needs "seasoning as a reporter." After expressing her displeasure to Miles in competitive terms ("I won't work with her on my story. I was an only child—I never learned to share"), Murphy finally agrees. She sends Corky on wild-goose chases, hoping to discourage her, but Corky eventually discovers a piece of information which proves meaningful.

Murphy dismisses the value of the information in front of Corky so that she can pursue the angle herself. Corky later discovers this maneuver but responds graciously, saying: "When I realized what you'd done with that crucial piece of information I gave you . . . there it was, the perfect example of what makes you the best . . . I have learned so much from you and I respect you so much. Thank you for allowing me to work by your side." Murphy assuages the guilt engendered by this reaction by telling Corky that she may introduce the story on the air before turning it over to Murphy.

However, Corky reads the entire story and takes full credit. After the show, Murphy is furious, but she must admit respect for Corky, saying: "You saw your brass ring and you went for it. It took a lot of *chutzpa*. I have to respect a person for that." This episode demonstrates the pattern on *Murphy Brown* of plot lines that censure Murphy for her extreme character. Murphy's aggressive, competitive personality creates the problem that leads to her comeuppance at Corky's hands. If, from the beginning, she had shared credit for the story with Corky, this episode would have turned out differently, and Murphy might have helped Corky to grow as a reporter.

Instead, Murphy rejected cooperation and nurturing (qualities of traditional femininity) in favor of competition and ruthlessness (qualities of the patriarchal public sphere). While the latter qualities have led to Murphy's past success, she is reproved for them in this situation, creating a classic double-bind for her. Through such plot-lines, *Murphy Brown* reiterates what it presents as an unresolvable conflict between femininity and professional success. Murphy, as the carrier of negative liberal feminist traits, is scapegoated for provoking the conflict.

This example of Murphy's failure to exhibit a "feminine" response, and the reproach she suffers, is not atypical for the series. Murphy's lack of traditionally feminine qualities, particularly domestic and interpersonal skills, are a consistent source of humor. She has no skill and no interest in such traditional tasks as cooking or child-care. Murphy also has none of the nurturing qualities so common in television's female characters. She is rarely physically affectionate, usually stiffening when others are demonstrative toward her. When Jim Dial comes to her for advice on a personal problem, her first response is "Don't you have a family priest or someone?"

Murphy's interpersonal difficulties extend to her private life, where she enacts the stereotype of a driven career woman with no time or talent for relationships. Unlike Mary Richards, Murphy has no close female friends. Outside of the newsroom, her closest relationship is with Eldin, her housepainter. When she is not invited to the inaugural ball, she ends up spending the evening with Eldin. When she is suspended from work, it appears that Eldin is the only person to keep her company. There is no real or implied romantic connection with Eldin, but Murphy seems to have no other friends outside her job. In "Baby Love" (1988), Murphy thinks of becoming a single mother. However, it proves difficult to find someone to father her child. Forty years old, Murphy fears her time for motherhood is running out, and she bemoans the fact that her "most enduring relationship is with the skycap at Dulles airport."

Unmarried, childless, and without a satisfying romantic relationship, Murphy's character embodies what many would consider the negative consequences of female independence. Although Jim Dial, who is closest to being Murphy's peer, has a successful marriage, such a choice is precluded for Murphy. Frank Fontana, while not married, does not lack for female companionship. Corky also has greater success with romance than Murphy, and is married at the end of the second season.

Several episodes of *Murphy Brown* comment on the effect of Murphy's life choices on her personal relations, offering the message that her professional ambition precludes lasting personal relationships. For example, in a 1988 episode ("Signed, Sealed, Delivered"), Murphy's ex-husband, to whom she was married for five days twenty years earlier, appears on "FYI." They reignite their attraction and decide to marry again. However, Murphy cannot find time for a wedding and they give up on the idea. Her excuses range from "I gotta fly to Moscow to interview Gorbachev" to "I can't plan that far in advance—I've got to be ready to hop a plane at a moment's notice." Murphy's devotion to her work seems extreme in this circumstance, with the result that she sacrifices her own personal happiness.

Murphy's most recent involvement has been with Jerry Gold, an abrasive talk show host. In their first try at a relationship, Murphy eventually called it off, saying "I'm good at a lot of things, but this isn't one of them. I start saying things I don't normally say, I start doing things I don't normally do. . . . Oh, God, I'm wearing an apron. See what I mean?" This remark comes after a failed dinner party that Murphy concocted to introduce Jerry to her colleagues. It is telling that Murphy equates her failure at the relationship with her unsuitability for a domestic role, reinforcing the dichotomy between the private and public spheres.

In the next season, Murphy and Jerry try once more for a relationship, but it ends when Jerry takes a job in California and Murphy is too busy to pursue a long-distance romance. Again, this episode creates an inverse relationship between Murphy's personal happiness and her professional success. Murphy and Jerry are brought together when a new "FYI" segment requires that they debate political issues each week. Their sharply contrasting political views make this a lively and popular segment. However, after they rekindle their romance, Murphy is no longer aggressive and sharp-witted in the debate segment; instead, she exhibits traditionally feminine qualities. She is supportive, polite, and willing to compromise with Jerry's extremist views. Her colleagues are horrified, concluding that her romance with Jerry has affected her professional performance.

Again, *Murphy Brown* reiterates that personal happiness and professional success are incompatible for Murphy, implicitly arguing that, for women, the qualities the public world requires are radically different from those necessary for success in the private world of relationships. Murphy simply cannot win. *Murphy Brown* implies that she must act one way to be professionally successful and another to be personally fulfilled. For many female viewers, Murphy's difficulties could strike a responsive chord. However, the episodes of *Murphy Brown* that deal with this issue are structured to encourage viewers to perceive such problems as Murphy's fault because she is unwilling to compromise career for relationships. The troublesome assumption that she must make such a choice in the first place is not addressed. While men in her position are accustomed to "having it all," Murphy's attempts to do so have problematic results.

A final example of the way in which patterns on *Murphy Brown* place Murphy in such double-binds again highlights Murphy's lack of traditional femininity. In "The Morning Show" (1989), the major plot line concerns Murphy's week-long stint as the substitute co-anchor of "Today America," a program much like "Good Morning

America." Murphy ridicules the "soft news" orientation of the program, and she is un-happy to discover that Corky is to be her co-host. Corky is excited by the assignment and spends significant time preparing. Murphy, in contrast, does not see the job as challenging and does not prepare.

The contrasts between Murphy and Corky as co-anchors are the context within which Corky's traditional feminine attributes are validated, while Murphy's aggres-sive competitiveness only creates difficulties. In the first morning show, they interview the male author of a popular children's book. Murphy asserts that the setting of the book, "the Land of the Woogies," emulates a male-dominated society, and that the story represents the larger culture's "struggle for sexual equality in the workplace." The author protests that his characters do not have a sex, but Murphy is relentless, claiming that the "Fifis," another group in the book, are female and represent "an op-pressed minority of sorts." At this point, Corky steps in, soothes the author, and ends the interview.

The contrast between Murphy's feminism and Corky's femininity is clear in this scene. Murphy personifies the intensity and humorlessness of the stereotypical femi-nist ideologue, refusing to enact the supportive, gracious role required in such a situa-tion. While her argument that the children's book is sexist indeed may be correct (and some viewers may see it as a salient point to make), within the context of the episode, the audience is encouraged to view her claim as absurd and her behavior as inappro-priate. Corky, in contrast, is at home in the "soft news" format that reflects tradition-ally female interests.

While Corky is praised for her performance, Murphy is described by colleagues as "acerbic, humorless, inflexible, and unprepared." The next day, Murphy panics when she hears that she must participate in a segment with a bake-off champion, and she moans, "The last time I tried to bake brownies, I had to call in an industrial cleaning service." During the segment, Corky startles Murphy by separating an egg with one hand. Corky's baking expertise is manifest, and Murphy is challenged. She becomes obsessed with learning to separate eggs and annoys the bake-off champion. Murphy ruins the segment as she and the bake-off champion do verbal (and nearly physical) battle and have to be pried apart by Corky. Murphy's choice of competition instead of cooperation leads to disaster and her dearth of culinary skills further demonstrates her lack of traditional femininity.

By the end of this episode, Murphy is humbled and she must admit that Corky did the better job. Murphy is humiliated because she is not traditionally feminine enough, in terms of social facilitation or cooking skills, to fulfill the assigned role. De-spite the fact that her particular traits have led to success in "hard news," when she fails at "soft news," she is punished. Again, Murphy is the victim of dual expectations. Corky, whose traditionally feminine skills are appropriate for the situation, shines on the morning show, although she has failed in the past at "hard news" assignments.

This episode adds strength to two major themes of *Murphy Brown*. The first is that a woman cannot both be professionally successful and retain traditional qualities of femininity. Murphy is rich and famous, but not a "real" woman in personality or per-sonal relationships. Corky, in contrast, is more traditionally feminine in appearance and behavior but she is professionally competent only in the typically female province of lower status, "soft" news situations. *Murphy Brown* only allows for polar concep-tions of womanhood, refusing to permit integration of traditionally bifurcated mascu-line and feminine qualities attached to the public and private spheres.

Second, this episode and others discussed in this essay demonstrate Murphy's function as comic scapegoat. By sacrificing Murphy through humiliation, embarrassment, or ridicule, *Murphy Brown* "turns the tables" on the basic project of liberal feminism, which is to critique how the public sphere excludes women. Instead, Murphy's dysfunctionality as an excessive representation of liberal feminism becomes the focus, and *Murphy Brown* is about how she fails to adjust adequately to the demands placed upon her, *even though those demands are inherently contradictory.*

Burke argues that the general attitude of classical comedy is "charitable," designed to promote cooperation and resolution of differences (Burke, 1959, p. 166). This is also the basic philosophy of television situation comedy narrative, which centers on the need to resolve some problem that threatens the situation. The way in which such problems are resolved says much about the values promoted by a series. For example, patriarchal authority is promoted in 1950s sitcoms like *Leave It to Beaver* or *Father Knows Best,* in which the correct resolution of a problem inevitably follows the wisdom of the father.

While they prefer to emphasize the progressive effects of comedy, both Burke and Duncan note the potential for social control as a function of comic strategies. The comic scapegoating in *Murphy Brown* is an example. While the qualities that cause problems for Murphy are endemic to and sustained by the patriarchy, the narrative of *Murphy Brown* makes it easier to view Murphy as the aggressor rather than the victim and to see the fault in her *character* as a representative of liberal feminism rather than in the *culture* which contains conflicting messages for women. Thus, resolution is achieved by censure of Murphy's actions.

Such a strategy works to naturalize patriarchal conceptions of "appropriate" behavior and gender roles and to make violation of such roles unappealing. As Burke notes, "Insofar as those for whom the frame is comparatively adequate are kept . . . from noting its limitations, it is the 'culturally dispossessed' whom they accuse of 'attitudinizing' " (1959, p. 40). As *Murphy Brown* tells it, Murphy is deviate and needs to be controlled. By controlling Murphy, feminism's threat to the patriarchy is contained. As I discuss in the final section, this interpretation of *Murphy Brown* has implications for understanding television's rhetorical function and for the role of feminist theory in assessing that function.

Conclusion

Murphy Brown is a highly rated, award-winning situation comedy entering its fourth season, and the interpretation offered in this essay can be used to understand the series' continuing popularity. For those who search for emancipatory images of women on television, Murphy Brown is exemplary on several levels. Her struggles make her sympathetic to an audience that empathizes with the contradictions that she faces. Such an audience may supplement the individualistic explanations of Murphy's problems offered by the series with an awareness of the difficulties that successful women face in a hostile culture. Indeed, some feminists may enjoy *Murphy Brown* precisely because they are willing to "fill in" information the series does not provide.

However, for an audience uncomfortable with the challenge that feminism presents to many cherished assumptions. Murphy's function as a comedic character, whose extreme personality traits are often the source of humor, provides the relief necessary to keep her character appealing. The fact that Murphy "suffers" for her success makes it easier to accept her rejection of traditional womanhood. For these viewers, Corky offers an alternative source for identification and reassurance that traditional femininity is a valid choice.

In short, it is possible to identify with Murphy and empathize with her problems or to find her a humorous object and rejoice in her comeuppances. Either decision reflects the value placed on the program's meaning by viewers (Condit, 1989). That *Murphy Brown* offers material open to divergent evaluations is an economic asset rather than a liability, especially within the competitive world of prime-time television entertainment.

As a feministic critic, however, I find it difficult to celebrate *Murphy Brown*'s qualified feminist vision. Like *TMTMS*, *Murphy Brown* illustrates a variation on television's general rhetorical strategy of coopting feminist content to serve patriarchal interests, a tactic also visible in other forms of cultural discourse.[4] Both *TMTMS* and *Murphy Brown* rely on liberal feminist premises that assume the erosion of barriers to women in the public sphere is the end goal of feminism. Once women receive equal opportunity, feminism has won.

This is the most common interpretation of feminism, and it is also the easiest for television to incorporate without a real challenge to patriarchal interests, because it "perpetuates the values of the status quo and limits the possibility of challenges to those values" (Jaggar, 1983, p. 197). This means that women who enter the public sphere are responsible for adjusting to its demands, even when those demands are contradictory. If a woman cannot adjust successfully, it is interpreted as individual failure rather than unfairness in the "system" that they had no role in creating.

Liberal feminism does not account for factors that limit a woman's ability to compete successfully, including race, class, or gender-role expectations. For example, Josephine Donovan notes that liberal feminism does not seriously consider "that the division of the world into public and private and the assumption that women uphold the domestic world—including the duty of child-rearing—might interfere with women's ability to enjoy equal rights and opportunities, even if they were granted" (1985, p. 27). Indeed, in its portrayal of a single, well-educated, upper-class woman with no dependents, *Murphy Brown* totally sidesteps such issues.

This analysis of the limitations of liberal feminism as interpreted in *Murphy Brown* illustrates two (of many) possibilities for future feminist rhetorical analysis. First, the study of television discourse *about* women enriches our understanding of patriarchal rhetorical strategies that function to interpret feminism and femininity for popular audiences. Second, this analysis indicates the need for critical engagement with feminist theory by rhetorical critics. For instance, my negative evaluation of the manipulation of liberal feminism in *Murphy Brown* is influenced by a radical feminist perspective, which defines women's problems "not as symptoms of individual failure but as symptoms of oppression by a system of male dominance" (Jaggar, 1983, pp. 85–86). Using this perspective, Murphy's problems are larger than her personality, reflecting instead the continuing dichotomy between the public and private spheres and between cultural valuations of masculine and feminine behavior.

However, such an evaluation is possible only when the adequacy of liberal feminist assumptions is questioned and alternatives are considered. Inevitably, this will lead to recognition that "feminism" is a contested term. While this realization may be disquieting, it also opens new possibilities for feminist rhetorical analysis, feminist rhetorical theory, and, ultimately, for genuine social change.

NOTES

1. For the purposes of this essay, I use patriarchy in the sense defined by Adrienne Rich: "Any form of group organization in which males hold dominant power and determine what part females shall and shall not play, and in which capabilities assigned to women are relegated generally to the mystical and aesthetic and excluded from the practical and political realms" (1979, p. 78).
2. Women's role on television has received some attention. A number of content analytic or descriptive studies have analyzed the inclusion, exclusion, and status of women in television programming (e.g., Meehan, 1983; Steeves & Smith, 1988; Tuchman, 1978). Moreover, some critics have taken a critical approach to symbolic representations of women on television (e.g., Kaplan, 1987; Modleski, 1982). Little work has taken an explicitly feminist rhetorical approach to television, an approach that I view as including two specific foci. First, such work is explicitly evaluative, concerned with how an artifact works rhetorically to aid or hinder feminist progress. Such evaluation depends on the critic's working definition of feminism. A second and related concern emphasizes rhetoric's probable function for an audience in a particular culture. To borrow Kenneth Burke's phrase, such a perspective sees television as "equipment for living" (1973, p. 304), an artifact to be studied not simply for its aesthetic dimensions but for its influence on the values that define a culture. Thus, television is not simply entertaining, it is persuasive, containing "strategies for selecting enemies and allies, for socializing losses, for warding off evil eye [sic], for purification, propitiation, and desanctification, consolation and vengeance, admonition and exhortation, implicit commands of one sort or another" (Burke, 1973, p. 304).
3. Episode titles were provided by the *Murphy Brown* production office.
4. For example, criticism of the rhetoric of ERA opponents has revealed strategies designed to depict feminist lifestyles as extremist, unattractive, and personally unfulfilling (Foss, 1979; Solomon, 1979). Murphy Brown closely parallels the "deviate" persona that Sonja Foss has argued was attributed to Equal Rights Amendment proponents by those who opposed the ERA: "Proponents are radical militant libbers (rather than feminine women); professional and executive women (rather than wives and mothers); masculine, aggressive women with personal problems (rather than feminine women who are content with their roles); and represent un-American values such as Communism and a hatred of children (rather than freedom and a love of children)" (1979, p. 286).

REFERENCES

Alley, R., & Brown, I. B. (1989). *Love is all around: The making of The Mary Tyler Moore Show.* New York: Delta.
Alley, R., & Brown, I. B. (1990). *Murphy Brown: Anatomy of a sitcom.* New York: Delta.
Burke, K. (1959). *Attitudes toward history* (2nd ed.). Berkeley, CA: University of California Press.

Burke, K. (1973). *The philosophy of literary form* (3rd ed.). Berkeley, CA: University of California Press.

Campbell, K. K. (1973). The rhetoric of women's liberation: An oxymoron. *Quarterly Journal of Speech, 59,* 74–86.

Campbell, K. K. (1980). "The solitude of self": A humanistic rationale for feminism. *Quarterly Journal of Speech, 66,* 304–312.

Campbell, K. K. (1985, January). The communication classroom: A chilly climate for women? *ACA Bulletin,* No. 51, 68–72.

Campbell, K. K. (1986). Style and content in the rhetoric of early Afro-American feminists. *Quarterly Journal of Speech, 72,* 434–445.

Campbell, K. K. (1989). *Man cannot speak for her, vol. 1: A critical study of early feminist rhetoric; vol 2: Key texts of the early feminists.* New York: Greenwood.

Campbell, K. K. (1991). Hearing women's voices. *Communication Education, 40,* 33–48.

Carlson, A. C. (1986). Gandhi and the comic frame: "Ad bellum purificandum." *Quarterly Journal of Speech, 72,* 446–455.

Cavett, D. (1989, December 23). Candice Bergen: She's no dummy. *TV Guide,* 7–9.

Chesebro, J. W. (1991). Communication, values, and popular television series—A seventeen year assessment. *Communication Quarterly, 39,* 197–225.

Condit, C. (1989). The rhetorical limits of polysemy. *Critical Studies in Mass Communication, 6,* 103–122.

Donovan. J. (1985). *Feminist theory: The intellectual traditions of American feminism.* New York: Frederick Ungar.

Dow, B. J. (1990). Hegemony, feminist criticism and *The Mary Tyler Moore Show. Critical Studies in Mass Communication, 7,* 261–274.

Dow, B. J. (1991). The "womanhood" rationale in the woman suffrage rhetoric of Frances E. Willard. *Southern Communication Journal, 56,* 298–307.

Duncan, H. D. (1962). *Communication and social order.* New York: Oxford University Press.

Elm, J. (1989, December 23). What TV's real newswomen think of Murphy Brown. *TV Guide,* 4–7.

Foss, K. A., & Foss, S. K. (1983). The status of research on women and communication. *Communication Quarterly, 31,* 220–223.

Foss, S. F. (1979). Equal rights amendment controversy: Two worlds in conflict. *Quarterly Journal of Speech, 65,* 275–288.

Hall, S. (1982). The rediscovery of "ideology": Return of the repressed in media studies. In M. Guretvitch, T. Bennett, & J. Wollacott (Eds.), *Culture, society, and the media* (pp. 56–90). London: Methuen.

Horowitz, J. (1989, April 9). On TV, Ms. Macho and Mr. Wimp. *New York Times,* 1H, 36H.

Jaggar, A. (1983). *Feminist politics and human nature.* Totowa, NJ: Rowman and Allanheld.

Japp, P. M. (1985). Esther or Isaiah? The abolitionist-feminist rhetoric of Angelina Grimké. *Quarterly Journal of Speech, 71,* 335–348.

Kaplan, E. A. (1987). Feminist criticism and television. In R. Allen (Ed.). *Channels of discourse: Television and contemporary criticism* (pp. 211–253). Chapel Hill, NC: University of North Carolina Press.

Lorde, A. (1984). *Sister outsider.* Trumansberg, NY: The Crossing Press.

Meehan, D. (1983). *Ladies of the evening: Women characters of prime-time television.* Metuchen, NJ: Scarecrow Press.

Modleski, T. (1982). *Loving with a vengeance: Mass-produced fantasies for women.* New York: Archon.

Murphy, J. M. (1989). Comic strategies and the American Covenant. *Communication Studies, 40,* 266–279.

Nightingale, V. (1990). Women as audiences. In M. E. Brown (Ed.). *Television and women's culture* (pp. 25–36). London: Sage.

O'Connor, J. (1989, November 27). An updated Mary Richards in "Murphy Brown." *The New York Times,* Y17.

O'Reilly, J. (1989, May 27). At last! Women worth watching. *TV Guide,* 18–21.

Panitt, M. (1989, February 4). Murphy Brown. *TV Guide,* 40.

Rich, A. (1979). *On lies, secrets, and silence: Selected prose, 1966–1978.* New York: W. W. Norton.

Rowland, R. (Ed.). (1984). *Women who do and women who don't join the feminist movement.* London: Routledge and Kegan Paul.

Solomon, M. (1979). The "positive woman's" journey: A mythic analysis of the rhetoric of Stop ERA. *Quarterly Journal of Speech, 65,* 262–74.

Spitzack, C. & Carter, K. (1987). Women in communication studies: A typology for revision. *Quarterly Journal of Speech, 73,* 401–423.

Spitzack, C. & Carter, K. (1989). Research on women's communication: The politics of theory and method. In Carter, K. & Spitzack, C. (Eds.). *Doing research on women's communication: Perspectives on theory and method* (pp. 11–39). Norwood, NJ: Ablex.

Steeves, H. L. (1987). Feminist theories and media studies. *Critical Studies in Mass Communication, 4,* 95–135.

Steeves, H. L. & Smith, M. C. (1987). Class and gender in prime-time television entertainment: Observations from a socialist feminist perspective. *Journal of Communication Inquiry, 11,* 48–62.

Tuchman, G., Daniels, A., & Benet, J. (Eds.). (1978). *Hearth and home: Images of women in the mass media.* New York: Oxford University Press.

Waters, H. F., & Huck, J. (1989, March 13). Networking women. *Newsweek,* p. 48–55.

Wisehart, B. (1989, December 24). Murphy and Mary: Similar but so unalike. *Star Tribune* (Mpls.), 39.

Zehme, B. (1989, November 6). Candice Bergen: Sitcom queen cracks the mold. *Chicago Tribune,* 2, 1–2.

Oliver Stone's Not-So-*Wild Palms*: A Postmodern Critique

A. Susan Owen and Peter Ehrenhaus

The texture of life in contemporary American society has undergone fundamental change during the second half of the twentieth century, such that the character of our lived experience differs significantly from that of the past. One way in which scholars and commentators have addressed this transformation is with the terms "modern" and "postmodern." In this selection, we introduce you to the general terrain of postmodern criticism through an analysis of a television mini-series, noteworthy for its style and substance as well as for the controversy surrounding its producer, Oliver Stone. Stone, an Academy Award-winning director, has achieved notoriety; viewed as both brilliant and disreputable, Stone has become a cultural artifact whose own significance intermingles with the ventures in which he is involved. In the pages that follow, we will discuss how the mini-series *Wild Palms* and Stone blend and blur to the point where each informs the other.

Assumptions About Television and Society

In a "modern" world view, purpose, reason, and coherence are the building blocks of progress; to progress, a society must create and have faith in a variety of institutions (e.g., government, education, religion, science, and technology) and the various hierarchical social relationships that accompany them (e.g., gender, family, class, race). While "modernity" offers great promise of a better world, it does so at a price of constraint and restriction: people must fit themselves within the range of preferred social roles and conduct themselves in ways that endorse and perpetuate the institutional and social structure of their society.

For example, much has been made recently of the phrase "family values." The phrase is bandied about as if it had a clear, agreed upon meaning; the demise of "family values" is viewed as the source of a litany of social ills. If only "it" were to regain its rightful stature, then society would regain its former harmony and function smoothly. From a modernist perspective, family values has clear and stable entailments: a two-parent family, traditional gender roles, a commitment to a particular set of moral tenets, and a middle-class standard of economic stability. We also can glimpse here two key assumptions of modernity. Language must have clear conceptual referents; words must signify things. Moreover, language use is indicative of thought, what the speaker has in mind, and therefore has entailments for future action. Thus, the old (sexist) maxim: "A man's word is his bond."

By contrast, a "postmodern" world view sees paradox, fragmentation, fatigue, and play. Why do some presume this shift? The answer can be found in at least two arenas. First, the primary institutions that have given structure, order, and reason to our world, and that have given us a sense of control over it, have faltered; public faith in institutions of government, education, religion, and science and technology to solve problems has eroded. As often as not, these institutions seem to operate in contradiction to the interests of those whom they ostensibly are designed to serve: Government lies to its citizens; education is driven increasingly by the narrow concerns of training and preparation for the workforce; religious dogma rings hollow in the face of everyday life's growing sense of pointlessness; and corporate science and technology privilege the pursuits of knowledge and profit at the expense of human welfare. In sum, the center, a core of rationally agreed upon commitments about what we should value and how we should structure our world, no longer seems to hold; the center has fractured. But all is not grim: With fragmentation comes liberation; the absence of a center means that there is no organized whole into which we must integrate ourselves, and opportunities for personal expression and forms of social organization proliferate. Here, family values is a highly contested concept, with no agreed upon referents. "Family," much less "family values," is continually open, perpetually able to be reshaped and redefined as diverse human needs and material conditions dictate. In postmodernity, meaning is endlessly mutable.

Another hallmark of postmodernity is the compression of experienced time and the reconstruction of space (Harvey, 1989). Once the printed word, the spoken word, and face-to-face conversation were the primary modes of social interaction; now, messages are mediated largely by electronics and telecommunications. When experienced time moved more slowly, we could meaningfully speak about the integrity of a single message, its substance, its influence, and its implications for future action. But now, amidst the clatter of competing voices and images, the integrity of a single message, and a single voice, becomes lost. The former luxury of a concern with substance has been supplanted by the demands of contending with a barrage of endlessly circulating images and intersecting message fragments. And our ability to gain access to an ever increasing array of mediated images is equaled by our ability to move among those images (e.g., channel surfing). Consider further that with the prospect of virtual reality technology, we will even be able to insert ourselves *into* the messages! Where once we assumed that the reader/viewer consumed whole messages created by others, we now see the reader/viewer actively assembling "the message" from the perpetual swirl of fragments in which she or he is awash (see McGee, 1990). For these reasons, we find it no longer valuable to refer to our society, or our time, as modern. We have moved beyond that into the postmodern condition. And television occupies a prominent place in that condition.

Television's significance is not merely technological. Because of the endless recirculation of programming (the replay of the already said), new expressions of human experience are possible. Viewed critically, old programming can reveal culturally entrenched prejudices of race, class, and gender; viewed ironically, we end up with *Nick at Nite* on the Nickelodeon cable network. For those who appreciate a playful treatment of classic American television programming from the 1960s, their framing of this material cannot help but color the manner in which they view equally dated programs on the Family Channel, which presents the same material as evidence of the wholesome "way we were" and ought to be again (Collins, 1992).

Assumptions About the Role of the Critic, Criticism, and the Audience

Television is a site where the strands of mass, popular culture intersect. As Barry Brummett (1994) observes, "[p]opular culture refers to those systems or artifacts that most people share and that most people know about." Moreover, he asserts that "television is an immensely rich world of popular culture" (p. 21). At a variety of levels, viewers cross reference their viewing experience; they bring to their viewing a sophisticated capacity for ironic interpretation, an ability to interpret their focus of attention by contextualizing it with other cultural fragments. This is not just a matter of being able to participate in in-jokes, but of experiencing the world seamlessly. As the quintessential postmodern medium, television is the central cultural site of "intertextual play," of the "already said" (Eco, 1984).

Like Stuart Hall (1980), we believe viewers are interactive participants in constructing their televisual experience. Thus, we advocate the perspective that texts are more and less "open" or "closed," enabling (or encouraging) a wide range of interpretations and viewpoints, or a restrictive, conventional interpretive frame. (We believe most texts actually are a combination of open and closed moments.) Further, viewers may opt to interact with the "preferred" reading of a text responding to the cues in the text which suggest how it is meant to be read (Seiter, 1992), or "oppositional" readings of the text, deliberately "reading against the grain" or reading in opposition to the "preferred" structure of the text. (See Chapter 6 on Text-Centered Approaches.) So, for example, one might read the relatively closed, annually televised Miss America pageant in a preferred manner, interpreting the broadcast as the achievement of highly valued status for women through goal setting, hard work, and talent. Or, one might read the pageant oppositionally as racist, sexist, and exclusionary—or view the program ironically as other fictional television characters might view it or participate in it. Imagine how the women of *Living Single, Cybill,* or *Ellen* might view the pageant, or how the Simpsons or the Bundys of *Married with Children* might disrupt the proceedings in Atlantic City. Keeping in mind that open/closed and preferred/oppositional always are relative to time, place, and viewing experience, viewers bring to their viewing experience cultural fragments from other television programs, other cultural forums, and their own situated cultural practices influenced by social role development.

Assumptions About the "Short Series" and Its Reception

Wild Palms, promoted as a television "event," was broadcast during the May 1993 sweeps week. Since the purpose of the short series was to garner ratings shares for ABC, we would expect programming to cater to sensationalism, popular with mainstream audiences. Traditionally, this translates as sex, money, power, and intrigue. Of course, all networks provide such spectacular programming, and the issue then becomes: How does one network differentiate its special programming from those of its competitors? In terms of product, *Wild Palms* sought distinction by wrapping its story in the high-tech cloak of virtual reality technology and the spectacle of charismatically powerful cults, two issues having received broad coverage by American mass media. In addition, the popular press touted this event as Oliver Stone's first venture into television. Stone recently had created a major stir among mainstream news journalists, historians, and the general public with his release of the film *JFK.* (We shall return to this point in our analysis.) Finally, the event was promoted as being the product of a number of different film directors; this strategy was designed to imbue the program with the legitimacy of cinematic art.

By attending to the economic parameters of the broadcast we can infer the underlying actual viewing audience that sponsors hoped to reach. In our analysis, we will expand "audience" to include the implied audience, by which we no longer mean audience-as-people, but audience as value orientation (i.e., what is good, normal, preferred), suggested by the narrative itself.

If television is the quintessential postmodern medium, then criticism should be sensitive to assumptions of postmodernity. In our approach, criticism operates as an interplay between two levels of analysis, the micro and the macro. By micro, we refer to the close analysis of the particular work itself. Here, we examine the televisual text (e.g., a scene, an episode, a series, or a genre) for evidence of structural or substantive features of postmodernity. Rather than approaching a televisual text as postmodern or not (again, the problem with essences, the presumed inherent meaning and stability of linguistic categories), we explore the extent to which a text exhibits features consistent with tenets of postmodernity. On the macro level, we locate a meaningful context within which to situate that televisual text; in this sense, the critic identifies the boundaries of the text, gleaned from fragments of broader cultural experience. By placing the televisual text (a cultural fragment) in context (constructed of other cultural fragments), the critic enables others to see how televisual texts fit into structures of institutional power that are not immediately apparent. In this manner, criticism enables viewers to become increasingly self-reflective so they can enter into a critical dialogue about the moral choices in their personal lives and in our collective life as members of a community.

We began this project with only four assumptions about Stone's work: (1) he upsets established media moguls; (2) his work seems to provoke controversy, and hence public examination, of painful episodes in American history; (3) the gender politics in all his films (including *Heaven and Earth*) are masculinist—meaning traditional, mainstream, and Anglo (see Jeffords, 1989; Sturken, 1997); and (4) his Vietnam combat experience appeared to have shattered his faith in modernist principles of reason, the common good, and civic virtue as anything more than rhetorical fictions. We were genuinely surprised to learn, as a result of our study, that Stone's work affirms the promises and illusions of modernity. We now see a deeply conflicted paradox in Stone's work; we shall explore that paradox in the following analysis.

Our criticism is developed in three sections. First, we provide an overview of the major characters, and lay out the general terrain of the narrative. Second, we discuss the manner in which *Wild Palms* reflects—and opposes—tenets of postmodernism (i.e., our micro analysis). Finally, we construct a broader cultural context within which *Wild Palms* may be placed, thus seeing it as one manifestation of a broader cultural struggle over the merits, promise, and dangers of modernism and postmodernism (i.e., our macro analysis).

Oliver Stone's *Wild Palms:* Postmodern Play, Sacred Cows, and Righteous Indignation

Partial Cast of Characters

Senator Tony Kreutzer (Robert Loggia): megalomaniac; U.S. Senator; charismatic founder of the Fathers; chair of the board, the Wild Palms Group

Josie (Angie Dickenson): psychotic; murderess sister to the Senator; Grace Wyckoff's mother; member of the inner circle of the Fathers

Harry Wyckoff (James Belushi): patent attorney; protagonist of the story; latecomer to the Friends, and the movement's eventual leader

Grace Wyckoff (Dana Delaney): Harry's wife; Josie's and Eli's daughter

Paige Katz (Kim Cattrall): the Senator's lover; kidnapped as a child by the Fathers; as adult, an agent of the Fathers and the Wild Palms Group; eventual member of the Friends

Cody: "son" of Grace and Harry; biological son of the Senator and Paige; switched at birth by the Fathers with Peter; charismatic child preacher for Church of Synthiotics

Deirdre: daughter of Grace and Harry

Peter: biological son of Grace and Harry; raised by the Friends; knows "the big picture," including identity of his parents

Tommy (Ernie Hudson): Harry's friend; apparent member of the Fathers; real member of the Friends; Tully's lover

Tully: artist; member of the Friends; Tommy's lover

Eli Levitt (David Warner): a leader of the Friends; Josie's ex-husband; Grace's father

Chickie Levitt: Eli's son (with his second wife, not with Josie); master technologist of virtual reality; Grace's half-brother

Dex Wyckoff: deceased cuckold "father" of Harry; inventor of Mimezine; former partner with the Senator

The Narrative

The story of *Wild Palms* is told over six hours, encompassing four episodes. The story is told in *analepsis,* in which information is given to the viewer out of chronological sequence; narrative events make sense to the viewer only after they have occurred. For example, the critical pieces of the narrative are provided only during the final episode, explaining events that transpired twenty years in the past. In our analysis we will examine how this apparently fragmented narrative structure provides the appearance of a postmodern text, and also serves the practical function of keeping the viewer involved and interested in demystifying the interwoven plot lines. Here we will explicate the narrative by introducing the mysteries set up in the first two-hour episode and presenting their resolution as revealed in the final episode.

The story opens in Los Angeles of 2007. We are first introduced to the family of Harry Wyckoff, a patent attorney hoping to make partner in his firm. His wife, Grace, is the quintessential good mother and wife, who works in boutique fashion. We next meet Josie, Grace's mother, as she comes home from her umpteenth face-lift. Harry and Grace have two beautiful children, Cody and Deirdre. They live in great comfort in a beautiful home, in an exclusive residential district. On the surface, all is well, but we soon discover that every relationship is fraught with mystery and tension. Harry and Grace are having sexual problems. Harry is plagued by inexplicable nightmares in which he sees a white rhinoceros; jolted awake from his nightmare he utters enigmatically, "So this is how it begins. . . ." Grace seems deeply menaced by Josie, viper-like beneath her veneer of gracious sophistication. Cody displays genuine affection for Josie, but is utterly cold toward his mother, forbidding even her touch. Deirdre, five years old, never speaks.

Problems are not limited to the Wyckoff family. Harry drives to work in his vintage Corvette, passing by incidents of beatings and muggings along the streets of upscale L.A. At the office, Harry is visited by Paige Katz, a lover from their college days, who asks Harry to find her missing son, Peter; he agrees to help her. Harry goes to lunch with his good friend, Tommy; while at a fashionable bistro, a patron is beaten and dragged from his table. No one but Harry attempts to intervene. Pulling him back, Tommy tells him to stay out of it. As Harry drives back to his office, he sees Paige and Josie driving together. Curious about how they know each other, he follows them to a presentation by the Wild Palms Group, a multimedia conglomerate. While Josie is nowhere to be seen, Paige introduces him to U.S. Senator Tony Kreutzer, chair of the board of the Wild Palms Group and founder of the Church of Synthiotics, a cult-like religion espousing the "New Realism," a "new, improved reality" based in the technologies of holography and virtual reality.

When we next return to Harry's firm, Paige has been identified by Harry's colleagues as an agent of the Wild Palms Group, which is a competitor of one of their clients. Because of their association, Harry is tainted, and he is denied partnership in the law firm. In a fit of rage, he quits. Harry returns home, where he learns that his son, Cody, will be an actor on *Church Windows*, a new virtual reality sitcom to appear on Channel 3, the Wild Palms network. That evening, Paige shows up at Harry's home, and invites him to Rancho Mirage, the Senator's retreat in the Palm Springs desert. Harry accepts and during their meeting the Senator offers Harry a position as chief of acquisitions for the Wild Palms Group at five times his old salary. Intrigued and flattered, he returns to L.A., discusses the offer with Grace, and takes the position.

We next find Tommy driving Harry to meet Chickie Levitt, a crippled computer whiz who has perfected the interactive virtual reality experience. As Tommy and Harry drive to Chickie's, they discuss rival political groups—the neo-fascist Fathers and the libertarian Friends. Tommy makes veiled references to mass child kidnappings during the 1990s. Along the way, we again see beatings and muggings in broad daylight. Chickie introduces himself to Harry; he reveals his hatred of the Fathers for crippling him and killing his mother. Here, Harry has his first virtual reality experience. He and Tommy don virtual reality glasses, and step into "cyberspace" where they encounter Chickie Levitt's fantasy world of 18th-century French royalty. In this world, Chickie dances effortlessly with a beautiful ballerina, herself (himself) a hologram simultaneously generated by another computer in Japan.

Shortly after this episode, Chickie is abducted by the Wild Palms Group in what is essentially a case of corporate raiding; the Group must have Chickie's technology. Chickie is drugged with Mimezine, an empathogen that floods the cerebral cortex creating the sensation of actual interaction with one's virtual reality experience. At this juncture, we are introduced to the ultimate prize, the Go-Chip. The Go-Chip is designed to be implanted in the human being, at which point the corporeal body is shed, and the human psyche takes the form of a hologram, unfettered by time or space, and capable of accessing all human consciousness. The Go-Chip is central to the Senator's plan for domination.

As this is transpiring, a woman is abducted by the Senator's operatives under the supervision of Paige. This is the same woman whose dining companion was beaten earlier in the bistro where Harry and Tommy lunched; she is the sister of Tully, a well-known artist. Following her abduction, her broken eyeglasses are then delivered to Tully's studio, at which point he goes berserk. A few scenes later, Tully confronts Josie in her home, demanding the return of his sister, almost strangling Josie to death. Shortly thereafter, Josie retaliates; she and her thugs break into Tully's studio. She tells him that his sister is dead. And as her thugs hold him down, she gouges out his eyes with her fingers.

Meanwhile, Grace slips into a serious depression, deeply troubled by her son's continued rejection and shaken by Harry's relationship to the mysterious Paige. Grace goes with Harry to the Perceptory, a psychiatric hospital/prison, to visit Eli Levitt, whom she describes to Harry as an old family friend. Grace asks Eli about harvesting, the abduction of the children of political enemies. We learn that Eli is really her father, a political prisoner for the past twenty years. Shortly after this, Grace confronts her mother, Josie, about the abduction of children, and demands to know whether Cody is her son. Josie dismisses her daughter as absurd. About this time, Harry begins to be shadowed by a dark-haired boy of about ten, a street urchin who seems to survive by his own wits.

In the final scene, a frantic Paige locates Harry. She tells him that she and her operatives have found her son's kidnapper, and implores him to join the chase. Despite his protestations that he is only a lawyer, Harry joins in the pursuit that reaches its climax on the beach. As they scramble from the cars, Paige forces a gun into Harry's hand, urging him to capture the fleeing kidnapper. Bewildered, Harry runs in pursuit, tackling his prey on the sand. Rolling the kidnapper over, he is astonished. It is Tommy, who utters the closing line of the episode: "So this is how it begins. . . ."

The relational clarification in the final episode enables all of the disparate fragments of action that we have viewed to fit together coherently. Harry Wyckoff is the Senator's son; he is not, as he had believed, the son of Dex Wyckoff, the inventor of Mimezine and the Senator's former partner. Furthermore, Harry's marriage to Grace was arranged by the Fathers. The college romance between Paige and Harry was stopped. Paige was being groomed as the Senator's wife; as a child she had been abducted by the Fathers because her father, a famous journalist, opposed the Senator. Through Paige, the Senator fathered Cody, who was switched at birth with Grace and Harry's actual son, Peter, the self-reliant street urchin. Cody, then, is really Harry's half-brother, not his son. We also learn that Josie is the Senator's sister and Eli Levitt's first wife. Moreover, Josie murdered Eli's second wife and crippled their child, Chickie Levitt; thus, Chickie and Grace are really half-brother and sister.

In the plot resolutions, the Friends defeat the Fathers, and characters receive their just rewards. The Senator has the Go-Chip implanted, but his hologram disintegrates; Peter and Harry tampered with the chip, putting a virus in it. Josie drowns Eli and strangles her daughter, Grace, to death. She, in turn, is killed at the hands of Tully, who then kills himself, because his lover, Tommy, has died of "image sickness," the result of Mimezine poisoning. Chickie Levitt dies of abuse suffered at the hands of his kidnappers. Cody, the classic bad seed child, dies in a raging inferno while preaching to the remnants of his following in the Church of Synthiotics. Harry becomes the new leader of the Friends. Paige is redeemed through her love for Harry, and survives to form a new family unit with Harry, Peter, and Deirdre. As the final episode concludes, we see the four of them driving to the beach in Harry's classic Corvette. Deirdre, united with her biological brother, speaks; she lavishes love on her father. At the beach, Harry and his new family lean against the car; our final view of them is in silhouette as the sunlight fades.

Postmodernity in Wild Palms

Wild Palms is filled with the stuff of postmodernity. To begin, the narrative develops in nontraditional fashion, with multiple, intersecting story lines, no central narrative voice, and the introduction of key information only after the fact. As the plot resolution reveals, nothing is as it appears. Visually, we find extensive use of cross-cutting between developing scenes, vibrant electric colors, stark contrast between intense brightness and near darkness, and surrealistic imagery and texture. Stylistically, the cyberpunk theme (e.g., the futuristic commingling of technology with nature and with religion) drives the narrative: The Senator seeks cultural domination through technologically achieved immortality. Semiotically, the style is bricolage, in which previously existing cultural signifiers are customized, recombined, and rearticulated (Collins, 1992). The well-dressed male business executive wears Edwardian-style suits and crisp white shirts with high starched collars; the music track is filled with vintage songs from the 1960s, offering allusions to the chaotic intensity of the drug culture and a society at war with itself over civil rights and Vietnam; Harry drives a classic Corvette convertible; and perhaps most postmodern of all, Oliver Stone parodies himself by appearing on a television program within the story, in which his conspiracy explanation of the Kennedy assassination finally is vindicated.

A measure of postmodernity's grasp on the American psyche is to be found in audiences' acceptance of any paranoid view of politics as plausible. Yet conspiracies and co-conspirators notwithstanding, television narratives must tread lightly when matters turn to the mythology of traditional American values. Plot lines can play with alternative lifestyles, "nonconventional" sexuality, and a litany of vices and social defects. But characters who personify those positions must be destroyed or devalued; those who personify even a modicum of redeeming social value may be saved, but only after recognizing their sins and seeking forgiveness. Television is a conservative medium because sponsors seek the widest range of lucrative consumers for their products and services.

Despite its stylized and high-tech trappings, *Wild Palms* is a cautionary tale of the evils, emptiness, and illusions of postmodernity. It reaffirms the virtues of modernism. We see this in three arenas. First, the story reaffirms the importance of having (and knowing) an immutable reality. The implicit message is that postmodernity ultimately is nihilistic and fascist; in the commingling of image and substance, in the endless play of signifiers, we lose our capacity to know what is "true" or "real," and thus fall prey to those who seek to dominate through the distractions and play that postmodernity offers. Second, it presumes that gender is biologically determined. True and good women are driven by their maternal instincts and need for fulfillment through a loving, monogamous, secure, and heterosexual relationship; men, good or bad, are driven by the need for power, achievement, and the desire to protect and control. And third, contentment is to be found in a Norman Rockwell vision of the family structure and society, more generally, much as we described earlier as "modern" family values.

The dangers of postmodernity are readily reflected in the tenets of New Realism and its Church of Synthiotics, which offer a new and improved reality. Once transformed by the Go-Chip, the Senator will "be able to reach into our dreams . . . he'll be like Christ." The movement's slogan, "Everything Must Go," portends the utter destabilization of society, to be replaced by image. Grace, the feminized pawn in this game of power politics, articulates the fascistic texture of postmodernity: "I don't know who to believe, what to believe . . . one day we're gonna find out in the middle of *Church Windows* our country no longer belongs to us . . . and nobody will even care!" And Josie, who is videotaped strangling to death her daughter, Grace, responds to a journalist's assertion that images don't lie ("But seeing is believing.") with deadpan dismissal: "You must be kidding." Here is the utter collapse of meaning, of stable relationships between signifier and signified, of perception and event: shades of Rodney King and O.J.

The story is also traditional in its assumptions about gender: Women compete for men; men compete for power and prestige. Women fight over husbands and children; men fight over affairs of state. Women are distorted by power politics; men express their true selves through it. Women are the victims of others' actions; men simply suffer the consequences of their deeds. Consider Grace and Josie. Grace is the good mother, wife, daughter, and friend; in the conflict of power politics, she is destroyed. Josie, the villainous woman, is masculinized in her hunger for power, her willingness to act violently in pursuit of those goals, her predatory sexual practices, and the utter lack of "natural" affection for her daughter. Her only natural affection is an unnatural love for her brother, the Senator—shades of Caligula. Paige, the distorted woman, is redeemable. Turned to evil by circumstance, she overcomes it by getting in touch with her "natural" womanliness; she renounces her place in the masculine world of power politics and sacrifices all to achieve personal salvation, taking her place by Harry's side as mate and mother to his (and Grace's) children. And Harry, the quintessential good guy, survives this tale of apocalyptic proportions unscathed: He gets the girl, he gets the car, he gets the beach house, and he gets to be the head of his family and the leader of the Friends.

Finally, we see the ultimate victory of modernism–stable, conventional relationships and firm grounding in an idyllic reality. As the battle is joined between the Friends (pluralistic modernists) and the Fathers (postmodern fascists), Harry becomes the story's dominant narrative voice. While the Senator disintegrates into cyberspace, Harry proclaims: "Paradise is here." By implication, paradise is not to be found in the nether-world of simulacra, free-floating holographic images (or in free-floating signifiers, for that matter). When pushed to take a political stand, he responds angrily, "These are *my* politics. I want my family back." Modernism sees the world as essentially apolitical; life is lived apart from ideology, not as its manifestation or instantiation. And in the key scene of the plot resolution, a kinder, gentler Paige turns to Harry and asks, "What's real?" With utter sincerity and conviction, Harry answers, "We are." What is entailed by Harry's "We"? A white, heterosexual family unit, traditional gender roles, and a politically and economically secure place in the capital culture.

Speaking with the authority of the narrative voice, Harry expresses his deepest longing as we see the couple in silhouette against a setting sun: "I want to find a Norman Rockwell-type town . . . a decent place . . . where people respect reality." There is nothing parodic in this scene's tone, despite the fact that the Rockwellian world that Harry seeks is illusory. It was never real. It was always already an image.

How is it possible for the enlightened virtues of modernity—personified by Harry and the redeemed Paige—to survive such apocalyptic confrontation? How can life return to normal after homicide, kidnapping, patricide, deviant sexuality, the murders of a spouse and daughter, and the incineration of an adolescent child? Narrative resolution of these horrors is essential if Harry and Paige are to live happily ever after in a reconstituted, heterosexual nuclear family unit. The distancing from Cody is crucial. Adults can die or be killed off because they are responsible for their courageous, evil, immoral, or even unfortunate choices. But the death of a child is different. Cody's character had to be drawn as innately evil and unredeemable. Moreover, the emotional bonds to Cody for Harry and Paige could not be what they initially appeared to be.

Harry could not simply dismiss the death of his son and then move on to a new family; but Cody turned out to be his depraved half-brother. Paige could not set aside the death of a child she bore in love; but it is quite another matter when one's body is used to incubate the satanic progeny of a megalomaniac.

Interestingly, the plot resolutions give us no idea about how the Friends will use the electronics and psycho-pharmacology of virtual reality. Again, by implication, we might assume that modernism's faith in rationality would be able to harness these technologies for some unspecified common good. However, we do know that Harry patented the technologies and then sold their rights to Channel 3's competitors, and we do know that these corporate competitors are driven by profit. Thus, we return to the quandaries of reconciling private gain with public good, and of determining whose voices may even be heard in that debate. And these matters aside, we, as critics, wonder: Is it even possible for humans to use such technology without precipitating even more slippage between reality and image?

Wild Palms *in Postmodernity*

As we noted earlier, one of the responsibilities of postmodern criticism is to bring to light struggles of institutional power that are not immediately apparent in the text. This task requires building a broader pastiche of cultural currents that shape the context. In this case, our context is shaped by what is essentially a dispute among modernists about truth, fact, history, and (ir)rational discourse. We should explore the central paradox in the dispute between Oliver Stone and that portion of the community whose domain is "truth" and "fact," journalists and historians. The paradox is this: In his attempt to recover the promise of modernism, Stone poses a direct threat to it. After exploring this paradox, we offer a postmodernist reading of the controversy, viewing it as a struggle for institutional control of the franchise over defining "truth" and shaping "reality."

Throughout Stone's film work, two themes recur: institutions lie and things are not as they appear. In various ways, these themes infuse *Salvador, Platoon, Wall Street,* and *Born on the Fourth of July, Nixon, JFK,* and *Talk Radio.* But they come together most prominently in *JFK,* and they do so in a way that has evoked vitriolic responses and heated criticism from the mainstream communities of journalists, political commentators, and academic historians. Stone's transgression is not that he is a modernist, for so, too, are members of the mainstream news media and many historians. Stone's sin is that he is an artist, a storyteller, and in his desire to see truth brought to light, to have the real story told, he has committed a wrong as great as any he may hope to right: he has blurred the boundaries between fact and fiction, between reality and fantasy.

Stone's motives are pure. His faith is in the promise of modernity; government can be as good, as moral, and as decent as the people it represents. Evident in *JFK,* one death knell of this promise was the assassination of President Kennedy. In Stone's view, the legacy of Kennedy's murder was the loss of Camelot, a fall from grace: America's Vietnam War, the murders of Robert Kennedy and Martin Luther King, Jr., and the demise of a coherent civil rights movement. As he sees it, the forces that killed John Kennedy were those of entrenched, institutionalized power (i.e., a government within the government), and corporate greed. Thus, by ferreting out those who distort the promise of modernism—based upon the ideals of enlightened pluralistic government and open, rational discourse—modernity's promise can be recovered. And what better way to begin than by refocusing the American public on the morass of uncertainties and inconsistencies surrounding the story of John F. Kennedy's assassination?

Stone dedicated *JFK* to "the young in whose spirit the search for truth marches on." But even during its production, the mainstream news media took aim at it. The *New York Times* wrote that the film was to be based upon " 'the far-out fringe' of conspiracy theories" (Bernstein, 1991, p. 9). Upon its release, Dan Rather of CBS News, Tom Wicker of the *New York Times*, George Lardner of the *Washington Post*, Kenneth Auchincloss of *Newsweek*, and syndicated columnist George Will all castigated Stone. They viewed *JFK* as propaganda, and accused Stone of a blatant disregard of fact and an unethical use of commercial filmmaking conventions (e.g., the misuse of semiotic conventions of documentary filmmaking), in which the lines between fact and conjecture were blurred (see Staples, 1991). The consequences of this irresponsibility, they argued, were the further erosion of public faith in society's primary institutions, and an irrational, conspiratorial paranoia resulting from what they viewed as Stone's disinformation. Wicker, in particular, accused Stone of "rewriting history," advancing the modernist claim that history is a set of knowable and known events, and that to conflate fact with fiction is an unpardonable secular sin, given the importance of history in securing social order and social integration (Wicker, 1991). George Will labeled the film a "travesty," a "celluloid diatribe," and a "three-hour lie." Stone fared worse, tarred by Will as "an intellectual sociopath, indifferent to truth," "combining moral arrogance with historical ignorance," "45 going on 8," and "a specimen of 1960s arrested development." The film "is an act of execrable history and contemptible citizenship by a man of technical skill, scant education and negligible conscience" (Will, 1991, p. B7). These comments offer just a sampling of the journalistic uproar. (Also see MacKenzie, 1991; Specter, 1991; "Twisted history," 1991.)

Stone's response reveals his commitments to modernist tenets of discoverable truths and a "real" reality. Of his critics, he wished that they had "applied the same passionate intensity of effort in trying to find out who *really* killed President Kennedy and why" (Stone, 1991a, p. 4, emphasis added). Moreover, he later observed that: "history may be too important to leave to newsmen. And that artists certainly have the right—and possibly the obligation—to step in and reinterpret the history of our times. . . . The issue of our times . . . is democracy. *Real democracy is not some illusion and must be based on truth told to the people*" (Stone, 1991b, p. B9, emphasis added).

Stone did not offer *JFK* as truth, but as provocation to dig deeper and discover that truth. By offering an "alternative mythology" of the Kennedy assassination—in contrast to the "official mythology" of the Warren Commission report—Stone hoped to compel the press to turn its spotlight again on the assassination, to force the early release of classified documents, and thus, to discover the "real" story.

Stone's film raised hackles in the academic community, as well, though some did find merit in Stone's political project. Writing in the *American Historical Review*, one academic saw the merit of the film this way:

> *JFK* is meant to use the assassination to force an audience to decide whether it wants to ground the American political process in the post-Cold War era with the same structures and habits of mind that governed it during the Cold War. Should, for example, we continue to have secrecy in government obscuring our understanding through the opaque shield of state security? (Raskin, 1992, p. 490)

Though Raskin found merit in Stone's motive, others in academe echoed the dominant, critical posture (see Cohen, 1992; Vogel, 1992).

What does all of this have to do with Oliver Stone and *Wild Palms?* A great deal, especially when one considers that Oliver Stone neither wrote nor directed the miniseries. He served as co-executive producer, a responsibility generally deemed to be "behind the scenes." Significantly, the label of "Oliver Stone's *Wild Palms*" was bestowed by the journalistic community, a designation which we find both intriguing and revealing. As a signifier, "Oliver Stone" often evokes associations with conspiracy, institutional deceit and duplicity, the blurring of fact and fiction, and societal paranoia. By the use of "Oliver Stone" as a modifier of *Wild Palms*, this mini-series becomes linked with the body of Stone's work that has made him controversial. As we have already established, most prominent of these other works is *JFK*, for which Stone was widely attacked for his "irresponsible" handling of history and for a cavalier disregard for accuracy. The fusion of Stone's name with the title of the mini-series also reveals something of the degree to which the mainstream journalistic community sees Stone's work as an attempt to usurp their rightful institutional position. The *New Republic* described the mini-series as "Oliver Stone's bewildering gift to network television" and "Oliver Stone's cyberkitsch" (Star, 1993, p. 32). The *Nation* was less generous in its characterization of Stone and his "technofascism," proclaiming the program as "a rehash of *JFK*, without the controversy; a story that reduces culture and politics to a conspiracy planned by creeps and endured by a passive public." The mini-series is "schizophrenic." Stone himself is a "false prophet of the apocalypse" who "turns his moral outrage on everyone but himself" (Cole, 1993, p. 715).

How can we explain such animosity? After all, this is just another television mini-series, not a major commercial film release. We believe that the hostility toward Stone is symptomatic of a major institutional crisis. From a postmodern perspective, we see these lingering antagonisms as part of a broad, cultural struggle for hegemonic control of public consciousness and the legitimation of the authority to tell the stories that a society chooses to label "reality." In this regard, columnist Ellen Goodman's insights are revealing: "Those of us who are print people—writers and readers—are losing ground to the visual people—producers and viewers. The younger generation gets its information and infotainment from television and movies. Less information. More infotainment. *The franchise over reality is passing hands*" (Goodman, 1991, p. C5, emphasis added).

We view Goodman's observations on the franchising of reality as a contest over power and institutional arrangements, where truth is a matter of authorship and authorship is a window on authority. Historians and the news media are culturally authorized as the keepers of facts and truths. Their legitimate role is to explain what those facts and truths mean, and how they are to be woven together into a coherent, morally positioned story that we can all understand (White, 1987).

Stone was accused of rewriting history, a grievous modernist sin. But as we view the dispute—from our postmodern perch—there is no original draft of the story. Thus, the search for the real story, much like the quest for ultimate truths or the "real" reality, is doomed to failure. What the dispute over *JFK* reveals is that the telling of truth is a matter of power and authority. This is not a matter of disputing the occurrence of events or of denying empirical evidence; it is, however, a matter of questioning that there is an essential and true meaning to those events or that evidence.

In conclusion, Oliver Stone and Harry Wyckoff both seek a Rockwellian world in which people have respect for reality. Both are committed to the fulfillment of modernity's promise, and where they see that promise jeopardized, both are moved to action. Thus, any elements of the postmodern that one finds in Stone's work are merely stylized trappings, tools of artistic license rather than evidence of a world view. What is significant is that the foundation of his work is quintessentially modern. Despite its trappings, *Wild Palms* is a highly conventional narrative, even a romantic myth. Distilled to its basics, it is just another story of the struggle between forces of good and evil, played out on both public (political) and private (domestic) stages. It is a conventionally gendered story about the pursuit of justice and liberty, in which the good guys profess faith in dominant political and social institutions of American culture, and win because of that faith. And despite all its gestures to the openness and play of postmodernism (and thus, to the implications of that openness for human relationships and social organization), when the dust finally settles, all that remains are the civic virtues personified by the white, middle-class nuclear family. Oliver Stone may be the "bad boy" of Hollywood who plays fast and loose with modernist divisions of labor (e.g., who has the right to tell history), with conventional signifiers of fact and fiction (e.g., as in *JFK*), and with the distinction between reality and image, but his heart is pure, for Oliver Stone longs for the promise of the American Dream.

REFERENCES AND RECOMMENDED READINGS

Ansen, D. (1991, Dec. 23). A troublemaker for our times. *Newsweek*, p. 50.

Baudrillard, J. (1983). *Simulations*. (P. Foss, P. Patton, & P. Beitchman, Trans.). New York: Semiotext(e).

Bernstein, R. (1991, July 28). Oliver Stone, under fire over the killing of J.F.K. *New York Times*, II, pp. 9–11.

Best, S. & Kellner, D. (1991). *Postmodern theory: Critical interrogation*. New York: Guilford.

Brummett, B. (1994). *Rhetoric in popular culture*. New York: St. Martin's.

Cohen, J. (1992, June). Yes, Oswald alone killed Kennedy. *Commentary, 93*(6), 32–40.

Cole, L. (1993, May 24). Wild palms. *Nation*, pp. 713–715.

Collins, J. (1992). Postmodernism and television. In R.C. Allen (Ed.), *Channels of discourse, reassembled* (2nd ed.). (pp. 327–353). Chapel Hill: University of North Carolina Press.

Eco, U. (1984). Postscript, *The name of the rose*. New York: Harcourt, Brace, Jovanovich.

Gergen, K. J. (1991). *The saturated self: Dilemmas of identity in contemporary life*. New York: Basic Books.

Goodman, E. (1992, Jan. 3). JFK raises questions; its answers raise doubts. *Oregonian*, p. B5.

Gronbeck, B. (1991). Mythic portraiture in the 1988 Iowa presidential caucus bio-ads. In L. Vande Berg & L. Wenner (Eds.), *Television criticism: Approaches and applications* (pp. 254–272). New York: Longman.

Grossberg, L. (1986). History, politics and postmodernism: Stuart Hall and cultural studies. *Journal of Communication Inquiry, 10*(2), 61–77.

Hall, S. (1980). Encoding/decoding. In S. Hall, D. Hobson, A. Lowe, & P. Willis (Eds.), *Culture, media language* (pp. 128–138). London: Hutchinson.

Harvey, D. (1989). *The condition of postmodernity*. Oxford, U.K.: Basil Blackwell.

Jeffords, S. (1989). *The remasculinization of America: Gender and the Vietnam war*. Bloomington: Indiana University Press.

Lyotard, J. (1984). *The postmodern condition: A report on knowledge.* Minneapolis: University of Minnesota Press.

MacKenzie, J. P. (1991, Dec. 20). Oliver Stone's patsy: JFK film revives a malicious prosecution [Editorial Notebook]. *New York Times,* p. A18.

McGee, M. C. (1990). Text, context, and the fragmentation of contemporary culture. *Western Journal of Speech Communication, 54,* 274–289.

Mumby, D. (Ed.). (1993). *Narrative and social control.* Newbury Park, CA: Sage.

Nicholson, L. J. (Ed.). (1990). *Feminism/postmodernism.* New York: Routledge.

Owen, A. S., & Ehrenhaus, P. (1993). Animating a critical rhetoric: On the feeding habits of American empire. *Western Journal of Communication, 57,* 169–177.

Raskin, M. (1992). JFK and the culture of violence. *American Historical Review, 97,* 487–499.

Rosenstone, R. A. (1992). JFK: Historical fact/historical film. *American Historical Review, 97,* 506–511.

Seiter, E. (1992). Semiotics, structuralism, and television. In R. C. Allen (Ed.), *Channels of discourse, reassembled* (2nd ed.). (pp. 31–66). Chapel Hill: University of North Carolina Press.

Spector, M. (1991, Dec. 23). Explosive imagery of J.F.K. igniting debate in audiences. *New York Times,* pp. A1, 14.

Staples, B. (1991, Dec. 25). Hollywood: History by default [Editorial Notebook]. *New York Times,* p. 30.

Star, A. (1993, June 14). Mild palms. *New Republic,* pp. 32–35.

Stone, O. (1991a, Dec. 20). Via the director's viewfinder [Letter to the editor]. *New York Times,* II, p. 4.

Stone, O. (1991b, Dec. 27). JFK: Media should not be sole interpreters of history. *Oregonian,* p. B9.

Stone, O. (Producer). (1993). *Wild palms: The dream begins and the dream concludes* [Telecast/Videotape]. New York: ABC.

Sturken, M. (1997). *Tangled memories: The Vietnam War, the AIDS epidemic, and the politics of remembering.* Berkeley: University of California Press.

Twisted history. (1991, Dec. 23). *Newsweek,* pp. 46–49.

Vogel, A. (1992). JFK: The question of propaganda. *Antioch Review, 50,* 578–585.

White, H. (1987). *The content of the form: Narrative discourse and historical representation.* Baltimore: Johns Hopkins University.

Wicker, T. (1991, Dec. 15). Does "J.F.K." conspire against reason? *New York Times,* II, pp. 1, 18.

Will, G. F. (1991, Dec. 26). JFK: No love of country, or truth. *Oregonian,* p. B7.

Williams, R. (1975). *Television: Technology and cultural form.* New York: Schocken Books.

Difference and Identity in *Northern Exposure*

Robert Hanke

In this selection, I offer some notes toward a multicultural analysis of the CBS network television series *Northern Exposure* (July 1990–July 26, 1995). While television is a site for multiple discourses (capitalism, patriarchy, sexuality, individualism, colonialism, etc.), this particular series allows us to explore the articulation of multicultural discourse into popular television fiction. At issue here is television's signification of cultural difference, its representation of subaltern groups, its thematization of identity, and its construction of multicultural community.

In attempting to develop multicultural television criticism, it seems clear that we need a different understanding of the role of popular television fiction in the hegemonic process. Cultural hegemony can no longer be understood in terms of single, dominant constructions of cultural identity, or as a strategy for incorporating everybody into the same, all encompassing national identity (Hall, 1991a). As Stuart Hall has aptly put it: "hegemony is not the disappearance or destruction of difference. It is the construction of a collective will through difference. It is the articulation of differences which do not disappear" (1991b, p. 58). Accordingly, multicultural television criticism enables us to grasp the "texture of hegemony/subalternity, the interlacing of resistance and submission, opposition and complicity" within contemporary, popular television culture (Martin-Barbero, 1988, p. 462).

First, I offer a brief sketch of multiculturalism within the university, and how the intellectual debate around cultural diversity spilled over into the mediated-public sphere by the early 1990s. In the second part, I offer a critical reading of *Northern Exposure* that examines its representation of place and diverse groups as a site that brings multiculturalism's struggle to win wider recognition into popular television fiction. I contend that *Northern Exposure*'s articulation of difference and identity constructs an imagined multicultural community in relation to, rather than in spite of, difference. While the series asserts an ideal that does not deny difference, it nevertheless works to diffuse the more progressive possibilities of the multicultural project and its rewriting of difference, identity, and political values. My discussion focuses upon the central and marginal characters who bear the weight of cultural difference, albeit in different proportions and with different meanings and implications. In this way, I hope to expose the series' discursive strategy for coming to terms with cultural diversity. In the closing section, I shall return to the question of hegemony/alterity/utopia, and try to speculate upon the relationship of *Northern Exposure*'s construction of multicultural community to the process of cultural hegemony.

Multiculturalism in the Academy

Multicultural discourse within higher education, which emerged, in part, as a response to the increasing demographic diversity of U.S. society, may be characterized as a project to reconstruct the relationship between cultural difference, identity, and experience. Within universities, the effort to diversify the curriculum represents a challenge to what counts as legitimate knowledge, culture (particularly the literary canon and the traditions of Western European civilization), and political values (Aronowitz, 1993).

At its core, multiculturalism is a struggle over the representation of the experiences, claims, values, and demands of subaltern groups. This counterhegemonic challenge to monoculturalism—to the *unum* in *e pluribus unum*—within the context of the rise of the new conservativism, and the decline of leftist working class-based politics, provided the theoretical foundations for identity politics—the politics of identity groups defined in terms of race, gender, ethnicity, and sexuality, and the struggle against racism, sexism, and heterosexism. By the 1990s, both the possibilities and limits of identity politics became a major focal point of contemporary intellectual debate (see Kauffman, 1991; Kraus, 1992; Carby, 1992).

Multicultural discourse invites us to rethink two basic assumptions (O'Sullivan *et al.*, 1994). First, it has challenged the notion that "American" identity represents a unity that transcends distinct cultural traditions. Multicultural studies have argued that such a unity has been historically constructed in ways that reproduce cultural hegemony, and that "Americanness" is centered on a mythical norm that "is usually defined as white, thin, male, young, heterosexual, christian, and financially secure" (Lorde, 1990, p. 282). Second, it attempts to rethink the liberal-pluralist framework of difference and identity, and its politics of assimilation and integration, by reconnecting distinct cultural traditions or practices to relations of power. Informed by contemporary social theory and its insights into the mechanisms of exclusion, oppression, marginalization, hierarchization, and normalization that operate in modern societies, multiculturalism challenges the limits of liberal pluralist model of power by highlighting the struggles for freedom, justice, and equality that have taken place to affirm identities and claim rights.

In the early 1990s, the critique of Western European cultural traditions going on inside the academy became a matter of debate and public controversy. By 1992, the internal debate over the multicultural agenda was joined by journalists and politicians, entering the mediated public sphere and public consciousness as "political correctness." This label was primarily used to characterize and discredit the attitudes and behaviors of those attempting to implement multicultural programs and policies within universities. While the responses of academic conservatives have served to frame multiculturalism in terms of a debate over "PC," we should not downplay the way in which multiculturalism has begun to permeate humanities education in general (see Giroux, 1992, 1993) and communication in particular (see Levy, 1992).

At the same time, multicultural themes and issues have become more visible in magazines, newspapers, advertising, movies, and television. Within the globalizing mediascape, cultural difference appears to proliferate, to be destigmatized, and occasionally celebrated. Cultural diversity, in this context, becomes an index of the contemporary and the marketable. This is not to deny that the industrial production of television culture is still a powerful homogenizing force that absorbs difference and otherwise divergent outlooks and sensibilities into an American cultural mainstream. But criticism informed by subaltern critical practices, and aware of intra- and international forces of cultural heterogenization, makes monocultural frameworks for difference and national identity even more difficult to sustain than in the past.

If multiculturalists, liberal-pluralists, and conservative individualists are the primary definers of multiculturalism within the university, and if the news media function as secondary definers of these debates, then it is not surprising that producers of television fiction, accustomed to referencing the news, would begin to take the conflicts over the propagation of cultural diversity even further into the terrain of popular culture. Large-scale, industrially organized, cultural production, such as network commercial television, is able to renew itself, and provide novel "quality" entertainment, by drawing upon somewhat more autonomous, restricted fields of cultural production such as the literary field, the art world, and popular music. Indeed, *Northern*

Exposure has been noted for its "quasi-literariness" and the "eclectic playlist" of the series' soundtrack (Chunovic, 1993), and it has been examined as an exemplar of "quality" television (Williams, 1994).

Multiculturalism and the Media

Historically, U.S. television networks' approach to cultural diversity adhered "to their well-worn philosophy of selling majority, not minority, audiences to advertisers and to their faith in the imagined community of the mainstream melting pot" (Ferguson, 1993, p. 51). However, the possibilities of, as well as the limitations of and resistance to, a multicultural agenda for the media industries are beginning to receive some attention (in journalism, see Gilliam, 1991; for the Public Broadcasting System, see Haddock & Lee, 1993). Alternative media have already explored the prospects for multicultural community (see Utne, 1992), and there appears to be more diversity of voices in television talk shows than in television news (Douglas, 1992). Fictional television series have also explored multicultural themes and issues, particularly science fiction (e.g., *Star Trek, Star Trek: The Next Generation, Star Trek: Deep Space Nine*).

Recent scholarly work has attempted to theorize television's representation of multiple identity groups, their interactions with one another, the televisual orchestration of signs of gender, race, class, ethnicity, and sexual orientation. Particularly noteworthy is *Frank's Place*, which addressed the specificity of African-American historical experience, as well as differences within the category "African-American."

Critics of *Frank's Place* have advanced two positions: the normalization/domestication argument, and the cultural hegemony argument. The first position, represented by White (1991), holds that television's "staging of difference is crucial to liberal democratic ideals—and ideology—of free market broadcasting, at least as long as it is expressed within the commercial/consumerist imperatives of the television apparatus as a whole" (p. 83). In this neo-Marxian reading, the representation of "ostensible otherness and difference" works ideologically to reclaim the logic of the same and its underlying universal values and goals. In this position, television normalizes and domesticates difference, disguising the forces of homogenization that organize the television apparatus on a global scale (Gray, 1993).

An alternative position, informed by feminist and African-American cultural studies, is represented by Byars and Dell (1992). In their reading, diversity is not reducible to an underlying commercial imperative or economic logic, nor is it simply a vehicle for dominant (liberal pluralist) ideology. *Frank's Place* is a site of struggle between residual, dominant, and emergent ideologies of race and gender. The major and minor characters articulate multiple differences (gender, class, and age), as well as intraracial, regional, and ethnic differences, in ways that do not simply reproduce dominant constructions of "blackness." So while the main character, Frank Parish, may often function to "recuperate the black Other for a largely white audience," he settles into his place in the community (and patriarchy) by questioning "retrogressive recuperation," such as skin color as a determinant of racial difference and identity. While the series explicitly addresses racial inequality from an African-American viewpoint, its representation of African-American women reproduces social codes that associate "whiteness" with feminine beauty. Such a reading highlights the text's opposition to dominant racial ideologies as well as its complicity with white hegemony.

Northern Exposure provides the opportunity to develop these positions further. Cultural studies, in coming to terms with multiculturalism, enables us to read this series not only in terms of a single identity group, but as an articulation of multiple differences into an imagined multicultural community. At the core of *Northern Exposure*'s ideological problematic is the meaning of difference and identity; what is at stake, then, is the text's imaginary resolution of the dialectic of belongingness and otherness, in the midst of the cultural relativization and hybridization of U.S. society.

Cicely, Alaska, as a Frontier of Cultural Relativism

Let's begin with the style in which producers Joshua Brand and John Falsey have imagined this particular American community. According to series' co-creator Joshua Brand, Cicely "is a nonjudgmental place. There's never any intent to hurt or expose" (quoted in Nance, 1992, p. 7). In contrast to *Twin Peaks, Northern Exposure* is a utopian vision of the cultural politics of difference. Geographically remote from the metropolitan centers of North America, and from most viewers of the series, Cicely is a fictional place where old borders of identity are being phased out and new codes for the representation of difference and identity are in the process of being phased in. Cicely stands, in this sense, on the frontier of cultural relativism in the current war of position over the meaning of "Americanness."

The main points of the articulation of difference, as in most television series, are the series' characters. Dr. Joel Fleischman may be, as some critics have suggested, our tour guide through this cultural borderland, but this functional conception of his role in the series is too static, and does not enable us to address the series' thematization of the shifting grounds of difference and identity. In this northwestern "dramedy" (see Vande Berg, 1991), executive producers Joshua Brand and John Falsey have drawn upon codes of "Americanness," such as melting pot and romantic love, that have long roots in ethnic literature and Hollywood films (Friedman, 1991).

Northern Exposure is premised upon the encounter between a transplanted urban Jew—Dr. Joel Fleischman—and the multiple others who are residents of Cicely. The series' pilot opens with Joel traveling from New York to Alaska, in order to fulfill his medical school financing obligations. Instead of metropolitan Anchorage, however, he ends up in Cicely, where he is obliged to remain and serve as the town physician.

As viewers, then, we are transported to Cicely, to imagine a place where two worlds, Joel's and the residents of Cicely, ours and theirs, stage their weekly encounters, verbal exchanges, and cultural translations. Joel's encounter with the otherness of Cicely, and his initial panic and "cultural shock" give way to subsequent encounters in which Joel comes to terms with Cicely's otherness. His position shifts from that of outsider and stranger to an insider who rediscovers, and learns to assert, his own unassimilated otherness, specifically his "Jewishness."

As Sobchack (1991) has pointed out, if multiculturalism has challenged the norms that define "Americanness," then "stable or sure notions of what it means to be ethnic also weakens" (Sobchack, 1991, p. 333). In one episode, for example, when Joel learns of an uncle's death, the townspeople engage in a search for a Jewish minyan to say

Kaddish. In the process, the very meaning of "Jewishness," particularly its emotional pull for Joel, is clouded in uncertainty. Signifiers of "Jewishness," such as surnames, appearance, accent, are no longer clear-cut markers of "Jewishness." In a dream sequence that resembles a scene from a Hollywood western, a posse consisting of white, black, and Indian "Jews" appears, revealing just how far borders of ethnicity and race have shifted.

It is significant that this ethnic subtext departs from the melting-pot image: Joel may be required to live and work in Cicely, but he is not forced to assimilate in order to belong to the community. For example, in an episode titled "Our Tribe," Joel's encounter with the "Indian" residents leads to his adoption as a member of an Indian "tribe." This suggests a dialectic of belonging and otherness that does not require Joel, or anyone, to completely divest themselves of their cultural difference.

Of course, the series' appeal does not depend upon viewers' recognition of semitic imagery or the decoding of this particular ethnic subtext. The burden of signifying difference does not rest on one character however central his point of view may be. Moreover, constructing a multicultural community requires a plurality of cultural codes of identity with multiple points of recognition and identification of difference. As Williams (1994) notes, the ensemble cast provides a range of perspectives to be expressed, at the same time that the series' hybrid style, use of backstories, and self-conscious "bardic" voice—particularly the philosophical, theological, literary, and artistic musings of local radio station disc jockey Chris Stevens—highlight the role of narrative in making sense of everyday and historical realities and in constructing culture(s).

Historically, women have been one of the main vehicles for the representation of difference and otherness in mass culture (Williamson, 1986). *Northern Exposure*'s major Euro-American female characters represent different generations of working "woman" in relation to personal and family relationships, love, and sex. Kray (1993) also points out that the series' pairing of Maggie O'Connell, a WASP woman, with a Jewish man is consistent with the annihilation of Jewish women in prime-time television.

However, it is the Native American characters, as radically different others, who seem to bear an even greater burden of representing difference and otherness. If we examine the series' image of Native Americans, especially in light of the representational history of "Indians" in U.S. television, *Northern Exposure* is a notable exception. Particularly remarkable is its "positive" image of Native Americans, its sympathetic admiration of the distinctiveness of Indian culture, and its acknowledgement of the pleasure of being non-European American and non-white. Native Americans make a reappearance outside of the convention of the western genre as regular characters, as minor characters, and as extras who provide local "background."

The coding of Indians as "primitive" feathered warriors on horseback or loyal "sidekicks" to white heroes yields here to a coding of Native Americans as "ex-primitives"—formerly "primitive" people who are acculturated to the industrial world (MacCannell, 1992). On the one hand, Marilyn Whirlwind and Ed Chigliak are seen participating in the private and public life of Cicely, their Indian culture is valorized, and their distinctiveness is allowed and affirmed. Moreover, signifiers of an Indian way of life, such as native language, dress, music, crafts, rituals, and ceremonies demonstrate the difference between Indian and non-Indian ways. They are "ex-primitives" who are completely at home in a postindustrial, consumer-oriented society.

On the other hand, their cultural difference is disconnected from historical and contemporary conflicts between indigenous and nonindigenous peoples over land and civil rights. Many non-Indian viewers would probably come away with the impression that today's "Indians" are maintaining a balance between traditional and modern ways of life. There is no hint of the racist attacks against Native Americans nor any suggestion of a Native American culture of resistance (as embodied, for example, in the American Indian Movement).

Northern Exposure also ironizes "Indianness," but not by setting Indian people's existence in Cicely against the legacies of colonialism and racism. Rather, the series displays how immersed in the mainstream, Euro-American culture Native Americans are. It is supposedly ironic, for example, that Marilyn Whirlwind is seen reading *The Face* magazine, or that she teaches non-Indians how to dance to Cajun zydeco music. Ed's passion for Hollywood films is another example if we are even dimly aware of the stereotyping of Indian people in those films. His documentary films about life in Cicely are an ironic reversal of the entire tradition of ethnographic filmmaking that documented everyday Native American cultural life. In an episode titled "Things Become Extinct," Ed makes a film about Ira Wingfeather's "dying art" of wooden flute-making, thereby perpetuating the cultural myth of "Indians" as a "Vanishing Race" and absolving the colonizing culture of any responsibility for the destruction of cultural diversity (George & Sanders, 1995).

The series' ironization of "Indianness" may be read as denaturalizing dominant constructions of "Indianness." Yet, as Aden and Cooks (1993) have argued, the distance that once defined the radical difference between non-Indian and Indian groups has apparently collapsed. As they put it, "the position of the show, to educate about difference—the expanse between a dominant culture's center and boundaries—works to *subvert* the center and boundaries, the defining moments of oppression, in Native American culture" (Aden & Cooks, 1993, p. 13). Moreover, in bearing the greatest proportion of difference (which is not pure Otherness) from the presumed mainstream Euro-American audience, Indian people are "made to be the voice of mainstream American culture" (George & Sanders, 1995, p. 448).

The problem with *Northern Exposure* is that the image of Indian peoples is still linked to mostly white, mostly European-American practices of consuming images of otherness in order to renew themselves and to display how inclusive of difference we, as a liberal democratic nation, really are. Referring to the commercial drama of otherness in recent advertising, hooks (1992) observes:

> In the cultural marketplace the Other is coded as having the capacity to be more alive, as holding the secret that will allow those who venture and dare to break cultural anhedonia . . . and experience sensual and spiritual renewal (p. 26).

It also cannot be overemphasized that even reconstructed "Indians" are "inscribed by historical traces of misinformation, cultural repression, and political domination" (George & Sanders, 1995, p. 434). For example, in an episode titled "Brains, Know–How and Native Intelligence," Joel treats Ed's Uncle Anku, who tests Joel's scientific medical expertise. We might appreciate Uncle Anku's refusal to submit to Joel's authority, even though Joel later admonishes him for holding onto his "stupid pride." In later episodes, Leonard Quinhagak, an Indian "healer," arrives to learn something about conventional medicine from Joel and ends up teaching Joel a lesson about combining scientific medicine with compassion. The Native American medicine-man character offers a more holistic view of the body, but this representation of "native" healing practices reduces it to "new age therapy," to "common sense pop psychology," or to a television doctor's "knowledge of and attention to human nature" (George & Sanders, 1995, p. 446).

Even though colonial discourse appears to shape the series' liberal humanist perspective on "Indianness," we should be careful to assume a critical position that leads to "devaluing or ignoring of the 'marginalized' challenges (aesthetic and political) of the 'ec-centric,' those relegated to the fringes of the dominant culture—the women, blacks, gays, Native Peoples, and others who have made us aware of the politics of all . . . representations" (Hutcheon, 1988, p. 17). Of course, this challenge has traditionally come from outside of the mainstream Hollywood film and U.S. network television, in the form of independent film and video production. Yet, it appears that even the most "ec-centric" others may find themselves approaching, if not actually occupying, the center of the field of mainstream televisual representation.

One of the most widely discussed episodes of *Northern Exposure,* which aired May 18, 1992, presented the story of Cicely's founding by two Euro-American lesbian women. The episode transcodes the familiar western story to thematize the collision of patriarchy with matriarchy and the transformation of the oppressed into self-actualized individuals (Aden & Cooks, 1993). While it is possible to read this episode as a "post-feminist" allegory whose definition of empowerment is finally individual rather than community-centered, this episode nevertheless does inscribe sexual difference into the origin myth of this community. So while the utopian lesbian founders of Cicely die and disappear, the recovery of this previously hidden past refracts the history actually being made (and rewritten) by gay and lesbian activists and scholars, and the struggle to remember past lesbian lives. Doubtless, this refraction is correlated with the series' plea for tolerance of gay and lesbian "lifestyles" but we should be careful not to minimize the significance of such subjugated memories when they do appear, even if they do not meet our criteria of "real" history.

If remembering lesbian women's founding of Cicely reveals something about the sexual politics of the 1990s, so too do the series' minor gay male characters. Ron and Erick own and operate the Sourdough Inn, a bed and breakfast inn on the outskirts of town. They appear to be accepted by everyone, except Maurice Minnifield, the town's patriarch and bigot. Ron and Erick appear amused, rather than bothered by, Maurice's homophobia. Over the course of their exchanges, Maurice tones down his homophobia, not out of an affirmative sense of their difference and identity, but out of a pragmatic appreciation of their small-business acumen. In general, the series presents Ron and Erick as good-natured, nonthreatening, nonactivist gay men. While they are presented outside of the conventions of AIDS stories, their image still reinforces, rather than challenges, the limits of television's images of gay men: "Sexual innuendoes and sexual activity between unmarried heterosexual couples are now routine . . . but overt display or discussion of physical and sexual behavior between homosexual characters is generally off limits; television homosexuals are de-sexed and without desire" (Fejes & Petrich, 1993, p. 402).

When the series does address the vicissitudes of sexual desire, it does so through heterosexual characters' romantic involvements and sexual activities. Joel and Maggie's "screwball" couplings, the physical consummation of their relationship, the antagonism which masks their underlying attraction, are central to the series' gender ideology (Scodari, 1995). While their "battle of sexes" defines gender difference in keeping with the conservative reintrenchment of gender "roles," Maggie's outward appearance of "masculinized" femininity, her history of having chosen the wrong type of men, her defense of celibacy, her forgetting of sex with Joel, express some ambivalence toward the obligatory nature of heterosexuality. Maggie's ambivalence, when viewed alongside the series' representation of multiple, cross-generational female friendships, may put dominant constructions of unfulfilled, incomplete, single women into question (e.g., Maggie decides not to join Joel when he leaves Cicely), even as other story lines (e.g., Maggie's crowning as homecoming queen of Cicely High School) work to recuperate patriarchal, heterosexual ideology.

Only one episode has gone beyond legitimating ambivalence in order to address the fluidity of sexual desire in a way that opens it up to a "queer reading" (Doty, 1993). Chris Stevens, who is characterized as sexually open and active with a variety of female partners, seeks "spiritual rejuvenation" by going to a monastery—a segregated world of men. Instead of realizing the virtues of chastity, he becomes intensely attracted to Brother Simon. His fantasies and exchanges become so infused with sexual desire that he begins to doubt his attraction to women. However, when Chris acts out his desire and kisses Brother Simon, "Brother Simon" is revealed to be a woman. In the end, Chris espouses poetic platitudes: "no spirituality, no sanctity, no truth without the female sex," and "Nature made thee to temper Man." This story line does not disavow the power, even the fluidity, of sexual desire, even though the episode concludes with a return to the centrality of heterosexual relations and binary oppositions that underwrite straight sexual identities and identifications. While the portrayal of Joel and Maggie's courtship perpetuates the myth of (hetero) "sexual tension" (Scodari, 1995), episodes such as this one begin to deconstruct the unity of gender and sexual desire, suggesting the degree to which sexual difference and identity is a site of current ambivalence and anxiety, as well as struggle.

Lastly but no less significant to the series' thematization of identity is its representation of racial differences and relations. A black male stranger arrives in the all-white town of Cicely, goes to the Brick (the town tavern), and gets involved in a conversation with Chris about the "collective unconscious." They begin to act, think, and speak alike. They discover that they have the same birthday and the same father—that they are "half brothers."

While black-white relations are initially defined in terms of sameness, subsequent episodes enunciate differences between Chris and his "half-brother" Bernard Stevens. Here the series references Alex Haley's *Roots*, the defining television text of popular African American ethnohistory, in order to address Afrocentric conceptions of black identity.

In *Northern Exposure*'s retelling of "Roots," Chris dreams about African music and dancers, where he and Bernard watch the dancers and speak in Swahili. When he awakes, Chris concludes he must go to Africa, and on KBHR, he announces that he is a "person of color." As it turns out, however, Chris has been having Bernard's dream, and it is Bernard, not Chris, who must go to Africa. In a follow-up episode, Bernard returns wearing "African" dress, but he and his half-brother Chris are no longer "in synch." Chris's speech becomes replete with inversions, skipped words, and missed sentences. Bernard takes over his announcing duties on KBHR, recounts his experiences in Africa, and urges listeners not to underestimate the "growing presence of the third world." Later, Bernard's dream of "Africa" is represented as incomplete—a half dream. Only after Chris and Bernard acknowledge their bond ("beyond the genetic coil"), and their mutual appreciation of the black culture of the African diaspora (juju music), does Chris return to his "normal" self.

In this story line, we may read an acknowledgement of black enthnohistory, which has helped to construct an affirmative sense of African American identity. At a time when more and more black Americans prefer to be called "African American," the racial subtext attempts to make sense of what this preference may mean for white Americans. On the one hand, Chris assumes some responsibility for his own racial location by learning how he is connected, rather than separated from, African Americans. Bernard also gives voice to anti-essentialist perspectives on race when responding to expressions of the old racism. On the other hand, the series' deliberations over what it means to be "black" puts a white, liberal, pluralist face on any construction of "blackness" that would insist on the specificity of African-American historical and cultural experience. The issue of racial identity is disconnected from neo-nationalist tendencies in black popular culture practices. Rather, Chris's declaration that he is a "person of color" is an alternative to white America's "fear of a black planet." The African-American presence in television, and popular culture more generally, gives rise here to a racial subtext that make persons of "white" color less invisible, but in a way that may reaffirm white viewers' presumption that it is not "normal" for whites to become more like "persons of color" because "melting pot" imagery has been predicated upon exactly the reverse.

"Quality Television" and New Age Otherness

We are now in a better position to see how this series attempts to come to terms with the increasing cultural diversity of American society and the counter-hegemonic thrust of multicultural discourse.

Within this imagined multicultural community, Maurice Minnifield, the very embodiment of cold-war, cultural imperialist, technological rationality, appears to be isolated as the last ethnocentric, sexist, racist, homophobic, "rugged individualist." The series frames this once-dominant ideology as a residual ideology, even as Maurice continues to imagine Cicely's future as an "Alaskan Riviera." In one episode, Maurice is even outsmarted in real estate dealings by another of Alaska's most wealthy men—an Alaskan Indian. The post-cold war era has also forced the former NASA astronaut to recognize former enemies (his South Korean son and his North Korean fiancée) as his own "flesh and blood." Another episode signals the end of this era of national and international politics when the annual chess match between Maurice and his Soviet counterpart escalates into a duel. The duel does not take place because the actors step out of character and stop acting; no longer believing in the cold-war "script," they simply agree to move onto the next scene.

Cicely is thus an imagined community of the American "nation" in a post-cold war era, but it is also a metaphor for unoppressive city life "defined as openness to unassimilated otherness" (Young, 1990, p. 319). In this sense, *Northern Exposure* is not a nostalgic glance backward, but a utopian vision of contemporary conflicts over difference and identity.

With this in mind, let us return to the question of hegemony/alterity. Based on my reading of the series, cultural hegemony does not operate solely through the exclusion or appropriation of homogeneous "woman" or any single subaltern group. What "Jewishness," "Indianness," "queerness" or "blackness" means is no less significant to this series' appeal, and its ability to make common sense of contemporary cultural experience and identity politics. This series' image of multicultural community may be seen as a reflection of the somewhat greater diversity of the professional middle-class, or as a recodification of liberal humanist "pluralism" that is inclusive of more cultural difference. But a discursive and conjunctural approach to popular television fictions suggests that *Northern Exposure*'s style of imagining community is shaped by the discursive context of multiculturalism, and its effort to disarticulate the imagined community of "America" from "melting pot" imagery.

While *Northern Exposure* shares a basic assumption of multicultural discourse—identity in relation to difference—and while it propagates cultural diversity as a worthy ideal, it does so within an individualizing framework and consensual model of culture that diffuses the challenges of "ec-centric" others to relations of power. Difference and identity, inscribed within social and cultural relations of power, violence, and exploitation, are reinscribed within an ideology of New Age Otherness, preempting multiculturalism's counter-hegemonic force. Any tension, polarizations, and conflicts based upon cultural difference are submerged in the structure of good-feeling, well-being, and harmonious coexistence. In fact, many episodes have concluded with scenes of the whole community coming together to marvel at Chris's performance art, to express the New Age wonder of life and awe of Nature, or to renew their faith in the workings of democracy and meritocracy in America. In this respect, embracing cultural diversity enables Cicelians to escape the banality and ordinariness of homogeneous, face-to-face, suburban, and increasingly gated communities, but it does not require any change in existing political values. If Cicely, as a multicultural community, is imagined in a style that erases the cultural politics and social divisions of contemporary urban life, we may tentatively conclude that *Northern Exposure* is part of a discursive strategy to contain the more progressive possibilities of a multicultural agenda and a radical politics of difference.

REFERENCES

Aden, R., & L. Cooks (1993, May). *Northern Exposure*'s sense of place: Constructing and marginalizing the matriarchal community. Paper presented at the meeting of the International Communication Association, Washington, DC.

Aronowitz, S. (1993). *Roll over Beethoven: The return of cultural strife.* Hanover: Wesleyan University Press.

Byars, J., & Dell, C. (1992). Big differences on the small screen: Race, class, gender, feminine beauty, and the characters at *Frank's Place.* In L. Rakow (Ed.), *Women making meaning* (pp. 191–209). New York: Routledge.

Carby, H. (1992). The multicultural wars. In G. Dent (Ed.), *Black popular culture* (pp. 187–199). Seattle: Bay Press.

Chunovic, L. (1993). *The Northern Exposure book.* New York: Citadel Press.

Doty, A. (1993). *Making things perfectly queer: Interpreting mass culture.* Minneapolis: University of Minnesota Press.

Douglas, S. (1992, July 8–21). Subverting the mainstream media. *In These Times,* 15.

Fejes, F., & Petrich, K. (1993). Invisibility, homophobia and heterosexism: Lesbian, gays and the media. *Critical Studies in Mass Communication, 10,* 396–422.

Ferguson, M. (1993). Invisible divides: Communication and identity in Canada and the U.S. *Journal of Communication, 43*(2), 42–57.

Friedman, L. (Ed.). (1991). *Unspeakable images: Ethnicity and the American cinema.* Urbana: University of Illinois Press.

George, D., with Sanders, S. (1995). Reconstructing Tonto: Cultural formations and American Indians in 1990s television fiction, *Cultural Studies, 9,* 427–452.

Gilliam, D. (1991). Harnessing the assets of a multicultural future. *Media Studies Journal, 5*(4), 127–135.

Giroux, H. (1992). *Border crossings: Cultural workers and the politics of education.* New York: Routledge.

Giroux, H. (1993). *Living dangerously: Multiculturalism and the politics of difference.* New York: Peter Lang.

Gray, H. (1993). The endless slide of difference: Critical television studies, television and the question of race. *Critical Studies in Mass Communication, 10,* 190–197.

Haddock, M., & Lee, C. (1993, Summer). Whose multiculturalism?: PBS, the public, and privilege. *Afterimage, 21,* 17–19.

Hall, S. (1991a). The local and the global: Globalization and ethnicity. In A. King (Ed.), *Culture, globalization and the world-system: Contemporary conditions for the representation of identity* (pp. 19–39). Binghamton: State University of New York.

Hall, S. (1991b). Old and new ethnicities. In A. King (Ed.), *Culture, globalization and the world-system: Contemporary conditions for the representation of identity* (pp. 41–68). Binghamton: State University of New York.

hooks, b. (1992). Eating the other: Desire and resistance. In *Black looks: race and representation* (pp. 21–39). Boston: South End Press.

Hutcheon, L. *The politics of postmodernism.* New York: Routledge.

Kauffman, L. A. (Ed.). (1991, July–December). Identities in search of a strategy: Envisioning a new radical politics [Special issue]. *Socialist Review, 21* (3, 4).

Kraus, R. *et al.* (Eds.). (1992, Summer). The identity in question [Special issue]. *October,* 61.

Kray, S. (1993). Orientalizing of an "almost white" woman: The interlocking effects of race, class, gender and ethnicity in American mass media. *Critical Studies in Mass Communication, 10,* 349–366.

Levy, M. (Ed.). (1992). Communication scholarship and political correctness [Special issue]. *Journal of Communication, 42,* 56–149.

Lorde, A. (1990). Age, race, class, and sex. In R. Ferguson, M. Gever, T. T. Minh-ha, & C. West (Eds.), *Out there: Marginalization and contemporary cultures* (pp. 281–287). New York and Cambridge: The New Museum of Contemporary Art and The MIT Press.

MacCannell, D. (1992). *Empty meeting grounds: The tourist papers.* New York: Routledge.

Martin-Barbero, J. (1988). Communication from culture: The crisis of the national and the emergence of the popular. *Media, Culture & Society, 10,* 447–465.

Nance, S. (1992). *Exposing Northern Exposure.* Las Vegas: Pioneer Books.

O'Sullivan, T., Hartley, J., Saunders, D., Montgomery, M., & Fiske, J. (1994). *Key concepts in communication and cultural studies.* New York: Routledge.

Scodari, C. (1995). Possession, attraction, and the thrill of the chase: Gendered mythmaking in film and television comedy of the sexes, *Critical Studies in Mass Communication, 12,* 23–39.

Sobchack, V. (1991). Postmodern modes of ethnicity. In L. Friedman (Ed.), *Unspeakable images: Ethnicity and American cinema* (pp. 329–352). Urbana: University of Illinois Press.

Utne, E. (Ed.). (1992, July/August). *Utne Reader,* 52.

Vande Berg, L. (1991). Dramedy: *Moonlighting* as an emergent generic hybrid. In L. Vande Berg & L. Wenner (Eds.), *Television criticism: Approaches and applications* (pp. 87–111). New York: Longman.

White, M. (1991). What's the difference? *Frank's Place* in television. *Wide Angle, 13,* 82–93.

Williams, B. (1994). North to the future: *Northern Exposure* and quality television. In H. Newcomb (Ed.), *Television, the critical view* (pp. 141–154). New York: Oxford University Press.

Williamson, J. (1986). Women is an island: Femininity and colonization. In T. Modleski (Ed.), *Studies in entertainment: Critical approaches to mass culture* (pp. 99–118). Bloomington: Indiana University Press.

Young, I. (1990). The ideal of community and the politics of difference. In L. Nicholson (Ed.), *Feminism/postmodernism* (pp. 300–323). New York: Routledge.

10

Institution-Centered Approaches to Television Criticism

We tend to think of television by what we can actually see and hear. However, if we examine only on-screen television, we get only part of the picture. Many important things in television happen behind the scenes to influence what shows up in our living rooms. Changes in ownership, responses to competition or regulation, and decisions made by producers and writers are all examples of institutional influences affecting television.

Institution-centered television criticism looks at television as an industry that is historically and culturally situated. From varying vantage points, this type of criticism seeks to answer questions about the significance of how and why television is produced. In the United States, television production occurs under the larger conditions of democratic capitalism. Television is an integral part of a larger multibillion dollar media and culture industry. Because television's economic well-being relates to its competitive position in a larger marketplace, the production of its product is necessarily strategic and politically contextualized. In other countries, such as China or the former Soviet Union, television's ties to governance, policy, and the politics of the state are firmer and the marketplace takes on a different character. In assessing the dynamics of institutions, organizations, and individuals that produce television, institution-centered television criticism examines the scenes behind the scenes.

Institutions, Industries, Organizations, and Individuals

When armchair critics rail against the problems and offenses of television, they often speak of television as if it were a coherent institutionalized monolith. Although television may be thought of as something that is institutionalized into American life, it is not in itself an institution. Rather television exists in culture at institutional crossroads where a variety of industries move traffic through organizations made up of people working both in groups and as individuals. Thus, institution-centered approaches look not only at the institutions that frame television as an industry, but also at the strategies, actions, and constraints of individual organizations and people who do television work.

Institutional arrangements that guide television are historically and culturally situated. In the United States, institutional-level arrangements dictate that the television industry is largely commercial and privately owned, as opposed to being run as a state-owned public service. Historically, this has been a centralized system that moves out from the core control of a limited amount of networks to local stations. Politically, the system has been insulated by a tradition of freedom of speech, within regulated bounds. Political control comes from a complex web of tensions between federal agencies, public advocacy, industry lobbying, and self-regulation. Economically, the system has been fueled by support and influence of advertisers, who in turn are influenced by audiences and viewing choices. The choices that viewers make in turn affect decisions that advertisers make about placements, and these decisions in turn affect strategies about the production of programming. All this happens in a competitive and changing environment. In more recent historical times, institutional dynamics in television have shifted as cable, satellite, computer, and other technologies offer new choices and forms of delivery.

This snapshot suggests that the institutional level of television is complex and fluid, presenting real challenges to the institution-centered television critic. As with other approaches to criticism, there is an inherent messiness that needs sorting through. To help position your critical efforts, some basic perspectives and their assumptions are introduced in the next section. This material is followed by two models you may find useful in analysis.

Perspectives and Assumptions

Perspectives on television can vary as they might in adjusting the focal length on a zoom lens. Wide-angle studies focus on the big picture, on how big strategies by the big players duking it out have effects. Some big-picture studies might follow industry trends in concentration of ownership and assess how it affects diversity in television programming. Other big-picture studies might provide a narrower view and focus, for example, on dueling fiefdoms of the corporate world such as the cable news service wars that pit Time-Warner's CNN, Disney's ABC, Rupert Murdoch's Fox (and News Corp), and General Electric's NBC (and its partner Microsoft) against each other. At the telephoto end of the lens are studies that provide a much tighter view of the action. These views might look closely at pressures that individual and groups of television workers face in doing their jobs. Somewhere between wide and telephoto perspectives are the more midrange studies, which often provide case studies or histories of the organizational dynamics within one company or niche of the industry.

Taking a perspective involves trade-offs that are willingly made in pursuit of answering a question. Wide-angle studies focus broadly but miss detail. Telephoto studies put individuals and organizations under the microscope but often discount broad structural factors that influence action. In each instance, pictures must not only be taken from some place, your point of view, but focus somewhere, your framing of the situation. You need to remember that something important may be happening just outside the edge of the frame.

Viewpoints and Control

Two major points of view characterize the poles of institution-centered television criticism. First are studies that rely on theories of capitalism and focus on political and economic implications. Second are studies that rely on theories of industrial society and focus on sociological and organizational relations (Giddens, 1979; Murdock, 1982; Schudson, 1991). Both kinds of studies can focus on a wide range of power and control issues at the macro and micro levels. However, studies coming from political economy often tend to be wide angle and focus on allocative control. Studies coming from industrial and organizational theorizing often tend to be more telephoto and focus on operational control.

Seen at higher levels, *allocative control* is the power to define an organization's scope and goals, and the ways in which resources will be used. In the corporate setting, allocative control is seen in policy and strategy formulation, decisions on expansion, financial policies, and patterns of profit distribution (Murdock, 1982). *Operational control* entails lower-level decisions about "the effective use of resources already allocated and the implementation of policies already decided upon at the allocative level" (Murdock, 1982, p. 122). In operational control, decision makers may be relatively autonomous and there is often much room for creativity. However, operational decision makers work within the constraints of the resources they have been allocated.

Murdock (1982) sees control as having actional and structural dimensions that influence the focus of analysis. *Actional analysis* focuses on power by looking at the ways people collectively or individually act to gain compliance with their demands and desires. Analysis of the action dimension often begins by identifying effective controllers and the persuasive and coercive strategies used to enlist support for their ideas, interests, and policies. *Structural analysis* focuses on issues of determination and often begins by examining the ways in which constraints in the economic, political, and organizational environments place limitations on effective controllers. Key features of political economy and industrial relations are discussed below in terms of how they approach issues of control.

Political Economy

Criticism in this tradition has grown out of a Marxist conception of the socioeconomic order. There is a focus on the base or underlying structures of elite economic power that promulgates a television system as a superstructure that reflects and reinforces dominant interests in its programming and advertising. The role that television (and the culture industry) plays in the relationship between economic and cultural power is thought to be "special" (Murdock, 1982). Critics of the approach attempt to discredit this special relationship by characterizing it as an unbelievable "conspiracy" of forces (Schudson, 1991). Still, there is little question that the economic and political interests of those that control the media industry are not served by producing messages at odds with their goals. More refined thinking suggests that economic interests can be maintained by domesticating rather than stifling social problems that raise questions about the legitimacy of prevailing arrangements (Gitlin, 1979). By showing the elasticity of consumer society, television produces consensus by presenting natural solutions that involve inconsequential give and take and do not challenge foundational control of the elites. Through this process, elites maintain social and ideological control through agreement and hegemony rather than confrontation. Regardless of the issue of how dominant power is maintained, critics with this perspective see prevailing economic and political arrangements as problematic for all but the ruling classes. Thus, the focus on how allocative control affects operational issues and has political and economic consequences.

In actional analysis, political economic critiques take an instrumentalist stance, seeing television product derived from industry economic structure. Much attention is given to the increasing concentration of ownership by conglomerates. Actional analysis examines the implications of centralization of ownership on allocative control and the policies and activities of corporations. At a specific level, analysis focuses on the actions of individual companies to advance their interests. At a more general level, consideration is given to how television (and its setting in the larger communication industries) operates to improve the position of the dominant classes.

In structural analysis, the political economic critiques often take a neo-Marxist stance, recognizing limits to instrumentality by corporations.

However, the focus is on another type of capitalist imperative: limitations dictated by marketplace conditions. Although structural analysis tends to center on the effects that competition in the communications industries has on television product, it also takes into account how television is constrained by the larger capitalist economy. It is important to recognize that in structural analysis, political economic critiques tend to look at limitations in the broader environment, rather than looking downward within the environment of television organizations for limitations on corporate power.

Industrial Relations

Criticism in this tradition is grounded in the larger traditions of organizational sociology as applied more specifically to the industrialization of cultural production (Peterson, 1976). In contrast to political economy, the focus is on the social organization of television work, the relative autonomy and power that managerial and creative personnel have in decision making, and constraints derived from consumer behavior. Criticism in this tradition starts with the organization of television production. It contrasts political economy with a focus on the dynamics of operational control and assessments of how these affect actions of allocative controllers. Key issues include the operational effects of professional values and standards, the bureaucratization of production, the maintenance of creativity and decisional autonomy in an organizational context, and the role the audience plays in television work.

In actional analysis, critiques of television production take a range of cultural pluralist stances. At one pole stands what might be called *managerialists,* at the other *culturalists,* with much terrain in between (see Murdock, 1982; Schudson, 1991; Turow, 1991). Managerialists stress a new industrial order with professional managers and popular creators commanding effective control over production. In television, this approach would stress managers as power brokers and the autonomy of star creative personnel. Managerialists are also interested in the power of these managers and creators relative to those in other institutional spheres, such as government, education, the legal system, and the military (Murdock, 1982). Culturalists stress a more relative autonomy of managers and creators working toward action but constrained by professional and organizational norms and practices. The focus here is on action as organizationally produced in the context of professional subcultures. Professionals in television occupations are seen as resourceful, creative, and change oriented individuals who are constrained by time, routines, professional standards, ethos, and the wider environments of the organization, industry, and culture. Organizations are viewed as dynamic, culturally situated, and constrained largely by practices at other referent organizations. The culturalist view, popular in diverse quarters in organizational analysis and in cultural studies, looks at professional work and organizational activity as socially and symbolically constructed performance constrained by interaction (see Molotch & Lester, 1974; Tuchman, 1978).

In structural analysis, industrial relations critiques rely on a consumerist stance. This is a laissez-faire model with organizational workers influenced by consumer's choices in a free market. Here, television is a product of the wants and demands of its audience. The range of television programs, the popularity of certain formats, creation of new forms, scheduling, and the like are all seen to be "limited by the power and veto of consumers" (Murdock, 1982, p. 129). This view of consumer choice and sovereignty is seen in many academic analyses that accept the assumption that marketplace forces are responsive and controlled by consumers. The consumerist stance is used by the television industry to justify its actions in terms of giving the public what it wants. Often this market-based argument is used to defend problematic programming.

Models for Institutional Analysis and Criticism

A difficulty in starting institution-centered television criticism is deciding exactly what needs to be included. Are you most concerned with macro- or micro-level issues or problems? Are you trying to understand larger issues of marketplace dynamics? Are you concerned about the strategies of one particular kind of organization? Are you interested in the production process for a certain television genre? Or are you interested in the trade-offs that creative personnel need to make to be successful? Assessing questions like these will help you get started.

Once settled on a central problem, look at how an effective analysis might spread out from your core focus. Two models are particularly useful in identifying the elements that you need to include in your critical efforts. One model (Dimmick & Coit, 1982, 1983) allows the critic to focus on the hierarchically ordered levels of decision making that are intertwined in the course of making the television product. A second model focuses on the "power roles" (Turow, 1992, 1984) played in producing television.

Depending on your concerns, you may find one model more useful or choose to use selected elements from both models. In almost all instances you will use only a portion of the models in any one critical effort. For instance, you may find it appropriate to look at the interrelationships between a fixed number of power roles. In another study, you may find it appropriate to examine one or two levels of decision making.

Hierarchies

Dimmick and Coit's (1982, 1983) hierarchy of media decision making provides a fine-grained structure to move beyond ambiguities in the broad macro- versus micro-level distinction. The approach borrows the analogy of a hierarchical taxonomy as used in the physical sciences and history. The framework will allow you to focus on levels of decision making that are key to your critical assessment and see interdependence amongst the "systems that shape television." The hierarchy poses nine levels of decision making, ordered from the most molar or supranational level to the molecular or individual level. Decisions made at one level affect decisions at others. Influence tends to pass down from molar to lower levels, but recognizes that decisions at lower levels also filter up with influence.

The approach extends the concept of "gatekeepers" (White, 1950) to interlevel relationships. Within the organization, gatekeepers such as news or story editors make individual decisions, and gatekeepers acting in sequence work to make organizational decisions by letting something pass through the progressively higher gates of the executive ranks (Dimmick & Coit, 1983, p. 363). Just as organizational decision making and policy start and stop with the executives at the apex of organizations such as television networks, actions at the organizational level are influenced by actions at a higher television industry level, and these at a yet higher societal level, and so on.

Dimmick and Coit (1982, 1983) focus on influence and power at and between hierarchical levels. They recognize that influence is exercised as a result of both formal and informal hierarchies. *Formal hierarchies* reflect the superior-subordinate patterns seen in an organizational chart; here influence comes largely from rank. *Informal hierarchies* reflect the influence patterns that come about through ongoing interaction; here influence is sociometrically constructed. Formal and informal hierarchies are associated with different forms of influence.

Normative social influence stems from formal hierarchical arrangements. Here, influence is exercised by A and accepted by B because A controls resources that B needs (King, 1975). This is a classic power model, where resources refer to a variety of rewards or sanctions that may be brought into play by the power holder. Normative power is often seen as an action-chain between hierarchical levels (Luhmann, 1979). For example, we might have the successive influence of (1) legislative action that (2) fuels FCC rulemaking that (3) affects strategies at a corporation that owns a television network that (4) affects a program decision at the network level that (5) affects the bottom line at an affiliated station. Normative social influence also occurs within organizations and is seen in formal ranks or reporting structures. In many instances no clear hierarchy exists between organizations or individuals. For example, ad agencies control buys of television time. Stations and networks depend on these monies, but the television–agency relationship is not a hierarchical dominant–subordinate relationship. Another example is the reporter–source relationship; each needs the other: dependency, rather than a hierarchical position, guides the exercise of normative influence.

Informational social influence stems from informal social networks (Rogers & Kincaid, 1981). Control of information and power in an organization may have little to do with formal hierarchies. Rather *liaison networks* form to get the job done. In television, these networks form both within production and support organizations and between those organizations. Networks between organization liaisons, such as good-ole-boys networks, often present complete packages of talent for shows to television networks (Shanks, 1976).

Dimmick and Coit's (1983) research strategy entails "an active search for between level influences" (p. 375). Often this approach involves studying at least at three levels: (1) the larger environment within which organizations function, (2) organizations themselves, and (3) organizations' members, both in groups and as individuals (Lorsch & Morse, 1974). Dimmick and Coit's (1982, 1983) approach is especially useful in comparative case studies. They suggest picking organizations and starting at a level of analysis where you would expect the organizations to be either "most similar" or "most different" (see Przeworski & Teune, 1970). Looks at similar organizations should isolate a limited amount of differences. Once key differences are found, a search for within-level or between-level explanations is the goal. The similar-systems design requires an a priori assumption about the most important level of operation. In contrast, a most-different systems approach doesn't require specification of a most important level but rather begins analysis at the most molecular (usually the individual) level. In contrast to the most-similar starting point, the most-different strategy expects differences but looks for similarities that can be explained as systemically shared by looking at levels up the hierarchy. Both kinds of analysis rely on the following levels of a taxonomy, which are briefly discussed in terms of doing television analysis.

Supranational- and Pan-National-Level Influences. In analyzing television, this most molar level of analysis asks how decision making is influenced by forces beyond the nation-state. In practice, these influences come about through actions and policies of international agencies and global agreements or tribunals by significant groups of nations. Agreements can involve technical standards that allow compatibility, legal issues such as reciprocity of copyrights, or policy issues with which organizations like UNESCO have been concerned. Although policy issues are sometimes framed at the supranational level, they often are aimed at controlling pannational influences by dominant communication producers. Studies such as that by Turnstall (1977) have demonstrated the dangers of "media imperialism." Others such as Luther (1988) and Short (1986) point to dangers in the "free flow" of information that comes with new technologies (DBS, videocassette recorders, etc.).

Societal Level Influences. At the societal level, television's role is defined and constrained in various ways. The influences of foundational laws (such as the First Amendment), pressures for new laws, and interpretations of new ones by the courts all influence decision making in television. In the United States, the Federal Communications Commission has licensing and rulemaking powers over television, and the Federal Trade Commission's authority shapes television advertising. Influence over television comes in other ways, such as attacks by members of the executive or legislative branches. Television is also affected at the societal level by diverse economic influences such as the deficit, tax rates, investment rules, and consumer spending.

Industry-Level/Interorganizational Relations Influences.   The industry system in which television organizations exist also shapes decisional processes. This large level includes, for example, the relationships among networks, local stations, advertisers, and program suppliers. The focus here is on competing organizations and their relationships with suppliers of resources necessary for television production, distribution, and exhibition. Two issues at the industry level are of particular interest to the critical understanding of television as an institution.

The first issue concerns the nature of competition. In television, program diversity decreases over time with limited oligopolistic competition (Dominick & Pearce, 1976). However, in today's broadened multichannel environment, with new networks and cable programming, what often appears to be competition is rather niche development, and the relationships between producers can often be synergistic or complementary.

The second issue concerns the nature of technology. Of interest are both the television industry's use of technology and its threats from new technology. Production organizations vie for an advantage through access to and innovative use of new technology. At the same time, a rule of thumb suggests that older media are displaced and change as new media alter the media mix. Some scholars have suggested that new media become the old and the old change (McLuhan, 1964). However, media strategists have become more sophisticated. Rather than battling new forms head to head, media corporations evolve with the punches and diversify, recombine, and reposition strategies. Thus, as traditional television networks lose market share, we see them taking on new partners, enhancing market position with new technology and new ventures in cable, information, theme park, and other synergistic businesses.

Supraorganizational Influences.   Responses to competition and technology have played an important role in the rise and continued growth of media conglomerates. Decision making in television is influenced by policy, budgeting, and other constraints at the supraorganizational level, for example, when a new owner changes the direction and character of a group of television stations. When a Disney or Westinghouse moves to take over an existing network, at least five *Ps* change: policies, procedures, programming, pricing, and personnel. Supraorganizational influences attempt to influence economies of scale and synergies with other products in the owner's stable. Concern over the problematic effects of the increasing concentration of television ownership into the hands of a limited group of big players is a driving force in much institution-centered television criticism (Bagdikian, 1989; Murdock, 1982). This issue has historically been difficult to sort out. It can be shown that increases in the conglomerization of television brings both reduced risk taking that leads to homogeneity of programming and to new financial resources to allow development in new marketplace niches (Turow, 1992).

Community or Market Influences.   In placing community and market influences at a subordinate level to societal, industry, and supraorganizational levels, Dimmick and Coit (1982, 1983) focus on specific actional influences of community pressures and marketplace conditions. For example, counterprogramming strategies fall into this fold. Establishing market position relative to media other than television may drive other decisions. Strategies or changes at a local newspaper or radio station may influence decisions of television station managers. Influences may be seen in other ways. Decision making about news can often be tied to pressures by a community group that believes its voice is being left out or misrepresented. News coverage may also be influenced by decision making to give coverage or favorable treatment to community organizations or issues that station executives or owners endorse. Influence on such decision making may be direct or indirect, with decision makers leaning in a direction that they do not have to be told is in their best interests.

Interorganizational Influences.   This level concerns organizational functioning. Here the influence of the organization's goals, formal structure, policies, work routines, and informal networks on decision making is assessed. The focus is often on gatekeepers (Breed, 1955) or key people who can make important decisions about the airing or character of programming. Television executives can be seen as power brokers who must make decisions in a climate of competing resources and political coalitions (Cyert & March, 1963). Often, however, it is not a person per se that influences decision making. Rather, decisions often come out of two key features of organizational life: policies and routines. Each of these has both a formal and an informal side.

Organizational policies often come out of debates for limited resources such as air time, budget, or personnel. Television programming is influenced by these departmental or subunit turf battles. In reality, these turf battles are often a working out of priorities to achieve larger organizational goals, such as achieving a 20 percent audience share or increasing advertising billings by 10 percent over a six-month period. Creative strategies, not seen in formal policy guidelines, often come into play in achieving these goals. Thus, informal policies such as leading the local newscast with blood and guts during a sweeps week might be consciously or unconsciously attended to.

Work routines also influence decisions throughout television organizations. Policies and goals are one thing, but work must get done in a timely and professional manner. Formal procedures or rules may be in place—for example, getting a required approval of the boss or cross-checking with two independent sources before running a news story. In attempting to simplify the work process, informal routines are often pragmatic practices. For example, the production staff of a situation comedy needs to allocate responsibilities and time to shoot a show before a studio audience at the end of week. Everything is "back timed" to the scheduled performance. Elements from read throughs to rewrites to camera blocking to dress rehearsal are slotted. In television news, a beat reporter learns to expedite covering a large bureaucracy by relying on tried-and-true sources, but the character of coverage is influenced by dependence on those sources. Thus, in various ways, work routines place real-life constraints on decisions and affect creativity, resourcefulness, and the aired television product.

Formal or Informal Group Influences.   Work done by groups on formal and informal bases affect television. Executives from different departments can come together to hammer out the program schedule (Brown, 1971). Section editors of a local newscast often meet as a group to decide the time allotted to national, local, sports, weather, and other news in a given day. Television beat reporters make decisions based on information and influence provided by reporters working the beat for the competition (Tuchman, 1973). The writing staff for a television show needs to work through a series of issues to come up with a ready-for-prime-time script (Pekurny, 1982). Studying group behavior in television means understanding the context, history, patterns of interaction, power relationships, and formal and informal forces. Although it is difficult to study a whole organization firsthand, studying decision making on the group level generally involves understanding the perspectives of all the participants and some actual observation.

Dyadic Communication Influences.   Some decisions are made on the basis of two people in a working relationship. Certainly many decisions about whether and how to cover a news story are made between an individual reporter and news editor. The relationship between a news reporter and individual sources is an important dyadic relationship that influences the character of television news. Agreements about the content of chat on a talk show are often negotiated with a guest by a segment producer (Tuchman, 1974). Relationships that individual powerful program producers have with key executives have their own unique and personal side. Thus, dyadic communication patterns that individuals in television have with others, both in and outside the industry, shape what we see on screen.

Intraindividual or Cognitive Level Influences.   Finally, what goes into an individual decision about television? What criteria come into play? Personal decisions can affect whether a show is produced, a news story runs, or whether a "final" cut needs reworking. Research in this area explores the elements involved in making different decisions. How are elements in a decision conceptualized, combined, weighted, and evaluated? How do models of decision making change by decision makers according to the situation? How do they change over time? How do two decision makers in comparable roles differ in their approach? This level of inquiry attempts to sort out decision criteria that are peculiar to the individual and distinguish them from elements that come from influences and conventions in the larger environment.

Power Roles

Turow's (1984, 1992) approach centers on struggles over power in interorganizational relations. Instead of focusing on decision making, Turow focuses on the varied power roles organizations in the media industry play. Organizations are seen to work within their boundaries or limitations to achieve goals. Because even the most diverse organizations tend to specialize in some areas and not others, they must negotiate with organizations in a larger environment to achieve goals and thrive. Each negotiation is an opportunity to gain or exercise power. The goal is to use resources strategically to gain control over resources needed from other organizations. From this vantage point, "power involves the use of resources by one organization to gain compliance by another organization" (Turow, 1992, p. 21). Money is a common resource used to gain this kind of compliance in using or affecting other's resources. However, resources can also come in the form of people and their talent and knowledge. Information, supplies, or services that are needed or valued are also examples of resources used to gain leverage. In television, there are many examples of resources that one organization has that another needs to succeed. Program producers have creative resources but need the distribution and exhibition services of a network for a program to see the light of day. Similarly, advertisers bring resources, investing money, because they need the creative, distribution, and exhibition resources of both producers and networks for marketplace gain.

Turow sees power roles as the purposeful roles that organizations (for the most part) play in employing resources to gain compliance. Players may emphasize certain aspects of their roles depending on their relationships with others. Some thirteen power roles can be distinguished by a label, typical activities, and the kind of leverage exerted in the television industry. Keep in mind that organizations are not the same as power roles. Rather, it is organizations that typically play most roles, and an organization can often play more than one role (such as when a network serving in the producer role also takes on the distributor and exhibitor roles). Some roles, such as the creator and public power roles, tend, more often than others, to be played by individuals.

The power role framework applied to television is an interorganizational system of activities. Interaction takes place continuously to gain influence over production and the marketplace. Whereas all role players sometimes engage in activities that do not bear on the production of television (like paying their utility bills), the power role framework focuses only on those activities that "affect the output of an organization taking on the producer power role" (Turow, 1992, p. 23). Because the approach centers on the producer role and influences on the producer role, it offers a tidy scheme to critics concerned about the scenes behind the scenes that influence television production. Each of the power roles is introduced briefly below in terms of doing institution-centered television criticism.

The Producer Power Role.   In television, the producer power role facilitates the creation of material for release to an audience. The material may be programming or advertising, but the key concepts here are powers to facilitate the creation and release of material. Thus, the producer power role is almost always played by a complex organization with vast resources with leverage to establish selection criteria for content, determine appropriate content, oversee and guide production of suitable material, and arrange for distribution and exhibition.

It is important to recognize that the producer power role is not the same as that played by creators of television content, such as television producers, directors, or writers who often do not have the power to determine, for example, whether a show makes or stays in a network's schedule. As will be discussed later, these and other creative personnel often have considerable leverage. Powerful creators, such as Aaron Spelling or Steven Bochco, can de facto play the producer power role through agreements with organizations responsible for selecting material. Sufficiently powerful creators can also alter selection criteria or change what is acceptable.

In television, the classic producer power role is played by television networks (and their entertainment, news, and other divisions) that have monies to contract for programming in line with corporate goals and programming strategy. Creative personnel in the form of television producers and their production companies pitch shows they would like to produce to organizations such as networks. However, these programs are not actually produced unless an agreement is made with an organization playing the producer power role. Consequently, organizations playing the producer power role control a host of creative personnel and, through them, the ideas that are presented on television.

The producer power role is played not only by television networks (and their parent corporations) but also by organizations such as local stations, program syndicators, cable networks, cable multiple system owners, and even local cable franchises. Critically oriented assessments of producer power roles reach out to assess the relationship of the producer role to other power roles. For example, studies that investigate the balance of power between the producer and stockholders or advertisers focus on financial tensions in the institutional climate. On the other hand, studies that examine the relationship between producers and creative personnel (such as writers and actors) look at tensions between creativity and constraint. Other studies might examine the tensions between public responsibility and private profit by looking at relationships between producers, public advocacy groups, and regulatory efforts.

The Authority Power Role.   The authority power role in television is played by government. Governmental agencies legislate, regulate, interpret, arbitrate, and enforce actions among the power role players. Authority roles are played at the federal, state, county, and city levels of government by organizations such as legislatures, courts, executive agencies, and the police. In the American television industry, the dominant authority is the Federal Communications Commission (FCC), which licenses and regulates local stations. The FCC also sets guidelines for cable television where the local franchise is granted and regulated at the local and/or state level. In television advertising, the Federal Trade Commission plays an important authority power role. In financial areas, tax code laws can influence investment in television. At a more basic level, the cooperation of the local police can affect the production schedule of a show.

Regulation provides leverage at three levels. At the *structural level,* regulations establish the character and bounds of organizations and their relationships. For example, the decisions to establish broadcasting as a commercial, rather than governmental, enterprise, or to limit the amount of stations owned by one owner are structural. On the *technical level,* the regulation of television's standards of transmission affect how programming is produced and distributed. And most important in terms of the producer power role and programming, television is regulated at the *content level.* Rulings on freedom of speech, copyright, and libelous, obscene, or deceptive materials are all examples of content regulation.

Critical assessments of the authority power role in television generally come from societal concerns over the powers of television. Regulations over station and cable system ownership, syndication, and children's programming all stem from such concern. In looking at the authority power role, the critic is often concerned about diversity issues and fairness. Thus, studies that assess concentration of ownership issues in television or dangers in deceptive advertising often start with baselines established by those playing authority power roles.

The Investor Power Role.   Organizations looking for a return on investment play a variety of power roles. Financial investments may be made at levels ranging from particular television programs to small production companies to multinational communication conglomerates. Diverse organizations such as investment banks, mutual fund managers, insurance companies, and private and government foundations all attempt to leverage their investments.

Some look for financial performance, whereas others, such as foundations, look to influence organizational plans or the production of certain kinds of programming. The ability to attract investors influences the viability of both television production organizations and certain kinds of programming.

The Client Power Role.   Looking for another type of return on investment, the advertising industry plays an important power role in television. Thought of as the producers' customers, clients in essence decide which television programming is released for public consumption. Clients provide money to producers in order to get their products before the public. This influx of money plays a critical role in determining what kinds of programming are produced and whether programming with borderline ratings continue.

Certain kinds of television programming are designed to appeal to those with the targeted demographics of the advertiser. Thus, children's programming garners the interest of cereal manufacturers, soap operas interest manufacturers of household cleaners trying to reach women, and beer advertisers go after males with sports programming. A variety of organizations are involved in the client product role. They range from product manufacturers and service providers who are the advertisers to the advertising agencies, media buyers, and production companies that support the client.

The influences of the client power role on television production can be considerable. When influential advertisers talk about creating the right program setting for their products, producers listen. Advertisers can enter into barter arrangements that underwrite the production costs of programming they want to sponsor. The television critic has many opportunities to examine the influence of the client power role. These opportunities range from econometrically based case studies of the buying strategies of major television advertisers to ethnographically inspired studies that examine the power relations between the sponsor and the network or local station.

The Auxiliary Power Role.   Organizations playing the auxiliary power role provide production and ancillary supplies and services to producers. Without these supplies and services, a television product could not be created. Sets need to be designed and constructed. Wardrobe, makeup, and hairdressing have to be just so. Cameras, sound, and lighting equipment need to be coordinated. Facilities with requisite office equipment, communication capabilities, and even plumbing and air conditioning need to be in place. All kinds of things need to be delivered and transported. Postproduction screening, editing, sound, and visual special effects call for another layer of auxiliary support. And throughout the process, such diverse services as maintenance, security, accounting, and insurance need to be attended to. These products and services are infrequently given attention in institution-centered television criticism. The effective handling of organizations that provide auxiliary power roles can make or break a production.

The Creator Power Role.   In television, individuals such as producers, directors, writers, actors, news reporters, stunt people, set designers, and film and videotape editors play the creator power role. These are key people who participate in the invention and execution of television's creative and artistic product. Individual creators gain leverage as they become highly recognized for distinct and superior talent that contributes to a pattern of success. This leverage, which might be thought of as *clout* (Turow, 1992), comes about not only because of the track record of success (Pekurny, 1982), but also because the creative individual can contribute something that is unique. Oftentimes, this star quality adds considerably to labor costs associated with television production, but it is seen as both an investment and a cost of doing business by those organizations playing the producer power role.

Once again it is important to distinguish the creator power role from the producer power role. As creators gain clout, this line may seem to blur. A good example of this situation can be seen by looking at the key creative figure in television production, the producer–writer (Newcomb & Alley, 1983). As particular writers like Stephen Bochco or Stephen J. Cannell establish successful track records, they often move into the producer role, forming production companies, with long-term deals with organizations such as networks or syndicators who play the producer power role. Another example might be an influential news anchor or personality, such as a Dan Rather or Barbara Walters, who has the personal clout to develop and shape the production of programming. Thus, even though these individuals may be employed by a network, their influence in creative roles is often sufficient to sway those playing the producer power role who technically hold the strings to production and distribution. Much of the power in the relationship between creators and production organizations comes from the need to keep star producer-writers and talent happy so they will stay in the stable and contribute to the ongoing success and identity of the production organization. Much institution-centered television criticism and popular attention have focused on the role of television creators, particularly producer–writers, and their ability to create in the face of corporate constraints. This line of criticism has much in common with analysis of the influence of the television auteur on the finished artistic product (see Chapter 5).

The Union Power Role.   Because creators and other production personnel have traditionally had little clout, job security, or control over working conditions, a guild system for creative and support workers developed to provide leverage over production organizations regarding the allocation of human resources and services. Television production companies negotiate agreements with union groups representing directors, writers, actors, technicians, musicians, art directors, designers, and other creative personnel. Examples of these groups include the Screen Actors Guild, American Federation of Television and Radio Artists, Directors Guild of America, Writers Guild of America,

National Association of Broadcast Employees and Technicians, International Alliance of Theatrical Stage Employees and Moving Picture Machine Operators, and the International Brotherhood of Electrical Workers.

Although Turow (1992) casts this attempt at leverage as the union power role, it is really the labor power role. One of the key issues in institutional relations in television production has been recent attempts by production organizations to evade the leverage exercised by stipulations in unionized agreements. These attempts accelerated during the 1980s with two main strategies. In Hollywood and New York, there was a movement to subcontract production with production companies that used many nonunionized employees. Second, there was a strategy to move production to places where labor costs were less than the norm in the two production capitals. As a result, attractive production climates in Canadian cities and in Florida drew production organizations interested in cutting labor costs. Although the ebb and flow of the influence of organized labor on television production has been little examined by television critics, these tensions influence the character of television product.

The Distributor and Exhibitor Power Roles.   In many media industries, including television, the distributor and exhibitor power roles are often merged or so interlinked as to be thought of as one. Technically, distributing television programming means making it available to an exhibitor. However, distribution through networks, syndicators, or other distribution firms does not necessarily ensure exhibition, or more important, ensure exhibition at a desirable time or place in the program schedule. For example, a television syndicator might arrange for programming to be distributed to a group of television stations, but the contractual arrangement may not stipulate the air time for the program. We see this contractual right exercised when a once popular syndicated program drops in a local station's ratings and is consequently moved from a prime-time access slot to the dead of night until the contract runs out.

One practice that has kept television networks powerful over the years has been their ability to control the distribution and exhibition of programming. Given that the networks also control production (through contracts and in-house efforts), this vertical integration of control over production, distribution, and exhibition has created powerful oligopolies. As distributors, networks rely on owned and operated stations as the basis for successful distribution and exhibition. Networks also elicit effective control of exhibition through contractual arrangements with their affiliated stations, although control waivers with increased competition (e.g., new networks such as Fox, WB, and UPN) or poor ratings.

Syndicators offer another distribution and exhibition mechanism to producers as an alternative to networks. Often syndicators can cut a more attractive deal with production organizations looking for a way to distribute and exhibit their product. Syndicators, however, rely on an often fragile group of stations; clout often comes in the form of including the syndication rights to a *hot* property (such as *The Cosby Show* in its heyday) with other shows the syndicator is trying to move. Leverage, such as a good place in the local station's line-up, is always negotiable.

Television product is also affected by the distribution and exhibition clout of movie studios, cable networks, and multiple system cable owners. Hollywood studios strike deals that put movie channels in competition with each other; cable networks compete for syndicated programming; and multiple system owners can control distribution channels by making or not making space available on their local cable systems for competitors or competitors of companies they have cut deals with. Much of the current action in the television marketplace concerns the ever-shifting arrangements between production organizations and those that control distribution and exhibition. The object is to get television product through the *gate* of distributors and exhibitors. Today, distribution and exhibition battles feature bigger and more interlocked conglomerates as warriors. For the television critic, the ways in which production organizations cope with the dynamics of distribution and exhibition play an essential part in explaining the nature of a specific television product (see Turow, 1992).

The Linking-Pin Power Role.   Distributors and exhibitors may play the primary gatekeeping role in deciding what and when programming airs, but a variety of linking-pin organizations also play a role in what gets through the gate. Linking-pin organizations move media material from another media industry to television, for example, people promoting a new book or movie on television. Often the same companies that own book publishers and movie studios also own television stations and networks or they produce syndicated programming. The placement of a media product from one arm of the media conglomerate to its television arm is one example of a synergistic relationship. Television stations and networks often exploit this synergy by promoting one program on another, such as interviewing the star of an upcoming TV movie on that network's morning show.

Many linking-pin organizations are involved in television. They help media cross-fertilize and bring together publics that sometimes share little else. Linking-pin power is often played by public relations or promotional agencies who are contracted by another media client. Yet much linking is not about public relations, but about necessary cooperation between media producers. For example, a talk show producer might need a movie clip to attract a wanted guest, or a local television station might need sports footage from ESPN for a story. In news, wire services and other news agencies link news from far away for distribution to individual television markets. In various ways, linking-pin organizations leverage resources that are needed in the production of television. These resources can be free when publicity is bartered or simply purchased.

The Facilitator Power Role.   Facilitator organizations differ from the linking pins that tend to move material to television programming from another media industry (or from another division of television). Organizations such as talent agencies, law firms, market research, and other consulting companies play the facilitator power role. Facilitators put together pieces of packages that can make proposals to production companies very attractive. By bringing together talent in their stable, a powerful talent agency such as William Morris or Creative Artists can offer a near complete package of creative talent to ensure success of television project. These packages can include name actors, producers, directors, writers, composers, and other talent. Packages of this sort leverage interest of organizations in the producer power role by simplifying the production task, saving time and money, and providing a safety net of talent with proven track records (Whiteside, 1981).

Other types of organizations provide information to help producers evaluate material and talent. Ratings research provided by firms such as A.C. Nielson and Arbitron facilitate decisions by clients such as advertisers about program *buys* and decisions about program continuance and counterprogramming. Other companies such as Preview House, Marketing Evaluations, the Stanford Research Institute, and Entertainment Response Analysts provide attitudinal, psychographic, and physiological research to aid pre- and postproduction decision making. Other consultants advise on programming, personnel, financial, technical, governmental, and public relations issues.

The Public and Public Advocacy Power Roles.   Individual members of the public make decisions about viewing television programming. Collectively, these decisions influence the strategies of production organizations through information provided by facilitators who collect and digest ratings data. Public advocacy organizations come about when individuals organize in collective action. Public advocacy organizations can make effective demands on producer, distributor, exhibitor, and client organizations that lead to change in television content. Diverse organizations such as the Moral Majority, Action for Children's Television, Mothers Against Drunk Driving, Partnership for a Drug-Free America, the National Association for the Advancement of Colored People, and the American Civil Liberties Union pressure local stations, networks, production companies, advertisers, and others in a variety of ways. The groups may lobby for legislation to control a certain kind of content. They may organize boycotts of products advertised in objectionable shows, or they may use public relations and advertising to directly expose or call attention to their problems or demands. The actions of public advocates are almost always evaluated in a cost-benefit analysis by organizations that can affect the producer power role. The expeditious nature of this kind of response has often led to temporary fixes to long-term problems. As a result, ongoing problem areas such as television treatment of violent and sexual material tend to ebb and flow with public advocacy efforts.

Permutations in Controlling Dependence and Risk.   Organizations often play more than one power role in attempting to reduce resource dependence and control risk. For example, television networks not only play producer, distributor, and exhibitor roles with regard to much of their product but also often bring some auxiliary, linking-pin, and facilitator services in-house. In an age of increasingly vertically integrated media conglomerates, almost any permutation of combined power roles is possible. When it is not possible or advantageous to bring power roles within the organization, interorganizational coalitions develop to reduce risk. Patterns in the shape and form of these interorganizational coalitions shift over time and circumstance. As these relationships change, centers of power shift in the television industry. For example, in the United States, as rule making by the FCC limited the abilities of networks to produce and syndicate their own programming, syndicators initiated relationships with cable networks and system owners and these new relationships tilted power away from the networks. As the consequences of this trend became clear, new rule making allowed the networks latitude in cable ownership, production, and syndication. Critical studies that assess the historical processes in changing power role relationships and the consequent shift in power centers can make real contributions to understanding television. Strategies for doing this and other types of studies are discussed in the next section.

Doing Institution-Centered Television Criticism

Doing institution-centered television criticism is complex. Like other forms of criticism, a central question gets you started. With this question in hand, think about your perspective. Do you want to study the big picture, or might you benefit from a close look at the inner workings of an organization or process? What viewpoint do you lean to? Are you interested in political-economic critique from an instrumentalist or neo-Marxist stance? Or are you more attracted to a viewpoint grounded in industrial relations? Are you a cultural pluralist? If so, are you more a managerialist or a culturalist? Or perhaps you are really a consumerist at heart? In deciding these questions, it is sometimes useful to look back at a wider range of critical approaches you were drawn to in analyzing television. You might want to blend a feminist leaning with a culturalist vantage point on organizational relations in studying story choice at a local television station. You might want to combine audience ethnographies to test the consumerist view that program development actually stems from market sensitivities.

There are other issues to decide upon. What levels in the decision making hierarchy are you most interested in studying? Which levels really need to be included for a complete analysis? Should you think about your institutional issue in terms of power roles? Which power-role relationships to the producer power role are most relevant in answering your question? In addition, there are some very practical issues. Often doing institution-centered criticism means getting access to organizations and spending time observing activities. In other instances, it means getting access to accurate economic data, much of which might be proprietary. You may find that you will need to backtrack, redefining and refining your research questions to focus on a television organization in your local area. Or you may need to rethink whether you can actually do a study because you just can't get your hands on the data that you need. Once you begin to resolve some of these issues, you should also think about your approach to gathering data and actually writing your critique.

Writing Institution-Centered Criticism

The approaches presented below tend to be linked to certain kinds of research questions at differing levels of analysis. Historical studies tend to use a wide-angle lens to look at the big picture. Ethnographic studies tend to put individual decision making and group dynamics under the microscope. Case studies take up the middle ground and are often used to study organizations. There are blurred lines among the approaches. For example, histories can be framed as case studies, and case studies can use ethnographic methods. All these approaches rely on historical sense and diversity of data. Most institutional critics of television are willing to trade off the benefits of being resourceful against the liabilities of being contained by methodological formalism.

Historical Approaches.   Histories of television institutions, organizations, and key people cannot help but have critical viewpoints. Viewpoints come in choosing certain subjects and events as significant, in interpreting what they mean, and most important, in attempting to explain causation. Readers and even chroniclers of history often seem to be unaware of a critical viewpoint. For example, authors of popular biographies, a common form of television history, might fail to recognize their own Horatio Alger driven beliefs in the individual's ability to succeed through hard work in a capitalist system as a pluralist or consumerist vantage point. Critical histories are more forthright, with critics in touch with the reasons they are interested in certain times, processes, organizations, or people. Critics may bring a viewpoint from political economy, industrial relations, or other areas to the study, or they may use a grounded-theory approach, where data informs the initial vantage point.

Histories share the purpose of presenting an explanation of the past. Good histories aim for fullness and truth; allegiance with a critical perspective should not obfuscate something being reported or fully analyzed. Topics should be significant, clearly defined, demarcated in terms of time and space, and have continuity. Topics may be broad, such as the development of U.S. television or the role of the sponsor (Barnouw, 1975, 1978), or be more narrowly focused, such as on a particular network or show (Metz, 1975, 1977).

Research should be bibliographically sound; a complete record of primary and secondary resources should be not only compiled but also evaluated in terms of their explicit and implicit meanings. Facts need to be purposively collected, accurate, verifiable, and clearly documented. Interpretation should stem from the facts at hand with generalizations made in context; generalizations should not overstep their logical bounds or be based on simplistic reductions. Causation similarly should be grounded in evidence, but proceed in an orderly fashion from a priori or grounded theory. Systematic attempts to distinguish causes (i.e., immediate vs. antecedent or paramount vs. contributory) often help in shaping theoretical explanations (Startt & Sloan, 1989).

Critical histories can bring a wide range of approaches and methods to the table. In the course of investigation, historians read others' accounts, do interviews, review institutional data, and even apply statistical and econometric methods to answering questions. A good historian is an adventurer with many tools at hand. In the end, the critical historian of television must make sense of a time, a situation, the nature of personal judgments, and structural constraints, all in the course of one analysis. Writing such histories presents real challenges. Foremost, historical narratives tell a story. Good critical histories read as literature; they are alive, present compelling and accurate evidence and examples, and rely on intuitive reasoning and an overarching structure. Successful structures for composition vary widely, but they all convey organizational clarity to the reader. For example, writing can follow a temporal logic or contrast parallel events happening in different places. Other successful approaches can organize around themes or tensions across time and place, as suggested below.

Case Study Approaches.   Just as histories may take a case study approach, case studies of more recent happenings may take the form of a history of the present. Similar to historical studies, case studies allow researchers to use a variety of evidence. Documents, interviews, direct observation, and even survey research methods may be used in framing the case, and triangulation of methods and types of data helps to build validity. The overarching goal of case studies is to use as many data sources as practical to systematically assess organizations, groups, individuals, policies, or events. Defining features of the case study come from its particularity in studying real life in context (Merriam, 1988). Thus, case studies are especially useful in studying the operational side of television. For example, case studies might be used to assess the making of a particular program (Stipp, Hill-Scott, & Dorr, 1987), compare television newsroom practices in different contexts (Browne, 1983), or examine the relationship between network profits and investment in new media technologies (Dimmick & Wallschlaeger, 1986). In studying such phenomena, the case study often relies on "thick" description, inductive reasoning, and an approach to theory that is grounded in data. Case studies are useful in exploration and suggesting explanations. However, the case study's particularity is also its weakness. While often serving as useful heuristic devices in explaining how things actually work, case studies risk painting idiosyncratic pictures that are unique and are not easily open to generalization.

There is no real cookbook for designing a case study. Your point of departure remains a significant and clearly defined topic. Case studies are often shaped by pragmatic issues, such as the power roles or decision-making levels you have interest in. Other times, your topic may be limited by organizations, individuals, and data that you can actually gain access to. Case studies often require the cooperation of television organizations. You will need to reach agreement early in the process about information you may access and people you may interview. Such limitations may influence beginning a case study, and undoubtedly, assessing inferences about phenomena you are trying to explain. Time or access issues may limit you to doing a single case study. Although you may be able to go into great depth in analyzing the single case, your generalizations may be limited. Multiple case studies offer opportunities to use pattern-matching strategies to assess similarities and differences in situations (Wimmer & Dominick, 1991). Pattern matching can guide you into using either a most-similar or most-different approach as discussed earlier in relation to Dimmick and Coit's (1983) decisional hierarchy model.

Similar to doing critical history, the case study method can often put massive amounts of information before the critic. Effectively summarizing data, coming up with coherent analytical strategies, and writing about both the process and your findings can present real challenges. Depending on the kinds of data that your study relies on, a traditional research report presenting problems, methods, findings, and discussion might be appropriate. Other cases may call for chronologically presented narratives, structural comparisons, or organization around selected themes.

Ethnographic Approaches.   Many times case studies use the ethnographic *impulse* in combination with other methods of data gathering to study overall organizational functioning. More purely ethnographic studies provide more detail about individuals and smaller groups within organizations. Issues in doing ethnographic studies to aid audience-centered criticism were discussed in some detail in Chapter 6. The issues here are largely the same. Ethnographic sensibilities are applied to studying individuals, groups, and organizations involved with television.

Going into the field when studying the audience means visiting the scene of the crime, where actual viewing takes place. Studying television work from this vantage point means getting inside television organizations. Gaining the trust of a viewer in doing an audience ethnography involves building a relationship and often participating in viewing and other household activities. Yet, however reticent a viewer may be in disclosing information and feelings to the researchers, trade secrets and other workplace dynamics are not at stake. Thus, studying the television workers in context presents many more marked difficulties in separating the wheat from the chaff. Workers may feel that candor over information would give a competitor an advantage. Disclosing true feelings about the work situation, bosses, or coworkers could create ill will and even put a person's job at risk. Thus, in studying the organizational context of television, you must take real care in being introduced into the organization, making your objectives clear, and providing ongoing reassurance about how the information gathered will be used. It is not uncommon for researchers to come to agreements about how the identity of the organization and individuals will be handled in research reports. Organizations may ask you to sign confidentiality agreements and to see (and even approve) research reports prior to release.

As is the case with audience study, gathering data means approaching the observational environment as though it were anthropologically strange. Observation should be inobtrusive and nonjudgmental. Efforts should be made to understand situations from the perspectives of the actors in the organizational setting. Focus on listening and understanding rules as perceived by participants, rather than imposing your own logic on situations. Work to triangulate data that can contribute to your understanding. Combine observation, depth interviewing, focus group interviews with mental-mapping exercises, institutional data, and a historical sense. The challenges of data reduction and presentation mirror those in audience-centered analysis. Outline your procedures clearly, work to present material efficiently in summary form, and explain your evaluative logic. Make the research report tell a story and think about whether it is best told as a realist or confessional tale (van Mannen, 1988; see Chapter 6). Often the best theorizing comes from an analytic induction process, revising your initial assumptions by grounding them in experiences as understood by television workers (Glaser & Strauss, 1967). As with histories and case studies, your ethnographically inspired critique should take on a literary quality. Thematic development, in areas such as those suggested below, often help the writer craft a tale of drama and struggle.

Themes and Tensions

Developing themes and confronting tensions in creative ways can make narrative critiques of television institutions come alive. A sample of often seen relational tensions in institution-centered criticism is presented below. The areas are not mutually exclusive and tensions exist between the themes. Although this list is by no means complete and you could easily add to it, you might be surprised to see how tensions of these types are almost universal and in evidence in both macro- and micro-level studies (see Ettema, Whitney, & Wackman, 1987).

Power and Equity.   The overarching tension in institution-centered television criticism is the one between power and equity. When one is concerned with power, one is at least implicitly concerned with equity. Questions about who has power beg other questions about who does not. Questions about the wielding of power suggest other questions about abuse and standards of fairness and equity. Thus, from a critical perspective, one cannot just analyze power in institutional relations, asking only about who has it and how it works. One has to go beyond analysis to evaluation of whether existing arrangements are fair from the vantage point of one's critical perspective. Power roles and decision making at all levels of television concern balances between those who have power and those who do not. Critical inquiry "interpellates" this relationship and searches for answers to questions of equity, fairness, and change.

Public Responsibility and Private Profit.   Struggles between power and equity in television are mirrored in the tensions between public responsibility and private profit. Often this tension is posed in terms of two philosophically distinct beliefs about regulation and the marketplace. In the first instance, many believe that we need regulation to protect us from the harms of television and the abuses of its operators. In the second case, others believe that government should stay out of the speech, ideas, and business of television and that a free marketplace will attend to issues of public responsibility. Interestingly, there are often ideological struggles even within a camp. For example, economic conservatives might advocate an unregulated marketplace, but social conservatives might be ill at ease with certain kinds of programming or ideas on television and call for regulation. Tensions between responsibility and profit are seen at almost every level of analysis, from the molar levels of policymaking, law, and regulation to most molecular levels of group and individual decision making, where ethical judgments based on professional and personal standards may be more significant.

News and Entertainment.   Related in no small way to the tension between responsibility and profit is television's tension between news and entertainment. One of television's basic definitional dilemmas is that it is a two-headed monster. There are market pressures for its news to be entertaining. Another complex issue is that its entertainment fare is necessarily informational, telling people much about how television sees the world. And in the blurry border between the two is television advertising. In a fundamentally persuasional form, commercials seek to inform viewers of products and their merits, but must do so in a way that leaves a warm afterglow. In television organizations, these issues are raised every day in varied contexts. Decisions about television reporters focus as much on personalities and good looks as they do on reportorial experience. Making television docudramas entails balancing an entertaining story with factual veracity. Overarching decisions about creating program schedules that are in the public interest beg questions about whether people are more interested in news or entertainment.

Global and Local. The conflicting demands of being interested in global markets but giving the appearance of meeting local needs poses a different kind of tension on television organizations. Once a television product has been produced, economies of scale encourage sale and distribution to the largest possible audience. Thus, television products with long shelf lives and the ability to cross national borders are attractive to investors. On the other hand, local interests may be served by community-specific programming that is temporally specific only to the here and now. Television-poor nations may cry out that problematic cultural invasion occurs when imported television dominates, homogenizes, and reprioritizes the local agenda. The pressures for globality of television programming refer to more than attempts at world-wide distribution. The market encourages national over regional programming and regional over local. Even in a local market, a station's broad reach often demands an area- as opposed to community-level focus. Regulatory philosophies intersect with these issues, and tensions are evident in production decisions. Sometimes local programming is produced in response to that produced at the national level, but the direction is almost never the other way around.

Conglomerization and Fragmentation. Television's built-in push toward globalization goes with its increasing conglomerization. With a pattern of mergers and acquisitions, television stations, production companies, cable-programming services, cable systems, and other television service companies are coming to be owned by a limited group of communications and general conglomerates. Goals to create vertical integration of production, distribution, and exhibition of television product and synergies among communication and other holdings are evident. With conglomerization comes a decrease in diversity of ownership and a homogeneity in approach. While conglomerization fuels a focus on globality of product, competition remains. Competition revolves around defining marketplace niches and competing in a fragmented market. Positioning strategies form around specialization with conglomerates moving to develop a suite of products that synergize nicely, and collectively control market share. Products like twenty-four-hour cable news or sports that develop as flagships of one corporate strategy are often challenged and repositioned by new corporate coalitions. The relationship between conglomerization and fragmentation in the television industry is as much synergy as tension and has raised questions about distinctions between specialization and diversity.

Diversity and Track Records. Opportunities for specialization in a fragmented marketplace do not automatically equate with diversity. Specialties may serve different parts of the consumer marketplace with essentially the same logic and value set. The dynamics of production may also remain the same. Here, the ongoing tension is between those people with track records of television success and those who want a place at the table. To control risk, industry decision makers lean to known people and products. Television is a risky business with many more failed shows than successes. There is always a push for something new in the marketplace, but not too new. As a result, new shows often look like old successful shows, produced by veteran creators, but with new twists. This system conspires to limit much creativity to a highly socialized (and over time, homogeneous) group with eyes pointed backward at television experience. For programmers and others in the managerial ranks, it is easier to defray failure by being surprised over the aberrance in a successful track record. The tension between diversity and track records also plays a hand in hiring practices within the television industry. Minorities and women are at a disadvantage in a system that values track records.

Routine and Creativity.   Dependence on track records is one way the television industry attempts to control risk. Workplace routines and dependence on formula are other ways that creativity is constrained. In many regards, producing television programming is much like producing any industrial product. In this case, workers on an assembly line produce a product in accordance with professional standards according to proven formulas. The resultant routinization dampens the need for bursts of creativity. Creativity is structurally constrained. Formulas set such things as episode and segment length, number of characters, plot structure, variants in theme, and breaks in the action. Much is predetermined. The show must be produced on budget and in a timely manner. Even in a news show, stories must fit into the sections of the program. Some stories are more likely to be seen than others. Stories with action and good pictures fit the formula. Stories about already famous people or leaders of established groups are more likely to be chosen (Tuchman, 1978). Professional standards about newsworthiness or the technical level of production also alleviate the need to make each decision a unique decision or creative event. In short, creativity is often in short supply because the routines and norms of professional practice dictate many decisions in television. Creativity can take precedence in unconventional situations or situations where organizations are forced to take risks. As a result, creativity is inversely related to market position; weak positions encourage creativity and risk taking.

Looking Ahead

In the selection that follows, one of the approaches to institution-centered television criticism can be seen. Tucker and Shah's study of the making of the miniseries *Roots* uses the *production of culture* research tradition, which is typically associated with an industrial relations approach as its point of departure. However, their strategy blends a decidedly culturalist version of this strategy with a larger look at the political economy of the television industry.

Their focus is very much on the structural mechanisms and social consequences of constraint.

REFERENCES

Bagdikian, B. (1989). *The media monopoly* (3rd ed.). Boston: Beacon.

Barnouw, E. (1975). *Tube of plenty: The development of American television.* New York: Oxford University Press.

Barnouw, E. (1977). *The sponsor: Notes on a modern potentate.* New York: Oxford University Press.

Breed, W. (1955). Social control in the newsroom: A functional analysis. *Social Forces, 32,* 326–335.

Brown, L. (1971). *Television: The business behind the box.* New York: Harcourt Brace Jovanovich.

Browne, D. (1983). The international newsroom. *Journal of Broadcasting, 27,* 205–231.

Cyert, R. M., & March, J. G. (1963). *A behavioral theory of the firm.* Englewood Cliffs, NJ: Prentice-Hall.

Dimmick, J., & Coit, P. (1982). Levels of analysis in mass media decision making: A taxonomy, research strategy, and illustrative data analysis. *Communication Research, 9,* 3–32.

Dimmick, J., & Coit, P. (1983). Levels of analysis in mass media decision making: A taxonomy, research strategy, and illustrative data analysis. In E. Wartella & D. C. Whitney (Eds.), *Mass communication review yearbook, volume 4* (pp. 361–390). Beverly Hills, CA: Sage.

Dimmick, J., & Wallschlaeger, M. (1986). Measuring corporate diversification: A case study of new media ventures by television network parent companies. *Journal of Broadcasting & Electronic Media, 30,* 1–14.

Dominick, J., & Pearce, M. C. (1976). Trends in network prime-time programming, 1953–74. *Journal of Communication, 26* (Winter), 70–80.

Ettema, J., Whitney, D. C., & Wackman, D. B. (1987). Professional mass communicators. In C. R. Berger & S. H. Chaffee (Eds.), *Handbook of communication science* (pp. 747–780). Newbury Park, CA: Sage.

Giddens, A. (1979). *Central problems in social theory: Action, structure, and contradiction in social analysis.* London: Macmillan.

Gitlin, T. (1979). *The whole world is watching.* Berkeley: University of California Press.

Glaser, B. G., & Strauss, A. L. (1967). *The discovery of grounded theory: Strategies for qualitative research.* Chicago: Aldine.

King, S. W. (1975). *Communication and social influence.* Reading, MA: Addison-Wesley.

Lorsch, J., & Morse, J. (1974). *Organizations and their members: A contingency approach.* New York: Harper & Row.

Luhmann, N. (1979). *Trust and power.* New York: John Wiley.

Luther, S. F. (1988). *The United States and direct broadcast satellite.* New York: Oxford University Press.

Mannen, J. Van (1988). *Tales of the field: On writing ethnography.* Chicago: University of Chicago Press.

McLuhan, M. (1964). *Understanding media: The extensions of man.* New York: McGraw-Hill.

Merriam, S. B. (1988). *Case study research in education.* San Francisco: Jossey-Bass.

Metz, R. (1975). *CBS: Reflections in a bloodshot eye.* Chicago: Playboy Press.

Metz, R. (1977). *The Today show: An inside look.* Chicago: Playboy Press.

Molotch, P., & Lester, M. (1974). News as purposive behavior: On the strategic use of routine events, accidents, and scandals. *American Sociological Review, 39,* 101–112.

Murdock, G. (1982). Large corporations and the control of the communications industries. In M. Gurevitch, T. Bennett, J. Curran, & J. Woolacott (Eds.), *Culture, society, and the media* (pp. 118–150). New York: Methuen.

Newcomb, H., & Alley, R. S. (1983). *The producer's medium.* New York: Oxford University Press.

Pekurny, R. (1982). Coping with television production. In D. C. Whitney & J. Ettema (Eds.), *Individuals in mass media organizations: Creativity and constraint* (pp. 131–143). Beverly Hills, CA: Sage.

Peterson, R. A. (1976). The production of culture: A prolegomenon. *American Behavioral Scientist, 19,* 7–22.

Przeworski, A., & Teune, H. (1970). *The logic of comparative social inquiry.* New York: Wiley.

Rogers, E. M., & Kincaid, D. L. (1981). *Communication networks: Toward a new paradigm for research.* New York: Free Press.

Schudson, M. (1991). The sociology of news production revisited. In J. Curran & M. Gurevitch (Eds.), *Mass media and society* (pp. 141–159). London: Edward Arnold.

Shanks, B. (1976). *The cool fire.* New York: Norton.

Short, K. R. M. (1986). *Western broadcasting over the iron curtain.* New York: St. Martin's Press.

Startt, J. D., & Sloan, W. D. (1989). *Historical methods in mass communication.* Hillsdale, NJ: Lawrence Erlbaum.

Stipp, H., Hill-Scott, K., & Dorr, A. (1987). Using social science to improve children's television. *Journal of Broadcasting & Electronic Media, 31,* 461–473.

Tuchman, G. (1973). Making news by doing work: Routinizing the unexpected. *American Journal of Sociology, 79,* 110–131.

Tuchman, G. (1974). Assembling a network talk show. In G. Tuchman (Ed.), *The TV establishment: Programming for power and profit.* Englewood Cliffs, NJ: Prentice-Hall.

Tuchman, G. (1978). *Making news: A study in the construction of reality.* New York: Free Press.

Turnstall, J. (1977). *The media are American.* New York: Columbia University Press.

Turow, J. (1984). *Media industries: The production of news and entertainment.* New York: Longman.

Turow, J. (1991). A mass communication perspective on entertainment industries. In J. Curran & M. Gurevitch (Eds.), *Mass media and society* (pp. 160–177). London: Edward Arnold.

Turow, J. (1992). *Media systems in society: Understanding industries, strategies, and power.* New York: Longman.

White, G. M. (1950). The gatekeeper: A case study in the selection of news. *Journalism Quarterly, 27,* 383–390.

Whiteside, T. (1981). *The blockbuster complex.* Middletown, CT: Wesleyan University Press.

Wimmer, R. D., & Dominick, J. R. (1991). *Mass media research: An introduction* (3rd ed.). Belmont, CA: Wadsworth.

Race and the Transformation of Culture: The Making of the Television Miniseries *Roots*

Lauren R. Tucker and Hemant Shah

First published in 1976, Alex Haley's *Roots* symbolized the cultural, social, economic, and political experience of the black community in America, an experience profoundly shaped by the brutality of slavery. *Roots* was a story about slavery told from a slave's point of view—an essentially African-American perspective. When ABC acquired the broadcast rights to Haley's epic slave story, however, *Roots* the television program (*TV Roots*) became a creation of an institution dominated largely by whites. *TV Roots* was produced, written, and directed by whites (with the exception of Gilbert Moses, who directed one episode), broadcast over a network whose programming was dominated by white characters, and shown to a predominantly white audience. As a result, Haley's novel was transformed from a critique of slavery and exposition of white cruelty and indifference into one that diluted, in many ways, the horror, complexities, and seriousness of slave holding.

Discrepancies between *Roots* and *TV Roots* resulted from specific creative choices that were influenced by concerns of the program's makers about reactions of the largely white audience to a story about slavery in America told from a black perspective. These considerations about race took place not in a vacuum but rather in the context of a complex process of producing television content—a process that itself took place in a specific understanding of social relations between black and white Americans. The transformation of *Roots* to *TV Roots* provides clues about how the U.S. television establishment views race in America.

Mass media represent important channels for cultural expression. They produce and spread symbols and images that describe and explain how and why the world works. Among the many representations of the social world mass media create is a perspective on race—what the term means, who it refers to, and how it will be understood (Omi & Winant, 1986, pp. 68–69). The key ideas embodied within the prevailing understanding of race in the United States are that a high level of homogeneity exists within a racial group, that there is a hierarchy of races (with whites at the top and other races and ethnic groups hovering at or near the bottom), and that the culture and sensitivities of blacks and other ethnic groups are subordinate to those of whites (see Fredrickson, 1988, pp. 189–205; Miles, 1989, pp. 42–50; Omi & Winant, 1986). By examining the discrepancies between *Roots* the novel and *TV Roots*, we can discover how and to what extent ideas about race informed creative choices made during the production process and are reflected in the program.

The Production of Television Content

The study of how television (and other mass media) content is produced, which generally comes under the rubric of "production of culture" research, has been informed and shaped by theories and methods used in the study of complex organizations. The general goal of production of culture research was laid out by Peterson (1976). This traditional approach focuses on the organizational structures, functions, and processes by which "creation, manufacture, marketing, distribution, exhibiting, inculcation, evaluation and consumption" of mass media content are undertaken and accomplished (p. 10).

In the traditional approach, television content is seen as the result of decisions made by powerful producers and a handful of associates. A variety of factors, of course, may affect those decisions. The research literature on the production of television programming suggests that factors at three levels—industrial/institutional, organizational, and individual (Ettema, Whitney, & Wackman, 1987)—have an impact on the program decisions and, ultimately, on material coming out of mass media organizations. The *industrial/institutional level* refers to factors such as market considerations and competition with other media organizations. At the *organizational level*, production techniques, product conventions, and casting decisions are some important factors. Television networks, like other businesses, try to reduce uncertainty in their production process. By routinizing certain creative decisions, networks bring control and stability to the creation of television programs. At the *individual level*, important factors include the perceptions, attitudes, and ideas of writers, directors, producers, and others involved in creating the television program.

Although far from mutually exclusive, these three levels can be conceptualized as a hierarchy, with the institutional/industrial level at the top, the organizational level in the middle, and the individual level at the bottom. Interaction among factors at various levels is complex, and it is not always easy to trace the impact of a particular factor at one level to a second factor at another level. But, generally, influence flows in a top-down fashion. Factors at the top level influence factors at the middle level, and top-level and middle-level factors influence bottom-level factors. This "trickle-down" process affects decision making and, ultimately, television content.

Although the traditional approach to production of culture is essentially apolitical in that it "would hold in abeyance the evaluation of cultural forms and focus on the mechanisms that reproduce these forms" (Ettema, Whitney, & Wackman, 1987, p. 748), it is far from non-ideological. Tuchman (1983), for example, has criticized this approach for taking for granted contemporary capitalism and thus obscuring the fact that cultural products emerge from specific sociopolitical and economic relations and tend to reinforce the status quo. By ignoring this dimension of the production of culture, the traditional approach leaves unquestioned and unexamined the relationship between the process of cultural production and the cultural products themselves, and the implications of that relationship for understanding race relations and other social phenomena.

By ignoring American capitalism, the traditional approach to the production of culture also ignores questions about race. One need only look at the importance of slavery to the economic strength of the southern United States in the nineteenth century (Williams, 1944), at the massacre of American Indians in the name of manifest destiny (Steinberg, 1989), and at interpretations of naturalization laws in the 1920s that prohibited Asian Indians from applying for U.S. citizenship (Helweg & Helweg, 1990; Takakai, 1989) to be convinced that the development of American capitalism is inextricably linked to views about race. By ignoring race, a traditional production of culture approach cannot fully explain how the processes involved in the transformation of Haley's novel into *TV Roots* resulted in the marginalization of the black cultural experience and the elevation of the white perspective on the black American experience. The more powerful and illuminating strategy for studying the production of culture, and specifically the transformation of *Roots* to *TV Roots*, is to combine the traditional approach, with its emphasis on the mechanisms and procedures of production, with a close examination of how ideas about race are embedded in the production process and are then reflected in cultural products.

From *Roots* to *TV Roots:* Race and the Transformation of Culture

Led by executive producer David Wolper, the predominantly white production team made creative choices and manufactured content that reflect the dominant understanding of race in the United States. In his book *The Inside Story of TV's "Roots"* (Wolper & Troupe, 1978), Wolper goes into edifying detail concerning the timidity of ABC network executives in developing *Roots* for network television. A dramatic series featuring a predominantly African-American cast had never been successful on American television. In addition, the story of Kunta Kinte and his family required more air time than was usually allotted to a network movie. Ultimately, network executives questioned whether Wolper could make a movie about an African slave acceptable to conservative advertisers and the predominately white audience. After three months of negotiations and Wolper's assurances, ABC finally agreed to finance the project (Wolper & Troupe, 1978).

For Haley, *Roots* symbolized more than one black family's struggle to maintain continuity and identity in the shadow of the dehumanizing institution of slavery. Haley's *Roots* offered an interpretation of American history that connected black Americans with a unique history, identity, and cultural experience that began in Africa. Haley's vision provides black America a connection not only with its past, but also with its present and future. In short, Haley's vision of the black American cultural experience is solidly rooted in the black, African-American perspective of the cultural experience of the black American community. When David Wolper and the network executives at ABC initiated negotiations for the television rights to *Roots*, Haley's vision began to be fundamentally altered.

Although thousands of black Americans viewed *TV Roots*, its producers primarily were concerned about attracting white viewers (Fishbein, 1983, pp. 288–289; Wolper & Troupe, 1978). ABC executive Larry Sullivan stated, "Our concern was to put a lot of white people in the promos. Otherwise, we felt the program would be a turnoff" (quoted in Bogle, 1988, p. 339). Brandon Stoddard, then in charge of ABC's novels for television, stated, "We made certain to use whites viewers had seen a hundred times before [Ed Asner, Lorne Greene] so they would feel comfortable" (quoted in Bogle, 1988, p. 340).

Transforming White Characters

Concern about the predominantly white audience (an institutional/industrial-level factor) motivated many of the changes that occurred during the transformation of Haley's novel into the television series. Some of these changes resulted in production decisions (organization- and individual-level factors) that led to the softening of the personalities of the white characters. During the opening episode of *TV Roots*, the sharp division between the white world of the slaveship captain and the pastoral world of Kunta Kinte's Gambia foreshadows how Haley's vision would be profoundly compromised throughout the production process.

Captain Davies, the slaveship captain portrayed by Asner, is introduced as an honorable, innocent, and naive participant in the thriving slave trade of the 1750s. The captain is characterized as a deeply religious family man and an intelligent and capable sailor, who begins his voyage on the Sabbath because it "seems the Christian thing to do."

His conscience-stricken demeanor is artfully contrasted with that of his godless and depraved first mate, Slater. Slater, no stranger to the slave trade, offers Davies the benefit of his expertise and experience. As they tour the lower decks where the slaves will be chained in a "loose pack" formation, each man evaluates the other's commitment to the task at hand. Viewing his first mate with a mixture of disgust and deference, Davies inquires about the number of times Slater has made the voyage. Upon hearing that Slater has participated in 18 such voyages, Davies responds, "Eighteen! That's seventeen more than I've made. So I'd be willing to admit Mr. Slater that below decks, let's say, you're the expert."

The interaction between Davies and Slater exemplifies the way in which the producers of *TV Roots* manufactured characterizations and content throughout the series to appeal to what they perceived were the needs and desires of white audience members. The inhumanity of Slater, and of the institution of slavery itself, is made more palatable by the humanity of Davies. Even when, longing for home and human warmth, he puts aside his morals and succumbs to temptation with a young African girl brought to him by Slater, Davies is made to appear even more human in his vulnerability and fallibility. Wolper and Troupe (1978) quote William Blinn, the head writer on the *TV Roots* project, offering his rationale for the Davies character:

> For our purposes, he was certainly not a sympathetic man. An understandable man yes—but it is clearly absurd to have a likable slaveship captain. It was equally unwise, we thought, to do four hours of television without showing a white person with whom we could identify. (p. 48)

In his reference to "a white person with whom *we* could identify," Blinn, who is white, clearly is alluding to his concern for the sensibilities of white audience members, which then apparently guided his characterization of Davies.

However, Davies, as the conscience-ridden slaveship captain of *TV Roots*, is in sharp contrast to the nameless, faceless "toubob" or white man that Haley (1976) describes in Kunta Kinte's first encounter with the slaveship crew:

> One of the new toubob was short and stout and his hair was white. The other towered over him, tall and huge and scowling, with deep knife scars across his face, but it was the white-haired one before whom the slatees and the other toubob grinned and all but bowed. . . . Looking at them all, the white-haired one gestured for Kunta to step forward, and lurching backward in terror, Kunta screamed as a whip seared across his back. . . . The white-haired toubob calmly spread Kunta's trembling lips and studied his teeth. (pp. 169–170)

Clearly, a slaveship captain with a conscience is not a part of Haley's narrative.

Blinn's characterization of Davies commences the profound alteration of the images conceived by Haley. Perhaps to accommodate the white television audience, the makers of *TV Roots* added substance and depth to many of the white characters, giving them complex personalities and important positions within the narrative. They also added white characters who did not appear in Haley's novel. Throughout *TV Roots*, white culture and community is given the substance and definition that Haley reserved for his African and black American subjects. The slave's perspective, central to Haley's novel, was subordinated in *TV Roots* so that multidimensional portrayals of white characters with whom the white audience could identify and empathize could be added to the story.

Transforming Black Characters

While expanding the content and characterizations of the white characters, the makers of *TV Roots* narrowed and consolidated many of the black characters developed by Haley. During the first two episodes, many of the black characters were eliminated, reduced, or homogenized by the miniseries' creators. The members of Kunta Kinte's TV family seem to be mere icons compared to the rich characterizations Haley developed. In the novel, Kunta Kinte's relationship with his parents, especially Binta, his mother, plays a significant role in his development. As a woman in a male-oriented society, Binta struggles with the difficult task of maintaining discipline and structure in her son's life without disrupting the social structure. The tension between the two grows as Kunta becomes a man and Binta faces the inevitability of his leaving home. However, Binta's character in *TV Roots*, played by Cicely Tyson, remains flat. Although the makers of *TV Roots* maintain the tension between Kunta Kinte and his mother, they do not provide the depth of characterization or context in which this tension makes logical sense.

According to Haley, Kunta Kinte's African heritage and history form the connective tissue between his homeland and his new home on the American continent. By not giving adequate time or attention to the full development of Kunta Kinte's life in Juffure, the makers of *TV Roots* broke the connection between Kunta Kinte's cultural experience in Africa and his subsequent experience as an American slave. As a result, the series' creators dismissed the uniqueness and complexity of Kunta Kinte's identity and heritage, and, on a broader level, the identity and heritage of all black Americans.

Once the series' makers consolidated and homogenized many of the black characters created by Haley, the rich diversity of slave life and culture described in the novel was lost. For example, the character of Fiddler in the television series was actually a composite of three of Haley's characters—the carriage driver Samson, the gardener, and the Fiddler. In Haley's narrative, each of these characters played a significant role in helping Kunta Kinte to manage life as a slave. In addition, each represented the variety of ways in which slaves adapted to the realities of the "peculiar institution." Each in some way revealed to Kunta different perspectives on slavery from the slaves' point of view.

The makers of *TV Roots* manufactured additions in content that are inconsistent with those portions of the series that remain faithful to the novel. The beauty of Haley's narrative lies in the way in which he intertwines the slave's crucial awareness of the white world with the routines of slave culture. Through their actions and conversations, the members of the slave population reveal their deep understanding of the social, political, and personal influence of slavery on their lives. By contrasting the white slave owners' general ignorance and fear of the activities of the slave population with the slave community's ability to obtain voluminous and insightful information concerning the white masters' world, Haley demonstrates with painstaking care that surviving life as an American slave required constant vigilance and informed awareness of white culture.

In the novel and the series, Kunta Kinte quickly comes to the important realization that a successful escape could be possible only through cautious observation of the white world and the careful control of his own behavior. Kunta Kinte learns to manage the duality of living in the white world and the slave world. However, in episode three, the producers add content that reveals their profound lack of understanding of Kunta Kinte's slave world. In this episode, Kunta Kinte plans the last of his many escape attempts, during which he wastes valuable time and energy by running to the next plantation to find his first love, Fanta, with whom he made the middle passage. The Fanta character loudly rebuffs Kunta Kinte's plea for her to escape with him. Her loud cries alert the slave catchers to Kunta Kinte's presence and, eventually, lead to his anguishing return to slavery.

But Haley's characterization of slave culture does not provide the logic for Fanta's behavior. As a monologue by Fiddler illustrates, the slaves in Haley's novel were painfully aware of the cruel sanctions awaiting those who forgot for a moment the repressiveness of the surrounding white world:

> Looka here, don't start me on white folks' laws. Startin' up a new settlement, dey firs' builds a courthouse, fo' passin' more laws. . . . It's a law niggers can't carry no gun, even no stick that look like a club. Law say twenty lashes you get caught widdout a travelin' pass, ten lashes if'n you looks white folks in dey eyes, thirty lashes if'n you raises your hand 'gainst a white Christian. Law say no nigger preachin' less'n a white man dere to listen; law say can't be no nigger funeral if dey think it's a meetin'. Law say they cut your ear off if'n white folks swear you lied, both ears if dey claim you lied twice. Law say you kill anybody white, you hang; kill 'nother nigger, you jes' gits whipped. Law say reward a Indian catchin' a 'scaped nigger wid all de tabacco dat Indian can carry. Law 'gainst teachin' any nigger to read or write, or givin' any nigger any book. Dey's even a law 'gainst niggers beatin' any drums—any dat African stuff. (Haley, 1976, p. 274)

Thus, Fanta's loud outburst clearly is inconsistent with Haley's view of slave culture, and the scene has little credibility. Although the structure of Haley's narrative could have allowed for Fanta's presence (in the novel there is a woman named Fanta in the village of Juffure), the hysterical nature of Fanta's television character is clearly more akin to that of the character played by Butterfly McQueen in *Gone with the Wind* than to the wary and discreet characters developed by Haley. According to critic Donald Bogle (1988):

> She was simply on television to titillate the viewer. . . . When she loudly argued with Kunta the morning after their night together, her idiotic explosion that led to

> his entrapment seemed blatantly fake because the very thing other parts of *Roots* pointed out (most notably with the characters Fiddler and Belle [sic]) was that the slave population never made a move without a terrifying awareness of the surrounding white world. (p. 340)

Thus, in one of the rare instances in which the makers of *TV Roots* added a black character to the story line, they did so in a way that revealed a lack of understanding of and sensitivity for the slave culture Haley described. Kunta's sensational romance with Fanta represents one of the many production techniques characteristic of the family of television spectaculars of which *TV Roots* was a member. Sex, greed, violence, and a star-studded cast comprise much of the recipe by which miniseries continue to be made. Bogle (1988) argues that these techniques aimed to attract and maintain the white viewer throughout the series. Manufactured by whites for whites, these enhancements compromised the cultural integrity of Haley's vision.

Casting Choices

The producers of *TV Roots* made careful casting choices designed to attract and maintain the white audience. Brandon Stoddard, the ABC executive, admitted that the network executives and the producers of *TV Roots* made a conscious decision to stack the supporting cast with well-known white actors as a means of attracting the white audience. The vast majority of these actors, such as Edward Asner, Lorne Greene, Sandy Duncan, Chuck Connors, Ralph Waite, and Robert Reed, were at the time strongly associated with the positive, good-natured television personas they had developed as the stars of regular television series. The audience's strong identification of these stars with their positive television personas became a cushion between the audience members and the characters portrayed by these stars. Robert Reed was recognized as the nice father of *The Brady Bunch*, who, for the moment, was portraying a slave master. Temporarily playing a slaveship captain, Edward Asner still seemed the gruff but lovable Lou Grant from *The Mary Tyler Moore Show*. The star status of these actors served as a means of putting psychological distance between white audience members and the negative white characters engaged in the cruel business of the slave trade.

The use of popular black actors served much the same purpose. With the exception of the young Kunta Kinte, played by the then unknown LeVar Burton, the majority of the black characters were portrayed by easily identifiable actors such as John Amos, Lou Gossett, Jr., Ben Vereen, and Leslie Uggams. Although no one can quarrel with the powerful, quality performances offered by the majority of *TV Roots'* actors, black and white, the star factor played an important role of distancing the audience from the cruel realities of slavery. A star's popularity provided a screen through which the audience could view a character's suffering or depravity. For this very reason, the makers of *TV Roots* chose not to cast a big-name star in the role of the young Kunta Kinte. According to ABC's Stoddard, "From a purely casting standpoint it was essential that Kunta Kinte be seen not as an actor being Kunta Kinte but this being Kunta Kinte, which is exactly what happened" (quoted in Fishbein, 1983, p. 288).

Transforming Africa

The makers' perceptions of their white audience, as well as their own white backgrounds, probably motivated the use of certain direction techniques as well. Although Haley's description of Africa approached a mythological ideal, his detailed description of African life, community, work, religion, and economy provided definition to Kunta Kinte's history and, ultimately, to the history of all black Americans. In contrast, *TV Roots* presented Africa as an American abstraction (the Africa scenes were filmed in Savannah, Georgia), more representative of an exhibit at the Smithsonian Institute than the living, breathing, thriving community Haley describes. The sparseness of the set, the isolation of the village, the primitiveness of the villagers' activities and conversations, and the limited amount of television time devoted to developing this part of Kunta Kinte's life offer viewers only a superficial glimpse of an African community, ignore the humanity and civility that Haley emphasizes in his novel, and trivialize and subordinate Africa and Africans.

The makers of *TV Roots* offered white audience members an image of Kunta Kinte's village that did not counter the audience's cultural perspective of Africa as the primitive and ancient dark continent (Fishbein, 1983). In his novel, Haley describes the thrill and consternation of Kunta and his classmates as they take on their school masters' rigorous challenges. Kunta also engages in the close observation of his village's civic and cultural life as he becomes more conscious of his role as a leader. However, the audience of *TV Roots* sees only the images of African children herding goats or running through the woods. As a result, Africa remains an uncivilized place, a place of natives and tribes, to which America seemed, naturally, a better alternative.

According to Stoddard, the tourist-eye view of the Gambia was necessary to maintain the attention of an ethnocentric white American audience: "What seems to interest Americans most are Americans. . . . In *Roots*, we got out of Africa as fast as we could. . . . I knew that as soon as we got Kunta Kinte to America we would be okay" (quoted in Fishbein, 1983, p. 289). As this and other statements suggest, the main goal of *TV Roots* was to capture the interest of white Americans. As a result, the scenes of Kunta Kinte's Africa met the requirements of the world view of the white audience members.

The plot emphasis and the direction of *TV Roots* offer additional insight into the efforts to make the series palatable to the white audience. In his novel, Haley draws strong connections between African culture and the cultural characteristics exhibited by the slaves. Frequently in the book Kunta Kinte notes with bewilderment and some degree of satisfaction the similarity between the slave community and Juffure:

> These heathen blacks wouldn't understand drumtalk any better than the toubob. Kunta was forced to concede though—if only with great reluctance—that these pagan blacks might not be totally irredeemable. Ignorant as they were, some of the things they did were purely African, and he could tell that they were totally unaware of it themselves. For one thing, he had heard all his life the very same sounds of exclamation, accompanied by the very same hand gestures and facial expressions. . . . And Kunta had been reminded of Africa in the way that black women here wore their hair tied up with strings into very tight plaits. . . . Kunta also saw Africa in the way that black children here were trained to treat their elders with politeness and respect. (Haley, 1976, p. 243)

The miniseries' creators de-emphasized the theme of African identity and community found within the slave culture in favor of highlighting the lives and activities of the white characters. Certainly, the development of the slave community's African identity would take additional airtime and require further effort. But just as the slave owners sought to erase the Africanness from Kunta Kinte, the makers of *TV Roots* sought to reduce the story's African focus to meet the perceived desires and needs of the white audience.

TV Roots clearly reflects the key ideas outlined earlier associated with the dominant understanding of race in the United States. The white producers of *TV Roots*, catering to a predominantly white audience, had little problem with adding white characters to the story or with giving them depth and agency not found in the novel. Black characters, on the other hand, movingly and intelligently sketched in Haley's novel, were either consolidated or eliminated altogether from the television series. Inevitably, the slave's perspective of slavery, much bally-hooed in ABC's promotional campaign for the miniseries, was subordinated in favor of the white interpretation of the black cultural experience and heritage in America.

Discussion

The foregoing analysis leads to several observations about the creation of *TV Roots*. The significance of Haley's story about the enslavement, freedom, and eventual success of a black family in America, all the while keeping alive its African heritage, was one that the white producers of *TV Roots* apparently did not fully grasp. Rather than a story that revealed how slaves kept a measure of dignity and self-esteem, and the social and cultural mechanisms they used to survive in the face of inhuman oppression, *TV Roots* became a generic tale of the classic immigrant success story in America (see Fishbein, 1983). What could be more appealing and understandable to American whites, in the audience and on the *TV Roots* production team, than a story about immigrant success in a new land? The story of Kunta Kinte's descendants is vintage rags-to-riches genre: His daughter Kizzy is sold to an unknown slave owner; his grandson Chicken George becomes an expert cock-fight trainer and eventually wins his freedom; his great-grandson Tom Moore earns respect as a skilled blacksmith and finally takes his family to Tennessee to live in freedom on their own land. But while Haley's novel presents the story as one of success in *spite* of the oppressive social system in which the family lived, *TV Roots* downplays the family's effort and determination and seems to attribute its success to the social system. In the context of the television production, the family couldn't have done it without the effort and sympathy of understanding whites.

TV Roots does little to enhance understanding of the black experience or the immigrant experience in America. By presenting the experience of Kunta Kinte's family as an immigrant story, *TV Roots* denies that slavery forced onto African blacks was a unique cultural experience different from that of most white immigrants, who came to the United States voluntarily (Fredrickson, 1988). White skin and the circumstances under which they arrived in America enabled white immigrants to assimilate into the mainstream of American life with relative ease (Steinberg, 1989). On the other hand, blacks, even after emancipation, remained outside the mainstream.

Part of the lore of the immigrant story is suffering and hard times in the new environment. Casting the story of slavery and freedom for blacks as an immigrant story, therefore, rationalizes the suffering of blacks as an inevitable step toward acceptance. In addition, because the suffering is set in the past, it does not impinge on contemporary white sensibilities (Willett, 1980).

TV Roots also "naturalized" slavery and the slave experience. The television drama masquerades as reality but describes conditions without analyzing the social context in which institutions such as slavery develop (Willett, 1980). Thus, slavery appears to be a naturally occurring phenomenon, an acceptable, inevitable, logical—and not at all peculiar—part of American history. By not examining social and economic conditions, both domestic and international, underlying the development of slavery, *TV Roots* appears to exonerate whites and white institutions of any moral or ethical responsibility for the exploitation and suffering of black slaves. In fact, by creating and emphasizing white characters who are caring and sensitive—kinder, gentler slave owners—*TV Roots* portrays slavery as not all that bad.

One of Haley's goals in writing *Roots* was to correct what has been termed a political amnesia about slavery in America (Fishbein, 1983). Popular, stereotypical images of slave life have downplayed the horror and cruelty associated with whites' treatment of black slaves (see Dates & Barlow, 1990; Wilson & Gutierrez, 1980; Woll & Miller, 1987). In his book, Haley provides an alternative understanding of slavery and slave life. His narrative offers an image of the black experience in America that counters the dominant American understanding of race.

Conclusion

Despite similarities of plot, themes, and focus, Haley's novel and *TV Roots* offer competing myths or cultural explanations of American slavery and race relations. The fundamental difference between Haley's *Roots* and the television series begins with the difference in the ideological perspective from which each was developed. In his novel, Haley presents the black American cultural experience as a distinct thread in the fabric of American and world history. Haley attributes most, if not all, of the success of Kunta Kinte, his family, and ultimately all black Americans to the resiliency and vitality of their African heritage. In his characterizations, content, and dialogue, Haley portrays the institution of slavery as a singular crime against humanity, clearly created and perpetuated by the white Euro-Americans for economic and social gain. Within the context of his epic slave narrative, Haley reveals his understanding of slavery as the forge that fashioned a unique yet tragic social, historical, and cultural experience that continues to affect the black community and the character of American race relations to the present day.

In the case of *TV Roots*, the white producers and network executives made several structural changes during the production process that altered the original characterizations, content, and theme of Haley's story in such a way as to promote an entirely different social meaning and ideology. By placing the black experience in the context of the classic immigrant story, the creators ignore the distinctiveness of Kunta Kinte's struggle—and the struggle of all black Americans—against the institution of slavery and oppression in favor of an emphasis on the idea of universal assimilation implicit in the immigrant myth.

Although the popular perspective of myth emphasizes the falsity of society's stories, a more useful view promotes the cultural role that myths play in conceptualizing historical or social events and relationships within a particular ideological framework (Fiske, 1990). For example, the pre–Civil Rights myths supported an ideology of race relations that favored racism and discrimination (see Omi & Winant, 1986). Fostered by works such as *Gone with the Wind* and D. W. Griffith's *Birth of a Nation*, a hierarchy of race was transmitted in terms of heroic, aristocratic whites, servile, contented black servants, and savage, lustful black freedmen. Against these images, which continued to linger in the media consciousness of the 1970s, Haley attempted to dramatically redefine and recode the black American experience from a black American perspective.

Once Haley's novel was adapted by the predominantly white television establishment, the explanation of slavery and race relations began to take on a different mythic flavor, reflecting the perspectives of the white producers and executives who controlled the production process. Content and characterizations were altered by the series' creators, obscuring any connection between Haley's collective indictment of the white establishment responsible for slavery and the identity of the white audience. The classic immigrant myth perpetuated by *TV Roots* invites white audience members to identify with the struggles of Kunta Kinte's family while relieving them of the responsibility to acknowledge the social and political contradictions underlying race relations in the United States.

REFERENCES

Bogle, D. (1988). *Blacks in American films and television: An encyclopedia.* New York: Garland.

Dates, J. L., & Barlow, W. (1990). *Split image: African Americans and the media.* Washington, D.C.: Howard University Press.

Ettema, J. S., Whitney, D. C., & Wackman, D. B. (1987). Professional mass communicators. In C. R. Berger and S. H. Chaffee (Eds.), *Handbook of communication science* (pp. 747–780). Newbury Park, CA: Sage.

Fishbein, L. (1983). *Roots:* Docudrama and the interpretation of history. In J. O'Connor (Ed.), *American history, American television: Interpreting the video past* (pp. 279–305). New York: Frederick Ungar.

Fiske, J. (1990). *Introduction to communication studies* (2nd ed.). London: Routledge.

Fredrickson, G. M. (1988). *The arrogance of race: Historical perspectives on slavery, racism and social inequality.* Middletown, CT: Wesleyan University Press.

Haley, A. (1976). *Roots: The saga of an American family.* New York: Dell.

Helweg, A. W., & Helweg, U. M. (1990). *An immigrant success story.* Philadelphia: University of Pennsylvania Press.

Miles, R. (1989). *Racism.* London: Routledge.

Omi, M., & Winant, H. (1986). *Racial formation in the United States from the 1960s to the 1980s.* London: Routledge.

Peterson, R. A. (1976). The production of culture: A prolegomenon. *American Behavioral Scientist, 19,* 7–22.

Steinberg, S. (1989). *The ethnic myth: Race, ethnicity and class in America.* Boston: Beacon Press.

Takaki, R. (1989). *Strangers from a different shore: A history of Asian Americans.* Boston: Little, Brown.

Tuchman, G. (1983). Consciousness industries and the production of culture. *Journal of Communication, 33*(3), 330–341.

Willett, R. (1980). Twisting the roots: Fiction, faction and recent TV drama. *UMOJA, 4,* 11–20.

Williams, E. (1944). *Slavery & capitalism.* Chapel Hill, NC: University of North Carolina Press.

Wilson, C. R., & Gutierrez, F. (1980). *Minorities and media: Diversity and the end of mass communication.* Beverly Hills: Sage.

Woll, A. L., & Miller, R. M. (1987). *Ethnic and racial images in American film and television: Historical essays and bibliography.* New York: Garland.

Wolper, D., & Troupe, Q. (1978). *The inside story of TV's "Roots."* New York: Warner Books.

11

Television and Criticism: Grasping the Future

Television has been with us for some time now. We have watched television reach for the sky and seemingly dig the same hole over and over again. Television, as a social and aesthetic force, has clearly entered middle age. Some wrinkles have been spotted, and it has been suggested that television's life is winding down. It is clear that television no longer is the new kid on the block or an unknown technology to be feared. Its beauties, strengths, liabilities, and open sores have now been pondered from almost every conceivable angle. It is understandable that anything subjected to such constant and critical scrutiny would not retain the luster of something bright, arriving in a shiny new box. Television and its criticism fit together as hand in glove.

The Stages of Television

Youth

If one dates mass television to 1948 and the splash of Uncle Miltie into contemporary consciousness, television is now "fiftysomething," a demographic target that its sponsors have long tried to avoid. Television's golden age came in the medium's infancy in the 1950s. The pressures of creating live television to fill time, with little latitude to record canned product, encouraged spontaneity and inventiveness. Rather than being the commonplace appliance it is seen as today, television sets were seen as rare and precious treasures. Soon, the big boxes with little tubes became shrines in upscale living rooms. With three or four national networks and little else, television was narrow and deep. Quality programs, competing with only two or three other offerings, attracted sizeable audiences. Hopes were high that serious drama and high culture would find a place in television.

By the 1960s a youthful and exuberant television scampered into almost every home. Although the tubes got bigger, the box still largely functioned as a hearth around which families gathered for warmth, sustenance, and shared amusement. We learned to turn to television as a first response. Television's day of fame came on America's day of shame as we watched President John F. Kennedy's assassination. During this decade, television's stark black and white scenes gave way to color. However, television continued to be a narrow and deep medium, broadened only by independent stations in the larger markets. We stayed tuned while color TV brought us *Bonanza* and *Green Acres*. *Beverly Hillbillies* dominated the ratings as we got used to watching assassinations and fights over race and power in the streets. Television's parade of images showed us Martin Luther King Jr. and Robert Kennedy gunned down, Watts burning, and the disenfranchised in the streets of Chicago.

Middle Age

By the 1970s television was moving into middle age with more sets, bigger tubes, and smaller boxes. Television, now a familiar member of the household, was invited into our bedrooms as well as living rooms, family rooms, and kitchens. Television became cultural wallpaper that marked the days of our lives. Day's end brought *Tonight* with Johnny competing with other passions, and the tone for both was increasingly being set by the slash-and-trash local news teams looking for the "live" as opposed to the significant. While news drifted toward happy talk and "infotainment," the decade's most significant television shows were comedies that made us confront prejudice in Archie Bunker's living room and the absurdities of Vietnam in the Korean guise of the *M*A*S*H* operating room. As the 1970s closed, television's superhighway had begun to develop some potholes. The happy days of network dominance stalled in nostalgia, seemingly unready to face the mounting assault from syndication and cable.

The 1980s brought us opportunities and illusions about controlling television. Television's landscape changed as antennae gave way to the cable. As we heard promises of two hundred channels, we often confronted television's wired universe with a confounding assortment of boxes, gadgets, and gizmos. Remote control devices became commonplace, and the home VCR entered the scene. We zapped and we zipped. We time shifted and we began to knit our own crazy quilts of video bricolage. Scanning the channels meant visiting television past and present. Along with visiting the CNNs, ESPNs, shopping networks, and other specialty stores in the televisual mall, American could still love Lucy, leave it to Beaver, and dream of Jeannie. Something old, something new, and something blue for the big three networks that were losing ground. Network television hung in there, its executives believing that a great hit, a *Cosby* or *Roseanne,* would help them carry the day. And sometimes it did. Still networks were being nibbled, if not to death, certainly into mere shadows of their former selves. They were vulnerable, steadfastly watching the gate for cable, while other network "foxes" hopped over the back fence.

Postmodern Maturity

In the 1990s we saw television under siege. However, amidst the claims that traditional television was dying, there was a stampede for seats on the bus. Warner Brothers and Paramount joined Fox in looking for seats with the big three commercial networks up front. Meanwhile the big three networks scampered to check out empty seats in the cabled off section at the back of the bus. Consolidations, partnerships, and the building of synergies became the order of the day. Battles of giants lurked at the center stages of news and sports. The concept of American networks gave way to world services, beamed, with economies of scale, across borders and continents.

Television was now truly both broad and shallow. Cynics scanned what now seemed like hundreds of channels and still saw "nothing on." Network program flow had turned to confetti. Navigating television was a virtual challenge in visual hyperreality. Television was a large discount fun house, a hugh carnival tent of competing brand killers. As consumers, our abilities to experience continuity in the multichannel environment were assaulted at almost every turn. As baby boomers cocooned in the surround of their home theaters, frenzied rumors circulated that Gen X's Internet promised to replace television and seemingly everything else. Something was happening here, and we really didn't know what it was: we had entered an electronic postmodern amusement park. A video pinball game had begun, and it wasn't clear whether we were the players or the balls. Was television as we knew it dead?

Climates of Criticism

Before we take a closer look at the rumors of television's death, it might be wise to take a step back and look at how television criticism has evolved in the face of changes in television and other cultural forms. In doing so, it is important to realize that television criticism does not exist in a vacuum. Cultural criticism, and more specifically, criticism of the arts in a cultural context, preceded television and will undoubtedly outlast it. One of the reasons that cultural criticism persists is its malleability. Critical stances change as cultural alignments reconfigure themselves. At any given time, different critics view the Rorschach blot of culture from different positions. To compound matters, critics are by definition moving objects that are attempting to assess the speed of other moving objects. When the "historiosity" of criticism is factored in, when critics look back at a point in culture from a time in the present, or when we try to compare the critical stances of two critics at different points in history, the critic-to-culture relationship seems even more complex. Simply put, critics and culture both move in a system that is in flux. Thus, to expect an unchanging stable system with inherent internal consistencies is unrealistic.

Therefore, in this book, we have argued that criticism is most usefully done and evaluated by taking a look at how it is centered. Television's pervasiveness in the latter portion of the twentieth century has made it a melting pot for critical inquiry. Indeed, the gloves worn by television critics come from many makers and serve many functions. Some critical gloves are worn for pragmatic purposes, others are adopted as fashion statements by critics boldly attempting to popularize some new approach. Picking out critical gloves and actually wearing them is a complex task. Some grab the nearest pair. They choose their gloves because they are chic, often disregarding whether the approach fits the critic's hands or the task of the moment. Others rely on a cherished and tattered old pair, seeing them suitable for all occasions. Some love always wearing something new and are never seen twice in the same outfit for their public writing. Others opt for a mismatched set out of convenience or as a way of getting attention.

Changing Climates

Many people keep more than one pair of critical-approaches gloves in their drawer. Changes in fashion, the challenge of the seasons, and the many occasions of life can lead to a full drawer. The colder the climate the more a good pair of gloves becomes a cherished commodity. The same is true for criticism. In cold, oppressive, or threatening times, good criticism becomes a cherished commodity.

It was the cold, in a sense, that brought out the critics in the early days of television. The shivering cultural elite wore boxing gloves in an attempt to give television, as an art form, a knockout punch. Of course, the knockout punch was never successfully delivered. For a while, it seemed that the elite critics were successfully battling the liberal apologists' defense of the popular back into the corner of the ring. However, while these two were slugging it out in the corner, television was very much alive and well: a snowstorm of activity on culture's center stage. Not surprisingly, the first critics to take notice of television were journalistic critics concerned with education in a larger sense. They attempted first to contextualize television as a social force and to take television programs on their own terms, not as something they were not: fine literature of another era, classic stage drama, or a symphonic concert. Soon a whole new set of academic critics emerged in the academy. They, too, realized that television needed to be taken seriously. It couldn't be ignored.

Like it or not, television seemed to be here to stay. So instead of standing in the cold, these academic critics moved inside and warmed their hands at television's hearth.

Getting Acclimated to Television Criticism

Many critics, however, saw that it was still cold outside. Some continued to see television as a significant culprit in the cultural cold front. Others focused on more significant structural problems, such as advanced capitalism, seeing television as a mere artifact in the political-economic mix. For some, the era of television was no more frigid than any other era. Although it might not be balmy, these critics didn't see the temperature gauge as the most useful to television study. Some studied the uniqueness of each snowflake. Others studied the mechanics of the snow machine. Still others wanted to study those who had their noses pressed against the window watching the flurries.

What emerged when the academic community warmed to television as a serious object of critical study was one large and continuing party, a moveable feast. Stepping inside and joining the television criticism party did not require an invitation. It was clear there was a party going on. After all, television was making a good deal of noise, and the door was open. One could clearly get inside. The party was made to be crashed. Still people worried over what to wear. This was no informal party. Gloves were in order. Thus, the challenge for good television criticism has always been what critical gloves to wear to the party.

As it is with any party, some arrive sooner and others come late. Some stay a while. Others make a quick appearance and leave. Some dominate conversation and like hearing their own voices. Some are self-righteous while others are gracious and accommodating. Some bullhorn single issues while others navigate broader terrain. So it has been with critics and the methods of analysis they use in doing television criticism. Debates over who came first to the party end up much like those over the chicken and the egg: the discussions can be interesting and loud but never completely resolved. Still, it might be argued that the party was being given by those in the context-centered camp who were most interested in sociocultural approaches to television. Television, after all, was a sociological phenomenon. Being able to deliver pictures and words to millions of homes was sure to put a kink in the social fabric. Indeed, aware of the critical knocks at its door, the television industry itself offered institution-centered explanations; some would say it crashed the party. Subsequently, this professional perspective was legitimized by those in the academy doing institution-centered criticism.

After these early arrivals came a critical onslaught. The television-criticism party was the new place to be seen. Genre and narrative-centered analysis crashed the television party from literary studies. Rhetoricians saw televised politics and advertising emerging as the center stage of persuasion.

Thus, they entered wearing gloves suitable for analyzing texts and mythical contexts. Film studies entered from another door wearing semiotic gloves and shook hands with the television producer as the auteur. Cultural studies entered from across the Atlantic, wearing a different set of semiological operating gloves, those that held a mixture of structural and ideological concerns.

Joining the party and jousting with cultural critics who had focused on race and class, but overlooked gender, were the feminist critics. The feminist gaze brought new eyes to interpretative studies and fueled realizations that the television text was polysemic. Next came the culturally based ethnographers and literary-based critics who brought explorations of ideal readers and the lived experiences of audience members. The postmodernists arrived fashionably late, arguing that the deluge of popular culture that had come before was recombined into new polyvalent textures, personal and indeterminate in meaning. Meanwhile, political economists hovered at the edges of the room, shaking their heads at the adaptability of swirling corporatization and globalism and wondering whether the bricolage of the postmodernists, modernists, and culturalists were apparitions. For them it was still cold outside.

Tomorrow's Weather

Critical inquiry into television has taken many turns. Diverse camps of critical approaches have come and gone. Strategic alliances have been formed and fractured. Old popular culture wars battle on, and new ones are started. Many of the methods discussed in this book came before television, and all have been applied to more than television. What now should be clear is that the critical methods applied to television have the ability to roll with changes in society and in a cultural form such as television. Even with the future of television clouded as we enter the twenty-first century, it is apparent that the fundamental forms of criticism will persist and usefully be applied to assess and understand television, however it evolves.

Creative forms will always have their auteurs. Television criticism has moved the focus from the film director to the television producer. However, the character of the auteur will surely change in the future. Perhaps as television becomes more interactive, all of us will become auteurs. With such changes, criticism will respond to new challenges. No matter how much television advances, it is not likely to become a text-free environment. There will be genres and narratives. Culturally, human beings have been telling stories and developing idioms and conventions for their telling for too long a time for us to believe that storytelling will disappear as new technological forms emerge as part of the television mix. We will surely see new and recombinant genres, and we may see some new twists on the narrative form. However, despite these changes, televisual texts will continue to have rhetorical and structural dimensions. We believe there is no need to fear that the forms of analysis discussed in this book will lose their value.

Similarly, audiences will certainly continue to be part of television criticism in the future. Audiences will continue to change, just as styles of spectatorship have changed from the hearing of stories around a campfire to visiting the Elizabethan theater, lounging in living rooms amid the first glow of television, and more recently, going online and being counted as someone who has surfed a World Wide Web television site. Television's culturally placed situational contexts will continue to be the sites where we confront our myths and ideological struggles. As television changes, context- and culture-centered criticism will adapt. We believe that the critical community will come to grips with what comes after postmodernism and what today looks like a uniquely fractured landscape. Finally, television is an institutional animal. It may do some cross-breeding and be changed by some new technological innovations, but it will evolve in significant ways because of its institutional relationships. Thus, we believe that continuing to study television from an institutional-centered perspective will be fruitful as we look into the future.

Rumors of Television's Death Greatly Exaggerated?

Earlier in this chapter, we used an anthropomorphic metaphor to sketch the relatively brief life of television. Although it was useful to look at television as a life cycle with infancy, youth, early adulthood, middle age, and on to graying years where it matters less and less and dies, television is not a human being. Television is a cultural form, inclusive of many others, including storytelling, theater, the newspaper, the photograph, moving pictures, and radio. Television has adapted to many environmental changes over the course of its life. Society has adapted to television, just as culture has undoubtedly been changed by television's presence.

As we near the twenty-first century, there are few signs that television is dying. It remains national advertisers' primary outlet to reach the masses in one fell swoop. Its big shows still leave a large cultural imprint. However, there is no question that traditional television is clearly atrophying. We are no longer in an era where the big three networks commandeer an audience share in the 90th percentile. But these days have long been gone. In fact, it is probably safe to say that television as we knew it is probably dead. However, television as we know it is alive and well.

It is this constantly evolving television that will provide the challenges for tomorrow's critics. Questions of how, and on whose terms, television will be transformed will be high on the critical agenda. Over the next few years we probably can expect to see a more fragmented and a more globalized television. New textual forms will emerge. Interactive narratives may become commonplace. Today's generic mutants may become tomorrow's discarded formulas. They will provide new challenges for audiences, and the term *audience* itself may well fade into the sunset. Institutional alignments of the major players will continue to require a road map. Television will be merged into fewer and fewer arms of the corporate oligarchy that will program our leisure and information access.

Television as we know it will not die; it will evolve. The critical strategies that we have outlined in this book will evolve with television. Television's bionic era has just begun. It will grow new parts and fuse with other cultural forms in heretofore unseen ways. Just as it was when television first entered the scene, this is a time of remarkable change. For the critic, it is cold outside. Put on your gloves.

 *About the Contributors*

Jane Banks (Ph.D., Ohio State University) is an Associate Professor of Communication at Indiana University/Purdue University, Ft. Wayne, Indiana. Her research and publications on gender ideology have included studies of Mary Kay cosmetics, science fiction, and television talk shows.

Bonnie J. Dow (Ph.D., University of Minnesota) is Assistant Professor of Communication at the University of Georgia, Athens, Georgia. Her research and publications, including her recent book *Prime-time Feminism: Television, Media Culture, and the Women's Movement Since 1970*, have examined images of women in film and television.

Peter Ehrenhaus (Ph.D., University of Minnesota) is Professor of Communication Studies at Portland State University, Portland, Oregon. His research and publications, including his book *Cultural Legacies of Vietnam: Uses of the Past in the Present*, coedited with Richard Morris, have focused on analyses of the Vietnam War, public memorials, nostalgia, and public memory.

Glenn C. Geiser-Getz (Ph.D., University of Iowa) is Assistant Professor of Communication Studies at East Stroudsburg University, East Stroudsburg, Pennsylvania. His areas of research include reality television, new electronic technologies, and comedy.

Bruce E. Gronbeck (Ph.D., University of Iowa) is Professor of Communication Studies and A. Craig Baird Distinguished Chair of Public Address at the University of Iowa, Iowa City, Iowa. He is a Fulbright Scholar, a past President of the Speech Communication Association (now the National Communication Association), and he has published widely on political rhetoric and media criticism. His extensive publications include eight books and cover subjects ranging from dramatism, British parliamentary address, and the works of Walter Ong to the television series *Family*, news, and political bio-ads. He authored *Writing Television Criticism* in the early 1980s, and he still watches prime-time TV on weeknights.

Rona Tamiko Halualani (ABD, Arizona State University) is a doctoral candidate in Communication Studies at Arizona State University, Tempe, Arizona. Her research and publications have examined images of Asian, Asian Pacific, and Asian American women in film and television, the Hawaiian Sovereignty Movement, and Pilipina Mail Order Brides.

Robert Hanke (Ph.D., Pennsylvania State University) is Assistant Professor at the University of Louisville, Louisville, Kentucky. His research and publications have focused on the representation of masculinity and masculine discourse in such television series as *thirtysomething, Northern Exposure, Home Improvement,* and *Quantum Leap* as well as on MTV Latino and sports.

Heather L. Hundley (ABD, University of Utah) is a doctoral candidate in the Department of Communication at the University of Utah, Salt Lake City, Utah. Her research and publications have included critical analyses of *Cheers*, as well as analyses of media law and regulation and the programming of the cable television network Lifetime.

Kent A. Ono (Ph.D., University of Iowa) is Assistant Professor of American Studies and Asian American Studies at the University of California, Davis, California. His research interests and publications include critical rhetoric and neo-colonial and poststructural analyses of race and gender in popular media. With Taylor Harrison, Sarah Projanksy, and Elyce Helford he has coedited *Enterprise Zones: Critical Positions on Star Trek.*

A. Susan Owen (Ph.D., University of Iowa) is Associate Professor and Chair of the Communication and Theatre Arts Department at the University of Puget Sound, Tacoma, Washington. In addition to her book *Parallels: Soldiers' Knowledge and the Oral History of Contemporary Warfare,* coauthored with the late Michael Madden and Tim Hansen, her research and publications focus on the social construction of gender, pornography, and representations of warfare and the warrior in mass media texts.

Michael J. Porter (Ph.D., University of Iowa) is Professor of Communication at the University of Missouri, Columbia, Missouri. His research and publications include structural, semiotic, aesthetic, narrative, and mythic analyses of such diverse television programs as *Hill Street Blues, thirtysomething, Cheers, Northern Exposure,* and *ER.*

Sarah Projansky (Ph.D., University of Iowa) is Assistant Professor of Women's Studies at the University of California, Davis, California. In addition to her book *Enterprise Zones: Critical Positions on Star Trek,* coedited with Taylor Harrison, Kent Ono, and Elyce Helford, her research and publications have examined the representation of rape in television programs, images of female sexuality, and postfeminist discourse in film and television.

Robert Schrag (Ph.D., Wayne State University) is Professor and Chair of the Department of Communication at North Carolina State University, Raleigh, North Carolina. His research interests and publications include analyses of values in such television series as *M*A*S*H, Cheers,* soap operas, children's Saturday morning cartoons, and Rabbit Ears Television. He has also written *Taming the Wild Tube: A Family's Guide to Television and Video.*

Ronald B. Scott (Ph.D., University of Utah) is Associate Professor and Assistant Chair in the Department of Mass Communication at Miami University, Oxford, Ohio. His research and publications have focused on representations of African Americans in film, television and entertainment news, and music videos.

Jonathan David Tankel (Ph.D., University of Wisconsin-Madison) is Associate Professor of Communication at Indiana University/Purdue University, Ft.

Wayne, Indiana. His research and publications have examined journalistic campaign practices, the recording industry, science fiction, and television talk shows.

Robert J. Thompson (Ph.D., Northwestern University) is Associate Professor at the S. I. Newhouse School of Public Communications at Syracuse University, Syracuse, New York. His books about television include analyses of the television programs of Stephen J. Cannell—*Adventures on Prime Time, Prime Time, Prime Movers: America's Greatest TV Shows and the People Who Created Them* (with David Marc), *Television Studies: Textual Analysis*, and *Making Television: Authorship and the Production Process*, the latter two coedited with Gary Burns.

Leah R. Vande Berg (Ph.D., University of Iowa) is Professor of Communication Studies at California State University, Sacramento, and editor of the *Western Journal of Communication* (1997–1999). Her research focuses on media and cultural values, and representations of women and men in television and other popular arts. With Nick Trujillo she has written *Organizational Life on Television*, and with Lawrence Wenner she coedited *Television Criticism: Approaches and Applications*. She currently is the editor of the *Western Journal of Communication*, and she, too, watches television on weeknights and weekends.

Lawrence A. Wenner (Ph.D., The University of Iowa) is Professor of Communication Arts and Director of the Graduate Program in Sports and Fitness Management at the University of San Francisco, San Francisco, California. He is the former editor of *Journal of Sport and Social Issues*. In addition to his books, *Media, Sport, & Society* and *MediaSport: Cultural Sensibilities and Sport in the Media Age*, his published articles have ranged from social scientific analyses of media uses and gratifications to critical analyses of sports, advertisements, and news.

With the permission of the National Communication Association, formerly the Speech Communication Association, and the copyright holder, we have reprinted a critical essay by **Lauren R. Tucker** and **Hemant Shah** published in *Critical Studies in Mass Communication*. We have been unable to ascertain additional information, however, about their current positions and areas of research.

Index